£24.95

000

00

2000

01

ARTIFICIAL INTELLIGENCE

Third Edition

Patrick Henry Winston

Professor of Computer Science
Director, Artificial Intelligence Laboratory
Massachusetts Institute of Technology

ADDISON-WESLEY PUBLISHING COMPANY
Reading, Massachusetts ■ Menlo Park, California
New York ■ Don Mills, Ontario ■ Wokingham, England
Amsterdam ■ Bonn ■ Sydney ■ Singapore ■ Tokyo
Madrid ■ San Juan ■ Milan ■ Paris

Library of Congress Cataloging-in-Publication Data
Winston, Patrick Henry.
    Artificial Intelligence / Patrick Henry Winston. — 3rd ed.
        p.   cm.
    Includes bibliographical references (p.   ) and index.
    ISBN 0-201-53377-4
    1. Artificial Intelligence.   I. Title.
    Q335.W56   1992   91–41385
    006.3—dc20   CIP

Reproduced by Addison-Wesley from camera-ready copy supplied by the author.

Reprinted with corrections June, 1992

2 3 4 5 6 7 8 9 10 HA 95949392

Contents

CHAPTER **12** ▬▬▬▬▬▬▬▬▬
Symbolic Constraints and Propagation   249

CHAPTER **13** ▬▬▬▬▬▬▬▬▬
Logic and Resolution Proof   283

Acknowledgments

The cover painting is by Karen A. Prendergast. The cover design is by Dan Dawson. The interior design is by Marie McAdam.

A draft of this book was read by Boris Katz, who has a special gift for rooting out problems and tenaciously insisting on improvements.

The following people also have made especially valuable suggestions: Johnnie W. Baker (Kent State University), Robert C. Berwick (MIT), Ronen Basri (MIT), Philippe Brou (Ascent Technology), David A. Chanen (MIT), Paul A. Fishwick (University of Florida), Robert Frank (University of Pennsylvania), W. Eric L. Grimson (MIT), Jan L. Gunther (Ascent Technology), James R. Harrington (Army Logistics Management College), Julie Sutherland-Platt (MIT), Seth Hutchinson (The Beckman Institute), Carl Manning (MIT), David A. McAllester (MIT), Michael de la Maza (MIT), Thomas Marill (MIT), Phillip E. Perkins (Army Logistics Management College), Lynn Peterson (University of Texas at Arlington), Tomaso Poggio (MIT), Oberta A. Slotterbeck (Hiram College), and Xiru Zhang (Thinking Machines, Inc.).

Finally, the following people identified errors that appeared in previous printings: Robert Gann, Gary Gu, George H. John, Martin Ruckert, and Peter Szolovits.

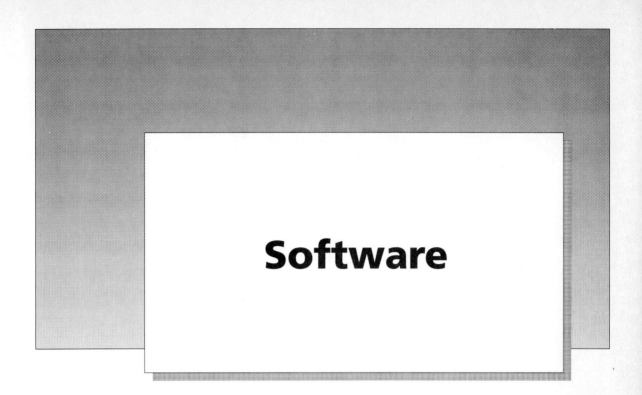

Software

Software in support of this book is available on diskettes from Gold Hill Computers, Inc., Cambridge, MA 02139 (617/621-3300).

Software in support of this book is also available via the INTERNET. To learn how to obtain this software, send a message to ai3@ai.mit.edu with the word "help" on the subject line. Your message will be answered by an automatic reply program that will tell you what to do next.

The automatic reply program also tells you how to report a bug or offer a suggestion via the INTERNET. If you wish to report a bug or offer a suggestion via ordinary mail, write to the author at the following address:

Patrick H. Winston
Room 816
Artificial Intelligence Laboratory
545 Technology Square
Cambridge, MA 02139

Preface

You Need to Know About Artificial Intelligence

This book was written for two groups of people. One group—computer scientists and engineers—need to know about artificial intelligence to make computers more useful. Another group—psychologists, biologists, linguists, and philosophers—need to know about artificial intelligence to understand the principles that make intelligence possible.

You do not need a computer-science education or advanced mathematical training to understand the basic ideas. Ideas from those disciplines are discussed, in a spirit of scientific glasnost, but those discussions are in optional sections, plainly marked and easily detoured around.

This Edition Reflects Changes in the Field

This edition of *Artificial Intelligence* reflects, in part, the steady progress made since the second edition was published. Some ideas that seemed good back then have faded, and have been displaced by newer, better ideas.

There have been more remarkable, more revolutionary changes as well. One of these is the change brought about by the incredible progress that has been made in computer hardware. Many simple ideas that seemed silly 10 years ago, on the ground that they would require unthinkable computations, now seem to be valid, because fast—often parallel—computing has become commonplace. As described in Chapter 19, for example, one good way to control a rapidly moving robot arm is to use a vast lookup table.

Another remarkable change, perhaps the most conspicuous, is the focus on learning—particularly the kind of learning that is done by neuronlike nets. Ten years ago, only a handful of people in artificial intelligence studied learning of any kind; now, most people seem to have incorporated a learning component into their work. Accordingly, about one-third of the chapters in this edition are devoted to various approaches to learning, and about one-third of those deal with neuronlike nets.

Still another remarkable change is the emergence of breakthroughs. As described in Chapter 26, for example, one good way to identify a three-dimensional object is to construct two-dimensional templates for the given object, in the given view, for each possible object class. Ten years ago, no one suspected that the required templates could be manufactured perfectly, simply, and on demand, no matter how the object is viewed.

Finally, there is the emphasis on scaling up. These days, it is hard to attract attention with an idea that appears suited to toy problems only. This difficulty creates a dilemma for a textbook writers, because textbooks need to discuss toy problems so that the complexities of particular real worlds do not get in the way of understanding the basic ideas. To deal with this dilemma, I discuss many examples of important applications, but only after I explain the basic ideas in simpler contexts.

This Edition Responds to Suggestions of Previous Users

Many readers of the first and second editions have offered wonderful suggestions. At one meeting in Seattle, on a now-forgotten subject, Peter Andreae and J. Michael Brady remarked, over coffee, that it was hard for students to visualize how the ideas could be incorporated into programs.

Similarly, feedback from my own students at the Massachusetts Institute of Technology indicated a need to separate the truly powerful ideas and unifying themes—such as the principle of least commitment and the importance of representation—from nugatory implementation details.

In response to such suggestions, this edition is peppered with several kinds of summarizing material, all set off visually:

- Semiformal procedure specifications
- Semiformal representation specifications
- Hierarchical specification trees
- Powerful ideas

You Can Decide How Much You Want to Read

To encourage my students to get to the point, I tell them that I will not read more than 100 pages of any dissertation. Looking at this book, it might seem that I have neglected my own dictum, because this book has grown to be many times 100 pages long. My honor is preserved, nevertheless, because several features make this edition easier to read:

- There are few essential chapter-to-chapter dependencies. Individual readers with bounded interests or time can get what they need from one or two chapters.
- The book is modular. Instructors can design their own subject around 200 or 300 hundred pages of material.
- Each chapter is shorter, relative to the chapters in the second edition. Many can be covered by instructors in one or two lectures.

If your want to develop a general understanding of artificial intelligence, you should read Chapters 2 through 12 from Part I; then you should skim Chapter 16 and Chapter 19 from Part II, and Chapter 26 from Part III to get a feel for what is in the rest of the book. If you are interested primarily in learning, you should read Chapter 2 from Part I to learn about representations; then, you should read all of Part II. If you are interested primarily in vision or in language, you can limit yourself to the appropriate chapters in Part III.

This Edition Is Supported by Optional Software

This book discusses ideas on many levels, from the level of issues and alternatives to a level that lies just one step short of implementation in computer programs. For those readers who wish to take that one extra step, to see how the ideas can be reduced to computer programs, there are two alternatives:

- For people who already know the LISP programming language, a large and growing number of programs written in support of this book are available via the INTERNET; see the software note that precedes this preface.
- For people who do not know the LISP programming language, the companion book *LISP*, by Patrick H. Winston and Berthold K. P. Horn, is a good introduction that treats many of the ideas explained in this book from the programming perspective.

This Edition Is Supported by an Instructor's Manual

A companion *Instructors Manual* contains exercise solutions and sample syllabuses.

P.H.W.

Part I
Representations
and Methods

In part I, you learn about basic representations and methods. These representations and methods are used by engineers to build commercial systems and by scientists to explain various kinds of intelligence.

In Chapter 1, **The Intelligent Computer**, you learn about *what artificial intelligence is*, *why artificial intelligence is important*, and *how artificial intelligence is applied*. You also learn about *criteria for judging success*.

In Chapter 2, **Semantic Nets and Description Matching**, you learn about the importance of good representation and you learn *how to test a representation* to see whether it is a good one. Along the way, you learn about *semantic nets* and about the *describe-and-match method*. By way of illustration, you learn about a geometric-analogy problem solver, a plot recognizer, and a feature-based object identifier.

In Chapter 3, **Generate and Test, Means-Ends Analysis, and Problem Reduction**, you learn about three powerful problem-solving methods: *generate and test*, *means–ends analysis*, and *problem reduction*. Examples illustrating these problem-solving methods at work underscore the importance of devising a good representation, such as a *state space* or a *goal tree*.

In Chapter 4, **Nets and Basic Search**, you learn about basic search methods, such as *depth-first search*, that are used in all sorts of programs, ranging from those that do robot path planning to those that provide natural-language access to database information.

In Chapter 5, **Nets and Optimal Search**, you learn more about search methods, but now the focus is on finding the *best* path to a goal, rather than just any path. The methods explained include *branch and bound*, *discrete dynamic programming*, and A*.

In Chapter 6, **Trees and Adversarial Search**, you learn still more about search methods, but here the focus shifts again, this time to games. You learn how *minimax search* tells you where to move and how *alpha–beta pruning* makes minimax search faster. You also learn how *heuristic continuation* and *progressive deepening* enable you to use all the time you have effectively, even though game situations vary dramatically.

In Chapter 7, **Rules and Rule Chaining**, you learn that simple *if–then rules* can embody a great deal of commercially useful knowledge. You also learn about using if–then rules in programs that do *forward chaining* and *backward chaining*. By way of illustration, you learn about toy systems that identify zoo animals and bag groceries. You also learn about certain key implementation details, such as *variable binding via tree search* and the *rete procedure*.

In Chapter 8, **Rules, Substrates, and Cognitive Modeling**, you learn how it is possible to build important capabilities on top of rule-based problem-solving apparatus. In particular, you learn how it is possible for a program *to explain* the steps that have led to a conclusion, *to reason in a variety of styles*, *to reason under time constraints*, *to determine a conclusion's probability*, and *to check the consistency of a newly proposed rule*. You also learn about *knowledge engineering* and about SOAR, a rule-based model of human problem solving.

In Chapter 9, **Frames and Inheritance**, you learn about *frames*, *classes*, *instances*, *slots*, and *slot values*. You also learn about *inheritance*, a powerful problem-solving method that makes it possible to know a great deal about *instances* by virtue of knowing about the *classes* to which the instances belong. You also learn how knowledge can be captured in certain procedures, often called *demons*, that are attached to classes.

In Chapter 10, **Frames and Commonsense**, you learn how frames can capture knowledge about how actions happen. In particular, you learn how *thematic-role frames* describe the action conveyed by verbs and nouns, and you learn about how *action frames* and *state-change frames* describe how actions happen on a deeper, syntax-independent level.

In Chapter 11, **Numeric Constraints and Propagation**, you learn how good representations often bring out constraints that enable conclusions to propagate like the waves produced by a stone dropped in a quiet pond. In particular, you see how to use *numeric constraint propagation* to propagate probability estimates through *opinion nets* and to propagate altitude measurements through *smoothness constraints*.

In Chapter 12, **Symbolic Constraints and Propagation**, you learn more about constraint propagation, but now the emphasis is on *symbolic* *constraint propagation.* You see how symbolic constraint propagation solves problems in *line-drawing analysis* and *relative time calculation.* You also learn about *Marr's methodological principles.*

In Chapter 13, **Logic and Resolution Proof**, you learn about *logic,* an important addition to your knowledge of problem-solving paradigms. After digesting a mountain of notation, you explore the notion of proof, and you learn how to use *proof by refutation* and *resolution theorem proving.*

In Chapter 14, **Backtracking and Truth Maintenance**, you learn how logic serves as a foundation for other problem-solving methods. In particular, you learn about *proof by constraint propagation* and about *truth maintenance.* By way of preparation, you also learn what *dependency-directed backtracking* is, and how it differs from *chronological backtracking,* in the context of numeric constraint propagation.

In Chapter 15, **Planning**, you learn about two distinct approaches to planning a sequence of actions to achieve some goal. One way, the STRIPS approach, uses *if–add–delete operators* to work on a single collection of assertions. Another way, the theorem-proving approach, rooted in logic, uses *situation variables* and *frame axioms* to tie together collections of expressions, producing a movielike sequence.

1

The Intelligent Computer

This book is about the field that has come to be called *artificial intelligence*. In this chapter, you learn how to define artificial intelligence, and you learn how the book is arranged. You get a feeling for why artificial intelligence is important, both as a branch of engineering and as a kind of science. You learn about some successful applications of artificial intelligence. And finally, you learn about *criteria* you can use to determine whether work in Artificial Intelligence is successful.

THE FIELD AND THE BOOK

There are many ways to define the field of Artificial Intelligence. Here is one:

Artificial intelligence is ...
▷ The study of the computations that make it possible to perceive, reason, and act.

From the perspective of this definition, artificial intelligence differs from most of **psychology** because of the greater emphasis on computation, and artificial intelligence differs from most of **computer science** because of the emphasis on perception, reasoning, and action.

From the perspective of goals, artificial intelligence can be viewed as part engineering, part science:

- The **engineering goal** of artificial intelligence is to solve real-world problems using artificial intelligence as an armamentarium of ideas about representing knowledge, using knowledge, and assembling systems.
- The **scientific goal** of artificial intelligence is to determine which ideas about representing knowledge, using knowledge, and assembling systems explain various sorts of intelligence.

This Book Has Three Parts

To make use of artificial intelligence, you need a basic understanding of how knowledge can be represented and what methods can make use of that knowledge. Accordingly, in Part I of this book, you learn about basic representations and methods. You also learn, by way of vision and language examples, that the basic representations and methods have a long reach.

Next, because many people consider learning to be the sine qua non of intelligence, you learn, in Part II, about a rich variety of learning methods. Some of these methods involve a great deal of reasoning; others just dig regularity out of data, without any analysis of why the regularity is there.

Finally, in Part III, you focus directly on visual perception and language understanding, learning not only about perception and language per se, but also about ideas that have been a major source of inspiration for people working in other subfields of artificial intelligence.[†]

The Long-Term Applications Stagger the Imagination

As the world grows more complex, we must use our material and human resources more efficiently, and to do that, we need high-quality help from computers. Here are a few possibilities:

- In farming, computer-controlled robots should control pests, prune trees, and selectively harvest mixed crops.
- In manufacturing, computer-controlled robots should do the dangerous and boring assembly, inspection, and maintenance jobs.
- In medical care, computers should help practitioners with diagnosis, monitor patients' conditions, manage treatment, and make beds.
- In household work, computers should give advice on cooking and shopping, clean the floors, mow the lawn, do the laundry, and perform maintenance chores.

[†]Sometimes, you hear the phrase *core AI* used by people who regard *language*, *vision*, and *robotics* to be somehow separable from the mainstream of artificial intelligence. However, in light of the way progress on language, vision, and robotics can and has influenced work on reasoning, any such separation seems misadvised.

■   In schools, computers should understand why their students make mistakes, not just react to errors. Computers should act as superbooks,
displaying planetary orbits and playing musical scores, thus helping
students to understand physics and music.

The Near-Term Applications Involve New Opportunities

Many people are under the false impression that the commercial goal of
artificial intelligence must be to save money by replacing human workers.
But in the commercial world, most people are more enthusiastic about new
opportunities than about decreased cost. Moreover, the task of totally
replacing a human worker ranges from difficult to impossible because we
do not know how to endow computers with all the perception, reasoning,
and action abilities that people exhibit.

Nevertheless, because intelligent people and intelligent computers have
complementary abilities, people and computers can realize opportunities
together that neither can realize alone. Here are some examples:

■   In business, computers can help us to locate pertinent information, to
schedule work, to allocate resources, and to discover salient regularities
in databases.

■   In engineering, computers can help us to develop more effective control
strategies, to create better designs, to explain past decisions, and to
identify future risks.

Artificial Intelligence Sheds New Light on
Traditional Questions

Artificial intelligence complements the traditional perspectives of psychology, linguistics, and philosophy. Here are several reasons why:

■   Computer metaphors aid thinking. Work with computers has led to a
rich new language for talking about how to do things and how to describe things. Metaphorical and analogical use of the concepts involved
enables more powerful thinking about thinking.

■   Computer models force precision. Implementing a theory uncovers conceptual mistakes and oversights that ordinarily escape even the most
meticulous researchers. Major roadblocks often appear that were not
recognized as problems at all before the cycle of thinking and experi-
menting began.

■   Computer implementations quantify task requirements. Once a program performs a task, upper-bound statements can be made about how
much information processing the task requires.

■   Computer programs exhibit unlimited patience, require no feeding, and
do not bite. Moreover, it is usually simple to deprive a computer
program of some piece of knowledge to test how important that piece
really is. It is almost always impossible to work with animal brains
with the same precision.

Note that wanting to make computers *be intelligent* is not the same as wanting to make computers *simulate intelligence*. Artificial intelligence excites people who want to uncover principles that must be exploited by all intelligent information processors, not just by those made of neural tissue instead of electronic circuits. Consequently, there is neither an obsession with mimicking human intelligence nor a prejudice against using methods that seem involved in human intelligence. Instead, there is a new point of view that brings along a new methodology and leads to new theories.

Artificial Intelligence Helps Us to Become More Intelligent

Just as psychological knowledge about human information processing can help to make computers intelligent, theories derived primarily with computers in mind often suggest useful guidance for human thinking. Through artificial intelligence research, many representations and methods that people seem to use unconsciously have been crystallized and made easier for people to deploy deliberately.

WHAT ARTIFICIAL INTELLIGENCE CAN DO

In this section, you learn about representative systems that were enabled by ideas drawn from artificial intelligence. Once you have finished this book, you will be well on your way toward incorporating the ideas of artificial intelligence into your own systems.

Intelligent Systems Can Help Experts to Solve Difficult Analysis Problems

During the early days of research in artificial intelligence, James R. Slagle showed that computers can work problems in integral calculus at the level of college freshmen. Today, programs can perform certain kinds of mathematical analysis at a much more sophisticated level.

The KAM program, for example, is an expert in nonlinear dynamics, a subject of great interest to scientists who study the equations that govern complex object interactions.

To demonstrate KAM's competence, Kenneth M. Yip, KAM's developer, asked KAM to reason about the implications of the following difference equations, which were developed by Michel Henon, a noted French astronomer, to study star motion:

$$x_{n+1} = x_n \cos\alpha - (y_n - x_n^2)\sin\alpha,$$
$$y_{n+1} = x_n \sin\alpha - (y_n - x_n^2)\cos\alpha.$$

First, KAM performed a series of simulations, tracing the progression of x and y from 10 sets of initial values selected by KAM. Figure 1.1 shows the resulting pattern of x–y values.

Then, using methods developed in computer-vision research, as well as its deep mathematical knowledge, KAM produced the following conclusions, which are presented here to give you a sense of KAM's sophistication:

Figure 1.1 Yip's program performs its own experiments, which it then analyzes using computer-vision methods and deep mathematical knowledge. Here you see a plot produced by Yip's program in the course of analyzing certain equations studied by astronomers. Images courtesy of Kenneth M. Yip.

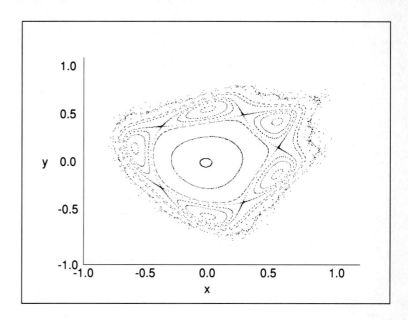

An Analysis ————————————————————

There is an elliptic fixed point at (0 0 0). Surrounding the fixed point is a regular region bounded by a KAM curve with a rotation number between 1/5 and 1/4. Outside the regular region lies a chain of 5 islands. The island chain is bounded by a KAM curve with rotation number between 4/21 and 5/26. The outermost region is occupied by chaotic orbits which eventually escape.

KAM's analysis is impressively similar to the original analysis of Henon.

Intelligent Systems Can Help Experts to Design New Devices

The utility of intelligence programs in science and engineering is not limited to sophisticated analysis; many recent programs have begun to work on the synthesis side as well.

For example, a program developed by Karl Ulrich designs simple devices and then looks for cost-cutting opportunities to reduce the number of components. In one experiment, Ulrich's program designed a device that measures an airplane's rate of descent by measuring the rate at which air pressure is increasing.

The first step performed by Ulrich's program was to search for a collection of components that does the specified task. Figure 1.2(a) shows the result. Essentially, a rapid increase in air pressure moves the piston to the right, compressing the air in back of the piston and driving it into a reservoir; once the increase in air pressure stops, the air in back of the piston and in the reservoir bleeds back through the return pipe, and the

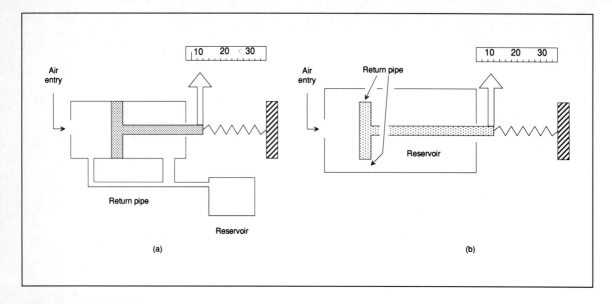

Figure 1.2 Ulrich's
program designs a
rate-of-descent device
in two steps. First,
as shown in (a), the
program discovers a
workable collection of
components. Then,
as shown in (b), the
program simplifies the
device by reducing the
number of components
required.

rate indicator returns to the zero position. Thus, in more sophisticated
language, Ulrich's program designed a device to differentiate air pressure.

The second step performed by Ulrich's program was to look for ways
for components to assume multiple functions, thus reducing the number
of components required. Figure 1.2(b) shows the result. The program
eliminated the return pipe by increasing the size of the small gap that
always separates a piston from its enclosing cylinder. Then, the program
eliminated the air reservoir by increasing the length of the cylinder, thus
enabling the cylinder to assume the reservoir function.

Intelligent Systems Can Learn from Examples

Most learning programs are either experience oriented or data oriented.
The goal of work on experience-oriented learning is to discover how programs can learn the way people usually do—by reasoning about new expe-
riences in the light of commonsense knowledge.

The goal of work on data-oriented learning programs is to develop practical programs that can mine databases for exploitable regularities. Among
these data-oriented learning programs, the most well-known is the ID3 system developed by J. Ross Quinlan. ID3 and its descendants have mined
thousands of databases, producing identification rules in areas ranging from
credit assessment to disease diagnosis.

One typical exercise of the technology, undertaken by Quinlan himself, was directed at a database containing information on patients with
hypothyroid disease. This information, provided by the Garvan Institute
of Medical Research in Sydney, described each of several thousand cases of
thyroid disease in terms of 7 continuous variables (such as the measured

level of thyroid-stimulating hormone, TSH), and 16 discrete variables, (such as whether or not the patient had already had thyroid surgery).

From this sea of data, Quinlan's program extracted three straightforward rules for classification of hypothyroid disease:

If	the patient's TSH level is less than 6.05 units
then	the patient's class is *negative*

If	the patient has not had thyroid surgery
	the patient's TSH level is greater than 6.05 units
	the patient's FTI level is less than 64.5 units
then	the patient's class is *primary hypothyroid*

If	the patient is not taking thyroxine
	the patient has not had thyroid surgery
	the patient's TSH level is greater than 6.05 units
	the patient's FTI level is greater than 64.5 units
	the patient's TT4 level is less than 150.5 units
then	the patient's class is *compensated hypothyroid*

Evidently, of the seven continuous and 16 discrete variables available, only five are useful in disease classification.

Intelligent Systems Can Provide Answers to English Questions Using both Structured Data and Free Text

As the Voyager 2 spacecraft concluded its 12-year grand tour of the outer planets, it sent back spectacular images of Neptune's moons and rings, much to the delight of journalists and scientists gathered to witness the event. In cooperation with researchers from the Jet Propulsion Laboratory, Boris Katz invited those journalists and scientists to use his START system to ask questions about the Neptune encounter, the Voyager spacecraft, and the Solar system.

To answer straightforward questions, START accessed a variety of tables, including a distance table supplied by the Voyager navigation team and a time-line table supplied by the Voyager sequencing group. Here are a few representative examples:

- When was Voyager launched?
  The Voyager Spacecraft was launched in Florida on August 20 1977.
- At what time will Voyager lose contact with Earth?
  The Voyager Spacecraft will lose the contact with Earth around 2014.
- How long is the year on Neptune?
  Neptune's period of revolution is about 165 Earth years.

START also answered questions by printing out English text drawn from various space publications, as illustrated by the following representative questions and answers. Note that the critical words in the questions—*color*, *talk*, and *weather*—do not appear in the answers:

- What color is Neptune?
  When you look at a photograph of Neptune, you see the planet's atmosphere and the tops of clouds. Neptune looks bluish because the methane in its atmosphere reflects blue and green frequencies of light. The methane absorbs red and yellow frequencies of sunlight.
- How does Voyager talk to Earth?
  Commands are sent from Earth to one of two receivers on the Voyager spacecraft. Engineering data and scientific information are sent to Earth over two channels. One channel is on all the time, but both channels are on during encounters with the planets. The radio transmitter on the Voyager transmits with about 25 watts of power, or with about the same power as a refrigerator lightbulb. These faint signals are picked up on Earth by ultrasensitive receivers known as the Deep Space Network.
- What's the weather on Neptune?
  Neptune receives about a thousand times less sunlight than the Earth. The temperatures there are thus quite low. Typically, the temperature is about −360 degrees Fahrenheit (−218 degrees Celsius).

Artificial Intelligence Is Becoming Less Conspicuous, yet More Essential

The first applications of artificial intelligence were mostly motivated by the desire of researchers to demonstrate that artificial intelligence is of practical value. Now, as the field is maturing, the development of applications is motivated increasingly by the desire of business people to achieve strategic business goals.

One example of a business-motivated application is the Airport Resource Information System—ARIS—developed by Ascent Technology, Inc., and used by Delta Airlines to help allocate airport gates to arriving flights.

The gate-allocation problem, illustrated in figure 1.3, is difficult at a busy airport, because ARIS must react immediately to arrival and departure changes, such as those imposed by bad weather, and because there are many constraints to consider. One obvious constraint is that you cannot park a large aircraft at a gate designed to handle only small aircraft. Another is that passengers want their connecting flights to be parked at gates that are within easy walking distance. Still another, less obvious constraint is that gate controllers want to avoid potential traffic jams as aircraft move to and from their assigned gates. ARIS handles all these constraints and many more using artificial intelligence methods that include rule-based reasoning, constraint propagation, and spatial planning.

Handling the constraints was not the principal challenge faced by ARIS's developers, however. Other difficult challenges were posed by the need to

Figure 1.3 ARIS helps determine how to manage gate resources at busy airport hubs.

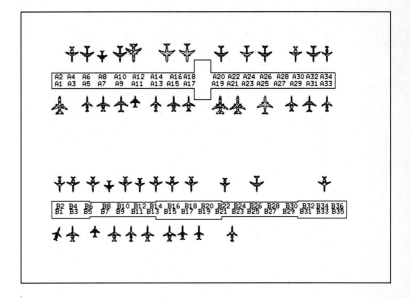

provide human decision makers with a transparent view of current operations, the need to exchange information with mainframe databases, the need to provide rapid, automatic recovery from hardware failures, and the need to distribute all sorts of information to personnel responsible for baggage, catering, passenger service, crew scheduling, and aircraft maintenance. Such challenges require considerable skill in the art of harnessing artificial intelligence ideas with those of other established and emerging technologies.[†]

CRITERIA FOR SUCCESS

Every field needs criteria for success. To determine if research work in artificial intelligence is successful, you should ask three key questions:

- Is the task defined clearly?
- Is there an implemented procedure performing the defined task? If not, much difficulty may be lying under a rug somewhere.
- Is there a set of identifiable regularities or constraints from which the implemented procedure gets its power? If not, the procedure may be an ad hoc toy, capable perhaps of superficially impressive performance on carefully selected examples, but incapable of deeply impressive performance and incapable of helping you to solve any other problem.

[†]Esther Dyson, noted industry analyst, has said that some of the most successful applications of artificial intelligence are those in which the artificial intelligence is spread like raisins in a loaf of raisin bread: the raisins do not occupy much space, but they often provide the principal source of nutrition.

To determine if an application of artificial intelligence is successful, you need to ask additional questions, such as the following:

- Does the application solve a real problem?
- Does the application open up a new opportunity?

Throughout this book, you see examples of research and applications-oriented work that satisfy these criteria: all perform clearly defined tasks; all involve implemented procedures; all involve identified regularities or constraints; and some solve real problems or open up new opportunities.

SUMMARY

- Artificial intelligence is the study of the computations that make it possible to perceive, reason, and act.
- The engineering goal of artificial intelligence is to solve real-world problems; the scientific goal of Artificial Intelligence is to explain various sorts of intelligence.
- Applications of artificial intelligence should be judged according to whether there is a well-defined task, an implemented program, and a set of identifiable principles.
- Artificial intelligence can help us to solve difficult, real-world problems, creating new opportunities in business, engineering, and many other application areas.
- Artificial intelligence sheds new light on questions traditionally asked by psychologists, linguists, and philosophers. A few rays of this new light can help us to be more intelligent.

BACKGROUND

Artificial intelligence has a programming heritage. To understand the ideas introduced in this book in depth, you need to see a few of them embodied in program form. A coordinated book, *LISP,* Third Edition [1989], by Patrick H. Winston and Berthold K. P. Horn, satisfies this need.

ID3 was developed by J. Ross Quinlan [1979, 1983].

KAM is the work of Kenneth M. Yip [1989]. The work on designing a rate-of-descent instrument is that of Karl T. Ulrich [1988].

The work on responding to English questions using both structured data and free text is that of Boris Katz [1990].

2

Semantic Nets and Description Matching

In this chapter, you learn about the role of *representation* in artificial intelligence, and you learn about *semantic nets*, one of the most ubiquitous representations used in artificial intelligence. You also learn about *describe and match*, an important problem-solving method.

By way of illustration, you see how one describe-and-match program, working on semantic-net descriptions, can solve geometric analogy problems of the sort found on intelligence tests. You also see how another describe-and-match program, again working on semantic-net descriptions, can recognize instances of abstractions, such as "mixed blessing" and "retaliation," in semantic nets that capture story plots. The pièce de résistance involves the analysis of O. Henry's intricate short story, "The Gift of the Magi." Both the analogy program and the abstraction program show that simple descriptions, conforming to appropriate representations, can lead to easy problem solving.

Also, you see that the describe-and-match method is effective with other representations, not just with semantic nets. In particular, you see how the describe-and-match method lies underneath the *feature-based approach* to object identification.

Once you have finished this chapter, you will know how to evaluate representations and you will know what representation-oriented questions you should always ask when you are learning how to deal with an unfamiliar class of problems. You will have started your own personal collection of representations and problem-solving methods by learning about semantic

nets, feature spaces, and the describe-and-match method. Finally, you will
have started your own personal collection of case studies that will serve as
useful precedents when you are confronted with new problems.

SEMANTIC NETS

In this section, you learn about what a representation is, a sense in which
most representations are equivalent, and criteria by which representations
can be judged. You also learn about semantic nets, a representation that
sees both direct and indirect service throughout artificial intelligence.

Good Representations Are the Key to Good Problem Solving

In general, a **representation** is a set of conventions about how to describe a class of things. A **description** makes use of the conventions of a
representation to describe some particular thing.

Finding the appropriate representation is a major part of problem solving. Consider, for example, the following children's puzzle:

> **The Farmer, Fox, Goose, and Grain** ─────────────────
> A farmer wants to move himself, a silver fox, a fat goose, and some
> tasty grain across a river. Unfortunately, his boat is so tiny he can
> take only one of his possessions across on any trip. Worse yet, an
> unattended fox will eat a goose, and an unattended goose will eat
> grain, so the farmer must not leave the fox alone with the goose or
> the goose alone with the grain. What is he to do?

Described in English, the problem takes a few minutes to solve because you
have to separate important constraints from irrelevant details. English is
not a good representation.

Described more appropriately, however, the problem takes no time at
all, for everyone can draw a line from the start to the finish in figure 2.1
instantly. Yet drawing that line solves the problem because each boxed
picture denotes a safe arrangement of the farmer and his possessions on the
banks of the river, and each connection between pictures denotes a legal
crossing. The drawing is a good description because the allowed situations
and legal crossings are clearly defined and there are no irrelevant details.

To make such a diagram, you first construct a **node** for each way the
farmer and his three possessions can populate the two banks of the river.
Because the farmer and his three possessions each can be on either of the
two river banks, there are $2^{1+3} = 16$ arrangements, 10 of which are safe in
the sense that nothing is eaten. The six unsafe arrangements place the fox,
the goose, and the grain, on one side or the other; or place the goose and
the grain on one side or the other; or place the fox and the goose on one
side or the other.

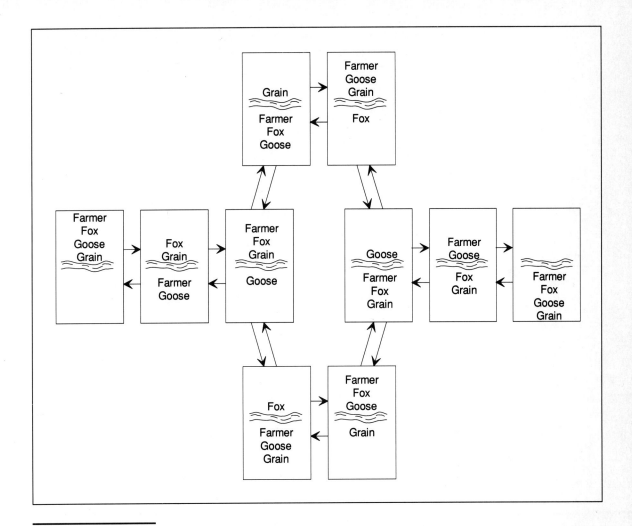

Figure 2.1 The problem of the farmer, fox, goose, and grain. The farmer must get his fox, goose, and grain across the river, from the arrangement on the left to the arrangement on the right. His boat will hold only him and one of his three possessions.

The second and final step is to draw a **link** for each allowable boat trip. For each ordered pair of arrangements, there is a connecting link if and only if the two arrangements meet two conditions: first, the farmer changes sides; and second, at most one of the farmer's possessions changes sides. Because there are 10 safe arrangements, there are $10 \times 9 = 90$ ordered pairs, but only 20 of these pairs satisfy the conditions required for links.

Evidently, the node-and-link description is a good description with respect to the problem posed, for it is easy to make, and, once you have it, the problem is simple to solve.

The important idea illustrated by the farmer, fox, goose, and grain problem is that a good description, developed within the conventions of a good representation, is an open door to problem solving; a bad description, using a bad representation, is a brick wall preventing problem solving.

In this book, the most important ideas—such as the idea that a good representation is important—are called **powerful ideas**; they are highlighted thus:

The **representation principle**:

▷ Once a problem is described using an appropriate representation, the problem is almost solved.

In the rest of this book, you learn about one or two powerful ideas per chapter.

Good Representations Support Explicit, Constraint-Exposing Description

One reason that the node-and-link representation works well with the farmer, fox, goose, and grain problem is that *it makes the important objects and relations explicit.* There is no bothering with the color of the fox or the size of the goose or the quality of the grain; instead, there is an explicit statement about safe arrangements and possible transitions between arrangements.

The representation also is good because *it exposes the natural constraints inherent in the problem.* Some transitions are possible; others are impossible. The representation makes it easy to decide which is true for any particular case: a transition is possible if there is a link; otherwise, it is impossible.

You should always look for such desiderata when you evaluate representations. Here is a list with which you can start, beginning with the two ideas just introduced:

- Good representations make the important objects and relations explicit: You can see what is going on at a glance.
- They expose natural constraints: You can express the way one object or relation influences another.
- They bring objects and relations together: You can see all you need to see at one time, as if through a straw.
- They suppress irrelevant detail: You can keep rarely used details out of sight, but still get to them when necessary.
- They are transparent: You can understand what is being said.
- They are complete: You can say all that needs to be said.
- They are concise: You can say what you need to say efficiently.
- They are fast: You can store and retrieve information rapidly.
- They are computable: You can create them with an existing procedure.

A Representation Has Four Fundamental Parts

With the farmer, fox, goose, and grain problem as a point of reference, you can now appreciate a more specific definition of what a representation is. A **representation** consists of the following four fundamental parts:

■ A **lexical** part that determines which symbols are allowed in the representation's **vocabulary**

■ A **structural** part that describes **constraints** on how the symbols can be arranged

■ A **procedural** part that specifies **access procedures** that enable you to create descriptions, to modify them, and to answer questions using them

■ A **semantic** part that establishes a way of associating **meaning** with the descriptions

In the representation used to solve the farmer, fox, goose, and grain problem, the **lexical** part of the representation determines that nodes and links are involved. The **structural** part specifies that links connect node pairs. The **semantic** part establishes that nodes correspond to arrangements of the farmer and his possessions and links correspond to river traversals. And, as long as you are to solve the problem using a drawing, the **procedural** part is left vague because the access procedures are somewhere in your brain, which provides constructors that guide your pencil and readers that interpret what you see.

Semantic Nets Convey Meaning

The representation involved in the farmer problem is an example of a **semantic net**.

From the lexical perspective, semantic nets consist of **nodes**, denoting objects, **links**, denoting relations between objects, and **link labels** that denote particular relations.

From the structural perspective, nodes are connected to each other by labeled links. In diagrams, nodes often appear as circles, ellipses, or rectangles, and links appear as arrows pointing from one node, the **tail node**, to another node, the **head node**.

From the semantic perspective, the meaning of nodes and links depends on the application.

From the procedural perspective, access procedures are, in general, any one of **constructor procedures**, **reader procedures**, **writer procedures**, or possibly **erasure procedures**. Semantic nets use constructors to make nodes and links, readers to answer questions about nodes and links, writers to alter nodes and links, and, occasionally, erasers to delete nodes and links.

By way of summary, the following specifies what it means to be a semantic net in lexical, structural, semantic, and procedural terms, using an informal specification format that appears throughout the rest of this book:

A **semantic net** is a representation

In which

▷ Lexically, there are nodes, links, and application-specific link labels.

▷ Structurally, each link connects a tail node to a head node.

▷ Semantically, the nodes and links denote application-specific entities.

With constructors that

▷ Construct a node

▷ Construct a link, given a link label and two nodes to be connected

With readers that

▷ Produce a list of all links departing from a given node

▷ Produce a list of all links arriving at a given node

▷ Produce a tail node, given a link

▷ Produce a head node, given a link

▷ Produce a link label, given a link

Such specifications are meant to be a little more precise and consistent than ordinary English phrases, but not stuffily so. In particular, they are not so precise as to constitute a specification of the sort you would find in an official standard for, say, a programming language.

Nevertheless, the specifications are sufficiently precise to show that many of the key representations in artificial intelligence form family groups. Figure 2.2, for example, shows part of the family of representations for which the semantic-net representation is the ultimate ancestor. Although this semantic-net family is large and is used ubiquitously, you should note that it is but one of many that have been borrowed, invented, or reinvented in the service of artificial intelligence.

There Are Many Schools of Thought About the Meaning of Semantics

Arguments about what it means to have a semantics have employed philosophers for millennia. The following are among the alternatives advanced by one school or another:

■ **Equivalence semantics**. Let there be some way of relating descriptions in the representation to descriptions in some other representation that already has an accepted semantics.

Figure 2.2 Part of the semantic-net family of representations. Although many programs explained in this book use one of the family members shown, others use important representations that lie outside of the family.

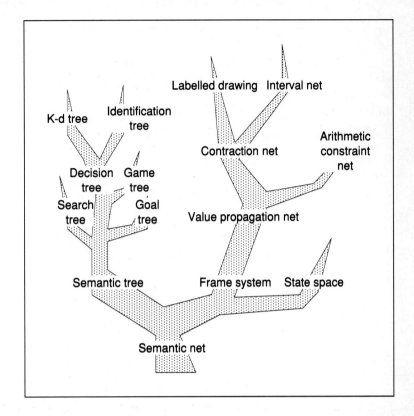

- **Procedural semantics**. Let there be a set of programs that operate on descriptions in the representation. Say that meaning is defined by what the programs do.
- **Descriptive semantics**. Let there be explanations of what descriptions mean in terms we understand intuitively.

From the perspective of descriptive semantics, the net on the left side of figure 2.3 is not a semantic net, because there is neither a prima facie description in terms you understand nor an explanation of what the link labels mean in terms you understand. The net on the right side of figure 2.3, however, is a semantic net, because you naturally tend to ascribe meaning to the links. Asked what the net means, most people would say immediately that it means that an object, known as the lintel, is supported by two other objects, known as posts.

Of course, the objects and relations involved in semantic nets need not be so concrete. The representation used in the farmer illustration is a semantic net because particular arrangements of the farmer and his possessions can be viewed as abstract objects, thereby meriting node status, and allowed river crossings can be viewed as abstract relations, thereby meriting link status.

Figure 2.3 An ordinary net (left) and a semantic net (right). Natural-language labels associate intuitive meanings with nodes and links, thereby producing an informal semantics.

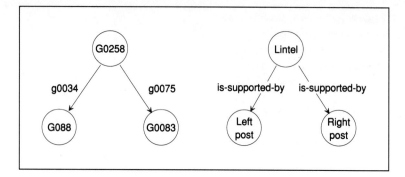

Ultimately, both equivalence semantics and procedural semantics lead back to descriptive semantics. In the case of equivalence semantics, descriptions have meaning because they are equivalent to something that means something to you. In the case of procedural semantics, descriptions have meaning because they cause a program to exhibit a behavior that means something to you. Thus, the alternatives all seem rooted in perceptions to which you ascribe meaning intuitively.

Theoretical Equivalence Is Different from Practical Equivalence

In some uninteresting theoretical sense, any computer-based representation can do anything that any other can do, because computer-based representations are based, ultimately, on arrangements of bits in memory. Consequently, any representation that can be used to represent arrangements of bits can be used as a substratum for the construction of any other representation.

In a practical sense, however, some representations help you to focus on the objects and relations you need to solve a class of problems. One representation, therefore, is more powerful than another because it offers you more convenience even though, theoretically, both can do the same work. *Convenience*, however, is perhaps too weak a word. In general, the good qualities of powerful representations make practicable what would be impracticable with weak representations.

THE DESCRIBE-AND-MATCH METHOD

In this section, you learn about the describe-and-match method; by way of illustration, you learn how the describe-and-match method can be used to identify two-dimensional objects.

As illustrated in figure 2.4 the basic idea behind the **describe-and-match method** is that you can identify an object by first describing it and then searching for a matching description in a description library. The objects involved may be simple physical entities such as the blocks with

Figure 2.4 The describe-and-match paradigm. To identify an object, you describe it, and then you look for a matching description in a description library.

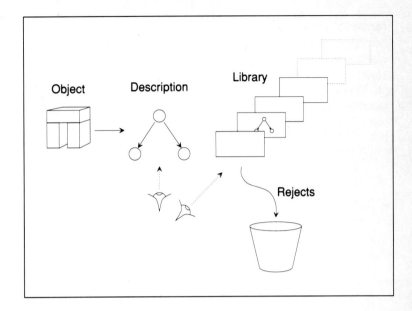

which children play, or complicated abstractions, such as those that emerge in the forthcoming examples.

As you move through this book, you will see many methods, such as the describe-and-match method, reduced to a specification cast in a form that is more precise than ordinary English, yet more transparent than a programming language—particularly a programming language that you do not happen to know. In this book, this informal, half-English, half-program form is called **procedural English**. Here is the describe-and-match method expressed in procedural English:

To identify an object using describe and match,

▷ Describe the object using a suitable representation.

▷ Match the object description against library descriptions until there is a satisfactory match or there are no more library descriptions.

▷ If you find a satisfactory match, announce it; otherwise, announce failure.

In general, procedural English allows all these programming constructs:

■ Steps and substeps, denoted by indentation, much after the fashion of an outline

■ Iterations, denoted by words such as *until* and *for each*

■ Conditional actions, denoted by words such as *if* and *otherwise*

■ Various sorts of tests, denoted variously

Figure 2.5 A feature space. An unknown object is identified according to the distances between its feature point and those of various models. Evidently the unknown is most likely to be a single-hole switch plate.

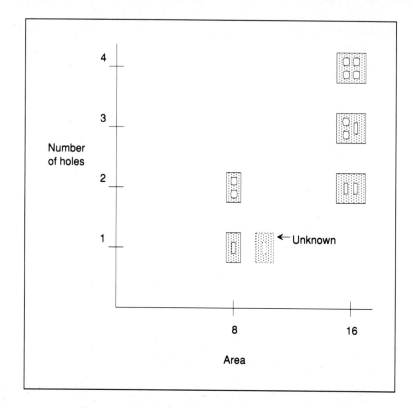

Many good programmers use a notation much like procedural English at the design stage, when they are deciding what a procedure will do. Much of the procedural English then survives in the form of illuminating comments.

Feature-Based Object Identification Illustrates Describe and Match

Feature-based object identification is one of the simplest applications of the describe-and-match method. Feature-based object identifiers consist of a **feature extractor** and a **feature evaluator**. The feature extractor measures simple characteristics such as an object's area. Values obtained by the feature extractor become the coordinates of a **feature point** in **feature space**, a multidimensional space in which there is one dimension for each feature measured. To identify an unknown object, you compare the distances between its feature point and the feature points of various idealized objects. The most likely identity of the unknown object is determined by the smallest distance. Figure 2.5 shows the points corresponding to an unknown object and a family of idealized electrical-box covers in a box-cover feature space.

Generally, speed and discrimination considerations determine which features are used in particular situations. Candidate features for objects

Figure 2.6 An easy problem for the ANALOGY program.

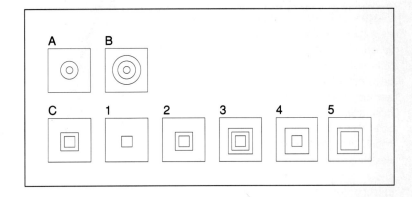

such as electrical-box covers include total object area, hole area, hole count, perimeter length, minimum distance from center of area to edge, maximum distance from center of area to edge, average distance from center of area to edge, length of major axis of ellipse of equal inertia moment, length of minor axis of ellipse of equal inertia moment, total area minus hole area, ratio of hole area to total area, and ratio of perimeter squared to area.

THE DESCRIBE-AND-MATCH METHOD AND ANALOGY PROBLEMS

In this section, you learn that the describe-and-match method, working in harness with a semantic-net representation, produces impressive performance on geometric analogy problems in which the problem, as shown in figure 2.6, is to select an answer figure, X, such that A is to B as C is to X gives the best fit.

One way to start is to *describe* rules that explain how A becomes B and how C becomes each of the answer figures. Then, you can *match* the rule that explains how A becomes B to each rule that explains how C becomes an answer. The best match between rules identifies the best answer. Thus, the describe-and-match paradigm can be used to solve analogy problems.

The key to solving such problems lies in good rule descriptions. The ANALOGY program, described in this section, does its job by matching rule descriptions together and measuring description similarity.

Geometric Analogy Rules Describe Object Relations and Object Transformations

ANALOGY uses two-part rules. One rule part describes how the objects are arranged in the source and destination figures. One object may be above, to the left of, or inside of another. The other rule part describes how the objects in the source figure are transformed into objects in the destination figure. An object may be scaled, rotated, or reflected, or may be subject

Figure 2.7 A rule described as a geometric analogy net, which is a kind of semantic net. Rule descriptions consist of object-relation descriptions and object-transformation descriptions. Links shown solid describe relations among source objects and among destination objects. Links shown dotted describe how objects are transformed between the source and the destination.

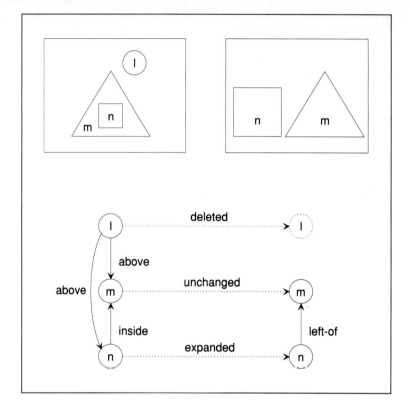

to some combination of these operations. Also, an object may be added or deleted.

A typical rule can be described using a semantic-net representation, as illustrated in figure 2.7. This representation is not just any semantic net, of course—it is one that is specialized to describe rules:

A **geometric analogy net** is a representation

That is a semantic net

In which

▷ The nodes denote dots, circles, triangles, squares, rectangles, and other geometric objects.

▷ Some links denote relations among figures objects, specifically inside, above, and to the left of.

▷ Other links describe how figure objects are transformed. The possibilities are addition, deletion, expansion, contraction, rotation, and reflection, and combinations of these operations.

Figure 2.8 Two circles, one
of which is inside a polygon.
One object is inside another if
a line drawn to infinity crosses
the boundary of the potentially
surrounding object an odd
number of times. Thus, one
circle is inside; the other is not.

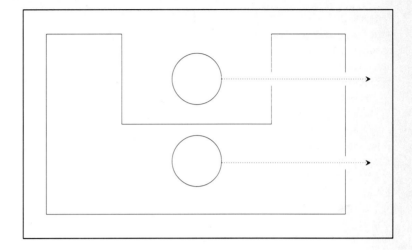

Figure 2.8 Two circles, one of which is inside a polygon. One object is inside another if a line drawn to infinity crosses the boundary of the potentially surrounding object an odd number of times. Thus, one circle is inside; the other is not.

You could write this specification for geometric analogy nets, of course, without any reference to semantic nets, by importing all the descriptive elements from the semantic-net specification. The alternative shown is better, not only because it saves space, but also because it focuses on exactly what you need to add to transform the general concept into a representation tailored to a particular circumstance. As you can see, transforming the semantic-net concept into a geometric analogy net requires only the application-specific recitation of which link labels are allowed and what the nodes and links denote.

ANALOGY uses a simple idea, illustrated in figure 2.8, to decide whether Inside, rather than either Left-of or Above, is the appropriate relation between objects. First, ANALOGY makes sure that the objects do not touch. Then, ANALOGY constructs a line from any point on one figure to infinity, as shown in figure 2.8. If the line crosses the second figure an odd number of times, then the second figure surrounds the first. Happily, this method involves only simple line-crossing tests, and it works even if the figures are extremely convoluted.

As shown in figure 2.9, ANALOGY uses another simple procedure to compute the spatial relationship between two objects. ANALOGY computes the center of area of each of the two objects, constructs diagonal lines through the center of area of one of them, and notes which region contains the center of area of the other object. Because the relations used are symmetric, it is not necessary to note both left and right relations.

Finally, ANALOGY uses a matching procedure to decide if an object in one figure can be transformed into an object in another figure by a combination of scaling, rotation, and reflection operations. The dotted links in figure 2.7 mark objects that pass this transformation test.

Now that you have seen how rules are constructed, you can see that the example in figure 2.10 is contrived so as to depend on only relations

Figure 2.9 A square to the left of a rectangle. Relations between objects are determined by comparing centers of area.

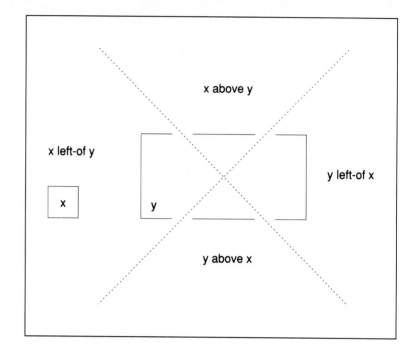

between objects. No object transformations can influence the solution, because no objects are transformed in the move from the source figure to the destination figure.

It is clear that the C-to-3 rule best matches the A-to-B rule because, with l associated with x and m associated with y, the two rules match exactly.

Note, however, that there is no a priori reason to associate l with x rather than with y. In going from the source figure to the destination figure, you want to be sure that squares go to squares, circles to circles, triangles to triangles, and so on. But this need to match one object to a geometrically similar object does not hold in comparing two rules. In the example, answer 3 is to be selected even though the objects in A and B are a triangle and a square, whereas in C and in all the answer figures, the objects are a circle and a dot. In general, ANALOGY must try all possible ways of associating the nodes when matching rules.

This one-for-one association of variables implies that the number of objects that move from the source figure to the destination figure must be the same in both of the two rules. The number of additions and deletions must be the same as well. Any attempt to match two rules for which the numbers are different fails immediately.

If n objects move from the source figure to the destination figure in each of two rules being compared, there will be $n!$ ways of associating the variables in searching for the best way to match the rules. More generally,

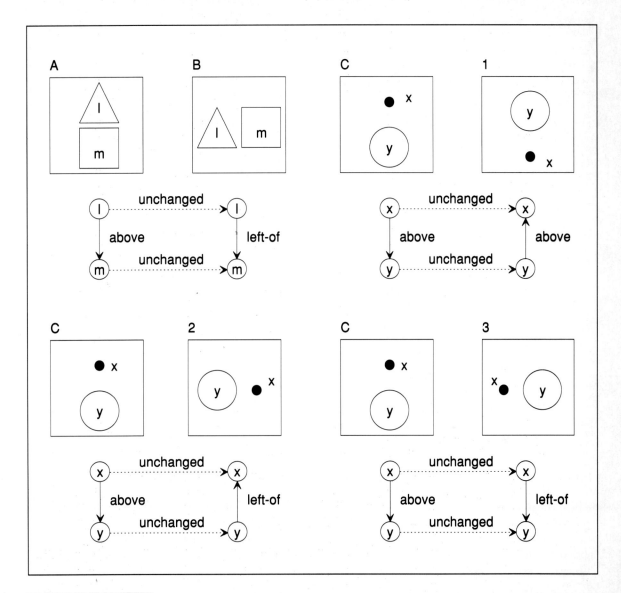

Figure 2.10 A problem whose solution is determined by relations only. Comparison of the rule descriptions verifies that the C-to-3 rule matches best.

if n_1 objects move, n_2 are added, and n_3 deleted, in going to the destination figure, then $n_1! \, n_2! \, n_3!$ is the number of possible associations. All must be tried.

In the example, there are two possible ways to associate the objects, because $n_1 = 2$, $n_2 = 0$, and $n_3 = 0$. Specifically, ANALOGY can associate l with x and m with y, or ANALOGY can associate l with y and m with x.

The previous example involves only relations between objects, because no objects are transformed. Symmetrically, for the problem in figure 2.11, there is only one object in each figure, so there are no relations between

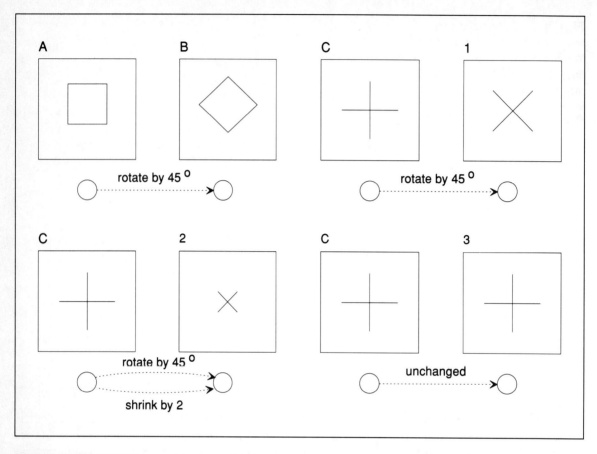

objects, and only object transformations can matter. ANALOGY concludes
that the C-to-1 rule best matches the A-to-B rule, because only answer 1
corresponds to a simple 45° rotation with no reflection or scale change.

Scoring Mechanisms Rank Answers

How should ANALOGY measure the similarity of two rules? So far, the
examples have been so simple that the best answer rule matches the A-to-
B rule exactly. But if an exact match cannot be found, then ANALOGY
must rank the inexact matches. One way to do this ranking is to count the
number of matching elements in the two rules involved in each match, as
shown in figure 2.12.

To tune the counting a bit, you can weight relations describing object transformations less heavily than you weight relations describing relations among objects. Assuming that relations among objects each add
one point to the total score, then less than one point should be added for
each object-transformation relation. Experimentally, the numbers shown
in figure 2.13 work well. A radically different set of numbers would reflect

Figure 2.12 Rule similarity, measured by degree of overlap. You determine the answers by finding the C-to-X rule with the maximum number of elements in common with the A-to-B rule.

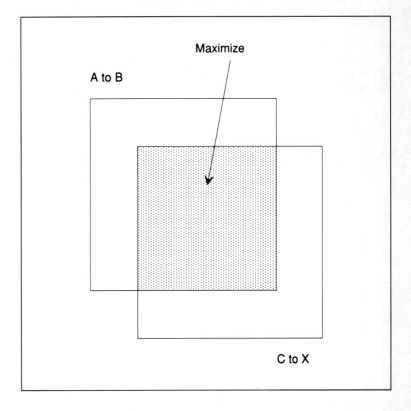

a different judgment about how the various possibilities should be ordered. The given set is biased toward rotations and against reflections. A different set might indicate the opposite preference. The corresponding variations on ANALOGY would occasionally disagree with one another about the answers.

Of course, it is possible to elaborate the measure of similarity in other directions. Suppose, for example, that S_{AB} is the set of elements in the A-to-B rule, and that S_{CX} is the set of elements in the C-to-X rule. Then, $S_{AB} \cap S_{CX}$ is the set of elements that appear in both rules, $S_{AB} - S_{CX}$ is the set of elements appearing in the A-to-B rule but not in the C-to-X rule, and $S_{CX} - S_{AB}$ is the set of elements appearing in only the C-to-X rule. With these sets in hand, you can use the following formula to measure similarity:

$$\text{Similarity} = \alpha \times \text{Size}(S_{AB} \cap S_{CX})$$
$$- \beta \times \text{Size}(S_{AB} - S_{CX})$$
$$- \gamma \times \text{Size}(S_{CX} - S_{AB})$$

where α, β, and γ are weights, and Size is the function that computes the number of elements in a set. If $\beta = 0$, $\gamma = 0$, and $\alpha = 1$, the formula reduces to counting the common elements. If β and γ are not the same, the formula gives asymmetric similarity judgments, allowing, for example,

Figure 2.13 Weights determine transformation-description contributions to similarity scores.

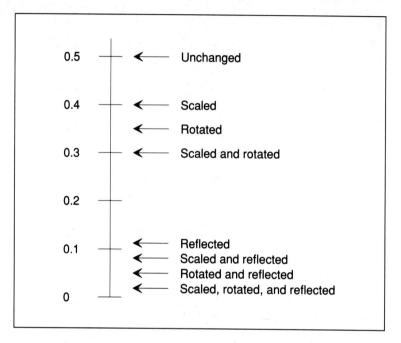

the A-to-B rule to be more similar to the C-to-X rule than the C-to-X rule is to the A-to-B rule.

Be skeptical about such formulas, however. Viewed as a representation for importance, a set of weights is not explicit and exposes little constraint.

Ambiguity Complicates Matching

So far, all the objects in the source and destination figures have distinct shapes. Consequently, it is easy to decide how to form the rule describing the transformation. In situations such as the one shown in figure 2.14, however, there is ambiguity because there is no way to know which of the two triangles has disappeared. Perhaps the larger one is gone; alternatively the smaller one may have been deleted and the larger one may have shrunk.

In fact, you cannot judge either explanation to be superior without considering the other figures given in the problem. Consequently, ANALOGY must construct two rules, one corresponding to each way the triangles in the source figure can be identified with triangles in the destination. In general, for each source and destination pair, many rules are possible; and, for each rule, there may be many ways to match it against another rule.

Good Representation Supports Good Performance

Examine figure 2.15. It shows three examples, drawn from intelligence tests, that are well within the grasp of the ANALOGY procedure. In the first example, the most reasonable theory about the rule for going from A to B is that the inside object is deleted. The C-to-3 rule is the same, and

Figure 2.14 An ambiguous change. The large triangle may have been deleted; alternatively, the small one may have been deleted and the large one shrunk.

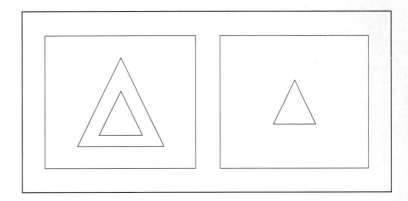

answer 3 is the best answer, with answer 4 a close second. Answer 4 would be the clear winner if answer 3 were not present.

In the second example, answer 3 is the correct answer. Actually, answer 3 is the only answer figure that ANALOGY considers seriously, because among the answer figures, only answer 3 has the same number of objects as B has. Remember that requiring the same number of objects is an indirect consequence of permitting a match only between rules for which the numbers of movements, additions, and deletions are the same.

In the third example, the A-to-B rule could be described as either a rotation or a reflection, with answer 2 being the best answer if the process prefers rotations, and with answer 1 being the best answer if it likes reflections better. ANALOGY prefers rotations, and judges answer 2 to be best.

THE DESCRIBE-AND-MATCH METHOD AND RECOGNITION OF ABSTRACTIONS

In this section, you learn that the describe-and-match method, again working in harness with a semantic-net representation, can be used to recognize abstractions in story plots. In combination with what you have already learned about the describe-and-match method and semantic nets, you see that both have a broad reach.

Story Plots Can Be Viewed as Combinations of Mental States and Events

To describe plots using a semantic net, you need a vocabulary of node types and link labels. Happily, you soon see that you can do a lot with a vocabulary of just three node types and three link labels. The three node types are mental states, denoted by MS in diagrams; positive events, denoted by $+$; and negative events, denoted by $-$. The link labels are i, an acronym for initiates, meaning that the mental state or event at the tail of an i link leads to the one at the head of the link; t, for terminates,

Figure 2.15 Three problems solved successfully by ANALOGY.

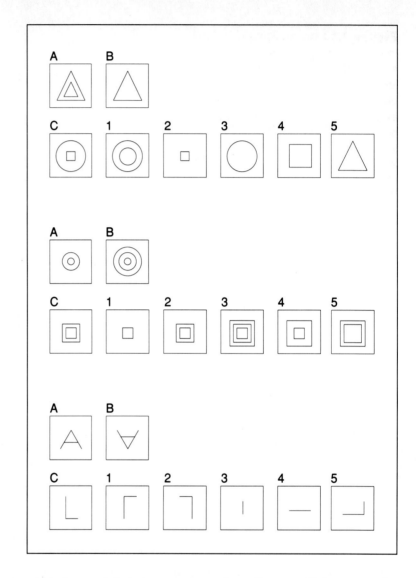

meaning that the mental state or event at the tail turns off the one at the head; and *c*, for corefers, meaning that the mental state or event at the tail refers to the same mental state or event as the one at the head. Links labeled with *c* have two heads: **double-headed links** are a notational shorthand for pairs of identically labeled single-headed links pointing in opposite directions.

With three node types and three link labels, there could be as many as $3 \times 3 \times 3 = 27$ node–link–node combinations. Of these 27 possibilities, 15 have a natural, easily stated interpretation, and each of these is called a **base unit**. In figure 2.16, for example, four base units are exhibited,

Figure 2.16 Combinations in which mental states and events initiate one another. Mental states may initiate positive events or negative events and vice versa. The four possible combinations constitute instances of *success*, *failure*, *enablement*, and *motivation*, all of which are base units.

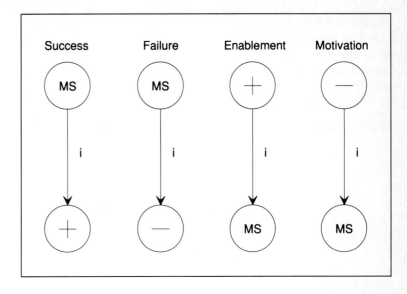

each of which involves a mental state that initiates an event, or vice versa. As shown, if a mental state initiates an event, you have what is casually called a *success* or a *failure*, depending on the sign of the event. If an event initiates a mental state, we witness *enablement* or *motivation*, again depending on the sign.

Another group of base units is shown in figure 2.17. This time, each of the base units involves two mental states. When one mental state initiates another, we say that *recursion* has occurred. When one terminates another, we have a *change of mind*. If a mental state persists over a period of time, the individual involved is exhibiting *perseverance*.

The final group of base units is shown in figure 2.18. Now there are no mental states at all; there are only events joined by termination or coreference. The eight combinations are *positive tradeoff* and *negative tradeoff*, *positive coreference* and *negative coreference*, *loss* and *resolution*, and *mixed blessing* and *hidden blessing*.

In descriptions, base units often overlap, producing recognizable aggregates. Let us call these aggregates **composite units**. Together, base units and composite units constitute **abstraction units**. Figure 2.19 shows a composite unit consisting of a *success* base unit joined, by its positive event, to a *loss* base unit. When a success is followed by a loss, in normal language we often say that "the success was fleeting," or use words to that effect. Hence, this composite unit is called *fleeting success*.

Other examples of composite units are shown in figure 2.20. Each composite unit in the figure consists of a negative event, followed by a mental state, followed by a positive event. The composite units differ because they involve different links, and, hence, different base units. Motivation followed by success yields *success born of adversity*; motivation followed by

Figure 2.17 Mental states joined by *initiate*, *terminate*, or *corefer* links. The three possible combinations constitute instances of *recursion*, *change of mind*, and *perseverance* base units.

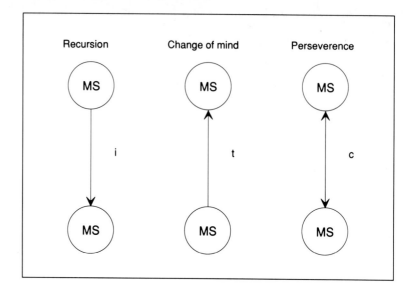

a positive event that terminates the motivation-producing negative event is a matter of *fortuitous success*; and finally, motivation followed by a success involving a positive event that terminates the motivation-producing negative event is *intentional problem resolution*.

When more than one person is involved, more elaborate arrangements are possible. In figure 2.21, for example, the situation from one person's perspective is a *success born of adversity*. In addition, however, the negative event from that person's perspective corefers to a positive event from the other person's perspective. Similarly, the positive event corefers to a negative event. These additions, together with the *success born of adversity*, constitute *retaliation*.

Abstraction-Unit Nets Enable Summary

To recognize abstractions in a story plot, you first *describe* the story plots in terms of nodes, representing mental states and events, and links, representing relations among those mental states and events. Then you *match* the nodes and links with items in a catalog of named abstraction units. Consider, for example, the following story about Thomas and Albert:

Thomas and Albert ————————————————————

Thomas and Albert respected each other's technical judgment and decided to form a company together. Thomas learned that Albert was notoriously absentminded, whereupon he insisted that Albert have nothing to do with the proposed company's finances. This angered Albert so much that he backed out of their agreement, hoping that Thomas would be disappointed.

Figure 2.18 Positive events and negative events joined by terminate or coreference links. The possible combinations constitute instances of eight base units: *positive tradeoff, loss, resolution, negative tradeoff, positive coreference, mixed blessing, hidden blessing,* and *negative coreference.*

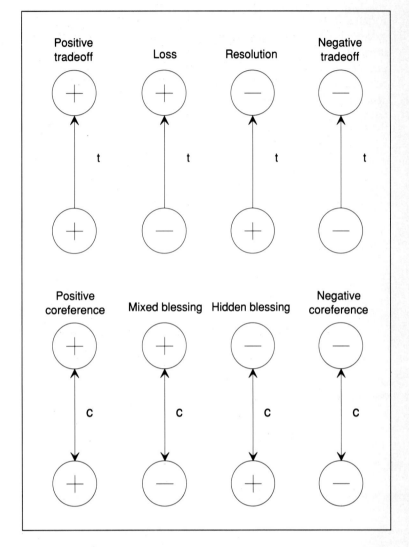

Figure 2.22 shows what "Thomas and Albert" looks like in semantic-net terms. The *respect* abstraction is captured by the two mental states at the top. Those mental states initiate the decision to form a company, a positive event from both Thomas's and Albert's points of view. Thomas's discovery about Albert is a negative event, which leads to a mental state in which Thomas thinks about the company's finances, which leads to his insistence that Albert keep out of them, a positive event as far as Thomas is concerned. The insistence is a negative event from Albert's perspective, however. For Albert, the insistence leads to a mental state that leads to backing out of the agreement, which Albert views now as a positive event and Thomas views as a negative one.

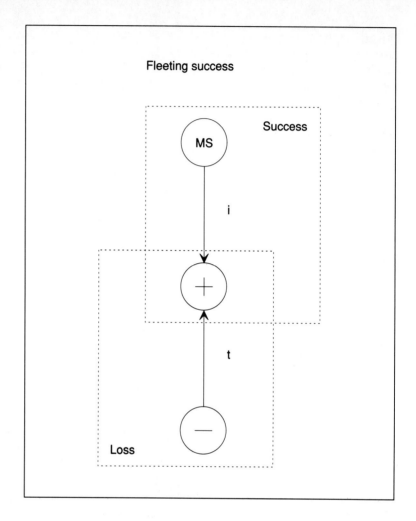

Figure 2.19 Base units joined to produce larger, composite units. In this illustration, a *success* unit and a *loss* unit, both basic, join to produce a *fleeting success* composite unit.

Now think of the diagram as a mine for abstraction units. Digging a little reveals that there are six abstraction units that are not wholly contained in some higher-level abstraction unit. These are called **top-level units**. In this particular example, the top-level units are connected to each other by exactly one shared mental state or one shared event.

Figure 2.23 shows the resulting arrangement of top-level units, in the form of a top-level abstraction net, with the top-level units shown in the same relative positions that their pieces occupied in figure 2.22.

To summarize a plot using a top-level abstraction net, you describe the central top-level unit first. Then, you describe the surrounding top-level units and explain how those top-level units are related to the central top-level unit. For the "Thomas and Albert" story, you would produce the following result:

Figure 2.20 Three different composite units. In this illustration, a negative event always is followed by a mental state that is followed by a positive event. In the first case, a *motivation* base unit is followed by a *success* base unit producing an instance of *success born of adversity*. In the second, the *success* unit disappears and a *resolution* unit appears, producing a *fortuitous success*. In the third, *success* reappears, joining the other two, producing an *intentional problem resolution*.

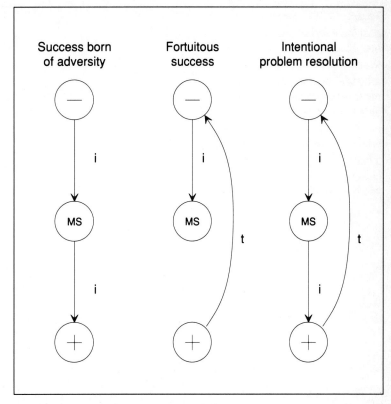

A Summary of Thomas and Albert ────────────────
Albert *retaliated* against Thomas because Thomas went through an *intentional problem resolution* that was bad for Albert. The *retaliation* caused a *loss* for Thomas and a *positive tradeoff* for Albert. The *loss* reversed Thomas's previous *success*, and the *positive tradeoff* reversed Albert's previous *success*.

In addition to enabling summary, top-level abstraction nets allow you to compare and contrast two situations, even when those two situations are superficially quite different. Consider the following story about John and Mary, for example:

John and Mary ────────────────────────────
John and Mary loved each other and decided to be married. Just before the wedding, John discovered that Mary's father was secretly smuggling stolen art through Venice. After struggling with his conscience for days, John reported Mary's father to the police. Mary understood John's decision, but she despised him for it nevertheless; she broke their engagement knowing that he would suffer.

Figure 2.21 Mental states, positive events, and negative events linked across perspectives. In this illustration, there are two perspectives. Each perspective involves a positive event that is seen as a negative event in the other. This particular combination of perspectives, events, and a mental state is called a *retaliation*.

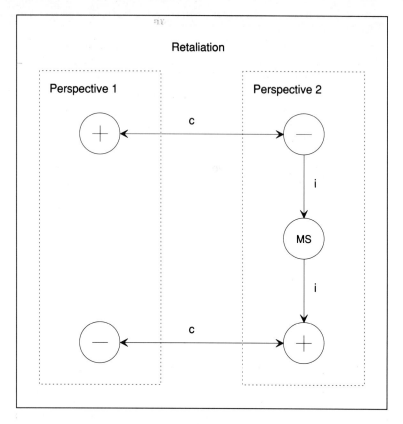

On the surface, "John and Mary" seems to have little resemblance to "Thomas and Albert." More abstractly, however, both involve a central *retaliation* brought on by an *intentional problem resolution* leading eventually to a *loss* and a *positive tradeoff*, both of which finish off a previous *success*. Such similarities are easy to see, once top-level abstraction nets are constructed: the stories' diagrams are exactly the same.

Of course, more complicated stories will have more complicated top-level abstraction nets. Consider, for example, "The Gift of the Magi," a story by O. Henry, with the following plot:

The Gift of the Magi ————————————————
Della and her husband, Jim, were very poor. Nevertheless, because Christmas was approaching, each wanted to give something special to the other. Della cut off and sold her beautiful hair to buy an expensive watch fob for Jim's heirloom gold watch. Meanwhile, Jim sold his watch to buy some wonderful combs for Della's hair. When they found out what they had done, they were sad for a moment, but soon realized that they loved each other so much, nothing else mattered.

Figure 2.22 Two stories viewed as aggregates of abstraction units, both base and composite. In this illustration, there are two perspectives, Thomas's and Albert's, and six top-level abstraction units.

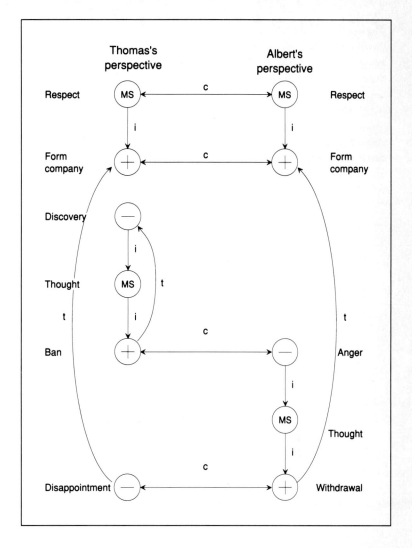

Figure 2.24 shows one plausible set of nodes and links for the story; those nodes and links lead to the top-level abstraction net shown in figure 2.25.

Abstraction Units Enable Question Answering

Abstraction units allow you to answer certain questions by matching. Here are examples:

■   What is the story about? Answer by naming the central abstraction unit in the top-level abstraction net. For example, "Thomas and Albert" is about *retaliation*.

■   What is the result? Answer by naming the abstraction units that are joined to earlier abstraction units in the top-level abstraction net, but

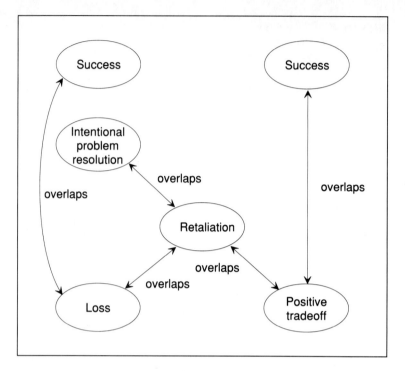

Figure 2.23 A top-level abstraction net formed from the top-level units of figure 2.22. This top-level abstraction net enables you to build a summary description around the most highly linked top-level unit, the *retaliation*.

not to later abstraction units. For example, the result in "Thomas and Albert" is a *loss* and a *positive tradeoff*.

■ Does the story involve a certain abstraction? Answer by checking for the appropriate abstraction unit. For example, "Thomas and Albert" does contain an instance of *intentional problem resolution*.

■ In what way is one story like another? Answer by naming the most highly connected abstraction unit that appears in both top-level abstraction nets. If hard pressed, enumerate the other abstraction units that appear in both. For example, "Thomas and Albert" is like "John and Mary" in that both involve *retaliation*. Moreover, both involve *success, intentional problem resolution, loss*, and *positive tradeoff*.

In all these examples, you could give more detailed answers by naming the people and the events involved in the abstraction units mentioned.

Abstraction Units Make Patterns Explicit

In this section, you have seen how a base-unit semantic net facilitates similarity analysis and summary by making mental states, events, and links between them explicit. Thus, the first criterion of good representation—that something important is made usefully explicit—is satisfied. Some people argue, however, that a base-unit semantic net does not yet pass the computability criterion for good representation because there is no fully specified way to translate text into abstraction-unit patterns.

Figure 2.24 The mental states, positive events, and negative events of "The Gift of the Magi."

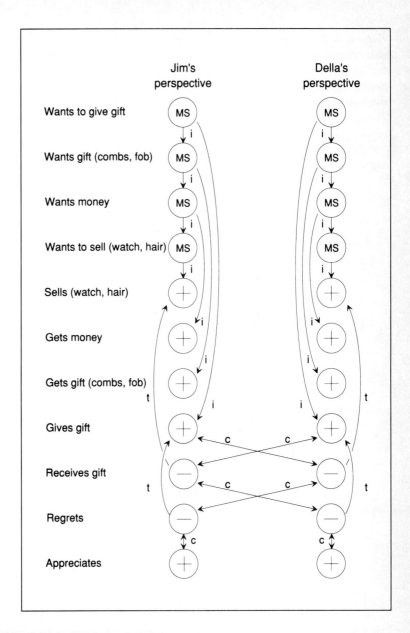

PROBLEM SOLVING AND UNDERSTANDING KNOWLEDGE

When approaching a new class of problems, to be solved either by you or by a computer, you always should start by asking yourself certain **questions about knowledge**. This section discusses a few questions about knowledge that are particularly important.

Figure 2.25 The top-level abstraction unit net for "The Gift of the Magi." All links are *overlaps* links.

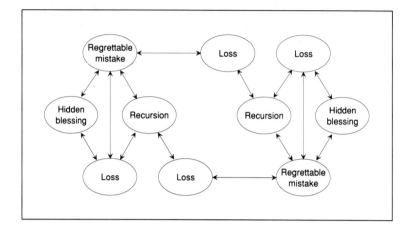

■   What kind of knowledge is involved?

Perhaps the important knowledge concerns the description of concrete or abstract objects. Alternatively, perhaps the important knowledge is about a problem-solving method.

■   How should the knowledge be represented?

Some knowledge may, for example, fit nicely within the semantic-net framework. Other knowledge is best embedded in a collection of procedures. There are many possibilities.

■   How much knowledge is required?

After learning what kind of knowledge is involved in a task, this question should be the one you ask. Are there 40 things to know, or 400, or 4,000?

One reason to ask about quantity is that you must consider the demand for sensible resource allocation among the various chores required. Another is that knowing the size of a problem builds courage; even if the size is large, digesting bad news is better than anticipating even worse news unnecessarily.

In any event, the tendency is to overestimate grossly; after seeing that a task is reasonably complicated, it is easy to suppose that it is unimaginably complicated. But many tasks can be performed with human-level competence using only a little knowledge.

■   What exactly is the knowledge needed?

Ultimately, of course, you need the knowledge. To do geometric analogy problems, you need to know what relations are possible between figure parts, and you need to know how parts can change. To recognize abstractions, you need a library of base and composite abstraction units. Much of learning any subject, from electromagnetic theory to genetics, is a matter of collecting such knowledge.

SUMMARY

- Once a problem has been described using an appropriate representation, the problem is almost solved.
- A representation consists of a lexical part, a structural part, a procedural part, and a semantic part.
- There are many schools of thought about the meaning of semantics. Ultimately, meaning always seems to be rooted in human perception and human intuition.
- Feature-based object identification illustrates the describe-and-match method. An unknown object is identified with an idealized object if their feature points are nearest neighbors in feature space.
- Geometric analogy rules describe object relations and object transformations. You solve geometric analogy problems by determining which rules are most similar.
- Story plots can be viewed as combinations of mental states and events.
- Abstraction-unit nets enable certain kinds of summary and question answering.
- Good representations make important objects and relations explicit, expose natural constraints, and bring objects and relations together.

BACKGROUND

The discussion of geometric analogy problems is based on work by Thomas Evans [1963]. The discussion of plot units is based on the work of Wendy Lehnert; the "John and Mary" story and the analysis of "The Gift of the Magi," in particular, are adapted from one of her highly influential papers [1981].

Feature vectors, and object identification using feature vectors, are described in more detail in *Robot Vision*, by Berthold K. P. Horn [1984].

3

Generate and Test
Means-Ends Analysis
and Problem Reduction

In this chapter, you learn about three powerful problem-solving methods: *generate and test*, *means–ends analysis*, and *problem reduction*. You also learn about two new representations, both of which can be viewed as special cases of the semantic-net representation introduced in Chapter 2. One is the *state-space representation*, introduced in the discussion of means–ends analysis, and another is the *goal tree*, introduced in the discussion of problem reduction.

By way of illustration, you see how a program can find the combination to a safe, plan a route from one city to another, and solve motion-planning problems in a world populated by a child's blocks.

Once you have finished this chapter, you will be able to identify and deploy three more problem-solving methods and two more representations, thus adding considerably to your personal representation and method collections. You will also begin to see that you yourself use similar representations and methods daily as you solve problems.

THE GENERATE-AND-TEST METHOD

Problem solvers adhering to the **generate-and-test paradigm** use two basic modules, as illustrated in figure 3.1. One module, the **generator**,

Figure 3.1 The generate-and-test method involves a generator and a tester.

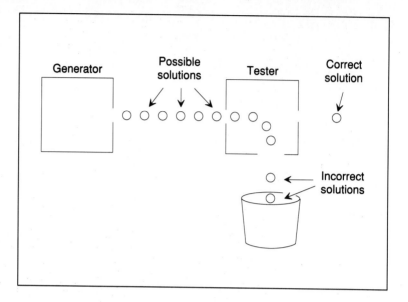

enumerates possible solutions. The second, the **tester**, evaluates each proposed solution, either accepting or rejecting that solution.

The generator may generate all possible solutions before the tester takes over; more commonly, however, generation and testing are interdigitated. Action may stop when one acceptable solution is found, or action may continue until some satisfactory number of solutions is found, or action may continue until all possible solutions are found. Here is the interdigitated, stop-when-acceptable version in procedural English:

To perform generate and test,

▷ Until a satisfactory solution is found or no more candidate solutions can be generated,

  ▷ Generate a candidate solution.

  ▷ Test the candidate solution.

▷ If an acceptable solution is found, announce it; otherwise, announce failure.

In the rest of this section, you learn more about the generate-and-test method, you learn which sort of problems the generate-and-test method solves, and you learn several criteria that good generators always satisfy.

Generate-and-Test Systems Often Do Identification

The generate-and-test paradigm is used most frequently to solve identification problems. In identification problems, the generator is said to produce *hypotheses.*

Figure 3.2 Burgling a safe using the generate-and-test paradigm. The generator is the procedure that the burglar uses to select and dial combinations. The tester is the procedure that the burglar uses to work the handle. Careful safecrackers make sure that they try all possibilities, without any repeats, until a twist of the handle opens the safe.

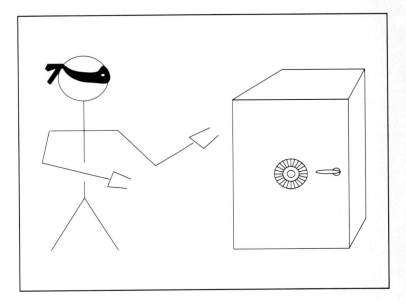

To use the generate-and-test paradigm to identify, say, a tree, you can reach for a tree book, then thumb through it page by page, stopping when you find a picture that looks like the tree to be identified. Thumbing through the book is the generation procedure; matching the pictures to the tree is the testing procedure.

To use generate and test to burgle a three-number, two-digit safe, you can start with the combination 00-00-00, move to 00-00-01, and continue on through all possible combinations until the door opens. Of course, the counting is the generation procedure, and the twist of the safe handle is the testing procedure.

The burglar in figure 3.2 may take some time to crack the safe with this approach, however, for there are $100^3 = 1$ million combinations. At three per minute, figuring that he will have to go through half of the combinations, on average, to succeed, the job will take about 16 weeks, if he works 24 hours per day.

Good Generators Are Complete, Nonredundant, and Informed

It is obvious that good generators have three properties:

- Good generators are complete: They eventually produce all possible solutions.
- Good generators are nonredundant: They never compromise efficiency by proposing the same solution twice.
- Good generators are informed: They use possibility-limiting information, restricting the solutions that they propose accordingly.

Informability is important, because otherwise there are often too many solutions to go through. Consider the tree-identification example. If it is winter and a tree you are trying to identify is bare, you do not bother going through a tree book's conifer section.

Similarly, if a burglar knows, somehow, that all of the numbers in a safe combination are prime numbers in the range from 0 to 99, then he can confine himself to $25^3 = 15625$ numbers, getting the safe open in less than 2 days, on the average, instead of in 16 weeks.

THE MEANS-ENDS ANALYSIS METHOD

The **state** of a system is a description that is sufficient to determine the future. In a **state space**, each node denotes a **state**, and each link denotes a possible one-step **transition** from one state to another state:

A **state space** is a representation

That is a semantic net

In which

▷ The nodes denote states.

▷ The links denote transitions between states.

Thus, a state space is a member of the semantic-net family of representations introduced in Chapter 2.

In the context of problem solving, states correspond to where you are or might be in the process of solving a problem. Hence, the **current state** corresponds to where you are, the **goal state** corresponds to where you want to be, and the problem is to find a sequence of transitions that leads from the **initial state** to the goal state.

In the rest of this section, you learn about means–ends analysis, a standard method for selecting transitions. You also learn about one popular way to implement means–ends analysis using a simple table.

The Key Idea in Means-Ends Analysis Is to Reduce Differences

The purpose of **means–ends analysis** is to identify a procedure that causes a transition from the current state to the goal state, or at least to an intermediate state that is closer to the goal state. Thus, the identified procedure reduces the observed **difference** between the current state and the goal state.

Consider the states shown in figure 3.3. Solid-line nodes identify the current state and the goal state. Dotted-line nodes correspond to states that are not yet known to exist. Descriptions of the current state, or of the goal state, or of the difference between those states, may contribute to the identification of a difference-reducing procedure.

In figure 3.4, a sequence of procedures $P1, \ldots, P5$ cause transitions from state to state, starting from the initial current state. Each of the

DENDRAL Analyzes Mass Spectrograms

DENDRAL is one of the great classic application programs. To see what it does, suppose that an organic chemist wants to know the chemical nature of some substance newly created in the test tube. The first step, not the one of concern here, is to determine the number of atoms of various kinds in one molecule of the stuff. This step determines the chemical formula, such as $C_8H_{16}O$. The notation indicates that each molecule has eight atoms of carbon, 16 of hydrogen, and one of oxygen.

Once a sample's chemical formula is known, the chemist may use the sample's mass spectrogram to work out the way the atoms are arranged in the chemical's structure, thus identifying the isomer of the chemical.

The spectrogram machine bombards a sample with high energy electrons, causing the molecules to break up into charged chunks of various sizes. Then, the machine sorts the chunks by passing them through a magnetic field that deflects the high-charge, low-weight ones more than it does the low-charge, high-weight ones. The deflected chunks are collected, forming a spectrogram like the following:

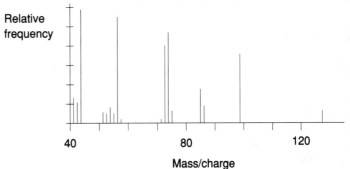

The purpose of DENDRAL is to work, like a knowledgeable chemist, from a chemical formula and spectrogram to a deduced structure, producing a chemical structure like this:

$$CH_3 - CH_2 - C - CH_2 - CH_2 - CH_2 - CH_2 - CH_3$$
$$\|$$
$$O$$

The DENDRAL program works out structures from chemical formulas and mass spectrograms using the generate-and-test method. The generator consists of a structure enumerator and a synthesizer that produces a synthetic mass spectrogram by simulating the action of a real mass spectrometer on each enumerated structure.

The structure enumerator ensures that the overall generator is complete and nonredundant because the structure enumerator uses a provably complete and nonredundant structure-enumeration procedure. The overall generator is also informed, because the structure enumerator uses the chemical formula and knowledge about necessary and forbidden substructures.

The tester compares the real mass spectrogram with those produced by the generator. The possible structures are those whose synthetic spectrograms match the real one adequately. The structure judged correct is the one whose synthetic spectrogram most closely matches the real one.

Figure 3.3 Means–ends analysis involves states and procedures for reducing differences between states. The current state and goal state are shown solid; other states, not yet encountered, are shown dotted.

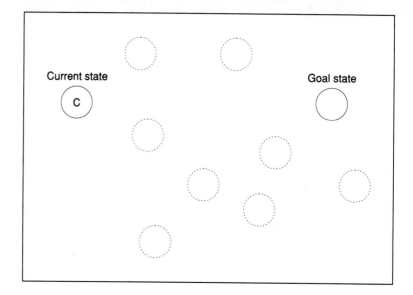

Figure 3.4 Means–ends analysis produces a path through state space. The current state, the goal state, and a description of their difference determine which procedure to try next. Note that the procedures are expected, but not guaranteed, to cause a transition to a state that is nearer the goal state than is the current state.

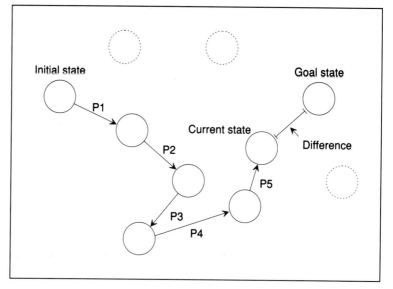

procedures is selected because it is believed to be relevant to reducing the difference between the state in which it was applied and the goal state. Note, however, that procedure P3 takes the problem solver farther away from the goal; there is no built-in mechanism preventing backward steps in the most general form of means–ends analysis. Fortunately, procedure P4 and procedure P5 take the problem solver back toward the goal.

In summary, here is the means–ends procedure expressed, more precisely, in procedural English:

To perform means–ends analysis,

▷ Until the goal is reached or no more procedures are available,

  ▷ Describe the current state, the goal state, and the difference between the two.

  ▷ Use the difference between the current state and goal state, possibly with the description of the current state or goal state, to select a promising procedure.

  ▷ Use the promising procedure and update the current state.

▷ If the goal is reached, announce success; otherwise, announce failure.

Difference-Procedure Tables Often Determine the Means

Whenever the description of the difference between the current state and the goal state is the key to which procedure to try next, a simple **difference-procedure table** may suffice to connect difference descriptions to preferred procedures.[†]

Consider, for example, a travel situation in which the problem is to find a way to get from one city to another. One traveler's preferences might link the preferred transportation procedure to the difference between states, described in terms of the distance between the cities involved, via the following difference-procedure table:

Distance	Airplane	Train	Car
More than 300 miles	√		
Between 100 and 300 miles		√	
Less than 100 miles			√

Thus, the difference-procedure table determines generally what to do, leaving descriptions of the current state and destination state with no purpose other than to specify the origin and destination for the appropriate procedure.

THE PROBLEM-REDUCTION METHOD

Sometimes, it is possible to convert difficult goals into one or more easier-to-achieve subgoals. Each subgoal, in turn, may be divided still more finely into one or more lower-level subgoals.

[†]Because transition-causing procedures are often called *operators*, a difference-procedure table is called a *difference-operator table* in some circles.

Figure 3.5 MOVER is a procedure for planning motion sequences in the world of bricks, pyramids, balls, and a robot hand.

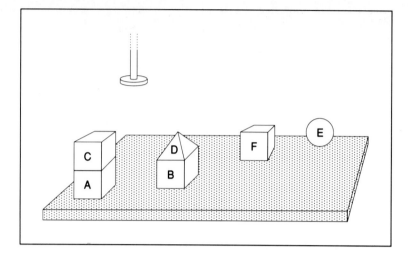

When using the **problem-reduction method**, you generally recognize goals and convert them into appropriate subgoals. When so used, problem reduction is often called, equivalently, **goal reduction**.

In the rest of this section, you learn more about the problem-reduction method, you learn which problems the problem-reduction method solves, and you learn how the problem-reduction method makes it easy to answer certain "why?" and "how?" questions.

Moving Blocks Illustrates Problem Reduction

The MOVER procedure solves problems in block manipulation and answers questions about its own behavior. MOVER works with blocks such as the one shown in figure 3.5, obeying commands such as the following:

> Put <block name> on <another block name>.

To obey, MOVER plans a motion sequence for a one-handed robot that picks up only one block at a time. MOVER consists of procedures that reduce given problems to simpler problems, thus engaging in what is called **problem reduction**. Conveniently, the names of these procedures are mnemonics for the problems that the procedures reduce. Figure 3.6 shows how the procedures fit together.

■ PUT-ON arranges to place one block on top of another block. It works by activating other procedures that find a specific place on the top of the target block, grasping the traveling block, moving it, and ungrasping it at the specific place.

■ GET-SPACE finds space on the top of a target block for a traveling block.

■ MAKE-SPACE helps GET-SPACE, when necessary, by moving obstructions until there is enough room for a traveling block.

■ GRASP grasps blocks. If the robot hand is holding a block when GRASP is invoked, GRASP must arrange for the robot hand to get rid of that

Figure 3.6 Specialists for moving blocks.

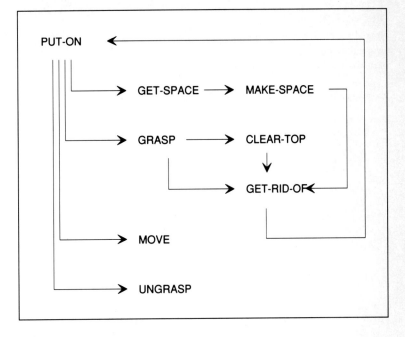

block. Also, GRASP must arrange to clear off the top of the object to be grasped.

■ CLEAR-TOP does the top clearing. It works by getting rid of everything on top of the object to be grasped.
■ GET-RID-OF gets rid of an obstructing object by putting it on the table.
■ UNGRASP makes the robot's hand let go of whatever it is holding.
■ MOVE moves objects, once they are held, by moving the robot hand.

Now imagine that there is a request to put block A on block B, given the situation shown in figure 3.5. Plainly, the following sequence suffices:

■ Grasp D.
■ Move D to some location on the table.
■ Ungrasp D.
■ Grasp C.
■ Move C to some location on the table.
■ Ungrasp C.
■ Grasp A.
■ Move A to some location on B.
■ Ungrasp A.

The question is, How do the procedures in MOVER find the appropriate sequence? Here is the answer:

First, PUT-ON asks GET-SPACE to identify a place for block A on top of block B. GET-SPACE appeals to MAKE-SPACE because block D is in the way.

Figure 3.7 A goal tree. Branches connect supergoals to simpler subgoals.

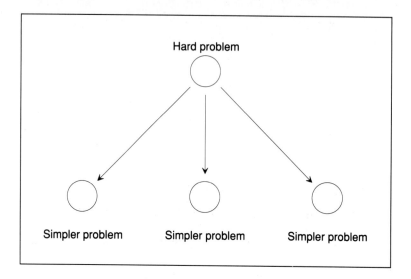

MAKE-SPACE asks GET-RID-OF to help by getting rid of block D. GET-RID-OF obliges by finding a place for block D on the table and by moving block D to that place using PUT-ON.

Note that PUT-ON, at work placing block A on block B, eventually produces a new job for PUT-ON itself, this time to put block C on the table. When a procedure uses itself, the procedure is said to **recurse**. Systems in which procedures use themselves are said to be **recursive**.

With block D gone, MAKE-SPACE can find a place for block A to go on top of block B. Recall that MAKE-SPACE was asked to do this by GET-SPACE because PUT-ON has the duty of putting block A on B. PUT-ON can proceed now, asking GRASP to grasp block A. But GRASP realizes that it cannot grasp block A because block C is in the way. GRASP asks CLEAR-TOP for help. CLEAR-TOP, in turn, asks GET-RID-OF for help, whereupon GET-RID-OF arranges for block C to go on the table using PUT-ON.

With block A cleared, CLEAR-TOP is finished. But if there were many blocks on top of block A, rather than just one, CLEAR-TOP would appeal to GET-RID-OF many times, rather than just once.

Now GRASP can do its job, and PUT-ON can ask MOVE to move block A to the place found previously on top of block B. Finally, PUT-ON asks UNGRASP to let block A go.

The Key Idea in Problem Reduction Is to Explore a Goal Tree

A **semantic tree** is a semantic net with special links, called **branches**, each of which connects two nodes:

A **semantic tree** is a representation

That is a semantic net

In which

▷ Certain links are called branches. Each branch connects two nodes; the head node is called the **parent node** and the tail node is called the **child node**

▷ One node has no parent; it is called the **root node**. Other nodes have exactly one parent.

▷ Some nodes have no children; they are called **leaf nodes**.

▷ When two nodes are connected to each other by a chain of two or more branches, one is said to be the **ancestor**; the other is said to be the **descendant**.

With constructors that

▷ Connect a parent node to a child node with a branch link

With readers that

▷ Produce a list of a given node's children

▷ Produce a given node's parent

A **goal tree**, like the one shown in figure 3.7, is a semantic tree in which nodes represent goals and branches indicate how you can achieve goals by solving one or more subgoals. Each node's children correspond to **immediate subgoals**; each node's parent corresponds to the **immediate supergoal**. The top node, the one with no parent, is the **root** goal.

Goal Trees Can Make Procedure Interaction Transparent

A goal tree, such as the one in figure 3.8, makes complicated MOVER scenarios transparent. Clearing the top of block A is shown as an immediate subgoal of grasping block A. Clearing the top of block A is also a subgoal of putting block A at a place on top of block B, but it is not an immediate subgoal.

All the goals shown in the example are satisfied only when all of their immediate subgoals are satisfied. Goals that are satisfied only when *all* of their immediate subgoals are satisfied are called And goals. The corresponding nodes are called And nodes, and you mark them by placing arcs on their branches.

Most goal trees also contain Or goals; these goals are satisfied when *any* of their immediate subgoals are satisfied. The corresponding, unmarked nodes are called Or nodes.

Finally, some goals are satisfied directly, without reference to any subgoals. These goals are called **leaf goals**, and the corresponding nodes are called **leaf nodes**.

Because goal trees always involve And nodes, or Or nodes, or both, they are often called And–Or trees.

To determine whether a goal has been achieved, you need a testing procedure. The key procedure, REDUCE, channels action into the REDUCE-AND and the REDUCE-OR procedures:

To determine, using REDUCE, whether a goal is achieved,

▷ Determine whether the goal is satisfied without recourse to subgoals:

  ▷ If it is, announce that the goal is satisfied.

  ▷ Otherwise, determine whether the goal corresponds to an And goal:

    ▷ If it does, use the REDUCE-AND procedure to determine whether the goal is satisfied.

    ▷ Otherwise, use the REDUCE-OR procedure to determine whether the goal is satisfied.

REDUCE uses two subprocedures: one deals with And goals, and the other deals with Or goals:

To determine, using REDUCE-AND, whether a goal has been satisfied,

▷ Use REDUCE on each immediate subgoal until there are no more subgoals, or until REDUCE finds a subgoal that is not satisfied.

▷ If REDUCE has found a subgoal that is not satisfied, announce that the goal is not satisfied; otherwise, announce that the goal is satisfied.

To determine, using REDUCE-OR, whether a goal has been satisfied,

▷ Use REDUCE on each subgoal until REDUCE finds a subgoal that is satisfied.

▷ If REDUCE has found a subgoal that is satisfied, announce that the goal is satisfied; otherwise, announce that the goal is not satisfied.

With REDUCE, REDUCE-AND, and REDUCE-OR in hand, it is a simple matter to test an entire And–Or tree: you just use REDUCE on the root node,

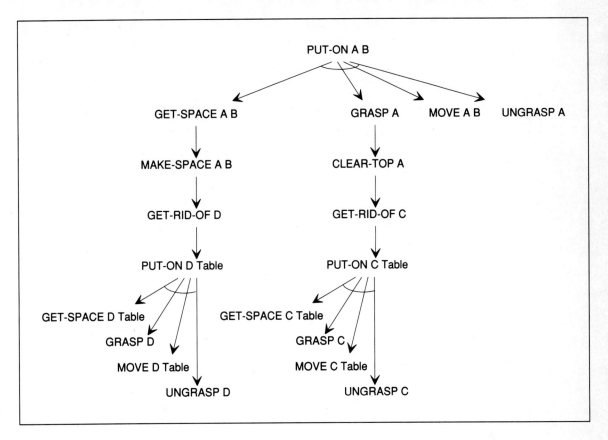

Figure 3.8 A goal tree. Branches joined by arcs are under And nodes; other branches are under Or nodes.

permitting the various procedures to call one another, as necessary, to work their way down the tree.

Goal Trees Enable Introspective Question Answering

The MOVER program is able to build And–Or trees because the specialists have a tight correspondence to identifiable goals. Indeed, MOVER's And–Or trees are so illuminating, they can be used to answer questions about *how* and *why* actions have been taken, giving MOVER a certain talent for introspection into its own behavior.

Suppose, for example, that MOVER has put block A on block B, producing the goal tree shown in figure 3.8.

Further suppose that someone asks, How did you clear the top of A? Plainly, a reasonable answer is, By getting rid of block C. On the other hand, suppose the question is, Why did you clear the top of A? Then a reasonable answer is, To grasp block A.

These examples illustrate general strategies. To deal with "how?" questions, you identify the goal involved in the And–Or tree. If the goal is an And goal, report all of the immediate subgoals. If the goal is an Or goal, you report the immediate subgoal that was achieved. To deal with "why?" questions, you identify the goal and report the immediate supergoal.

Problem Reduction Is Ubiquitous in Programming

From a programming point of view, MOVER consists of a collection of specialized procedures. Each time one specialized procedure calls another, it effects a problem-reduction step.

More generally, whenever one procedure calls a subprocedure, there is a problem reduction step. Thus, problem reduction is the problem-solving method that all but the shortest programs exhibit in great quantity.

Problem-Solving Methods Often Work Together

Few real problems can be solved by a single problem-solving method. Accordingly, you often see problem-solving methods working together.

Suppose, for example, that you want to go from your house near Boston to a friend's house near Seattle. Earlier in this chapter, you learned that you can use means–ends analysis to decide what sort of transportation is most preferred for reducing the distance between where you are and where you want to be. Because the distance between Boston and Seattle is large, means–ends analysis doubtlessly would suggest that you take an airplane, but taking an airplane solves only part of your problem: You still have to figure out how get to the Boston airport from your house, and how to get from the Seattle airport to your friend's house. Thus, the initial goal, as shown in figure 3.9, becomes three subgoals, each of which can be handled, perhaps, by means–ends analysis.

SUMMARY

- Generate-and-test systems often do identification. Good generators are complete, nonredundant, and informed.
- The key idea in means–ends analysis is to reduce differences. Means–ends analysis is often mediated via difference-procedure tables.
- The key idea in problem reduction is to explore a goal tree. A goal tree consists of And goals, all of which must be satisfied, and Or goals, one of which must be satisfied.
- Problem reduction is ubiquitous in programming because subprocedure call is a form of problem reduction.
- The MOVER program uses problem reduction to plan motion sequences. While MOVER is at work, it constructs a goal tree that enables it to answer *how* and *why* questions.

Mathematics Toolkits Use Problem Reduction to Solve Calculus Problems

Because problem reduction is such an obvious, yet powerful, problem-solving method, it is among the first to be put to use. One application of problem reduction, the SAINT program, pioneered the use of artificial intelligence in mathematical problem solving.

Basically, SAINT was a program that integrated symbolic expressions in one variable. For example, when given

$$\int \frac{x^4}{(1-x^2)^{5/2}}\, dx$$

as the integrand, SAINT produced the dazzling result:

$$\int \frac{x^4}{(1-x^2)^{5/2}}\, dx = \frac{1}{3}\tan^3(\arcsin x) - \tan(\arcsin x) + \arcsin x.$$

SAINTlike programs perform variable substitutions and other algebraic manipulations to transform difficult integrands into one or more simpler integrands, thus exhibiting problem reduction, with the hope of eventually producing integrands so simple that the answers are given directly in integral tables.

To do the work, SAINT reduced the integrand to a function of sines and cosines by a substitution:

$$\int \frac{\sin^4 y}{\cos^4 y}\, dy.$$

Next, SAINT reduced the integrand to a function of the tangent of y using a trigonometric identity:

$$\int \tan^4 y\, dy.$$

SAINT reduced the integrand to a rational function with another substitution:

$$\int \frac{z^4}{1+z^2}\, dz.$$

Then, SAINT divided out the two polynomials, producing the following:

$$\int z^2 - 1 + \frac{1}{1+z^2}\, dz.$$

The first two of the integrand expressions are easy to integrate:

$$\int z^2\, dz = \frac{z^3}{3} \qquad \int -1\, dz = -\int -1\, dz = -z$$

Finally, another reduction takes care of the third expression:

$$\int \frac{1}{1+z^2}\, dz = \int \frac{1}{w}\, dw = \frac{w^2}{2}$$

Thus, the original integrand is reduced to three separate integrands, all readily handled by reference to an integral table. The results—$z^3/3$, z, and w—produce the desired result once the variable substitutions are reversed.

Figure 3.9 Frequently, problem-solving methods work together. Here, a travel problem is split apart, using problem reduction, into pieces susceptible to solution using means–ends analysis.

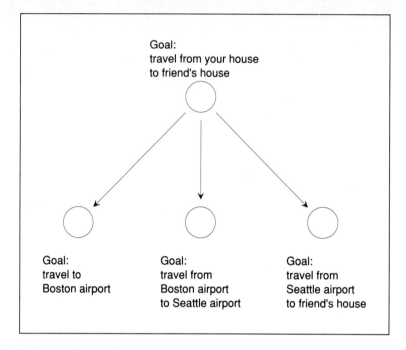

BACKGROUND

Means–ends analysis became conspicuous through pioneering work on GPS, the general problem solver system. Early work on GPS is described by Allen Newell et al. [1957].

The discussion of MOVER is based on part of a system built by Terry Winograd [1971]. The main thrust of Winograd's early work was to show how a computer can be made to accept commands and questions expressed in English.

DENDRAL was developed primarily by Edward A. Feigenbaum, Bruce Buchanan, and Joshua Lederberg and their students. DENDRAL is described in great detail by Robert Lindsay et al. [1969].

SAINT was conceived and developed by James R. Slagle [1961]. SAINT was subsequently superseded by programs based on SIN, a program written by Joel Moses [1967].

4

Nets and
Basic Search

In this chapter, you learn how to find paths through nets, thus solving *search* problems.[†] In particular, you learn about *depth-first search* and *breath-first search*, both of which are methods that involve blind groping. You also learn about *hill-climbing*, *beam search*, and *best-first search*, all of which are methods that are guided by heuristic quality estimates.

Search problems pop up everywhere. In this chapter, you see examples involving map traversal and recipe discovery. Other chapters offer many other examples of the basic search methods in action, including an example, in Chapter 29, of how depth-first search can be used to provide natural-language access to a database.

Once you have finished this chapter, you will know that you must think about several questions if you are to use search methods wisely; these are examples:

- Is search the best way to solve the problem?
- Which search methods solve the problem?
- Which search method is most efficient for this problem?

[†]Many problem-solving paradigms, like search, require only a weak understanding of the domains to which they are applied. Consequently, some people call such problem-solving paradigms *weak methods*. The term *weak method* is not used in this book because it can be taken to mean *low powered*.

Figure 4.1 A basic search problem. A path is to be found from the start node, S, to the goal node, G. Search procedures explore nets such as these, learning about connections and distances as they go.

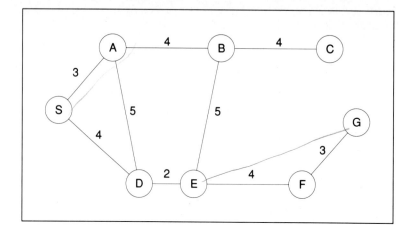

BLIND METHODS

Suppose you want to find some path from one city to another using a highway map such as the one shown in figure 4.1. Your path is to begin at city S, your starting point, and it is to end at city G, your goal. To find an appropriate path through the highway map, you need to consider two different costs:

- First, there is the computation cost expended when *finding* a path.
- And, second, there is the travel cost expended when *traversing* the path.

If you need to go from S to G often, then finding a really good path is worth a lot of search time. On the other hand, if you need to make the trip only once, and if it is hard to find any path, then you may be content as soon as you find some path, even though you could find a better path with more work.

In this chapter, you learn about the problem of finding one path. In the rest of this section, you learn about finding one path given no information about how to order the choices at the nodes so that the most promising are explored earliest.

Net Search Is Really Tree Search

The most obvious way to find a solution is to look at all possible paths. Of course, you should discard paths that revisit any particular city so that you cannot get stuck in a loop—such as S–A–D–S–A–D–S–A–D–....

With looping paths eliminated, you can arrange all possible paths from the start node in a **search tree**, a special kind of semantic tree in which each node denotes a path:

Figure 4.2 A search tree
made from a net. Each node
denotes a path. Each child
node denotes a path that is
a one-step extension of the
path denoted by its parent. You
convert nets into search trees
by tracing out all possible paths
until you cannot extend any of
them without creating a loop.

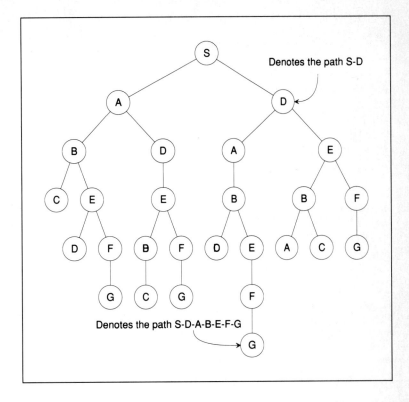

A **search tree** is a representation

That is a semantic tree

In which

▷ Nodes denote paths.

▷ Branches connect paths to one-step path extensions.

With writers that

▷ Connect a path to a path description

With readers that

▷ Produce a paths's description

Figure 4.2 shows a search tree that consists of nodes denoting the possible
paths that lead outward from the start node of the net shown in figure 4.1.

Note that, although each node in a search tree denotes a path, there
is no room in diagrams to write out each path at each node. Accordingly,
each node is labeled with only the terminal node of the path it denotes.
Each **child** denotes a path that is a one-city extension of the path denoted
by its **parent**.

In Chapter 3, the specification for the semantic-tree representation indicated that the node at the top of a semantic tree, the node with no parent, is called the **root node**. The nodes at the bottom, the ones with no children, are called **leaf nodes**. One node is the **ancestor** of another, a **descendant**, if there is a chain of two or more branches from the ancestor to the descendant.

If a node has b children, it is said to have a **branching factor** of b. If the number of children is always b for every nonleaf node, then the tree is said to have a branching factor of b.

In the example, the root node denotes the path that begins and ends at the start node S. The child of the root node labeled A denotes the path S-A. Each path, such as S-A, that does not reach the goal is called a **partial path**. Each path that does reach the goal is called a **complete path**, and the corresponding node is called a **goal node**.

Determining the children of a node is called **expanding** the node. Nodes are said to be **open** until they are expanded, whereupon they become **closed**.

Note that search procedures start out with no knowledge of the ultimate size or shape of the complete search tree. All they know is where to start and what the goal is. Each must expand open nodes, starting with the root node, until it discovers a node that corresponds to an acceptable path.

Search Trees Explode Exponentially

The total number of paths in a tree with branching factor b and depth d is b^d. Thus, the number of paths is said to **explode exponentially** as the depth of the search tree increases.

Accordingly, you always try to deploy a search method that is likely to develop the smallest number of paths. In the rest of this section, you learn about several search methods from which you can choose.

Depth-First Search Dives into the Search Tree

Given that one path is as good as any other, one simple way to find a path is to pick one of the children at every node visited, and to work forward from that child. Other alternatives at the same level are ignored completely, as long as there is hope of reaching the goal using the original choice. This strategy is the essence of **depth-first search**.

Using a convention that the alternatives are tried in left-to-right order, the first thing to do is to dash headlong to the bottom of the tree along the leftmost branches, as shown in figure 4.3.

But because a headlong dash leads to leaf node C, without encountering G, the next step is to back up to the nearest ancestor node that has an unexplored alternative. The nearest such node is B. The remaining alternative at B is better, bringing eventual success through E in spite of another dead end at D. Figure 4.3 shows the nodes encountered.

Figure 4.3 An example of depth-first search. One alternative is selected and pursued at each node until the goal is reached or a node is reached where further downward motion is impossible. When further downward motion is impossible, search is restarted at the nearest ancestor node with unexplored children.

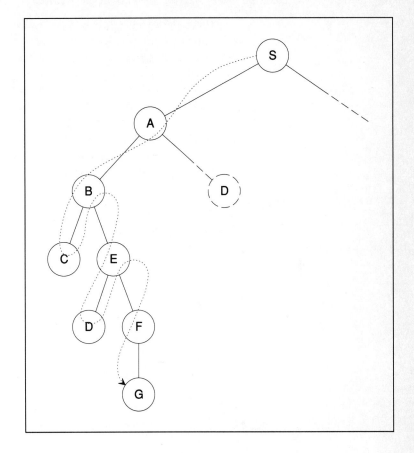

Figure 4.4 An example of breadth-first search. Downward motion proceeds level by level, until the goal is reached.

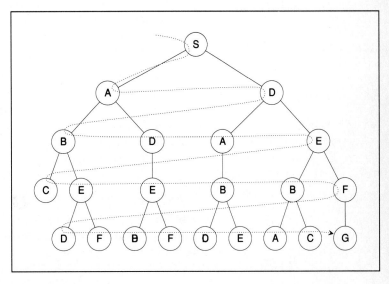

If the path through E had not worked, then the procedure would move still farther back up the tree, seeking another viable decision point from which to move forward. On reaching A, the procedure would go down again, reaching the goal through D.

Having learned about depth-first search by way of an example, you can see that the procedure, expressed in procedural English, is as follows:

To conduct a depth-first search,

▷ Form a one-element queue consisting of a zero-length path that contains only the root node.

▷ Until the first path in the queue terminates at the goal node or the queue is empty,

    ▷ Remove the first path from the queue; create new paths by extending the first path to all the neighbors of the terminal node.

    ▷ Reject all new paths with loops.

    ▷ Add the new paths, if any, to the *front* of the queue.

▷ If the goal node is found, announce success; otherwise, announce failure.

Breadth-First Search Pushes Uniformly into the Search Tree

As shown in figure 4.4, **breadth-first search** checks all paths of a given length before moving on to any longer paths. In the example, breadth-first search discovers a complete path to node G on the fourth level down from the root level.

A procedure for breadth-first search resembles the one for depth-first search, differing only in where new elements are added to the queue:

To conduct a breadth-first search,

▷ Form a one-element queue consisting of a zero-length path that contains only the root node.

▷ Until the first path in the queue terminates at the goal node or the queue is empty,

    ▷ Remove the first path from the queue; create new paths by extending the first path to all the neighbors of the terminal node.

    ▷ Reject all new paths with loops.

    ▷ Add the new paths, if any, to the *back* of the queue.

▷ If the goal node is found, announce success; otherwise, announce failure.

The Right Search Depends on the Tree

Depth-first search is a good idea when you are confident that all partial paths either reach dead ends or become complete paths after a reasonable number of steps. In contrast, depth-first search is a bad idea if there are long paths, even infinitely long paths, that neither reach dead ends nor become complete paths. In those situations, you need alternative search methods.

Breadth-first search works even in trees that are infinitely deep or effectively infinitely deep. On the other hand, breadth-first search is wasteful when all paths lead to the goal node at more or less the same depth.

Note that breath-first search is a bad idea if the branching factor is large or infinite, because of exponential explosion. Breadth-first search is a good idea when you are confident that the branching factor is small. You may also choose breadth-first search, instead of depth-first search, if you are worried that there may be long paths, even infinitely long paths, that neither reach dead ends nor become complete paths.

Nondeterministic Search Moves Randomly into the Search Tree

You may be so uninformed about a search problem that you cannot rule out either a large branching factor or long useless paths. In such situations, you may want to seek a middle ground between depth-first search and breadth-first search. One way to seek such a middle ground is to choose **nondeterministic search**. When doing nondeterministic search, you expand an open node that is chosen at random. That way, you ensure that you cannot get stuck chasing either too many branches or too many levels:

To conduct a nondeterministic search,

▷ Form a one-element queue consisting of a zero-length path that contains only the root node.

▷ Until the first path in the queue terminates at the goal node or the queue is empty,

    ▷ Remove the first path from the queue; create new paths by extending the first path to all the neighbors of the terminal node.

    ▷ Reject all new paths with loops.

    ▷ Add the new paths at random places in the queue.

▷ If the goal node is found, announce success; otherwise, announce failure.

HEURISTICALLY INFORMED METHODS

Search efficiency may improve spectacularly if there is a way to order the choices so that the most promising are explored earliest. In many situations, you can make measurements to determine a reasonable ordering. In the rest of this section, you learn about search methods that take advantage of such measurements; they are called **heuristically informed methods**.

Quality Measurements Turn Depth-First Search into Hill Climbing

To move through a tree of paths using **hill climbing**, you proceed as you would in depth-first search, except that you order your choices according to some heuristic measure of the remaining distance to the goal. The better the heuristic measure is, the better hill climbing will be relative to ordinary depth-first search.

Straight-line, as-the-crow-flies distance is an example of a heuristic measure of remaining distance. Figure 4.5 shows the straight-line distances from each city to the goal; Figure 4.6 shows what happens when hill climbing is used on the map-traversal problem using as-the-crow-flies distance to order choices. Because node D is closer to the goal than is node A, the children of D are examined first. Then, node E appears closer to the goal than is node A. Accordingly, node E's children are examined, leading to a move to node F, which is closer to the goal than node B. Below node F, there is only one child: the goal node G.

From a procedural point of view, hill climbing differs from depth-first search in only one detail; there is an added step, shown in italic type:

To conduct a hill-climbing search,

▷ Form a one-element queue consisting of a zero-length path that contains only the root node.

▷ Until the first path in the queue terminates at the goal node or the queue is empty,

  ▷ Remove the first path from the queue; create new paths by extending the first path to all the neighbors of the terminal node.

  ▷ Reject all new paths with loops.

  ▷ *Sort the new paths, if any, by the estimated distances between their terminal nodes and the goal.*

  ▷ Add the new paths, if any, to the *front* of the queue.

▷ If the goal node is found, announce success; otherwise, announce failure.

Figure 4.5 Figure 4.1 revisited. Here you see the distances between each city and the goal. If you which to reach the goal, it is usually better to be in a city that is close, but not necessarily; city C is closer than all but city F, but city C is not a good place to be.

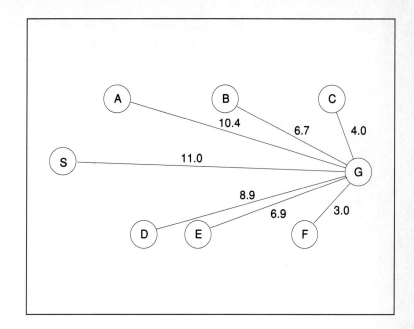

Figure 4.6 An example of hill climbing. Hill climbing is depth-first search with a heuristic measurement that orders choices as nodes are expanded. The numbers beside the nodes are straight-line distances from the path-terminating city to the goal city.

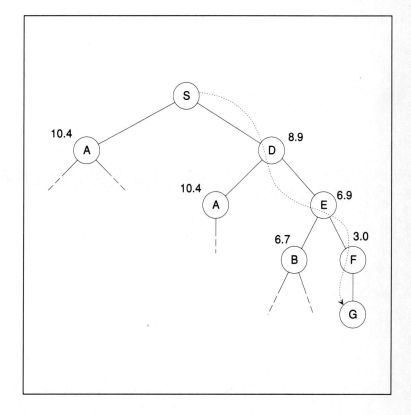

Generally, exploiting knowledge, as in hill climbing, reduces search time, a point worth elevating to the status of a powerful idea:

Whenever faced with a search problem, note that,

▷ More knowledge generally leads to reduced search time.

Sometimes, knowledge reduces search time by guiding choices, as in the example. Sometimes, knowledge reduces search time by enabling you to restate a problem in terms of a smaller, more easily searched net; this observation leads directly to another powerful idea:

When you think you need a better search method,

▷ Find another space to search instead.

Although search is involved in many tasks, devising a fancy, finely tuned search procedure is rarely the best way to spend your time. You usually do better if you improve your understanding of the problem, thereby reducing the need for fanciness and fine tuning.

Foothills, Plateaus, and Ridges Make Hills Hard to Climb

Although it is simple, hill climbing suffers from various problems. These problems are most conspicuous when hill climbing is used to optimize parameters, as in the following examples:

■ On entering a room, you find that the temperature is uncomfortable. You decide to adjust the thermostat.

■ The picture on your television set has deteriorated over time. You decide to adjust the color, tint, and brightness controls for a better picture.

■ You are climbing a mountain when a dense fog rolls in. You have no map or trail to follow, but you do have a compass, an altimeter, and a determination to get to the top.

Each of these problems conforms to an abstraction in which there are *adjustable parameters* and a *measured quantity* that tells you about the quality or performance associated with any particular setting of the adjustable parameters.

In the temperature example, the adjustable parameter is the thermostat setting, and your comfort determines how well the parameter has been set. In the television example, the various controls are the parameters, and your subjective sense of the picture's quality determines how well the parameters have been set.

In the mountaineering example, your location is the adjustable parameter, and you can use your altimeter to determine whether you are progressing up the mountain. To get to the top using **parameter-oriented**

hill climbing, you tentatively try a step northward, then you retreat and try a step eastward. Next you try southward and westward as well. Then you commit to the step that increases your altitude most. You repeat until all tentative steps decrease your altitude.

More generally, to perform parameter-oriented hill climbing, you make a one-step adjustment, up and down, to each parameter value, move to the best of the resulting alternatives according to the appropriate measure of quality or performance, and repeat until you find a combination of parameter values that produces better quality or performance than all of the neighboring alternatives.

But note that you may encounter severe problems with parameter-oriented hill climbing:

- The **foothill problem** occurs whenever there are secondary peaks, as in the example at the top of figure 4.7. The secondary peaks draw the hill-climbing procedure like magnets. An optimal point is found, but it is a **local maximum**, rather than a **global maximum**, and the user is left with a false sense of accomplishment or security.

- The **plateau problem** comes up when there is a mostly flat area separating the peaks. In extreme cases, the peaks may look like telephone poles sticking up in a football field, as in the middle example of figure 4.7. The local improvement-operation breaks down completely. For all but a small number of positions, all standard-step probes leave the quality measurement unchanged.

- The **ridge problem** is more subtle, and, consequently, is more frustrating. Suppose you are standing on what seems like a knife edge contour running generally from northeast to southwest, as in the bottom example of figure 4.7. A contour map shows that each standard step takes you down, even though you are not at any sort of local or global maximum. Increasing the number of directions used for the probing steps may help.

Among these problems, the foothill problem is particularly vexing, especially as the number of parameter dimensions increases. When you reach a point from which all steps lead down, you could retreat to a previous choice point and do something else, as hill climbing prescribes, but there may be millions of paths back to the same local maximum. If there are, you are really stuck if you stick to ordinary hill climbing.

Accordingly, you may want to do a bit of nondeterministic search when you detect a local maximum. The reason for using this strategy is that a random number of steps, of random size, in random directions, may shield you from the magnetlike attraction of the local maximum long enough for you to escape.

Figure 4.7 Hill climbing is a bad idea in difficult terrain. In the top example, foothills stop progress. In the middle example, plains cause aimless wandering. In the bottom example, with the terrain described by a contour map, all ridge points look like peaks because both east–west and north–south probe directions lead to lower-quality measurements.

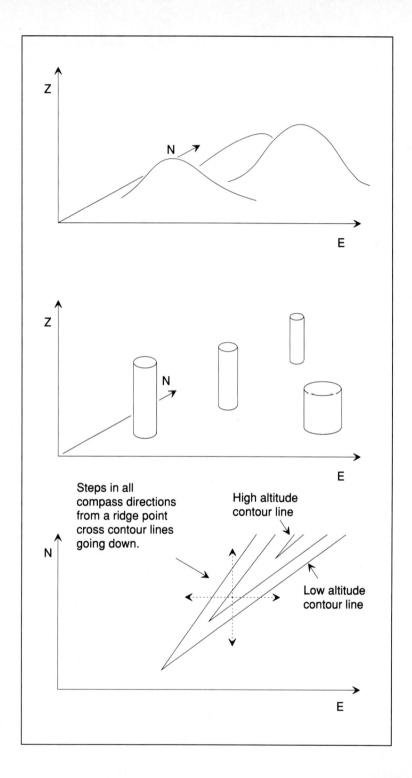

Beam Search Expands Several Partial Paths and Purges the Rest

Beam search is like breadth-first search in that it progresses level by level. Unlike breadth-first search, however, beam search moves downward only through the best w nodes at each level; the other nodes are ignored. Consequently, the number of nodes explored remains manageable, even if there is a great deal of branching and the search is deep. Whenever beam search is used, there are only w nodes under consideration at any depth, rather than the exponentially explosive number of nodes with which you must cope whenever you use breadth-first search. Figure 4.8 illustrates how beam search would handle the map-traversal problem.

Best-First Search Expands the Best Partial Path

Recall that, when forward motion is blocked, hill climbing demands forward motion from the most recently created open node. In **best-first search**, forward motion is from the best open node so far, no matter where that node is in the partially developed tree.

In the example map-traversal problem, hill climbing and best-first search coincidentally explore the search tree in the same way.

The paths found by best-first search are likely to be shorter than those found with other methods, because best-first search always moves forward from the node that seems closest to the goal node. Note that *likely to be* does not mean *certainly are*, however.

Search May Lead to Discovery

Finding physical paths and tuning parameters are only two applications for search methods. More generally, the nodes in a search tree may denote abstract entities, rather than physical places or parameter settings.

Suppose, for example, that you are wild about cooking, particularly about creating your own omelet recipes. Deciding to be more systematic about your discovery procedure, you make a list of *ingredient transformations* for varying your existing recipes:

- Replace an ingredient with a similar ingredient.
- Double the amount of an ingredient.
- Halve the amount of an ingredient.
- Add a new ingredient.
- Eliminate an ingredient.

Naturally, you speculate that most of the changes suggested by these ingredient transformations will turn out to taste awful, and thus to be unworthy of further development.

Figure 4.8 An example of beam search. Investigation spreads through the search tree level by level, but only the best w nodes are expanded, where $w = 2$ here. The numbers beside the nodes are straight-line distances to the goal node.

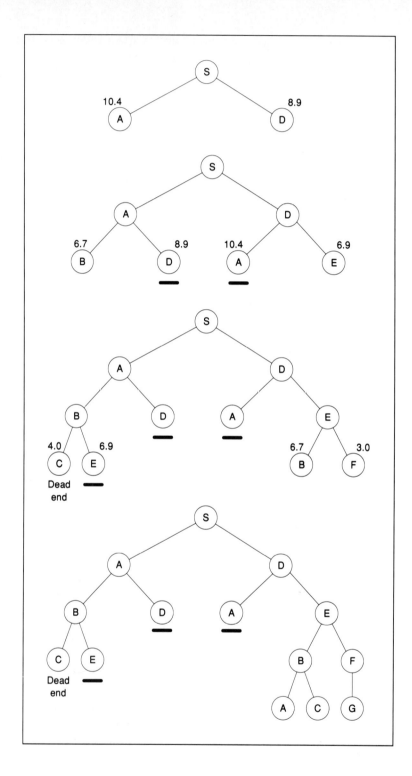

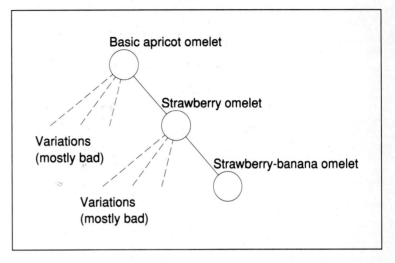

Figure 4.9 A search tree with recipe nodes. Ingredient transformations build the tree; interestingness heuristics guide the best-first search to the better prospects.

Consequently, you need **interestingness heuristics** to help you to decide on which recipes to continue to work. Here are four interestingness heuristics:

■ It tastes good.
■ It looks good.
■ Your friends eat a lot of it.
■ Your friends ask for the recipe.

Interestingness heuristics can be used with hill climbing, with beam search, or with best-first search.

Figure 4.9 shows part of the search tree descending from a basic recipe for an apricot omelet, one similar to a particular favorite of Rex Stout's fictional detective and gourmand Nero Wolfe:

Ingredients for Apricot Omelet Recipe

1   ounce kümmel
1   cup apricot preserves
6   eggs
2   tablespoons cold water
1/2   teaspoon salt
2   teaspoons sugar
2   tablespoons unsalted butter
1   teaspoon powdered sugar

As shown in figure 4.9, you can discover a strawberry omelet recipe using the substitution transformation on the basic apricot omelet recipe. Once you have a strawberry omelet, you can go on to discover a strawberry-peach recipe, using the addition transformation.

Of course, to be a real recipe generator, you would have to be skilled at generating plausible transformations, for you would waste too many

Figure 4.10 Part of the search family of procedures.

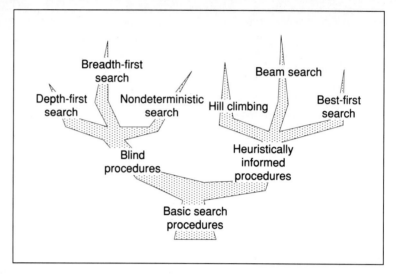

eggs otherwise. Essentially, you need to remember that more knowledge generally leads to reduced search time.

Search Alternatives Form a Procedure Family

You have seen that there are many ways for doing search, each with advantages:

■ Depth-first search is good when unproductive partial paths are never too long.

■ Breadth-first search is good when the branching factor is never too large.

■ Nondeterministic search is good when you are not sure whether depth-first search or breadth-first search would be better.

■ Hill climbing is good when there is a natural measure of distance from each place to the goal and a good path is likely to be among the partial paths that appear to be good at each choice point.

■ Beam search is good when there is a natural measure of goal distance and a good path is likely to be among the partial paths that appear to be good at all levels.

■ Best-first search is good when there is a natural measure of goal distance and a good partial path may look like a bad option before more promising partial paths are played out.

All these methods form part of the search family of procedures, as shown in figure 4.10.

SUMMARY

■ Depth-first search dives into the search tree, extending one partial path at a time.

- Breadth-first search pushes uniformly into the search tree, extending many partial paths in parallel.
- Nondeterministic search moves randomly into the search tree, picking a partial path to extend at random.
- Heuristic quality measurements turn depth-first search into hill climbing. Foothills, plateaus, and ridges make hills hard to climb.
- Heuristic quality measurements also are used in beam search and best-first search. Beam search expands a fixed number of partial paths in parallel and purges the rest. Best-first search expands the best partial path.
- Heuristically guided search may lead to discovery, as in the example of recipe improvement.
- Search alternatives form a procedure family.
- More knowledge generally means less search.
- When you think you need a better search method, try to find another space to search instead.

BACKGROUND

Artificial intelligence is but one of many fields in which search is an important topic. Artificial intelligence's particular contribution lies largely in the development of heuristic methods such as those discussed in this chapter, in Chapter 6, and in many of the chapters in Part II.

You can learn more about the contributions of other fields to search from many books. Look for those with titles that include words such as *algorithms*, *linear programming*, *mathematical programming*, *optimization*, and *operations research*.

You can learn more about heuristic search from *Principles of Artificial Intelligence*, by Nils J. Nilsson [1980].

The discussion of omelet-recipe generation is based on ideas introduced in the work of Douglas B. Lenat [1977]. Lenat's AM program, a breakthrough in learning research, discovered concepts in mathematics. AM developed new concepts from old ones using various transformations, and it identified the most interesting concepts for further development.

5

Nets and Optimal Search

In this chapter, you learn how to deal with search situations in which the cost of traversing a path is of primary importance. In particular, you learn about the *British Museum procedure, branch and bound, discrete dynamic programming*, and A*. All but the British Museum procedure aspire to do their work efficiently.

By way of illustration, you see how it is possible to find the shortest route from one city to another using an ordinary highway map, and you see how a robot-planning system can find the most efficient way to move an object using *configuration space*.

Once you have finished this chapter, you will know what to do when you do not care as much about how long it takes to find a path as you do about finding the best path.

THE BEST PATH

In this section, you learn more about the map-traversal problem that emerged in Chapter 4; here, however, you pay attention to path length.

The British Museum Procedure Looks Everywhere

One procedure for finding the shortest path through a net is to find all possible paths and to select the best one from them. This plodding procedure, named in jest, is known as the **British Museum procedure**.

If you wish to find all possible paths, either a depth-first search or a breadth-first search will work, with one modification: Search continues until every solution is found. If the breadth and depth of the tree are small, as in the map-traversal example, then there are no problems.

Unfortunately, the size of search trees is often large, making any procedure for finding all possible paths extremely unpalatable. Suppose that, instead of the number of levels being small, it is moderately large. Suppose further that the branching is completely uniform and that the number of alternative branches at each node is b. Then, in the first level, there will be b nodes. For each of these b nodes, there will be b more nodes in the second level, or b^2. Continuing this analysis leads to the conclusion that the number of nodes at depth d must be b^d. For even modest breadth and depth, the number of paths can be large: $b = 10$ and $d = 10$ yields 10 billion paths. Fortunately, there are strategies that enable optimal paths to be found without all possible paths being found first.

Branch-and-Bound Search Expands the Least-Cost Partial Path

One way to find optimal paths with less work is to use **branch-and-bound search**. The basic idea is simple. Suppose an optimal solution is desired for the highway map shown Chapter 4. Also suppose that an oracle has told you that S–D–E–F–G is the optimal solution. Being a scientist, however, you do not trust oracles.

Nevertheless, knowing that the length of S–D–E–F–G is 13, you can eliminate some work that you might otherwise do. For example, as shown in figure 5.1, there is no need to consider paths that start with S–D–A–B, because their length has to be at least 13, given that the length of S–D–A–B is already 13.

More generally, the branch-and-bound scheme always keeps track of all partial paths contending for further consideration. The shortest one is extended one level, creating as many new partial paths as there are branches. Next, these new paths are considered, along with the remaining old ones: again, the shortest is extended. This process repeats until the goal is reached along some path. Because the shortest path was always the one chosen for extension, the path first reaching the goal is likely to be the optimal path.

To turn *likely* into *certain*, you have to extend all partial paths until they are as long as or longer than the complete path. The reason is that the last step in reaching the goal may be long enough to make the supposed solution longer than one or more partial paths. It might be that only a tiny step would extend one of the partial paths to the solution point. To be sure that this is not so, instead of terminating when a path is found, you terminate when the shortest partial path is longer than the shortest complete path.

Here, then, is the procedure; it differs from the basic search procedures you learned about in Chapter 4 only in the steps shown in italic type:

Figure 5.1 The length of the complete path from S to G, S–D–E–F–G is 13. Similarly, the length of the partial path S–D–A–B also is 13 and any additional movement along a branch will make it longer than 13. Accordingly, there is no need to pursue S–D–A–B any further because any complete path starting with S–D–A–B has to be longer than a complete path already known. Only the other paths emerging from S and from S–D–E have to be considered, as they may provide a shorter path.

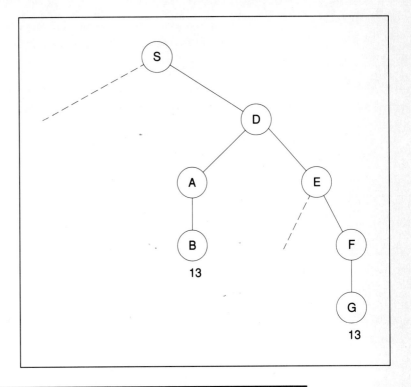

To conduct a branch-and-bound search,

▷ Form a one-element queue consisting of a zero-length path that contains only the root node.

▷ Until the first path in the queue terminates at the goal node or the queue is empty,

  ▷ Remove the first path from the queue; create new paths by extending the first path to all the neighbors of the terminal node.

  ▷ Reject all new paths with loops.

  ▷ *Add the remaining new paths, if any, to the queue.*

  ▷ *Sort the entire queue by path length with least-cost paths in front.*

▷ If the goal node is found, announce success; otherwise, announce failure.

Now look again at the map-traversal problem, and note how branch-and-bound works when started with no partial paths. Figure 5.2 illustrates the exploration sequence. In the first step, the partial-path distance of S–A is found to be 3, and that of S–D is found to be 4; partial path S–A is therefore selected for expansion. Next, S–A–B and S–A–D are generated from S–A with partial path distances of 7 and 8.

Now S–D, with a partial path distance of 4, is expanded, leading to partial paths to S–D–A and S–D–E. At this point, there are four partial paths, with the path S–D–E being the shortest.

After the seventh step, partial paths S–A–D–E and S–D–E–F are the shortest partial paths. Expanding S–A–D–E leads to partial paths terminating at B and F. Expanding S–D–E–F, along the right side of the tree, leads to the complete path S–D–E–F–G, with a total distance of 13. This path is the shortest one, but if you wish to be absolutely sure, you must extend two partial paths: S–A–B–E, with a partial-path distance of 12, and S–D–E–B, with a partial-path distance of 11. There is no need to extend the partial path S–D–A–B, because its partial-path distance of 13 is equal to that of the complete path. In this particular example, little work is avoided relative to exhaustive search, British Museum style.

Adding Underestimates Improves Efficiency

In some cases, you can improve branch-and-bound search greatly by using guesses about distances remaining, as well as facts about distances already accumulated. After all, if a guess about distance remaining is good, then that guessed distance added to the definitely known distance already traversed should be a good estimate of total path length, e(total path length):

$$e(\text{total path length}) = d(\text{already traveled}) + e(\text{distance remaining}),$$

where d(already traveled) is the known distance already traveled, and where e(distance remaining) is an estimate of the distance remaining.

Surely it makes sense to work hardest on developing the path with the shortest estimated path length until the estimate is revised upward enough to make some other path be the one with the shortest estimated path length. After all, if the guesses were perfect, this approach would keep you on the optimal path at all times.

In general, however, guesses are not perfect, and a bad overestimate somewhere along the true optimal path may cause you to wander away from that optimal path permanently.

Note, however, that *underestimates* cannot cause the right path to be overlooked. An underestimate of the distance remaining yields an underestimate of total path length, u(total path length):

$$u(\text{total path length}) = d(\text{already traveled}) + u(\text{distance remaining}),$$

where d(already traveled) is the known distance already traveled, and where u(distance remaining) is an underestimate of the distance remaining.

Now, if you find a total path by extending the path with the smallest underestimate repeatedly, you need to do no further work once all partial-path distance estimates are longer than the best complete path distance so far encountered. You can stop because the real distance along a complete path cannot be less than an underestimate of that distance. If all estimates

Figure 5.2 Branch-and-bound search determines that path S–D–E–F–G is optimal. The numbers beside the nodes are accumulated distances. Search stops when all partial paths to open nodes are as long as or longer than the complete path S–D–E–F–G.

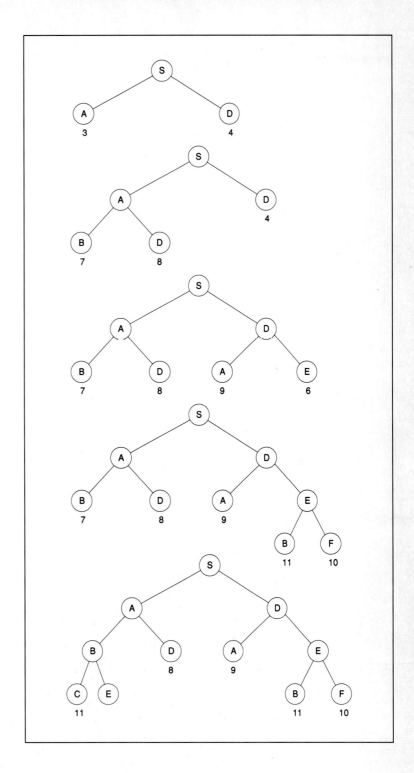

Figure 5.2 Continued.

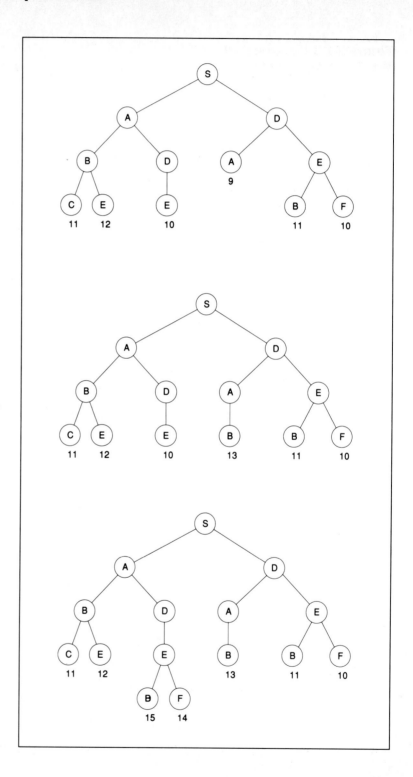

Figure 5.2 Continued.

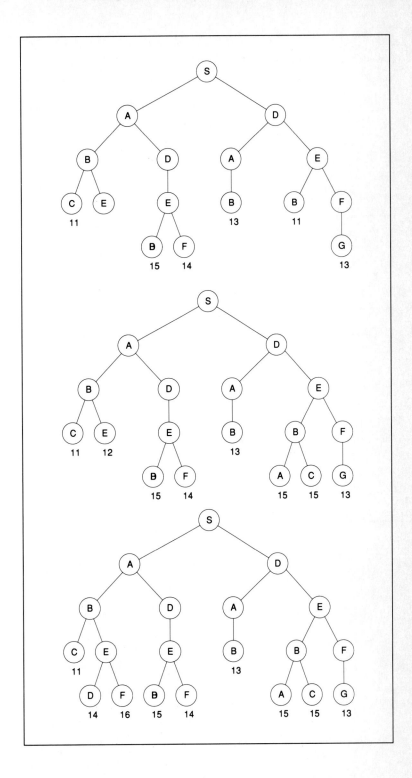

of remaining distance can be guaranteed to be underestimates, you cannot blunder.

When you are working out a path on a highway map, straight-line distance is guaranteed to be an underestimate. Figure 5.3 shows how straight-line distance helps to make the search efficient. As before, A and D are generated from S. This time, D is the node from which to search, because D's underestimated path length is 12.9, which is shorter than that for A, 13.4.

Expanding D leads to partial path S–D–A, with an underestimated path length of 19.4, and to partial path S–D–E, with a underestimated path length of 12.9. S–D–E is therefore the partial path to extend. The result is one path to B with a distance estimate of 17.7, and another path to F with a distance estimate of 13.0.

Expanding the partial path to F is the correct move, because it is the partial path with the minimum underestimated path length. This expansion leads to a complete path, S–D–E–F–G, with a total distance of 13.0. No partial path has a lower-bound distance so low, so no further search is required.

In this particular example, a great deal of work is avoided. Here is the modified procedure, with the modification in italic:

To conduct a branch-and-bound search with a lower-bound estimate,

▷ Form a one-element queue consisting of a zero-length path that contains only the root node.

▷ Until the first path in the queue terminates at the goal node or the queue is empty,

    ▷ Remove the first path from the queue; create new paths by extending the first path to all the neighbors of the terminal node.

    ▷ Reject all new paths with loops.

    ▷ Add the remaining new paths, if any, to the queue.

    ▷ Sort the entire queue by *the sum of the path length and a lower-bound estimate of the cost remaining*, with least-cost paths in front.

▷ If the goal node is found, announce success; otherwise, announce failure.

Of course, the closer an underestimate is to the true distance, the more efficiently you search, because, if there is no difference at all, there is no chance of developing any false movement. At the other extreme, an underestimate may be so poor as to be hardly better than a guess of zero,

Figure 5.3 Branch-and-bound search augmented by underestimates determines that the path S–D–E–F–G is optimal. The numbers beside the nodes are accumulated distances plus underestimates of distances remaining. Underestimates quickly push up the lengths associated with bad paths. In this example, many fewer nodes are expanded than would be expanded with branch-and-bound search operating without underestimates.

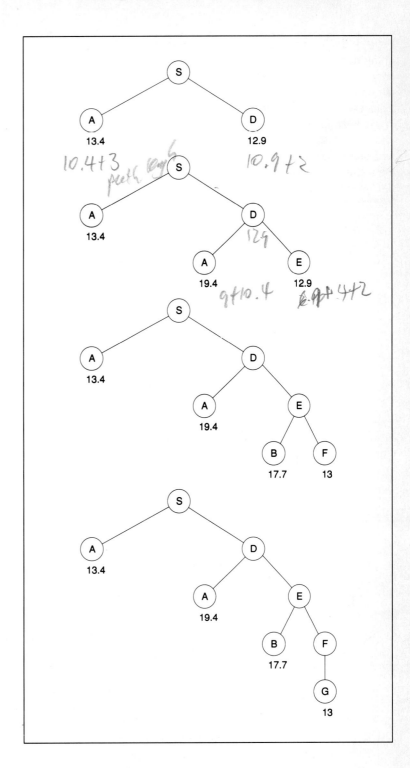

Figure 5.4 An illustration of the dynamic-programming principle. The numbers beside the nodes are accumulated distances. There is no point in expanding the instance of node D at the end of S–A–D, because getting to the goal via the instance of D at the end of S–D is obviously more efficient.

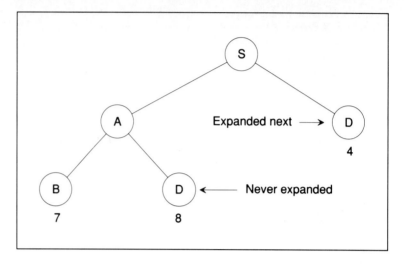

which certainly must always be the ultimate underestimate of remaining distance. In fact, ignoring estimates of remaining distance altogether can be viewed as the special case in which the underestimate used is uniformly zero.

REDUNDANT PATHS

In this section, you learn still more about the map-traversal problem that emerged in Chapter 4, but now you look at it with a view toward weeding out redundant partial paths that destroy search efficiency. In the end, you learn how to bring together several distinct ideas to form the A* procedure, and you see how A* can be put to work on a robot planning problem.

Redundant Partial Paths Should Be Discarded

Now let us consider another way to improve on basic branch-and-bound search. Look at figure 5.4. The root node, S, has been expanded, producing partial paths S–A and S–D. For the moment, let us use no underestimates for remaining path length.

Because S–A is shorter than S–D, S–A is extended first, leaving three paths: S–A–B, S–A–D, and S–D. Then, S–D will be extended, because it is the partial path with the shortest length.

But what about the path S–A–D? Will it ever make sense to extend it? Clearly, it will not. Because there is one path to D with length 4, it cannot make sense to work with another path to D with length 8. The path S–A–D should be forgotten forever; it cannot produce a winner.

This example illustrates a general principle. Assume that the path from a starting point, S, to an intermediate point, I, does not influence the choice of paths for traveling from I to a goal point, G. Then the minimum distance from S to G through I is the sum of the minimum distance from S to I and the minimum distance from I to G. Consequently, the strangely named **dynamic-programming principle** holds that, when you look for the best path from S to G, you can ignore all paths from S to any intermediate node, I, other than the minimum-length path from S to I:

The **dynamic-programming principle**:

▷ The best way *through* a particular, intermediate place is the best way *to it* from the starting place, followed by the best way *from it* to the goal. There is no need to look at any other paths to or from the intermediate place.

The branch-and-bound procedure, with dynamic programming included, is as follows:

To conduct a branch-and-bound search with dynamic programming,

▷ Form a one-element queue consisting of a zero-length path that contains only the root node.

▷ Until the first path in the queue terminates at the goal node or the queue is empty,

  ▷ Remove the first path from the queue; create new paths by extending the first path to all the neighbors of the terminal node.

  ▷ Reject all new paths with loops.

  ▷ Add the remaining new paths, if any, to the queue.

  ▷ *If two or more paths reach a common node, delete all those paths except the one that reaches the common node with the minimum cost.*

  ▷ Sort the entire queue by path length with least-cost paths in front.

▷ If the goal node is found, announce success; otherwise, announce failure.

Figure 5.5 shows the effect of using the dynamic-programming principle, together with branch-and-bound search, on the map-traversal problem. Four paths are cut off quickly, leaving only the dead-end path to node C and the optimal path, S–D–E–F–G.

Figure 5.5 Branch-and-bound
search, augmented by dynamic
programming, determines
that path S–D–E–F–G is
optimal. The numbers beside
the nodes are accumulated
path distances. Many paths,
those shown terminated with
underbars, are found to be
redundant. Thus, dynamic
programming reduces the
number of nodes expanded.

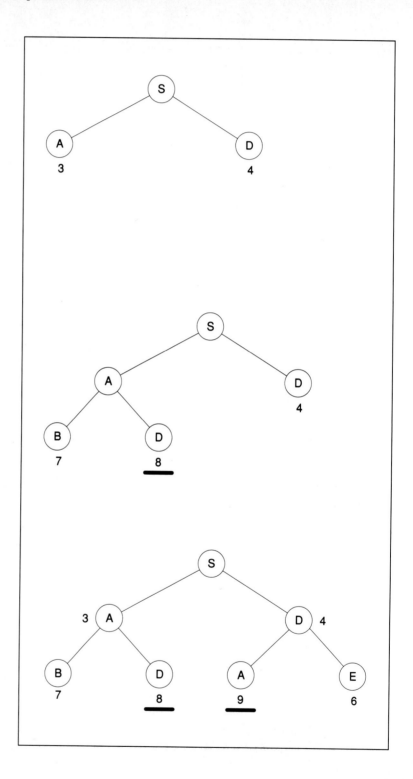

Figure 5.5 Continued.

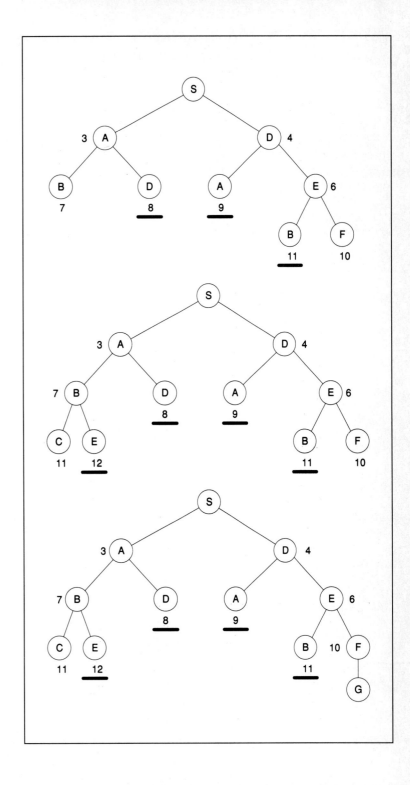

Underestimates and Dynamic Programming Improve Branch-and-Bound Search

The A* **procedure** is branch-and-bound search, with an estimate of remaining distance, combined with the dynamic-programming principle. If the estimate of remaining distance is a lower-bound on the actual distance, then A* produces optimal solutions. Generally, the estimate may be assumed to be a lower bound estimate, unless specifically stated otherwise, implying that A*'s solutions are normally optimal. Note the similarity between A* and branch-and-bound search with dynamic programming:

To conduct A* search,

▷ Form a one-element queue consisting of a zero-length path that contains only the root node.

▷ Until the first path in the queue terminates at the goal node or the queue is empty,

  ▷ Remove the first path from the queue; create new paths by extending the first path to all the neighbors of the terminal node.

  ▷ Reject all new paths with loops.

  ▷ If two or more paths reach a common node, delete all those paths except the one that reaches the common node with the minimum cost.

  ▷ Sort the entire queue by the sum of the path length and a lower-bound estimate of the cost remaining, with least-cost paths in front.

▷ If the goal node is found, announce success; otherwise, announce failure.

Several Search Procedures Find the Optimal Path

You have seen that there are many ways to search for optimal paths, each of which has advantages:

■   The British Museum procedure is good only when the search tree is small.

■   Branch-and-bound search is good when the tree is big and bad paths turn distinctly bad quickly.

■   Branch-and-bound search with a guess is good when there is a good lower-bound estimate of the distance remaining to the goal.

■   Dynamic programming is good when many paths converge on the same place.

■   The A* procedure is good when both branch-and-bound search with a guess and dynamic programming are good.

Figure 5.6 An obstacle-avoidance problem. The problem is to move the small triangular robot to a new position, shown dotted, without bumping into the pentagon or the octagon.

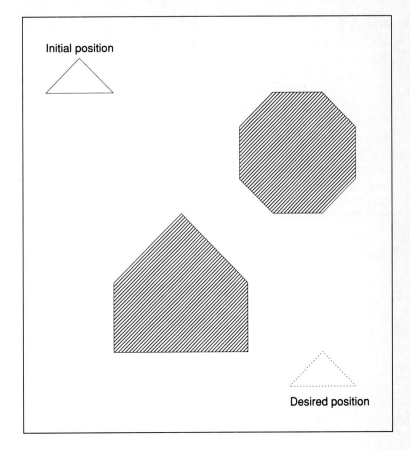

Robot Path Planning Illustrates Search

To see how the A* search procedure can be put to use, consider the collision-avoidance problem faced by robots. Before a robot begins to move in a cluttered environment, it must compute a collision-free path between where it is and where it wants to be. This requirement holds for locomotion of the whole robot through a cluttered environment and for robot hand motion through a component-filled workspace.

Figure 5.6 illustrates this motion-planning problem in a simple world inhabited by a triangular robot. The robot wants to move, without turning, from its initial position to the new position indicated by the dashed-line triangle. The question is, Can the robot make it through the gap between the pentagon and the octagon?

In two dimensions, a clever trick makes the problem easy. The general idea is to redescribe the problem in another, simpler representation, to solve the simpler problem, and to redescribe the solution in the original representation. Overall, taking this approach is like doing multiplication by moving back and forth between numbers and their logarithms or like

Figure 5.7 The configuration-space transformation. The heavy line shows the locus of the small triangle's lower-left corner as the small triangle is moved around the big one. Numbered positions are the starting points for each straight-line run. Keeping the lower-left corner away from the heavy line keeps the small triangle away from the pentagon.

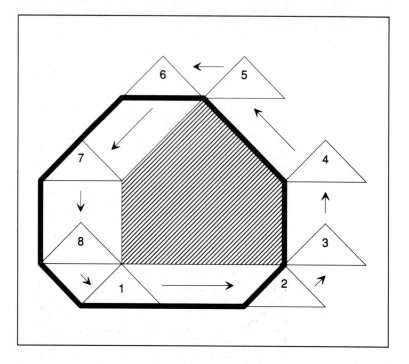

analyzing linear systems by moving back and forth between signals and their Fourier transforms.

For obstacle avoidance, the original representation involves a moving object and stationary obstacles, and the new representation involves a moving point and larger, virtual obstacles called **configuration-space obstacles**.

Figure 5.7 shows how you can transform an ordinary obstacle into a configuration-space obstacle using the object to be moved and the obstacle to be avoided. Basically, you slide the object around the obstacle, maintaining contact between them at all times, keeping track of one arbitrary tracing point on the moving object as you go. As the tracing point moves around the obstacle, it builds an eight-sided fence. Plainly, there can be no collision between object and obstacle as long as the tracing point stays outside the fence that bounds the configuration-space obstacle associated with the original obstacle.

Figure 5.8 shows both of the configuration-space obstacles made from the original triangle and the pentagon and octagon shown in figure 5.6. The lower-left vertex of the triangular robot was used. Evidently, the robot can get through the gap, because the configuration-space obstacles are not large enough to close up the space.

It is not entirely clear that the shortest path is through the gap, however. To be sure that it is, you have to search.

Figure 5.8 The configuration space for the problem shown in figure 5.6. No collision occurs if the point is kept out of the shaded area.

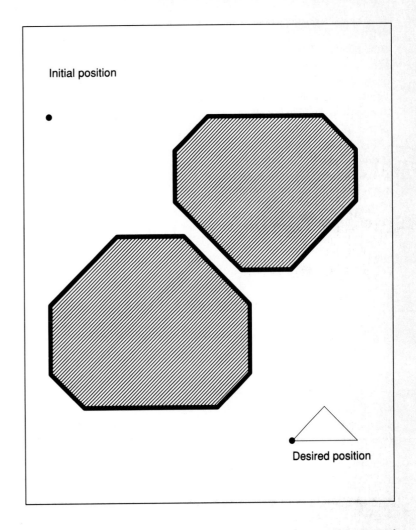

Initial position

Desired position

As yet, there is no net through which to search. The construction of a net is easy, however, for two-dimensional configuration-space problems. To see why it is easy, suppose that you are at any point in a configuration space. From where you are, you either can see the desired position or you cannot see it. If you can, you need to think no more, for the shortest path is the straight line between you and the desired position.

If you cannot see the desired position from where you are, then the only move that makes sense is a move to one of the vertexes that you can see. Accordingly, all motion is confined to motion from vertex to vertex, except at the beginning, when motion is from initial position to a vertex, and at the end, when motion is from a vertex to the desired position. Thus, the initial position, desired position, and vertexes are like the nodes in a net. Because the links between nodes are placed only when there is an

Figure 5.9 In a two-dimensional configuration space, the point robot moves along the straight lines of a visibility graph. An A* search through the visibility graph produces the shortest path from the initial position to the desired position. The heavy arrow shows the shortest path.

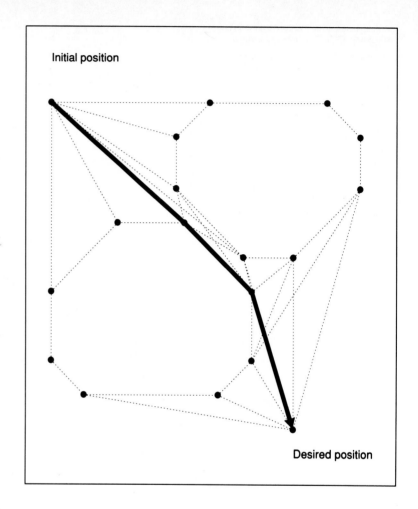

unobstructed line of sight between the nodes, the net is call a **visibility graph**.

Figure 5.9 illustrates the visibility graph for the robot-motion example, along with the result of performing an A* search to establish the shortest path for the configuration-space robot, a point, through the space of configuration-space obstacles, all oddly shaped. Figure 5.10 shows motion of the actual robot, along with the actual obstacles it circumnavigates, all superimposed on the solution in configuration space.

If you allow the moving object to rotate, you can make several configuration spaces corresponding to various degrees of rotation for the moving object. Then, the search involves motion not only through individual configuration spaces, but also from space to space.

Still more generally, when you need to move an arm, holding an object, in three dimensions, rather than just two, the construction of a suitable con-

Figure 5.10 The robot's movement is dictated by the shortest path found in the visibility graph. The lower-left corner of the triangular robot—the one used to produce configuration-space obstacles—is moved along the shortest path. Note that the triangular robot never collides with either the pentagon or the octagon.

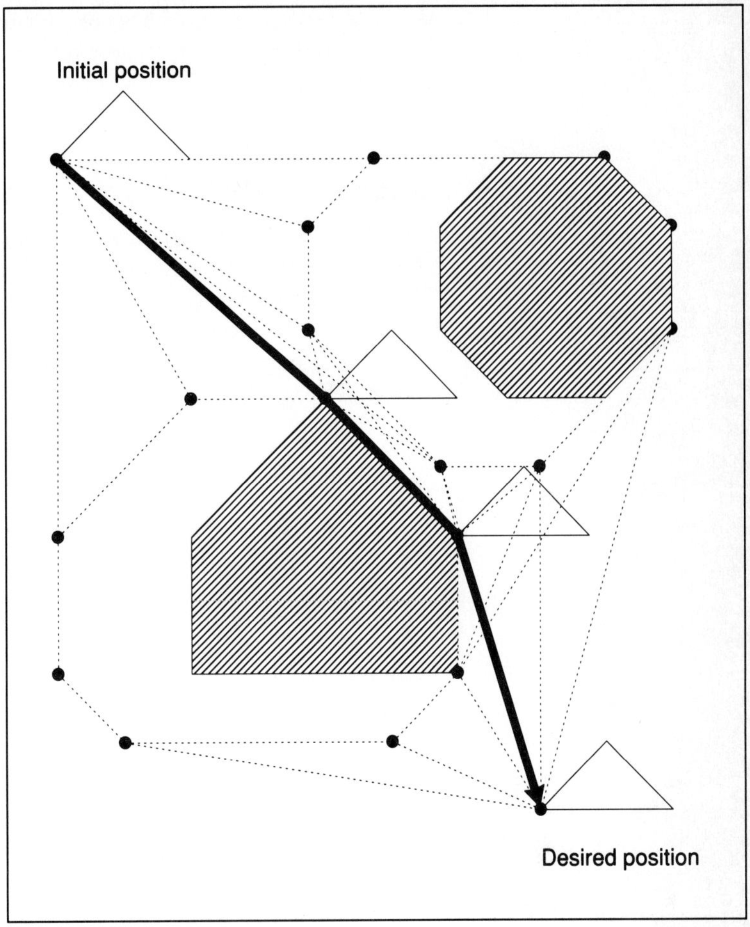
Initial position
Desired position

figuration space is extremely complicated mathematically. Complication-loving mathematicians have produced a flood of literature on the subject.

SUMMARY

- The British Museum procedure is one of many search procedures oriented toward finding the shortest path between two points. The British Museum procedure relies on working out all possible paths.
- Branch-and-bound search usually saves a lot of time relative to the British Museum procedure. It works by extending the least-cost partial path until that path reaches the goal.
- Adding underestimates to branch-and-bound search improves efficiency. Deleting redundant partial paths, a form of dynamic programming, also improves efficiency. Adding underestimates and deleting redundant partial paths converts branch-and-bound search into A* search.

■   The configuration-space transformation turns object-obstacle problems
    into point-obstacle problems. So transformed, robot path-planning
    problems succumb to A* search.

BACKGROUND

Optimal search methods are discussed in great detail in many books on
algorithms. In particular, see the textbook, *Introduction to Algorithms*, by
Thomas H. Cormen, Charles E. Leiserson, and Ronald L. Rivest [1990] for
an excellent treatment.

The discussion of configuration space is based on the work of Tomás
Lozano-Pérez [1980].

6

Trees and
Adversarial Search

In this chapter, you learn about how programs can play board games, such as checkers and chess, in which one choice leads to another producing a tree of choices. In contrast with the choices in Chapter 4 and Chapter 5, the choices here are the interdigitated choices of two adversaries.

In particular, you learn about *minimax search*, the basic method for deciding what to do, and about *alpha–beta pruning*, an idea that greatly reduces search by *stopping work on guaranteed losers*. You also learn about *progressive deepening* and *heuristic continuation*, both of which help programs to allocate search effort more effectively.

Once you have finished this chapter, you will know that you should not waste time exploring alternatives that are sure to be bad, and that you should spend a lot of time buttressing conclusions that are based on only flimsy evidence.

ALGORITHMIC METHODS

In this section, you learn how game situations can be represented in trees, and you learn how those trees can be searched so as to make the most promising move.

Figure 6.1 Games raise a new issue: competition. The nodes in a game tree represent board configurations, and the branches indicate how moves can connect them.

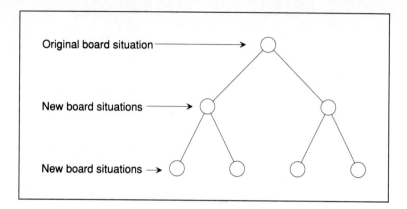

Nodes Represent Board Positions

As shown in figure 6.1, the natural way to represent what can happen in a game is to use a **game tree**, which is a special kind of semantic tree in which the nodes denote board configurations, and the branches indicate how one board configuration can be transformed into another by a single move. Of course, there is special twist in that the decisions are made by two adversaries who take turns making decisions.

The **ply** of a game tree, p, is the number of levels of the tree, including the root level. If the depth of a tree is d, then $p = d + 1$. In the chess literature, a **move** consists of one player's choice and another player's reaction. Here, however, we will be informal, referring to each choice as a *move*.

Exhaustive Search Is Impossible

Using something like the British Museum procedure, introduced in Chapter 5, to search game trees is definitely out. For chess, for example, if we take the effective branching factor to be 16 and the effective depth to be 100, then the number of branches in an exhaustive survey of chess possibilities would be on the order of 10^{120}—a ridiculously large number. In fact, if all the atoms in the universe had been computing chess moves at picosecond speeds since the big bang (if any), the analysis would be just getting started.

At the other end of the spectrum, if only there were some infallible way to rank the members of a set of board situations, it would be a simple matter to play by selecting the move that leads to the best situation that can be reached by one move. No search would be necessary. Unfortunately, no such situation-ranking procedure exists. When one board situation is enormously superior to another, a simple measure, such as a piece count, is likely to reflect that superiority, but always relying on such a measure to rank the available moves from a given situation produces poor results. Some other strategy is needed.

One other strategy is to use a situation analyzer only after several rounds of move and countermove. This approach cannot be pursued too far because the number of alternatives soon becomes unthinkable, but if search terminates at some reasonable depth, perhaps the leaf-node situations can be compared, yielding a basis for move selection. Of course, the underlying presumption of this approach is that the merit of a move clarifies as the move is pursued and that the lookahead procedure can extend far enough that even rough board-evaluation procedures may be satisfactory.

The Minimax Procedure Is a Lookahead Procedure

Suppose we have a situation analyzer that converts all judgments about board situations into a single, overall quality number. Further suppose that positive numbers, by convention, indicate favor to one player, and negative numbers indicate favor to the other. The degree of favor increases with the absolute value of the number.

The process of computing a number that reflects board quality is called **static evaluation**. The procedure that does the computation is called a **static evaluator**, and the number it computes is called the **static evaluation score**.

The player hoping for positive numbers is called the **maximizing player** or the **maximizer**. The other player is called the **minimizing player** or **minimizer**.

A **game tree** is a representation

That is a semantic tree

In which

▷ Nodes denote board configurations

▷ Branches denote moves

With writers that

▷ Establish that a node is for the maximizer or for the minimizer

▷ Connect a board configuration with a board-configuration description

With readers that

▷ Determine whether the node is for the maximizer or minimizer

▷ Produce a board configuration's description

The maximizer looks for a move that leads to a large positive number, and assumes that the minimizer will try to force the play toward situations with strongly negative static evaluations.

Thus, in the stylized, miniature game tree shown in figure 6.2, the maximizer might hope to get to the situation yielding a static score of 8. But the maximizer knows that the minimizer can choose a move deflecting the play toward the situation with a score of 1. In general, the decisions of the maximizer must take cognizance of the choices available to the minimizer at the next level down. Similarly, the decisions of the minimizer must take cognizance of the choices available to the maximizer at the next level down.

Eventually, however, the limit of exploration is reached and the static evaluator provides a direct basis for selecting among alternatives. In the example, the static evaluations at the bottom determine that the minimizer can choose between effective scores of 2 and 1 at the level just up from the static evaluations. Knowing these effective scores, the maximizer can make the best choice at the next level up. Clearly, the maximizer chooses to move toward the node from which the minimizer can do no better than to hold the effective score to 2. Again, the scores at one level determine the action and the effective score at the next level up.

The procedure by which the scoring information passes up the game tree is called the MINIMAX **procedure**, because the score at each node is either the minimum or the maximum of the scores at the nodes immediately below:

To perform a minimax search using MINIMAX,

▷ If the limit of search has been reached, compute the static value of the current position relative to the appropriate player. Report the result.

▷ Otherwise, if the level is a minimizing level, use MINIMAX on the children of the current position. Report the minimum of the results.

▷ Otherwise, the level is a maximizing level. Use MINIMAX on the children of the current position. Report the maximum of the results.

Note that the whole idea of minimaxing rests on the translation of board quality into a single, summarizing number, the static value. Unfortunately, a number is a poor summary.

Also note that minimaxing can be expensive, because either the generation of paths or static evaluation can require a lot of computation. Which costs more depends on how the move generator and static evaluator have been implemented.

The Alpha-Beta Procedure Prunes Game Trees

At first, it might seem that the static evaluator must be used on each leaf node at the bottom of the search tree. But, fortunately, this is not so.

Figure 6.2 Minimaxing is a method for determining moves. Minimaxing employs a static evaluator to calculate advantage-specifying numbers for the game situations at the bottom of a partially developed game tree. One player works toward the higher numbers, seeking the advantage, while the opponent goes for the lower numbers.

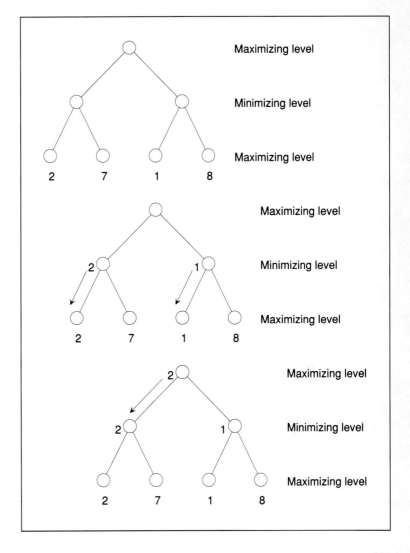

There is a procedure that reduces both the number of tree branches that must be generated and the number of static evaluations that must be done, thus cutting down on the work to be done overall. It is somewhat like the branch-and-bound idea in that some paths are demonstrated to be bad even though not followed to the lookahead limit.

Consider the situation shown at the top of figure 6.3, in which the static evaluator has already been used on the first two leaf-node situations. Performing the MINIMAX procedure on the scores of 2 and 7 determines that the minimizing player is guaranteed a score of 2 if the maximizer takes the left branch at the top node. This move in turn ensures that the maximizer is guaranteed a score at least as good as 2 at the top. This guarantee

Figure 6.3 The ALPHA–BETA procedure at work. There is no need to explore the right side of the tree fully, because there is no way the result could alter the move decision. Once movement to the right is shown to be worse than movement to the left, there is no need to see how much worse.

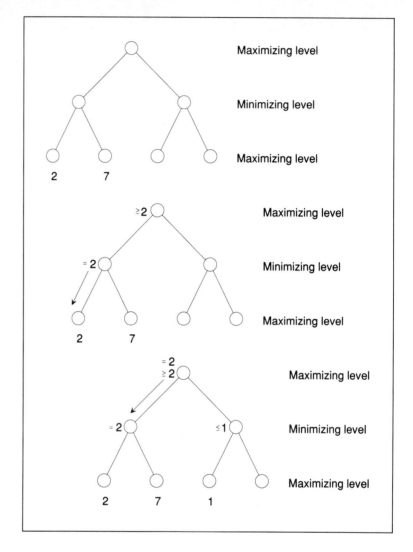

is clear, even before any other static evaluations are made, because the maximizer can certainly elect the left branch whenever the right branch turns out to result in a lower score. This situation is indicated at the top node in the middle of figure 6.3.

Now suppose the static value of the next leaf node is 1. Evidently, the minimizer is guaranteed a score at least as low as 1 by the same reasoning that showed that the maximizer is guaranteed a score at least as high as 2 at the top. At the maximizer levels, a *good* score is a larger value; at the minimizer levels, a *good* score is a smaller value.

Look closely at the tree. Does it make sense to go on to the board situation at the final node? Can the value produced there by the static evaluator possibly matter? Strangely, the answer is No. For surely if the maximizer knows that it is guaranteed a score of 2 along the left branch, it needs to know no more about the right branch other than that it can get a score of no higher than 1 there. The last node evaluated could be +100, or −100, or any number whatever, without affecting the result. The maximizer's score is 2, as shown in the bottom of figure 6.3.

On reflection, it is clear that, if an opponent has one response establishing that a potential move is bad, there is no need to check any other responses to the potential move. More generally, you have an instance of the following powerful idea:

The **alpha–beta principle**:

▷ If you have an idea that is surely bad, do not take time
  to see how truly awful it is.

This idea is called the alpha–beta principle because, as you see later, it is embodied in the ALPHA–BETA *procedure*, which uses two parameters, traditionally called alpha and beta, to keep track of expectations.

In the special context of games, the alpha–beta principle dictates that, whenever you discover a fact about a given node, you should check what you know about ancestor nodes. It may be that no further work is sensible below the parent node. Also, it may be that the best that you can hope for at the parent node can be revised or determined exactly.

With the alpha–beta principle translated into instructions for dealing with score changes, you can work through a larger example. Unfortunately, it is a bit difficult to see how static evaluations intermix with conclusions about node values on paper. We must make do with boxed event numbers placed beside each conclusion showing the order in which the conclusions are determined. These numbers are shown in the example of figure 6.4, in which we look at another stylized tree with a depth of 3 and a uniform branching factor of 3:

1–2.   Moving down the left branch at every decision point, the search penetrates to the bottom where a static value of 8 is unearthed. This 8 clearly means that the maximizer is guaranteed a score at least as high as 8 with the three choices available. A note to this effect is placed by step 2.

3–5.   To be sure no score higher than 8 can be found, the maximizer examines the two other moves available to it. Because 7 and 3 both indicate inferior moves, the maximizer concludes that the highest score achievable is exactly 8 and that the correct move is the first one examined.

6.   Nailing down the maximizer's score at the lowest node enables you to draw a conclusion about what the minimizer can hope for at

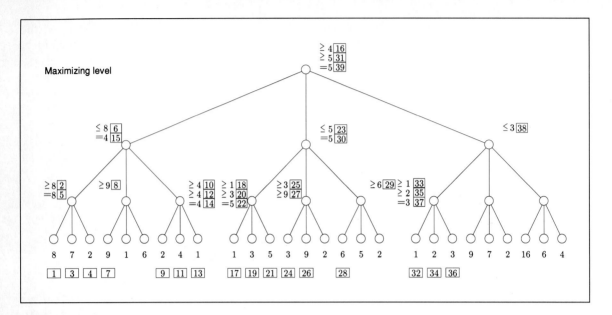

Maximizing level

Figure 6.4 A game tree of depth 3 and branching factor 3. The boxed numbers show the order in which conclusions are drawn. Note that only 16 static evaluations are made, rather than the 27 required without alpha–beta pruning. Evidently the best play for the maximizer is down the middle branch.

the next level up. Because one move is now known to lead to a situation that gives the maximizer a score of 8, you know that the minimizer at the next level up can achieve a score of 8 or lower.

7–8. To see whether the minimizer can do better at the second level, you must examine his two remaining moves. The first leads to a situation from which the maximizer can score at least a 9. Here cutoff occurs. By taking the left branch, the minimizer forces a score of 8; but by taking the middle branch, the minimizer allows a score that is certainly no lower than 9 and will be higher if the other maximizer choices are higher. Hence, the middle branch is bad for the minimizer, there is no need to go on to find out how bad it is, and there is consequently no need for two static evaluations. There is no change in the minimizer's worst-case expectation; it is still 8.

9–14. The minimizer must still investigate its last option, the one to the right. You need to see what the maximizer can do there. The next series of steps bounces between static evaluations and conclusions about the maximizer's situation immediately above them. The conclusion is that the maximizer's score is 4.

15. Discovering that the right branch leads to a forced score of 4, the minimizer would take the right branch, because 4 is less than 8, the previous low score.

16. Now a bound can be placed at the top level. The maximizer, surveying the situation there, sees that its left branch leads to a score of 4, so it now knows it will score at least that high, and

	perhaps better. To see if it can do better, it must look at its middle and right branches.
17–22.	Deciding how the minimizer will react at the end of the middle branch requires knowing what happens along the left branch descending from there. Here, the maximizer is in action, discovering that the best play is to a position with a score of 5.
23.	Until something definite was known about what the maximizer could do, no bounds could be placed on the minimizer's potential. Knowing that the maximizer scores 5 along the left branch, however, is knowing something definite. The conclusion is that the minimizer can obtain a score at least as low as 5.
24–27.	In working out what the maximizer can do below the minimizer's middle branch, you discover partway through the analysis that the maximizer can reach a score of 9. But 9 is a poor choice relative to the known option of the minimizer that ensures a 5. Cutoff occurs again. There is no point in investigating the other maximizer option, so you avoid one static evaluation.
28–29.	Looking at the minimizer's right branch quickly shows that it, too, gives the maximizer a chance to force the play to a higher score than the minimizer can achieve along the left branch. Cutoff saves two static evaluations here.
30.	Because there are no more branches to investigate, the minimizer's score of 5 is no longer merely a bound; 5 is the actual value achievable.
31.	The maximizer at the top, seeing a choice leading to a higher score through the middle branch, chooses that branch tentatively and knows now that it can score at least as high as 5.
32–37.	Now the maximizer's right-branch choice at the top must be explored. Diving into the tree, bouncing about a bit, leads to the conclusion that the minimizer sees a left-branch choice ensuring a score of 3.
38.	The minimizer can conclude that the left-branch score is a bound on how low a score it can obtain.
39.	Knowing the minimizer can force play to a situation with a score of 3, the maximizer at the top level concludes that there is no point in exploring the right branch farther. After all, a score of 5 follows a middle-branch move. Note that this saves six static evaluations, as well as two move generations.

It is not unusual to get lost in this demonstration. Even seasoned game specialists still find magic in the ALPHA–BETA procedure. Each individual conclusion seems right, but somehow the global result is strange and hard to believe.

Note that, in the example, you never had to look more than one level up to decide whether or not to stop exploration. In deeper trees, with four or more levels, so-called **deep cutoffs** can occur, forcing a longer look.

One way to keep track of all the bookkeeping is to use a procedure with parameters, alpha and beta, that record all the necessary observations. The ALPHA–BETA procedure is started on the root node with an alpha value of −∞ and a beta value of +∞; ALPHA–BETA then calls itself recursively with a narrowing range between the alpha and beta values:

To perform minimax search with the ALPHA–BETA procedure,

▷ If the level is the top level, let alpha be −∞ and let beta be ∞.

▷ If the limit of search has been reached, compute the static value of the current position relative to the appropriate player. Report the result.

▷ If the level is a minimizing level,

  ▷ Until all children are examined with ALPHA–BETA or until alpha is equal to or greater than beta,

    ▷ Use the ALPHA–BETA procedure, with the current alpha and beta values, on a child; note the value reported.

    ▷ Compare the value reported with the beta value; if the reported value is smaller, reset beta to the new value.

  ▷ Report beta.

▷ Otherwise, the level is a maximizing level:

  ▷ Until all children are examined with ALPHA–BETA or alpha is equal to or greater than beta,

    ▷ Use the ALPHA–BETA procedure, with the current alpha and beta value, on a child; note the value reported.

    ▷ Compare the value reported with the alpha value; if the reported value is larger, reset alpha to the new value.

  ▷ Report alpha.

Alpha-Beta May Not Prune Many Branches from the Tree

One way deepen your understanding of the ALPHA–BETA procedure is to ask about its the best-case and worst-case performance.

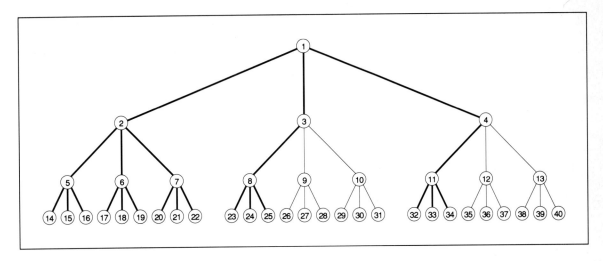

Figure 6.5 An ideal situation from the perspective of the ALPHA–BETA procedure. The ALPHA–BETA procedure cuts the exponent of exponential explosion in half, because not all the adversary's options need to be considered in verifying the left-branch choices. In a tree with depth 3 and branching factor 3, the ALPHA–BETA procedure can reduce the number of required static evaluations from 27 to 11.

In the worst case, for some trees, the branches can be ordered such that the ALPHA–BETA procedure does nothing. For other trees, however, there is no way to order the branches to avoid all alpha–beta cutoff.

For trees ordered by a cooperative oracle, the ALPHA–BETA procedure does a great deal. To see why, suppose a tree is ordered with each player's best move being the leftmost alternative at every node. Then, clearly, the best move of the player at the top is to the left. But how many static evaluations are needed for the topmost player to be sure that this move is optimal? To approach the question, consider the tree of depth 3 and branching factor 3 shown in figure 6.5.

Presuming that the best moves for both players are always to the left, then the value of the leftmost move for the maximizing player at the top is the static value of the board situation at the bottom left. This static value provides the maximizer with a concrete measurement against which the quality of the alternatives can be compared. The maximizer does not need to consider all the minimizer's replies to those alternatives, however.

To verify the correct move at a given node in an ordered tree, a player needs to consider relatively few of the leaf nodes descendant from the immediate alternatives to the move to be verified. All leaf nodes found below nonoptimal moves by the player's opponent can be ignored.

Why is it necessary to deal with all the options of the moving player while ignoring all but one of the moving-player's opponent's moves? This point is a sticky one. To understand the explanation, you need to pay close attention to the alpha–beta principle: if an opponent has some response that makes a move bad no matter what the moving player does subsequently, then the move is bad.

The key to understanding lies in the words *some*, and *no matter what*. The *some* suggests that the moving player should analyze its opponent's moves wherever the opponent has a choice, hoping that the selected move certifies the conclusion. But to be sure that the conclusion holds no matter what the moving player might do, the moving player must check out all its choices.

Thus, the hope in the example in figure 6.5 is that only the leftmost branch from node 3 to node 8 will need exploration. All the maximizer's counterresponses to that move must be checked, so static evaluations need to be made at nodes 23, 24, and 25.

These evaluations establish that the maximizer's score at node 8, which in turn sets a bound on what the minimizer can do at node 3, which, by comparison with the minimizer's score at node 2, should show that no further work below node 3 makes any sense. Similar reasoning applies to node 4, which leads to static evaluations at node 32, node 33, and node 34.

Now, however, the question is, How can the maximizer be sure that the score transferred up the left edge is valid? Surely, it must verify that an intelligent minimizer at node 2 would select the leftmost branch. It can do this verification by assuming the number coming up the left edge from node 5 is correct and then rejecting the alternatives as efficiently as possible. But, by the same arguments used at node 1, it is clear that not all the minimizer's opponent's options need to be examined. Again, branching occurs only at every second level, working out from the choice to be verified along the left edge. Static evaluations must be done at nodes 17 and 20.

Finally, there is the question of the minimizer's assumption about the number coming up from node 5. Answering this question requires exploring all of the maximizer's alternatives, resulting in static evaluations at node 15 and node 16 to ensure that the static evaluation done at node 14 yields the correct number to transfer up to node 5.

You need to make only 11 of the 27 possible static evaluations to discover the best move when, by luck, the alternatives in the tree have been nicely ordered. In deeper trees with more branching, the saving is more dramatic. In fact, it can be demonstrated that the number of static evaluations, s, needed to discover the best move in an optimally arranged tree is given by the following formula, where b is the branching factor and d is the depth of the tree:

$$ s = \begin{cases} 2b^{d/2} - 1 & \text{for } d \text{ even;} \\ b^{(d+1)/2} + b^{(d-1)/2} - 1 & \text{for } d \text{ odd.} \end{cases} $$

A straightforward proof by induction verifies the formula. You need only to generalize the line of argument used in the previous example, focusing on the idea that verification of a choice requires a full investigation of only every second level. Note that the formula is certainly correct for $d = 1$, because it then simplifies to b. For $d = 3$ and $b = 3$, the formula yields 11, which nicely resonates with the conclusion reached for the example.

But be warned: The formula is valid for only the special case in which a tree is perfectly arranged. As such, the formula is an approximation to what can actually be expected; if there were a way of arranging the tree

Figure 6.6 Explosive growth. The ALPHA–BETA procedure reduces the rate of explosive growth, but does not prevent it. The branching factor is assumed to be 10.

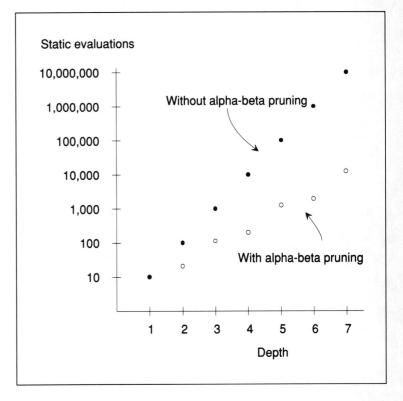

with the best moves on the left, clearly there would be no point in using alpha–beta pruning. Noting this fact is not the same as saying that the exercise has been fruitless, however. It establishes the lower bound on the number of static evaluations that would be needed in a real game. It is a lower bound that may or may not be close to the real result, depending on how well the moves are, in fact, arranged. The real result must lie somewhere between the worst case, for which static values must be computed for all b^d leaf nodes, and the best case, for which static values must be computed for approximately $2b^{d/2}$ leaf nodes. In practice, the number of static evaluations seems nearer to the best case than the worst case, nature proving unusually beneficent.

Still, the amount of work required becomes impossibly large with increasing depth. The ALPHA–BETA procedure merely wins a temporary reprieve from the effects of the explosive, exponential growth. The procedure does not prevent the explosive growth, as figure 6.6 shows.

HEURISTIC METHODS

In this section, you learn how to search game trees under time pressure so you can make a reasonable move within allowed time limits. You also learn how to allocate computational effort so you are as confident as possible that the best choice found is at least a good choice.

Progressive Deepening Keeps Computing Within Time Bounds

In tournaments, players are required to make a certain number of moves within time limits enforced by a relentless clock. This rule creates a problem, because the time required to search to any fixed depth depends on the situation. To search to a fixed depth, independent of the evolving game, you have to use a conservative choice for the fixed depth. Otherwise, you will lose games by running out of time. On the other hand, a conservative choice means that you have to be content to do less search than you could most of the time.

The way to wriggle out of this dilemma is to analyze each situation to depth 1, then to depth 2, then to depth 3, and so on until the amount of time set aside for the move is used up. This way, there is always a move choice ready to go. The choice is determined by the analysis at one level less deep than the analysis in progress when time runs out. This method is called **progressive deepening**.

At first, it might seem that a great deal of time would be wasted in extra analysis at shallow levels. Curiously, however, little time is wasted. To see why, let us suppose, for simplicity, that the dominant cost in analysis is that for static evaluation. The number of nodes requiring static evaluation at the bottom of a tree with depth d and effective branching factor b is b^d. With a bit of algebra, it is easy to show that the number of nodes in the rest of the tree is

$$b^0 + b^1 + \cdots + b^{d-1} = \frac{b^d - 1}{b - 1}.$$

Thus, the ratio of the number of nodes in the bottom level to the number of nodes up to the bottom level is

$$\frac{b^d(b - 1)}{b^d - 1} \approx b - 1.$$

For $b = 16$, the number of static evaluations needed to do minimaxing at every level up to the bottom level is but one-fifteenth of the static evaluation needed to do minimaxing at the bottom level. Insurance against running out of time is a good buy.

Heuristic Continuation Fights the Horizon Effect

You can get a false sense of euphoria if your analysis stops just before your opponent captures one of your pieces; symmetrically, you can get a false sense of depression if your analysis stops just before you capture one of the opponent's pieces. To avoid such false senses, you have to explore the search tree until no captures are imminent.

When a capture is imminent, often only one move makes sense, and that move is said to be **forced**. Interestingly, you can usually determine whether a move is forced by analyzing the local static-value situation. In forced-moved situations, the child node involving a capture generally has a static value that stands out from the rest, because most static evaluators weight piece count heavily.

The **singular-extension heuristic** dictates that search should continue as long as one move's static value stands out, indicating a likely capture. As shown by figure 6.7, for example, the maximizer's capture at the top of the tree produces a static value that is very different from that of other moves. Similarly, the minimizer's responding capture produces a static value that is much different from the other moves. Eventually, however, all available moves have static values within a narrow range, suggesting that there is no capture opportunity at that point; hence, there is no forced move, and no further search is dictated by the singular-extension heuristic.

If you do not use the singular-extension heuristic, or a similar procedure, you risk harm from the **horizon effect**. Early chess programs searched all paths to the same depth, thus establishing an horizon beyond which disasters often lurked. As a result, those early programs often seized low-valued pieces along paths that led to the loss of high-valued pieces farther on.

In figure 6.7, for example, if the maximizer fails to look beyond the horizon shown, then the maximizer is seduced into a move that leads to a node with a static value of +6. Unfortunately, that move proves to be less advantageous than other moves with lower static values.

Heuristic Pruning Also Limits Search

Pruning procedures are used occasionally, albeit not often, in combination with alpha–beta search to limit tree growth by reducing the effective branching factor.

One way to prune a game tree is to arrange for the branching factor to vary with depth of penetration, possibly using **tapered search** to direct more effort into the more promising moves. You can perform tapered search by ranking each node's children, perhaps using a fast static evaluator, and then deploying the following formula:

$$b(\text{child}) = b(\text{parent}) - r(\text{child}),$$

where $b(\text{child})$ is the number of branches to be retained at some child node, $b(\text{parent})$ is the number of branches retained by the child node's parent, and $r(\text{child})$ is the rank of the child node among its siblings. If a node is one of five children and ranks second most plausible among those five, then it should itself have $5 - 2 = 3$ children. An example of a tree formed using this approach is shown in figure 6.8.

Another way of cutting off disasters is to stop search from going down through apparently bad moves no matter what. If only one line of play makes any sense at all, that line would be the only one pursued.

Figure 6.7 An example of the horizon effect. All numbers shown are static values. Looking ahead by only one level, the leftmost branch looks best, for it has a static value of 6. The minimax score, developed after looking ahead until there are no capture moves, is +1. The singular-extension heuristic prevents such blunders.

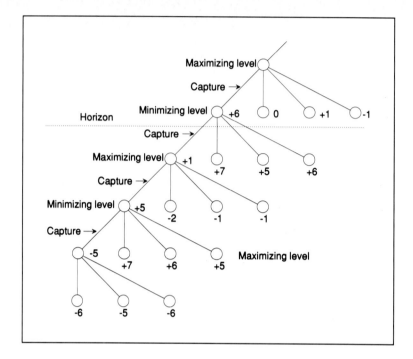

Figure 6.8 Tapering search gives more attention to the more plausible moves. Here, the tapering procedure reduces the search with increases in depth and decreases in plausibility.

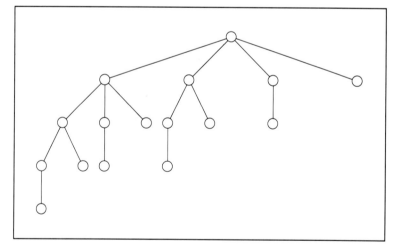

Needless to say, any heuristic that limits branching acts in opposition to lines of play that temporarily forfeit pieces for eventual position advantage. Because they trim off the moves that appear bad on the surface, procedures that limit branching are unlikely to discover spectacular moves that seem disastrous for a time, but then win back everything lost and more. There will be no queen sacrifices.

DEEP THOUGHT Plays Grandmaster Chess

To the surprise of many chess experts, an extremely good game of chess can be played by a search-based chess program, as long as the program can search deeply enough. The best such program at this writing, the DEEP THOUGHT program, uses a sophisticated special-purpose computer to perform the search. Using a special-purpose computer, and exploiting the alpha–beta procedure, DEEP THOUGHT usually is able to search down to about 10 ply.

Using the singular extension heuristic, DEEP THOUGHT often goes much further still, shocking some human opponents with its ability to penetrate complicated situations.

DEEP THOUGHT's static evaluator considers piece count, piece placement, pawn structure, passed pawns, and the arrangement of pawns and rooks on columns, which are called files in the chess vernacular.

Curiously, the playing strength of several generations of search-oriented chess programs seems proportional to the number of ply that the programs can search. In the following illustration, program strength, as measured by the U.S. Chess Federation's rating scale, is plotted against search depth in ply:

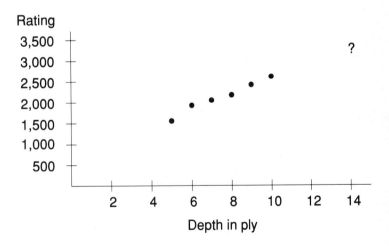

A successor to DEEP THOUGHT, projected to be 1000 times faster, is under development. Given a real branching factor of 35 to 40 for chess, the effective branching factor is about 6. Thus, 1000 times more speed should enable DEEP THOUGHT's successor to search to about 14 ply. If the relation between ply and rating continues to hold, this next-generation machine should have a rating in the vicinity of 3400, which is well above the 2900 rating of Gary Kasparov, the current world champion.

SUMMARY

- In the context of board games, nodes represent board positions, and branches represent moves.
- The depth, d, of a game tree is the number of moves played. The ply, p, is the depth plus one. The branching factor, b, is the average number of moves available at each node. You cannot play most games by working out all possible paths to game conclusion, because the number of paths, b^d, is too large.
- The MINIMAX procedure is based on the analysis of numeric assessments computed by a static evaluator at the bottom of a game tree.
- The ALPHA–BETA procedure prunes game trees, often cutting the effective branching factor in half, enabling search to go twice as far. The ALPHA–BETA procedure embodies the idea that you should not waste time analyzing options that you know are bad.
- Progressive deepening finds a move with one-move lookahead, then two-move, then three-move, and so on, until time runs out. Progressive deepening both guarantees that there is always a move ready to play and ensures that no time is squandered.
- Chess-playing programs now perform so well that many people believe they will soon overpower all human opponents. All the best chess-playing programs use a form of heuristic continuation to play out capture sequences.

BACKGROUND

The basic minimax approach to games was laid out by Claude E. Shannon [1950], who anticipated most of the subsequent work to date. The classic papers on checkers are by Arthur L. Samuel [1959, 1967]. They deal extensively with tree-pruning heuristics, schemes for combining evidence, and methods for adaptive parameter improvement.

The term *horizon effect* was coined by Hans J. Berliner [1973, 1978]. Berliner's work on chess is complemented by seminal progress on backgammon [Berliner, 1980].

DEEP THOUGHT was developed by Teng-hsiung Hsu, Thomas Anantharaman, Murray Campbell, and Andreas Nowatzyk [1990]. Hsu conceived the singular-extension idea for searching game trees beyond normal depth.

David A. McAllester has proposed an extremely clever approach to growing search trees sensibly without using alpha–beta pruning [1988]. McAllester's approach introduces the notion of a *conspiracy number*, which is the minimum number of static values that you must change to change what the moving player will do. In general, small conspiracy numbers indicate a need for further search.

7

Rules and Rule Chaining

In this chapter, you learn about the use of easily-stated *if–then rules* to solve problems. In particular, you learn about *forward chaining* from assertions and *backward chaining* from hypotheses.

By way of illustration, you learn about two toy systems; one identifies zoo animals, the other bags groceries. These examples are analogous to influential, classic systems that diagnose diseases and configure computers.

You also learn about how to implement rule-based systems. You learn, for example, how search methods can be deployed to determine which of many possible rules are applicable during backward chaining, and you learn how the *rete procedure* does efficient forward chaining.

When you have finished this chapter, you will understand the key ideas that support many of the useful applications of artificial intelligence. Such applications are often mislabeled **expert systems**, even though their problem-solving behavior seems more like that of human novices, rather than of human experts.

RULE-BASED DEDUCTION SYSTEMS

Rule-based problem-solving systems are built using rules like the following, each of which contains several *if* patterns and one or more *then* patterns:

Figure 7.1 A convenient graphical notation for antecedent–consequent rules. The symbol, appropriately, is the same as the one used in digital electronics for AND gates.

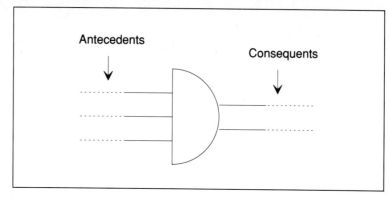

$$\text{R}n \qquad \text{If} \qquad if_1$$
$$if_2$$
$$\vdots$$
$$\text{then} \qquad then_1$$
$$then_2$$
$$\vdots$$

In this section, you learn how rule-based systems work.

Many Rule-Based Systems Are Deduction Systems

A statement that something is true, such as "Stretch has long legs," or "Stretch is a giraffe," is an **assertion**.[†] In all rule-based systems, each *if* pattern is a pattern that may match one or more of the assertions in a collection of assertions. The collection of assertions is sometimes called **working memory**.

In many rule-based systems, the *then* patterns specify new assertions to be placed into working memory, and the rule-based system is said to be a **deduction system**. In deduction systems, the convention is to refer to each *if* pattern as an **antecedent** and to each *then* pattern as a **consequent**. Figure 7.1 shows a graphical notation for deduction-oriented **antecedent–consequent rules**.

Sometimes, however, the *then* patterns specify actions, rather than assertions—for example, "Put the item into the bag"—in which case the rule-based system is a **reaction system**.

In both deduction systems and reaction systems, **forward chaining** is the process of moving from the *if* patterns to the *then* patterns, using the *if* patterns to identify appropriate situations for the deduction of a new assertion or the performance of an action.

[†]Facts and assertions are subtly different: A *fact* is something known to be true; an assertion is a statement that something is a fact. Thus, assertions can be false, but facts cannot be false.

During forward chaining, whenever an *if* pattern is observed to match an assertion, the antecedent is **satisfied**. Whenever all the *if* patterns of a rule are satisfied, the rule is **triggered**. Whenever a triggered rule establishes a new assertion or performs an action, it is **fired**.

In deduction systems, all triggered rules generally fire. In reaction systems, however, when more than one rule is triggered at the same time, usually only one of the possible actions is desired, thus creating a need for some sort of *conflict-resolution procedure* to decide which rule should fire.

A Toy Deduction System Identifies Animals

Suppose that Robbie, a robot, wants to spend a day at the zoo. Robbie can perceive basic features, such as color and size, and whether an animal has hair or gives milk, but his ability to identify objects using those features is limited. He can distinguish animals from other objects, but he cannot use the fact that a particular animal has a long neck to conclude that he is looking at a giraffe.

Plainly, Robbie will enjoy the visit more if he can identify the individual animals. Accordingly, Robbie decides to build ZOOKEEPER, an identification-oriented deduction system.

Robbie could build ZOOKEEPER by creating one if–then rule for each kind of animal in the zoo. The consequent side of each rule would be a simple assertion of animal identity, and the antecedent side would be a bulbous enumeration of characteristics sufficiently complete to reject all incorrect identifications.

Robbie decides, however, to build ZOOKEEPER by creating rules that produce intermediate assertions. The advantage is that the antecedent–consequent rules involved need have only a few antecedents, making them easier for Robbie to create and use. Using this approach, ZOOKEEPER produces chains of conclusions leading to the identification of the animal that Robbie is currently examining.

Now suppose that Robbie's local zoo contains only seven animals: a cheetah, a tiger, a giraffe, a zebra, an ostrich, a penguin, and an albatross. This assumption simplifies ZOOKEEPER, because only a few rules are needed to distinguish one type of animal from another. One such rule, rule Z1, determines that a particular animal is a mammal:

Z1   If $?x$ has hair
        then $?x$ is a mammal

Note that antecedents and consequents are patterns that contain *variables*, such as x, marked by question-mark prefixes. Whenever a rule is considered, its variables have no values initially, but they acquire values as antecedent patterns are matched to assertions.

Suppose that a particular animal, named Stretch, has hair. Then, if the working memory contains the assertion *Stretch has hair*, the antecedent pattern, *?x has hair*, matches that assertion, and the value of *x* becomes *Stretch*. By convention, when variables become identified with values, they are said to be **bound** to those values and the values are sometimes called **bindings**. Thus, *x* is bound to *Stretch* and *Stretch* is *x*'s binding.

Once a variable is bound, that variable is replaced by its binding wherever the variable appears in the same or subsequently processed patterns. Whenever the variables in a pattern are replaced by variable bindings, the pattern is said to be **instantiated**. For example, the consequent pattern, *?x is a mammal* becomes *Stretch is a mammal* once instantiated by the variable binding acquired when the antecedent pattern was matched.

Now let us look at other ZOOKEEPER rules. Three others also determine biological class:

Z2   If   *?x* gives milk
      then   *?x* is a mammal

Z3   If   *?x* has feathers
      then   *?x* is a bird

Z4   If   *?x* flies
               ?x lays eggs
      then   *?x* is a bird

The last of these rules, Z4, has two antecedents. Although it does not really matter for the small collection of animals in ZOOKEEPER's world, some mammals fly and some reptiles lay eggs, but no mammal or reptile does both.

Once ZOOKEEPER knows that an animal is a mammal, two rules determine whether that animal is carnivorous. The simpler rule has to do with catching the animal in the act of having its dinner:

Z5   If   *?x* is a mammal
               ?x eats meat
      then   *?x* is a carnivore

If Robbie is not at the zoo at feeding time, various other factors, if available, provide conclusive evidence:

Z6   If   *?x* is a mammal
               ?x has pointed teeth
               ?x has claws
               ?x has forward-pointing eyes
      then   *?x* is a carnivore

All hooved animals are ungulates:

Z7	If	$?x$ is a mammal
		$?x$ has hoofs
	then	$?x$ is an ungulate

If Robbie has a hard time looking at the feet, ZOOKEEPER may still have a chance because all animals that chew cud are also ungulates:

Z8	If	$?x$ is a mammal
		$?x$ chews cud
	then	$?x$ is an ungulate

Now that Robbie has rules that divide mammals into carnivores and ungulates, it is time to add rules that identify specific animal identities. For carnivores, there are two possibilities:

Z9	If	$?x$ is a carnivore
		$?x$ has tawny color
		$?x$ has dark spots
	then	$?x$ is a cheetah

Z10	If	$?x$ is a carnivore
		$?x$ has tawny color
		$?x$ has black strips
	then	$?x$ is a tiger

Strictly speaking, the basic color is not useful because both of the carnivores are tawny. However, there is no need for information in rules to be minimal. Moreover, antecedents that are superfluous now may become essential later as new rules are added to deal with other animals.

For the ungulates, other rules separate the total group into two possibilities:

Z11	If	$?x$ is an ungulate
		$?x$ has long legs
		$?x$ has long neck
		$?x$ has tawny color
		$?x$ has dark spots
	then	$?x$ is a giraffe

Z12	If	$?x$ is an ungulate
		$?x$ has white color
		$?x$ has black stripes
	then	$?x$ is a zebra

Three more rules are needed to handle the birds:

Z13   If   *?x* is a bird
               ?x does not fly
               ?x has long legs
               ?x has long neck
               ?x is black and white
       then   *?x* is an ostrich

Z14   If   *?x* is a bird
               ?x does not fly
               ?x swims
               ?x is black and white
       then   *?x* is a penguin

Z15   If   *?x* is a bird
               ?x is a good flyer
       then   *?x* is an albatross

Now that you have seen all the rules in ZOOKEEPER, note that the animals evidently share many features. Zebras and tigers have black stripes; tigers, cheetahs, and giraffes have a tawny color; giraffes and ostriches have long legs and a long neck; and ostriches and penguins are black and white.

To learn about how forward chaining works, suppose that Robbie is at the zoo and is about to analyze an unknown animal, Stretch, using ZOO-KEEPER. Further suppose that the following six assertions are in working memory:

Stretch has hair.
Stretch chews cud.
Stretch has long legs.
Stretch has a long neck.
Stretch has tawny color.
Stretch has dark spots.

Because Stretch has hair, rule Z1 fires, establishing that Stretch is a mammal. Because Stretch is a mammal and chews cud, rule Z8 establishes that Stretch is an ungulate.

At this point, all the antecedents for rule Z11 are satisfied. Evidently, Stretch is a giraffe.

Rule-Based Systems Use a Working Memory and a Rule Base

As you have seen in the ZOOKEEPER system, one of the key representations in a rule-based system is the working memory:

A **working memory** is a representation

In which

▷ Lexically, there are assertions and application-specific symbols. There are also patterns that contain application-specific symbols mixed with pattern symbols.

▷ Structurally, the assertions are lists of application-specific symbols.

▷ Semantically, the assertions denote facts in some world.

With constructors that

▷ Add an assertion to working memory

With readers that

▷ Produce a list of the matching assertions in working memory, given a pattern

Another key representation is the rule base:

A **rule base** is a representation

In which

▷ There is a working memory.

▷ Lexically, there are rules.

▷ Structurally, the rules consist of patterns. Some of these patterns constitute the rule's *if* patterns; the others constitute the rule's *then* pattern.

▷ Semantically, rules denote constraints that enable procedures to seek new assertions or to validate a hypothesis.

With constructors that

▷ Construct a rule, given an ordered list of *if* patterns and a *then* pattern

With readers that

▷ Produce a list of a given rule's *if* patterns

▷ Produce a list of a given rule's *then* patterns

Thus, ZOOKEEPER uses instances of these representations that are specialized to animal identification. ZOOKEEPER itself can be expressed in procedural English, as follows:

Figure 7.2 Knowing something about an unknown animal enables identification via forward chaining. Here, the assertions on the left lead to the conclusion that the unknown animal is a giraffe.

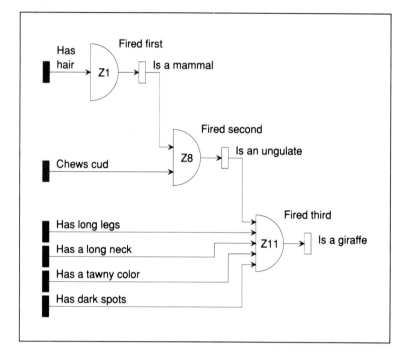

To identify an animal with ZOOKEEPER (forward-chaining version),

▷ Until no rule produces a new assertion or the animal is identified,

   ▷ For each rule,

      ▷ Try to support each of the rule's antecedents by matching it to known facts.

      ▷ If all the rule's antecedents are supported, assert the consequent unless there is an identical assertion already.

      ▷ Repeat for all matching and instantiation alternatives.

Thus, assertions flow through a series of antecedent–consequent rules from given assertions to conclusions, as shown in the history recorded in figure 7.2. In such diagrams, sometimes called **inference nets**, the D–shaped objects represent rules, whereas vertical bars denote given assertions and vertical boxes denote deduced assertions.

Deduction Systems May Run Either Forward or Backward

So far, you have learned about a deduction-oriented rule-based system that works from given assertions to new, deduced assertions. Running this way, a system exhibits forward chaining. *Backward chaining* is also possible: A rule-based-system can form a hypothesis and use the antecedent–consequent rules to work backward toward hypothesis-supporting assertions.

For example, ZOOKEEPER might form the hypothesis that a given animal, Swifty, is a cheetah and then reason about whether that hypothesis is viable. Here is a scenario showing how things work out according to such a backward-chaining approach:

■ ZOOKEEPER forms the hypothesis that Swifty is a cheetah. To verify the hypothesis, ZOOKEEPER considers rule Z9, which requires that Swifty is a carnivore, that Swifty has a tawny color, and that Swifty has dark spots.

■ ZOOKEEPER must check whether Swifty is a carnivore. Two rules may do the job, namely rule Z5 and rule Z6. Assume that ZOOKEEPER tries rule Z5 first.

■ ZOOKEEPER must check whether Swifty is a mammal. Again, there are two possibilities, rule Z1 and rule Z2. Assume that ZOOKEEPER tries rule Z1 first. According to that rule, Swifty is a mammal if Swifty has hair.

■ ZOOKEEPER must check whether Swifty has hair. Assume ZOOKEEPER already knows that Swifty has hair. So Swifty must be a mammal, and ZOOKEEPER can go back to working on rule Z5.

■ ZOOKEEPER must check whether Swifty eats meat. Assume ZOO-KEEPER cannot tell at the moment. ZOOKEEPER therefore must abandon rule Z5 and try to use rule Z6 to establish that Swifty is a carnivore.

■ ZOOKEEPER must check whether Swifty is a mammal. Swifty is a mammal, because this was already established when trying to satisfy the antecedents in rule Z5.

■ ZOOKEEPER must check whether Swifty has pointed teeth, has claws, and has forward-pointing eyes. Assume ZOOKEEPER knows that Swifty has all these features. Evidently, Swifty is a carnivore, so ZOOKEEPER can return to rule Z9, which started everything done so far.

■ Now ZOOKEEPER must check whether Swifty has a tawny color and dark spots. Assume ZOOKEEPER knows that Swifty has both features. Rule Z9 thus supports the original hypothesis that Swifty is a cheetah, and ZOOKEEPER therefore concludes that Swifty is a cheetah.

Thus, ZOOKEEPER is able to work backward through the antecedent–consequent rules, using desired conclusions to decide for what assertions it should look. A backward-moving chain develops, as dictated by the following procedure:

Figure 7.3 Knowing something about an unknown animal enables identification via backward chaining. Here, the hypothesis that Swifty is a cheetah leads to assertions that support that hypothesis.

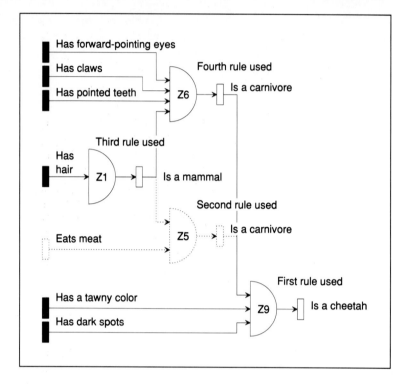

To identify an animal with ZOOKEEPER (backward-chaining version),

▷ Until all hypotheses have been tried and none have been supported or until the animal is identified,

    ▷ For each hypothesis,

        ▷ For each rule whose consequent matches the current hypothesis,

            ▷ Try to support each of the rule's antecedents by matching it to assertions in working memory or by backward chaining through another rule, creating new hypotheses. Be sure to check all matching and instantiation alternatives.

            ▷ If all the rule's antecedents are supported, announce success and conclude that the hypothesis is true.

In the example, backward chaining ends successfully, verifying the hypothesis, as shown in figure 7.3. The chaining ends unsuccessfully if any required antecedent assertions cannot be supported.

The Problem Determines Whether Chaining
Should Be Forward or Backward

Many deduction-oriented antecedent–consequent rule system can chain either forward or backward, but which direction is better? This subsection describes several rules of thumb that may help you to decide.

Most important, you want to think about how the rules relate facts to conclusions. Whenever the rules are such that a typical set of facts can lead to many conclusions, your rule system exhibits a high degree of **fan out**, and a high degree of fan out argues for backward chaining. On the other hand, whenever the rules are such that a typical hypothesis can lead to many questions, your rule system exhibits a high degree of **fan in**, and a high degree of fan in argues for forward chaining.

■ If the facts that you have or may establish can lead to a large number of conclusions, but the number of ways to reach the particular conclusion in which you are interested is small, then there is more fan out than fan in, and you should use backward chaining.

■ If the number of ways to reach the particular conclusion in which you are interested is large, but the number of conclusions that you are likely to reach using the facts is small, then there is more fan in than fan out, and you should use forward chaining.

Of course, in many situations, neither fan out nor fan in dominates, leading you to other considerations:

■ If you have not yet gathered any facts, and you are interested in only whether one of many possible conclusions is true, use backward chaining.

Suppose, for example, that you do not care about the identity of an animal. All you care about is whether it is a carnivore. By backward chaining from the carnivore hypothesis, you ensure that all the facts you gather are properly focused. You may ask about the animal's teeth, but you will never ask about the animal's color.

■ If you already have in hand all the facts you are ever going to get, and you want to know everything you can conclude from those facts, use forward chaining.

Suppose, for example, that you have had a fleeting glimpse of an animal that has subsequently disappeared. You want to know what you can deduce about the animal. If you were to backward chain, you would waste time pursuing hypotheses that lead back to questions you can no longer answer because the animal has disappeared. Accordingly, you are better off if you forward chain.

RULE-BASED REACTION SYSTEMS

In deduction systems, the *if* parts of some if–then rules specify combinations of assertions, and the *then* part specifies a new assertion to be deduced

Mycin Diagnoses Bacterial Infections of the Blood

ZOOKEEPER is based on MYCIN, a well-known rule-based deduction system. Historically, the MYCIN system played a major role in stimulating research interest in rule-based expert systems.

MYCIN's expertise lies in the domain of bacterial infections. Physicians usually must begin antibiotic treatment for patients who have bacterial infections without knowing exactly which organism is the culprit. There is no time to wait for definitive laboratory culture evidence, which accumulates too slowly. For the desperately sick, therapy must begin at once—not 2 days from at once. This requirement leaves two choices: the physician can either prescribe a broad-spectrum drug that covers all possibilities, or she can prescribe a better, disease-specific drug.

MYCIN helps the physician to prescribe disease-specific drugs. MYCIN informs itself about particular cases by requesting information from the physician about a patient's symptoms, general condition, history, and laboratory-test results that can be obtained easily and quickly. At each point, the question MYCIN asks is determined by MYCIN's current hypothesis and the answers to all previous questions. Thus, the questions start as though taken from a checklist, but the questions then vary as evidence builds. Here is an excerpt from a sample session:

> What is the patient's name?
>
> John Doe.
>
> Male or female?
>
> Male.
>
> Age?
>
> He is 55.
>
> Have you obtained positive cultures indicating general type?
>
> Yes.
>
> What type of infection is it?
>
> Primary bacteremia.
>
> When did symptoms first appear?
>
> May 5.
>
> Let's call the most recent positive culture C1. From what site was C1 taken?
>
> From the blood.
>
> When?
>
> May 9.
>
> Let's call the first significant organism from this culture U1. Do you know the identity of U1?
>
> No.
>
> Is U1 a rod or a coccus or something else?
>
> Rod.
>
> What is the gram stain of U1?
>
> Gram-negative.
>
> Have there been positive cultures from sites that are not associated with the infections about which you are seeking advice?
>
> No.
>
> Did U1 grow aerobically?
>
> Yes.

⋮

When it is satisfied that it has a reasonably good grasp of the situation, MYCIN announces its diagnosis:

> My recommendation will be based on the opinion that the identity of U1 may be
> 1. Pseudomonas-aeruginosa
> 2. Klebsiella-pneumoniae
> 3. E. coli
> 4. Bacteroides-fragilis
> 5. Enterobacter
> 6. Proteus-nonmirabilis.

After asking a few more questions about the patient, MYCIN announces its recommendation:

> On a scale of 0 to 4, where higher numbers indicate greater severity, how would you rate the patient's degree of sickness?
> 3.
> Does the patient have a clinically significant allergic reaction to any antimicrobial agent?
> No.
> How much does the patient weigh?
> 70 kilograms.
> My first recommendation is as follows: to cover for items 1, 2, 3, 5, and 6, give gentamycin using a dose of 119 mg (1.7 mg/kg) q8h IV [or IM] for 10 days. Modify dose in renal failure. Also, to cover for item 4, give clindamycin using a dose of 595 mg (8.5 mg/kg) q6h IV [or IM] for 14 days. If diarrhea or other gastrointestinal symptoms develop, check for pseudomembranous colitis.

MYCIN's pool of knowledge consists of approximately 500 antecedent–consequent rules, which give MYCIN the ability to recognize about 100 causes of bacterial infections. The following rule is typical:

M88   If $?x$'s type is primary bacteremia
               the suspected entry point of $?x$ is the gastrointestinal tract
               the site of the culture of $?x$ is one of the sterile sites
       then   there is evidence that $?x$ is bacteroides

MYCIN is a backward-chaining system, because physicians prefer to think about one hypothesis at a time. By sticking with the questions that are relevant to a particular hypothetical conclusion, the questioning is guaranteed to remain relevant to that hypothesis. A forward-running system can jump around, working first toward one conclusion and then toward another, seemingly at random.

Another reason why MYCIN was designed to be a backward-chaining system is that backward chaining simplifies the creation of an English-language interface. The interface needs to deal only with answers to specific questions, rather than with free-form, imaginative text.

directly from the triggering combination. In reaction systems, which are introduced in this section, the *if* parts specify the *conditions* that have to be satisfied and the *then* part specifies an *action* to be undertaken. Sometimes, the action is to *add* a new assertion; sometimes it is to *delete* an existing assertion; sometimes, it is to execute some procedure that does not involve assertions at all.

A Toy Reaction System Bags Groceries

Suppose that Robbie has just been hired to bag groceries in a grocery store. Because he knows little about bagging groceries, he approaches his new job by creating BAGGER, a rule-based reaction system that decides where each item should go.

After a little study, Robbie decides that BAGGER should be designed to take four steps:

1   The check-order step: BAGGER analyzes what the customer has selected, looking over the groceries to see whether any items are missing, with a view toward suggesting additions to the customer.
2   The bag-large-items step: BAGGER bags the large items, taking care to put the big bottles in first.
3   The bag-medium-items step: BAGGER bags the medium items, taking care to put frozen ones in freezer bags.
4   The bag-small-items step: BAGGER bags the small items.

Now let us see how this knowledge can be captured in a rule-based reaction system. First, BAGGER needs a working memory. The working memory must contain assertions that capture information about the items to be bagged. Suppose that those items are the items listed in the following table:

Item	Container type	Size	Frozen?
Bread	plastic bag	medium	no
Glop	jar	small	no
Granola	cardboard box	large	no
Ice cream	cardboard carton	medium	yes
Potato chips	plastic bag	medium	no
Pepsi	bottle	large	no

Next, BAGGER needs to know which step is the current step, which bag is the current bag, and which items already have been placed in bags. In the following example, the first assertion identifies the current step as the check-order step, the second identifies the bag as Bag1, and the remainder indicate what items are yet to be bagged:

Step is check-order
Bag1 is a bag
Bread is to be bagged
Glop is to be bagged
Granola is to be bagged
Ice cream is to be bagged
Potato chips are to be bagged

Note that working memory contains an assertion that identifies the step. Each of the rules in BAGGER's rule base tests the step name. Rule B1, for example, is triggered only when the step is the check-order step:

B1	If	step is check-order
		potato chips are to be bagged
		there is no Pepsi to be bagged
	then	ask the customer whether he would like a bottle of Pepsi

The purpose of rule B1 is to be sure the customer has something to drink to go along with potato chips, because potato chips are dry and salty. Note that rule B1's final condition checks that a particular pattern *does not* match any assertion in working memory.

Now let us move on to a rule that moves BAGGER from the check-order step to the bag-large-items step:

B2	If	step is check-order
	then	step is no longer check-order
		step is bag-large-items

Note that the first of rule B2's actions deletes an assertion from working memory. Deduction systems are assumed to deal with static worlds in which nothing that is shown to be true can ever become false. Reaction systems, however, are allowed more freedom. Sometimes, that extra freedom is reflected in the rule syntax through the breakup of the action part of the rule, marked by *then*, into two constituent parts, marked by *delete* and *add*. When you use this alternate syntax, rule B2 looks like this:

B2 (add–delete form)

	If	step is check-order
	delete	step is check-order
	add	step is bag-large-items

The remainder of BAGGER's rules are expressed in this more transparent **add–delete syntax**.

At first, rule B2 may seem dangerous, for it looks as though it could prevent rule B1 from doing its legitimate and necessary work. There is no problem, however. Whenever you are working with a reaction system, you adopt a suitable *conflict-resolution procedure* to determine which rule to fire among many that may be triggered. BAGGER uses the simplest conflict-resolution strategy, *rule ordering*, which means that the rules are arranged in a list, and the first rule triggered is the one that is allowed to fire. By placing rule B2 after rule B1, you ensure that rule B1 does its job before rule B2 changes the step to bag-large-items. Thus, rule B2 changes the step only when nothing else can be done.

Use of the rule-ordering conflict resolution helps you out in other ways as well. Consider, for example, the first two rules for bagging large items:

B3	If	step is bag-large-items
		a large item is to be bagged
		the large item is a bottle
		the current bag contains < 6 large items
	delete	the large item is to be bagged
	add	the large item is in the current bag

B4	If	step is bag-large-items
		a large item is to be bagged
		the current bag contains < 6 large items
	delete	the large item is to be bagged
	add	the large item is in the current bag

Big items go into bags that do not have too many items already, but the bottles—being heavy—go in first. The placement of rule B3 before rule B4 ensures this ordering.

Note that rules B3 and B4 contain a condition that requires counting, so BAGGER must to do more than assertion matching when looking for triggered rules. Most rule-based systems focus on assertion matching, but provide an escape hatch to a general-purpose programming language when you need to do more than just match an antecedent pattern to assertions in working memory.

Evidently, BAGGER is to add large items only when the current bag contains fewer than six items.[†] When the current bag contains six or more items, BAGGER uses rule B5 to change bags:

B5	If	step is bag-large-items
		a large item is to be bagged
		an empty bag is available
	delete	the current bag is the current bag
	add	the empty bag is the current bag

Finally, another step-changing rule moves BAGGER to the next step:

[†]Perhaps a better BAGGER system would use volume to determine when bags are full; to deal with volume, however, would require general-purpose computation that would make the example unnecessarily complicated, albeit more realistic.

B6	If	step is bag-large-items
	delete	step is bag-large-items
	add	step is bag-medium-items

Let us simulate the result of using these rules on the given database. As we start, the step is check-order. The order to be checked contains potato chips, but no Pepsi. Accordingly, rule B1 fires, suggesting to the customer that perhaps a bottle of Pepsi would be nice. Let us assume that the customer goes along with the suggestion and fetches a bottle of Pepsi.

Inasmuch as there are no more check-order rules that can fire, other than rule B2, the one that changes the step to bag-large-items, the step becomes bag-large-items.

Now, because the Pepsi is a large item in a bottle, the conditions for rule B3 are satisfied, so rule B3 puts the Pepsi in the current bag. Once the Pepsi is in the current bag, the only other large item is the box of granola, which satisfies the conditions of rule B4, so it is bagged as well, leaving the working memory in the following condition:

Step is bag-medium-items
Bag1 contains Pepsi
Bag1 contains granola
Bread is to be bagged
Glop is to be bagged
Ice cream is to be bagged
Potato chips are to be bagged

Now it is time to look at rules for bagging medium items.

B7	If	step is bag-medium-items
		a medium item is frozen, but not in a freezer bag
	delete	the medium item is not in a freezer bag
	add	the medium item is in a freezer bag

B8	If	step is bag-medium-items
		a medium item is to be bagged
		the current bag is empty or contains only medium items
		the current bag contains no large items
		the current bag contains < 12 medium items
	delete	the medium item is to be bagged
	add	the medium item is in the current bag

B9	If	step is bag-medium-items
		a medium item is to be bagged
		an empty bag is available
	delete	the current bag is the current bag
	add	the empty bag is the current bag

Note that the fourth condition that appears in rule B8 prevents BAGGER from putting medium items in a bag that already contains a large item. If there is a bag that contains a large item, rule B9 starts a new bag.

Also note that rule B7 and rule B8 make use of the rule-ordering conflict-resolution procedure. If both rule B7 and rule B8 are triggered, rule B7 is the one that fires, ensuring that frozen things are placed in freezer bags before bagging.

Finally, when there are no more medium items to be bagged, neither rule B7 nor rule B8 is triggered; instead, rule B10 is triggered and fires, changing the step to bag-small-items:

B10	If	step is bag-medium-items
	delete	step is bag-medium-items
	add	step is bag-small-items

At this point, after execution of all appropriate bag-medium-item rules, the situation is as follows:

Step is bag-small-items
Bag1 contains Pepsi
Bag1 contains granola
Bag2 contains bread
Bag2 contains ice cream (in freezer bag)
Bag2 contains potato chips
Glop is to be bagged

Note that, according to simple rules used by BAGGER, medium items do not go into bags with large items. Similarly, conditions in rule B11 ensure that small items go in their own bag:

B11	If	step is bag-small-items
		a small item is to be bagged
		the current bag contains no large items
		the current bag contains no medium items
		the bag contains < 18 small items
	delete	the small item is to be bagged
	add	the small item is in the current bag

BAGGER needs a rule that starts a new bag:

B12	If	step is bag-small-items
		a small item is to be bagged
		an empty bag is available
	delete	the current bag is the current bag
	add	the empty bag is the current bag

Finally, BAGGER needs a rule that detects when bagging is complete:

B13   If   step is bag-small-items
        delete step is bag-small-items
        add   step is done

After all rules have been used, everything is bagged:

Step is done
Bag1 contains Pepsi
Bag1 contains granola
Bag2 contains bread
Bag2 contains ice cream (in freezer bag)
Bag2 contains potato chips
Bag3 contains glop

Reaction Systems Require Conflict Resolution Strategies

Forward-chaining deduction systems do not need strategies for conflict resolution because every rule presumably produces reasonable assertions, so there is no harm in firing all triggered rules. But in reaction systems, when more than one rule is triggered, you generally want to perform only one of the possible actions, thus requiring a **conflict-resolution strategy** to decide which rule actually fires. So far, you have learned about rule ordering:

■ *Rule ordering.* Arrange all rules in one long prioritized list. Use the triggered rule that has the highest priority. Ignore the others.

Here are other possibilities:

■ *Context limiting.* Reduce the likelihood of conflict by separating the rules into groups, only some of which are active at any time.
■ *Specificity ordering.* Whenever the conditions of one triggering rule are a superset of the conditions of another triggering rule, use the superset rule on the ground that it deals with more specific situations.
■ *Data ordering.* Arrange all possible assertions in one long prioritized list. Use the triggered rule that has the condition pattern that matches the highest priority assertion in the list.
■ *Size ordering.* Use the triggered rule with the toughest requirements, where *toughest* means the longest list of conditions.
■ *Recency ordering.* Use the least recently used rule.

Of course, the proper choice of a conflict resolution strategy for a reaction system depends on the situation, making it difficult or impossible to rely on a fixed conflict resolution strategy or combination of strategies. An alternative is to think about which rule to fire as another problem to be solved. An elegant example of such problem solving is described in Chapter 8 in the introduction of the SOAR problem solving architecture.

PROCEDURES FOR FORWARD AND BACKWARD CHAINING

In this section, you learn more about rule-based systems. The focus is on how to do forward and backward chaining using well-known methods for exploring alternative variable bindings.

Depth-First Search Can Supply Compatible Bindings for Forward Chaining

One simple way to do forward chaining is to cycle through the rules, looking for those that lead to new assertions once the consequents are instantiated with appropriate variable bindings:

To forward chain (coarse version),

▷ Until no rule produces a new assertion,

  ▷ For each rule,

    ▷ For each set of possible variable bindings determined by matching the antecedents to working memory,

      ▷ Instantiate the consequent.

      ▷ Determine whether the instantiated consequent is already asserted. If it is not, assert it.

For an example, let us turn from the zoo to the track, assuming the following assertions are in working memory:

Comet	is-a	horse
Prancer	is-a	horse
Comet	is-a-parent-of	Dasher
Comet	is-a-parent-of	Prancer
Prancer	is	fast
Dasher	is-a-parent-of	Thunder
Thunder	is	fast
Thunder	is-a	horse
Dasher	is-a	horse

Next, let us agree that a horse who is the parent of something fast is valuable. Translating this knowledge into an if–then rule produces the following:

Parent Rule
    If $?x$ is-a horse
             $?x$ is-a-parent-of $?y$
             $?y$ is fast
    then $?x$ is valuable

XCON Configures Computer Systems

BAGGER is based on XCON, a well-known rule-based deduction system. Historically, the XCON system played a major role in stimulating commercial interest in rule-based expert systems.

XCON's domain is computer-system components. When a company buys a big mainframe computer, it buys a central processor, memory, terminals, disk drives, tape drives, various peripheral controllers, and other paraphernalia. All these components must be arranged sensibly along input–output buses. Moreover, all the electronic modules must be placed in the proper kind of cabinet in a suitable slot of a suitable backplane.

Arranging all the components is a task called *configuration*. Doing configuration can be tedious, because a computer-component family may have hundreds of possible options that can be organized in an unthinkable number of combinations.

To do configuration, XCON uses rules such as the following:

X1   If   the context is doing layout and assigning a power supply
    an sbi module of any type has been put in a cabinet
    the position that the sbi module occupies is known
    there is space available for a power supply
    there is no available power supply
    the voltage and frequency of the components are known
    then   add an appropriate power supply

X2   If   the context is doing layout and assigning a power supply
    an sbi module of any type has been put in a cabinet
    the position the sbi module occupies is known
    there is space available for a power supply
    there is an available power supply
    then   put the power supply in the cabinet in the available space

The first rule, X1, acts rather like the one in BAGGER that asks the customer whether he wants a bottle of Pepsi if the order contains potato chips but no beverage. The second rule, X2, is a typical insertion rule. The context mentioned in both rules is a combination of the top-level step and a substep. The context is changed by rules such as the following:

X3   If   the current context is x
    then   deactivate the x context
    activate the y context

Rule X3 has the effect of deleting one item from the context designation and adding another. It fires only if no other rule associated with the context triggers.

XCON has nearly 10,000 rules and knows the properties of several hundred component types for VAX computers, made by Digital Equipment Corporation. XCON routinely handles orders involving 100 to 200 components. It is representative of many similar systems for marketing and manufacturing.

Figure 7.4 During forward chaining, binding commitments can be arranged in a tree, suggesting that ordinary search methods can be used to find one or all of the possible binding sets. Here, the parent rule's first antecedent leads to four possible bindings for *x*, and the rule's second antecedent, given that *x* is bound to Comet, leads to two possible bindings for *y*.

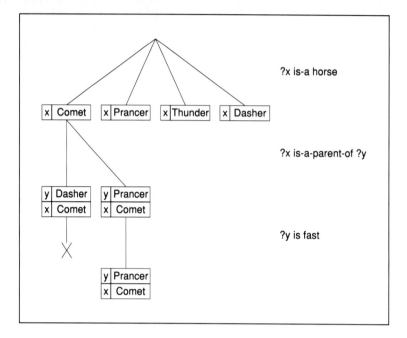

Now, if there is a binding for *x* and a binding for *y* such that each antecedent corresponds to an assertion when the variables are replaced by their bindings, then the rule justifies the conclusion that the thing bound to *x* is valuable. For example, if *x* is bound to Comet and *y* is bound to Prancer, then each of the antecedents corresponds to an assertion—namely *Comet is-a horse*, *Comet is-a-parent-of Prancer*, and *Prancer is fast*. Accordingly, Comet must be valuable.

To conduct a search for binding pairs, you can start by matching the first antecedent against each assertion. As shown in figure 7.4, there are four matches and four corresponding binding choices for *x* in the antecedent *?x is-a horse*, because Comet, Prancer, Thunder, and Dasher are all horses.

Next, proceeding in the depth-first search style, assume that *x*'s binding should be Comet, which is the binding produced by the first match. Then, with *x* bound to Comet, the second assertion, after instantiation, is *Comet is-a-parent-of ?y*. Matching this second instantiated antecedent against each assertion produces two matches, because Comet is a parent of both Dasher and Prancer. Thus, there are two binding choices for *y* given that *x* is bound to Comet.

Figure 7.4 show how the *x* and *y* choices fit together. Evidently, each of the two antecedents examined so far produces binding choices that can be arranged in a search tree.

Traveling along the leftmost branch, with *x* bound to Comet and *y* bound to Dasher, you proceed to the third antecedent, which becomes *Dasher is fast* when instantiated with *y*'s binding. This instantiated an-

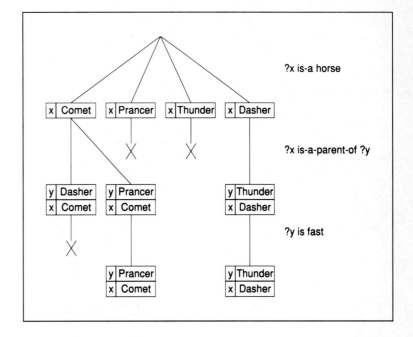

Figure 7.5 Two paths extend from the root down through the levels corresponding to three rule antecedents. Evidently, there are two binding sets that satisfy the rule.

tecedent fails to match any assertion, however, so you have to look farther for an acceptable combination. You do not have to look far, because the combination with x bound to Comet, as before, and y bound to Prancer leads to the instantiation of the third antecedent as *Prancer is fast*, which does match an assertion. Accordingly, you can conclude that the combination with x bound to Comet and y bound to Prancer is a combination that jumps over all the antecedent hurdles. You can use this combination to instantiate the consequent, producing *Comet is valuable*.

As shown in figure 7.4, there are three other choices for x bindings. Among these, if x is bound to Prancer or Thunder, then the second assertion, once instantiated, becomes *Prancer is-a-parent-of ?y* or *Thunder is-a-parent-of ?y*, both of which fail to match any assertion. If Dasher is the proper binding, then *Dasher is-a-parent-of ?y* matches just one assertion, *Dasher is-a-parent-of Thunder*, leaving only Thunder as a choice for y's binding. With x bound to Dasher and y bound to Thunder, the third instantiated antecedent is *Thunder is fast*, which matches an assertion, leading to the conclusion, as shown in figure 7.5, that the Dasher–Thunder combination also jumps over all the hurdles, suggesting that Dasher is valuable too.

From this example, several points of interest emerge. First, you can see that each path in the search tree corresponds to a set of binding commitments. Second, each antecedent matches zero or more assertions given the bindings already accumulated along a path, and each successful match produces a branch. Third, the depth of the search tree is always equal to the number of antecedents. Fourth, you have a choice, as usual, about how you search the tree. Exhaustive, depth-first, left-to-right search is the usual method when the objective is to find all possible ways that a rule can be deployed. This method is the one exhibited in the following procedure:

To forward chain (detailed version),

▷ Until no rule produces a new assertion,

  ▷ For each rule,

    ▷ Try to match the first antecedent with an existing assertion. Create a new binding set with variable bindings established by the match.

    ▷ Using the existing variable bindings, try to match the next antecedent with an existing assertion. If any new variables appear in this antecedent, augment the existing variable bindings.

    ▷ Repeat the previous step for each antecedent, accumulating variable bindings as you go, until,

      ▷ There is no match with any existing assertion using the binding set established so far. In this case, back up to a previous match of an antecedent to an assertion, looking for an alternative match that produces an alternative, workable binding set.

      ▷ There are no more antecedents to be matched. In this case,

        ▷ Use the binding set in hand to instantiate the consequent.

        ▷ Determine if the instantiated consequent is already asserted. If not, assert it.

        ▷ Back up to the most recent match with unexplored bindings, looking for an alternative match that produces a workable binding set.

      ▷ There are no more alternatives matches to be explored at any level.

Depth-First Search Can Supply Compatible Bindings for Backward Chaining

You learned that forward chaining can be viewed as searching for variable-binding sets such that, for each set, all antecedents correspond to assertions once their variables are replaced by bindings from the set.

Backward chaining can be treated in the same general way, but there are a few important differences and complications. In particular, you start by matching a hypothesis both against existing assertions and against rule consequents.

Suppose, for example, that you are still working with horses using the same rules and assertions in working memory as before. Next, suppose that you want to show that Comet is valuable; in other words, suppose that you want to verify the hypothesis, *Comet is valuable*. You fail to find a match for *Comet is valuable* among the assertions, but you succeed in matching the hypothesis with the rule consequent, *?x is valuable*. The success leads you to attempt to match the antecedents, presuming that x is bound to Comet.

Happily, the instantiated first antecedent, *Comet is-a horse*, matches an assertion, enabling a search for the instantiated second antecedent, *Comet is-a-parent-of y*. This second antecedent leads to two matches, one with the assertion *Comet is-a-parent-of Dasher* and one with the assertion *Comet is-a-parent-of Prancer*. Accordingly, the search branches, as shown in figure 7.6.

Along the left branch, y is bound to Dasher, leading to a futile attempt to match the third antecedent *Dasher is fast* to an assertion. Along the right branch, however, y is bound to Prancer, leading to a successful attempt to match *Prancer is fast* to an assertion.

Evidently, the hypothesis, *Comet is valuable*, is supported by the combination of the given rule and the given assertions because a binding set, discovered by search, connects the hypothesis with the assertions via the rule.

The search is more complicated, however, when the hypothesis itself contains a variable. Suppose that the question is "Who is valuable?" rather than "Is Comet valuable?" Then, the hypothesis itself, *?z is valuable*, contains a variable, z.

This new hypothesis, like the hypothesis *Comet is valuable*, matches no assertions but does match the consequent, *?x is valuable*. Now, however, you have a match between two variables, z and x, instead of a constant, Comet, and a variable, x.

Accordingly, now that it is time to match the first antecedent with the assertions, you go into the match with z bound to x. The variable x is not bound to anything, however, so the match of the first antecedent proceeds unfettered, as though the chaining were forward. There are four possible matches of the first antecedent to assertions, with x bound to any one of Comet, Prancer, Thunder, or Dasher. Then, assuming x's binding should be Comet, and working through the bindings allowed by the next two assertions, you are led to one of the results shown in figure 7.7, with z bound to x, x bound to Comet, and y bound to Prancer.

The fact that z, the variable in the hypothesis, matches x, a variable in a rule, need cause you no serious pause. The only additional task you need to perform is to instantiate all the way to constants whenever you have an

Figure 7.6 During backward chaining, as during forward chaining, binding commitments can be arranged in a tree, but the first binding commitments are established by the consequent, rather than by the first antecedent. Here, the consequent establishes one binding for *x*, and the second antecedent establishes two bindings for *y*. The binding for *x* and one of the two bindings for *y* establish that Comet is valuable.

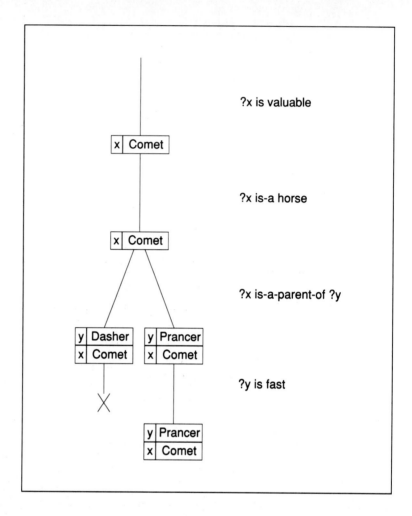

option to continue instantiating. Thus, you first replace *z* by *x*, and then you replace *x* by Comet, producing an instantiated hypothesis of *Comet is valuable.*

At this point, you could, if you wished, continue to look for other ways to bind variables so as to find other valuable horses.

The search is still more complicated when more than one rule can provide a variable binding. Suppose, for example, that you have the hypothesis with the variable, *?z is valuable*, but that you now add a new rule and two new assertions:

Winner Rule
  If   *?w* is-a winner
  then *?w* is fast

Figure 7.7 During backward chaining, hypothesis variables can be bound not only to assertion constants but also to consequent variables. Here, the hypothesis variable *z* is bound to the consequent variable *x*. Ultimately, two binding sets are found, establishing that two horses are valuable.

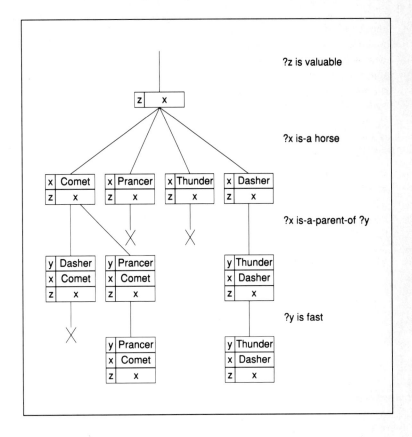

Dasher	Is-a	Winner
Prancer	Is-a	Winner

Now, the search proceeds as before, as shown in figure 7.8, until it is time to find a match for the third antecedent, *?y is fast*. The first time, with *y* bound to Dasher, there is no matching assertion, but there is a match between the second rule's consequent *w is fast* and the instantiated first-rule antecedent, *Dasher is fast*. Consequently, *w* becomes bound to Dasher, and an effort is made to find a match between the second rule's instantiated antecedent, *Dasher is-a winner*, against an assertion. Because there is a match with one of the two new assertions, you can conclude that Dasher is indeed fast, which means that the original hypothesis, *?z is valuable*, can be connected via rules to assertions using the binding set with *w* and *y* bound to Dasher, *x* bound to Comet, and *z* bound to *x*. To instantiate the hypothesis with this binding set, you first replace *z* with *x*, and then replace *x* with Comet.

Note that you can gain nothing by trying to find a second match for the instantiated antecedent, *Comet is-a-parent-of y*, because the ultimate conclusion, that Comet is valuable, has already been reached. Nevertheless,

Figure 7.8 During backward chaining, rules chain together whenever the antecedent of one matches the consequent of another. Here, an antecedent, *?y is fast*, in one rule matches a consequent, *?w is fast* in another rule.

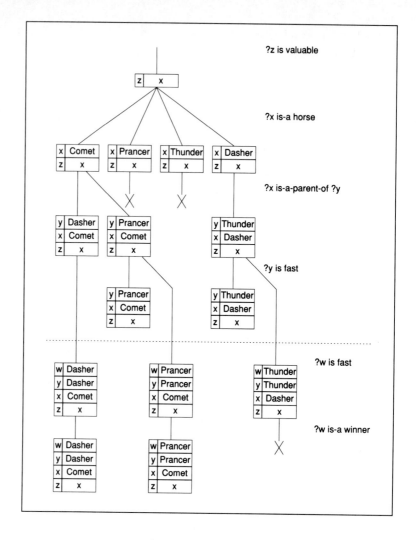

most binding-set programs are not smart enough to realize that nothing is to be gained, so they look for other ways to bind *y* using *Comet is-a-parent-of y*.

As shown in figure 7.8, *y* can be bound to Prancer, which leads to an attempt to match the third antecedent, *Prancer is fast* with an assertion; the match succeeds, reaffirming, with a different binding set, that Comet is valuable.

Displaying even more energy, most binding programs not only note that the instantiated antecedent, *Prancer is fast*, is in the database; they also note, as shown in figure 7.8, that there is a rule that links *Prancer is fast* to the assertion *Prancer is-a winner*, thus reaffirming, for a third time, with a binding set that includes a binding for *w*, that Comet is valuable.

Similarly, when searching for evidence that Dasher is valuable, the instantiated antecedent, *Thunder is fast*, is not only matched to an assertion, it is matched to the consequent, *w is fast*, in the second rule. This time, however, the instantiated antecedent in the second rule, *w is-a winner*, does not match any assertion, so there remains just one way of showing that Dasher is valuable.

In summary, the backward-chaining procedure moves from the initial hypothesis, through rules, to known facts, establishing variable bindings in the process. When the initial hypothesis matches the consequent of a rule, you create a binding set. Additional bindings are added to the initial binding set as the backward-chaining procedure works on the antecedents, and still more bindings are added when the procedure chains through an antecedent to the consequent of another rule. The following procedure summarizes:

To backward chain,

▷ Find a rule whose consequent matches the hypothesis (or antecedent) and create a binding set (or augment the existing binding set).

▷ Using the existing binding set, look for a way to deal with the first antecedent,

　▷ Try to match the antecedent with an existing assertion.

　▷ Treat the antecedent as an hypotheses and try to support it by backward chaining through other rules using the existing binding set.

▷ Repeat the previous step for each antecedent, accumulating variable bindings, until,

　▷ There is no match with any existing assertion or rule consequent using the binding set established so far. In this case, back up to the most recent match with unexplored bindings, looking for an alternative match that produces a workable binding set.

　▷ There are no more antecedents to be matched. In this case, the binding set in hand supports the original hypothesis.

　　▷ If all possible binding sets are desired, report the current binding set, and back up, as if there were no match.

　　▷ If only one possible binding set is desired, report the current binding set and quit.

　▷ There are no more alternative matches to be explored at any level.

Relational Operations Support Forward Chaining

Now it is time to look at another approach to forward chaining. First, you learn how relational database operations can handle the bookkeeping required for forward chaining. Then, you learn how the relational database operations can be arranged to produce high-speed operation.

All that you need to know about relational databases in this section is introduced as you need it. If you have not studied relational databases elsewhere, and find the introduction in this section to be too brief, read the appendix, which describes relational databases in more detail.

Now consider the Parent Rule and assertions previously used to demonstrate the search-oriented approach. Here, again, is the Parent Rule.

Parent Rule
> If $?x$ is-a horse
> $?x$ is-a-parent-of $?y$
> $?y$ is fast
> then $?x$ is valuable

Now think of the assertions as though they were part of a table. In the language of relations, the assertions are recorded in a **relation**, named Data, whose columns are labeled with **field names**—namely First, Second, and Third:

First	Second	Third
Comet	is-a	horse
Prancer	is-a	horse
Comet	is-a-parent-of	Dasher
Comet	is-a-parent-of	Prancer
Prancer	is	fast
Dasher	is-a-parent-of	Thunder
Thunder	is	fast
Thunder	is-a	horse
Dasher	is-a	horse

To determine what values of x and y trigger the rule, you first determine which of the relation's records match the first antecedent in the rule, *?x is-a horse*. In the language of relations, you need to find those records whose Second field value is *is-a* and whose Third field value is *horse*. Conveniently, relational database systems include an access procedure, SELECT, that extracts records with specified field values from one relation to produce a new relation with fewer records. You can ask SELECT to pick the horses out of the Data relation, for example:

SELECT Data with Second = is-a and Third = horse

The result is the new relation:

First	Second	Third
Comet	is-a	horse
Prancer	is-a	horse
Thunder	is-a	horse
Dasher	is-a	horse

All you really want to know, however, is which bindings of x produce matches. Accordingly, you use another relational database access procedure, PROJECT, to isolate the appropriate field:

PROJECT Result over First

At this point, the field named First is renamed X to remind you that it consists of bindings for the x variable. The result, a single-field relation, is as follows:

A1
X
Comet
Prancer
Thunder
Dasher

Next, you determine which of the records in the data relation match the second antecedent in the rule, *?x is-a-parent-of ?y.* You need to select those records whose Second field value is *is-a-parent-of.* Then you project the results over the First and Third fields:

PROJECT   [SELECT Data with Second = is-a-parent-of]
           over First and Third

After renaming the field named First to X and the field named Third to Y, you have the following table:

A2
X	Y
Comet	Dasher
Comet	Prancer
Dasher	Thunder

Finally, you need to determine which of the records in the data relation match the third antecedent in the rule, *?y is fast*. Accordingly, you select those records whose Second field value is *is* and whose Third field value is *fast*, and you project the result over the First field:

PROJECT   [SELECT Data with Second = is and Third = fast]
           over First

After renaming the field named First to Y, reflecting the fact that the field values are possible bindings for *y*, you have the following table:

A3

Y
Prancer
Thunder

You now have three new relations–A1, A2, and A3—corresponding to the three antecedents in the rule. The next question is, What bindings of *x* satisfy both the first and second antecedents? Or, What field values are found both in A1's X field and in A2's X field?

    The JOIN operation builds a relation with records constructed by concatenating records, one from each of two source tables, such that the records match in prescribed fields. Thus, you can join A1 and A2 over their X fields to determine which values of *x* are shared. Here is the required JOIN operation:

JOIN A1 and A2 with X = X

The result is a relation in which field-name ambiguities are eliminated by concatenation of ambiguous field names with the names of the relations that contribute them:

B1 (preliminary)

X.A1	X.A2	Y
Comet	Comet	Dasher
Comet	Comet	Prancer
Dasher	Dasher	Thunder

All you really want, of course, is to find the pairs of bindings for *x* and *y* that satisfy the first two antecedents. Accordingly, you can project the preliminary B1 relation over, say, X.A1 and Y, with the following result, after renaming of the fields:

B1	X	Y
	Comet	Dasher
	Comet	Prancer
	Dasher	Thunder

B1 now contains binding pairs that simultaneously satisfy the first two antecedents in the rule. Now you can repeat the analysis to see which of these binding pairs also satisfy the third antecedent.

To begin, you join A3 and B1 over their Y fields to determine which values of y are shared:

JOIN A3 and B1 with Y = Y

The result is as follows:

B2 (preliminary)	Y.A3	X	Y.B1
	Prancer	Comet	Prancer
	Thunder	Dasher	Thunder

Now you project to determine the pairs of bindings for x and y that satisfy not only the first two antecedents, but also the third:

B2	X	Y
	Comet	Prancer
	Dasher	Thunder

At this point, you know that there are two binding pairs that simultaneously satisfy all three antecedents. Inasmuch as the *then* part of the rule uses only the binding of x, you project B2 over the X field:

B2	X
	Comet
	Dasher

Thus, the parent rule is triggered in two ways: once with x bound to Comet, and once with x bound to Dasher. In a deduction system, both binding sets can be used. In a reaction system, a conflict-resolution procedure would be required to select the next action.

The only problem with the procedure that you just learned about is that it consumes a large amount of computation. If a rule has n antecedents, then it takes n SELECT and n PROJECT operations to produce the A relations along with $n-1$ JOIN and $n-1$ PROJECT operations to produce the B relations. If there happen to be m rules, and if you check out each rule whenever a new assertion is added to the data relation, then you have to perform mn SELECTs, $m(2n-1)$ PROJECTs, and most alarmingly, $m(n-1)$ expensive JOINs each time a new assertion is added. Fortunately, there is another way to search for variable bindings that does not use so many operations.

The Rete Approach Deploys Relational Operations Incrementally

You have just learned how to use relational operations to find binding sets, but the method described is an expensive way to do forward chaining, because a great deal of work has to be done to trigger a rule. Now you are ready to learn that the relational operations can be performed incrementally, as each new assertion is made, reducing both the total amount of work and the time it takes to trigger a rule once all the triggering assertions are in place.

Ordinarily, the word *rete* is an obscure synonym for net, found only in large dictionaries. In the context of forward chaining, however, the word **rete procedure** names a procedure that works by moving each new assertion, viewed as a relational record, through a rete of boxes, each of which performs a relational operation on one relation or on a few, but never on all the relations representing accumulated assertions.

The arrangement of the rete for the valuable-horse example is shown in figure 7.9.

As a new assertion is made, it becomes a single-record relation. That single-record relation is then examined by a family of SELECT operations, each of which corresponds to a rule antecedent.

In the example, the first assertion is *Comet is-a horse*. Accordingly, the following single-record relation is constructed:

New-assertion

First	Second	Third
Comet	is-a	horse

This relation is examined by three SELECT operations:

SELECT new-assertion with Second = is-a and Third = horse
SELECT new-assertion with Second = is-a-parent-of
SELECT new-assertion with Second = is and Third = fast

Next, whenever the record in the single-record relation makes it past a SELECT operation, the single-record relation endures a PROJECT operation that picks off the field or fields that contain bindings.

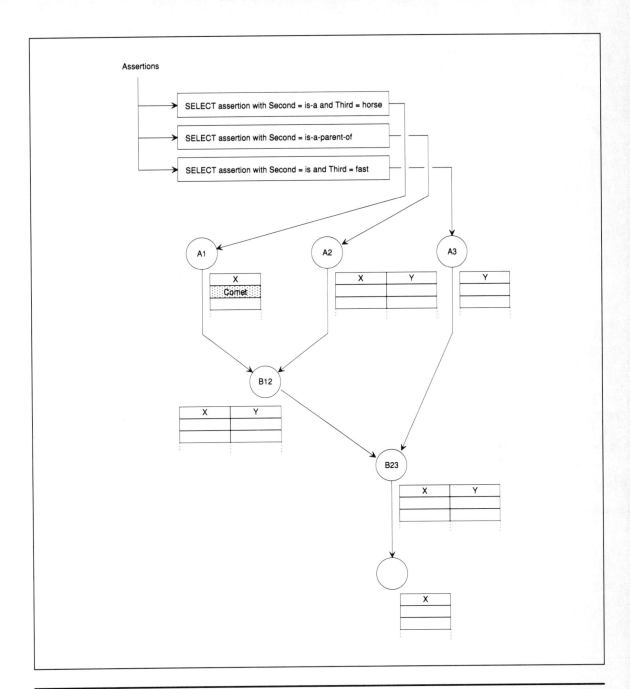

Figure 7.9 The rete for a simple rule about horses with fast offspring. Here the state of the rete is captured just following the addition made in response to the first assertion. In this and other figures, the most recent changes are shown shaded.

In the example, the record makes it past the first of the three SELECT operations, whereupon the PROJECT and renaming operations produce the following:

New-assertion

X
Comet

Once a record has gone past the SELECT, PROJECT, and renaming operations, it is added to a relation associated with a rule antecedent. Each antecedent-specific relation is located at an **alpha node** created specifically for the antecedent. Each alpha-node relation accumulates all the assertions that make it through the corresponding, filterlike SELECT operation. In the example, the selected, projected, and renamed record is added to the A1 node—the one attached to the first antecedent.

The second assertion, *Prancer is-a horse*, follows the first through the rete, and also ends up as a record in the relation attached to the A1 node. Then, the third assertion, Comet is-a-parent-of Dasher, following a different route, ends up as a record in the relation attached to the A2 node.

Each addition to an alpha node's relation inspires an attempt to join the added record, viewed as a single-record relation, with another relation. In particular, an addition to either A1's relation or A2's relation leads to joining of the added record, viewed as a single-record relation, with the relation attached to the other alpha node. Importantly, the JOIN operation is done with a view toward determining whether the variable binding expressed in the added record corresponds to a variable binding already established in the other relation.

In the example, the added record—the one added to A2's relation—produces the following single-record relation:

X	Y
Comet	Dasher

Meanwhile, A1's relation has accumulated two records:

A1

X
Comet
Prancer

Joining the two relations over the X field and projecting to eliminate one of the redundant X fields yields a one-record, two-field relation:

X	Y
Comet	Dasher

This new relation is then added to a relation attached to a **beta node**—the B12 node—so named because it is the JOIN of the A1 and A2 relations. B12's relation contains a single record that records a pair of bindings for x and y that satisfies the first and second antecedents.

Thus, an addition to either A1's relation or A2's relation leads to a JOIN operation that may add one or more records to B12's relation reflecting variable bindings that satisfy the first two rule antecedents simultaneously.

The next assertion—the fourth—*Comet is-a-parent-of Prancer*, produces the wave of activity in the rete shown by the shading in figure 7.10.

The wave starts with the addition of a second record to A2's relation. This new record, viewed as a single-record relation, is joined to A1's relation, producing a second record for B12's relation.

Because it is tiresome to append the phrase, *viewed as a relation*, each time a record, viewed as a relation, is joined with another relation, let us agree to speak of joining records with a relation, even though, strictly speaking, only relations are joined.

Next, the fifth assertion, *Prancer is fast*, initiates a wave of additions to the records in the rete and leads to a record in A3's relation. In general, an addition to A3's relation leads to joining the added record with B12's relation. This JOIN operation is done with a view toward determining whether the variable binding expressed in the added record corresponds to a variable binding already established in B12's relation.

The result is added to B23's relation. In this example, the JOIN operation is over the Y fields, and the JOIN operation produces—after doing a PROJECT to eliminate one of the redundant Y fields—an initial record for B23's relation:

B23

X	Y
Comet	Prancer

Projecting this new record over the X field yields a possible binding for x in the rule's *then* part:

Parent-Rule Bindings B23

X
Comet

Thus, an addition to A3's relation has led to joining the added record with B12's relation. Symmetrically, of course, any new records added to B12's

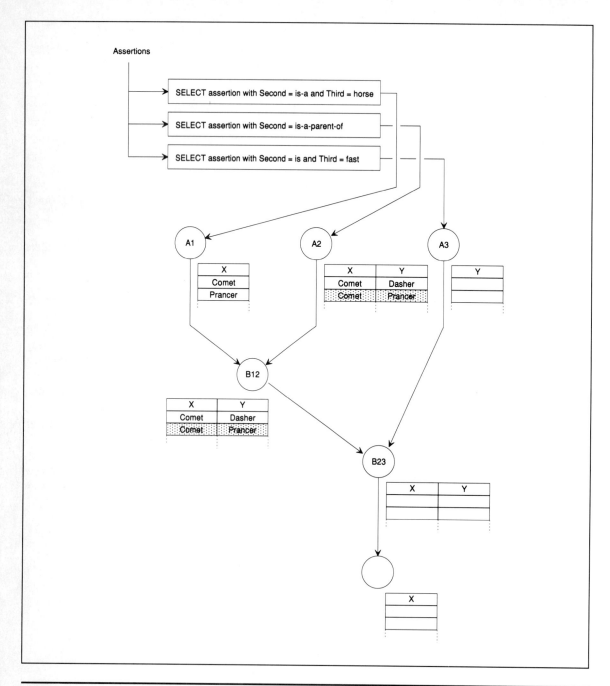

Figure 7.10 Here, the state of the rete is captured just following the additions made in response to the fourth assertion, *Comet is-a-parent-of Prancer*. The additions are shown shaded.

relation are joined to A3's relation. As before, the JOIN operation is done to determine whether the variable bindings expressed in the added records correspond to variable bindings already expressed in the other relation involved in the JOIN operation.

Now consider the state of the rete after you add three more assertions— *Dasher is-a-parent-of Thunder, Thunder is fast,* and *Thunder is-a horse.* A1's relation indicates that there are three horses:

A1

X
Comet
Prancer
Thunder

A2's relation indicates that Comet is a parent of two children, and Dasher is a parent of one child:

A2

X	Y
Comet	Dasher
Comet	Prancer
Dasher	Thunder

A3's relation indicates that Prancer and Thunder are fast:

A3

Y
Prancer
Thunder

Next, the information in the alpha-node relations is joined to form the beta-node relations:

B12

X	Y
Comet	Dasher
Comet	Prancer

B23

X	Y
Comet	Prancer

Next, the ninth assertion, *Dasher is-a horse*, initiates another wave of additions to the records in the rete—the additions indicated by the shading in figure 7.11.

The first of these additions is the new record in A1's relation. This new record is joined to A2's relation, producing a new record in B12's relation:

B12 (increment)

X	Y
Dasher	Thunder

But now this new B12 record is joined to A3's relation producing a new record for B23's relation:

B23 (increment)

X	Y
Dasher	Thunder

Projection of this new record over the X field yields another possible binding for x in the rule's consequent:

Parent-Rule Bindings (increment) B23

X
Dasher

Thus, after all nine assertions are processed, the possible bindings for x in the rule's consequent are given by the following relation:

Parent-Rule Bindings B23

X
Comet
Dasher

As you have seen, adding a new relation produces a wavelike phenomenon that continues through the rete as long as JOIN operations produce new records. Note that all the relational operations involve only small relations containing a few assertions; they never involve the entire accumulated database of assertions.

Although the example may seem complicated, the procedures for building and using a rete are straightforward:

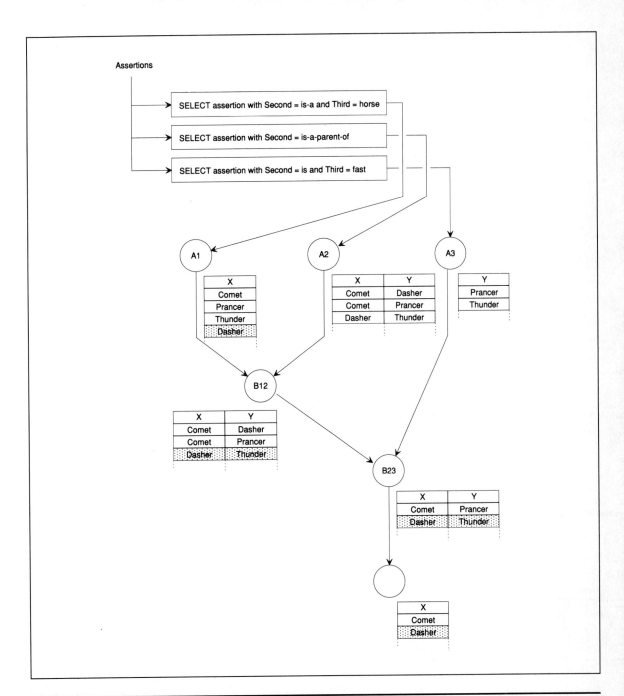

Figure 7.11 Here, the state of the rete is captured just following the additions made in response to the ninth assertion, *Dasher is-a horse*. The most recent changes are shown shaded.

To construct a rete,

▷ For each antecedent pattern that appears in the rule set, create a SELECT operation that examines new assertions.

▷ For each rule,

  ▷ For each antecedent,

    ▷ Create an alpha node and attach it to the corresponding SELECT operation, already created.

▷ For each alpha node, except the first,

  ▷ Create a beta node.

  ▷ If the beta node is the first beta node, attach it to the first and second alpha nodes.

  ▷ Otherwise, attach the beta node to the corresponding alpha node and to the previous beta node.

▷ Attach a PROJECT operation to the final beta node.

To use a rete,

▷ For each assertion, filter the assertion through the SELECT operations, passing the assertion along the rete to the appropriate alpha nodes.

▷ For each alpha node receiving an assertion, use the PROJECT operation to isolate the appropriate variable bindings. Pass these new bindings, if any, along the rete to the appropriate beta nodes.

▷ For each beta node receiving new variable bindings on one of its inputs, use the JOIN operation to create new variable binding sets. Pass these new variable binding sets, if any, along the rete to the next beta node or to the final PROJECT operation.

▷ For each rule, use the PROJECT operation to isolate the variable bindings needed to instantiate the consequent.

SUMMARY

■ Rule-based systems were developed to take advantage of the fact that a great deal of useful knowledge can be expressed in simple if–then rules.

■ Many rule-based systems are deduction systems. In these systems, rules consist of antecedents and consequents. In one example, a toy deduction system identifies animals.

- Deduction systems may chain together rules in a forward direction, from assertions to conclusions, or backward, from hypotheses to questions. Whether chaining should be forward or backward depends on the problem.

- Many rule-based systems are reaction systems. In these systems, rules consist of conditions and actions. A toy reaction system bags groceries.

- Reaction systems require conflict-resolution strategies to determine which of many triggered rules should be allowed to fire.

- Depth-first search can supply compatible bindings for both forward chaining and backward chaining.

- Relational operations support breadth-first search for compatible bindings during forward chaining. The rete procedure performs relational operations incrementally as new assertions flow through a rule-defined rete.

BACKGROUND

The rete procedure was developed by C. L. Forgy [1982].

MYCIN was developed by Edward Shortliffe and colleagues at Stanford University [1976].

XCON was developed to configure the Digital Equipment Corporation's VAX computers by John McDermott and other researchers working at Carnegie Mellon University, and by Arnold Kraft, Dennis O'Connor, and other developers at the Digital Equipment Corporation [McDermott 1982].

8

Rules Substrates and Cognitive Modeling

In this chapter, you learn that you can build important capabilities on top of the rule-chaining problem-solving method. In particular, simple ideas enable rule-based systems *to explain the steps* that have led to a conclusion, *to reason in a variety of styles*, *to reason under time constraints*, *to determine a conclusion's probability*, and *to check the consistency of a newly proposed rule*.

You learn about *knowledge engineering*, and about two key heuristics that knowledge engineers use to acquire rules from human experts.

You also learn that rule-based systems have limits, when viewed from an engineering perspective, that render them too weak to be a universal tool for implementers who desire to capture all the characteristics of human experts. Accordingly, you will know that you should avoid the misnomer **expert system**, which commonly is used for rule-based systems that really perform at a level more like that of a novice.

Nevertheless, some cognitive scientists believe rules and rule chaining constitute part of a larger explanation of human information processing. By way of illustration, you learn about the SOAR *problem-solving architecture*.

RULE-BASED SYSTEMS VIEWED AS SUBSTRATE

In this section, you learn about the benefits and limitations that follow from using rules to represent knowledge and using rule chaining to solve problems. You also learn how to extract knowledge in general and rules in particular from human experts.

163

Explanation Modules Explain Reasoning

One way to show what a set of antecedent–consequent rules can do is to draw an **inference net** like those introduced in Chapter 7: one showed how forward chaining led to the conclusion that a particular animal is a giraffe; and another led to the verification of an hypothesis that a particular animal is a cheetah.

Sometimes, it is useful to look at part of an inference net to answer questions about *why* an assertion was used or about *how* an assertion was established. Much of this ability stands on the simple, highly constrained nature of rules. To decide how a given assertion was concluded, a rule-based deduction system needs to reflect only on the antecedent–consequent rules it has used, looking for those that contain the given assertion as a consequent. The required answer is just an enumeration of those antecedent–consequent rules, perhaps accompanied by information about their triggering assertions.

Consider, for example the cheetah example from Chapter 7. In that example, rule Z6 was used as shown in figure 8.1. Accordingly, if you ask ZOOKEEPER "How did you show that Swifty is a carnivore?" then ZOO-KEEPER can determine the answer by moving to the left, saying, "By using rule Z6 and by knowing that Swifty is a mammal, has pointed teeth, claws, and forward-pointing eyes." If you ask "Why did you show that Swifty is a mammal?" then ZOOKEEPER can determine the answer by moving to the right, saying, "Because I wanted to use rule Z6 to show that the animal is a carnivore." Here, by way of summary, is the procedure ZOOKEEPER uses:

To answer a question about the reasoning done by a rule-based deduction system,

▷ If the question is a *how* question, report the assertions connected to the *if* side of the rule that established the assertion referenced in the question.

▷ If the question is a *why* question, report the assertions connected to the *then* sides of all rules that used the assertion referenced in the question.

Other questions, such as "Did you use rule Z6?" and "When did you use rule Z6?" are also easy to answer.

Of course, this ability to answer questions is not a surprise: you learned in Chapter 3 that goal trees always enable you to answer simple *how* and *why* questions, and an inference net always contains an implied goal tree. Figure 8.2 shows the goal tree that reaches from assertions at the bottom, through antecedent–consequent rules, to the cheetah conclusion at the top.

Figure 8.1 Rule-based systems retain a history of how they have tied assertions together, enabling a kind of introspection. The system answers *How did you show . . . ?* by moving one step backward, mentioning rules and antecedents; it answers *Why did you show . . . ?* questions by moving one step forward.

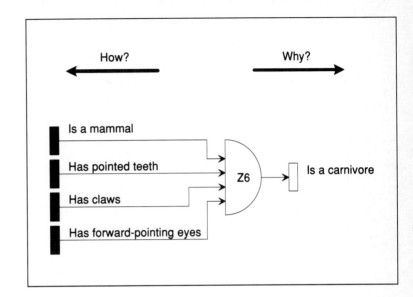

Figure 8.2 An inference net can be used to produce a goal tree. Each node in this goal tree corresponds to the application of an antecedent–consequent rule.

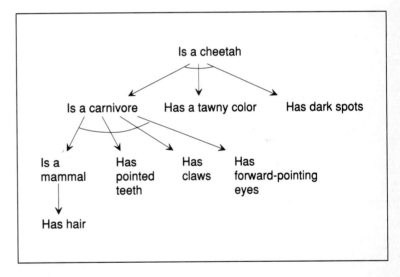

Reasoning Systems Can Exhibit Variable Reasoning Styles

Rule-based systems are often used in domains in which some assertions are almost certainly true and others are almost certainly false.

In the horse-evaluation system, taken up in Chapter 7, the principal rule says that a horse is valuable if it has parented something fast, which is a way of saying that a horse qualifies as a good stud or brood mare.

Nevertheless, the conclusion breaks down if a horse happens to become sterile, so a more reliable rule should say something about fertility:

Fertile-Parent Rule

> If $?x$ is-a horse
>
> $?x$ is-a-parent-of $?y$
>
> $?y$ is fast
>
> $?x$ is fertile
>
> then $?x$ is valuable

If you try to use a system containing this rule at an auction, however, you will not buy many horses, because it is time consuming and expensive to determine whether a horse is fertile. Accordingly, you might well elect to assume that all horses are fertile, banishing the *$?x$ is fertile* antecedent to a new part of the rule where **providing assumptions** are collected:

Modified Fertile-Parent Rule

> If $?x$ is-a horse
>
> $?x$ is-a-parent-of $?y$
>
> $?y$ is fast
>
> then $?x$ is valuable
>
> providing $?x$ is fertile

Now you can arrange, easily, for your system to run in two modes:

- **Show-me mode**: Treat the providing assumptions as though they were ordinary antecedents; thus, refuse to accept anything that is not shown.
- **Ask-questions-later mode**: Ignore all providing assumptions. This mode is good in situations in which rapid response is more important than careful analysis.

You can even incorporate **unless assumptions** into your rules to complement the providing assumptions. Here is fanciful example:

Live-Horse Rule

> If $?x$ is-a horse
>
> $?x$ is-a-parent-of $?y$
>
> $?y$ is fast
>
> $?x$ is alive
>
> then $?x$ is valuable

Taking the likelihood of thinking about the value of a dead horse to be small, you can rewrite the Live-Horse Rule as follows, moving the *$?x$ is alive* assertion to a new part of the rule where unless assumptions are collected:

Modified Live-Horse Rule

> If $?x$ is-a horse
>
> $?x$ is-a-parent-of $?y$
>
> $?y$ is fast
>
> then $?x$ is valuable
>
> unless $?x$ is dead

In ask-questions-later mode, unless assumptions are ignored, but in show-me mode, unless patterns are treated as ordinary antecedents, except that they appear in negated form. Thus, *?x is dead* becomes *?x is alive.*

Of course, there are other ways to treat providing assumptions and unless assumptions, in addition to show-me mode and ask-questions-later mode. Essentially, each way specifies whether you work on providing assumptions and unless assumptions using assertions or rules or neither or both. Here are representative examples:

- **Decision-maker mode**: Assume that providing assumptions are true. Assume that unless assumptions are false, unless they match existing assertions.

- **Trusting-skeptic mode**: Assume that providing assumptions are true and that unless assumptions are false, unless you can show otherwise with a single rule. This mode is called the trusting-skeptic mode because you assume that the likelihood of overturning providing and unless assumptions is small and therefore trying to overturn them is worthy of but little effort.

- **Progressive-reliability mode**: Produce an answer in ask-questions-later mode, and then, as time permits, explore more and more of the providing and unless assumptions, producing a more and more reliable answer. This mode is reminiscent of the progressive deepening idea, introduced in Chapter 6, in connection with adversarial search.

Probability Modules Help You to Determine Answer Reliability

Rule-based deduction systems used for identification usually work in domains where conclusions are rarely certain, even when you are careful to incorporate everything you can think of into rule antecedents. Thus, rule-based deduction system developers often build some sort of certainty-computing procedure on top of the basic antecedent–consequent apparatus. Generally, certainty-computing procedures associate a probability between 0 and 1 with each assertion. Each probability reflects how certain an assertion is, with 0 indicating that an assertion is definitely false and 1 indicating that an assertion is definitely true.

Two Key Heuristics Enable Knowledge Engineers to Acquire Knowledge

A **domain expert** is a person who has accumulated a great deal of skill in handling problems in a particular area called the **domain of expertise**. **Knowledge engineering** is the extraction of useful knowledge from domain experts for use by computers. Often, albeit far from always, knowledge engineers expect to cast the acquired knowledge in the form of rules for rule-based systems.

To some extent, knowledge engineering is an art, and some people become more skilled at it than do others. Nevertheless, there are two key heuristics that enable any knowledge engineer to do the job well.

The first of the key knowledge-engineering heuristics is the *heuristic of specific situations*. According to this heuristic, it is dangerous to limit inquiry to office interviews, asking only the general question, "How do you do your job?" Instead, a knowledge engineer should go into the field to watch domain experts proceed about their normal business, asking copious questions about specific situations as those situations are witnessed.

Suppose, for example, that you are a knowledge engineer and that you are working on new rules to be used by the BAGGER system introduced in Chapter 7. If you ignore the heuristic of specific situations, you would have just asked a few real grocery-store baggers to describe what they do. But no matter how cooperative your domain experts are, they are unlikely to be able to help you much unless you provide more evocative stimulation. You might well learn nothing about what to do with, for example, eggs. On the other hand, if you adhere to the heuristic of specific situations, you would get yourself into a grocery store so as to watch baggers handle specific situations, like the one shown in figure 8.3, asking questions like, "Do you always put the eggs on top?"

The second of the key knowledge-engineering heuristics is the *heuristic of situation comparison*. The idea is to ask a domain expert for clarification whenever the domain expert's behavior varies in situations that look identical to the knowledge engineer. The purpose is to help the knowledge engineer to acquire a vocabulary that is sufficiently rich to support the necessary acquisition of knowledge.

Again, if you were the knowledge engineer charged with acquiring the knowledge needed to support BAGGER, you would need to understand the important characteristics of groceries from the bagging perspective. Noting, for example, that a real bagger handles the two items in figure 8.4 differently, you would ask why, whereupon the bagger would say something about frozen food, thus signaling that *frozen* is a word that should be in BAGGER's vocabulary.

Note that ideas for extracting knowledge for computers also apply when your motive is to extract knowledge for your own use. Accordingly, the two key heuristics for knowledge engineering deserve powerful-idea status:

To learn from an expert,

▷ Ask about specific situations to learn the expert's general knowledge.

▷ Ask about situation pairs that look identical, but that are handled differently, so that you can learn the expert's vocabulary.

Figure 8.3 Knowledge engineers generally start their work by asking domain experts a few general questions about what experts do. Eventually, most knowledge-engineering jobs require knowledge engineers to use the heuristic of specific situations, watching domain experts at work on concrete examples.

Figure 8.4 Knowledge engineers often ask why similar-looking situations are different, thus building essential vocabulary via the heuristic of situation comparison. Here, the domain expert will note that the essential difference is that one item is frozen.

Figure 8.5 The rules in a rule-based deduction system form natural groups according to the conclusions expressed in their consequents.

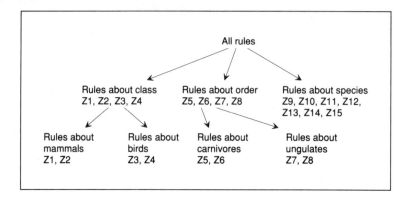

Acquisition Modules Assist Knowledge Transfer

When you represent knowledge using if–then rules, you lose flexibility and power, but you gain the opportunity to add interesting capabilities to your basic problem-solving apparatus. To add a question-answering superprocedure, for example, you need to deal with only rules and rule histories.

Another relatively easy capability to add is a rule-transfer superprocedure that helps knowledge engineers to make new rules.

Suppose, for example, that you are a knowledge engineer and that you are working on new rules to be used by the ZOOKEEPER system introduced in Chapter 7. Further suppose that you have determined that another rule is needed, one that captures the idea that an animal is a carnivore if it is seen stalking another animal.

The knowledge engineer therefore proposes the following new rule:

Z16a   If $?x$ stalks a different kind of animal
         then $?x$ is a carnivore

There is evidence an antecedent is missing, however. When compared with the other rules that conclude that an animal is a carnivore, this proposed rule lacks an antecedent requiring that the animal is a mammal. Noting this lack, it makes sense to ask whether the omission is intended. The answer would lead to a refined rule:

Z16b   If $?x$ is a mammal
               $?x$ stalks a different kind of animal
         then $?x$ is a carnivore

Suppose Robbie creates PROCRUSTES, a knowledge-acquisition assistant, to automate the search for omissions.

To encourage knowledge engineers to construct new rules that look like old ones, PROCRUSTES makes heavy use of natural rule groups. It forms these natural rule groups by filtering all existing rules down through a tree like the one shown in figure 8.5.

For each rule group, PROCRUSTES forms a typical member by combining all antecedents and all consequents that occur in, say, 30 percent of the group's rules. For the group of those rules that conclude that an animal is a carnivore, there is one such antecedent (that the animal is a mammal), and one such consequent (that the animal is a carnivore).

Typical-carnivore
>   If   the animal is a mammal
>   then   it is a carnivore

All PROCRUSTES needs to do, then, is to compare proposed rules with the typical rules of the applicable rule groups, asking the knowledge engineer for a decision whenever something in a typical rule is not in a proposed rule. In the example, the carnivore rule group is applicable. Because the only antecedent of the typical carnivore rule is missing from the proposed rule, Z16a, PROCRUSTES would suggest that antecedent, leading to the more reliable rule, Z16b.

Thus, procedures such as PROCRUSTES can do a lot by *helping you to transfer* rulelike knowledge from knowledge engineers to rule-based systems. In Chapter 17, you learn about another procedure that can do even more by *directly producing* rulelike knowledge from precedents and exercises.

Rule Interactions Can Be Troublesome

It would seem that rule-based systems allow knowledge to be tossed into systems homogeneously and incrementally without concern for relating new knowledge to old. Evidently, rule-based systems should permit knowledge engineers to focus their attention on the rules, letting the rule chainer control rule interactions.

There are problems about which to worry, however. One particular problem is that the *advantage* of bequeathing control becomes the *disadvantage* of losing control, as King Lear failed to foresee.

Rule-Based Systems Can Behave Like Idiot Savants

Rule-based systems do some things so well, they can be said to be **savants** with respect to those things:

■   Rule-based systems solve many problems.
■   Rule-based systems answer simple questions about how they reach their conclusions.

Still, basic rule-based systems lack many of the characteristics of domain experts, qualifying them to be *idiot savants*:

■   They do not reason on multiple levels.
■   They do not use constraint-exposing models.
■   They do not look at problems from different perspectives.
■   They do not know how and when to break their own rules.

■   They do not have access to the reasoning behind their rules.

In principle, there is nothing to prevent building more humanlike systems using rules, because rules can be used as a sort of programming language. When used as a programming language, however, rules have to be measured against alternative programming languages; when so measured, rules have little to offer.

RULE-BASED SYSTEMS VIEWED AS MODELS FOR HUMAN PROBLEM SOLVING

Do computational theories of problem solving have promise as psychological models of human reasoning? The answer is yes, at least to many computationally-oriented psychologists who try to understand ordinary human activity using metaphors shared with researchers who concentrate on making computers smarter.

Rule-Based Systems Can Model Some Human Problem Solving

In the human-modeling world, if–then rules are called **productions** and rule-based systems are called **production systems**. Hard-core rule-based-system enthusiasts believe that human thinking involves productions that are triggered by items in **short-term memory**. They also believe that short-term memory is inhabited by only a few simple symbolic **chunks**, whereas **long-term memory** holds all the productions. Specific combinations of the short-term memory items trigger the long-term memory's productions.

Protocol Analysis Produces Production-System Conjectures

To learn how people solve problems, information-processing psychologists pore over transcripts of subjects talking their way through problems. These transcripts are called **protocols**. The psychologists who study protocols generally think in terms of two important concepts:

■   The **state of knowledge** is what the subject knows. Each time the subject acquires knowledge through his senses, makes a deduction, or forgets something, the state of knowledge changes.

■   The **problem-behavior graph** is a trace of a subject moving through states of knowledge as he solves a problem.

The problem-behavior graph is important because it helps you to unravel characteristics of the subject who produces it. By analyzing the way one state of knowledge becomes another, you can draw inferences about the productions that cause those state changes. Consider, for example, the following protocol fragment:

A Protocol for Robbie ——————————————————

Let's see, I want to identify this animal, I wonder if it's a cheetah—
I have nothing to go on yet, so I think I'll start by looking into
the possibility that it is a carnivore—I had better check to see if
it is a mammal first—yes, that is OK—hair—it doesn't seem to
be eating anything so I can't tell if it is a carnivore—but oh, yes,
it has pointed teeth, claws, and forward-pointing eyes, so it is a
carnivore all right—now where was I—it's a carnivore, and I also
see that it has a tawny color and dark spots—surely it must be a
cheetah!

It would seem that assertions accumulate in the following order: hair, mammal, pointed teeth, claws, forward-pointing eyes, carnivore, tawny color,
dark spots, and cheetah. From observations such as these, the information-
processing psychologists would probably deduce that Robbie's production
system is a backward-chaining one with rules much like those used in the
ZOOKEEPER examples.

SOAR Models Human Problem Solving, Maybe

In artificial intelligence, an **architecture** is an integrated collection of representations and methods that is said to handle a specified class of problems
or to model insightfully a form of natural intelligence.

SOAR[†] is an elaborate, production-centered architecture that was developed both to explain human problem solving and to support the implementation of applied systems. SOAR features a long-term memory for
productions and a short-term memory for items that trigger the productions.

In the rest of this section, you learn about SOAR's key architectural
features, but you learn only a bit, as a full treatment would require a book,
not a section of a chapter.

SOAR Searches Problem Spaces

First, SOAR developers are committed to the idea that all problems can be
formulated in terms of a search through a **problem space**, a net consisting of situation-describing **problem states**. SOAR starts from an initial
situation, the **current state**, in the expectation that it will arrive at an
identifiable **goal state** eventually. One such net is shown in figure 8.6.

SOAR moves from problem state to problem state in three-step cycles:
First, SOAR establishes a **preference net**, a net in which preference labels
and preference links describe the merits of various choices. Second, SOAR
translates the preference labels and preference links into dominance relations among the states. Third, SOAR uses the dominance relations to select

---

[†] "SOAR" is an acronym for state, operator, and result, which together constitute
one basic search step in SOAR. "SOAR" is an obscure acronym, however; many
SOAR researchers cannot tell you its derivation.

Figure 8.6 A problem space. At this point in the search, there are no links to indicate which problem states are considered neighbors.

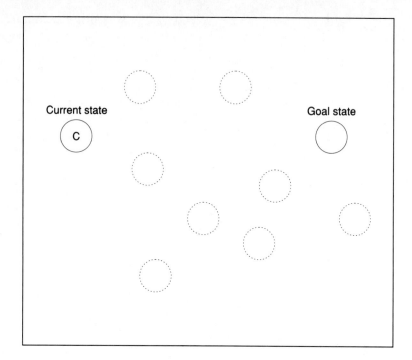

Figure 8.7 A preference net uses preference labels and preference links to describe the absolute and relative merits of a state and its neighbors.

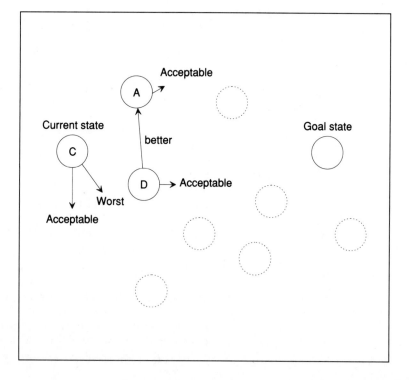

the next current state. Then, SOAR repeats the cycle, placing new links, determining new dominance relations, and updating the current state, until SOAR reaches the goal state.

One example of a preference net is shown in figure 8.7. State C is the current state. The links labeled *acceptable*, *worst*, and *better* carry preference information. More generally, the links that can appear in a preference net are given in the following specification:

A **preference net** is a representation

That is a state space

In which

▷ Absolute preferences are identified by Is links that connect states to *acceptable*, *rejected*, *best*, and *worst* nodes.

▷ Relative preferences are identified by *better*, *worse*, and *indifferent* links that connect states to each other.

SOAR Uses an Automatic Preference Analyzer

To use preference labels and links, SOAR uses an **automatic preference analyzer**—one that resolves inconsistencies caused by rules with limited vision.

To see how SOAR's automatic preference analyzer works, consider the nodes and links shown in figure 8.7. SOAR's automatic preference analyzer first collects problem states C, A, and D, as those are labeled *acceptable*. Next, SOAR establishes that state D dominates state A because there is a *better* link from state D to state A. Then, SOAR establishes that state C is dominated by both of the other states because state C is labeled *worst* and it does not dominate any other state.

At this point, all dominated states are rejected, leaving only state D. Consequently, SOAR selects state D to be the next problem state, leaving SOAR ready to start another cycle of preference marking, preference analysis, and state selection.

While discovering new problem states and labeling known problem states with preference information, SOAR uses no conflict-resolution strategy to decide which triggered rule should fire. Instead, SOAR fires all triggered rules and decides what to do by looking at what they all do, rather than by using some rigidly prescribed, result-ignorant conflict-resolution strategy that suppresses all but one of the triggered rules.

On a higher level, in addition to determining which new problem state should replace the current state, SOAR's automatic preference analyzer looks for opportunities to reformulate the problem in terms of a better set of problem states in which to search for the goal, thereby replacing the current **problem space**. On a lower level, SOAR's automatic preference analyzer looks for opportunities to replace the method, called the **current operator**, that discovers new problem states.

Finally, whenever SOAR gets stuck—finding no unambiguous way to replace any current problem space, problem state, or operator—SOAR's automatic preference analyzer announces an impasse, and SOAR's **universal subgoaling mechanism** creates a subgoal to resolve the impasse. SOAR users are expected to anticipate various sorts of problem-specific impasses so as to provide the appropriate productions for setting up subgoal-handling problem spaces, problem-space–dependent problem states, and problem-state–dependent operators.

In summary, the detailed behavior of SOAR's automatic preference analyzer is dictated by the following procedure:

To determine the preferred state using SOAR's automatic preference analyzer,

▷ Collect all the states that are labeled *acceptable*.

▷ Discard all the acceptable states that are also labeled *rejected*.

▷ Determine dominance relations as follows:

   ▷ State A dominates state B if there is a *better* link from A to B but no *better* link from B to A.

   ▷ State A dominates state B if there is a *worse* link from B to A but no *worse* link from A to B.

   ▷ A state labeled *best*, and not dominated by another state, dominates all other states.

   ▷ A state labeled *worst*, which does not dominate any other state, is dominated by all other states.

▷ Discard all dominated states.

▷ Select the next state from among those remaining as follows:

   ▷ If only one state remains, select it.

   ▷ Otherwise, if no states remain, select the current state, unless it is marked *rejected*.

   ▷ Otherwise, if all the remaining states are connected by *indifferent* links,

      ▷ If the current state is one of the remaining states, keep it.

      ▷ Otherwise, select a state at random.

   ▷ Otherwise, announce an impasse.

SUMMARY

- The simplicity of rule-based deduction systems enables you to build extremely useful modules on top of a basic chaining procedure.
- Explanation modules explain reasoning by using a goal tree to answer *how* and *why* questions. Probability modules help you to determine answer reliability. Acquisition modules assist knowledge engineers in knowledge transfer from a human expert to a collection of rules.
- Variable-precision reasoning systems exhibit variable reasoning styles, ranging from quick and superficial to slow and careful.
- Two key heuristics enable knowledge engineers to acquire knowledge from human experts. One is to work with specific situations; another is to ask about situation pairs that look identical, but are handled differently.
- Rule-based systems can behave like idiot savants. They do certain tasks well, but they do not reason on multiple levels, they do not use constraint-exposing models, they do not look at problems from different perspectives, they do not know how and when to break their own rules, and they do not have access to the reasoning behind their rules.
- Rule-based systems can model some human problem solving. SOAR, the most highly developed rule-based model of human problem solving, uses an automatic preference analyzer to determine what to do, instead of using a fixed conflict-resolution strategy.

BACKGROUND

The discussion of reasoning styles is based on the work of Ryszard S. Michalski and Patrick H. Winston [1986]. The discussion of PROCRUSTES is based on the work of Randall Davis [1976].

A system for propagating certainties is discussed in Chapter 11.

SOAR was developed by Allen Newell and his students [Laird et al. 1987; Newell 1990].

9

Frames and Inheritance

In this chapter, you learn about *frames*, *slots*, and *slot values*, and you learn about *inheritance*, a powerful problem-solving method that makes it possible to know a great deal about the slot values in *instances* by virtue of knowing about the slot values in the *classes* to which the instances belong.

With basic frame-representation ideas in hand, you learn that frames can capture a great deal of commonsense knowledge, informing you not only about what assumptions to make, but also about for what information to look and how to look for that information. You learn that much of this knowledge is often embedded in *when-constructed procedures*, *when-requested procedures*, *when-read procedures*, *when-written procedures*, and *with-respect-to procedures*.

By way of illustration, you see how to use frames to capture the general properties of various kinds of dwarfs, and you see how to use frames to capture the properties of various kinds of newspaper stories.

Once you have finished this chapter, you will understand that frames can capture a great deal of commonsense knowledge, including knowledge about various sorts of objects ranging from individuals to events. You will also know how the CLOS inheritance procedure determines a precedence ordering among multiple classes.

FRAMES, INDIVIDUALS, AND INHERITANCE

In this section, you learn about frames and their relation to semantic nets. In particular, you learn how to capture general knowledge that holds for

179

most of the individuals in a class. This capability enables you to make use of the following general knowledge about fairy-tale dwarfs:

- Fairy-tale competitors and gourmands are fairy-tale dwarfs.
- Most fairy-tale dwarfs are fat.
- Most fairy-tale dwarfs' appetites are small.
- Most fairy-tale gourmands' appetites are huge.
- Most fairy-tale competitors are thin.

You also learn the details of one particularly good mechanism for deciding which general knowledge about classes to transfer to individuals.

Frames Contain Slots and Slot Values

At this point, it is convenient to introduce a few terms that make it easier to think about semantic nets at a level slightly higher than the lowest level, where there are just nodes and links.

As shown in figure 9.1, each node and the links that emanate from it can be collected together and called a **frame**. Graphically, frames may be shown in an alternate, rectangle-and-slot notation. Each frame's name is the same as the name of the node on which the frame is based. The names attached to the slots are the names of the links emanating from that frame's node. Accordingly, you can talk about a **slot**, rather than about a link that emanates from a node. Similarly, you can talk about **slot values** rather than about the destinations of links emanating from a node. Thus, the language of frames, slots, and slot values is sometimes more concise, and hence clearer, than is the language of nodes and links, although both describe the same concepts.

Frames may Describe Instances or Classes

Many frames describe individual things, such as Grumpy, an individual dwarf. These frames are called **instance frames** or **instances**. Other frames describe entire classes, such as the dwarf class. These frames are called **class frames** or **classes**.

As soon as you know the class to which an instance belongs, you generally assume a lot. Unless you know you are dealing with an exception, you assume, for example, that dwarfs are fat.

A special slot, the Is-a slot, short for is-a-member-of-the-class, ties instances to the classes that they are members of. In figure 9.2, for example, a dwarf named Blimpy is identified as a member of the Managers class.

Another special slot, the Ako slot, short for a-kind-of, ties classes together. The Managers class is a subclass of the Competitors class, for example. The Managers class is also a **direct subclass** of the Competitors class because there is an Ako slot in the Managers class that is filled with the Competitors class. The Managers class is just a subclass of the Dwarfs class, however, because you have to traverse more than one Ako slot to get from the Managers class to the Dwarfs class. Symmetrically,

Figure 9.1 A semantic net can be viewed either as a collection of nodes and links or as a collection of frames. At the top, a semantic net is viewed as a collection of nodes and links. In the middle, the same semantic net is divided into chunks, each of which consists of a node and the links that emanate from it. Next, at the bottom, each chunk is shown as a frame with slots and slot values. As the Grumpy frame illustrates, slot values may be shown as frame names or as links connected to frames.

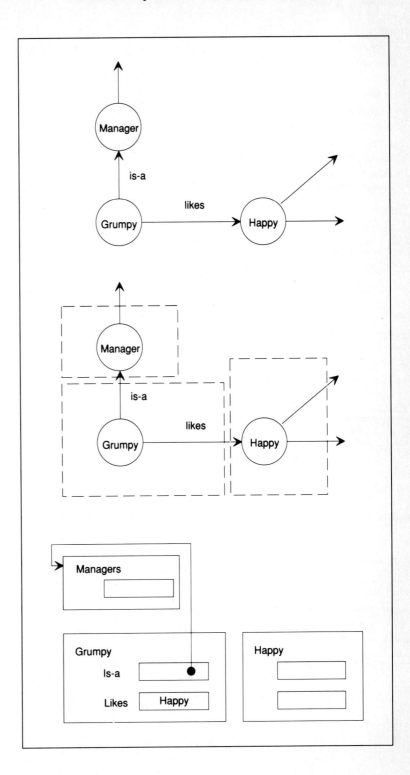

Figure 9.2 A simple class hierarchy. Blimpy is a member of the Managers class, which is a direct subclass of the Competitors class and a subclass of the Dwarfs class. Every class is considered to be, ultimately, a subclass of the Everything class.

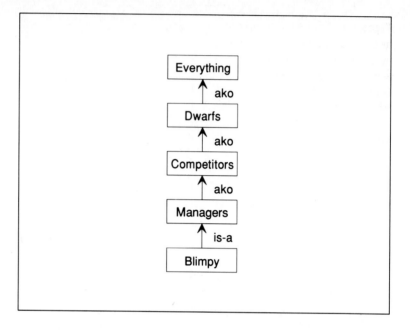

the Competitors class is said to be a **direct superclass** of the Managers class, and the Dwarfs class is said to be a superclass of the Managers class.

Note that it is convenient to draw class hierarchies with Is-a and Ako links connecting frames that are actually connected via values in Is-a and Ako slots. Thus, the vocabulary of nodes and links is often mixed with the vocabulary of frames and slots.

Frames Have Access Procedures

To make and manipulate instances and classes, you need access procedures, just as you do for any representation. In figure 9.3, the **class constructor** makes a Manager frame that has one direct superclass, the Competitors class, which appears in the Ako slot. In general, the class constructor can make class frames that contain other slots and more than one direct superclass.

An **instance constructor** makes instance frames. Its input consists of the name of the class to which the instance belongs; its output is an instance that belongs to those classes. The new instance is connected automatically to the class frames via an Is-a slot in the new instance.

A **slot writer** installs slot values. Its input is a frame, the name of a slot, and a value to be installed. Finally, a **slot reader** retrieves slot values. Its input is a frame and the name of a slot; its output is the corresponding slot value.

Figure 9.3 Instance frames and class frames are data types that are made and accessed with various constructors, writers, and readers.

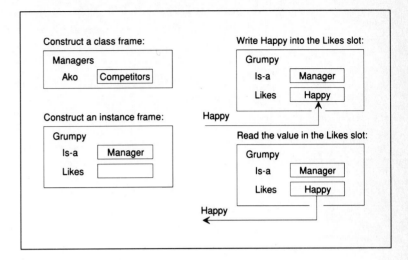

Inheritance Enables When-Constructed Procedures to Move Default Slot Values from Classes to Instances

The slots in an instance are determined by that instance's superclasses. If a superclass has a slot, then the instance **inherits** that slot.

Sometimes, slot values are specified after an instance is constructed. After Blimpy is constructed, for example, you can indicate that Blimpy is smart by inserting the value Smart in Blimpy's Intelligence slot.

Alternatively, the slot values of an instance may be specified, somehow, by the classes of which the instance is a member. It might be, for example, that Dwarfs are fat in the absence of contrary information; also it might be that Competitors are thin, again in the absence of contrary information.

By writing down, in one place, the knowledge that generally holds for individuals of that class, you benefit from the following characteristics of shared, centrally located knowledge:

Shared knowledge, located centrally, is

▷ Easier to construct when you write it down

▷ Easier to correct when you make a mistake

▷ Easier to keep up to date as times change

▷ Easier to distribute because it can be distributed automatically

---

One way to accomplish knowledge sharing is to use **when-constructed procedures** associated with the classes of which the instance is a member. Here is an example that supplies a value for the physique slot of individual dwarfs:

To fill the Physique slot when a new Dwarf is constructed,

▷ Write Fat in the slot.

The expectations established by when-constructed procedures are called **defaults**.

In the simplest class hierarchies, no more than one when-constructed procedure supplies a default for any particular slot. Often, however, several when-constructed procedures, each specialized to a different class, supply default values for the same slot. Here, for example, a second when-constructed procedure provides a default value for the Physique slot of individual Competitors:

To fill the Physique slot when a new Competitor is constructed,

▷ Write Thin in the slot.

Whenever an individual is both a Competitor and Dwarf, both procedures compete to supply the default value. Of course, you could specify an inheritance procedure that allows multiple procedures to supply defaults, but the usual practice is to allow just one procedure.

How can you decide which when-constructed procedure is the winner? First, you learn about the special case in which no individual has more than one Is-a link and no class has more than one Ako link. Once this foundation is in place, you learn about more complicated hierarchies in which individuals and class have multiple inheritance links.

One way to decide which when-constructed procedure to use, albeit a way limited to single-link class hierarchies, is to think of classes themselves as places where procedures can be attached. One of the sample procedures, because it deals with new Dwarfs, is attached to the Dwarf class; the other is attached to the Competitors class. That way, you can find both by a search up from the new instance through Is-a links and Ako links.

Because each class in the class hierarchy in the example has only one exiting Ako link, it is easy to form an ordered list consisting of Blimpy and the classes to which Blimpy belongs. This ordered list is called the **class-precedence list**:

Blimpy
Managers class
Competitors class   ← procedure stored here
Dwarfs class   ← procedure stored here
Everything class

A procedure that is specialized to one of the classes on the class-precedence list is said to be **applicable**.

Suppose, for example, that you have just constructed Blimpy. You have Blimpy's class-precedence list, which supplies two procedures for computing values for the Physique slot. The procedure attached to the Competitor's class says that Blimpy is Thin and the procedure attached to the Dwarf class says that Blimpy is Fat. This kind of ambiguity is always resolved in favor of the most specific applicable procedure—the one that is encountered first on the class-precedence list. In the example, as shown by the class-precedence list, the first of the procedure-supplying classes encountered is the Competitors class, so the procedure attached there is the one that determines Blimpy's physique when Blimpy is constructed. Evidently, Blimpy is Thin.

A Class Should Appear Before All Its Superclasses

When there is more than one Is-a link above an instance or more than one Ako link above a class, then the class hierarchy is said to **branch**.[†] Because branching class hierarchies are more difficult to handle, yet are ubiquitous in intelligent systems, the rest of this section is devoted to explaining the issues involved, and to presenting an procedure that deals with those issues.

As an illustration, consider the class hierarchy shown in figure 9.4. Suppose that there are two procedures for computing Appetite:

To fill the Appetite slot when a new Dwarf is constructed,

▷ Write Small in the slot.

To fill the Appetite slot when a new Gourmand is constructed,

▷ Write Huge in the slot.

Because the class hierarchy branches, you must decide how to flatten the class hierarchy into an ordered class-precedence list.

One choice is to use depth-first search. Depth-first search makes sense because the standard convention is to assume that information from specific classes should override information from more general classes. Left-to-right search makes sense too, but only because you need some way to specify the priority of each direct superclass, and the standard convention is to specify

---

[†]Generally, the treatment of frames in this chapter follows the conventions of the Common Lisp Object System, also known as CLOS. However, in contrast to the conventions of CLOS, multiple Is-a connections are allowed—CLOS forbids them for the sake of efficient implementation. There is no loss of generality in CLOS, however, because an instance can be attached to a class that is wholly dedicated to that instance and that has multiple Ako connections to the desired superclasses.

Figure 9.4 Another class hierarchy. Because Blimpy belongs to both the Gourmands class and to the Diarists class, as well as the Managers class, the class hierarchy branches upward. Because the Dwarfs class has three subclasses— Competitors, Gourmands and Diarists—the class hierarchy branches downward as well.

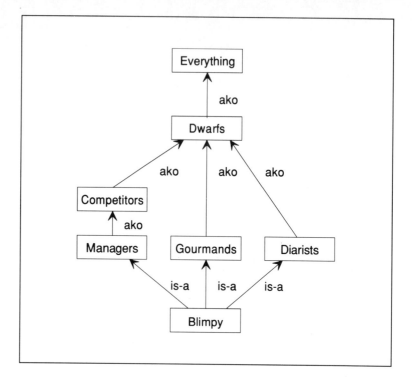

priority through the left-to-right superclass order provided to the class-constructor procedure.

Note, however, that you must modify depth-first search slightly, because you want to include all nodes exactly once on the class-precedence list. To perform **exhaustive depth-first search**, you explore all paths, depth first, until each path reaches either a leaf node or a previously-encountered node.

To search the class hierarchy shown in figure 9.4, using exhaustive depth-first search, you first follow the left branch at each node encountered; the resulting path includes Blimpy, Managers, Competitors, Dwarfs, and Everything. Then, you follow Blimpy's middle branch to Gourmands; the resulting path terminates at Gourmands, however, because you have already encountered the Dwarfs node. Finally, you follow Blimpy's right branch to Diarists, where you terminate the path.

Thus, exhaustive depth-first, left-to-right search produces the following class-precedence list for Blimpy:

Blimpy
Managers class
Competitors class
Dwarfs class   ← procedure stored here
Everything class
Gourmands class   ← procedure stored here
Diarists class

You can see that the first Appetite-computing when-constructed procedure encountered for Blimpy is the one attached to the Dwarfs class—the one that would indicate that Blimpy's appetite is small. This conclusion seems at odds with intuition, however, because the Gourmands class is a subclass of the Dwarfs class. Surely a class should supply more specific procedures than any of its superclasses. Rephrasing, you have a rule:

■   Each class should appear on class-precedence lists before any of its superclasses.

To keep a class's superclasses from appearing before that class, you can modify depth-first, left-to-right search by adding the **up-to-join proviso**. The up-to-join proviso stipulates that any class that is encountered more than once during the depth-first, left-to-right search is ignored until that class is encountered for the last time.

Using this approach, the construction of Blimpy's class-precedence list proceeds as before until the Competitors class is added and the Dwarfs class is encountered. Because there are three paths from Blimpy to the Dwarfs class, the Dwarfs class is ignored the first and second times it is encountered. Consequently, the Gourmands class is the next one added to the class-precedence list, followed by the Diarists class. Then, the Dwarfs class is encountered for the third and final time, whereupon it is noted for the first time, enabling it and the Everything class to be added to the class-precedence list. Thus, the Gourmands class appears before the Dwarf class, as desired:

Blimpy
Managers class
Competitors class
Gourmands class   ← procedure stored here
Diarists class
Dwarfs class   ← procedure stored here
Everything class

Now the first appetite-computing procedure encountered is the one that says Blimpy's appetite is huge.

A Class's Direct Superclasses Should Appear in Order

The depth-first, left-to-right, up-to-join procedure for computing class-precedence lists still leaves something to be desired. Consider, for example,

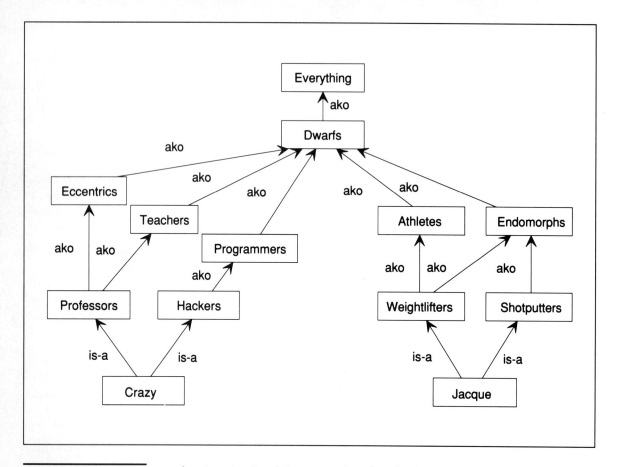

Figure 9.5 Another class hierarchy, with Is-a and Ako links shown. The depth-first, left-to-right, up-to-join approach produces appropriate class-precedence lists for both Crazy and Jacque.

the situation involving two other dwarfs, Crazy and Jacque, shown in figure 9.5.

The depth-first, left-to-right, up-to-join approach produces the following class-precedence lists for Crazy and Jacque:

Crazy	Jacque
Professors class	Weightlifters class
Eccentrics class	Athletes class
Teachers class	Shotputters class
Hackers class	Endomorphs class
Programmers class	Dwarfs class
Dwarfs class	Everything class
Everything class	

Nothing is amiss. No class appears after any of its own superclasses. Moreover, each class's direct superclasses appear in their given left-to-right order: The Professors class appears before the Hackers class; the Eccentrics class appears before the Teachers class; the Weightlifters class appears

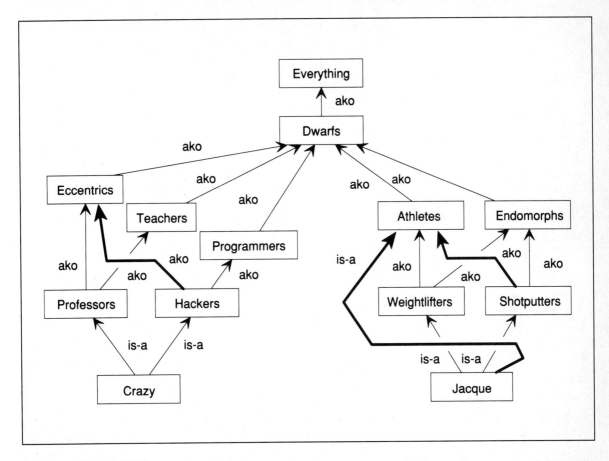

Figure 9.6 Still another class hierarchy, with one new Is-a link and two new Ako links shown by thick lines. This time, the depth-first, left-to-right, up-to-join approach does not produce appropriate class-precedence lists for either Crazy or Jacque.

before the Shotputters class; and the Athletes class appears before the Endomorphs class.

But suppose one Is-a link and two Ako links are added, as in figure 9.6. Now the class-precedence lists for Crazy and Jacque are different:

Crazy	Jacque
Professors class	Weightlifters class
Teachers class	Shotputters class
Hackers class	Endomorphs class
Eccentrics class	Athletes class
Programmers class	Dwarfs class
Dwarfs class	Everything class
Everything class	

Again, no class appears after any of its own superclasses, but the Eccentrics and Teachers classes—direct superclasses of the Professors class—are now out of the left-to-right order prescribed by the Ako links exiting from the Professors class. Similarly, the Athletes and Endomorphs classes—direct superclasses of the Weightlifters class—are now out of the left-to-right order prescribed by the Ako links exiting from the Weightlifters class. In both instances, the order changes are caused by the addition of Ako links connected to other classes. These order changes are bad because left-to-right order, by convention, is supposed to indicate priority. You need a still better way to compute class-precedence lists that conforms to the following rule:

■ Each direct superclass of a given class should appear on class-precedence lists before any other direct superclass that is to its right.

The Topological-Sorting Procedure Keeps Classes in Proper Order

The **topological-sorting procedure**, to be described in this section, is definitely more complicated than the depth-first, left-to-right, up-to-join procedure. The extra complexity is worthwhile, however, because the topological-sorting procedure keeps direct superclasses in order on class-precedence lists. Thus, you know the order of a class's direct superclasses on the class's class-precedence list as soon as you know how the direct superclasses are ordered: You do not need to know the entire structure of the class hierarchy.

Before you learn the details of the topological sorting procedure, however, you will find it helpful to see what happens when a path through a class hierarchy is expressed as a list of adjacent pairs. For example, the simple, nonbranching class hierarchy in figure 9.2 can be represented as three pairs of adjacent classes, Managers–Competitors, Competitors–Dwarfs, and Dwarfs–Everything.

Note that the order in which the pairs appear can be scrambled without hindering your ability to reconstruct the original path. First, you look for a class that occupies the left side of a pair but that does not occupy the right side of any other pair. There will always be such a class; once you find it, you need only to add it to the end of a list, to strike out the pair in which it appears, and to repeat.

Next consider the classes to which Blimpy belongs, as shown in figure 9.4. Blimpy is not just a Manager; he is also a Gourmand and a Diarist, in that left-to-right order. Now you can express that left-to-right order as a list of adjacent pairs, just as you previously expressed a path up a class hierarchy as a set of left-to-right pairs. This time, you get Managers–Gourmands and Gourmands–Diarists.

As before, you can scramble the order of the pairs without hindering your ability to reconstruct the original left-to-right order. Again, all you need to do is to look for a class that occupies the left side of a pair but that does not occupy the right side of a pair. Once you find it, you add it to the end of a list, strike out the pair in which it appears, and repeat.

Thus, you can reconstruct either a nonbranching path up a class hierarchy or the left-to-right order across a set of direct superclasses from appropriately constructed lists of pairs. In one instance, you ensure that no class is listed before any of its superclasses; in the other instance, you ensure that the left-to-right order of direct superclasses is preserved.

Now you already understand the key idea behind the topological-sorting procedure; all that remains is to learn about a clever way of constructing a list of pairs such that both the upward and rightward constraints are expressed.

The first step in forming a class-precedence list for an instance using topological sorting is to form an exhaustive list consisting of the instance itself and all classes that can be reached via Is-a and Ako links from that instance. For Crazy, for example, this list contains Crazy, Professors, Eccentrics, Dwarfs, Everything, Teachers, Hackers, and Programmers. Note that this list constitutes raw material for building the class precedence list; it is not the class-precedence list itself.

The next step is to form a list of pairs for the one instance and the many classes on the raw-materials list. To make discussion easier, let us refer to both the instance and the classes on the raw-materials list as *items*.

To form a list of pairs for an item on the raw-materials list, think of passing a fish hook through the item and that item's direct superclasses, as shown in figure 9.7. Next, walk along the fish hook from barb to eyelet while making a list of pairs of adjacent items encountered on the hook. Following the fish hook for Crazy produces Crazy–Professors and Professors–Hackers. Following the fish hook for Professors produce Professors–Eccentrics and Eccentrics–Teachers; following the fish hook for Hackers produce Hackers–Eccentrics and Eccentrics–Programmers.

Following fish hooks for all the items on the raw materials list for Crazy yields the following pairs:

Node	Fish-hook pairs
Crazy	Crazy–Professors, Professors–Hackers
Professors	Professors–Eccentrics, Eccentrics–Teachers
Eccentrics	Eccentrics–Dwarfs
Dwarfs	Dwarfs–Everything
Teachers	Teachers–Dwarfs
Hackers	Hackers–Eccentrics, Eccentrics–Programmers
Programmers	Programmers–Dwarfs
Everything	Everything

The next step is to look for an item that occupies the left side of one or more pairs, but does not occupy the right side of any pair. To make it easier to refer to such an item, let us say that it is **exposed**. In our example, Crazy is exposed by virtue of the pair Crazy–Professors and the absence of any pair with Crazy on the right side.

Whenever you find an exposed item, you add it to the end of the class-precedence list and strike out all pairs in which it occurs. For the example, this means starting the class-precedence list with Crazy and striking out Crazy–Professors:

Node	Fish-hook pairs
Crazy	~~Crazy–Professors~~, Professors–Hackers
Professors	Professors–Eccentrics, Eccentrics–Teachers
Eccentrics	Eccentrics–Dwarfs
Dwarfs	Dwarfs–Everything
Teachers	Teachers–Dwarfs
Hackers	Hackers–Eccentrics, Eccentrics–Programmers
Programmers	Programmers–Dwarfs
Everything	Everything

Class-precedence list: Crazy

Now, with the pair Crazy–Professors struck out, the Professors class is exposed, leading to the next addition to the class-precedence list and to the accompanying strike-out action:

Node	Fish-hook pairs
Crazy	~~Crazy–Professors~~, ~~Professors–Hackers~~
Professors	~~Professors–Eccentrics~~, Eccentrics–Teachers
Eccentrics	Eccentrics–Dwarfs
Dwarfs	Dwarfs–Everything
Teachers	Teachers–Dwarfs
Hackers	Hackers–Eccentrics, Eccentrics–Programmers
Programmers	Programmers–Dwarfs
Everything	Everything

Class-precedence list: Crazy, Professors

Now the Hackers class is exposed, so you add Hackers and strike Hackers–Eccentrics:

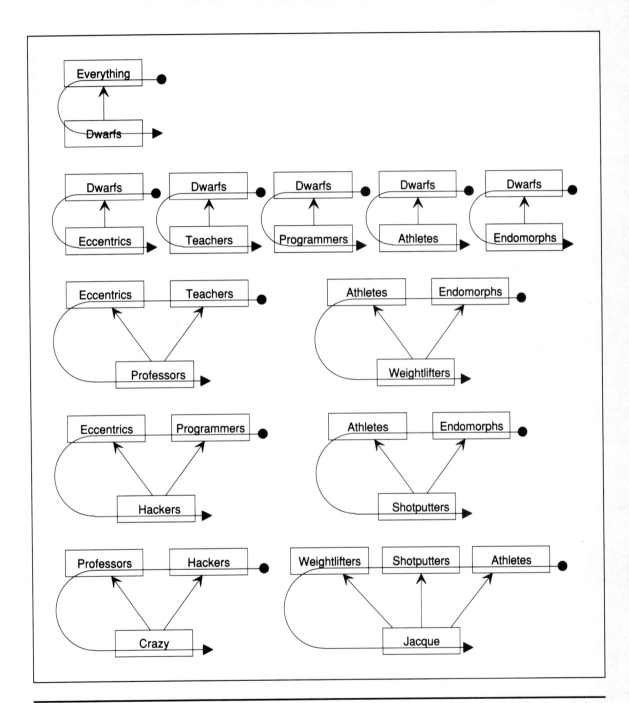

Figure 9.7 Fish hooks for Crazy and the classes reachable from Crazy. These fish hooks yield lists of class pairs that enable the computation of a class-precedence list via the topological-sorting procedure.

Node	Fish-hook pairs
Crazy	~~Crazy–Professors~~, ~~Professors–Hackers~~
Professors	~~Professors–Eccentrics~~, Eccentrics–Teachers
Eccentrics	Eccentrics–Dwarfs
Dwarfs	Dwarfs–Everything
Teachers	Teachers–Dwarfs
Hackers	~~Hackers–Eccentrics~~, Eccentrics–Programmers
Programmers	Programmers–Dwarfs
Everything	Everything

Class-precedence list: Crazy, Professors, Hackers

Now the Eccentrics class is exposed, so you add Eccentrics and strike Eccentrics–Teachers, Eccentrics–Dwarfs, and Eccentrics–Programmers:

Node	Fish-hook pairs
Crazy	~~Crazy–Professors~~, ~~Professors–Hackers~~
Professors	~~Professors–Eccentrics~~, ~~Eccentrics–Teachers~~
Eccentrics	~~Eccentrics–Dwarfs~~
Dwarfs	Dwarfs–Everything
Teachers	Teachers–Dwarfs
Hackers	~~Hackers–Eccentrics~~, ~~Eccentrics–Programmers~~
Programmers	Programmers–Dwarfs
Everything	Everything

Class-precedence list	Crazy
	Professors
	Hackers
	Eccentrics

At this point, there are two exposed classes, Teachers and Programmers. Accordingly, you need a way to break ties. One possible tie breaker—one that tends to prevent erratic movement through the tree—is to select the class that is a direct superclass of the rightmost class on the emerging class precedence list.

In the example, however, neither the Teachers class nor the Hackers class is a direct superclass of the rightmost class on the class-precedence list, the Eccentrics class.

Generalizing a bit, you move from right to left on the emerging class-precedence list, encountering the Hackers class. Because the Programmers class is a direct superclass of the Hackers class, but the Teachers class is not, the tie is broken and you can proceed:

Node	Fish-hook pairs
Crazy	~~Crazy–Professors~~, ~~Professors–Hackers~~
Professors	~~Professors–Eccentrics~~, ~~Eccentrics–Teachers~~
Eccentrics	~~Eccentrics–Dwarfs~~
Dwarfs	Dwarfs–Everything
Teachers	Teachers–Dwarfs
Hackers	~~Hackers–Eccentrics~~, ~~Eccentrics–Programmers~~
Programmers	~~Programmers–Dwarfs~~
Everything	Everything

Class-precedence list	
	Crazy
	Professors
	Hackers
	Eccentrics
	Programmers

From here on, progress is uneventful, with the following result:

Node	Fish-hook pairs
Crazy	~~Crazy–Professors~~, ~~Professors–Hackers~~
Professors	~~Professors–Eccentrics~~, ~~Eccentrics–Teachers~~
Eccentrics	~~Eccentrics–Dwarfs~~
Dwarfs	~~Dwarfs–Everything~~
Teachers	~~Teachers–Dwarfs~~
Hackers	~~Hackers–Eccentrics~~, ~~Eccentrics–Programmers~~
Programmers	~~Programmers–Dwarfs~~
Everything	~~Everything~~

Class-precedence list		
	Crazy	
	Professors	
	Hackers	← procedure to be stored here
	Eccentrics	← procedure to be stored here
	Programmers	
	Teachers	
	Dwarfs	
	Everything	

Now, suppose you create two personality-determining when-constructed procedures, one for Hackers and one for Eccentrics. The when-constructed procedure that is specialized to the Hacker class indicates that hackers are shy:

To fill the Personality slot when a new Hacker is constructed,

▷ Write Shy in the slot.

On the other hand, the when-constructed procedure that is specialized to the Eccentrics class indicates that eccentrics are weird:

To fill the Personality slot when a new Eccentric is constructed,

▷ Write Weird in the slot.

Now suppose that the Crazy instance is constructed after these when-constructed procedures are defined. Is Crazy Shy or Weird? Evidently, Crazy is Shy, because Hackers appears before Eccentrics on Crazy's class-precedence list.

In summary, when new individuals are created, when-constructed procedures supply default slot values. The class-precedence list determines which when-constructed procedures are appropriate:

To fill the slots in a new instance,

▷ Compute the class-precedence list for the new instance using the topological-sorting procedure.
▷ For each slot,
   ▷ Collect all when-constructed procedures for that slot.
   ▷ Move along the class-precedence list, from the most specific end. Stop when you encounter a class that is referred to by one of the slot-specific when-constructed procedures. Call this when-constructed procedure the most specific when-constructed procedure for the slot.
   ▷ Use that most specific when-constructed procedure.

To compute the class-precedence list, you can use the topological sorting procedure, which honors the subclass–superclass principle and the left-to-right principle:

To compute an instance's class-precedence list,

  ▷ Create fish-hook pairs

  ▷ Until all the fish-hook pairs are eliminated

  ▷ Find the exposed classes.

  ▷ Select the exposed class that is a direct superclass of the rightmost class on the emerging class-precedence list.

  ▷ Add the selected class to the emerging class-precedence list.

  ▷ Strike all fish-hook pairs that contain the newly added class.

DEMON PROCEDURES

So far, you have seen that slot values can be established by inheritance when instances are constructed, or by the direct use of a writer for slots. In this section, you see that reading or writing can activate **when-requested procedures**, **when-read procedures**, or **when-written procedures**. Sometimes these procedures are called **demons** because they lurk about doing nothing unless they see the request, read, or write operations they were designed to look for. In contrast to ordinary demons, these when-requested, when-read, and when-written demons are entirely friendly.

When-Requested Procedures Override Slot Values

After an instance has been constructed, you can replace slot values installed at creation time. If you like, you can go one step further, overriding any existing slot values altogether, using when-requested procedures. One such when-requested procedure indicates that athletes generally exercise as a hobby:

When a value for the Hobby slot of an Athlete is requested,

  ▷ Return Exercise.

Thus, Exercise becomes a sort of virtual slot value. No slot actually has Exercise in it, but it seems as though the Hobby slots of all Athletes have Exercise in them nevertheless.

When-requested procedures do not need be as simple as the when-requested, hobby-determining procedure for Athletes. They can, for example, take advantage of slot values already established by when-constructed procedures:

When a value for the Hobby slot of a Dwarf is requested,

▷ If the dwarf's Personality slot is filled with Shy, return
Reading.

▷ Otherwise, return Dancing.

Now that there are two hobby-determining procedures, you need a way to
choose between them. Naturally, it makes sense to use the same precedence-
determining topological-sorting procedure that you have seen already in the
context of choosing among when-constructed procedures.

For Crazy's Hobby slot, the governing procedure is the when-requested,
hobby-determining procedure for Dwarfs that examines the dwarf's Personality slot. Inasmuch as Crazy's Personality slot was filled with Shy when the
Crazy instance was constructed, Crazy's hobby must be reading. On the
other hand, for Jacque's Hobby slot, the governing procedure is the when-
requested procedure for Athletes that straightaway indicates the Athlete's
Hobby is Exercise.

When-Read and When-Written Procedures Can Maintain Constraints

When-read and when-written procedures are activated when slot values
are, respectively, read and written. The following when-written procedure
is activated whenever a value is written into the Physique slot of an Athlete
after the Athlete is constructed:

When a value is written in the Physique slot of an Athlete,

▷ If the new value is Muscular, write Large in the Athlete's
Appetite slot.

Evidently, this when-written procedure captures a constraint relating an
Athlete's Physique to the Athlete's Appetite: If the new slot value is Muscular, then Large is written into the Appetite slot. Thus, Muscular Athletes
have Large Appetites, in contrast to Gourmands, who have Huge Appetites,
and ordinary Dwarfs, who have Small Appetites.

As the example illustrates, when-read and when-written procedures
can be used to ensure that a change in one slot's value is reflected in an
appropriate, automatic change to another slot's value. In this role, they
perform as constraint-enforcing bookkeepers.

In contrast to when-constructed and when-requested procedures, all
applicable when-read and when-written procedures always are activated—
rather than only the one with the highest precedence as determined by
the topological sorting procedure. Given that all applicable when-read
and when-written procedures are activated, however, there is a question

of order. Sophisticated frame systems provide you with a variety of options.

With-Respect-to Procedures Deal with Perspectives and Contexts

Sometimes, the proper way to think about an instance is determined by a particular perspective. A particular dwarf, Blimpy, may be considered big for a dwarf, but small when viewed from the perspective of, say, **Snow White**. At other times, the proper way to think about an instance is conditioned by the context in which instance lies. A particular person, for example, may be happy when hiking in the mountains, yet grumpy when traveling on an airplane.

To deal with these dependencies, you use **with-respect-to procedures**, which are when-requested procedures that are specialized to more than one class. The following, for example, are two with-respect-to size-determining procedures, each of which is specialized to two classes, the first being the class to which an instance belongs, and the second being the reference class:

When a value for the Size slot of Blimpy, from the perspective of a typical dwarf, is requested,

▷ Return Big.

When a value for the Size slot of Blimpy, from the perspective of a typical person, is requested,

▷ Return Small.

Similarly, you can define with-respect-to procedures that involve context:

When a value for the Mood slot of Patrick, in the context of Mountain Hiking, is requested,

▷ Return Happy.

When a value for the Mood slot of Patrick, in the context of Airplane Travel, is requested,

▷ Return Grumpy.

Inheritance and Demons Introduce Procedural Semantics

When no demons are used, frame systems can be viewed as semantic nets.
When demons are used, however, a great deal of procedural knowledge can
be incorporated into a particular frame system. Accordingly, the mechanisms that enable the incorporation of procedural knowledge are prominent
in the specification for frame systems:

A **frame system** is a representation

That is a semantic net

In which

▷ The language of nodes and links is replaced by the language
of frames and slots.

▷ Ako slots define a hierarchy of class frames.

▷ Is-a slots determine to which classes an instance frame belongs.

▷ Various when-constructed, when-requested, when-read, when-
written, and with-respect-to procedures supply default values, override slot values, and maintain constraints.

▷ A precedence procedure selects appropriate when-constructed,
when-requested, when-read, when-written, and with-respect-
to procedures by reference to the class hierarchy.

With constructors that

▷ Construct a class frame, given a list of superclasses, and a
list of slots

▷ Construct an instance frame, given a list of direct superclasses

▷ Construct a when-requested, when-read, when-written, or
with-respect-to procedure

With writers that

▷ Establish a slot's value, given an instance, a slot, and a value

With readers that

▷ Produce a slot's value, given an instance and a slot

Recall that you have an example of procedural semantics when meaning
is defined by a set of procedures that operate on descriptions in a representation. Those procedures often lie outside the representation. In a frame
system, however, powerful procedures are brought into the representation
itself, becoming part of it.

One kind of incorporated procedural knowledge lies in the procedures
for computing class precedence and using class-precedence to determine

default slot values, thus contributing to the meaning of the Is-a and Ako slots. Another kind of incorporated procedural knowledge lies in demon procedures, many of which are permanent parts of whole classes of frame systems.

The idea of incorporating procedural knowledge into a representation is extremely powerful. In subsequent chapters, you see that you can build powerful problem solvers merely by adding some class definitions and constraint-enforcing demons to an off-the-shelf, generic frame system. Little is left to be done from scratch, other than the description of particular problems or situations.

Object-Oriented Programming Focuses on Shared Knowledge

You can benefit from the virtues of knowledge sharing, not only when creating, writing, and reading slot values, but also when performing actions in general.

Consider, for example, the problem you face when you have to decide how to eat various foods at a fancy dinner. You can capture the advice offered by a typical etiquette book in *when-applied procedures* such as the following:

To *eat* when Soup is to be eaten,

▷ Use a big spoon.

To *eat* when Salad is to be eaten,

▷ Use a small fork.

To *eat* when the Entree is to be eaten,

▷ Use a big fork and a big knife.

Thus, a **when-applied procedure** is a procedure that helps you to perform an action in a manner suited to the object acted on.

Note that when-applied procedures, like other demon procedures, are shared among subclasses automatically. Accordingly, you do not need to write and maintain separate procedures for every possible subclass of the soup, salad, and entree classes. If, however, some soup, salad, or entree subclass calls for an unusual or special tool, you can construct another when-applied procedure easily, specialize it to the appropriate subclass, an thereby ensure that your new, specific procedure will displace the old, general one:

To *eat* when the Entree is a Lobster,

▷ Use a tiny fork and a nutcracker.

Essentially, an **object-oriented programming language** enables knowledge sharing by providing mechanisms for defining object classes, creating individuals, and writing when-applied procedures. The virtues of knowledge sharing have made object-oriented programming languages increasingly popular.

FRAMES, EVENTS, AND INHERITANCE

In the previous section, you learned how you can capture general knowledge about individuals by using frames. In this section, you learn how frames can capture general knowledge about events of the sort described in newspapers.

Digesting News Seems to Involve Frame Retrieving and Slot Filling

Any news report of an earthquake probably will supply the place; the time; the number of people killed, injured, and homeless; the amount of property damage; the magnitude on the Richter scale; and possibly the name of the geological fault that has slipped. To represent this kind of knowledge in frames, you need the Earthquake, Disaster, and Event frames shown in figure 9.8.

Now suppose you have a news story freshly arrived from a wire service. You want to use that story to fill in the slots in an appropriate instance frame. Curiously, for many news stories—earthquake stories in particular— primitive when-constructed procedures can fill in the slots by looking in the story for various sorts of numbers:

To fill the Time slot when a new Event is constructed,

▷ Find a number with a colon in it and write it in the slot.

To fill the Fatalities slot when a new Disaster is constructed,

▷ Find an integer near a word with a root such as *kill* or *die*, and write it in the slot.

To fill the Damage slot when a new Disaster is constructed,

▷ Find a number next to a dollar sign, and write it in the slot.

Figure 9.8 A net connecting frames for news stories. By inheritance on two levels, it is clear that earthquake stories typically have seven slots to be filled. All may have slot-filling procedures attached.

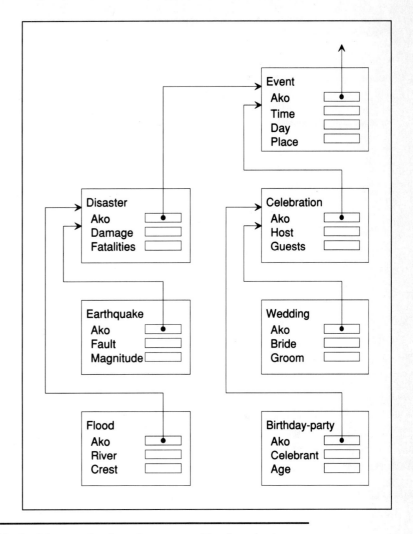

To fill the Magnitude slot when a new Earthquake is constructed,

▷ Find a decimal number between 1.0 and 10.0, and write it in the slot.

Other simple procedures can fill in nonnumeric slots:

To fill the Day slot when a new Event is constructed,

▷ Find a word such as *today, yesterday, tomorrow,* or the name of one of the days of the week, and write it in the slot.

Figure 9.9 A frame produced
by two news stories. One news
story, correctly analyzed, is
about a genuine earthquake.
The other news story, muffed, is
about earthquake research.

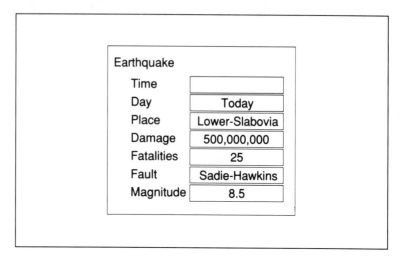

To fill the Place slot when a new Event is constructed,

▷ Find a name that appears in a dictionary of geographical
   places and write that name in the slot.

To fill the Fault slot when a new Earthquake is constructed,

▷ Find a proper name near the word *fault* and write it in
   the slot.

Consequently, analyzing stories such as the following can be easy, given
that the title evokes the Earthquake frame:

Earthquake Hits Lower Slabovia ───────────────
Today, an extremely serious earthquake of magnitude 8.5 hit Lower
Slabovia, killing 25 people and causing $500 million in damage.
The President of Lower Slabovia said that the hard-hit area near
the Sadie Hawkins fault has been a danger zone for years.

In Chapter 7, you learned that, whenever a pattern is filled in with appropriate variable values, it is said to be *instantiated*. Figure 9.9 shows the
instantiated frame constructed for the earthquake story. Once the frame is
instantiated, the frame's slot values can be used to instantiate a summary
pattern such as the following:

Earthquake Summary Pattern —————————————
An earthquake occurred in <*value in Location slot*> <*value in Day slot*>. There were <*value in Fatalities slot*> fatalities and $<*value in Damage slot*> in property damage. The magnitude was <*value in Magnitude slot*> on the Richter scale; the fault involved was the <*value in Fault slot*>.

Thus, you get the following summary by instantiating the earthquake summary pattern using data transferred in from an instantiated Earthquake frame:

Instantiated Earthquake Summary Pattern ——————
An earthquake occurred in *Lower Slabovia today*. There were *25* fatalities and $500 *million* in property damage. The magnitude was *8.5* on the Richter scale; the fault involved was the *Sadie Hawkins*.

Evidently, the Earthquake frame stands between the story and its summary, helping to bridge the gap, so to speak.

Note, however, that slot filling using simple, special-purpose procedures can lead to silly results, given that the special-purpose procedures really do not understand stories. Consider this example:

Earthquake Study Stopped ————————————————
Today, the President of Lower Slabovia killed 25 proposals totaling $500 million for research in earthquake prediction. Our Lower Slabovian correspondent calculates that 8.5 research proposals are rejected for every one approved. There are rumors that the President's science advisor, Sadie Hawkins, is at fault.

Shudder to think: This story could be summarized, naively, as though it were the story about an actual earthquake, producing the same frame shown before in figure 9.9 and the same instantiated earthquake summary pattern.

Of course, creating procedures for general news is much harder than creating procedures for specialized news. Interestingly, good news writers seem to use certain conventions that help:

- The title of a news story and perhaps the first sentence or two evoke a central frame.
- Subsequent material fills slots in the central frame. The slot-filling process evokes other frames introducing more open slots.
- Cause-effect relations are given explicitly. Readers do not need to deduce causes, because words such as *because* appear frequently.
- Few pronouns, if any, are used. In political news, for example, the nation's legislature may be referred to as "Congress," or "Capitol Hill," or "Washington's lawmakers," according to fancy.

■ Few new frames, if any, need to be constructed. Creating new frames requires reflection, and reflection is discouraged.

Event-Describing Frames Make Stereotyped Information Explicit

You have seen that the information in event frames and when-constructed procedures make certain expectations and procedures explicit:

■ The slots in event frames make explicit what you should expect to know about them.

■ The when-constructed procedures associated with event frames make explicit how you can try to acquire what you expect to know.

By making explicit appropriate knowledge—what you expect to know and how to acquire what you expect to know—event frames and their associated procedures satisfy an important criterion for good representation.

SUMMARY

■ A frame system can be viewed as a generalized semantic net. When you speak about frames, however, your language stresses instances or classes, rather than nodes, and stresses slots and slot values, rather than links and link destinations.

■ Inheritance moves default slot values from classes to instances through the activation of the appropriate when-constructed procedure.

■ To determine which when-constructed procedure dominates all other applicable when-constructed procedures, you have to convert a class hierarchy into a class-precedence list. Generally, the conversion should be such that each class appears before all that class's superclasses and each class's direct superclasses appear in order.

■ When-requested procedures override slot values. When-read and when-written procedures maintain constraints. With-respect-to procedures deal with perspectives and contexts.

■ Digesting news seems to involve inheritance. Your understanding of an earthquake news story, for example, benefits from your knowledge of the connection between earthquakes and disasters and your knowledge of the connection between disasters and events in general.

■ Shared knowledge, located centrally, is easier to construct when you write it down, easier to correct when you make a mistake, easier to keep up to date as times change, and easier to distribute because it can be distributed automatically.

BACKGROUND

Marvin Minsky is largely responsible for defining and popularizing many of the notions connected with frames [1975]. Other important contributions have been made via the many frame-oriented representation languages patterned after Minsky's ideas.

For a discussion of inheritance as embodied in a programming language, see the monumental reference work *Common Lisp, The Language*, by Guy L. Steel, Jr. [1990]

The discussion of news is based on the work of Gerald F. DeJong II [1979].

10
Frames and Commonsense

In Chapter 9, you learned how frames can capture the properties of individuals and events. In this chapter, you learn how frames can capture detailed knowledge about how acts happen.

First, you learn about how *thematic-role frames* describe the action conveyed by the verbs and nouns appearing in typical declarative sentences. Next, you learn how *action frames*, *state-change frames*, *subaction links* and *result links* describe what happens on a deeper, syntax-independent level that is more suited to question answering, sentence paraphrasing, and language translating.

Once you have finished this chapter, you will understand that frames make it possible to capture and exploit some of the knowledge carried, both explicitly and implicitly, by human language.

THEMATIC-ROLE FRAMES

Much of what happens in the world involves actions, and objects undergoing change. It is natural, therefore, that many of the sentences in human language amount to descriptions that specify actions, identify the object undergoing change, and indicate which other objects are involved in the change. In this section, you learn about one representation for that kind of knowledge, you learn how to build descriptions using that representation, and you learn how to use those descriptions to answer questions.

An Object's Thematic Role Specifies the Object's Relation to an Action

In linguistic terms, verbs often specify actions, and noun phrases identify the objects that participate in the action. Each noun phrase's **thematic role** specifies how the object participates in the action. You speak, for example, of the *agent, thematic object*, and *instrument* thematic roles.[†]

The sentence, "Robbie hit a ball with a racket," for example, carries information about how Robbie, a ball, and a racket relate to the verb *hit*. A procedure that understands such a sentence must discover that Robbie is the **agent** because he performs the action of hitting, that the ball is the **thematic object** because it is the object hit, and that the racket is the **instrument** because it is the tool with which hitting is done.

Thus, sentence analysis requires, in part, the answers to these questions:

- What thematic roles are to be filled by a sentence?
- How is it possible to determine the thematic roles of the noun phrases in a sentence?

The number of thematic roles embraced by various theories varies considerably. Some people use a half-dozen thematic roles. Others use three or four times as many. The exact number does not matter much, as long as it is great enough to expose natural constraints on how verbs and thematic-role instances form sentences.

For illustration, let us confine ourselves to a world for which the thematic roles shown in figure 10.1 are adequate.

- **Agent**. The agent causes the action to occur. Volition is generally implied, as in "*Robbie* hit the ball," but there are exceptions: "*The moon* eclipsed the sun." The agent is often the surface subject, but in a passive sentence, the agent also may appear in a prepositional phrase: "The ball was hit *by Robbie.*"
- **Coagent**. The word *with* may introduce a noun phrase that serves as a partner to the principal agent. The two carry out the action together: "Robbie played tennis *with Suzie.*"
- **Beneficiary**. The beneficiary is the person for whom an action is performed: "Robbie bought the balls *for Suzie.*"
- **Thematic object**. The thematic object is the object the sentence is really all about—typically the object undergoing a change. Often, the thematic object is the same as the syntactic direct object, as in "Robbie hit *the ball.*" On the other hand, in a passive sentence, the thematic object appears as the syntactic subject as in "*The ball* was hit by Robbie."

[†]Some people use the term *object* instead of *thematic object*. Using *thematic object* avoids confusion with the syntactic direct and indirect objects.

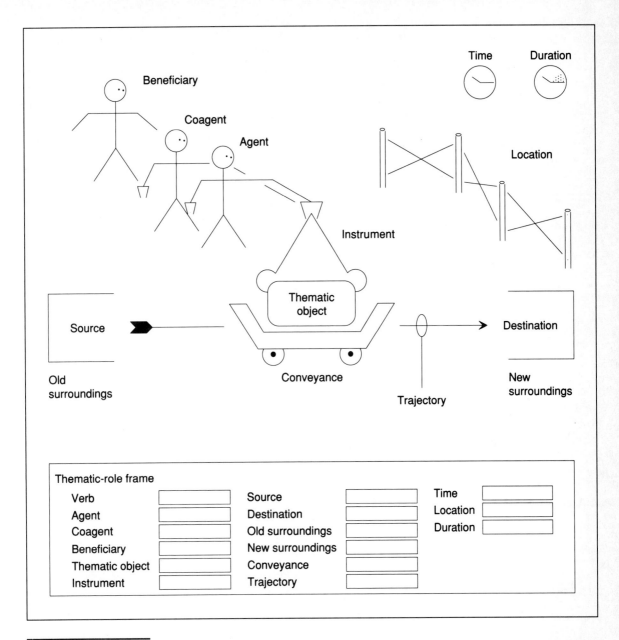

Figure 10.1

Thematic roles focus on how noun phrases relate to actions.

■ **Instrument**. The instrument is a tool used by the agent. The preposition *with* typically introduces instrument noun phrases: "Robbie hit a ball *with a racket.*"

■ **Source and destination**. Changes are often simple changes in physical position. The source is the initial position, and the destination is the final position: "Robbie went *from the dining room to the kitchen.*"

- **Old surroundings and new surroundings**. The old surroundings is the location out of which something comes, and the new surroundings is the location in which it goes: "Robbie took the cereal out *of the box* and put it *into the bowl*."
- **Conveyance**. The conveyance is something in which or on which one travels: "Robbie always goes *by train*."
- **Trajectory**. Motion from source to destination takes place over a trajectory. In contrast to the other role possibilities, several prepositions can serve to introduce trajectory noun phrases: "Robbie and Suzie went in *through the front door;* he carried her *over the threshold*."
- **Location**. The location is where an action occurs. As in the trajectory role, several prepositions are possible, each of which conveys meaning in addition to serving as a signal that a location noun phrase is coming: "Robbie and Suzie studied *in the library, at a desk, by the wall, under a picture, near the door*."
- **Time**. Time specifies when an action occurs. Prepositions such as *at, before*, and *after* introduce noun phrases serving as time role fillers. "Robbie and Susie left *before noon*."
- **Duration**. Duration specifies how long an action takes. Prepositions such as *for* indicate duration. "Robbie and Susie jogged *for an hour*."

Another way of summarizing all this information about thematic roles is to use the representation specification form, noting that all the thematic roles involved in a particular action can be viewed as slot values for a thematic-role frame:

A **thematic-role system** is a representation

That is a frame system

In which

▷ The slots are, typically, *verb, agent, coagent, beneficiary, thematic object, instrument, source, destination, old surroundings, new surroundings, conveyance, trajectory, time, location,* and *duration*.

▷ Each frame describes an action. The verb slot identifies the action. Other slots identify objects that play various roles with respect to the action.

Filled Thematic Roles Help You to Answer Questions

Because thematic-role frames make certain roles explicit, many questions are easy to answer once values for thematic-role slots are worked out. Consider this sentence:

Robbie made coffee for Suzie with a percolator.

Figure 10.2 A filled thematic-role frame. The slot values provide answers to a variety of questions about what happened.

Thematic-role frame	
Verb	Make
Agent	Robbie
Beneficiary	Suzie
Thematic Object	Coffee
Instrument	Percolator

Figure 10.3 Another filled thematic-role frame. Again, the slot values provide answers to a variety of questions about what happened.

Thematic-role frame	
Verb	Go
Agent	Robbie
Coagent	Suzie
Destination	Theater
Conveyance	Car

There are four noun phrases, each of which fits into a particular role, as shown in figure 10.2. Four corresponding questions can be answered:

What was made?	→	thematic object	→	coffee
Who made it?	→	agent	→	Robbie
With what was it made?	→	instrument	→	a percolator
For whom was it made?	→	beneficiary	→	Suzie

Similar results follow from another sentence:

Robbie went to the theater with Suzie by car.

Again there are four noun phrases, each of which fits into a particular role, as shown in figure 10.3.

Who went?	→	agent	→	Robbie
With whom did he go?	→	coagent	→	Suzie
To where did he go?	→	destination	→	the theater
By what means did they travel?	→	conveyance	→	car

Thus, thematic roles roughly correspond to some of the simple questions about actions.

Although such question answering is important, you must keep in mind that it is only one of the functions of front-line semantic analysis. Presumably, the results of thematic-role identification are the fodder for still deeper mechanisms that understand the relations among individual sentences, evolving contexts, and global knowledge about the world.

Various Constraints Establish Thematic Roles

Of course, slot values have to be ferreted out by a language-understanding program before they can support question analysis. Fortunately, for simple English sentences, many constraints help you to establish the thematic role of any given noun phrase:

■ Each verb carries strong preferences about what thematic roles can appear and where the noun phrases that fill those thematic roles can be placed, relative to the verb.

■ Prepositions limit a noun phrase's role possibilities.

Here is the relation between prepositions and role possibilities:

Preposition	Allowable thematic role
by	agent or conveyance or location
with	coagent or instrument
for	beneficiary or duration
from	source
to	destination

Thus, the preposition *by* signals that you can expect an agent, a conveyance, or a location, but not a coagent, beneficiary, instrument, source, or destination.

■ The noun itself may limit possible role identifications.

For example, you get a different picture from "Robbie was sent to the scrap heap by parcel post," than from "Robbie was sent to the scrap heap by Marcel Proust," because parcel post is more likely to be a conveyance, whereas Marcel Proust is more likely to be an agent.

■ Only one filler is allowed in any sentence for most thematic roles.

If, somehow, the thematic role of one noun phrase is determined, then the other noun phrases in the sentence are forced to fill other thematic roles.

Note, however, that a filler may involve more than one object if the objects are conjoined explicitly by *and*. In "Robbie ate with a fork with a gazerkle," it is not clear whether the gazerkle is a coagent, because **gazerkle** is a made-up word. It is clear, however, that the gazerkle is not an instrument because the fork has a lock on that. On the other hand, if the sentence were, "Robbie ate with a fork and a gazerkle," the fork and gazerkle would fill the instrument thematic role together, and hearing such a sentence, you would learn that a gazerkle can be an instrument.

Time, trajectory, and location are exceptions to the one-filler rule because more than one noun phrase may be involved in their description. It is perfectly reasonable to say, for example, "Robbie ate at noon on Monday."

A Variety of Constraints Help Establish Verb Meanings

Verbs and verb phrases in isolation exhibit meaning ambiguity just as noun phrases exhibit thematic-role ambiguity. Conveniently, meaning-selection constraints often seem to resolve the ambiguity.

The noun phrase in the thematic-object thematic role can help considerably. Consider the following examples:

He shot the rabbit.
He shot the picture.

Shooting a rifle and shooting a camera are very different kinds of shooting, even though there are similarities at a certain level of abstraction. The words *rifle* and *camera* are not specifically mentioned; information found in the words *rabbit* and *picture* is apparently enough to guide your interpretation toward one meaning or the other.

Another way verb meanings are selected is through a small family of words called **particles**. For example, see how particles select meanings for *throw* and *pick*:

He threw some food.
He threw away some food.
He threw up some food.
She picked up some candy.
She picked out a nice assortment.

One other strong influence on meaning derives from the overall context. Curiously, quite a lot can be gained from a very coarse categorization of life's subjects into a few worlds:

- **The physical world**.

Objects change position, and they acquire and lose various properties and relations to other objects. Other worlds seem to relate to the physical world through analogy.

- **The mental world**.

The objects in the mental world are facts, ideas, and concepts. You sometimes think about them with actions, properties, and relations borrowed from the physical world, just as though the abstractions were physical things. Consider these examples:

The theory is supported by facts.
The overall concept is solid.
The idea was exposed in the class.

Figure 10.4 Many constraints help determine noun-phrase thematic roles and verb-phrase meanings. Among the noun phrases, the one in the thematic object role has a strong influence on verb meaning.

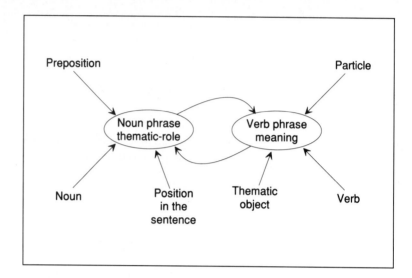

■   **The ownership world.**

In the ownership world, the objects are abstract certificates of control, possession, or ownership, whose locations are in the hands of people or organizations. Again, the events in this world often are communicated in language that is analogous to that of the physical world:

Robbie took the ball away from Bozo.
The bank took the house back.

Note that transfer of a physical thing is not necessarily implied. Robbie is probably holding the ball he took control of, but the bank probably never moves a physical house.

Constraints Enable Sentence Analysis

As suggested in figure 10.4, many constraints help you to assign thematic roles to the noun phrases in simple sentences. To see how they do so, you need to agree to a few assumptions.

First, assume you have a dictionary of stored information about nouns and verbs. Also, assume, for the sake of simplicity, that all noun phrases help you to describe the action; no noun phrase helps you to describe another noun phrase.

Of course, in addition to determining noun-phrase thematic roles, you also need to determine the verb phrase's meaning. Several constraints enable you to hack away at the potential meanings, ultimately determining a unique interpretation, or, at worst, a small number of interpretations. Noting the presence of a particle helps you considerably. You can instantly throw out verb meanings that are inconsistent with an observed particle, or that are inconsistent with the absence of a particle.

If you wish to determine the noun-phrase thematic roles, the first step is to locate the thematic object among the noun phrases without prepositions. If the verb phrase is passive, then the thematic object—the thing the sentence is about—must occupy a spot in front of the verb. It is what you learned in grammar school to call the **syntactic subject**.

If the verb is active, then the thematic object follows the verb. If there is only one noun phrase after the verb, possibly accompanied by one or more prepositional phrases, then that noun phrase is the thematic object. In the rest of this chapter, such noun phrases are called **preposition-free noun phrases** to distinguish them from noun phrases that are part of larger prepositional phrases.

If there are two preposition-free noun phrases following the verb, then the second is the thematic object, as long as the verb requires a thematic object. Assume that it does, constraining sentence construction, just to keep illustrative analysis manageable.

With the thematic object in hand, there is an opportunity to weed out unlikely verb meanings—namely, those whose stored meanings are incompatible with the thematic object.

At this point, it is conceivable that more than one verb meaning remains. Accordingly, you must carry more than one interpretation forward in parallel. Fortunately, in human communication, as the number of interpretations seems about to explode, some powerful constraint appears to keep the number of interpretations small. Note, incidentally, that strength in one dimension allows flexibility in another. It is easy to imagine how a language might have a larger number of prepositions than English has, with an offsetting reduction in word-order constraint. Finnish is an example of such a language.

Now you can nail down the thematic roles for other noun phrases, starting with those without prepositions. Again, the surviving verb meanings may state preferences about what is needed and where what is needed can be found. Many active verbs, for example, demand an explicit agent and prefer to find that agent in the syntactic subject position. Such verb-carried demands are ordinarily sufficient to fix the role for the one or two preposition-free noun phrases that may be found in addition to the thematic object. Knowing the roles for the preposition-free noun phrases greatly simplifies the analysis of other noun phrases, because those other noun phrases cannot be assigned to thematic roles that are already spoken for.

Consider, for example, a sentence containing a noun phrase introduced by the word *by*. This word typically introduces either the agent role or the conveyance or the location. If you have already determined that agent role is spoken for by the syntactic subject, then only the conveyance and location possibilities remain. Generally, you can resolve this remaining ambiguity either by using knowledge about the words in the noun phrase or by deferring to the dictionary-stated needs of the verb.

Finally, once the thematic roles are known for all noun phrases, certain roles may be present that help you to resolve remaining verb-meaning ambiguity.

Whew! It is time to capture all these steps by restating them in procedural English:

To determine thematic roles,

▷ Obtain possible verb meanings from the dictionary. Throw away those verb meanings that are inconsistent with the verb's particle, if there are any.

▷ Find the thematic object among the preposition-free noun phrases.

▷ Throw away the verb meanings that the dictionary says are inconsistent with the thematic object.

▷ For each remaining noun phrase, determine the thematic role.

▷ Throw away the verb meanings that the dictionary says are inconsistent with the observed thematic roles.

Although there are more complicated procedures, the one introduced here is powerful enough to handle the forthcoming examples.

Examples Using Take Illustrate How Constraints Interact

Suppose Robbie and Suzie communicate using a simple subset of English. To keep the illustration simple, they talk only about the things shown in figure 10.5. The verbs may have more than one meaning, but they certainly do not have all of the meanings possible in unrestricted English.

Robbie and Suzie move objects, get sick, engage in business activities, and date. Consequently, the verb *take* has a variety of meanings:

- *Take1* means transport. Either a source or a destination or both should appear.
- *Take2* means swindle. The source and destination roles are absent when this meaning is intended. Only people can be swindled.
- *Take3* means to swallow medicine. The available medicines include aspirin. The beneficiary is the same as the agent.
- *Take4* means to steal. People are not stolen.
- *Take5* means to initiate and execute a social event with another person. The particle *out* is always used.
- *Take6* means to remove. The particle *out* is always used. People cannot be removed.
- *Take7* means to assume control. The particle *over* signals this meaning.
- *Take8* means to remove from the body. The particle *off* is always used.

Figure 10.5 A small world used to illustrate the effect of various sentence constraints.

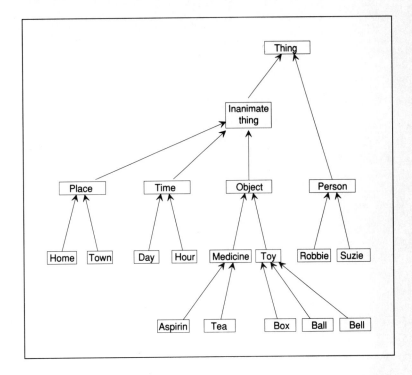

These various meanings of *take* combine with noun phrases according to the thematic-role constraints you have been studying. Assume all passive sentences have exactly one preposition-free noun phrase, the syntactic subject, and that preposition-free noun phrase appears before the verb. Also assume that thematic roles are subject to the constraints given in the following table:

Thematic role	Preposition	Allowed class
agent	by	person
coagent	with	person
beneficiary	for	person
thematic object	—	—
instrument	with	inanimate
source	from	—
destination	to	—
old surroundings	out of	inanimate
new surroundings	into	inanimate
conveyance	by	inanimate
duration	for	a time

Now you can examine a few sentences with a view toward better understanding the way various constraints interact.

Robbie took aspirin.

The verb meanings *Take5* through *Take8* are eliminated, because there is no particle. Evidently Robbie is the agent and aspirin is the thematic object by virtue of word order and the lack of alternatives. *Take1* is unlikely, because there are no noun phrases that can be either the source or the destination of a transporting action. *Take2* is out, because aspirin is not a subclass of people and hence cannot be swindled. Thus, the sentence means that Robbie either swallowed or stole aspirin.

Robbie took aspirin for Suzie.

Robbie is the agent and aspirin is the thematic object by the same word-order argument used before. Again only *Take3* and *Take4* survive particle and thematic object considerations. *For* can flag either the beneficiary or duration, but because Suzie is not time, she must be the beneficiary. This observation, in turn, eliminates the *Take3* interpretation—swallowing medicine—because swallowing medicine requires the agent and beneficiary to be the same. Robbie has stolen. Of course, Robbie may have swallowed aspirin because Suzie begged and pleaded with him to do so, but that conclusion is incompatible with our assumptions here.

Robbie took out Suzie.

The particle limits the verb meaning to *Take5* and *Take6*, to date or to remove. *Take6* requires an inanimate thematic object, so Robbie dated Suzie.

Robbie took out the box.

A box is inanimate; hence it is removed, not dated.

Robbie took the ball to Suzie.

The ball is the thematic object, so *Take1*, to transport, and *Take4*, to steal, are the alternatives. Because a destination is given, *Take1* is preferred.

Robbie took Suzie.

Suzie being the thematic object, *Take1* and *Take2*, to transport and to swindle, are possible. Because there is no source or destination, Robbie has probably swindled Suzie.

Robbie took Suzie to town.

With a destination, the swindle conclusion is unlikely. Robbie has transported Suzie.

The bell was taken out of town by Robbie by car for a day for Suzie.

Because the sentence is passive, the bell is the thematic object. Because a bell is both inanimate and not a medicine, the verb meaning must be *Take1* or *Take4*. The compound preposition *out of* can flag old surroundings. Knowing that a town is a place and places are possible old surroundings resolves the ambiguity in favor of *Take1*. *Car* is an unknown word, so it could be either the agent or a conveyance. But because Robbie is animate, he must be an agent, thus filling the agent role, forcing the car to be a conveyance. Finally, *Suzie* and *day* are easily resolved into beneficiary and duration, because Suzie cannot be a time and a day cannot be a beneficiary.

EXPANSION INTO PRIMITIVE ACTIONS

In the previous section, you learned how thematic-role frames deal with the verbs and nouns in sentences. In this section, you learn how to go underneath the words, searching for more meaning. Here are some examples of what your search enables you to do:

- You can guess what happens when an action is taken. You can guess, for example, that comforting someone probably implies that the person emotional state improves.
- You can guess the details of how an action is done. You can know, for example, that eating probably involves moving a fork or a spoon, requiring the movement of a hand.

Primitive Actions Describe Many Higher-Level Actions

How many primitives are needed to describe the actions denoted by English verbs? The answer may be a surprisingly small number. It seems that many ordinary verbs are used as a sort of shorthand for ideas that can be expressed as well by combinations of basic primitives and default slot fillers. The combination process, called **telescoping**, accounts for an amazing number of superficially distinct verbs.

During the 1930s, champions of **Basic English** as a world language argued persuasively that people can get by with a vocabulary of only 1000 words by depending heavily on *come*, *get*, *give*, *go*, *keep*, *let*, *make*, *put*, *take*, *have*, *say*, *see*, and *send*. In Basic English, the verb *eat*, for example, is translated, from the thematic-role perspective, into *put*, together with a new surroundings thematic role prefilled with something such as the eater's stomach. Indeed, the eater's stomach is so much a part of the definition of *eat* that it seems strange to have it mentioned explicitly: one does not say, "I am eating a sandwich *into my stomach*."

The following list of primitives is similar to the list in Basic English, but it was originally constructed for the benefit of computer programs, rather than for human communication. The list includes actions in the physical world, the mental world, and the ownership world:

Move-body-part	Move-object
Expel	Ingest
Propel	Speak
See	Hear
Smell	Feel
Move-possession	Move-concept
Think-about	Conclude

Figure 10.6 Much of the meaning of simple sentences is captured by Action frames and State-change frames tied together through Result slots. Here putting a wedge on a red block makes Robbie happy.

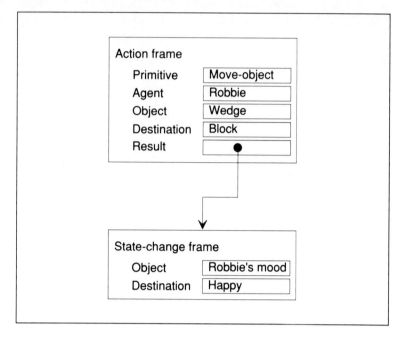

A variety of examples in the rest of this section show how these primitives help you to capture the meaning of simple sentences.

Actions Often Imply Implicit State Changes and Cause-Effect Relations

Many sentences are about a primitive action connected to a state change by a Result link. Consider this sentence:

Robbie enjoyed putting the wedge on the red block.

Evidently, the action caused Robbie to be in the state of being happy. Nothing is known about how he felt before he moved the block, but while he moved it, he was happy. It is convenient to represent such sentences as combinations of Action frames and State-change frames. Figure 10.6, for example, pictures what happens when Robbie puts the wedge onto the red block. Note the Result link; it indicates that the action causes the state change.

Of course, one action also can cause another action. You indicate this relation by placing a Result link between the two things involved. Consider this sentence, for example:

Suzie told Robbie to put the wedge on the red block.

For this sentence, the diagram of figure 10.7 is appropriate.

Some sentences announce only state changes, leaving the actions that cause the state changes unspecified. Suppose someone says this:

Suzie comforted Robbie.

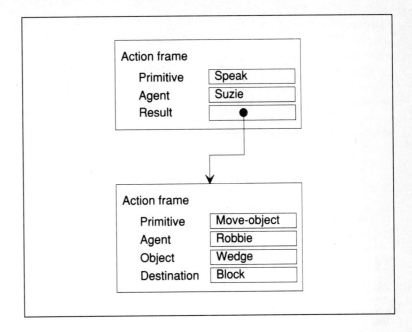

Figure 10.7 One action can cause another as when Suzie tells Robbie to do something.

There is a state change because Robbie is less sad than he was, assuming *comfort* implies original sadness. But what exactly did Suzie do? She caused Robbie to be less sad, certainly, but by what action? Did she talk with him, take him for a walk, or just help him move the wedge? There is no way of knowing from the sentence, so all that can be done is to represent what is known, as shown in figure 10.8. Note the use of the maximally nonspecific Do in the Primitive slot.

Let us look at one more example showing how actions and state changes can interdigitate:

Robbie was gored by the test.

This language is metaphoric. The test itself presumably did no damage to poor Robbie; it was getting a bad grade that hurt him. Moreover, no one stuck a horn in his gut; something merely made him feel as though a horn had been thrust into him.

The real idea conveyed, when stripped of the color, is represented in figure 10.9. Note that Do is used because it is hard to guess precisely what Robbie did or perhaps failed to do. Overall, the example again demonstrates that a sentence's verb may imply a state-change rather than an action.

Actions Often Imply Subactions

The Subaction slot is used to indicate that an action involves one or more subactions. Through Subaction slots, actions reveal their pieces, and then the pieces themselves reveal their pieces, ad nauseum.

Figure 10.8 Some sentences specify only state change even though they seem to be about actions. Saying "Suzie comforted Robbie" gives no clue about how Robbie's improved state is achieved.

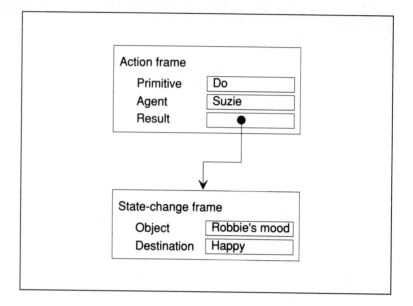

Putting a wedge on a red block involves a Move-object action with three Move-body-part subactions, as indicated in figure 10.10. Moving the hand employs one Move-body-part, whereas grasping and ungrasping employ two others, each dealing with finger movements.

As another example, suppose that Robbie eats some ice cream. Figure 10.11 shows how the basic action, Ingest, calls to mind a Move-object involving a spoon. Of course, there is no way of knowing that Robbie eats the ice cream with a spoon, given only "Robbie eats ice cream." He may eat an ice-cream cone or drink a milk shake. Using a spoon is only a default presumption, a general image called up if explanation is demanded and nothing specific to the situation is known.

Primitive-Action Frames and State-Change Frames Facilitate Question Answering and Paraphrase Recognition

Like thematic-role frames, primitive-action frames and state-change frames make it possible to answer certain questions directly. Here are some examples:

- How is an action done? Answer by expanding the action into primitive actions and state changes. Give more detail by working through Subaction slots.

For example, Robbie eats ice cream by ingesting it (indicated by Ingest). He ingests it by moving a spoon (indicated by Move-object). He moves the spoon by moving his hand (indicated by Move-body-part).

Figure 10.9 Considerable knowledge may be needed to expand simple-sounding metaphors into an arrangement of primitive-action and state-change frames. The diagram here represents a statement that Robbie was gored by a test.

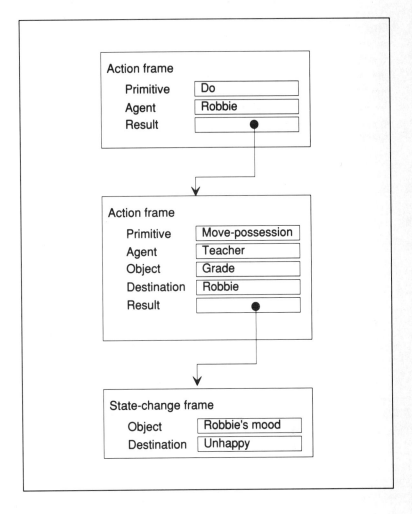

■ What will happen if an action is done? Answer by first expanding the action into primitive-action and state-change frames. Then you may be able to find a similar, but more complete expansion in a database of remembered precedents.

For example, if Suzie hits Robbie (by Move-body-part her fist to his body), a remembered precedent may indicate, via a Result link, that he is likely either to hit her back (by Move-body-part his fist to her body) or to cry (by Expel tears). A remembered precedent, consisting of tightly coupled, expectation-suggesting primitive-action and state-change frames, is called a **script**.

■ Does one sentence have the same meaning as another? Answer by expanding both into primitives and checking to see whether the results match.

Figure 10.10 Subaction slots offer another way of tying together action frames. This simple arrangement shows that moving a wedge is ultimately accomplished by a sequence of Move-body-part primitives.

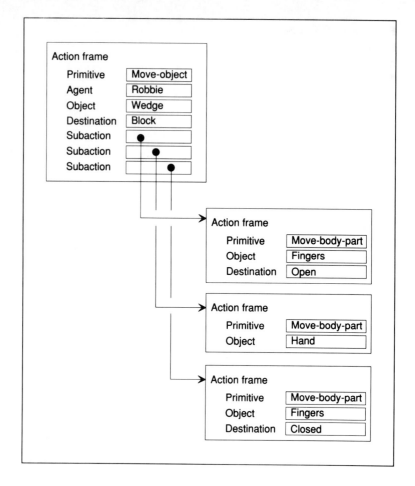

For example, "Suzie comforted Robbie" has the same meaning as "Suzie did something to make Robbie happy," because both expand into an action frame with an unspecified action and a state-change frame with Robbie's mood improving. Evidently, the sentences are paraphrases of each other.

The assumption behind the paraphrase test is that sentences have the same meaning if and only if they expand into the same primitive-action and state-change frames—a gigantic, heavily contested assumption. Some people deny that primitive-action and state-change frames are good canonical forms for describing the meanings of sentences. Other people contend that even if primitive-action and state-change frames do qualify as a good canonical form, there is still no reason to believe that there is a procedure that will transform sentences with the same meaning into the same primitive-action and state-change descriptions. Still other people do not care, arguing that paraphrase recognition is only a small, rather insignificant part of commonsense reasoning.

Figure 10.11 In this example, Robbie eats ice cream by moving a spoon to the mouth.

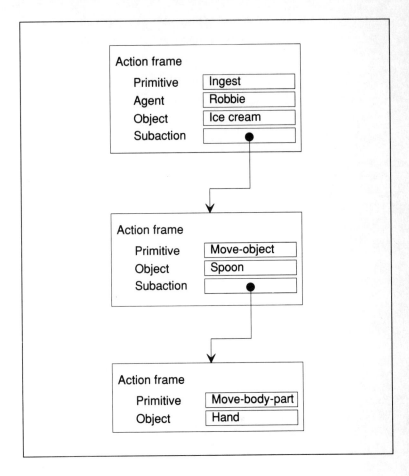

Thematic-Role Frames and Primitive-Action Frames Have Complementary Foci

You have seen that primitive-action and state-change frames make explicit certain action-describing details:

■ The primitive actions in Primitive slots make explicit what actions occur.

■ The slot values in state-change frames make explicit what state changes occur.

■ The frames in Result and Subaction slots make explicit what consequences and methods are assumed.

Note that primitive-action and state-change frames complement thematic-role frames with respect to what is made explicit. The specification of thematic-role frames, as given, places no constraint on the values allowed in the verb slot, but the specification makes a fuss over the names of the other slots. In contrast, in a specification for a primitive-action and state-change system, the emphasis is on Subaction and Result slots and on the vocabulary of values allowed in the Primitive slot; everything else is loose:

A **primitive action system** is a representation

That is a frame system

In which

▷ Action frames contain a Primitive slot that must be filled by a value drawn from a small, canonical set, such as Move-body-part, Move-object, Expel, Ingest, Propel, Speak, See, Hear, Smell, Feel, Move-possession, Move-concept, Think-about, Conclude, and Do.

▷ State-change frames contain an Object slot that is filled with an application-specific object or quantity.

▷ An Action frame may be connected to one or more other Action frames via a Subaction slot.

▷ Action frame and State-change frames may be connected to each other via Result slots.

▷ Other slots and slot values are application specific.

SUMMARY

- A thematic-role frame is an action-oriented representation focused on identifying the roles played by various objects.
- Primitive-action frames and state-change frames constitute an action-oriented representation focused on using background knowledge to identify primitive actions and infer subactions and state changes.
- Various constraints establish thematic roles and verb meanings. Once a thematic-role frame is instantiated, it can be used to answer questions about who or what played what role in an action.
- Instantiated primitive-action frames and state-change frames can be used to answer questions about what probably was done or what probably happened next.

BACKGROUND

C. J. Fillmore is closely associated with thematic-role grammar, which he called **case grammar** [1968]. Many of the ideas in this chapter were more directly influenced by the late William A. Martin. Most of his work was never published, regrettably.

CYC Captures Commonsense Knowledge

The most ambitious knowledge-representation effort in artificial intelligence is the CYC project, so named because one main goal of the project is to recast much of the knowledge you would find in a desk encyclopedia so as to make that knowledge accessible to reasoning programs.

Believing there is no way to be intelligent without knowing a lot, the developers of CYC have created a vast network of concept-describing frames. A tiny fraction of the frames in that vast network, along with a tiny fraction of the links connecting the frames in that tiny fraction, is shown here:

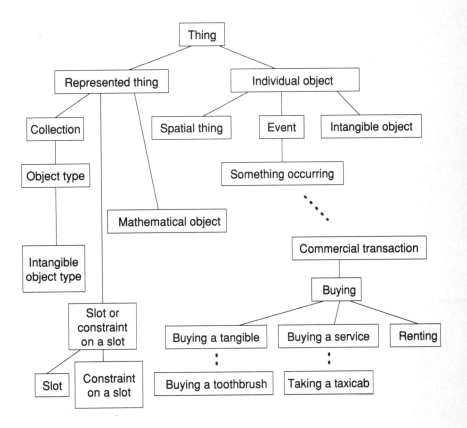

Various specialized reasoning modules work with many types of links, not just with the inheritance links shown in the illustration. Thus, inheritance is just one of many methods that CYC can use to reach conclusions. At the moment, CYC has more than 4000 link types and dozens of specialized reasoning modules.

Knowledge is entered by **ontological engineers**, who use a sophisticated human-machine interface to increase the speed and reliability of knowledge entering. So far, they have entered more than 5,000 distinct, but richly interconnected frames.

The basic book on Basic English is *Basic English: International Second Language*, by C. K. Ogden [1968]. It is a delightful book, which demonstrates that a small vocabulary can convey a lot of information. The purpose was to promote a subset of English to solve the tower-of-Babel problem.

Yorick A. Wilks contributed importantly to establishing the value of canonical primitives for representing what sentences say on a deeper level [1972]. The work of Roger C. Schank is better known, however, and the discussion of action and state-change frames is based on his work [Shank and Colby 1973].

For arguments against canonical primitives see William A. Woods's classic paper, "What's in a Link" [1975].

The Cyc project was conceived, championed, and developed by Douglas B. Lenat. For a comprehensive review, see *Building Large Knowledge-Based Systems* [Lenat and R. V. Guha 1990].

11

Numeric Constraints and Propagation

In this chapter, you learn about how *propagation procedures* move numeric values through *constraint boxes*, thus performing what has come to be called, somewhat idiomatically, *numeric constraint propagation*.

By way of illustration, you see how a procedure can propagate probabilities through *opinion nets*. You also see, indirectly, how numeric constraint propagation solves problems in image understanding by way of an example involving elevation estimates.

When you have finished this chapter, you will understand that numeric constraint propagation can achieve *global consistency* through *local computation*.

PROPAGATION OF NUMBERS THROUGH NUMERIC CONSTRAINT NETS

In this section, you learn how simple arithmetic constraints can be enforced in nets, thus enabling fresh information to have far-reaching consequences.

Numeric Constraint Boxes Propagate Numbers through Equations

Numeric constraints can be represented in a number of ways. One way, of course, is by a set of equations. Alternatively, constraints can be represented by a net consisting of **variable boxes** and **multiplier boxes**.

For example, the net shown in figure 11.1 corresponds to the following equations:

$$B1 = 1.1$$
$$B5 = 3000$$
$$C5 = B1 \times B5$$
$$D5 = B1 \times C5$$

Each multiplier constrains its terminals' values such that the value at the product terminal is the product of the values at the multiplicand terminals. Note that it is better to talk of multiplicands and products, rather than of inputs and outputs, because the multiplier box allows information to flow toward any terminal. Knowing the two multiplicands of a three-terminal multiplier, you can compute the product; knowing the product and one multiplicand, you can compute the other multiplicand.

Similarly, **adder boxes** constrain their terminals' values such that the value at the sum terminal is the sum of the numbers on addend terminals. As with multipliers, a conclusion can be reached at any terminal.

One way to arrange for these computations is to represent numeric constraint boxes as a frame system. That way, you can use demon procedures to enforce constraints. Here is the specification:

A **value-propagation net** is a representation

That is a frame system

In which

▷ Variable boxes are frames that hold variable values.

▷ Operation boxes are frames that enforce constraints.

▷ Application-specific demon procedures, specialized to particular operation-box classes, compute unknown terminal values whenever enough information is available at the other terminals of the same operation box.

With the specification for a value-propagation net in hand, it is easy to specialize the idea into a specification for an arithmetic constraint net:

An **arithmetic constraint net** is a representation

That is a value-propagation net

In which

▷ Variable boxes hold numbers.

▷ Operation boxes enforce arithmetic constraints.

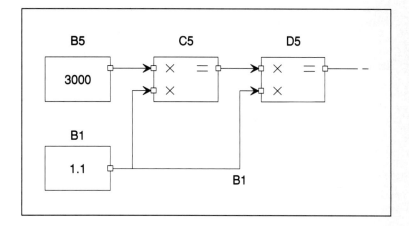

Figure 11.1 A numeric constraint net representing a set of numeric constraints.

The following, for example, is a when-written procedure for an arithmetic constraint net that insists that the value in the product terminal of a multiplier is the product of the values at the multiplicand terminals:

When a value is written into the Multiplicand1 terminal of a multiplier,

▷ When there is a value at the Multiplicand2 terminal of the multiplier,

   ▷ If there is no value at the product terminal, write the product of the multiplicand values into the product terminal.

   ▷ Otherwise, compare the value in the product terminal with the product of the multiplicands,

      ▷ If they are the same, do nothing.

      ▷ Otherwise, complain.

In the example of figure 11.1, this when-written procedure produces a value at the first multiplier's product terminal as soon as values are available at the terminals of both ports, box B1 and box B5. Once that is done, the same when-written procedure will place a value at the second multiplier's product terminal inasmuch as both of its multiplicands are available. You can determine the result by interrogating the value of the product terminal of box D5.

In the rest of this chapter and in subsequent chapters, you see that several other representations can be built on top of arithmetic constraint nets. As shown in figure 11.2, these representations include opinion nets, discussed in this chapter, as well as various kinds of neural nets, discussed in several chapters in Part II.

Figure 11.2 The arithmetic-
constraint net family of
representations.

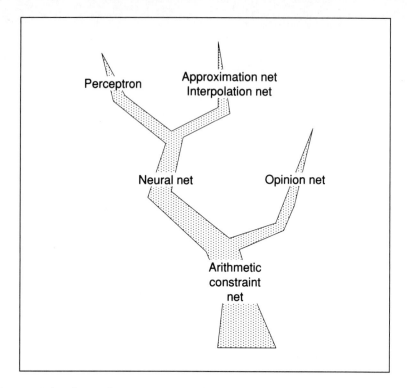

Figure 11.2 The arithmetic-
constraint net family of
representations.

In principle, the arithmetic-constraint-net family tree could be grafted
onto the semantic-net family tree shown in Chapter 2 because arithmetic-
constraint nets are a kind of value-propagation net, which, in turn, can
be viewed as a kind of frame system. On the other hand, the switch
from propagating symbolic descriptions to propagating mere numbers is
extremely radical. Accordingly, the arithmetic-constraint-net family is best
regarded as completely separate from the semantic-net family.

PROPAGATION OF PROBABILITY
BOUNDS THROUGH OPINION NETS

In the previous section, you learned how simple arithmetic constraints can
be enforced in nets. In this section, you learn that the same ideas enable
you to keep track of a conclusion's probability.

Probability Bounds Express Uncertainty

Suppose you like to buy stocks just before splits are announced. To decide
whether a stock is about to split, you habitually consult four advisors: two
stock brokers and two mystics. You consider the brokers, as a group, to
believe that a stock will split if either of the brokers believes that it will;
similarly, you consider the mystics, as a group, to believe that a stock will

Spreadsheets Propagate Numeric Constraints
Through Numeric-Constraint Nets

The enormously successful electronic financial spreadsheet systems can be viewed
as constraint-propagation systems. You have probably seen what a spreadsheet
system looks like in **equation mode**:

	A	B	C	D
1	Ratio X	1.1		
2	Ratio Y	1.0		
3				
4		1st year	2nd year	3rd year
5	Income X	3000	B1×B5	B1×C5
6	Income Y	5000	B2×B6	B2×C6
7	Expenses	9000	B7	C7
8		——	——	——
9		B5+B6−B7	C5+C6−C7	D5+D6−D7

Each array location contains a title, a constant, or an equation. The array locations with numbers correspond to the constants in numeric-constraint nets. The
array locations with equations describe the constraints that tie numbers together
and correspond to collections of numeric-constraint boxes. In **what-if mode**,
the implications of the constants are propagated throughout the spreadsheet, as
in the following example, in which a company becomes profitable after a 1-year
startup phase:

	A	B	C	D
1	Ratio X	1.1		
2	Ratio Y	1.0		
3				
4		1st year	2nd year	3rd year
5	Income X	3000	3600	4320
6	Income Y	5000	5500	6050
7	Expenses	9000	9000	9000
8		——	——	——
9		−1000	100	1370

For this example, the procedure for numeric constraint propagation nets could
be used.

Figure 11.3 Upper and lower bounds on probability allow greater flexibility when expressing certainty.

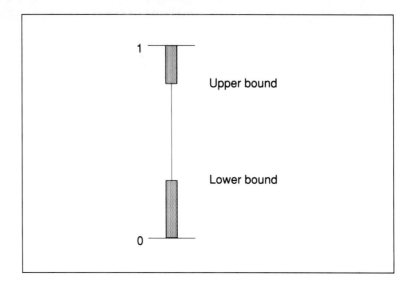

split if either of the mystics believes that it will. Being conservative, you believe that a stock will split only if both the brokers group and the mystics group believe that it will.

There are many approaches to representing as numbers opinions such as those of the brokers and the mystics. Most approaches translate opinions into probability numbers that indicate how frequently an assertion is true. Probability numbers range from 0 to 1, with 1 representing the idea that an assertion is certainly true, and 0 representing the idea that an assertion is certainly false.

The approach explained here is more sophisticated, because each opinion is translated into a range of probability numbers, rather than into only one value. The range is specified by a lower bound on assertion probability and an upper bound, as shown in figure 11.3.

Upper and lower bounds enable you to deal with advisors who refuse to be pinned down precisely. With upper and lower bounds, you can capture statements such as, "I do not know enough to give you a probability that the stock will split, but I do know enough to say that the probability is definitely between one-quarter and three-quarters" Of course, the upper and lower bounds converge to one number if an advisor is willing to express an exact probability.

Individual opinions can be tied together in various ways. Figure 11.4 shows how the various opinions in our stock-split example fit together with constraint boxes in between.

Of course, these constraint boxes are more complicated than those in the arithmetic boxes, being based on probability theory, rather than arithmetic. The following constraint equations, for example, govern the action of *or* boxes. For any such *or* box, suppose A represents an input, B

Figure 11.4 The opinion of the broker group is that the stock will split if either group thinks this will happen. Similarly, the opinion of the mystic group is that the stock will split if either group thinks this will happen. However, your opinion is that the stock will split only if both the broker group and the mystic group think this will happen.

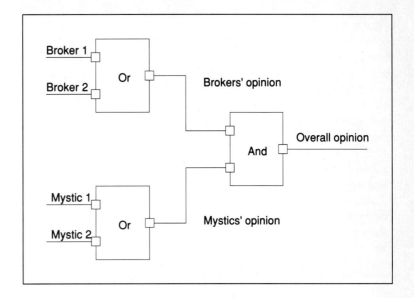

represents another input, and A or B represents the output. Then, $l(A)$, $l(B)$, and $l(A$ or $B)$ represent lower bounds on probability. Similarly $u(A)$, $u(B)$, and $u(A$ or $B)$ represent upper bounds on probability. Then, as you soon learn, the following equations hold:

$$u(A) \leq u(A \text{ or } B),$$
$$l(A) \geq l(A \text{ or } B) - u(B),$$
$$u(B) \leq u(A \text{ or } B),$$
$$l(B) \geq l(A \text{ or } B) - u(A),$$
$$u(A \text{ or } B) \leq u(A) + u(B),$$
$$l(A \text{ or } B) \geq \max[l(A), l(B)].$$

When you combine assertions and boxes that constrain probabilities, the result is an **opinion net**. When you deal with opinion nets, the words *input* and *output* are used loosely because the constraint inequalities enable propagation from any terminal to any terminal. You see **forward propagation**, from input to output, in the upper part of figure 11.5, as upper and lower probability bounds propagate through an Or box; in the lower part of figure 11.5, you see **backward propagation**, as upper and lower probability bounds propagate through an Or box from the output to the two inputs.

Venn Diagrams Explain Bound Constraints

To understand probability bound constraints, you need to think about diagrams such as the one shown in figure 11.6. In that diagram, each dot denotes an event. Some of the events belong to class A; these are denoted

Figure 11.5 The upper part shows forward propagation through a constraint box. New bounds on the lower of the two inputs, together with the existing bounds on the other input, constrain the output probability to lie between 0.3 and 0.8. The lower part shows backward propagation through a constraint box. New bounds on an output probability, indicating that the probability must lie between 0.3 and 0.8, constrain both input probabilities to lie between 0 and 0.4.

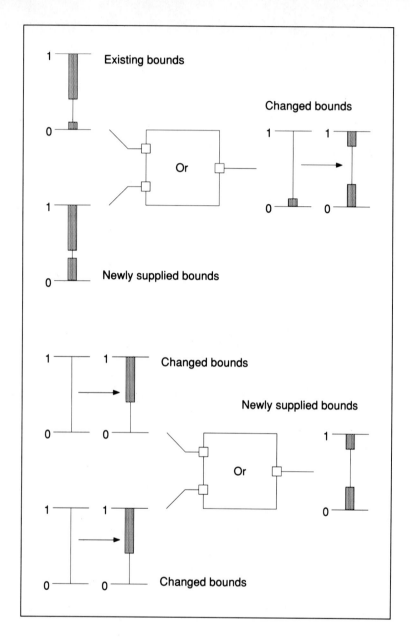

by dots inside the rectangle labeled A. Other events belong to class B, and they are denoted by dots inside rectangle B.

All events are inside a rectangle, called the *universe*, that contains all events. If there are any events that belong to both class A and class B, the corresponding rectangles overlap. The result is called a **Venn diagram** or an **event diagram**.

Figure 11.6 A Venn diagram.
Some of the events are in
A, others are in B, and still
others are in both. To reduce
clutter, you normally draw Venn
diagrams without the event-
denoting dots.

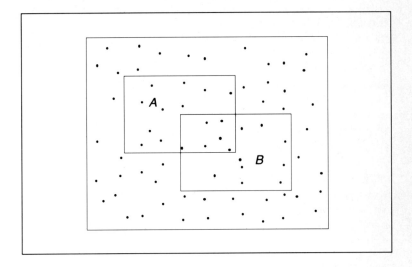

The purpose of Venn diagrams is to help you visualize a key idea in probability theory: if you increase the number of events in a class, corresponding to an increase in the area allocated to the class in a Venn diagram, the probability of the class must either stay the same or increase. The probability will stay the same only if the added events have zero probability.

Now suppose you want to know how the probability of the events in either class A or class B, written $p(A$ or $B)$, relates to the probabilities of the classes themselves, $p(A)$ and $p(B)$. Four situations have to be considered, because as shown in figure 11.7, class A and class B may share no events, some events, or all events, or all events in one class may be in the other.

The heavy black lines in figure 11.7 enclose all the events in either class A or class B. As you see, no matter with which of the four situations you are faced, the area enclosed by the black line is at least as large as the larger of the areas enclosed by the rectangles for class A and for class B. Evidently then, $p(A$ or $B) \geq \max[p(A), p(B)]$. It is also clear that the area enclosed by the black line is not larger than the sum of the areas enclosed by class A and class B. Thus, $p(A$ or $B) \leq p(A) + p(B)$. In summary, there are lower and upper bounds on $p(A$ or $B)$:

$$\max[p(A), p(B)] \leq p(A \text{ or } B) \leq p(A) + p(B).$$

Now you are just a step or two away from two of the Or box-constraint equations. You know that $p(A)$ cannot be any less than the lower bound given for the probability of A—namely, $l(a)$. Similarly, $p(B)$ cannot be less than $l(B)$. Thus, $\max[p(A), p(B)]$ cannot be any less than $\max[l(A), l(B)]$. Thus, $p(A$ or $B)$ certainly must be greater than or equal to $\max[l(A), l(B)]$, which means that $l(A$ or $B) \geq \max[l(A), l(B)]$, which is one of the constraint equations.

Figure 11.7 Venn diagrams
for thinking about the probability
that an event is either in class
A or in class B.

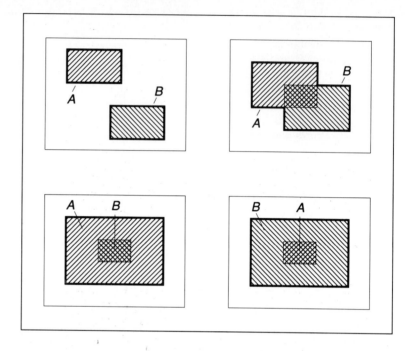

Also, you know that $p(A)$ cannot be any more than the upper bound,
$u(A)$. Thus, $p(A) + p(B)$ cannot be any more than $u(A) + u(B)$. Furthermore, $p(A$ or $B)$ certainly must be less than or equal to $u(A) + u(B)$, which
means that $u(A$ or $B) \leq u(A) + l(B)$, which is another of the constraint
equations.

So far, you have considered the probability that an event is in either
class A or class B. For the other four constraint equations, you need to
focus on one of the individual classes—class A, for example.

From another look at the Venn diagram in figure 11.7, you can see
that the area enclosed by class A cannot be smaller than the area enclosed by both class A and class B minus the area of class B. Thus,
$p(A) \geq p(A$ or $B) - p(B)$. Similarly, the area enclosed by class A cannot be larger than the area enclosed by both class A and class B. Thus,
$p(A) \leq p(A$ or $B)$. In summary, the lower and upper bounds on $p(A)$ are
as follows:

$$p(A \text{ or } B) - p(B) \leq p(A) \leq p(A \text{ or } B).$$

Now $p(A$ or $B)$ cannot be any smaller than $l(A$ or $B)$, and $p(B)$ cannot
be any larger than $u(B)$. Thus, $p(A$ or $B) - p(B)$ cannot be any smaller
than $l(A$ or $B) - u(B)$. Consequently, $p(A)$ must be at least as large as
$l(A$ or $B) - u(B)$, which means that $l(A) \geq l(A$ or $B) - u(B)$, which is
another of the constraint equations.

Finally, $p(A$ or $B)$ cannot be any larger than $u(A$ or $B)$. Thus, $p(A)$
cannot be larger than $u(A$ or $B)$, which means that $u(A) \leq u(A$ or $B)$,

which is still another of the constraint equations. The remaining two equations are constraints on $p(B)$ that mirror those just worked out for $p(A)$.

Having seen how to work out equations for Or boxes, you could carry on yourself, producing constraint equations for, say, And boxes:

$$u(A) \le u(A \text{ and } B) - l(B) + 1,$$
$$l(A) \ge 0,$$
$$u(B) \le u(A \text{ and } B) - l(A) + 1,$$
$$l(B) \ge 0,$$
$$u(A \text{ and } B) \le \min[u(A), u(B)],$$
$$l(A \text{ and } B) \ge l(A) + l(B) - 1.$$

Propagation Moves Probability Bounds Closer Together

Now everything is in place for the advisors example. To begin, you assume that none of the four advisors have submitted opinions. Then, the probability bounds associated with a stock split are between 0 and 1, written $[0, 1]$.

Next, suppose that you learn that your first broker thinks that the probability of a stock split is between 0.25 and 0.75, written $[0.25, 0.75]$. With this information from your first broker, and general knowledge of how to propagate probability bounds through Or boxes, you conclude that the lower-bound probability expressed by the broker group must be $\max[0.25, 0] = 0.25$. As in the rest of this example, the upper bound remains at 1.

When you learn the opinion of the second broker, expressed as the bounds $[0.33, 0.66]$, the lower-bound probability expressed by the broker group becomes $\max[0.25, 0.33] = 0.33$.

The first mystic expresses his opinion as the bounds $[0.15, 0.15]$, causing the lower-bound probability of the mystic group to be 0.15. The second mystic expresses his opinion as the bounds $[0.85, 0.85]$, causing the lower-bound probability to be 0.85. The change in the lower-bound probability of the mystic group causes, at last, a change in the lower-bound probability of the overall conclusion; that value moves from 0 to 0.18 because $0.33 + 0.85 - 1 = 0.18$, as shown in figure 11.8.

PROPAGATION OF SURFACE ALTITUDES THROUGH ARRAYS

In the previous sections, you learned how arithmetic constraints can be enforced in nets, thus enabling fresh information to have far-reaching consequences. In this section, you learn how arithmetic constraints on the elements of an array can lead to far-reaching consequences as well. This kind of constraint propagation is particularly useful when you are looking

Figure 11.8 The opinion net after all opinions are known.

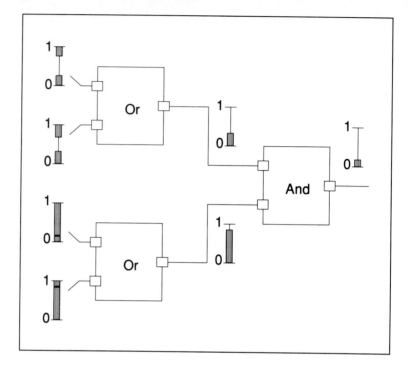

at images to determine surface properties such as distance and direction. Here, however, you learn about the ideas through an example in another, simpler domain.

Local Constraints Arbitrate between Smoothness Expectations and Actual Data

Suppose that you want to make a digital terrain map—that is, a map that indicates altitude. To keep the illustration simple, let us confine ourselves to an east–west line along which you happen to have a collection of altitude estimates that you have obtained by sending out people with barometers to a few accessible places.

Assume the barometer readings, b, are sparse. Further assume that each instrument is identified with a confidence level, c. The confidence level ranges from 0, meaning worthless, to 1, meaning perfectly reliable.

At the top of figure 11.9, you see some actual terrain, along with altitude estimates produced by the barometers. At the bottom of the figure, you see the confidence levels associated with each measurement.

When you make your estimates, you should honor two principles: each estimate should be close to the value indicated by the barometer if there is one; and the altitude should be close to the average of the altitudes at neighboring points, given that the terrain is fairly smooth. From these two principles, it is only a small step to an equation that gives altitude, a_i, at

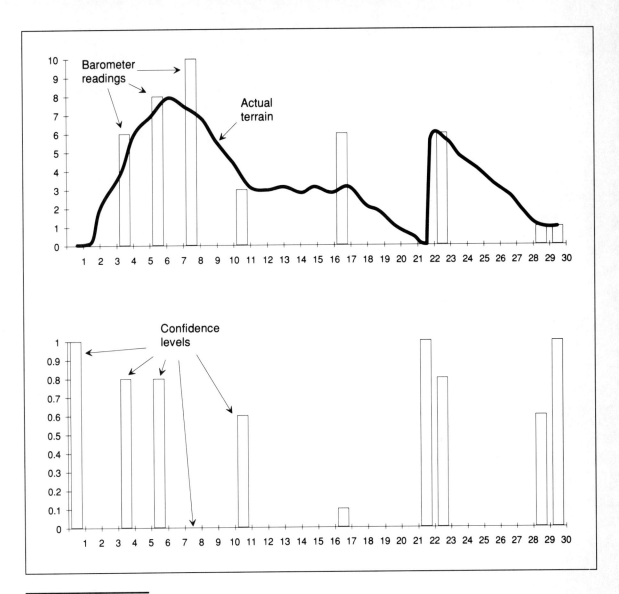

Figure 11.9 The problem is to find good altitude estimates for the terrain using barometric measurements in which you have varying confidence.

point i, as a weighted sum of the barometer reading there, the b_i, and the average of the neighbors' altitudes. Using the confidence factor, c_i, and $1 - c_i$ as the weights, the equation slants the result toward the barometer measurement in proportion to the judged reliability of the measurement. To deal with places where there is no barometer reading, you take both b_i and c_i to be 0:

$$a_i = c_i b_i + (1 - c_i) \frac{a_{i+1} + a_{i-1}}{2}.$$

Because there is one equation like this for each value of the subscript i, it is time consuming to use the standard, sequential procedures for solving sets of linear equations. Instead, you can find an approximate solution by numeric constraint propagation.

The first step is to find initial altitude estimates, a_i, using only the b_i and c_i values (remember that both are taken to be 0 where no barometer readings exist):

$$a_i = c_i b_i + (1 - c_i)\frac{b_{i+1} + b_{i-1}}{2}.$$

Next, using the initial altitude estimates, you form a second, improved set of altitude estimates. You use the same equation as before, except that the neighbors' altitudes are those computed as initial estimates, rather than the barometer readings. So that you can keep the estimates straight, superscripts specify the iteration number, with 0 representing the initial estimates:

$$a_i^1 = c_i b_i + (1 - c_i)\frac{a_{i+1}^0 + a_{i-1}^0}{2}.$$

In general, then, for the nth refinement, you have the following equation:

$$a_i^n = c_i b_i + (1 - c_i)\frac{a_{i+1}^{n-1} + a_{i-1}^{n-1}}{2}.$$

This kind of numeric constraint is called a **relaxation formula**, a term inherited from mathematics. Procedures that use relaxation formulas are called **relaxation procedures**. The general structure of a relaxation-based propagation procedure is as follows:

To propagate numeric constraints through arrays using relaxation,

▷ Call the initial array the current array.

▷ Until all values in the array change sufficiently slowly,

  ▷ For each element in the current array, calculate an element for a new array using the relaxation formula.

  ▷ Make the new array the current array.

Figure 11.10 shows altitude estimates at various stages. Note that the influence of the high, totally unreliable peak at $i = 8$ eventually dies out. By the tenth iteration, things have just about settled down. After the fortieth iteration, changes are too small to see.

Altitude values converge to their asymptotic values slowly because our propagation procedure is too myopic. Constraint travels slowly when it travels in tiny steps. Using a larger separation between points helps you to reach convergence faster, but then the result lacks fine detail.

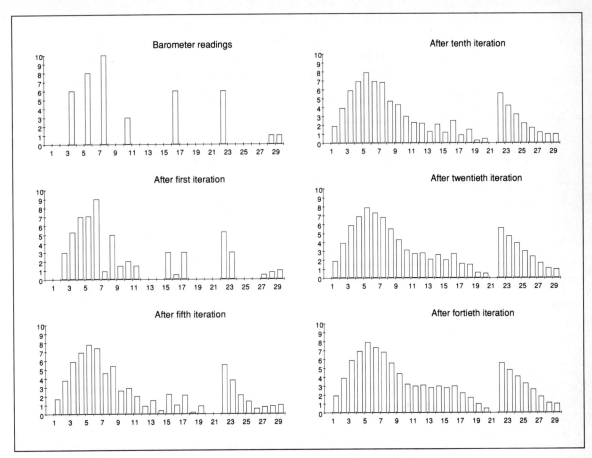

Figure 11.10 Raw altitude data and data processed by numeric constraint propagation. For each iteration, you obtain a new value for each point by computing a weighted average of the point's original raw-data value and the point's neighbors' values during the previous iteration.

Constraint Propagation Achieves Global Consistency through Local Computation

The overall objective of numeric-constraint-propagation procedures is to find values that are consistent everywhere with some stipulated constraints. When numeric-propagation procedures use constraints that link only a few numbers in small neighborhoods, they are said to be doing **local computation**. When constraints are satisfied everywhere, the consistency is said to be **global consistency**. Hence, the point of numeric constraint propagation is to achieve *global consistency through local computation*.

SUMMARY

- Numeric constraint boxes propagate numbers through equations.
- One kind of numeric propagation operates on probability bounds attached to various assertions connected together in an opinion net. Venn diagrams help you to explain the constraints involved.

GENINFER Helps Counselors to Provide Precise Genetic Advice

Many people in artificial intelligence borrow heavily from other, more established disciplines, probability theory in particular. One important example is GENINFER, a system constructed to help genetic counselors provide advice to prospective parents.

The purpose of GENINFER is to determine the likelihood that a future child will have an inherited disorder. For the following family tree, GENINFER determines the probability that a future child will be a hemophiliac.

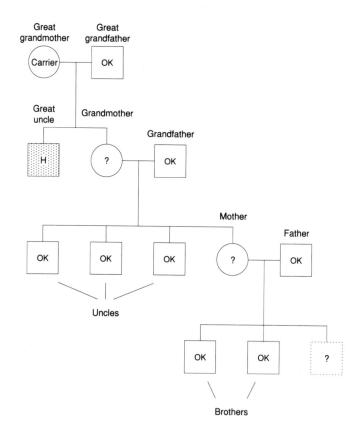

Hemophilia is an interesting genetic disease because it is an example of a recessive genetic defect carried on the X chromosome.

Females have two paired X chromosomes; males have one X chromosome paired with a Y chromosome. Because the hemophilia defect is recessive and is carried on the X chromosome, a female with one defective X chromosome can pass on hemophilia, but shows no sign of the disease herself. If a male has a defective X chromosome, however, he is a hemophiliac.

Every child inherits one of its mother's X chromosomes, but which one is a matter of chance. Thus, a female child of a carrier mother and a normal father has a probability of 0.5 of becoming a carrier. A male child has a probability of 0.5 of being a hemophiliac.

Computing the probabilities for family trees, such as the one shown on the previous page, is difficult, however, so many genetic counselors rely on coarse approximations. GENINFER does not need to rely on approximations, because it works out the exact probabilistic implications of all the facts. In the example, GENINFER states that the probability that a future male child will be a hemophiliac, given only the knowledge that the great uncle is a hemophiliac, is 12.5 percent, an uncomfortably high probability. Informed that there are three normal uncles, GENINFER revises its calculations, and restates the probability as only 2.8 percent. Finally, further informed that there are two normal brothers, GENINFER concludes that the probability is only 0.7 percent, a comfortably low probability. The following graph summarizes GENINFER's calculations:

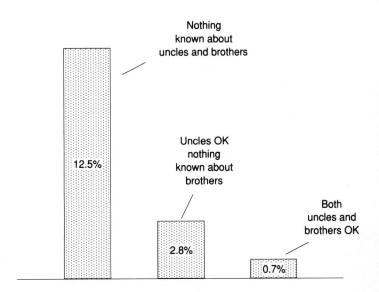

To do such calculations, GENINFER treats the family tree as a **Bayesian net** and performs Bayesian probability analysis. Because GENINFER is intended for interactive use, GENINFER uses a variety of program-optimization methods to do the necessary calculations with acceptable speed.

Versions of GENINFER under development now go further in that they combine traditional Bayesian analysis with reasoning modules that look for peculiarities in the Bayesian analysis so as to identify probable errors in the construction of the family tree.

■   Another kind of numeric propagation operates in altitude arrays. Local constraints arbitrate between smoothness expectations and actual data.

BACKGROUND

The discussion of probability bounds is based on the work of Ross Quinlan [1983].

A system for propagating numbers through arrays is discussed in the context of image understanding in Chapter 27.

Methods for dramatically increasing the speed of numeric constraint propagation in the context of surface reconstruction from stereo images have been introduced by Demetri Terzopoulos [1983].

Interestingly, simple nets of voltage sources, current sources, resistors, and transistors can be modeled as numeric constraint nets. Thus, the procedure for propagating numeric constraints in nets, with generalizations, can do certain kinds of electronic-circuit analysis. The generalized procedure seems to work through circuits the way human engineers often do, producing a similar analysis, as described, for example, in a landmark paper by Richard M. Stallman and Gerald J. Sussman [1977].

The discussion of GENINFER is based on the work of Peter Szolovits [1992].

12

Symbolic Constraints and Propagation

In this chapter, you learn how *symbolic constraint-propagation procedures* can determine the consequences of interacting constraints.

By way of illustration, you learn about a program that interprets drawings, and about another program that finds relations among time intervals.

Once you have finished this chapter, you will know that, when a domain is well understood, it is often possible to describe the objects in the domain in a way that uncovers useful, interacting constraints. You will also know how to use *Marr's methodological principles* when you work on difficult problems.

PROPAGATION OF LINE LABELS THROUGH DRAWING JUNCTIONS

In this section, you learn about propagating symbolic labels through nets. In particular, you learn about symbolic constraint propagation in the context of understanding drawings of plane-faced objects, such as those in figure 12.1. The main problem is to determine which lines are boundary lines that separate objects. You see that boundary, convex, concave, shadow, and crack lines come together at junctions in only a few ways, and then you see that this restriction on junction combinations determines the proper physical interpretation for each line in a drawing. Once correct line interpretations are known, it is easy to use known boundary lines to divide

Figure 12.1 Part of drawing analysis is to decide how each line in a drawing should be interpreted.

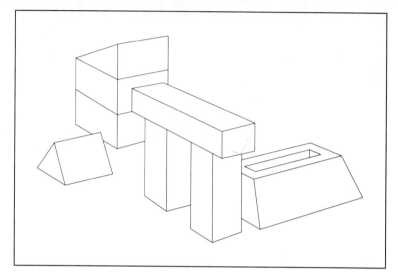

the drawing into objects. Along the way, you see that some impossible drawings can be detected, because there is no way to interpret all the lines consistently.

There Are Only Four Ways to Label a Line in the Three-Faced-Vertex World

Consider a world populated by crack-free polyhedra with lighting arranged to eliminate all shadows. The lines in drawings of this world represent various naturally occurring edge types. A simple partitioning of these lines is shown in figure 12.2.

All lines are divided into boundary lines and interior lines. **Boundary lines** occur where one object face hides the other. The two regions in the drawing separated by a boundary line *do not* abut along the boundary line. **Interior lines** are those for which the two separated regions *do abut* one another. The interior lines are those that are associated with concave edges and those that are associated with convex edges.

For notational convenience, line interpretations are identified on drawings by **line labels**. There are three such labels:

Line	Label
Convex	+
Concave	−
Boundary	>

You determine the direction of the boundary line label by noting which side of the line corresponds to a face of the object causing the boundary line. Imagine taking a stroll along the line, keeping the boundary-line object on the right. The direction of walking is the direction of the boundary label.

Figure 12.2 Drawings consist of boundary lines and interior lines. The interior lines may be concave or convex.

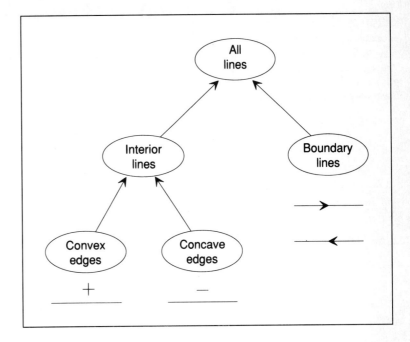

Figure 12.3 An L–shaped solid illustrates the three basic line interpretations: convex lines, marked with plus labels; concave lines, marked with minus labels; and boundary lines, marked with boundary labels.

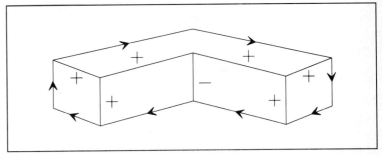

Combinations of line labels surrounding junctions are called **junction labels**. Natural constraints severely limit the number of junction labels that are physically realizable.

It is easy to label each of the lines in figure 12.3 such that all the junction labels are physically realizable by using your intuition. By so labeling a drawing, you exploit your understanding of the physical situation to arrive at interpretations for the lines. The key idea to pursue now is that of turning the process around, using knowledge about allowable junction labels to derive an understanding of the physical reality.

Accordingly, you need a catalog of physically realizable junctions. To keep straight the distinction between a drawing and the actual physical world, note that **junctions** in drawings denote physical **vertexes** in the world, and **lines** denote physical **edges**.

Figure 12.4 The common junctions. Those on the right are excluded if vertexes are all three-faced vertexes and there are no shadows or cracks.

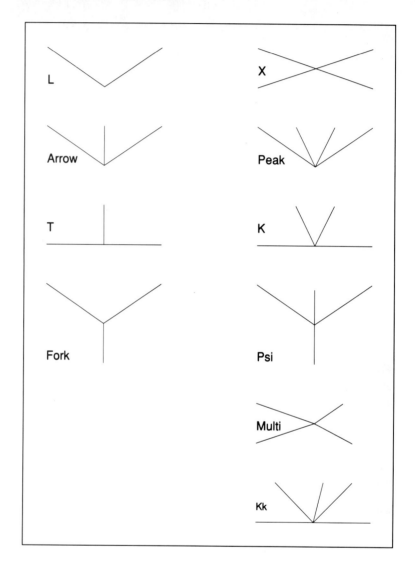

Junctions can be categorized according to the number of lines coming together and the size of the angles between the lines. Figure 12.4 assigns mnemonic names to the common categories.

Fortunately, the following simple assumptions exclude all junctions other than Forks, Arrows, Ls, and Ts:

■   Limited line interpretations: There are no shadows or cracks.
■   Three-faced vertexes: All vertexes are the intersection of exactly three object faces. The vertexes at the top of the Great Pyramids of Egypt are forbidden. The vertexes in figure 12.5 are allowed.

Figure 12.5 Some objects with exclusively three-faced vertexes.

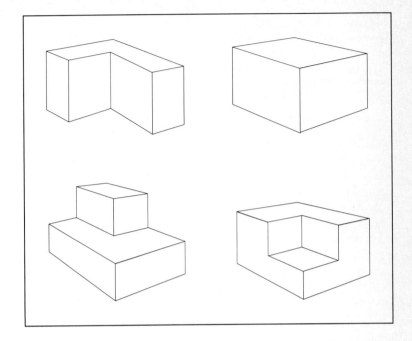

Figure 12.6 The criterion of general viewing position excludes both of these configurations because any perturbation of the viewing position changes the junctions indicated. On the left, you see the front and top of a cube, viewed without perspective.

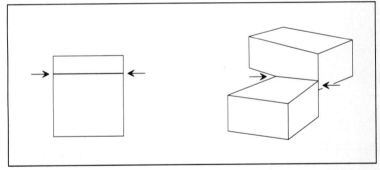

■ General position: The choice of viewpoint is such that no junctions change type with a small change of viewpoint. The viewpoints in figure 12.6 are forbidden.

These assumptions are in force only temporarily; later, they will be relaxed. The reason that these assumptions help you is that they reduce the number of junction possibilities and hence the number of interpretations possible for junction-surrounding lines.

Now, because there are four ways to label any given line, there must be $4^2 = 16$ ways to label an L. Similarly, there must be $4^3 = 64$ ways to label any particular Fork, Arrow, or T. Thus, the upper bound on the number of junction labels is 208. Curiously, only 18 of these combinations are physically realizable. It is not possible, for example, to find the junc-

Figure 12.7 Some junction labels not found in drawings of polyhedra with three-faced vertexes.

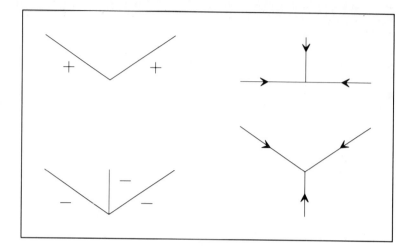

tion labels of figure 12.7 in drawings of real polyhedral objects, given our assumptions.

The next job is to collect the junction labels that are possible. There are only six for Ls, five for Forks, four for Ts, and three for Arrows. Once you have them, analyzing drawings is like working easy jigsaw puzzles.

There Are Only 18 Ways to Label a Three-Faced Junction

At first, it might seem crazy to think that you can build a junction catalog containing all physically realizable junction labels by looking at every possible three-faced physical vertex from every possible direction. Fortunately, forbidding all but general viewing positions makes the task manageable, and assuming that drawings contain only three-faced vertexes makes the task easy.

The three faces of any three-faced vertex define three intersecting planes, and three intersecting planes divide space into eight octants, as shown in figure 12.8. An object forming a vertex plainly must occupy one or more of the eight octants so formed. Accordingly you can make a complete junction catalog by a two-step process: consider all ways of filling up eight octants with object material; and view each of the resulting vertexes from the unfilled octants.

Of course, if no octants are filled, or if all are filled, then there is no vertex, and consequently, there is nothing to consider. But suppose seven of the eight are filled, as in the left half of figure 12.9. Evidently, the seven-octant situation validates a Fork junction label in which each of the three lines involved bears a minus label. Note that the only junction of interest in the drawing is the one in the center. The surrounding drawing is only a visual aid to understanding how the seven filled octants produce a single drawing junction. Note further that, because seven octants are filled, there can be only one octant from which to look at the vertex. The junction

Figure 12.8 The three faces
of a three-faced vertex divide
space into eight octants. Here
the planes meet at right angles.
They need not.

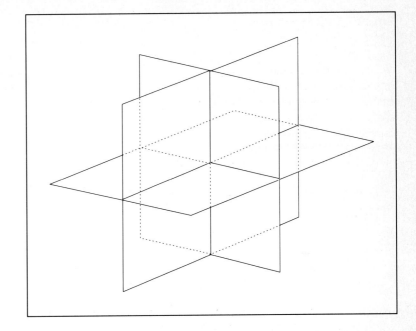

Figure 12.8 The three faces
of a three-faced vertex divide
space into eight octants. Here
the planes meet at right angles.
They need not.

Figure 12.9 Junctions seen
when seven octants are filled
or when one is. On the left,
the three concave lines are
seen, no matter where the
viewer stands within the one
available viewing octant. On
the right, the view from one
octant is such that there is a
Fork surrounded by convex
labels.

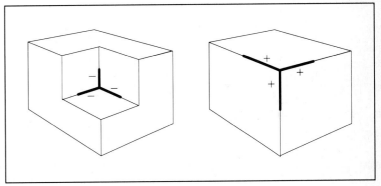

type seen is a Fork, no matter what particular position is taken within the
viewing octant. Also, the planes forming the octants do not need to be at
right angles.

Fortunately, invariance within a viewing octant and indifference to
plane angle hold in general. The junction type does not change as the
viewpoint moves within one viewing octant or as the angles between the
planes change.

So far, the junction catalog has but one entry, a Fork. One new entry is
suggested by the right half of figure 12.9, in which the junction of interest is
surrounded again by a drawing that provides a visual aid to understanding
just what is filled and what is empty. From the point of view shown,

Figure 12.10 Stick figures help to show what a one-octant vertex looks like from various viewpoints. Because of symmetry, the seven viewing octants yield only three different labels. These three viewpoints yield one L and one Arrow.

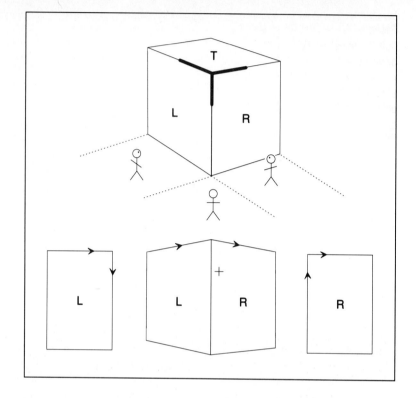

the vertex appears as a Fork junction with each line labeled with a plus. Because only one octant is filled, however, there must be seven from which to look, and so far you have seen only the junction label derived from the octant diagonally opposite the stuff of the object.

Consequently, positions must be taken in the six other octants. Three of these are the positions occupied by the stick figures in figure 12.10. Two stick figures on stilts, shown in figure 12.11, occupy two positions above the plane defined by the top of the cube. And one final stick figure, standing on top of the cube, occupies the final position. All six stick-figure views provide only two new junction labels, because three of the views produce one kind of Arrow, and the other three produce one kind of L.

Now consider the situations with two, four, or six octants filled. All are excluded by the initial three-faced presumption. Suppose, for example, that two octants are to be filled. If the two were adjacent, then the edges between them would be cracks, there would be four object faces at the central vertex, and the vertex would not be three-faced. If the two filled octants were not adjacent, then they would meet either along an edge or at a common point. Either way, there would be more than three faces at the central vertex. Similar arguments exclude the four- and six-octant cases, leaving only the three- and five-octant cases to be considered.

Figure 12.11 Stick figures help to show what a one-octant vertex looks like from various viewpoints. Because of symmetry, the seven viewing octants yield only three different labels.

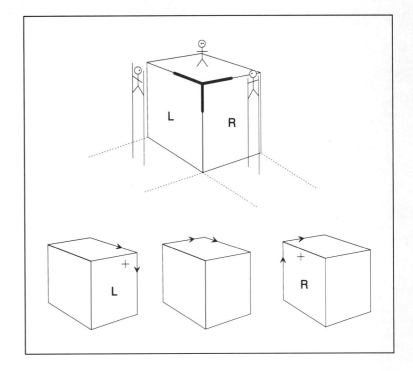

In the three-octant case, each of the five viewing octants provides a unique junction label, as shown in figure 12.12. Of course, one of the viewing octants produces the view shown, which yields an Arrow. In one of the other octants, the vertex looks like a Fork; in each of the other three remaining octants, it looks like an L. Each of the L labels observed is unique.

Figure 12.13 illustrates what five filled octants do. There are three junction labels, each of which is different from those seen before.

Finally, because cracks are forbidden, Ts can be labeled in only four ways, all of which are consequences of partial occlusion. Thus, the total number of ways to label a junction is now 18, as collected together in figure 12.14.

Note that there are three junction labels in the Fork column that include boundary labels. All three could be considered rotated versions of one another. Three distinct labels appear, to emphasize that there are three distinct ways for a Fork to be labeled with boundary lines.

Now, all possible ways in which three-faced vertexes can be formed have been enumerated, and you have viewed each such vertex from all possible directions. You conclude that the 18 junction labels are all that there can be. Any other label cannot correspond to a physically realizable three-faced vertex.

Figure 12.12 If three octants are filled, the remaining five viewing octants each supply a junction label. There are three unique Ls, one Fork, and one Arrow.

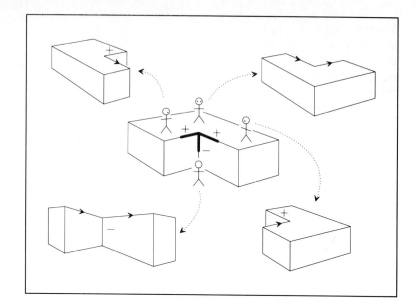

Figure 12.13 If five octants are filled, the three viewing octants supply two Ls and one Arrow.

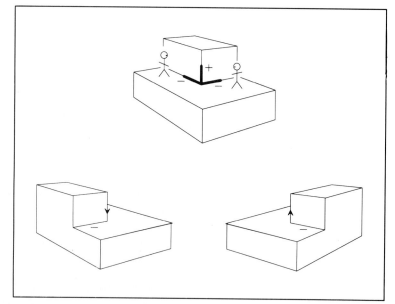

Finding Correct Labels Is Part of Line-Drawing Analysis

Now let us examine examples showing how the junction catalog can be used. At first, assume that each object is suspended in space. Consequently, each object's background border has only boundary labels. Also note that there is only one kind of Arrow junction in the junction catalog that has boundary labels on its barbs. For any such Arrow, the shaft must be labeled with a

Figure 12.14 Eighteen
junction configurations are
possible. Were it not for natural
constraints, there would be 208.

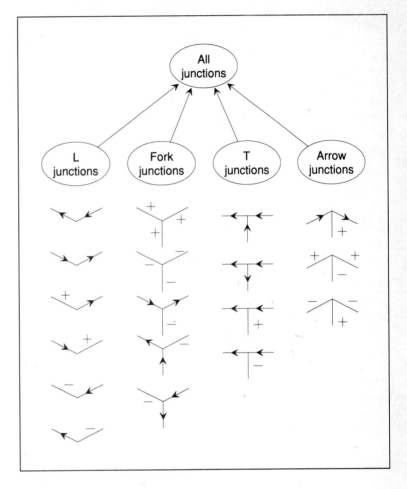

plus. Furthermore, there is only one kind of Fork with any plus label. For any such Fork, all the lines are forced to be labeled with plus labels.

Now consider the cube shown in figure 12.15. Because you are to imagine that the cube is suspended in space, the lines bordering on the background certainly can be labeled with boundary labels. Next, each of the Arrow's shafts is forced to be labeled with a plus because the barbs already have boundary labels. Now, only the central Fork remains to be investigated. Because all the Fork junction's lines already have plus labels assigned through previous considerations, it remains only to check that a Fork with three plus labels is in the junction catalog. It is.

Now consider the slightly harder example in figure 12.16, which is a sort of two-tiered, double L–shaped figure. Again, it is useful to begin by labeling the background border. Then, it is easy to move toward the interior using the Arrows with boundary labels on their barbs, together with the fact that a plus on any Fork line forces two more plus labels. To

Figure 12.15 Labeling begins by placing boundary labels pointing clockwise on the border of the drawing. Next, it is usually convenient to label the shafts of the Arrow junctions whose barbs lie on the border. In this example, a consistent labeling of all lines is possible, of course.

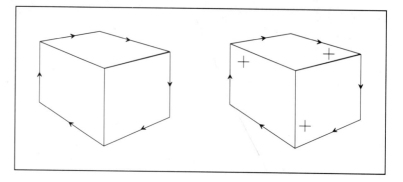

move still further, you must return to the junction catalog to pick up the other two Arrow junction labels. These other two Arrow junction labels force all of the remaining junction labeling, as shown.

Starting from interior junctions is more difficult. Unlike border lines, internal lines can get any label. In general, some ambiguity remains until analysis reaches a border, at which time the ambiguity is usually resolved.

The border seems important to human analysis of drawings as well. Consider the example shown in figure 12.17. By covering up the sides and a little of the top, you can see either a series of ordinary steps or a row of saw blades. This ambiguity may occur because the interior junctions, separated by occlusion from the powerful border constraints, undergo reversals in which concave, minus labels, switch with convex, plus labels.

Thus, symbolic constraint propagation offers a plausible explanation for one kind of human information processing, as well as a good way for a computer to analyze drawings. This idea suggests the following principle:

The principle of **convergent intelligence**:

▷ The world manifests constraints and regularities. If a computer is to exhibit intelligence, it must exploit those constraints and regularities, no matter of what the computer happens to be made.

It is also interesting that the theory is useful not only in analyzing normal drawings, but also in identifying illegal drawings—those that cannot correspond to real objects. The drawing in figure 12.18 is illegal, a conclusion you can reach through a labeling argument. Proceeding as before, background lines, Arrow junctions with plus-marked barbs, and Fork junctions with plus labels can be exploited as shown. But now one junction is illegally labeled. The Arrow on the end of one arm insists on a minus label for that arm, whereas the Fork on the other arm demands a plus label for that arm. But because there is no L with one minus arm and one plus arm, the drawing cannot be a view of a polyhedron with three-faced vertexes.

Figure 12.16 Labeling of this two-tiered figure begins with the background border. Next the shafts of the border Arrows begin a propagation of plus labels that continues through all Forks encountered. The rest of the job requires use of two other Arrow junctions found in the junction catalog.

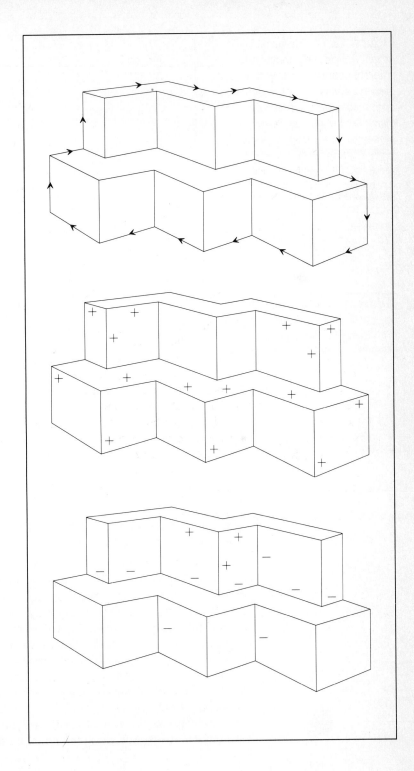

Figure 12.17 The background border contributes considerable constraint to line-drawing analyses. If the border of this object is covered up, the disconnected central portion is perceived in a variety of ways.

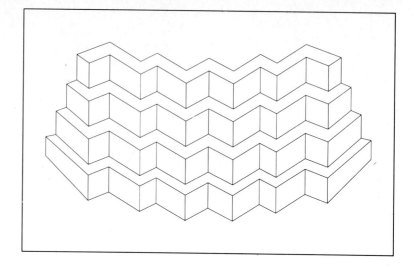

Figure 12.18 An impossible object. The indicated junction is not among the legal ones.

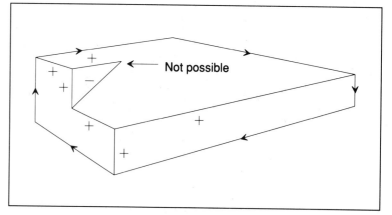

Waltz's Procedure Propagates Label Constraints through Junctions

Now you are ready to learn about **Waltz's procedure**, a powerful procedure for propagating symbolic constraints. To see how Waltz's procedure works, first consider the drawing-labeling problem abstractly, in figure 12.19, without getting into the details of the actual labels. Think of keeping piles of label possibilities for each junction. These piles are created when a junction is visited for the first time, and they are reexamined each time an adjacent junction pile is altered.

In the illustration, junction A is the first junction visited, so you pile on A all of the label possibilities allowed from the junction catalog, as shown in the upper left of figure 12.19.

Now suppose junction B is the next junction visited. Again, you pile on junction labels, but the total set is reduced immediately to those that

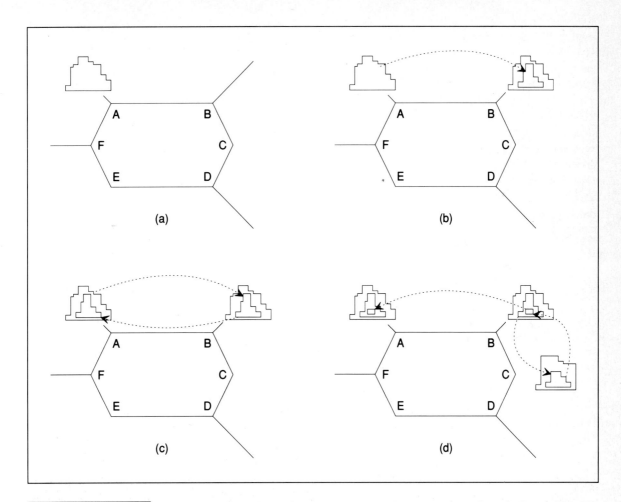

Figure 12.19
Label propagation in
networks. At first, an
initial junction pile is
placed at an arbitrary
junction. Propagation
continues as long
as reduction occurs
at each junction pile
encountered.

are compatible with at least one junction in the piles of all neighboring
junctions with piles. In figure 12.19, junction A's label pile constrains
what can be in junction B's pile.

Once a pile is created and has been reduced by neighboring piles, it is
time to see whether those same neighboring piles contain junction labels
that are incompatible with every junction label at the newly installed pile.
In figure 12.19, the reduced pile at junction B constrains what can be in
the pile at junction A.

Once set in motion, constraint propagation continues as long as the
junction piles encountered continue to be reduced. In figure 12.19, for
example, after the junction pile at junction C is installed and reduced,
the outward-moving part of the process starts, travels through the pile at
junction B, and terminates at the pile at junction A.

If there were no change at junction B, the propagation initiated at
junction C would have terminated at junction B. On the other hand, if there

Figure 12.20 An example illustrating constraint propagation in drawings. Junction A is visited first, followed by B, C, and D. The Arrows placed at A limit the choices for Ls at B, which in turn limit the choices for Arrows at C. At C, automatic neighbor reexamination has an effect, eliminating all but one label at B and A. Finally, the C boundary label limits the Fork choices at D to the one shown.

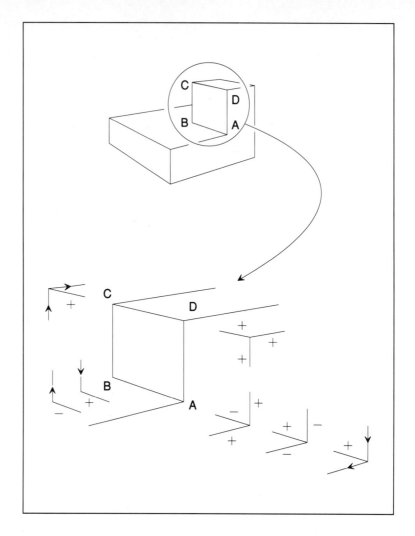

already were label piles at all junctions in the illustration, a pile reduction at junction C could initiate a propagation series that would travel all the way around the loop, reduce the piles at each junction, and ultimately lead to further reduction at junction C, the junction where the round-the-loop propagation was initiated. Looping cannot continue forever, however.

Now let us move from the abstract to the concrete. Look at figure 12.20, in which two Arrows, a Fork, and an L are buried in a drawing. Suppose, further, that these four junctions are lifted out of the drawing and are analyzed with the plus, minus, and boundary line labels.

If junction A is the first junction visited and none of its neighbors have been visited, then the first step is to bring in all the possible Arrow junction labels, piling them on junction A.

Suppose junction B is the next junction investigated. There are six junction labels for Ls in the junction catalog, but only two of these are compatible with the possibilities known for the adjacent Arrow, junction A. The other four are therefore rejected immediately.

After labels are placed at junction B, the next step is to investigate the neighboring junctions that have been examined previously to see whether any junction labels can be thrown out because of the new labels at junction B. For this situation, nothing happens, because all three of the Arrow junction labels at junction A are compatible with one of the two L labels at junction B.

Moving on to junction C, the junction catalog supplies three entries as before; for this Arrow, however, only one is compatible with the neighbors already analyzed. The other two are rejected immediately.

The last time the neighbor of a newly visited junction was revisited, nothing happened. This time, however, looking afresh at junction B reveals that only one of the two remaining junction labels is compatible with the adjacent Arrow, junction C. The list for junction B having been revised, the adjacent Arrow, junction A, must be revisited as well. Of the three original possibilities, only one survives.

Finally, looking at the Fork, junction D, the constraints from either of its analyzed neighbors force all but one of the five Fork entries in the junction catalog to be rejected.

Thus, the constraint is sufficient to interpret each line uniquely in this group of four junctions, even though the group is lifted out of its surrounding context and is analyzed separately.

Of course, one way to implement Waltz's procedure is to use demons reminiscent of those in the arithmetic constraint nets introduced in Chapter 11. To see how that would work, first consider the following specification for a **contraction net**.

A **contraction net** is a representation

That is a frame system

In which

▷ Lexically and structurally, certain frame classes identify a finite list of application-specific interpretations.

▷ Procedurally, demon procedures enforce compatibility constraints among connected frames.

Starting with contraction nets, it is easy to specify a **labeled drawing**. Here is one such specification—one that happens to be limited to the original four line labels:

Figure 12.21 Without shadows, there are several ways to interpret a cube: It may be suspended, it may be supported by the floor, or it may be attached to a wall.

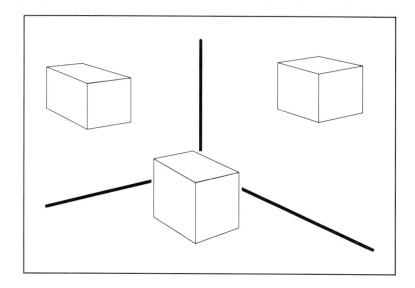

A **labeled drawing** is a representation

That is a contraction net

In which

▷ Lexically, there are line frames and junction frames. Lines may be convex, concave, or boundary lines. Junctions may be L, Fork, T, or Arrow junctions.

▷ Structurally, junction frames are connected by line frames. Also, each junction frame contains a list of interpretation combinations for its connecting lines.

▷ Semantically, line frames denote physical edges. Junction frames denote physical vertexes.

▷ Procedurally, demon procedures enforce the constraint that each junction label must be compatible with at least one of the junction labels at each of the neighboring junctions.

Many Line and Junction Labels Are Needed to Handle Shadows and Cracks

So far, by assumption, all the examples involve objects that are hanging suspended in space. If a cube is resting on a table, however, the bottom lines represent concave edges; they do not represent boundaries. If a cube is stuck against a wall, as figure 12.21 shows, other lines represent concave edges. Without an additional clue or assumption, several interpretations are equally plausible.

Figure 12.22 Shadows help determine where an object rests against others.

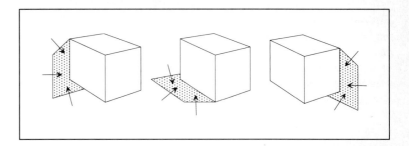

Note, however, that introducing shadows resolves the ambiguity. The block in the middle of figure 12.22 definitely seems supported by a horizontal surface, whereas the ones to the left and right, although less familiar, seem attached vertically. Evidently, expanding labeling theory to include labels for shadows should add further constraint and reduce ambiguity.

Take note that the shadow labels introduced in figure 12.22 indicate a direction, just as boundary labels do: shadow labels are small arrows placed so that they point into the shadowed region.

Now let us reconsider concave lines. Because concave lines are often found where objects come together, the concave-label category can be split into subcategories, indicating the number of objects involved and identifying which object is in front. Suppose a concave edge represents a place where two objects come together. Then, imagine pulling apart the two objects slightly. The concave edge becomes a boundary edge with the label pointing in one of two possible directions, as shown on the left and in the middle of figure 12.23. The two possibilities are indicated by compound symbols made up of the original minus label and the new boundary label. If, by chance, there are three objects, again a compound symbol is used, reflecting what is seen when the objects are pulled apart, as shown on the right in figure 12.23.

Cracks lying between two objects can be treated analogously: Each crack is labeled with a *c*, together with a boundary label that indicates how the two objects involved fit together. With cracks between objects allowed, you have the possibilities shown in figure 12.24. There are now 11 ways that any particular line may be labeled.

Illumination Increases Label Count and Tightens Constraint

The illumination on any face of an object can be classified, as shown in figure 12.25, as directly illuminated, shadowed by another object, or shadowed because it faces away from the light. The three possibilities are denoted by I, for directly illuminated, S for shadowed by another object, and SS for facing away from the light—that is, self-shadowed.

Line labels can carry knowledge about these illumination states in addition to information about edge type. If the illumination states and line interpretations were to combine freely, there would be $3^2 = 9$ illumination

Figure 12.23 Concave edges often occur where two or three objects meet. It is useful to distinguish among the possibilities by combining the minus label with the one or two boundary labels that are seen when the objects are separated.

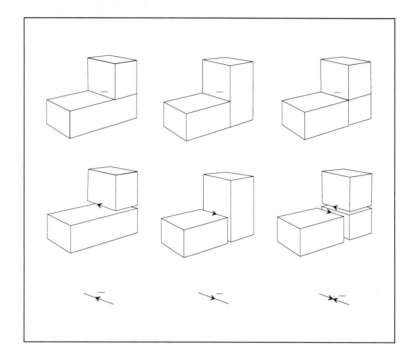

Figure 12.24 The eleven line interpretations and the corresponding labels.

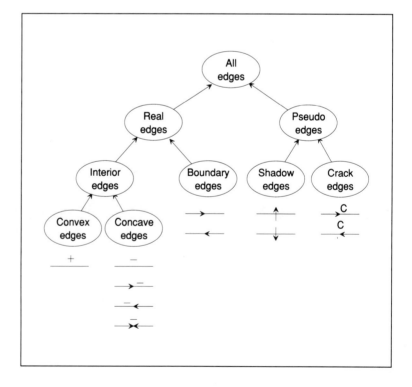

Figure 12.25 Illumination information often provides useful constraint. If there is a single light source, it is convenient to recognize three surface categories: illuminated; shadowed by intervening objects; and self-shadowed by virtue of facing away from the light source.

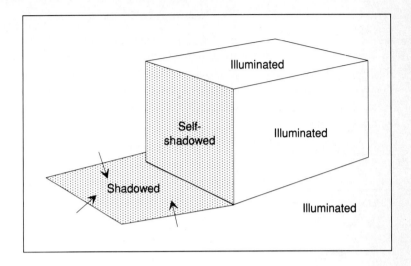

combinations for each of the 11 line interpretations, giving 99 total possibilities. Only about 50 of these combinations, however, are possible. Some combinations are forbidden because they would require an incredible coincidence, like the projection of a shadow line exactly onto a concave edge. Other combinations are excluded by definition; there cannot be, for example, a combination in which both sides of a shadow line are illuminated.

Now, let us review. Initially, only basic lines were considered: boundary lines, and interior concave and convex lines. Then, shadows were added. Concave lines were split up to reflect the number of objects coming together and the way those objects obscure one another. Cracks between objects were introduced and handled analogously. Finally, line information was combined with illumination information. Just over 50 line labels emerge from this final expansion.

These changes make the number of physically realizable junctions large, both for the original Fork, Arrow, L, and T types, and for other vertex types allowed by relaxing the three-faced-vertexes and general position constraints. What is gained in return for this increased number?

First, consider how the set of physically realizable junction labels compares to that of the unconstrained junction labels. The following table gives the results for the original set of line labels:

Vertex type	Number of unconstrained possible junctions	Number of physically realizable junctions	Ratio (%)
L	16	6	37.5
Fork	64	5	7.8
T	64	4	6.2
Arrow	64	3	4.7

The percentages shown all indicate constraint, but they do not indicate extraordinary constraint. When the line categories are expanded, however, all numbers grow large and the constraint becomes incredible. The number of junction labels in the expanded set, known as **Waltz's set**, is large absolutely, but the number is small compared with what it might be:

Vertex type	Approximate number of unconstrained possible junctions	Approximate number of physically realizable junctions	Ratio (%)
L	2.5×10^3	80	3.2
Fork	1.2×10^5	500	4.0×10^{-1}
T	1.2×10^5	500	4.0×10^{-1}
Arrow	1.2×10^5	70	5.6×10^{-2}
Psi	6.2×10^6	300	4.8×10^{-3}
K	6.2×10^6	100	1.6×10^{-3}
X	6.2×10^6	100	1.6×10^{-3}
Multi	6.2×10^6	100	1.6×10^{-3}
Peak	6.2×10^6	10	1.6×10^{-4}
Kk	3.1×10^8	30	9.6×10^{-6}

Figure 12.4 shows what all these junction types look like. For the Kk junction, only about one junction label in 10 million is physically realizable. To be sure, the total number of labels has increased to a size too large to use by hand, but still the constraints are so extreme that a computer program using the large set can converge on an unambiguous solution.

In this progression from small set, large fraction to large set, small fraction, you can observe the following powerful idea at work:

The **describe-to-explain principle**:

▷ The act of detailed description may turn probabilistic regularities into entirely deterministic constraints.

The Flow of Labels Can Be Dramatic

Watching a film is the best way to appreciate what can happen when Waltz's set, instead of the dwarfish set for the three-faced vertex world, is used to label a drawing.

Lacking a film, glancing at the drawing in figure 12.26 and at the trace in table 1 provides some feel for how the Waltz procedure works with Waltz's set. It would be tedious to follow the trace in detail, but some overall points are obvious without much effort.

In each of the 80 steps, the step number is followed by a letter denoting the junction involved. The letter is followed by the old number of junction labels in the pile and the new number in the pile.

Figure 12.26 A drawing analyzed successfully by Waltz's labeling procedure.

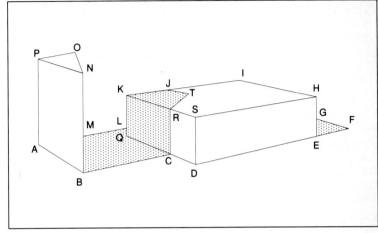

Table 1. A trace of Waltz's labeling procedure in action.

#			→		#			→		#			→	
1	A	–	→	123	31	C	20	→	2	61	P	5	→	1
2	A	123	→	76	32	B	14	→	2	62	O	2	→	1
3	B	–	→	79	33	A	20	→	2	63	Q	–	→	123
4	B	79	→	52	34	H	–	→	79	64	Q	123	→	5
5	A	76	→	32	35	H	79	→	1	65	Q	5	→	1
6	C	–	→	388	36	I	–	→	123	66	L	3	→	1
7	C	388	→	78	37	I	123	→	2	67	K	5	→	2
8	B	52	→	34	38	J	–	→	593	68	R	–	→	388
9	A	32	→	26	39	J	593	→	9	69	R	388	→	20
10	D	–	→	79	40	K	–	→	79	70	R	20	→	4
11	D	79	→	15	41	K	79	→	7	71	J	6	→	4
12	C	78	→	20	42	J	9	→	8	72	K	2	→	1
13	B	34	→	14	43	L	–	→	593	73	S	–	→	1391
14	A	26	→	20	44	L	593	→	12	74	S	1391	→	5
15	E	–	→	79	45	K	7	→	5	75	S	5	→	1
16	E	79	→	33	46	J	8	→	6	76	T	–	→	123
17	D	15	→	14	47	I	2	→	1	77	T	123	→	4
18	F	–	→	123	48	M	–	→	593	78	T	4	→	1
19	F	123	→	28	49	M	593	→	4	79	J	4	→	1
20	G	–	→	593	50	M	4	→	1	80	R	4	→	1
21	G	593	→	42	51	L	12	→	3					
22	G	42	→	18	52	B	2	→	1					
23	F	28	→	11	53	A	2	→	1					
24	E	33	→	7	54	C	2	→	1					
25	D	14	→	6	55	N	–	→	79					
26	F	11	→	2	56	N	79	→	1					
27	G	18	→	1	57	O	–	→	123					
28	E	7	→	1	58	O	123	→	2					
29	D	6	→	1	59	P	–	→	79					
30	F	2	→	1	60	P	79	→	5					

Note that the border junctions are visited first. This order exploits the extra constraint available at the border. Further inspection shows that convergence is rapid. After only two or three visits, most of the junctions have only one unique junction label associated with them. In step 74, for example, junction S starts with 1391 possibilities. The number is reduced to 5 by constraints coming in from one neighbor. Then, constraints from another neighbor reduce the number to 1, leaving but a single interpretation.

The Computation Required Is Proportional to Drawing Size

Experiments using Waltz's set show that the work required to analyze a drawing grows in roughly linear proportion with the number of lines in the drawing. To see why, informally, suppose that drawings can be split into areas of more or less fixed size in terms of the lines and junctions contained in each area. If the areas are such that constraint does not flow across their frontiers, then the total time required to analyze a drawing is linearly proportional to the number of areas, and hence is linearly proportional to the number of junctions.

Flow-impeding frontiers exist because the T junctions, common at object boundaries, have little ability to transmit constraint: An obscuring boundary can lie in front of any kind of edge.

PROPAGATION OF TIME-INTERVAL RELATIONS

In this section, you learn about another example of symbolic constraint propagation; this one involves time intervals and the relations among time intervals. The general idea is to use existing information about the relations among time intervals to reach conclusions about other relations. For example, if interval A is before interval B, and interval B is before interval C, then plainly interval A has to be before C.

Time relations are easier to understand visually, especially as they become more complicated. As shown in the upper part of figure 12.27, time intervals can be depicted as objects resting on a time line. Alternatively, as shown in the lower part of figure 12.27, a pair of time intervals and the relation that lies between them can be depicted as two nodes, and a labeled link.

There Are 13 Ways to Label a Link between Interval Nodes Yielding 169 Constraints

Assuming that no interval is allowed to start and stop at the same time, then the interval *before* relation is just one of 13 possible relations between two intervals, seven of which are shown in figure 12.28. The other six are members of symmetric pairs. One such symmetric pair is the *before* pair, because interval A may be before interval B or interval B may be before interval A.

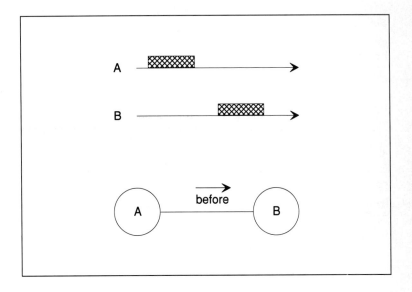

Figure 12.27 Two time intervals and the relation between them. In the upper part, two time intervals are shown as objects resting on a time line, with the object representing interval A preceding the one for interval B. In the lower part, the two time intervals are shown as nodes, and the relation between them is expressed as a link label.

Notationally, an arrow is drawn over each label to indicate the direction in which a relation is to be read. Thus, A $\overrightarrow{\text{before}}$ B means interval A is before interval B, whereas A $\overleftarrow{\text{before}}$ B means interval B is before interval A. Attaching arrows to labels is necessary, rather than making the links directional, because several labels, with arrows in opposite directions, may be attached to one link.

Using this notation, figure 12.29 illustrates the idea that the labels on each of a pair of links can constrain the labels on a third link. As shown, three interval nodes are involved, one of which lies between the two links in the link pair. The third link—the one constrained—spans the other two interval nodes.

If two $\overrightarrow{\text{before}}$ labels point in the same direction, the constraint is severe, allowing only a $\overrightarrow{\text{before}}$ label on the spanning relation. Curiously, however, if the $\overrightarrow{\text{before}}$ labels both point toward the central interval, there is no constraint whatsoever, because all the 13 ways of labeling the spanning relation remain possible.

Of course, there are $13 \times 13 = 169$ pairs of relations that can connect interval A to interval B and interval B to interval C. The key idea is that each such pair, joined at the central interval, interval B, has something to say about which relations can possibly connect interval A directly to interval C. Just what each pair has to say is something you can work out on the back of an envelope or two, producing the table shown in figure 12.30.

All the constraints captured by the tables in figure 12.30 can be enforced, of course, by way of demon procedures in an **interval net**, which is a special kind of contraction net:

Figure 12.30 Half of the table constraining the labels between X and Z when the labels between X and Y (the rows) and between Y and Z (the columns) are known. So as to fit the table on two book-sized pages, all labels are abbreviated by their first letter. Empty entries correspond to no constraint; all 13 labels are possible.

	b→	m→	o→	s→	d→	f→	b←	m←	o←	s←	d←	f←
b→	b	b	b	b	b m o s d	b m o s d		b m o s d	b m o s d	b	b	b
m→	b	b	b	m	o→ s→ d→	o→ s→ d→	b← m← o← s← d←	f→ f← =	o→ s→ d→	m	b	b
o→	b	b	b→ m→ o→	o	o→ s→ d→	o→ s→ d→	b← m← o← s← d←	o← s← d←	o→ s→ d→ o← s← d← f→ f← =	o→ d← f←	b→ m→ o→ d← f←	b→ m→ o→
s→	b	b	b→ m→ o→	s	d	d	b←	m←	d→ f→ o←	s→ s← =	b→ m→ o→ d← f←	b→ m→ o→
d→	b	b	b→ m→ o→ s→ d→	d	d	d	b←	b←	d→ f→ b← m← o←	d→ f→ b← m← o←		b→ m→ o→ s→ d→
f→	b	m	o→ s→ d→	d	d	f	b←	b←	b← m← o←	b←	b← m← o← s← d←	f→ f← =

Time Constraints Can Propagate across Long Distances

Given a chain of relations, it may be possible to use the table in figure 12.30 to reach a long-distance conclusion about the relation between two widely separated intervals. Figure 12.31 shows how. First, the pair of relations connecting interval A, interval B, and interval C enable a conclusion about which relations can connect interval A to interval C.

Next, the relation that connects interval A to interval C is used in concert with the relation that connects interval C to interval D to determine which

Figure 12.29 In the top half, interval A is before interval B, and interval B is before interval C. These relations force the conclusion that interval A is before interval C. On the other hand, as shown in the bottom half, nothing can be concluded about the relation between interval A and interval C given only that interval A is before interval B and interval C is before interval B.

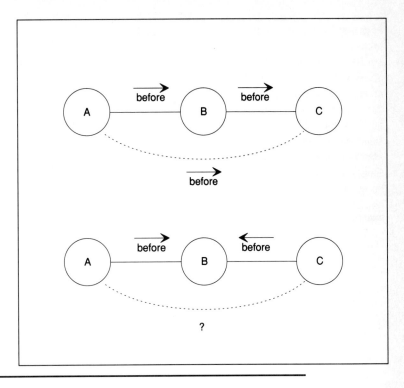

An **interval net** is a representation

That is a contraction net

In which

▷ Lexically and semantically there are interval frames denoting time intervals and link frames denoting time relations, specifically $\overrightarrow{\text{before}}$, $\overleftarrow{\text{before}}$, $\overrightarrow{\text{during}}$, $\overleftarrow{\text{during}}$, $\overrightarrow{\text{overlaps}}$, $\overleftarrow{\text{overlaps}}$, $\overrightarrow{\text{meets}}$, $\overleftarrow{\text{meets}}$, $\overrightarrow{\text{starts}}$, $\overleftarrow{\text{starts}}$, $\overrightarrow{\text{finishes}}$, $\overleftarrow{\text{finishes}}$, and $\overrightarrow{\text{is equal to}}$.

▷ Structurally, interval frames are connected by link frames.

▷ Procedurally, demon procedures enforce the constraint that the interpretations allowed for a link frame between two intervals must be consistent with the interpretations allowed for the two link frames joining the two intervals to a third interval.

Time Constraints Can Propagate across Long Distances

Given a chain of relations, it may be possible to use the table in figure 12.30 to reach a long-distance conclusion about the relation between two widely

Figure 12.30 Half of the table constraining the labels between X and Z when the labels between X and Y (the rows) and between Y and Z (the columns) are known. So as to fit the table on two book-sized pages, all labels are abbreviated by their first letter. Empty entries correspond to no constraint; all 13 labels are possible.

	$\vec{b}$	$\vec{m}$	$\vec{o}$	$\vec{s}$	$\vec{d}$	$\vec{f}$	$\overleftarrow{b}$	$\overleftarrow{m}$	$\overleftarrow{o}$	$\overleftarrow{s}$	$\overleftarrow{d}$	$\overleftarrow{f}$
$\vec{b}$	$\vec{b}$	$\vec{b}$	$\vec{b}$	$\vec{b}$	$\vec{b}\,\vec{m}\,\vec{o}\,\vec{s}\,\vec{d}$	$\vec{b}\,\vec{m}\,\vec{o}\,\vec{s}\,\vec{d}$		$\vec{b}\,\vec{m}\,\vec{o}\,\vec{s}\,\vec{d}$	$\vec{b}\,\vec{m}\,\vec{o}\,\vec{s}\,\vec{d}$	$\vec{b}$	$\vec{b}$	$\vec{b}$
$\vec{m}$	$\vec{b}$	$\vec{b}$	$\vec{b}$	$\vec{m}$	$\vec{o}\,\vec{s}\,\vec{d}$	$\vec{o}\,\vec{s}\,\vec{d}$	$\overleftarrow{b}\,\overleftarrow{m}\,\overleftarrow{o}\,\overleftarrow{s}\,\overleftarrow{d}$	$\vec{f}\,\overleftarrow{f}\,=$	$\vec{o}\,\vec{s}\,\vec{d}$	$\vec{m}$	$\vec{b}$	$\vec{b}$
$\vec{o}$	$\vec{b}$	$\vec{b}$	$\vec{b}\,\vec{m}\,\vec{o}$	$\vec{o}$	$\vec{o}\,\vec{s}\,\vec{d}$	$\vec{o}\,\vec{s}\,\vec{d}$	$\overleftarrow{b}\,\overleftarrow{m}\,\overleftarrow{o}\,\overleftarrow{s}\,\overleftarrow{d}$	$\overleftarrow{o}\,\overleftarrow{s}\,\overleftarrow{d}$	$\vec{o}\,\vec{s}\,\vec{d}\,\overleftarrow{o}\,\overleftarrow{s}\,\overleftarrow{d}\,\vec{f}\,\overleftarrow{f}\,=$	$\vec{o}\,\overleftarrow{d}\,\overleftarrow{f}$	$\vec{b}\,\vec{m}\,\vec{o}\,\overleftarrow{d}\,\overleftarrow{f}$	$\vec{b}\,\vec{m}\,\vec{o}$
$\vec{s}$	$\vec{b}$	$\vec{b}$	$\vec{b}\,\vec{m}\,\vec{o}$	$\vec{s}$	$\vec{d}$	$\vec{d}$	$\overleftarrow{b}$	$\overleftarrow{m}$	$\vec{d}\,\vec{f}\,\overleftarrow{o}$	$\vec{s}\,\overleftarrow{s}\,=$	$\vec{b}\,\vec{m}\,\vec{o}\,\overleftarrow{d}\,\overleftarrow{f}$	$\vec{b}\,\vec{m}\,\vec{o}$
$\vec{d}$	$\vec{b}$	$\vec{b}$	$\vec{b}\,\vec{m}\,\vec{o}\,\vec{s}\,\vec{d}$	$\vec{d}$	$\vec{d}$	$\vec{d}$	$\overleftarrow{b}$	$\overleftarrow{b}$	$\vec{d}\,\vec{f}\,\overleftarrow{b}\,\overleftarrow{m}\,\overleftarrow{o}$	$\vec{d}\,\vec{f}\,\overleftarrow{o}$		$\vec{b}\,\vec{m}\,\vec{o}\,\vec{s}\,\vec{d}$
$\vec{f}$	$\vec{b}$	$\vec{m}$	$\vec{o}\,\vec{s}\,\vec{d}$	$\vec{d}$	$\vec{d}$	$\vec{f}$	$\overleftarrow{b}$	$\overleftarrow{b}$	$\overleftarrow{b}\,\overleftarrow{m}\,\overleftarrow{o}$	$\overleftarrow{b}\,\overleftarrow{m}\,\overleftarrow{o}$	$\overleftarrow{b}\,\overleftarrow{m}\,\overleftarrow{o}\,\overleftarrow{s}\,\overleftarrow{d}$	$\vec{f}\,\overleftarrow{f}\,=$

separated intervals. Figure 12.31 shows how. First, the pair of relations connecting interval A, interval B, and interval C enable a conclusion about which relations can connect interval A to interval C.

Next, the relation that connects interval A to interval C is used in concert with the relation that connects interval C to D to determine which relations can connect interval A to D. Continued iteration may eventually provide some constraint on the relation between interval A and Z.

Figure 12.30 Continued. The other half of the table constraining the labels between X and Z when the labels between X and Y (the rows) and between Y and Z (the columns) are known. Empty entries correspond to no constraint; all 13 labels are possible.

	$\vec{b}$	$\vec{m}$	$\vec{o}$	$\vec{s}$	$\vec{d}$	$\vec{f}$	$\overleftarrow{b}$	$\overleftarrow{m}$	$\overleftarrow{o}$	$\overleftarrow{s}$	$\overleftarrow{d}$	$\overleftarrow{f}$
$\overleftarrow{b}$		$\vec{d}\,\vec{f}\,\overleftarrow{b}\,\overleftarrow{m}\,\overleftarrow{o}$	$\vec{d}\,\vec{f}\,\overleftarrow{b}\,\overleftarrow{m}\,\overleftarrow{o}$	$\vec{d}\,\vec{f}\,\overleftarrow{b}\,\overleftarrow{m}\,\overleftarrow{o}$	$\vec{d}\,\vec{f}\,\overleftarrow{b}\,\overleftarrow{m}\,\overleftarrow{o}$	$\overleftarrow{b}$	$\overleftarrow{b}$	$\overleftarrow{b}$	$\overleftarrow{b}$	$\overleftarrow{b}$	$\overleftarrow{b}$	$\overleftarrow{b}$
$\overleftarrow{m}$	$\vec{b}\,\vec{o}\,\vec{m}\,\vec{d}\,\overleftarrow{f}$	$\overleftarrow{s}\,\overleftarrow{s}\,=$	$\vec{d}\,\vec{f}\,\overleftarrow{o}$	$\vec{d}\,\vec{f}\,\overleftarrow{o}$	$\vec{d}\,\vec{f}\,\overleftarrow{o}$	$\overleftarrow{m}$	$\overleftarrow{b}$	$\overleftarrow{b}$	$\overleftarrow{b}$	$\overleftarrow{b}$	$\overleftarrow{b}$	$\overleftarrow{m}$
$\overleftarrow{o}$	$\vec{b}\,\vec{m}\,\vec{o}\,\vec{d}\,\overleftarrow{f}$	$\vec{o}\,\vec{d}\,\vec{f}$	$\vec{o}\,\vec{d}\,\overleftarrow{o}\,\vec{d}\,=$	$\vec{o}\,\vec{f}\,\overleftarrow{o}\,\vec{d}$	$\vec{d}\,\vec{f}\,\overleftarrow{o}$	$\overleftarrow{o}$	$\overleftarrow{b}$	$\overleftarrow{b}$	$\overleftarrow{b}\,\overleftarrow{m}\,\overleftarrow{o}$	$\overleftarrow{b}\,\overleftarrow{m}\,\overleftarrow{o}$	$\overleftarrow{b}\,\overleftarrow{m}\,\overleftarrow{o}\,\overleftarrow{s}\,\overleftarrow{d}$	$\overleftarrow{o}\,\overleftarrow{s}\,\overleftarrow{d}$
$\overleftarrow{s}$	$\vec{b}\,\vec{m}\,\vec{o}\,\vec{d}\,\overleftarrow{f}$	$\vec{o}\,\vec{d}\,\vec{f}$	$\vec{o}\,\vec{d}\,\vec{f}$	$\vec{s}\,\overleftarrow{s}\,=$	$\vec{d}\,\vec{f}\,\overleftarrow{o}$	$\overleftarrow{o}$	$\overleftarrow{b}$	$\overleftarrow{m}$	$\overleftarrow{o}$	$\overleftarrow{s}$	$\overleftarrow{d}$	$\overleftarrow{d}$
$\overleftarrow{d}$	$\vec{b}\,\vec{m}\,\vec{o}\,\vec{d}\,\overleftarrow{f}$	$\vec{o}\,\vec{d}\,\vec{f}$	$\vec{o}\,\vec{d}\,\vec{f}$	$\vec{o}\,\vec{d}\,\vec{f}$	$\vec{o}\,\vec{d}\,\vec{f}\,\overleftarrow{o}\,\vec{d}\,=$	$\overleftarrow{o}\,\vec{d}\,\vec{f}$	$\overleftarrow{b}\,\overleftarrow{m}\,\overleftarrow{o}\,\overleftarrow{d}\,\overleftarrow{f}$	$\overleftarrow{o}\,\overleftarrow{s}\,\overleftarrow{o}\,\overleftarrow{d}$	$\overleftarrow{o}\,\overleftarrow{s}\,\overleftarrow{d}$	$\overleftarrow{d}$	$\overleftarrow{d}$	$\overleftarrow{d}$
$\overleftarrow{f}$	$\vec{b}$	$\vec{m}$	$\vec{o}$	$\vec{o}\,\overleftarrow{s}\,\vec{d}$	$\vec{o}\,\overleftarrow{s}\,\vec{d}$	$\vec{f}\,\overleftarrow{f}\,=$	$\overleftarrow{b}\,\overleftarrow{m}\,\overleftarrow{o}\,\overleftarrow{s}\,\overleftarrow{d}$	$\overleftarrow{o}\,\overleftarrow{s}\,\overleftarrow{d}$	$\overleftarrow{o}\,\overleftarrow{s}\,\overleftarrow{d}$	$\overleftarrow{d}$	$\overleftarrow{d}$	$\overleftarrow{f}$

A Complete Time Analysis Is Computationally Expensive

Now suppose you want to do a complete analysis, ensuring that you have used whatever link labels are given to determine the absolute minimum number of labels at every link in a net of n time intervals.

Because you are free to place a link between any two nodes, if there are n nodes, there can be as many as $n-1$ links emerging from each. Avoiding double counting by dividing by two, there must be $\frac{n \times (n-1)}{2}$ links.

For each link between two nodes, there are $n-2$ other nodes that can serve as a central interval. Thus, there are $n-2$ link pairs that can, in

Figure 12.31 A chain of time-interval relations labeled $\overrightarrow{\text{before}}$ enables the placement of other $\overrightarrow{\text{before}}$ labels, including the placement of a $\overrightarrow{\text{before}}$ label between the ends of the chain.

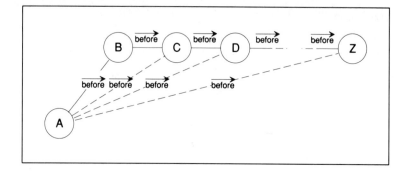

principle, force a reduction in the number of labels on a link. Each time you cycle through all the links, you have to examine $\frac{n \times (n-1)}{2} \times (n-2)$ link pairs.

If no labels are eliminated during a cycle, you stop. But if any labels are eliminated, you have to continue.

In the worst case, only one label of one link is eliminated during a cycle. Because each of the $\frac{n \times (n-1)}{2}$ links may have as many as 13 labels, you may have to cycle through all the links, in the worst case, $13 \times \frac{n \times (n-1)}{2}$ times. Thus, the worst-case number of pair examinations is $13 \times \frac{n \times (n-1)}{2} \times \frac{n \times (n-1)}{2} \times (n-2)$, which is order n^5. This is not good if n is large.

Reference Nodes Can Save Time

Because a complete time analysis is computationally expensive, it may be important to single out some of the time-interval nodes to serve as *reference nodes*. When you want to determine the possible labels on a link between two given interval nodes, you start by looking for paths between the two nodes such that all links, except for the first and last, must connect reference node pairs. Then you collect all the nodes in all such paths and perform a complete analysis using those nodes.

Suppose, for example, that you single out interval nodes that represent the morning and the afternoon. Further suppose that each is connected to three other nodes as shown in figure 12.32.

Next, suppose you want to know the possible links between interval X, attached to the morning node, and interval Y, attached to the afternoon node. There is only one path between them through interval nodes, and that path happens to contain four nodes. Accordingly, you need to do a complete analysis of only a four-node, six-link net. Without reference nodes, you would have to do a complete analysis of an eight-node, 28-link net.

Of course, there is a price for confining your analysis to reference nodes: you may overlook a constraint now and then. Generally, however, with carefully selected reference intervals, little or nothing is lost.

Figure 12.32 Reference nodes can reduce dramatically the amount of computation required to do constraint propagation. As shown in the upper part, only the nodes on reference-node paths are considered. As shown in the lower part, an analysis involving the four reference-path nodes quickly indicates that interval X is before interval Y.

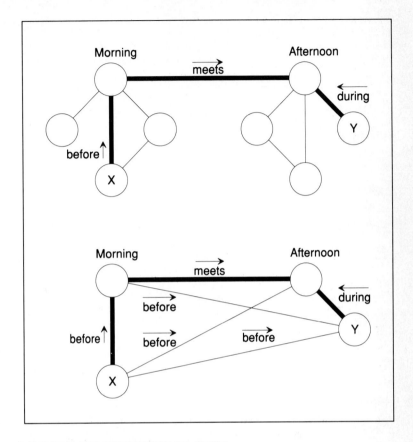

FIVE POINTS OF METHODOLOGY

History shows that many of the methods of artificial intelligence are like sirens, seducing you into misapplication. Consequently, to keep yourself focused on solving problems, rather than on showing off particular methods, you should follow Marr's methodological principles—those championed by the late David Marr:

To follow **Marr's methodological principles**:

▷ First, *identify the problem.*
▷ Then, *select or develop an appropriate representation.*
▷ Next, *expose constraints or regularities.*
▷ Only then, *create particular procedures.*
▷ Finally, *verify via experiments.*

You can easily imagine that the original developers of drawing-analysis and interval-calculation procedures could have followed such methodological principles; in both cases, there is a clearly identified problem, a carefully worked-out representation, and exposed constraints. Furthermore, in both cases, there were implemented procedures that enabled convincing experiments to be performed.

SUMMARY

- In general terms, symbolic constraint boxes propagate information that is used to reduce the sizes of collections of possible interpretations.
- In line drawing analysis, for example, information propagating along lines and through junctions leads to a steady reduction in the number of interpretations possible for the connected junctions.
- There are only four ways to label a line in the three-faced-vertex world: as a convex line, a concave line, or a boundary line with two possible orientations. The three-faced-vertex world permits only 18 ways of arranging such line labels around a junction.
- Waltz's procedure propagates label constraints by eliminating all junction labels at each junction that fail to be compatible with at least one junction labeling at each neighboring junction.
- Many additional line and junction labels are needed to handle shadows and cracks. Illumination also increases label count.
- In the world of time intervals, there are 13 ways to label a link between interval nodes, yielding 169 possible constraints on links that bridge link pairs. These constraints can propagate time information across long distances.
- A complete time analysis is computationally expensive, but much of the expense can be avoided if reference nodes are used, albeit with some reduction in capability.
- The world manifests many constraints and regularities. For a computer to exhibit intelligence, it is necessary to exploit those constraints and regularities no matter of what the computer happens to be made.
- The act of detailed description may turn probabilistic regularities into deterministic constraints.
- Marr's approach specifies five steps. First, you identify the problem. Then, you select or develop an appropriate representation. Next, you expose constraints or regularities. After that, you create particular procedures. Finally, you verify via experiments.

BACKGROUND

Early ad hoc methods for line-drawing analysis, such as those developed by Adolfo Guzman [1968], stimulated much of the subsequent work on line-drawing analysis, including David Waltz's seminal thesis on drawing analysis, on which this chapter is largely based [Waltz 1972]. Waltz dealt not only with the labeling scheme explained here, but also with similar schemes involving line and surface directions. David Huffman [1971] and Maxwell Clowes [1971], working independently, devised labeling schemes directly antecedent to Waltz's. Their work was limited to the simplified domain of three-faced vertexes with no shadows. Later work by Alan K. Mackworth shows how constraints like Waltz's can be derived automatically [Mackworth 1973]. Subsequently, the work of Kokichi Sugihara has come to be regarded as a tour de force [Sugihara 1978].

The idea of using constraint propagation to reason about time was introduced in a seminal paper by James Allen [1983].

For an interesting use of symbolic constraint propagation in quite another domain, see the work of Mark Stefik on a program that plans gene-cloning experiments in molecular genetics [1980]. For a domain-independent treatment of symbolic constraint propagation, see the work of Eugene C. Freuder [1978, 1982].

The development of the PROLOG programming language can be viewed as an effort to design a programming language around the idea of constraint expression. PROLOG programmers try to express only knowledge, rather than precise prescriptions of how knowledge is to be used. More often, however, PROLOG is viewed as a programming language based on logic. For an excellent introduction to PROLOG, see PROLOG *Programming for Artificial Intelligence*, by Ivan Bratko [1986].

13

Logic and Resolution Proof

In this chapter, you learn about *logic*, an important addition to your knowledge of problem-solving paradigms.

Like the other paradigms, logic has both seductive advantages and bothersome disadvantages. On the positive side, the ideas of logic, having matured for centuries, are concise and universally understood, like Latin. Moreover, until recently, logicians have focused on proving theorems about what can be proved. Consequently, when a problem can be attacked by logic successfully, you are in luck, for you know exactly what you can and cannot do.

On the negative side, logic can be a procrustean bed, for concentrating on logic can lead to concentrating on the mathematics of logic, deflecting attention away from valuable problem-solving methods that resist mathematical analysis.

First, you learn how to handle the notation used in logic; building on that notation, you see how rules of inference, such as *modus ponens*, *modus tolens*, and *resolution*, make it possible to create new expressions from existing ones. Then, you explore the notion of proof, and you use *proof by refutation* and *resolution theorem proving*.

In the course of learning about logic, you are exposed to a blizzard of new concepts. Accordingly, the key points in this chapter are illustrated with ridiculously simple examples designed to keep human intuition fully engaged. These examples stick to the blocks world, showing how one relation can be deduced from others.

RULES OF INFERENCE

You know that something is a bird if it has feathers or if it flies and lays
eggs. This knowledge was expressed before, in Chapter 7, in the form of
if–then rules:

I3   If   the animal has feathers
        then   it is a bird

I4   If   the animal flies
                it lays eggs
        then   it is a bird

In this section, you see the same sort of knowledge expressed in the language
of logic, and you learn about the rules of inference that make it possible to
use knowledge expressed in that language.

Logic Has a Traditional Notation

In logic, to express the sense of the antecedent–consequent rule concerning
feathers and birds, you need a way to capture the idea that something has
feathers and that something is a bird. You capture such ideas by using
predicates, for predicates are **functions** that map object **arguments**
into true or false values.

For example, with the normal way of interpreting the object Albatross
and the predicates Feathers and Bird, you can say, informally, that the
following are true expressions:

Feathers(Albatross)

Bird(Albatross)

Now suppose you say that the following is a true expression:

Feathers(Squigs)

Evidently, Squigs is a symbol that denotes something that has feathers, constraining what Squigs can possibly name, for Squigs satisfies the Feathers
predicate.

You can express other constraints with other predicates, such as Flies
and Lays-eggs. In fact, you can limit the objects that Squigs can name to
those objects that satisfy *both* predicates together by saying that both of
the following expressions are true:

Flies(Squigs)

Lays-eggs(Squigs)

There is a more traditional way to express this idea, however. You simply
combine the first expression and the second expression and say that the
combination is true:

Flies(Squigs) and Lays-eggs(Squigs)

Of course, you can also insist that Squigs names something that satisfies either of the two predicates. You specify this constraint as follows:

Flies(Squigs) or Lays-eggs(Squigs)

Logicians prefer a different notation, however. They like to write *and* as & and *or* as ∨.[†]

Now you can rewrite the expressions you wrote before, recasting them as a logician would write them:

Flies(Squigs)&Lays-eggs(Squigs)

Flies(Squigs) ∨ Lays-eggs(Squigs)

When expressions are joined by &, they form a **conjunction**, and each part is called a **conjunct**. Similarly, when expressions are joined by ∨, they form a **disjunction**, and each part is called a **disjunct**.

Note that & and ∨ are called **logical connectives** because they map combinations of true and false to true or false.

In addition to & and ∨, there are two other essential connectives: one is *not*, written as ¬, and the other is *implies*, written as ⇒. Consider this:

¬Feathers(Suzie)

For this expression to be true, Suzie must denote something for which Feathers(Suzie) is not true. That is, Suzie must be something for which the predicate Feathers is *not satisfied*.

Moving on, using ⇒, here is an expression that resembles one of the antecedent–consequent rules:

Feathers(Suzie) ⇒ Bird(Suzie)

Saying that the value of this expression is true constrains what Suzie can denote. One allowed possibility is that Suzie is something for which both Feathers(Suzie) and Bird(Suzie) are true. Naturally, the definition of ⇒ also allows both Feathers(Suzie) and Bird(Suzie) to be false. Curiously, another possibility, allowed by the definition of ⇒, is that Feathers(Suzie) is false but Bird(Suzie) is true. If Feathers(Suzie) is true and Bird(Suzie) is false, however, then the expression Feathers(Suzie) ⇒ Bird(Suzie) is false.

Perhaps it is time to be more precise about the ⇒, &, ∨, and ¬ connectives, before it is too late. Thinking of them as functions, it is easy to define them by listing the approved value for each possible combination of arguments. Such a list is shown in figure 13.1, which contains diagrams that are called **truth tables**.

Note that the connectives have an accepted **precedence**. In ordinary arithmetic, a unary minus sign has precedence higher than that of a plus sign, so you can write $-a + b$, meaning $(-a) + b$, not $-(a + b)$. Similarly, because ¬ has precedence higher than that of ∨, you can write $¬E_1 ∨ E_2$, meaning $(¬E_1) ∨ E_2$, without any possibility of confusion with $¬(E_1 ∨ E_2)$.

[†]Actually, most logicians write *and* as ∧, instead of as &. In this book, & is used because it is easy for beginners to distinguish & from ∨.

Figure 13.1 Truth tables show what $\Rightarrow$, &, $\vee$, and $\neg$ do.

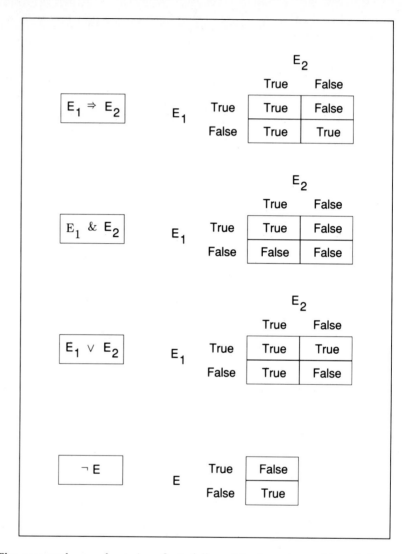

The accepted precedence is $\neg$ first, followed by & and $\vee$, with $\Rightarrow$ bringing up the rear. A good habit is to use parentheses liberally, even when not strictly necessary, to reduce the likelihood of a mistake.

Note that the truth-table definition for $\Rightarrow$ indicates that the values of $E_1 \Rightarrow E_2$ are the same as the values of $\neg E_1 \vee E_2$ for all combinations of values for E_1 and E_2. Consequently, and important to note, $\neg E_1 \vee E_2$ can be substituted for $E_1 \Rightarrow E_2$, and vice versa, at any time. Rules for reversible substitution are expressed by a $\Leftrightarrow$ symbol:

$$E_1 \Rightarrow E_2 \Leftrightarrow \neg E_1 \vee E_2$$

Truth tables also demonstrate other useful properties of logical connectives, which are listed here, partly for the sake of completeness and partly because you need some of them to deal with forthcoming examples. First, the & and ∨ connectives are **commutative**:

$$E_1 \& E_2 \Leftrightarrow E_2 \& E_1$$
$$E_1 \vee E_2 \Leftrightarrow E_2 \vee E_1$$

Next, they are **distributive**:

$$E_1 \& (E_2 \vee E_3) \Leftrightarrow (E_1 \& E_2) \vee (E_1 \& E_3)$$
$$E_1 \vee (E_2 \& E_3) \Leftrightarrow (E_1 \vee E_2) \& (E_1 \vee E_3)$$

In addition, they are **associative**:

$$E_1 \& (E_2 \& E_3) \Leftrightarrow (E_1 \& E_2) \& E_3$$
$$E_1 \vee (E_2 \vee E_3) \Leftrightarrow (E_1 \vee E_2) \vee E_3$$

They obey **de Morgan's laws**:

$$\neg(E_1 \& E_2) \Leftrightarrow (\neg E_1) \vee (\neg E_2)$$
$$\neg(E_1 \vee E_2) \Leftrightarrow (\neg E_1) \& (\neg E_2)$$

And finally, two ¬ symbols annihilate each other:

$$\neg(\neg E_1) \Leftrightarrow E_1$$

Quantifiers Determine When Expressions Are True

To signal that an expression is universally true, you use a symbol meaning *for all*, written as ∀, as well as a variable standing in for possible objects. In the following example, the expression, when true, says that any object having feathers is a bird:

$$\forall x [\text{Feathers}(x) \Rightarrow \text{Bird}(x)]$$

Like other expressions, $\forall x [\text{Feathers}(x) \Rightarrow \text{Bird}(x)]$ can be true or false. If true, a ∀ expression means that you get a true expression when you substitute any object for x inside the square brackets. For example, if $\forall x [\text{Feathers}(x) \Rightarrow \text{Bird}(x)]$ is true, then certainly Feathers(Squigs) ⇒ Bird(Squigs) is true and Feathers(Suzie) ⇒ Bird(Suzie) is true.

When an expression is surrounded by the square brackets associated with a quantifier, the expression is said to lie within the **scope** of that quantifier. The expression Feathers(x) ⇒ Bird(x) therefore lies within the scope of the ∀ quantifier.

Because true expressions starting with ∀ say something about all possible object-for-variable substitutions within their scope, they are said to be **universally quantified**. Consequently, ∀ is called the **universal quantifier**.

Some expressions, although not always true, are true at least for some objects. Logic captures this idea using a symbol meaning *there exists*, written as ∃, used like this:

$$\exists x [\text{Bird}(x)]$$

When true, this expression means that there is at least one possible object, that, when substituted for x, makes the expression inside the square brackets true. Perhaps Bird(Squigs) is true; in any case, something like Bird(Squigs) is true.

Expressions with $\exists$ are said to be **existentially quantified**. The symbol $\exists$ is called the **existential quantifier**.

Logic Has a Rich Vocabulary

One problem with logic is that there is a large vocabulary to keep straight. For reference, let us gather together and complete the common elements of that vocabulary now, by way of figure 13.2 and the following definitions:

- A world's **objects** are terms.
- **Variables** ranging over a world's objects are terms.
- **Functions** are terms. The arguments to functions and the values returned are terms.

Terms are the only things that appear as arguments to predicates.

- **Atomic formulas** are individual predicates, together with arguments.
- **Literals** are atomic formulas and negated atomic formulas.
- **Well-formed formulas**, generally referred to, regrettably, by the abbreviation *wffs*, are defined recursively: literals are wffs; wffs connected together by $\neg$, $\&$, $\vee$, and $\Rightarrow$ are wffs; and wffs surrounded by quantifiers are also wffs.

For wffs, there are some special cases:

- A wff in which all the variables, if any, are inside the scope of corresponding quantifiers is a **sentence**. These are sentences:

$$\forall x[\text{Feathers}(x) \Rightarrow \text{Bird}(x)]$$
$$\text{Feathers(Albatross)} \Rightarrow \text{Bird(Albatross)}$$

Variables such as x, appearing within the scope of corresponding quantifiers, are said to be **bound**. Variables that are not bound are **free**. The following expression is not a sentence, because it contains a free variable, y:

$$\forall x[\text{Feathers}(x) \vee \neg\text{Feathers}(y)]$$

Note carefully that variables can represent objects only; variables cannot represent predicates. Consequently, this discussion is limited to a kind of logic called **first-order predicate calculus**. A more advanced topic, **second-order predicate calculus** permits variables representing predicates. A less advanced topic, **propositional calculus**, permits no variables of any kind.

- A wff consisting of a disjunction of literals is a **clause**.

Generally, the word *expression* is used interchangeably with wff, for using a lot of wffs makes it difficult to think about logic, instead of kennels.

Figure 13.2 The vocabulary of logic. Informally, the sample well-formed formula says this: Stating that the unspecified object, x, satisfies the predicate Feathers implies that x is satisfies the predicate Bird.

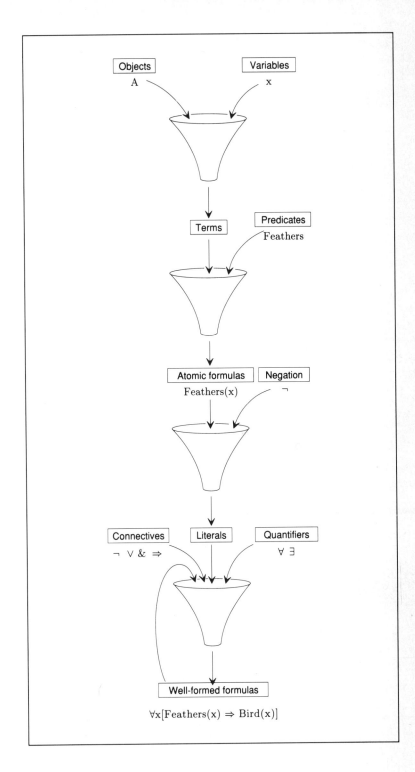

Figure 13.3 An interpretation is an accounting for how objects and relations map to object symbols and predicates.

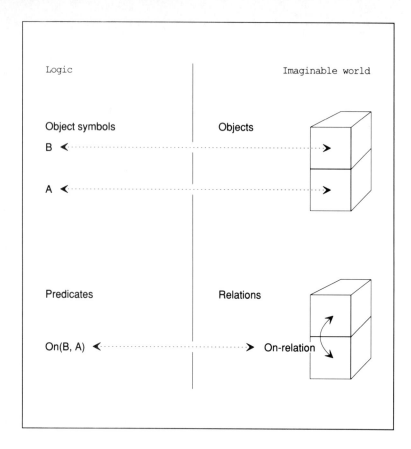

Interpretations Tie Logic Symbols to Worlds

Ultimately, the point of logic is to say something about an imaginable world. Consequently, object symbols and predicates must be related to more tangible things. As figure 13.3 illustrates, the two symbol categories correspond to two world categories:

- Objects in a world correspond to object symbols in logic. In the example shown in figure 13.3, the object symbols A and B on the left correspond to two things in the imaginable world shown on the right.

- Relations in a world correspond to predicates in logic. Whenever a relation holds with respect to some objects, the corresponding predicate is true when applied to the corresponding object symbols. In the example, the logic-world predicate, On, applied to object symbols B and A, is true because the imaginable-world relation, On-relation, holds between the two imaginable-world objects.

An **interpretation** is a full accounting of the correspondence between objects and object symbols, and between relations and predicates.

Proofs Tie Axioms to Consequences

Now you are ready to explore the notion of **proof**. Suppose that you are told that both of the following expressions are true:

$$\text{Feathers}(\text{Squigs})$$

$$\forall x[\text{Feathers}(x) \Rightarrow \text{Bird}(x)]$$

From the perspective of interpretations, to say that such expressions are true means that you are restricting the interpretations for the object symbols and predicates to those objects and relations for which the implied imaginable-world relations hold. Any such interpretation is said to be a **model** for the expressions.

When you are told Feathers(Squigs) and $\forall x[\text{Feathers}(x) \Rightarrow \text{Bird}(x)]$ are true, those expressions are called **axioms**. Now suppose that you are asked to show that all interpretations that make the axioms true also make the following expression true:

$$\text{Bird}(\text{Squigs})$$

If you succeed, you have **proved** that Bird(Squigs) is a **theorem** with respect to the axioms:

■ Said in the simplest terms, you prove that an expression is a theorem when you *show* that the theorem must be true, *given* that the axioms are true.

■ Said in the fanciest terms, you prove that an expression is a theorem when you show that any model for the axioms is also a model for the theorem. You say that the theorem **logically follows** from the axioms.

The way to prove a theorem is to use a **proof procedure**. Proof procedures use manipulations called **sound rules of inference** that produce new expressions from old expressions such that, said precisely, models of the old expressions are guaranteed to be models of the new ones too.

The most straightforward proof procedure is to apply sound rules of inference to the axioms, and to the results of applying sound rules of inference, until the desired theorem appears.

Note that proving a theorem is not the same as showing that an expression is **valid**, meaning that the expression is true for all possible interpretations of the symbols. Similarly, proving a theorem is not the same as showing that an expression is **satisfiable**, meaning that it is true for some possible interpretation of the symbols.

The most straightforward sound rule of inference used in proof procedures is *modus ponens*. **Modus ponens** says this: If there is an axiom of the form $E_1 \Rightarrow E_2$, and there is another axiom of the form E_1, then E_2 logically follows.

If E_2 is the theorem to be proved, you are done. If not, you might as well add E_2 to the axioms, for it will always be true when all the rest of the axioms are true. Continuing with *modus ponens* on an ever-increasing list of axioms may eventually show that the desired theorem is true, thus proving the theorem.

For the feathers-and-bird example, the axioms are just about right for the application of *modus ponens*. First, however, you must specialize the second expression. You have $\forall x[\text{Feathers}(x) \Rightarrow \text{Bird}(x)]$. Because you are dealing with interpretations for which $\text{Feathers}(x) \Rightarrow \text{Bird}(x)$ is true for all x, it must be true for the special case where x is Squigs. Consequently, $\text{Feathers}(\text{Squigs}) \Rightarrow \text{Bird}(\text{Squigs})$ must be true.

Now, the first expression, $\text{Feathers}(\text{Squigs})$, and the specialization of the second expression, $\text{Feathers}(\text{Squigs}) \Rightarrow \text{Bird}(\text{Squigs})$, fit *modus ponens* exactly, once you substitute $\text{Feathers}(\text{Squigs})$ for E_1 and $\text{Bird}(\text{Squigs})$ for E_2. You conclude that $\text{Bird}(\text{Squigs})$ must be true. The theorem is proved.

Resolution Is a Sound Rule of Inference

One of the most important rules of inference is *resolution*. **Resolution** says this: If there is an axiom of the form $E_1 \vee E_2$, and there is another axiom of the form $\neg E_2 \vee E_3$, then $E_1 \vee E_3$ logically follows. The expression $E_1 \vee E_3$ is called the **resolvent** of $E_1 \vee E_2$ and $\neg E_2 \vee E_3$.

Let us look at the various possibilities to see whether resolution is believable. First, suppose E_2 is true; then $\neg E_2$ must be false. But if $\neg E_2$ is false, from the second expression, then E_3 must be true. But if E_3 is true, then surely $E_1 \vee E_3$ is true. Second, suppose that E_2 is false. Then, from the first expression, E_1 must be true. But if E_1 is true, then surely $E_1 \vee E_3$ is true. You conclude that the resolvent, $E_1 \vee E_3$, must be true as long as both $E_1 \vee E_2$ and $\neg E_2 \vee E_3$ are true.

It is easy to generalize resolution such that there can be any number of disjuncts, including just one, in either of the two resolving expressions. The only demand is that one resolving expression must have a disjunct that is the negation of a disjunct in the other resolving expression. Once generalized, you can use resolution to reach the same conclusion about Squigs that you reached before with *modus ponens*.

The first step is to specialize the quantified expression to Squigs. The next step is to rewrite it, eliminating $\Rightarrow$, producing these:

$$\text{Feathers}(\text{Squigs})$$

$$\neg\text{Feathers}(\text{Squigs}) \vee \text{Bird}(\text{Squigs})$$

So written, resolution obviously applies, dropping out $\text{Feathers}(\text{Squigs})$ and $\neg\text{Feathers}(\text{Squigs})$, producing $\text{Bird}(\text{Squigs})$.

As a matter of fact, this example suggests a general truth: *Modus ponens* can be viewed as a special case of resolution, because anything concluded with *modus ponens* can be concluded with resolution as well. To see why, let one expression be E_1, and let the other be $E_1 \Rightarrow E_2$. According to *modus ponens*, E_2 must be true. But you know that $E_1 \Rightarrow E_2$ can be rewritten as $\neg E_1 \vee E_2$. So rewritten, resolution can be applied, dropping out the E_1 and the $\neg E_1$, producing E_2, which is the same result that you obtained using *modus ponens*.

Similarly, resolution subsumes another rule of inference called *modus tolens*. **Modus tolens** says this: If there is an axiom of the form $E_1 \Rightarrow E_2$, and there is another axiom of the form $\neg E_2$, then $\neg E_1$ logically follows.

RESOLUTION PROOFS

To prove a theorem, one obvious strategy is to search forward from the axioms using sound rules of inference, hoping to stumble across the theorem eventually. In this section, you learn about another strategy, the one used in resolution theorem proving, that requires you to show that the negation of a theorem cannot be true:

■ Assume that the negation of the theorem is true.
■ Show that the axioms and the assumed negation of the theorem together force an expression to be true that cannot be true.
■ Conclude that the assumed negation of the theorem cannot be true because it leads to a contradiction.
■ Conclude that the theorem must be true because the assumed negation of the theorem cannot be true.

Proving a theorem by showing its negation cannot be true is called **proof by refutation**.

Resolution Proves Theorems by Refutation

Consider the Squigs example again. Recall that you know from the axioms the following:

$$\neg\text{Feathers}(\text{Squigs}) \vee \text{Bird}(\text{Squigs})$$

$$\text{Feathers}(\text{Squigs})$$

Adding the negation of the expression to be proved, you have this list:

$$\neg\text{Feathers}(\text{Squigs}) \vee \text{Bird}(\text{Squigs})$$

$$\text{Feathers}(\text{Squigs})$$

$$\neg\text{Bird}(\text{Squigs})$$

Resolving the first and second axiom, as before, permits you to add a new expression to the list:

$$\neg\text{Feathers}(\text{Squigs}) \vee \text{Bird}(\text{Squigs})$$

$$\text{Feathers}(\text{Squigs})$$

$$\neg\text{Bird}(\text{Squigs})$$

$$\text{Bird}(\text{Squigs})$$

But now there is a contradiction. All the things in the list are supposed to be true. But it cannot be that $\text{Bird}(\text{Squigs})$ and $\neg\text{Bird}(\text{Squigs})$ are both true. Consequently, the assumption that led to this contradiction must be

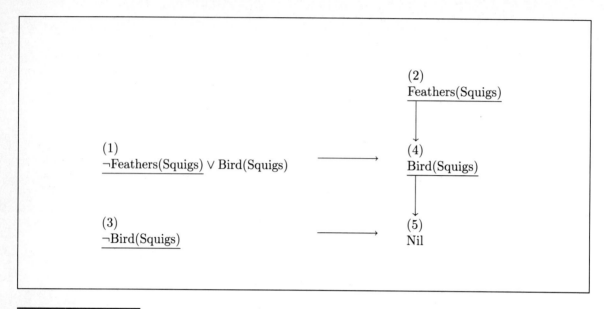

Figure 13.4 A
tree recording the
resolutions needed
to prove Bird(Squigs).

false; that is, the negation of the theorem, ¬Bird(Squigs), must be false;
hence, the theorem, Bird(Squigs), must be true, which is what you set out
to show.

The traditional way to recognize that the theorem is proved is to wait
until resolution happens on a literal and that literal's contradicting negation. The result is an empty clause—one with nothing in it—which by
convention is written as **Nil**. When resolution produces Nil, you are guaranteed that resolution has produced manifestly contradictory expressions.
Consequently, production of Nil is the signal that resolution has proved the
theorem.

Usually, it is illuminating to use a treelike diagram to record how
clauses get resolved together on the way to producing an empty clause.
Figure 13.4 is the tree for the proof.

Using Resolution Requires Axioms to Be in Clause Form

Now that you have the general idea of how proof by resolution works, it is
time to understand various manipulations that make harder proofs possible.
Basically, the point of these manipulations is to transform arbitrary logic
expressions into a form that enables resolution. Specifically, you need a
way to transform the given axioms into equivalent, new axioms that are all
disjunctions of literals. Said another way, you want the new axioms to be
in **clause form**.

An axiom involving blocks illustrates the manipulations. Although the
axiom is a bit artificial, so as to exercise all the transformation steps, the
axiom's message is simple. First, a brick is on something that is not a
pyramid; second, there is nothing that a brick is on and that is on the

brick as well; and third, there is nothing that is not a brick and also is the same thing as the brick:

$$\forall x[\text{Brick}(x) \Rightarrow (\exists y[\text{On}(x, y)\&\neg\text{Pyramid}(y)]$$
$$\&\neg\exists y[\text{On}(x, y)\&\text{On}(y, x)]$$
$$\&\forall y[\neg\text{Brick}(y) \Rightarrow \neg\text{Equal}(x, y)])]$$

As given, however, the axiom cannot be used to produce resolvents because it is not in clause form. Accordingly, the axiom has to be transformed into one or more equivalent axioms in clause form. You soon see that the transformation leads to four new axioms and requires the introduction of another function, Support:

$$\neg\text{Brick}(x) \vee \text{On}(x, \text{Support}(x))$$
$$\neg\text{Brick}(w) \vee \neg\text{Pyramid}(\text{Support}(w))$$
$$\neg\text{Brick}(u) \vee \neg\text{On}(u, y) \vee \neg\text{On}(y, u)$$
$$\neg\text{Brick}(v) \vee \text{Brick}(z) \vee \neg\text{Equal}(v, z)$$

Next, let us consider the steps needed to transform arbitrary logical expressions into clause form. Once explained, the steps will be summarized in a procedure.

■ Eliminate implications.

The first thing to do is to get rid of all the implications. This step is easy: All you need to do is to substitute $\neg E_1 \vee E_2$ for $E_1 \Rightarrow E_2$. For the example, you have to make two such substitutions, leaving you with this:

$$\forall x[\neg\text{Brick}(x) \vee (\exists y[\text{On}(x, y)\&\neg\text{Pyramid}(y)]$$
$$\&\neg\exists y[\text{On}(x, y)\&\text{On}(y, x)]$$
$$\&\forall y[\neg(\neg\text{Brick}(y)) \vee \neg\text{Equal}(x, y)])]$$

■ Move negations down to the atomic formulas.

Doing this step requires a number of identities, one for dealing with the negation of & expressions, one for $\vee$ expressions, one for $\neg$ expressions, and one each for $\forall$ and $\exists$:

$$\neg(E_1\&E_2) \rightarrow (\neg E_1) \vee (\neg E_2)$$
$$\neg(E_1 \vee E_2) \rightarrow (\neg E_1)\&(\neg E_2)$$
$$\neg(\neg E_1) \rightarrow E_1$$
$$\neg\forall x[E_1(x)] \rightarrow \exists x[\neg E_1(x)]$$
$$\neg\exists x[E_1(x)] \rightarrow \forall x[\neg E_1(x)]$$

For the example, you need the third identity, which eliminates the double negations, and you need the final identity, which eliminates an $\exists$ and introduces another $\forall$, leaving this:

$$\forall x[\neg\text{Brick}(x) \vee (\exists y[\text{On}(x, y)\&\neg\text{Pyramid}(y)]$$
$$\&\forall y[\neg\text{On}(x, y) \vee \neg\text{On}(y, x)]$$
$$\&\forall y[\text{Brick}(y) \vee \neg\text{Equal}(x, y)])]$$

■   Eliminate existential quantifiers.

Unfortunately, the procedure for eliminating existential quantifiers is a little obscure, so you must work hard to understand it. Let us begin by looking closely at the part of the axiom involving ∃:

$$\exists y[On(x,y)\&\neg Pyramid(y)]$$

Reflect on what this expression means. Evidently, if someone gives you some particular object x, you will be able to identify an object for y that makes the expression true. Said another way, there is a function that takes argument x and returns a proper y. You do not necessarily know how the function works, but such a function must exist. Let us call it, for the moment, Magic(x).

Using the new function, you no longer need to say that y exists, for you have a way of producing the proper y in any circumstance. Consequently, you can rewrite the expression as follows:

$$On(x, Magic(x))\&\neg Pyramid(Magic(x))$$

Functions that eliminate the need for existential quantifiers are called **Skolem functions**. Note carefully that the Skolem function, Magic(x), must depend on x, for otherwise it could not produce a y that depends on a particular x. The general rule is that the universal quantifiers determine which arguments Skolem functions need: There is one argument for each universally quantified variable whose scope contains the Skolem function.

Here then is the evolving axiom, after eliminating the ∃ and introducing the Skolem function, which you now can call the Support function:

$$\forall x[\neg Brick(x) \vee ((On(x, Support(x))\&\neg Pyramid(Support(x)))$$
$$\&\forall y[\neg On(x,y) \vee \neg On(y,x)]$$
$$\&\forall y[Brick(y) \vee \neg Equal(x,y)])]$$

■   Rename variables, as necessary, so that no two variables are the same.

The quantifiers do not care what their variable names are. Accordingly, you can rename any duplicates so that each quantifier has a unique name. You do this renaming because you want to move all the universal quantifiers together at the left of each expression in the next step, without confounding them. In the example, the substitutions leave this:

$$\forall x[\neg Brick(x) \vee ((On(x, Support(x))\&\neg Pyramid(Support(x)))$$
$$\&\forall y[\neg On(x,y) \vee \neg On(y,x)]$$
$$\&\forall z[Brick(z) \vee \neg Equal(x,z)])]$$

■   Move the universal quantifiers to the left.

This step works because, by now, each quantifier uses a unique variable name—no confusion results from leftward movement. In the example, the result is as follows:

$$\forall x \forall y \forall z [\neg \text{Brick}(x) \lor ((\text{On}(x, \text{Support}(x)) \& \neg \text{Pyramid}(\text{Support}(x)))$$
$$\& \neg \text{On}(x, y) \lor \neg \text{On}(y, x)$$
$$\& \text{Brick}(z) \lor \neg \text{Equal}(x, z))]$$

■   Move the disjunctions down to the literals.

This step requires you to move the ∨s inside the &s; to do this movement, you need to use one of the distributive laws:

$$E_1 \lor (E_2 \& E_3) \Leftrightarrow (E_1 \lor E_2) \& (E_1 \lor E_3)$$

For the example, let us do the work in two steps:

$$\forall x \forall y \forall z [(\neg \text{Brick}(x) \lor (\text{On}(x, \text{Support}(x)) \& \neg \text{Pyramid}(\text{Support}(x))))$$
$$\& (\neg \text{Brick}(x) \lor \neg \text{On}(x, y) \lor \neg \text{On}(y, x))$$
$$\& (\neg \text{Brick}(x) \lor \text{Brick}(z) \lor \neg \text{Equal}(x, z))]$$
$$\forall x \forall y \forall z [(\neg \text{Brick}(x) \lor \text{On}(x, \text{Support}(x)))$$
$$\& (\neg \text{Brick}(x) \lor \neg \text{Pyramid}(\text{Support}(x)))$$
$$\& (\neg \text{Brick}(x) \lor \neg \text{On}(x, y) \lor \neg \text{On}(y, x))$$
$$\& (\neg \text{Brick}(x) \lor \text{Brick}(z) \lor \neg \text{Equal}(x, z))]$$

■   Eliminate the conjunctions.

Actually, you do not really eliminate them. Instead, you simply write each part of a conjunction as though it were a separate axiom. This way of writing a conjunction makes sense, because each part of a conjunction must be true if the whole conjunction is true. Here is the result:

$$\forall x [\neg \text{Brick}(x) \lor \text{On}(x, \text{Support}(x))]$$
$$\forall x [\neg \text{Brick}(x) \lor \neg \text{Pyramid}(\text{Support}(x))]$$
$$\forall x \forall y [\neg \text{Brick}(x) \lor \neg \text{On}(x, y) \lor \neg \text{On}(y, x)]$$
$$\forall x \forall z [\neg \text{Brick}(x) \lor \text{Brick}(z) \lor \neg \text{Equal}(x, z)]$$

■   Rename all the variables, as necessary, so that no two variables are the same.

There is no problem with renaming variables at this step, for you are merely renaming the universally quantified variables in each part of a conjunction. Because each of the conjoined parts must be true for any variable values, it does not matter whether the variables have different names for each part. Here is the result for the example:

$$\forall x [\neg \text{Brick}(x) \lor \text{On}(x, \text{Support}(x))]$$
$$\forall w [\neg \text{Brick}(w) \lor \neg \text{Pyramid}(\text{Support}(w))]$$
$$\forall u \forall y [\neg \text{Brick}(u) \lor \neg \text{On}(u, y) \lor \neg \text{On}(y, u)]$$
$$\forall v \forall z [\neg \text{Brick}(v) \lor \text{Brick}(z) \lor \neg \text{Equal}(v, z)]$$

■   Eliminate the universal quantifiers.

Actually, you do not really eliminate them. You just adopt a convention whereby all variables at this point are presumed to be universally quantified. Now, the example looks like this:

$$\neg\text{Brick}(x) \lor \text{On}(x, \text{Support}(x))$$

$$\neg\text{Brick}(w) \lor \neg\text{Pyramid}(\text{Support}(w))$$

$$\neg\text{Brick}(u) \lor \neg\text{On}(u, y) \lor \neg\text{On}(y, u)$$

$$\neg\text{Brick}(v) \lor \text{Brick}(z) \lor \neg\text{Equal}(v, z)$$

The result is now in clause form, as required when you wish to use resolution. Each clause consists of a disjunction of literals. Taking the whole set of clauses together, you have an implied & on the top level, literals on the bottom level, and ∨s in between. Each clause's variables are different, and all variables are implicitly universally quantified. To summarize, here is the procedure for translating axioms into clause form:

To put axioms into clause form,

▷ Eliminate the implications.

▷ Move the negations down to the atomic formulas.

▷ Eliminate the existential quantifiers.

▷ Rename the variables, if necessary.

▷ Move the universal quantifiers to the left.

▷ Move the disjunctions down to the literals.

▷ Eliminate the conjunctions.

▷ Rename the variables, if necessary.

▷ Eliminate the universal quantifiers.

Here is the procedure for doing resolution proof:

To prove a theorem using resolution,

▷ Negate the theorem to be proved, and add the result to the list of axioms.

▷ Put the list of axioms into clause form.

▷ Until there is no resolvable pair of clauses,

  ▷ Find resolvable clauses and resolve them.

  ▷ Add the results of resolution to the list of clauses.

  ▷ If Nil is produced, stop and report that the theorem is true.

▷ Stop and report that the theorem is false.

Figure 13.5 Some fodder for a proof.

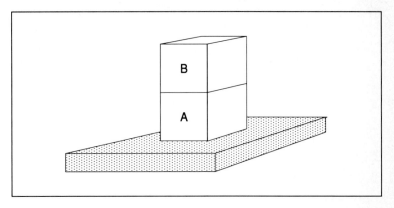

Before discussing which clause pairs to resolve at any given point, let us work out an example. The following axioms account for the observed block relations in figure 13.5:

$$On(B, A)$$
$$On(A, Table)$$

These axioms, of course, are already in clause form. Let us use them to show that B is above the table:

$$Above(B, Table)$$

To show this, you need the clause form of two universally quantified expressions. The first says that being on an object implies being above that object. The second says that one object is above another if there is an object in between:

$$\forall x \forall y [On(x, y) \Rightarrow Above(x, y)]$$
$$\forall x \forall y \forall z [Above(x, y) \& Above(y, z) \Rightarrow Above(x, z)]$$

After you go through the procedure for reduction to clause form, these axioms look like this:

$$\neg On(u, v) \vee Above(u, v)$$
$$\neg Above(x, y) \vee \neg Above(y, z) \vee Above(x, z)$$

Recall that the expression to be proved is Above(B, Table). No conversion is needed after negation:

$$\neg Above(B, Table)$$

Next, all the clauses need identifying numbers to make it easy to refer to them:

$$\neg On(u, v) \vee Above(u, v) \tag{1}$$
$$\neg Above(x, y) \vee \neg Above(y, z) \vee Above(x, z) \tag{2}$$
$$On(B, A) \tag{3}$$
$$On(A, Table) \tag{4}$$
$$\neg Above(B, Table) \tag{5}$$

Now you can start. First, you resolve clause 2 and clause 5 by specializing x to B and z to Table so that the final part of clause 2 looks exactly like the expression negated in clause 5, producing clause 6:

$$\neg\text{Above}(B, y) \lor \neg\text{Above}(y, \text{Table}) \lor \underline{\text{Above}(B, \text{Table})} \qquad (2)$$

$$\underline{\neg\text{Above}(B, \text{Table})} \qquad (5)$$

$$\neg\text{Above}(B, y) \lor \neg\text{Above}(y, \text{Table}) \qquad (6)$$

Now, you can resolve (1) with clause 6 by replacing u with y and specializing v to Table:

$$\neg\text{On}(y, \text{Table}) \lor \underline{\text{Above}(y, \text{Table})} \qquad (1)$$

$$\neg\text{Above}(B, y) \lor \underline{\neg\text{Above}(y, \text{Table})} \qquad (6)$$

$$\neg\text{On}(y, \text{Table}) \lor \neg\text{Above}(B, y) \qquad (7)$$

Curiously, it pays to use (1) again with clause 7, with u specialized to B and v replaced by y:

$$\neg\text{On}(B, y) \lor \underline{\text{Above}(B, y)} \qquad (1)$$

$$\neg\text{On}(y, \text{Table}) \lor \underline{\neg\text{Above}(B, y)} \qquad (7)$$

$$\neg\text{On}(B, y) \lor \neg\text{On}(y, \text{Table}) \qquad (8)$$

Now, let us use clause 3 and clause 8, specializing y to A:

$$\underline{\text{On}(B, A)} \qquad (3)$$

$$\underline{\neg\text{On}(B, A)} \lor \neg\text{On}(A, \text{Table}) \qquad (8)$$

$$\neg\text{On}(A, \text{Table}) \qquad (9)$$

Now, clause 4 and clause 9 resolve to Nil, the empty clause.

$$\underline{\text{On}(A, \text{Table})} \qquad (4)$$

$$\underline{\neg\text{On}(A, \text{Table})} \qquad (9)$$

$$\text{Nil} \qquad (10)$$

You must be finished: You have arrived at a contradiction, so the negation of the theorem, $\neg\text{Above}(B, \text{Table})$, must be false. Hence, the theorem, $\text{Above}(B, \text{Table})$, must be true.

Proof Is Exponential

One big question is, How can you be so shrewd as to pick just the right clauses to resolve? The answer is that you take advantage of two ideas:

■ First, you can be sure that every resolution involves the negated theorem or a clause derived—directly or indirectly—using the negated theorem.

■ Second, you know where you are, and you know where you are going, so you can note the difference and use your intuition.

Unfortunately, there are limits to what you can express if you restrict yourself to the mathematically attractive concepts in pure logic. For example, pure logic does not allow you to express concepts such as difference, as required by means–ends analysis, or heuristic distances, as required by best-first search. Theorem provers can use such concepts, but then a large fraction of the problem-solving burden rests on knowledge lying outside the statement, in logical notation, of what is known and what is to be done.

Although some search strategies require you to separate yourself considerably from pure logic, others do not. One such strategy, the **unit-preference strategy**, gives preference to resolutions involving the clauses with the smallest number of literals. The **set-of-support strategy** allows only resolutions involving the negated theorem or new clauses derived—directly or indirectly—using the negated theorem. The **breadth-first strategy** first resolves all possible pairs of the initial clauses, then resolves all possible pairs of the resulting set together with the initial set, level by level. All these strategies are said to be **complete** because they are guaranteed to find a proof if the theorem logically follows from the axioms. Unfortunately, there is another side:

■ All resolution search strategies, like many searches, are subject to the **exponential-explosion problem**, preventing success for proofs that require long chains of inference.

■ All resolution search strategies are subject to a version of the **halting problem**, for search is not guaranteed to terminate unless there actually is a proof.

In fact, all complete proof procedures for the first-order predicate calculus are subject to the halting problem. Complete proof procedures are said to be **semidecidable** because they are guaranteed to tell you whether an expression is a theorem only if the expression is indeed a theorem.

Resolution Requires Unification

To resolve two clauses, two literals must match exactly, except that one is negated. Sometimes, literals match exactly as they stand; sometimes, literals can be made to match by an appropriate substitution.

In the examples so far, the matching part of resolution was easy: The same constant appeared in the same place, obviously matching, or a constant appeared in the place occupied by a universally quantified variable, matching because the variable could be the observed constant as well as any other.

You need a better way to keep track of substitutions, and you need the rules by which substitutions can be made. First, let us agree to denote substitutions as follows:

$$\{v_1 \rightarrow C; v_2 \rightarrow v_3; v_4 \rightarrow f(\ldots)\}$$

This expression mean that the variable v_1 is replaced by the constant C, the variable v_2 is replaced by the variable v_3, and the variable v_4 is replaced by a function, f, together with the function's arguments.[†] The rules for

---

[†]Other authors denote the same substitution by $\{C/v_1, v_3/v_2, f(\ldots)/v_4\}$, which is easier to write but harder to keep straight.

such substitutions say that you can replace a variable by any term that does not contain the same variable:

■ You may replace a variable by a constant. That is, you can have the substitution $\{v_1 \rightarrow C\}$.

■ You may replace a variable by a variable. That is, you can have the substitution $\{v_2 \rightarrow v_3\}$.

■ You may replace a variable by a function expression, as long as the function expression does not contain the variable. That is, you can have the substitution $\{v_4 \rightarrow f(\ldots)\}$.

A substitution that makes two clauses resolvable is called a **unifier**, and the process of finding such substitutions is called **unification**. There are many procedures for unification. For the examples, however, inspection will do.

Traditional Logic Is Monotonic

Suppose that an expression is a theorem with respect to a certain set of axioms. Is the expression still a theorem after the addition of some new axioms? Surely it must be, for you can do the proof using the old axioms exclusively, ignoring the new ones.

Because new axioms only add to the list of provable theorems and never cause any to be withdrawn, traditional logic is said to be **monotonic**.

The monotonicity property is incompatible with some natural ways of thinking, however. Suppose that you are told all birds fly, from which you conclude that some particular bird flies, a perfectly reasonable conclusion, given what you know. Then, someone points out that penguins do not fly, nor do dead birds. Adding these new facts can block your already-made conclusion, but cannot stop a theorem prover; only amending the initial axioms can do that.

Research on this sort of problem has led to the development of logics that are said to be **nonmonotonic**.

Theorem Proving Is Suitable for Certain Problems, but Not for All Problems

Logic is terrific for some jobs, and is not so good for others. But because logic is unbeatable for what it was developed to do, logic is seductive. People try to use logic for all hard problems, rather than for only those for which it is suited. That is like using a hammer to drive screws, just because hammers are good at dealing with nails, which are simply one kind of fastener.

Consequently, when using logic and a theorem prover seems unambiguously right, review these caveats:

■ Theorem provers may take too long.

Complete theorem provers require search, and the search is inherently exponential. Methods for speeding up search, such as set-of-support resolution, reduce the size of the exponent associated with the search, but do not change the exponential character.

■ Theorem provers may not help you to solve practical problems, even if they do their work instantaneously.

Some knowledge resists embodiment in axioms. Formulating a problem in logic may require enormous effort, whereas solving the problem formulated in another way may be simple.

■ Logic is weak as a representation for certain kinds of knowledge.

The notation of pure logic does not allow you to express such notions as heuristic distances, or state differences, or the idea that one particular approach is particularly fast, or the idea that some manipulation works well, but only if done fewer than three times. Theorem provers can use such knowledge, but you must represent that knowledge using concepts other than those of pure logic.

SUMMARY

■ Logic concentrates on using knowledge in a rigorous, provably correct way; other problem-solving paradigms concentrate on the knowledge itself.

■ Logic has a traditional notation, requiring you to become familiar with the symbols for *implies, and, or,* and *not.* These symbols are ⇒, &, ∨, and ¬.

■ A universally quantified expression is true for all values of the quantified variable. An existentially quantified expression is true for at least one value.

■ An interpretation is an account of how object symbols, predicates, and functions map to objects, relations, and functions in some imaginable world. A model of a set of expressions is an interpretation for which the implied imaginable-world relations hold.

■ A theorem logically follows from assumed axioms if there is a series of steps connecting the theorem to the axioms using sound rules of inference.

■ The most obvious rule of inference is *modus ponens.* Another, more general rule of inference is resolution.

■ Resolution theorem proving uses resolution as the rule of inference and refutation as the strategy. Resolution requires transforming axioms and the negated theorem to clause form. Resolution also requires a variable substitution process called unification.

■ The set-of-support strategy dictates using only resolutions in which at least one resolvent descends from the negation of the theorem to be proved.

■   Logic is seductive, because it often works neatly. There are caveats that you must obey, however, for logic is just one of many tools that you should have in your workshop.

BACKGROUND

The development of the resolution method for theorem proving is generally credited to J. A. Robinson [1965, 1968].

PROLOG is a popular programming language based on logic. For an excellent introduction to PROLOG, see PROLOG *Programming for Artificial Intelligence* (second edition), by Ivan Bratko [1990]. PROLOG was developed by Alain Colmerauer and his associates [Colmerauer, H. Kanoui, R. Pasero, and P. Roussel 1973; Colmerauer 1982].

For an excellent treatment of the role of logic in artificial intelligence, see the papers of Patrick J. Hayes [1977].

14

Backtracking and Truth Maintenance

In this chapter, you see how logic serves as a foundation for other problem-solving methods. In particular, you learn to *prove statements by constraint propagation*. Although ordinary resolution theorem proving is more powerful in some ways, proof by constraint propagation offers distinctive benefits. For one thing, proof by constraint propagation makes it easy to keep track of *justifications* enabling *truth-maintenance procedures* to withdraw assumptions simply, without deriving still-true expressions all over again.

First, however, you learn what *dependency-directed backtracking* is, and how it differs from *chronological backtracking*. The key idea is illustrated through a scheduling example involving exercise, entertainment, and study time.

CHRONOLOGICAL AND DEPENDENCY-DIRECTED BACKTRACKING

In Chapter 11, you learned how arithmetic constraints can be enforced in nets. In this section, you learn about **dependency-directed backtracking**, which makes it possible to find the sources of inconsistencies.

Limit Boxes Identify Inconsistencies

Imagine that each day of the week involves a set of choices. Some choices involve entertainment, others involve exercise, and still others involve study. The choices are constrained by weekly objectives: There must be enough entertainment, enough exercise, enough study, and not too much money spent. To make things specific, let us assume these are the options:

- Tuesday, Wednesday, and Thursday are study days. You can study 2, 4, or 6 hours, or not at all.

- Monday and Friday are exercise days. One choice is to take a walk, producing 5 exercise units; another is to jog 10 kilometers, producing 10 exercise units; another is to work out at a health club, producing 15 exercise units; and still another is to do nothing. The health club costs $20 per use in fees and taxi fares.

- Monday and Friday are also entertainment days. One choice is to go out to eat, which costs $20 and returns 2 pleasure units. Another is to read a library book, which costs nothing and returns 1 pleasure unit. Another is to do nothing, which costs nothing and returns 0 pleasure units.

Further assume that, each week, to stay stimulated and healthy, you must have 6 hours of study, 2 units of pleasure, and 20 units of exercise. To keep your budget in line, you must limit your expenses to $30 per week.

All these assumptions can be expressed in the slightly generalized numeric constraint net shown in figure 14.1. The daily choices are expressed in **choice boxes**. Numbers are propagated through **adder boxes**. The weekly needs are expressed in **limit boxes**. If the value at the terminal of a limit box is outside the allowed range, the plan is unacceptable. Now suppose you plan the week as follows:

- On Monday, you expect snow, making walking and jogging difficult, so you plan to go to the health club. This takes time, so you will not have time for entertainment.
- You plan to study 2 hours on Tuesday.
- You plan to study 2 more hours on Wednesday.
- You plan to study 2 more hours on Thursday.
- On Friday, you plan to take a walk and to read a library book.

Now, propagating these choices through the numeric constraint net to the limit boxes, you see that you have met your study needs, for you have studied 6 hours, yielding 6 study units. Exercise is also under control, for you have managed to get 20 exercise units. On the other hand, you are in trouble with entertainment. Worse yet, you cannot correct the problem by going out to dinner because that would put you over your budget, because you have already spent $20 on visiting your health club.

You must alter a choice to fix the plan. The question is, How can you find a good plan quickly, preserving as much of the bad plan as possible?

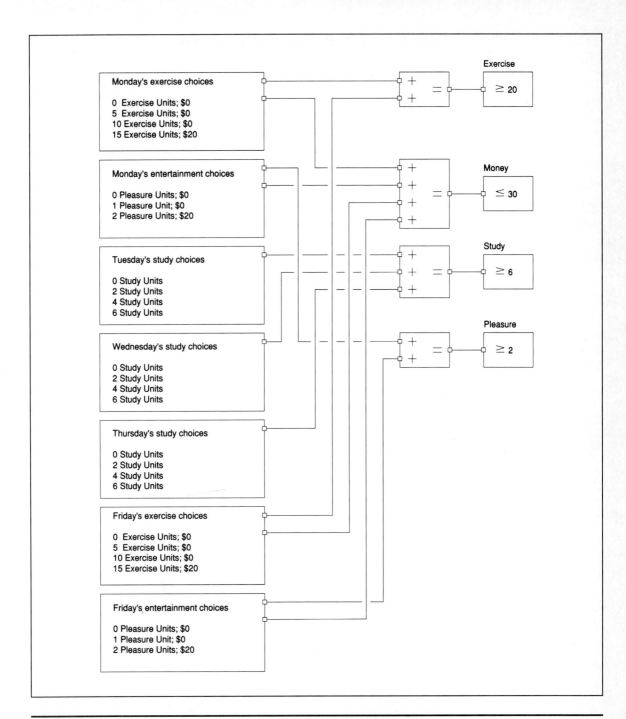

Figure 14.1 A numeric constraint net expressing activity-planning constraints.

Chronological Backtracking Wastes Time

One way to work on a faulty plan is to withdraw the most recently made choice, and its consequences, to select an alternative at that choice point, and to move ahead again. If all the alternatives at the last choice point have been explored already, then go further back until an unexplored alternative is found.

The whole process resembles what you do when you work your way through a maze: you come to dead ends, you retreat, you go forward again. As you learned in Chapter 4, this procedure is called *depth-first search*. That part of the procedure that responds to dead ends is called **chronological backtracking**, to stress that everything is *undone* as you move back in *time*.

Chronological backtracking normally begins as soon as a dead end is detected, as stipulated in the following procedure description:

To backtrack chronologically,

▷ Whenever you reach a dead end,

  ▷ Until you encounter a choice point with an unexplored alternative,

    ▷ Withdraw the most recently made choice.

    ▷ Undo all consequences of the withdrawn choice.

    ▷ Move forward again, making a new choice.

The problem with chronological backtracking is clear: Many of the withdrawn choices may have nothing whatever to do with why the dead end is a dead end. In the activity-planning example, chronological backtracking would begin on Friday, when the problem of meeting the entertainment objective is detected. After quickly withdrawing and trying both of the remaining entertainment choices, chronological backtracking works its way back in time, trying other exercise alternatives for Friday, and then going through all of Thursday's, Wednesday's, and Tuesday's study alternatives, none of which have anything to do with the entertainment problem that initiated the backup. Chronological backtracking must work its way through $4^3 = 64$ study combinations before reaching back to the choice point that matters.

Thus, chronological backtracking can be inefficient. In real problems, the inefficiency can make a problem-solving system absurdly impractical.

Nonchronological Backtracking Exploits Dependencies

Another way to work on the faulty plan is to withdraw the choices *that matter*. To identify the choices that matter, you need only to keep track of how propagation reaches from choice boxes to the limit boxes that announce dead ends.

The highlighted lines in figure 14.2 show that the entertainment limit box complains because the choices made on Monday and Friday are incompatible with the weekly entertainment requirement. Only those choices are candidates for change.

The procedure for identifying relevant choices is called **dependency-directed backtracking**, to emphasize that the choices to be withdrawn are those on which the dead end *depends*. The procedure is also called **nonchronological backtracking**, to stress that *time* does *not* determine which choices are to be withdrawn:

To backtrack nonchronologically,

▷ Whenever you reach an impasse,

   ▷ Trace back through dependencies, identifying all choice points that may have contributed to the impasse.

   ▷ Using depth-first search, find a combination of choices at those choice points that break the impasse.

With nonchronological backtracking, only the relevant choices are withdrawn. In the activity-planning example, none of the Tuesday, Wednesday, and Thursday choices are withdrawn before, during, or after the entertainment problem is fixed. Instead, Monday's entertainment choice—doing nothing—can be changed to reading, which yields one pleasure unit at no cost. Friday's choice can be reading again, satisfying both the pleasure and budget constraints for the week.

Thus, nonchronological backtracking is an efficient way to find compatible choices, as long as there is a way of tracing back over dependencies to find the relevant choice points.

PROOF BY CONSTRAINT PROPAGATION

In the previous section, you learned about *chronological backtracking* and *dependency-directed backtracking* in situations where numeric values have to be kept consistent.

Now you revisit the same general ideas about backtracking in a different context. In Chapter 13, you viewed the logical connectives, &, ∨, ¬, and ⇒, as predicates that accept arguments and return true or false. In this section, you use expressions to build a **truth-propagation net** consisting of truth boxes, which contain true and false **truth values**, and **truth-propagation boxes**, which propagate truth values.

Truth Can Be Propagated

There are several reasons to combine logic with the idea of constraint propagation. First, truth-propagation nets highlight the point that theorem proving can be viewed as a way of exploiting constraints. Second,

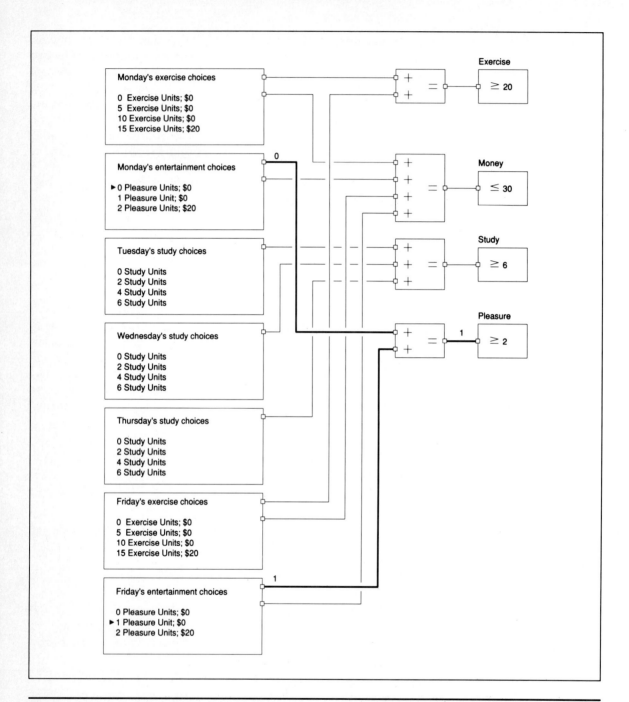

Figure 14.2 A numeric constraint net enabling nonchronological backtracking. You identify the causes of the unmet objectives by tracing back through adder boxes in this situation.

truth propagation nets make it easy to keep track of what happens as assumptions are made or withdrawn; this record-keeping feature is why truth-propagation nets are associated with the notion of *truth maintenance*. Third, truth propagation nets make it easy to see how dependency-directed, nonchronological backtracking can help you to correct the contradictions that occur when assumptions are incompatible.

To see how logic and constraint propagation can be combined, consider two acquaintances, A and B. Suppose that B likes A, so if A is happy, so is B. If you assume that A is happy, you readily conclude that B is happy too. The question is, How can you use constraint propagation to make such deductions about who is happy?

First, you need to create a truth box for every logical expression and subexpression that may be true or false. In the example, Happy(A) $\Rightarrow$ Happy(B) is an expression which may be true or false, so you need a truth box for it. In addition, Happy(A) $\Rightarrow$ Happy(B) contains two subexpressions, the literals Happy(A) and Happy(B), which may be true or false, so you need truth boxes for them as well.

All three truth boxes are shown in figure 14.3(a). Note that the truth value of the truth box for the expression is true, indicating that if A is happy, B is too. The truth value of the other two truth boxes, however, is unknown, indicating that you do not know whether the corresponding literals are true or false.

If you further assume that A is happy, then the truth value of Happy(A) is true, and the truth value of Happy(B) must be true too. Thinking in terms of propagation through constraints, you expect the truth value of the truth box for Happy(A), together with the truth value of the truth box for Happy(A) $\Rightarrow$ Happy(B), to constrain the truth value of the truth box for Happy(B). This constraint on Happy(B) is enforced by the truth-propagation box shown in figure 14.3(b). Thus, truth-propagation nets contain both truth boxes and truth-propagation boxes.

In general, each logical connective holds together a pair of subexpressions and determines how the truth values of those subexpressions constrain the truth value of their combination. Thus, to implement a truth-propagation net given a set of logical expressions, you need a truth-propagation box for each logical connective that appears in those logical expressions.

Also, you need to know how each kind of truth-propagation box enforces constraint. Then, a value determined for one truth box may help you to determine values for others.

In a moment, you will see that the definition of $E_1 \Rightarrow E_2$ has the following logical consequences:

$$\neg E_1 \lor E_2 \lor \neg(E_1 \Rightarrow E_2)$$
$$E_1 \lor (E_1 \Rightarrow E_2)$$
$$\neg E_2 \lor (E_1 \Rightarrow E_2)$$

Figure 14.3 In (a), literals and logical expressions become truth boxes in a truth propagation net. In (b), the truth box for an implication expression is connected to the literals that it contains by way of a truth-propagation box. Assuming that the expression is true and that Happy(A) is true, the truth-propagation box forces Happy(B) to be true.

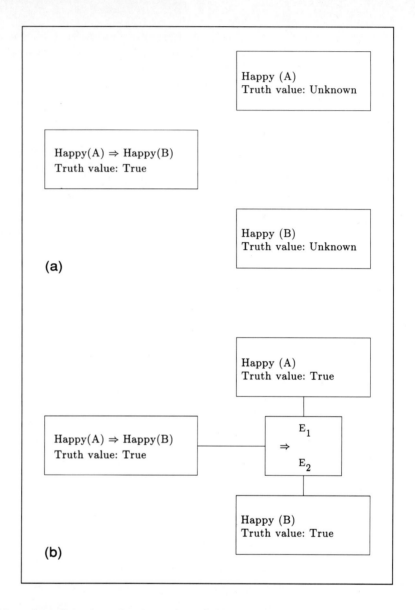

Note that the value of at least one of the literals on each line must be true. To highlight this point, you can rewrite the expressions as follows:

Require E_1 is false *or* E_2 is true *or* $(E_1 \Rightarrow E_2)$ is false

Require E_1 is true *or* $(E_1 \Rightarrow E_2)$ is true

Require E_2 is false *or* $(E_1 \Rightarrow E_2)$ is true

Written this way, the expressions are said to be **syntactically sugared**, because syntactic sugar makes the expressions easier to deal with, just as sugar makes medicine easier to take. Looking at the syntactically sugared form, you can see that at least one of the subexpressions on each line must match the stipulated true or false value. Hence, if all but one subexpression mismatches, the remaining subexpression is *required* to match. Each line, therefore, is a constraint on the values of expressions appearing in that line. Consequently, each line is called a **constraint expression**.

Conveniently, you can implement the constraints associated with the truth-propagation boxes using when-written procedures of the sort introduced in Chapter 9:

A **truth-propagation net** is a representation

That is a value-propagation net

In which

▷ Truth boxes contain truth values. Each truth box corresponds to a literal or expression.

▷ Truth-propagation boxes enforce logical constraints via when-written procedures.

Using constraint expressions, you easily can construct when-written procedures that define what each kind of constraint-propagation box must do. Here is a when-written procedure that captures the first of the constraint expressions for implication truth boxes:

When a value is written into any terminal of an implication truth box,

▷ If E_1 is true and E_2 is false, write false in the implication slot.

▷ Otherwise, if E_1 is true and the implication is true, write true in the E_2 slot.

▷ Otherwise, if E_2 is false and the implication is true, write false in the E_1 slot.

Now you are ready to return to the definition of $E_1 \Rightarrow E_2$ to see how that definition leads to the three logical consequences that lead, in turn, to three constraint expressions. The rest of this subsection is devoted to this somewhat tedious task; you may choose to skip to the next subsection.

From the truth-table definition of $\Rightarrow$, you know that $E_1 \Rightarrow E_2$ allows only the following combinations:

E_1	E_2	$E_1 \Rightarrow E_2$
true	false	false
false	false	true
false	true	true
true	true	true

But there are eight possible combinations of three true or false values. Consequently, these four remaining combinations must be forbidden:

E_1	E_2	$E_1 \Rightarrow E_2$
true	false	true
false	false	false
false	true	false
true	true	false

Saying the same thing another way, the following must be true, for each line excludes one of the four forbidden combinations:

$$\neg(E_1 \& \neg E_2 \& (E_1 \Rightarrow E_2))$$
$$\& \neg(\neg E_1 \& \neg E_2 \& \neg(E_1 \Rightarrow E_2))$$
$$\& \neg(\neg E_1 \& E_2 \& \neg(E_1 \Rightarrow E_2))$$
$$\& \neg(E_1 \& E_2 \& \neg(E_1 \Rightarrow E_2))$$

Taking the outside negations inside, you can rewrite the expression this way:

$$(\neg E_1 \vee E_2 \vee \neg(E_1 \Rightarrow E_2))$$
$$\&(E_1 \vee E_2 \vee (E_1 \Rightarrow E_2))$$
$$\&(E_1 \vee \neg E_2 \vee (E_1 \Rightarrow E_2))$$
$$\&(\neg E_1 \vee \neg E_2 \vee (E_1 \Rightarrow E_2))$$

Now, you can simplify by combining the second and third lines and the third and fourth lines, producing the following equivalent expression:

$$(\neg E_1 \vee E_2 \vee \neg(E_1 \Rightarrow E_2))$$
$$\&(E_1 \vee (E_1 \Rightarrow E_2))$$
$$\&(\neg E_2 \vee (E_1 \Rightarrow E_2))$$

Aha! These are the consequences of $\Rightarrow$ that you assumed before. You could, tiresomely, repeat for $\&$, $\vee$, and $\neg$. Instead, be content with these summary results:

For $\Rightarrow$ truth boxes, you have each of the following constraint expressions:

Require E_1 is false   *or* E_2 is true   *or* $(E_1 \Rightarrow E_2)$ is false

Require E_1 is true   *or* $(E_1 \Rightarrow E_2)$ is true

Require E_2 is false   *or* $(E_1 \Rightarrow E_2)$ is true

For & truth boxes, you have each of the following constraint expressions:

> *Require* E_1 is false   *or* E_2 is false   *or* $(E_1 \& E_2)$ is true
>
> *Require* E_1 is true   *or* $(E_1 \& E_2)$ is false
>
> *Require* E_2 is true   *or* $(E_1 \& E_2)$ is false

For ∨ truth boxes, you have each of the following constraint expressions:

> *Require* E_1 is true   *or* E_2 is true   *or* $(E_1 \vee E_2)$ is false
>
> *Require* E_1 is false   *or* $(E_1 \vee E_2)$ is true
>
> *Require* E_2 is false   *or* $(E_1 \vee E_2)$ is true

For ¬ truth boxes, you have the following constraint expressions:

> *Require* E_1 is true   *or* $\neg E_1$ is true
>
> *Require* E_1 is false   *or* $\neg E_1$ is false

Truth Propagation Can Establish Justifications

In the acquaintance example, if A is happy, so is B. Now, to expand on the example slightly, suppose that there are two more acquaintances, C and D. C likes B, so if B is happy, so is C. Finally, assume that A and D are happy. Thus, you have the following assumptions:

$$\text{Happy(A)} \Rightarrow \text{Happy(B)}$$
$$\text{Happy(B)} \Rightarrow \text{Happy(C)}$$
$$\text{Happy(A)}$$
$$\text{Happy(D)}$$

These four expressions and literals produce the four truth boxes and two truth-propagation boxes shown in figure 14.4. The first two assumptions, each of which contains a ⇒, provide the constraint expressions that determine how the truth-propagation boxes behave:

> *Require*   Happy(A) is false
>
>   *or*   Happy(B) is true
>
>   *or*   (Happy(A) ⇒ Happy(B)) is false
>
> *Require*   Happy(A) is true   *or*   (Happy(A) ⇒ Happy(B)) is true
>
> *Require*   Happy(B) is false   *or*   (Happy(A) ⇒ Happy(B)) is true
>
> *Require*   Happy(B) is false
>
>   *or*   Happy(C) is true
>
>   *or*   (Happy(B) ⇒ Happy(C)) is false
>
> *Require*   Happy(B) is true   *or*   (Happy(B) ⇒ Happy(C)) is true
>
> *Require*   Happy(C) is false   *or*   (Happy(B) ⇒ Happy(C)) is true

At this point, the truth-propagation boxes conclude that Happy(B) and Happy(C) are both true. Moreover, as truth propagation takes place,

Figure 14.4 Constraint expressions govern the propagation of truth values through truth boxes in a truth-propagation net.

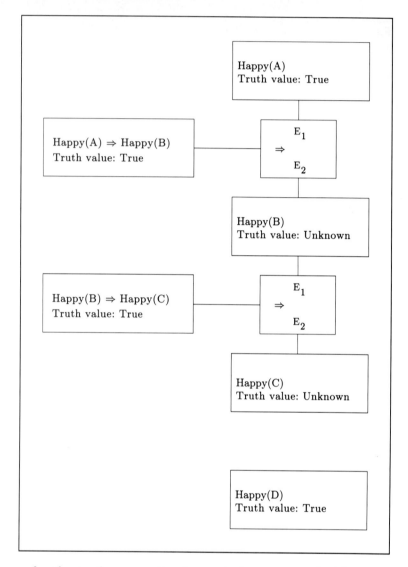

it is easy for the truth-propagation boxes to keep a record of how the truth values are determined. In the record, **justification links** point from each truth value to the truth-box values on which that truth value directly depends. The justification links for the example are shown in figure 14.5.

Justification Links Enable Programs to Change Their Minds

Now assume, tentatively, that C dislikes D, so if D is happy, C is not happy:

$$\text{Happy(D)} \Rightarrow \neg\text{Happy(C)}$$

This new expression produces two additional truth boxes and two additional truth-propagation boxes, as shown in figure 14.6.

Figure 14.5 Justification links indicate how each truth value is established.

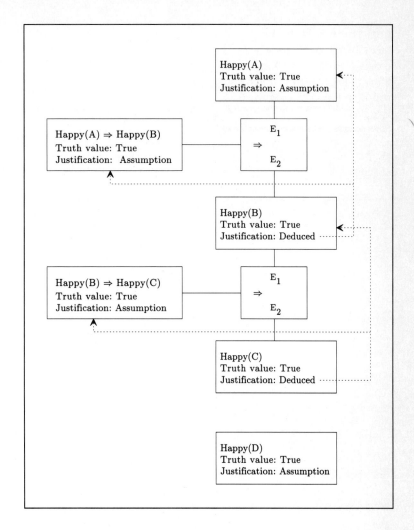

The constraint expressions for the $\Rightarrow$ truth-propagation box are as follows:

Require Happy(D) is false

      or ¬Happy(C) is true

      or (Happy(D) $\Rightarrow$ ¬Happy(C)) is false

Require Happy(D) is true *or* (Happy(D) $\Rightarrow$ ¬Happy(C)) is true

Require ¬Happy(C) is false *or* (Happy(D) $\Rightarrow$ ¬Happy(C)) is true

Here are the constraint expressions for the ¬ truth-propagation box:

      Require Happy(C) is true *or* ¬Happy(C) is true

      Require Happy(C) is false *or* ¬Happy(C) is false

Figure 14.6 Truth values move through a truth-propagation net from Happy(D) through implication and negation truth boxes to contradict Happy(C).

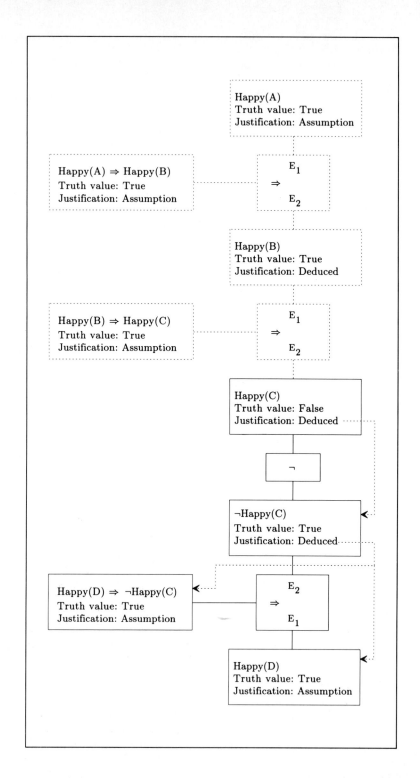

Note, however, that the enforcement of these new constraint expressions, by the corresponding truth-propagation boxes, leads to a contradiction. The first constraint expression of the $\Rightarrow$ set forces $\neg$Happy(C) to be true, because Happy(D) is true, rather than false, and because (Happy(D) $\Rightarrow$ $\neg$Happy(C)) is assumed to be true. But if $\neg$Happy(C) is true, then the second constraint expression of the $\neg$ set forces Happy(C) to be false, contradicting the previous conclusion that Happy(C) is true. Something is wrong.

Fortunately, however, the justification links make it easy to trace back from the truth value for Happy(C) to assumptions about A, D, and various happiness and lack-of-happiness influences.

Consequently, when something goes wrong—if one line of reasoning says something is true and another says that that something is false—it is possible to track down the assumptions that lead to the contradiction. Said another way, justification links enable you to use dependency-directed backtracking.

In the example, tracing back from the true value for C brings you to three assumptions:

$$\text{Happy(A)} \Rightarrow \text{Happy(B)}$$
$$\text{Happy(B)} \Rightarrow \text{Happy(C)}$$
$$\text{Happy(A)}$$

Tracing back from the false value for C leads to two more assumptions:

$$\text{Happy(D)} \Rightarrow \neg\text{Happy(C)}$$
$$\text{Happy(D)}$$

Having traced back to all the contributions to the contradiction, it is time to consider what should be done. One option is to withdraw Happy(A).

Once an assumption is withdrawn, it is easy to track down the consequences that depend on the withdrawn assumption so that they too can be withdrawn, if necessary. Sometimes, of course, more than one argument supports a conclusion, and withdrawing one of them leaves the conclusion intact.

Suppose, for example, that Happy(A) implies that another person, E, is happy. With Happy(A) withdrawn, Happy(E) might have to be withdrawn as well. However, suppose that Happy(D) also makes E happy, by operating through an $\vee$ constraint box, as shown in figure 14.7. With that second, independent way to show that Happy(E) is true, Happy(E) remains true, even when the assumption that Happy(A) is true is withdrawn.

Proof by Truth Propagation Has Limits

Truth propagation deals with propositional calculus only. Accordingly, you cannot use truth propagation to deal with expressions containing variables, unless the problem is such that there is a way to transform the variable-containing expressions into a finite number of variable-free expressions.

Figure 14.7 Given a second path establishing Happy(E), Happy(E) remains true after a critical assumption in the first path is withdrawn.

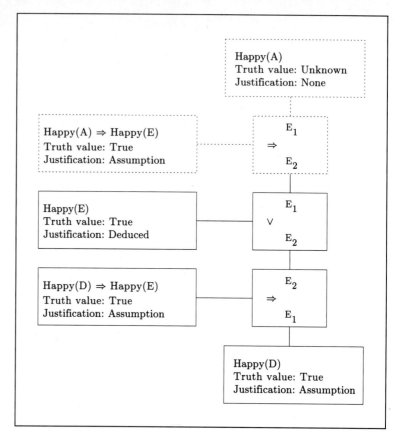

Also, it can be shown that truth propagation cannot prove all true expressions. Accordingly, truth propagation is not a complete proof procedure.

SUMMARY

- Numeric choices can lead to problems identified by limit boxes. Backing up over those choices chronologically can waste time prodigiously.
- Nonchronological backtracking focuses on dependencies, allowing you to zero in on those choices that actually make a difference.
- Using the constraint-propagation approach to logic, you can propagate truth values through nodes using constraints supplied by logical expressions. Sometimes, propagated truth values lead to inconsistencies that force you to withdraw an assumption.
- Using constraint propagation, you can easily keep track of justifications for all conclusions. These justifications make it easy for you to deal with withdrawn assumptions nonchronologically.

BACKGROUND

Mechanisms for nonchronological backtracking were originally developed when constraint propagation was applied to the problem of understanding electronic circuits. Because the transistors in a circuit may be in any of four states, there are many combinations of choices, most of which are incompatible. Finding the valid choice combinations using chronological backtracking is inconceivably tedious. This problem led Richard M. Stallman, in collaboration with Gerald J. Sussman, to invent nonchronological backtracking [1977].

The discussion of truth-maintenance ideas in the context of logic is based loosely on the work of David A. McAllester [1980].

15

Planning

In this chapter, you learn about two distinct approaches to planning a sequence of actions to achieve some goal. One way, the STRIPS approach, uses *if–add–delete operators* to work on a single collection of assertions. The other way, using logic, requires the introduction of *situation variables* and *frame axioms* that deal with linked collections of logical statements.

Both approaches are presented in this chapter; their differences and complementary strengths are highlighted through juxtaposition. Fortunately, however, you can study them independently, if you wish.

By way of illustration, you see how to plan simple blocks-world movement sequences.

First, you learn about the much more transparent STRIPS approach, and how you can use notions like *establishes* and *threatens* to prevent potentially interfering actions from destroying each other's work. Next, you learn that logic requires you to use *frame axioms* whenever you want to deal with a changing world.

PLANNING USING IF-ADD-DELETE OPERATORS

In the physical world, a **plan** is a prescription for a sequence of actions that, if followed, will change the relations among objects so as to achieve a desired goal. One way to represent a plan is by way of a sequence of assertion additions and deletions that reflect physical movements. Thus, the deletion of ON(A, C) and addition of ON(A, B) means move object A from object C to object B.

One way to create a plan is to search for a sequence of operators that lead from the assertions that describe the initial state of the world to assertions that describe your goal. In this section, you learn how to perform such a search.

Operators Specify Add Lists and Delete Lists

Figure 15.1 shows an example of an initial situation and a goal situation in which block A is on block B, and block B is on block C. A little more precisely, part of the initial situation description consists of the following axioms:

ON(A, C)
ON(C, Table)
ON(D, B)
ON(B, Table)

In addition, you need a way of expressing that two of the objects support nothing. One way is to introduce the idea that a block is clear, and hence is capable of having something placed on it only if there is nothing on it to start with. In contrast to the blocks world discussed in Chapter 3, here no block can directly support more than one other block. The axioms are

CLEAR(A)
CLEAR(D)

The goal is to arrange for the following to be part of the situation description:

ON(A, B)
ON(B, C)

For this particular example, you are to assume that nothing can be moved if it is supporting something; said another way, you cannot move x unless x's top is clear.

To plan, you need to capture what the various actions accomplish when they are actually deployed. One approach is to specify each action in terms of when it can be used, what new assertions it makes true, and what previous assertions it withdraws. These specifications can be packaged into if–add–delete rules, introduced previously in Chapter 7. In this chapter, some labels change in honor of the language that is used in the planning literature: In the context of planning, if–add–delete rules are called **operators** and the *if* conditions of each operator are called its **prerequisites**. Here is the description of an operator that describes the action of moving a block:

Figure 15.1 An initial
situation and a goal situation.

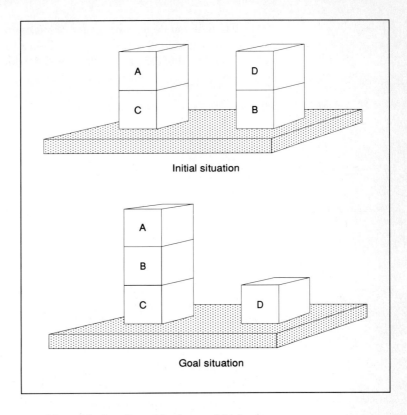

Operator 1: Move block x from block y to block z
    If: ON(x, y)
                     CLEAR(x)
                     CLEAR(z)
    Add list   ON(x, z)
                     CLEAR(y)
    Delete list: ON(x, y)
                     CLEAR(z)

Now suppose you instantiate the move-block-from-block-to-block operator
with x bound to block A, y to block C, and z to block D:

Operator 1: Move block A from block C to block D
    If: ON(A, C)
                     CLEAR(A)
                     CLEAR(D)
    Add list   ON(A, D)
                     CLEAR(C)
    Delete list: ON(A, C)
                     CLEAR(D)

Then, if you deploy this instantiated operator in the example's initial situation, you will alter the situation description such that it appears as follows, with two deleted assertions struck out and two new assertions at the end:

~~ON(A, C)~~
ON(C, Table)
ON(D, B)
ON(B, Table)
CLEAR(A)
~~CLEAR(D)~~
ON(A, D)
CLEAR(C)

You can, of course, move a block onto the table even though there are other blocks on the table already. Also, the table does not become clear when a block is moved off it. Accordingly, you need two extra operators specialized for movements in which the table is involved:

Operator 2: Move block x from block y to Table
If:	ON(x, y)
	CLEAR(x)
Add list	ON(x, Table)
	CLEAR(y)
Delete list:	ON(x, y)

Operator 3: Move block x from Table to block z
If:	ON(x, Table)
	CLEAR(x)
	CLEAR(z)
Add list	ON(x, z)
Delete list:	ON(x, Table)
	CLEAR(z)

You Can Plan by Searching for a Satisfactory Sequence of Operators

Once you have a problem description, planning is, in a certain silly sense, simple. You need only to try everything, using breadth-first search, where *try everything* means try every operator, instantiated in every possible way, as long as the operators' prerequisites are satisfied. If you use this strategy for the example, you discover a satisfactory plan after four moves, as demonstrated by the breadth-first search tree shown in figure 15.2.

Unfortunately, this approach forces you to fight a battle against exponential tree growth—a battle you would probably lose for any problem of practical size. For the example, you can manage, because there is a maximum of 12 branches under any node and because there is a solution after

Figure 15.2 A simple, but bad approach to planning. You try every possible operator sequence, using breadth-first search. The heavy line marks a plan that reaches the goal.

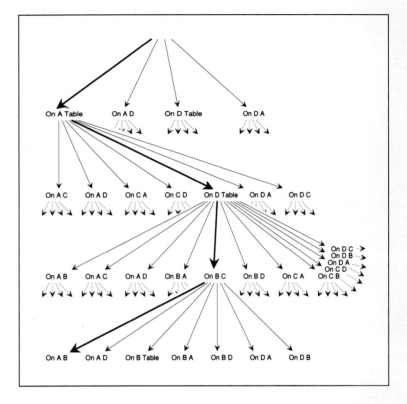

just four moves, but if you were to scatter, say, eight irrelevant two-block towers on the table, then there would be 100 alternatives for the first move alone.

Plainly, you need to be smarter about how to conduct a search for a suitable operator sequence.

Backward Chaining Can Reduce Effort

Usually, the goal is described by only a few assertions that must hold for a problem to be solved, whereas any full description of a situation involves many more assertions. Accordingly, you may want to chain backward through operators, rather than forward. To backward chain, you look for an operator that, when instantiated, has an *add* pattern that matches your goal. Then, if that operator's prerequisites are not satisfied, you backward chain through other operators until you reach assertions that describe the initial state of the world.

For example, consider that part of the example problem that requires block A to be on block B. For the moment, forget about getting block B on block C.

At the top of figure 15.3, you see the initial state on the left, the single goal assertion on the right, and an attempt to start bridging the gap between the two by moving block A from block C to block B. More specifically, an Establishes link extends from the ON(A, B) assertion in the add list of the instantiated movement operator to the ON(A, B) assertion in the goal description.

Moving block A from block C to block B is not the only choice, of course; it is just one of three possibilities, because block A could, in principle, come from block D or the table. If moving it to its goal position from block C does not work out, those other possibilities could be checked by breadth-first search.

Given that moving block A from block C to block B is the choice to be considered, two prerequisites have to be satisfied: both block A and block B must be clear. One way to clear block B is to move block D to the table. As shown in the middle of figure 15.3, this move links together two instantiated operators; an Establishes link joins the CLEAR(B) assertion in the add list of operator 2's instantiation to the CLEAR(B) prerequisite in operator 1's instantiation.

Again, satisfying the CLEAR(B) prerequisite using an instantiated operator that moves block D to the table is just one of many choices. In principle, any other block could be in the way.

Note that the Establishes link means that the operator that establishes an assertion must appear in the final plan before the operator that needs the assertion. The establisher does not need to appear right before the establishee, however. There may be other operators in between, as long as none of those interposed operators add or delete the established assertion.

Once block B is clear, no other operator is needed, for the remaining prerequisites of both operators are satisfied in the initial situation, as shown at the bottom of figure 15.3. Once again, this way of dealing with those prerequisites is not the only one. It is the direct way, and it is a reasonable way under the circumstances, but in principle, you could, for example, uselessly stall by moving block D on and off block B many times to create a longer bridge between the initial state and the movement of block A to block B.

Alternative choices have been mentioned frequently in this discussion to emphasize that search is involved. What you see in figure 15.3 is just one path through a search tree.

In general, a partial path may involve choices that cannot possibly lead to a workable plan because of devastating operator interactions. To see why, consider the full example, with a goal involving two assertions, ON(A, B) and ON(B, C), rather than only ON(A, B). If you temporarily ignored the second of the goal assertions, you could certainly make the choices that previously led to the placement of block A on block B, leading to the partial plan shown at the top of figure 15.4.

With the problem of moving A onto B solved, you could then attempt to enable the movement of B onto C by moving B from the table onto C.

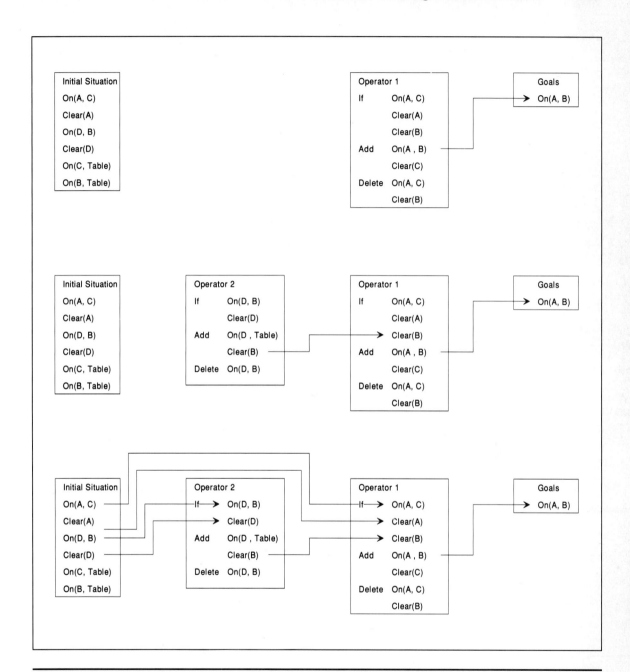

Figure 15.3 Three steps toward constructing a plan for achieving a simple goal using backward chaining. All links shown are Establishes links. Most of them tie an addition in one instantiated operator to a prerequisite in another instantiated operator, thus creating an ordering constraint between the two operators. Other Establishes links are connected to initial-situation assertions or goal assertions.

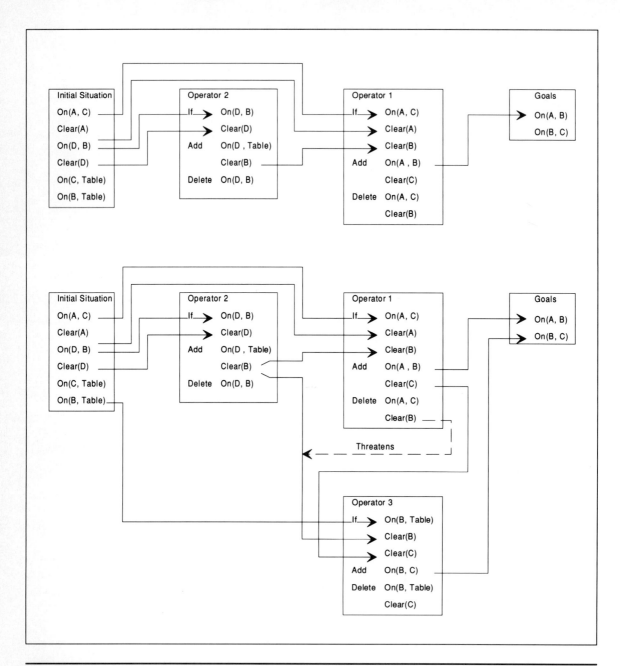

Figure 15.4 Construction of a plan for achieving two goal assertions using backward chaining. All links shown are Establishes links. The top portion deals with moving block A onto block B; the bottom portion adds an operation intended to move block B onto block C. The plan is flawed because operator 1 interferes with an Establishes link between operator 2 and operator 3.

Then, to satisfy the prerequisites required to move block B from the table onto block C, you have to be sure that both blocks are clear. At first glance, looking only at the diagram and forgetting about real blocks, you might think you could satisfy these prerequisites by taking advantage of the initial situation and the additions to it made by other operators. Using Establishes links to establish order, you might think you could move block D onto the table, move block A onto block B, and finally move block B onto block C. But too bad for first-glance looks: Moving block A onto block B interferes with moving block B anywhere.

Thus, you are faced with a major problem. As you try to add an assertion demanded by the prerequisites of one operator, you may withdraw an assertion that you added previously to satisfy a goal or to establish a prerequisite for another operator. Clearly, you need a method for detecting such interference as soon as possible, so that you can terminate useless partial plans without further work.

Impossible Plans Can Be Detected

Fortunately, it is easy to identify potential problems in the plan itself, without appealing to your knowledge of blocks. You simply monitor each Establishes link, checking for operators that could invalidate the link. When you find such a link-invalidating operator, you impose an additional ordering constraint that prevents the operator from doing any damage.

In the bottom of figure 15.4, for example, there is an Establishes link between operator 2 and operator 3, because operator 2 adds CLEAR(B) and operator 3 needs CLEAR(B). Operator 1 deletes CLEAR(B), however, and if operator 1 were allowed to occur after operator 2 and before operator 3, then operator 1 would invalidate the Establishes link. Accordingly, operator 1 is said to be a **threat** to the link.

To contain such threats, you need only to introduce an additional ordering constraint: The threatening operator must appear before the establisher or after the establishee, and may not appear between them. In the example, this constraint means that operator 1 must appear in the plan either before operator 2 or after operator 3.

Unfortunately, neither choice works, as shown by figure 15.5, in which implied Before links replace Establishes links, creating a kind of simple **ordering net**. As shown in the left portion of the figure, operator 1 cannot appear before operator 2, because the Establishes link from operator 2 to operator 1 has already established that operator 2 appears before operator 1. Similarly, as shown in the right portion of the figure, operator 3 cannot appear before operator 1, because an Establishes link from operator 1 to operator 3 has already established that operator 1 appears before operator 3. The only possible conclusion is that the choices made so far cannot lead to a workable plan.

The possibility of interference is not the certainty of interference, however. Consider figure 15.6. In the top portion, you see the initial state on

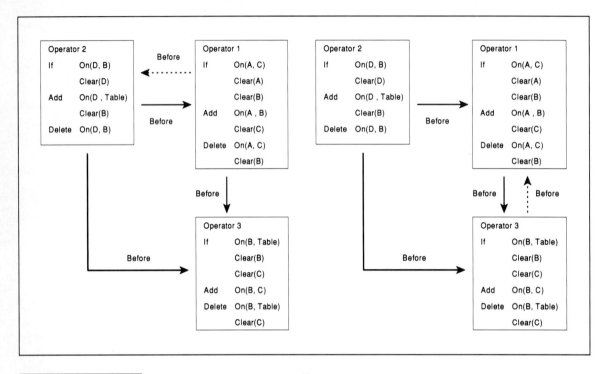

Figure 15.5 You can protect a threatened Establishes link by installing an additional Before link. Here, however, operator 1 cannot appear before operator 2, as in the left portion, or after operator 3, as in the right portion, without creating a Before loop.

the left, the goal assertions on the right. This time, the choice is to move block A from the table to block B, instead of from its initial resting place on block C. In the bottom portion, you see how the prerequisites of the operator that moves block A from the table can be satisfied by the assertions in the initial state augmented by assertions placed by one instantiation of operator 2 that moves block A from block C to the table, and by another instantiation of operator 2 that moves block D from block B to the table. At this point, there are no threats.

Although there are no threats, there is a question of how to get block B onto block C. One choice is to instantiate operator 3 again, as shown in the top portion of figure 15.7, thereby moving block B from the table, where it lies initially. Following that choice, you need only to decide how to satisfy the prerequisites that require block B to be on the table and both block B and block C to have clear tops. One set of choices is shown in the bottom portion of figure 15.7.

Note, however, that there is, once again, a threat to which you must attend. Operator 3a, the first of the two instantiations of operator 3, deletes the CLEAR(B) assertion that operator 2a adds and that operator 3b needs. Thus, operator 3a threatens the Establishes link between operator 2a and operator 3b. Evidently, operator 3a must be placed before operator 2a or after operator 3b. Plainly, operator 3a cannot be placed before operator 2a, because operator 2a establishes one of operator 3a's prerequisites.

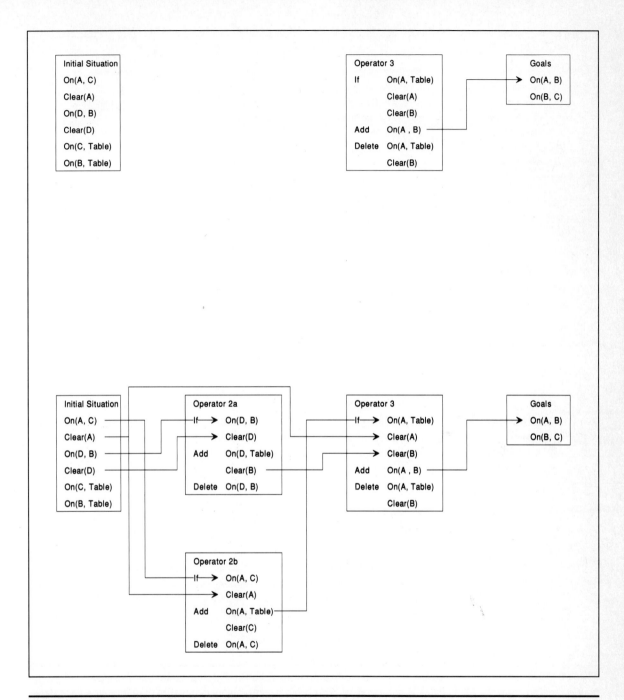

Figure 15.6 In the top portion, planning begins with an instantiation of operator 3; in the bottom, two instantiations of operator 2 are added to deal with operator 3's prerequisites.

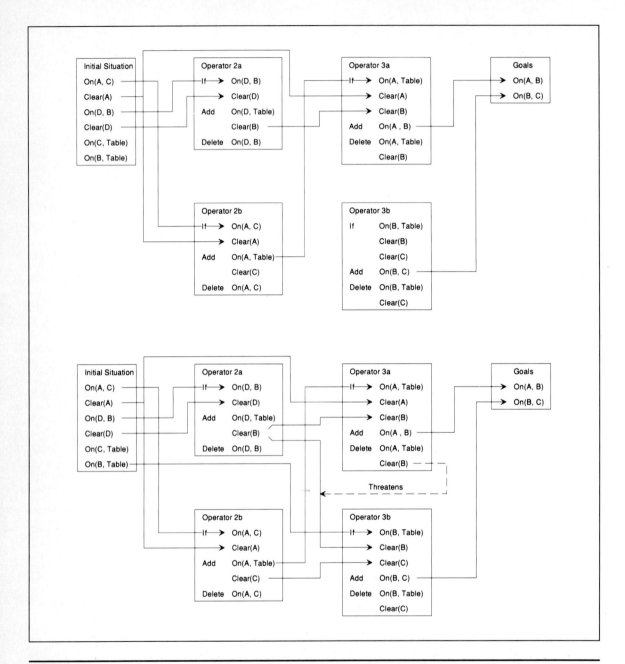

Figure 15.7 Completion of a plan for achieving two goal assertions. The top portion shows how work might start on the problem of getting block B onto block C. The bottom portion shows how the plan might be completed by addition of operator 3b, which is a second instantiation of operator 3. Because of the addition, operator 3a threatens the Establishes link that extends from operator 2a to operator 3b.

Figure 15.8 You can protect the threatened Establishes link shown in figure 15.7 by installing an additional Before link. Here, a new Before link forcing operator 3b to occur before operator 3a prevents trouble.

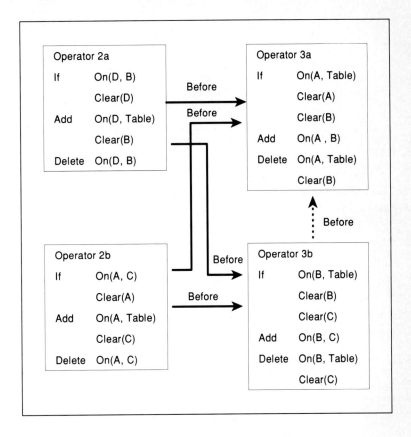

Fortunately, as shown in figure 15.8, operator 3a can be after operator 3b without creating any impossible chain of Before links.

The plan shown in the bottom of figure 15.8 is called a **complete plan** because all goal assertions are asserted, all operator prerequisites are satisfied, and the implied Before links form no loops. A **partial plan** is any other plan in which the implied Before links form no loops.

Note that a complete plan does not completely specify an exact ordering of steps. Block A can be moved to the table before block D, or vice versa, whichever you like:

Plan 1	Plan 2
Move A to the table	Move D to the table
Move D to the table	Move A to the table
Move B to C	Move B to C
Move A to B	Move A to B

At this point, you might wonder whether there is always at least one way to write out a sequence of operators consistent with the ordering constraints implied by a complete plan's Establishes links, forming a **linear plan**. Be comforted: A version of the topological sorting procedure, introduced in Chapter 9, always can produce at least one linear plan from each complete plan.

In summary, the procedure for constructing a plan is a search procedure that extends partial plans until one is complete:

To construct a plan,

▷ Extend a partial plan containing no operators until you discover a satisfactory complete plan.

To extend a partial plan,

▷ If the plan has a Before loop, announce failure.

▷ If the plan is a complete plan, announce success.

  ▷ If there is an operator that threatens an Establishes link between operators o_1 and o_2, call the threat o_t, and do one of the following:

    ▷ Place a Before link from o_t to o_1 and extend the plan.

    ▷ Place a Before link from o_2 to o_t and extend the plan.

  ▷ Otherwise, pick an unsatisfied prerequisite, and do one of the following:

    ▷ Find an existing operator that adds the unsatisfied prerequisite, install an Establishes link, and extend the plan.

    ▷ Instantiate and add an operator that adds the unsatisfied prerequisite and extend the plan.

Partial Instantiation Can Help Reduce Effort Too

Even with backward chaining, extra blocks scattered here and there are a nuisance. In the example, block A does not need to be parked on the table while you arrange for block B to be on block C. It could be parked on any block other than block B or block C, thus increasing the branching involved in your search with each addition of a new block.

One way to cope with this sort of branching is to instantiate operators only insofar as necessary. To see how you do that, suppose that you have one additional block on the table, block E. Further suppose that you decide to move block A from a parking block to block B, rather than from the table. This decision can lead to another decision between two full instantiations of operator 1:

Operator 1, full instantiation 1
 If: ON(A, D)
       CLEAR(A)
       CLEAR(B)
 Add list   ON(A, B)
       CLEAR(D)
 Delete list: ON(A, D)
       CLEAR(B)

Operator 1, full instantiation 2
 If: ON(A, E)
       CLEAR(A)
       CLEAR(B)
 Add list   ON(A, B)
       CLEAR(E)
 Delete list: ON(A, E)
       CLEAR(B)

Alternatively, you could limit instantiation to x and z, placing just one, partially instantiated operator, with a fresh variable to avoid variable confusion, into the plan:

Operator 1, partial instantiation 1
 If: ON(A, y_1)
       CLEAR(A)
       CLEAR(B)
 Add list   ON(A, B)
       CLEAR(y_1)
 Delete list: ON(A, y_1)
       CLEAR(B)

Then, you can deal with the prerequisites of this partially instantiated operator using another partially instantiated operator, with another fresh variable, to get block A from block C to wherever it is supposed to go:

Operator 1, partial instantiation 2
 If: ON(A, C)
       CLEAR(A)
       CLEAR(z_1)
 Add list   ON(A, z_1)
       CLEAR(C)
 Delete list: ON(A, C)
       CLEAR(z_1)

Note that you do not need to decide on bindings for y_1 or z_1 to be sure that the two operators work together; you need only to insist that they are bound to the same thing.

This idea of partial instantiation is a special case of a generally good idea:

The **principle of least commitment**:

▷ When there is uncertainty about what commitment is right, commit to as little as possible.

You still search, and so you are still vulnerable to the tyranny of exponential tree growth, but you fight back with an approach that reduces the branching factor enormously.

PLANNING USING SITUATION VARIABLES

In ordinary logic, once a statement has been shown to be true, that statement cannot become false, because ordinary logic does not deal with the passage of time. Accordingly, it would seem that logic would have trouble supporting the development of a plan of action, for each action in a plan surely must make something true that was not true, or make something not true that was true.

One way to wiggle out of this apparent dilemma, as you learn in this section, is to think in terms of a sequence of situations, with each action taking one situation to the next in the sequence. Accordingly, it may be that block A is on block B initially, so $\text{ON}(A, B)$ is true in situation s_i; but then block A can be put on the table, creating a new situation, s_{i+1}, in which $\neg \text{ON}(A, B)$ is true. Thus, the truth of $\text{ON}(A, B)$ may change from situation to situation, but within each situation, no time passes, nothing changes, and $\text{ON}(A, B)$ is either true or false.

Finding Operator Sequences Requires Situation Variables

The ideas in this section are more difficult to understand than are those in most of this book. Accordingly, the example is even simpler than usual, so that distracting clutter is minimized. Instead of moving a block from one support to another, the task is to put a clear block on the table, as suggested in figure 15.9.

Clearly, $\text{ON}(A, B)$ is not true in the initial situation of the problem world, but it could be true in other situations with different block arrangements. Consequently, it is incomplete to say that some expression is true; to be complete, you must specify the situation in which it is true.

You could do the necessary bookkeeping by indicating the expressions that are known to be true in various situations, such as the following:

Initial situation   Final situation
$\text{ON}(B, A) \& \text{ON}(A, \text{Table})$ $\text{ON}(B, \text{Table}) \& \text{ON}(A, \text{Table})$

Figure 15.9 A simple initial situation and final situation involving blocks. The problem is to find a sequence of operators that transforms the initial situation into the final situation.

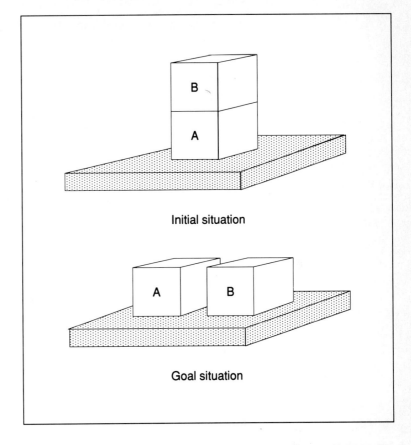

Initial situation

Goal situation

A better alternative is to add a situation argument to the predicates. To say that block B is on block A in situation S, the initial situation, and block A is on the table, you insert S as the value of an extra argument:

$$\text{ON}(B, A, S) \& \text{ON}(A, \text{Table}, S)$$

Note that the initial situation, S, is a known, constant situation, not an unknown, variable situation. Hence, an upper-case Roman character is used.

What you want is a final situation, s_f, such that block B is on the table:

$$\exists s_f [\text{ON}(B, \text{Table}, s_f)]$$

Note that s_f is an unknown, variable situation, not a known, constant situation. Hence, you use a lower-case italic character.

Now imagine an operation, STORE, that changes situations by putting an object on the table. More specifically, STORE takes two arguments, x and s_i, and produces a new situation, s_{i+1}, in which $\text{ON}(x, \text{Table})$ is true. Thus, STORE's value is a situation, and STORE must be a function, rather than a predicate, because a predicates's values are either true or false.

Because STORE's value is a situation, STORE can appear as the situation argument in an ON expression. In fact, STORE can be defined this way:

$$\forall s \forall x [\neg \text{ON}(x, \text{Table}, s) \Rightarrow \text{ON}(x, \text{Table}, \text{STORE}(x, s))]$$

To use this definition, you need a way to know when something is not on the table. Clearly, something is not on the table if it is on something that is not the table. This expression says the same thing:

$$\forall s \forall y \forall z [\text{ON}(y, z, s) \& \neg \text{Equal}(z, \text{Table}) \Rightarrow \neg \text{ON}(y, \text{Table}, s)]$$

Now you can use what you know to show that there is a way to move block B onto the table. You simply add the definition of STORE and the not-on-table expression to the list of axioms, and turn the resolution crank. The initial axioms are

$$\text{ON}(B, A, S) \& \text{ON}(A, \text{Table}, S)$$

$$\forall s \forall x [\neg \text{ON}(x, \text{Table}, s) \Rightarrow \text{ON}(x, \text{Table}, \text{STORE}(x, s))]$$

$$\forall s \forall y \forall z [\text{ON}(y, z, s) \& \neg \text{Equal}(z, \text{Table}) \Rightarrow \neg \text{ON}(y, \text{Table}, s)]$$

The desired expression, the theorem, is

$$\exists s_f [\text{ON}(B, \text{Table}, s_f)]$$

Now, negating the desired expression, you have

$$\neg \exists s_f [\text{ON}(B, \text{Table}, s_f)]$$

Moving the negation down to the atomic formula, you have

$$\forall s_f [\neg \text{ON}(B, \text{Table}, s_f)]$$

Adding this expression to the list of axioms, larding with some expressions about object–object equality, putting everything in clause form, and taking care to use unique variables in each clause, you have

$$\text{ON}(B, A, S) \tag{1}$$

$$\text{ON}(A, \text{Table}, S) \tag{2}$$

$$\text{ON}(x, \text{Table}, s_3) \lor \text{ON}(x, \text{Table}, \text{STORE}(x, s_3)) \tag{3}$$

$$\neg \text{ON}(y, z, s_4) \lor \text{Equal}(z, \text{Table}) \lor \neg \text{ON}(y, \text{Table}, s_4) \tag{4}$$

$$\neg \text{Equal}(B, A) \tag{5}$$

$$\neg \text{Equal}(B, \text{Table}) \tag{6}$$

$$\neg \text{Equal}(A, \text{Table}) \tag{7}$$

$$\neg \text{ON}(B, \text{Table}, s_f) \tag{8}$$

Note that subscripted variables, such as s_3, have been used, rather than new letters. This convention helps you to remember that these variables all represent situations. To avoid repeating a subscript by accident, you use subscripts that correspond to the clause number.

From here, proof is easy, as shown by figure 15.10. You can resolve clause 3 and clause 8, using $\{x \rightarrow B; s_f \rightarrow \text{STORE}(x, s_3)\}$, producing the following, after renaming the variable:

$$\text{ON}(B, \text{Table}, s_9) \tag{9}$$

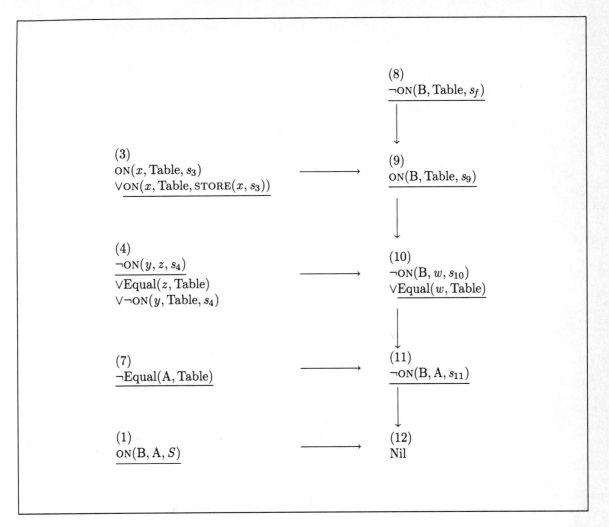

Now you work with clause 9 and clause 4, using $\{y \rightarrow B; s_4 \rightarrow s_9\}$ and renaming the variables:

$$\neg \text{ON}(B, w, s_{10}) \lor \text{Equal}(w, \text{Table}) \tag{10}$$

Resolving clause 10 with clause 7, using $\{w \rightarrow A\}$ and renaming, you get the following:

$$\neg \text{ON}(B, A, s_{11}) \tag{11}$$

Finishing by resolving clause 11 with clause 1, using $\{s_{11} \rightarrow S\}$, you have Nil, the empty clause:

$$\text{Nil} \tag{12}$$

But you know only that it is possible to have a situation where block B is on the table. You do not know how to reach that situation. Knowledge about how to get where you want to be is implicitly locked into all the unifications, however. Looking back over what you have done, you see this sequence of substitutions:

$$s_f \rightarrow \text{STORE}(\text{B}, s_3)$$
$$s_3 \rightarrow s_9$$
$$s_9 \rightarrow s_{10}$$
$$s_{10} \rightarrow s_{11}$$
$$s_{11} \rightarrow \text{S}$$

Plugging through all the substitutions, evidently the desired situation, s_f, is the situation you get to by using the STORE operation on block B in the initial situation, S.

Tracing the situation history is a tedious, error-provoking chore for problems involving many operations. Consequently, the usual practice is to use something called **Green's trick**. The basic idea is to add an extra term to the negation of the desired result. This extra term, called the **answer term**, exploits the ordinary unification apparatus to keep track of situation information. Instead of $\neg\text{ON}(\text{B}, \text{Table}, s_f)$, you write $\neg\text{ON}(\text{B}, \text{Table}, s_f) \lor \text{Answer}(s_f)$. Let us then repeat the steps in the proof:

$$\neg\text{ON}(\text{B}, \text{Table}, s_f) \lor \text{Answer}(s_f) \tag{8}$$
$$\text{ON}(\text{B}, \text{Table}, s_9) \lor \text{Answer}(\text{STORE}(\text{B}, s_9)) \tag{9}$$
$$\neg\text{ON}(\text{B}, w, s_{10}) \lor \text{Equal}(w, \text{Table}) \lor \text{Answer}(\text{STORE}(\text{B}, s_{10})) \tag{10}$$
$$\neg\text{ON}(\text{B}, \text{A}, s_{11}) \lor \text{Answer}(\text{STORE}(\text{B}, s_{11})) \tag{11}$$
$$\text{Answer}(\text{STORE}(\text{B}, \text{S})) \tag{12}$$

Note that, because Answer is inserted only once, without negation, into the axioms, it can never appear negated. Consequently, the Answer term can never be the basis of a resolution. On the other hand, it is carried along with every clause that can be traced to the desired situation through a series of resolutions. Moreover, Answer's argument is always a record of the situation changes involved in the series of resolutions endured.

Of course, instead of terminating when you have Nil, you now terminate when you have a clause containing only Answer. The resolution steps are shown in figure 15.11. The revised resolution procedure is as follows.

To prove a single-literal existentially quantified theorem using resolution with Green's trick,

▷ Negate the theorem, convert it to clause form, and add the answer term.

▷ Put the list of axioms into clause form. Add the clause derived from the theorem and the answer term.

▷ Until a clause with only the answer term is produced or there is no resolvable pair of clauses,

  ▷ Find resolvable clauses.

  ▷ Resolve them.

  ▷ Add the results of resolution to the list of clauses.

  ▷ If a clause with only the answer term is produced, report that the sequence of operations in the answer term is the required answer. If there are no resolvable clauses, report that the required action cannot be done.

This procedure can be generalized to handle proofs for theorems with multiple literals and universal quantification.

Frame Axioms Address the Frame Problem

Now suppose you try a problem similar to the previous one, but requiring both block B and block A to be on the table in the final situation. That is, the goal is

$$\exists s_f [\text{ON}(B, \text{Table}, s_f) \& \text{ON}(A, \text{Table}, s_f)]$$

You know that the same operation, putting block B on the table, suffices. After all, block A is already on the table. To prove that putting block B on the table suffices, you negate and transform to clause form, as shown in the following step:

$$\neg \exists s_f [\text{ON}(B, \text{Table}, s_f) \& \text{ON}(A, \text{Table}, s_f)]$$
$$\forall s_f [\neg (\text{ON}(B, \text{Table}, s_f) \& \text{ON}(A, \text{Table}, s_f))]$$
$$\forall s_f [\neg \text{ON}(B, \text{Table}, s_f) \lor \neg \text{ON}(A, \text{Table}, s_f)]$$
$$\neg \text{ON}(B, \text{Table}, s_f) \lor \neg \text{ON}(A, \text{Table}, s_f)$$

The last expression is the one to number and to add to the axioms:

$$\neg \text{ON}(B, \text{Table}, s_f) \lor \neg \text{ON}(A, \text{Table}, s_f) \tag{8}$$

Using $\{x \to B; s_f \to \text{STORE}(x, s_3)\}$ and renaming, as in the previous proof, you can resolve clause 3 and clause 8, producing clause 9.

$$\text{ON}(B, \text{Table}, s_9) \lor \neg \text{ON}(A, \text{Table}, \text{STORE}(B, s_9)) \tag{9}$$

Using clause 9 and clause 4, with the substitution $\{y \to B; s_4 \to s_9\}$ and renaming:

$$\neg \text{ON}(B, w, s_{10}) \lor \text{Equal}(w, \text{Table}) \lor \neg \text{ON}(A, \text{Table}, \text{STORE}(B, s_{10})) \tag{10}$$

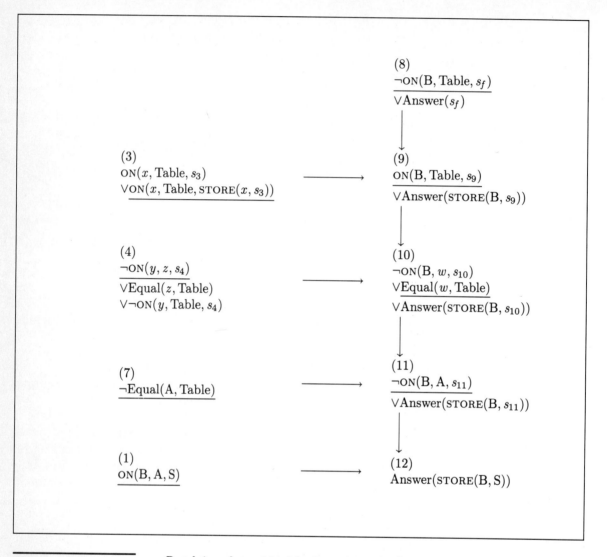

Figure 15.11 You append an answer term to the goal expression to keep track of the situation-change operations using the standard unification apparatus.

Resolving clause 10 with clause 7, using $\{w \to A\}$ and renaming, you get

$$\neg\text{ON}(B, A, s_{11}) \vee \neg\text{ON}(A, \text{Table}, \text{STORE}(B, s_{11})) \qquad (11)$$

Finishing by resolving clause 11 with clause 1, using $\{s_{11} \to S\}$, you have:

$$\neg\text{ON}(A, \text{Table}, \text{STORE}(B, S)) \qquad (12)$$

At this point, you may be tempted to resolve clause 12 with clause 2, ON(A, Table, S). That would be a terrible blunder, however, for resolving these two would require the substitution $\{S \to \text{STORE}(B, S)\}$. But S is a situation, rather than a variable, so no such substitution is possible.

At first, this prohibition may seem strange, for if block A is on the table in the initial situation, surely it remains on the table after block B is put on the table too. You know block A stays put, but your knowledge is not in the logic. The STORE axiom says what happens to the object being moved, but it does not say what happens to other objects. Without knowing more, there is no way to know which predicate's values are unchanged in going from one situation to another. After all, some do change. This dilemma is known as the **frame problem**.

Consequently, to get both block B and block A on the table, you need to inform your resolution theorem prover about preserved relations. One popular way to do this is to introduce **frame axioms**. A frame axiom is a statement about how predicates survive operations. Here is one explaining how ON survives STORE:

$$\forall s \forall x \forall y \forall z [\text{ON}(x, y, s) \& \neg \text{Equal}(x, z) \Rightarrow \text{ON}(x, y, \text{STORE}(z, s))]$$

In English, this expression says that if x is on y before a STORE operation, then x remains on y afterward, as long as x was not the object put on the table.

Now, converting the frame axiom to clause form, and changing the variable names as required, you have this frame axiom:

$$\neg \text{ON}(p, q, s_0) \vee \text{Equal}(p, r) \vee \text{ON}(p, q, \text{STORE}(r, s_0)) \tag{0}$$

Remember that you were stuck in the proof at the point where you had

$$\neg \text{ON}(A, \text{Table}, \text{STORE}(B, S)) \tag{12}$$

But now you are no longer stuck, for the new frame axiom comes to the rescue. Using the substitutions $\{p \rightarrow A; q \rightarrow \text{Table}; r \rightarrow B; s_0 \rightarrow S\}$ to resolve clause 12 with clause 0, you have

$$\neg \text{ON}(A, \text{Table}, S) \vee \text{Equal}(A, B) \tag{13}$$

Quickly resolving clause 13 with clause 5 and the result, clause 14, with clause 2, you obtain Nil, completing the proof:

$$\neg \text{ON}(A, \text{Table}, S) \tag{14}$$

$$\text{Nil} \tag{15}$$

If you desire, you can use Green's trick again, producing the required operator sequence.

At this point, you have managed to get two blocks on the table, but it took quite a bit of doing. In general, the approach illustrated requires a baggage of not-equal axioms and frame axioms. You need one not-equal axiom for each pair of distinct objects, and you need one frame axiom for most predicate–operator pairs.

SUMMARY

- When following the STRIPS approach to planning, you deal with operators that consist of prerequisites, add lists, and delete lists.
- Planning can be viewed as a matter of searching for operator sequences that lead to a collection of desired assertions.

- Like any search process, planning is expensive. Accordingly, it is important to detect when a partial plan cannot be completed. It is also helpful to limit instantiation to those variables for which instantiation is necessary.
- When following an approach to planning derived from logic, you deal with operators expressed as logical implications.
- Using logical deduction to search for operator sequences requires you to keep track of situations. The usual method is to annotate predicates with situation-denoting arguments.
- Once situation-denoting arguments are introduced, you need a method to keep track of those predicates whose values are unchanged as operators are applied. Using frame axioms is one approach.
- When there is uncertainty about what commitment is right, commit to as little as possible.

BACKGROUND

The pioneering STRIPS problem solver was developed largely by Richard E. Fikes, Nils J. Nilsson, and Peter Hart [Fikes and Nilsson 1971]. The discussion of STRIPS-based planning in this chapter is based on an idea conceived by David A. McAllester [McAllester and David Rosenblitt 1991], which is closely related to an idea introduced by Austin Tate [1977].

   C. Cordell Green introduced situation variables and Green's trick into logic in his influential thesis, making it possible to derive operator sequences [1969]. Green's thesis also introduced the idea of logic programming.

Part II
Learning and
Regularity
Recognition

In Part II, you learn about two kinds of learning. The first kind of learning is based on coupling new information to previously acquired knowledge. Usually, a great deal of reasoning is involved.

In Chapter 16, **Learning by Analyzing Differences**, you learn how it is possible to deploy *induction heuristics*, such as *require-link* and *drop-link*, to analyze the differences that appear in a sequence of observations. The induction heuristics make it possible to use *near misses* to learn about arches. You also learn about *felicity conditions*, which are the implied covenants between teachers and students that make learning possible.

In Chapter 20, **Learning by Managing Multiple Models**, you learn about an elegant way to use positive and negative examples to create a *version space*, which in turn helps you to zero in on what it takes to be a member of a class. You see that there may be no need for negative examples to be near-miss examples if it is possible to keep track of many descriptions.

In Chapter 17, **Learning by Explaining Experience**, you learn how it is possible to *learn from experience* by working exercises. In particular, you learn about MACBETH, a procedure that works on précis of Shakespeare's plays, performing one kind of *explanation-based learning*. You also see how MACBETH learns to relate *form and function*, learning what cups look like from a functional definition, from prior knowledge of other objects, and from a physical description of a particular cup.

In Chapter 18, **Learning by Correcting Mistakes**, you learn how a procedure can *repair previously acquired knowledge* by exploiting its own errors. In particular, you learn how a knowledge-repair program deals with a model that incorrectly allows pails to be identified as cups. The program notes that pails are not cups, that cups have to be oriented, that fixed handles enable orientation, and that cups therefore have to have fixed handles, not hinged ones.

A second kind of learning is based on digging useful regularity out of data, a practice sometimes referred to as *database mining*.

In Chapter 19, **Learning by Recording Cases**, you see how to *learn by recording situations as is*, doing nothing to the information in those situations until they are used. You learn about the *consistency heuristic*, and you learn how it is possible to find nearest neighbors in a feature space quickly using K-D *trees*.

In Chapter 21, **Learning by Building Identification Trees**, you read about the most widely used learning method—a method by which tests are assembled into an *identification tree*. You also learn how an identification tree can be transformed into a *perspicuous set of antecedent-consequent rules*.

In Chapter 22, **Learning by Training Neural Nets**, you see how *neuronlike elements, arranged in nets*, can be used to recognize instances of patterns, and you learn how neural nets can learn using the *back-propagation procedure*.

In Chapter 23, **Learning by Training Perceptrons**, you learn about *perceptrons*, which can be viewed as a special kind of neural net, and you learn about the remarkable *perceptron convergence procedure*, which is guaranteed to find a set of perceptron weights to solve a given problem if such a set of weights exists.

In Chapter 24, **Learning by Training Approximation Nets**, you learn about *interpolation and approximation nets*, which also can be viewed as a special case of the general notion of neural net. Interpolation and approximation nets are completely general, and are capable of anything a multilayer neural net can do; yet they have only two layers of nodes.

In Chapter 25, **Learning by Simulating Evolution**, you learn how search can be done using procedures that are inspired by natural evolution. These procedures, commonly called *genetic algorithms*, rest on ideas that are analogous, in some ways, to *individuals, mating, chromosome crossover, gene mutation, fitness*, and *natural selection*. You also learn that one way to avoid entrapment by local maxima is to populate them, rather than to wonder how to escape from them.

16

Learning by Analyzing Differences

In this chapter, you learn how it is possible to learn by analyzing the differences that appear in a sequence of observations. Along the way, you learn about *induction heuristics* that enable procedures to learn *class descriptions* from *positive and negative examples*. These induction heuristics make it possible, for example, to learn that an arch consists of one brick that must be supported by two others that must not touch each other.[†] Among the heuristics needed are the *require-link* and *forbid-link* heuristics, which enable learning about classes from *near-miss* examples that miss being class members for a small number of reasons.

You also learn about *felicity conditions*, which are the implied covenants between teachers and students that make learning possible.

By way of illustration, you learn about a simple learning program that expects a cooperative teacher to present carefully chosen examples, one after another. The procedure learns whatever it can from each example as the example is presented, and then forgets the example forever.

Once you have finished this chapter, you will have accumulated an armamentarium of induction heuristics, and you will have an understanding of the covenants that must hold between a teacher and a student. You will be able to use these ideas not only to build learning programs, but also to make yourself a more perceptive student and a more effective teacher.

[†]Properly speaking, one brick supported by two others is a lintel and pair of posts; for our purpose, however, that is just a nugatory detail.

Figure 16.1 A sequence of positive examples and near-miss negative examples for learning about arches.

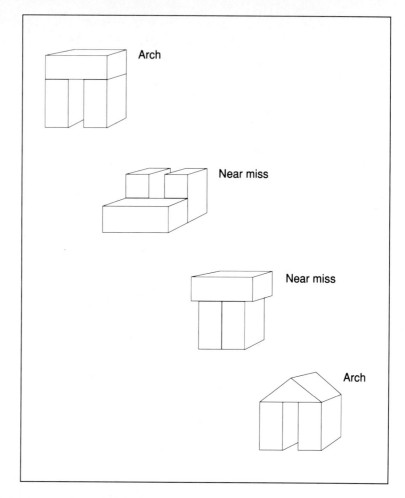

INDUCTION HEURISTICS

Induction occurs when you use particular examples to reach general conclusions. In this section, you learn about the **induction heuristics** used by a procedure, W, that learns about arches from the Arch and nonArch sequence shown in figure 16.1. You also learn about several powerful learning ideas that apply to human learning, as well as computer learning.

From the first example in figure 16.1, procedure W derives a general idea of what an arch is. In particular procedure W learns that an arch consists of two standing bricks that support a lying brick.

Each subsequent example drives home another point. In the second example, procedure W sees the same objects as before, but in a different configuration. Told that the pieces are not an arch, procedure W takes the example to be a **negative example**, and concludes that the support links must be an important aspect of the general arch concept. Note that the idea is conveyed by a single, well-chosen negative example, rather than by extended, tedious training exercises.

In the third example, the two standing bricks touch. Again, procedure W is told that the structure is not an arch. Nothing else is significantly different from the first arch in the example sequence. Evidently, the standing bricks must not touch if there is to be an arch. Procedure W makes progress once again by way of a good negative example.

A teacher may or may not claim the fourth example is an arch, according to personal taste. If it is given as an arch, then procedure W notes that having a brick on top is not essential. At the very least, either a brick or a wedge will do; procedure W may even guess that any simple parallelepiped is acceptable.

Responding to Near Misses Improves Models

To do its job, procedure W needs to start with a typical member of the class to be learned. From that example, procedure W constructs an **initial description**, as shown in figure 16.2(a). During learning, the initial description is augmented by information indicating which links are important. The augmented description is called the **evolving model**.

A **near miss** is a negative example that, for a small number of reasons, is not an instance of the class being taught. The description shown in figure 16.2(b) is not a description of an arch, but, because it is only a little different from the arch description in figure 16.2(a), it is a **near miss**. Its purpose is to teach the importance of the Support links.

Because the Support links are missing, comparing the two descriptions leads procedure W to the conclusion that arches require Support links. Thus, procedure W synthesizes the two descriptions into a new, refined description in which the Support links are replaced by the emphatic form, Must-support, as in figure 16.2(c). Used in this way, the near miss is said to supply information for the **require-link** heuristic. After procedure W uses the require-link heuristic, no group of blocks is identified as an arch unless Support links are in place.

Note that the two missing Support links associated with the near miss in figure 16.2(b) receive identical treatment. Generally, procedure W uses only one difference—either the only one or the one procedure W decides is most important. Sometimes, however, two or more differences are so similar, that they are handled as though they were just one difference. Procedure W's reaction is to suppose that the teacher intended the two differences to be handled in the same way. Thus, both Support links are replaced by Must-support.

The next comparison, the one between the evolving model in figure 16.3(a) and the near-miss in figure 16.3(b), also involves two similar differences because two new Touch links lie between the arch's sides. Now, however, the near miss fails to be an arch because links are present

Figure 16.2 The require-link generalization rule. Compared with the Arch description in (a), the near-miss description in (b) lacks Support links. The conclusion is that Support links are essential, so the Support links in the Arch model are altered, indicating that they are required in all arches, as shown in (c). The Left-of link is shown to emphasize the need for evidence that is sufficient to establish the correct correspondence between the parts of the arch and the parts of the near miss. Many links have been omitted from the drawing to prevent distraction from those that matter.

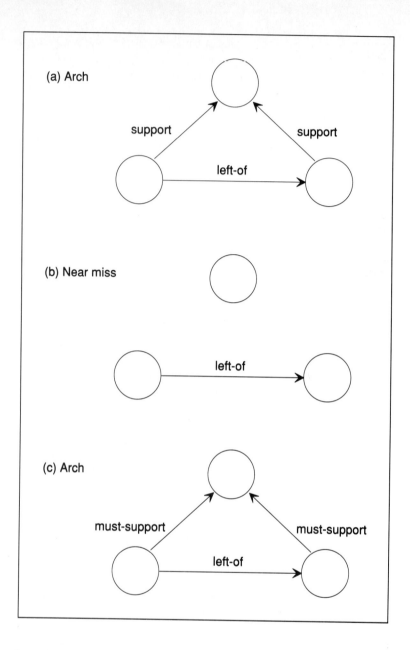

rather than absent. Procedure W concludes that the new links should be forbidden, and converts each Touch link to the negative emphatic link, Must-not-touch, as shown in figure 16.3(c). In so doing, procedure W is said to make use of the **forbid-link** heuristic.

Note that the require-link and forbid-link heuristics work because the descriptions contain essential information and because description compar-

Figure 16.3 The forbid-link generalization rule. Compared with the Arch description in part (a), the near-miss description in part (b) differs because it has Touch links. The conclusion is that the Touch links must not be present, so Must-not-touch links are added to the Arch description as shown in part (c). Many links have been omitted from the drawing to prevent distraction from those that matter.

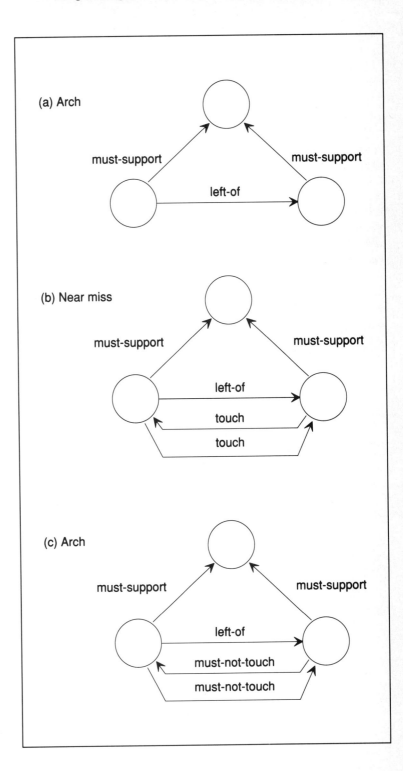

ison provides a way of zeroing in on the proper conclusions. These points bear elevation to principles:

You cannot learn if you cannot know.

▷ Good teachers help their students by being sure that their students acquire the necessary representations.

You cannot learn if you cannot isolate what is important.

▷ Good teachers help their students by providing not only positive examples, but also negative examples and near misses.

Responding to Examples Improves Models

So far, both near-miss examples *restrict* the model, limiting what can be an arch. Positive examples *relax* the model, expanding what can be an arch. Consider the situation of figure 16.4. Compared to the evolving model in figure 16.4(a), the example configuration in figure 16.4(b) has a wedge on top instead of a brick. If this is to be an arch, procedure W must make a change in the model that reflects a loosened constraint. At the very least, procedure W should cut the Is-a connection between the top of the arch and Brick, and replace that connection by a Must-be-a link to a more general class, as shown in figure 16.4(c). Procedure W is said to use the **climb-tree** heuristic.

Using the most specific common class is only one alternative, however. In the example, replacing Brick by Block represents a conservative position with respect to how much generalization procedure W should do, because bricks and wedges are also polyhedra, physical objects, and things. The new target for the top's Must-be-a link could be anything along the chain of Ako links, depending on how aggressive procedure W is to be.

Sometimes, however, there is no classification tree to climb. For example, if bricks and wedges were not known to be members of any common class, the climb-tree heuristic would not be of any use. In such a case, procedure W forms a new class, the Brick-or-wedge class, and joins the top part of the arch to this new class with Must-be-a, thereby using the **enlarge-set** heuristic.

If there are no objects other than bricks and wedges, however, procedure W gets rid of the Is-a link completely, and is said to use the **drop-link** heuristic.

Procedure W also uses the drop-link heuristic when a link in the evolving model is not in the example. If the initiating example has color information for some blocks and the other examples do not, procedure W ignores color, dropping all color references from the evolving model.

Figure 16.4 The climb-tree heuristic. The top of the Arch description in part (a) is a brick, while the corresponding object in the example description in part (b) is a wedge. Evidently, the difference does not matter. The Is-a link in the Arch description is changed to a Must-be-a link and redirected from Brick to Block, as shown in part (c), which is the most specific common generalization of Brick and Wedge. Many links have been omitted from the drawing to prevent distraction from those that matter.

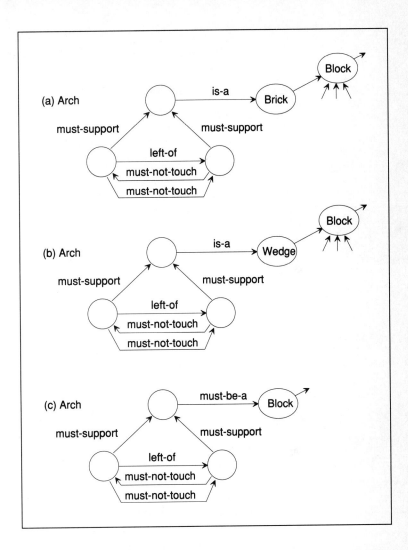

Finally, procedure W uses another heuristic if a difference involves numbers. If one example exhibits a 10-centimeter brick, and another exhibits a 15-centimeter brick, then procedure W supposes that bricks of any length between 10 centimeters and 15 centimeters will do, thus using the **close-interval** heuristic.

Near-Miss Heuristics Specialize; Example Heuristics Generalize

Having seen how procedure W uses induction heuristics, it is time to summarize. Note that the near-miss heuristics, require link and forbid link, both specialize the model, making it more restrictive. The positive-example heuristics all generalize the model, making it more permissive.

- The **require-link** heuristic is used when an evolving model has a link in a place where a near miss does not. The model link is converted to a Must form.

- The **forbid-link** heuristic is used when a near miss has a link in a place where an evolving model does not. A Must-not form is installed in the evolving model.

- The **climb-tree** heuristic is used when an object in an evolving model corresponds to a different object in an example. Must-be-a links are routed to the most specific common class in the classification tree above the model object and the example object.

- The **enlarge-set** heuristic is used when an object in an evolving model corresponds to a different object in an example and the two objects are not related to each other through a classification tree. Must-be-a links are routed to a new class composed of the union of the objects' classes.

- The **drop-link** heuristic is used when the objects that are different in an evolving model and in an example form an exhaustive set. The drop-link heuristic is also used when an evolving model has a link that is not in the example. The link is dropped from the model.

- The **close-interval** heuristic is used when a number or interval in an evolving model corresponds to a number in an example. If the model uses a number, the number is replaced by an interval spanning the model's number and the example's number. If the model uses an interval, the interval is enlarged to reach the example's number.

Here then are the procedures that use these heuristics:

To use SPECIALIZE to make a model more restrictive,

▷ Match the evolving model to the example to establish correspondences among parts.

▷ Determine whether there is a single, most important difference between the evolving model and the near miss.

  ▷ If there is a single, most important difference,

    ▷ If the evolving model has a link that is not in the near miss, use the require-link heuristic.

    ▷ If the near miss has a link that is not in the model, use the forbid-link heuristic.

  ▷ Otherwise, ignore the example.

To use GENERALIZE to make a model more permissive,

▷ Match the evolving model to the example to establish correspondences among parts.

▷ For each difference, determine the difference type:

  ▷ If a link points to a class in the evolving model different from the class to which the link points in the example,

    ▷ If the classes are part of a classification tree, use the climb-tree heuristic.

    ▷ If the classes form an exhaustive set, use the drop-link heuristic.

    ▷ Otherwise, use the enlarge-set heuristic.

  ▷ If a link is missing in the example, use the drop-link heuristic.

  ▷ If the difference is that different numbers, or an interval and a number outside the interval, are involved, use the close-interval heuristic.

  ▷ Otherwise, ignore the difference.

Note that SPECIALIZE does nothing if it cannot identify a most important difference. One way to identify the most important difference is to use a procedure that ranks all differences by difference type and by link type. Another way is described in Chapter 18.

Note also that both SPECIALIZE and GENERALIZE involve matching. For now, be assured that there are matching procedures that tie together the appropriate nodes. One such matching procedure is described in Chapter 17.

Learning Procedures Should Avoid Guesses

As described, procedure W uses examples supplied by a teacher in an order decided on by that teacher. The learner analyzes each example as it is given; the learner does not retain examples once they are analyzed:

To learn using procedure W,

▷ Let the description of the first example, which must be an example, be the initial description.

▷ For all subsequent examples,

  ▷ If the example is a near miss, use procedure SPECIALIZE.

  ▷ If the example is an example, use procedure GENERALIZE.

As given, procedure W never unlearns something it has learned once. In principle, procedure W could unlearn, but deciding exactly what to unlearn, such that nothing breaks, is hard. Consequently, it is better not to learn something that may have to be unlearned:

The **wait-and-see principle**:

▷ When there is doubt about what to do, do nothing.

It may seem excessively conservative to refuse to act because no act is absolutely safe. There is a point, however, where risk taking becomes fool-hardiness. Honoring the wait-and-see principle, a learner is not condemned to eternal stupidity; the learner is merely expecting to encounter difficult situations again, later, when the learner is better prepared.

Procedure W honors the wait-and-see principle when it ignores negative examples for which it cannot identify a single or most-important difference.

Procedure W's teacher can help procedure W to avoid the need to ignore negative examples by ensuring that the negative examples are bona fide near misses. Alternatively, the teacher and the student can agree on how difference types should be ranked so that the difference that seems most important to the student actually is important from the perspective of the teacher. Learning-facilitating teacher–student agreements are called **felicity conditions**, especially if they are implied, rather than expressed.

Even with elaborate felicity conditions, however, there will be situations when a model is not consistent with an example, even though the model is basically correct. Penguins, for example, are birds, even though penguins cannot fly. In such situations, the way out is to honor another principle:

The **no-altering principle**:

▷ When an object or situation known to be an example fails to match a general model, create a special-case exception model.

Thus, the wait-and-see principle says to avoid building a model that will be wrong, and the no-altering principle says to avoid changing a model, even if it is wrong, again because fixing a general model in one way is likely to break it in another.

Learning Usually Must Be Done in Small Steps

Procedure W works because it exploits the knowledge it has, adding to that knowledge in small steps using new examples.

Skillful teachers know that people learn mostly in small steps, too. If there is too much to figure out, there is too much room for confusion and error:

Martin's law:

▷ You cannot learn anything unless you almost know it already.

IDENTIFICATION

In the previous section, you saw what procedure W can learn about objects. In this section, you learn how identification methods can use what has been learned by matching unknown objects to appropriate models.

Must Links and Must-Not Links Dominate Matching

One way to determine whether an unknown matches a model adequately is to see whether the unknown is compatible with the model's emphatic links. Any links with names prefixed by Must must be in the unknown; and links prefixed by Must-not must not be in the unknown.

More flexible match evaluation requires a procedure that can judge the degree of similarity between an unknown and a model. To implement such a procedure, you have to translate the abstract notion of *similarity* between an *unknown* and a *model*, $s(U, M)$, into a concrete measurement. One simple way of doing this translation, by a weighted counting of corresponding links, was described in Chapter 2 in connection with a geometric-analogy procedure. Note, however, that any counting scheme for combining evidence is limited, because all information is compressed into a singularly inexpressive number.

Models May Be Arranged in Lists or in Nets

Given a mechanism for matching an unknown with a model, the next issue is how to arrange the models for testing. We consider two of many possibilities: model lists and similarity nets.

Matching the unknown with the models in a model list was called the describe-and-match method in Chapter 2. It is a reasonable approach only if the number of models is small.

Another approach to arranging models is to use a **similarity net**. Imagine a set of models organized into a net in which the links connect model pairs that are very similar. Now suppose that an unknown object is to be identified. What should be done when the first comparison with a particular model in the net fails, as it ordinarily will? If the match does not fail by much—that is, if the unknown seems like the model in many respects—then surely other similar models should be tried next. These new similar models are precisely the ones connected by similarity links to the just-tried model.

ARIEL Learns about Proteins

Increasingly, an impressive demonstration on a real problem is the sine qua non of successful research in artificial intelligence. Sometimes, the demonstration involves a program and a human expert working in tandem to do some task that neither could do independently.

In molecular biology, for example, the ARIEL program acts as a partner to human biologists, helping them to improve patterns that predict protein function. Before you learn how ARIEL works, you may find it helpful to review a little elementary protein biology.

First, **proteins** consist of one or a few long chains called **polypeptides**. Each link in a polypeptide chain is one of the 20 **amino acids**.

The **primary structure** of a protein is a specification of how the various amino acids are arranged in the polypeptide chain.

Here, for example, is a fragment a polypeptide produced by an AIDS virus:

-a-g-k-k-k-s-v-t-v-l-d-v-g-d-a-y-f-s-v-p-l-d-k-d-f-r-k-y-t-a-f-t-i-p-

The **secondary structure** is a specification of how various short segments in the chain fold up into small configurations, which have names such as alpha helix, beta strand, and beta turn. The example polypeptide fragment happens to contain several alpha helixes, beta strands, and beta turns.

The enzymatic activity of a protein is determined by its **tertiary structure**, a complete description of how it folds up in space—which ultimately depends, of course, on the primary structure of the polypeptides in the protein. As yet, however, no one knows how to use the primary structure to predict exactly how a protein will fold up. Nevertheless, a molecular biologist can predict that a protein will have certain functional properties by looking for characteristic patterns in the primary and secondary structure. One such characteristic pattern, refined with help from ARIEL, determines that a matching protein is likely to help duplicate **DNA molecules**, the ones that carry the genetic code:

DNA polymerase rule
> If   There is a small amino acid followed by
>   a beta strand followed by
>   a hydrophobic amino acid followed by
>   an aspartic acid followed by
>   a hydrophobic amino acid followed by
>   an aromatic amino acid followed by
>   a beta strand followed by
>   a beta strand
> then   the protein is likely to be a DNA polymerase

Note that the pattern involves primary structure, in that it specifies amino-acid classes, as well as secondary structure, in that it specifies beta strands, which are identified, in turn, by an analysis of primary structure. The pattern happens to match the example primary-structure fragment from the AIDS virus.

ARIEL is able to improve such recognition patterns by artfully deploying induction heuristics, beam search, and parallel testing. The induction heuristics are used to perturb an existing pattern in the hope of producing a more reliable pattern. Typically, a human biologist asks ARIEL to try a variation on the climb-tree heuristic on a particular amino acid specified in the pattern, producing one new pattern for each of the many possible generalizations in the amino-acid classification tree.

None of these new patterns is perfect when tested on a database of about 50 examples and several hundred nonexamples. Instead, each pattern recognizes some fraction of the examples and rejects some fraction of the nonexamples. In the diagram that follows this text, you see that the seed pattern, indicated by the black dot, recognizes about 89 percent of the examples, and rejects about 80 percent of the nonexamples.

Also shown, by open circles, are the places occupied by new patterns derived from the seed pattern. Among these, the best are the ones that are closest to the upper-right corner, where all examples are recognized and all nonexamples are rejected.

Of course, it can take a lot of time to locate all the patterns on the recognize–reject diagram, for each induction heuristic can produce tens of possible patterns, each of which has to be tested on hundreds of examples and near-miss negative examples. In practice, given today's technology, this kind of pattern testing is best done on a parallel computer, such as a Connection Machine^{TM}.

Once all the patterns are evaluated, a few of the best are kept for further analysis, and the rest are rejected. Then the human biologist specifies another induction heuristic for ARIEL to try on the surviving patterns. Thus, ARIEL and the human biologist work their way through the space of derivative patterns using beam search.

After moving through a few layers of the beam search, ARIEL and the human biologist usually can do no more, halting with a family of patterns that are better than the seed pattern originally supplied by the human biologist.

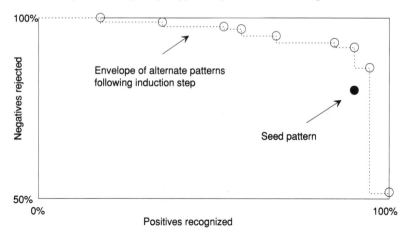

Figure 16.5 Identification using a similarity net. Progress from hypothesis to hypothesis is guided by comparison of difference descriptions. M80 is presumed to be the first hypothesis tried. M12 is next if the difference between M12 and M80 is much like the difference between the unknown, U, and M80.

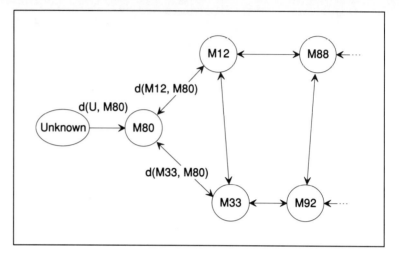

In an obvious improvement, the similarity links between models can not only convey similarity, but also describe the difference, as stipulated in the following representation specification:

A **similarity net** is a representation

That is a semantic net

In which

▷ Nodes denote models.

▷ Links connect similar models.

▷ Links are tied to difference descriptions.

Figure 16.5 illustrates a similarity net. If an unknown differs from a test model in the same way that a neighbor of the test model differs from the test model, then that neighbor is a particularly good model to test next. Thus, attention moves not only to a family of likely candidates, but also to the particular member of that family that is most likely to lead toward success. Accordingly, the initial match is not so much a failure as it is an enlightening **knowledge probe**.

Finally, note that the procedure for moving through a similarity net is a hill-climbing procedure because movement is to the immediate neighbor that seems most likely to yield an improved match with the unknown.

SUMMARY

■ One way to learn is to declare an initial example to be your initial model. Then, you improve the initial model incrementally using a series of examples.

- Some examples should be negative, near-miss examples. These examples enable you to zero in on just what it is about the evolving model that is essential, thus specializing the model.
- Require link and forbid link are specialization heuristics.
- Some examples should be positive examples. These enable you to generalize the model.
- Climb tree, enlarge set, drop link, and close interval are generalization heuristics.
- You cannot learn if you cannot isolate what is important. Good teachers help you by providing not only positive examples, but also negative examples and near misses.
- You should avoid guessing when you learn, because a bad guess may be hard to root out later on. One way to avoid guessing is to create a special-case exception when an object or idea known to be an example fails to match a general model.
- Martin's law says that you cannot learn anything unless you almost know it already.

BACKGROUND

The work described in this chapter is based on early work by Patrick H. Winston that introduced many induction heuristics, along with the near-miss idea [Winston 1970].

Subsequently, other researchers have offered improved procedures for using specializing and generalizing induction heuristics. In particular, most of the induction-heuristic names are adapted from the work of Ryszard S. Michalski [1980]. Michalski's INDUCE system includes several additional induction heuristics, many of which deal with chains of links and properties of groups.

The *no-altering principle* is my name for one of Marvin Minsky's **laws of noncompromise** discussed in *The Society of Mind*, Minsky's seminal book on artificial intelligence [1985].

Martin's law is an idea that was expressed by William A. Martin in Dubrovnik, Yugoslavia, in 1979.

The discussion of similarity nets is based on an idea by Winston [1970], subsequently developed by David L. Bailey [1986].

ARIEL is the work of Richard H. Lathrop [1990].

17

Learning by Explaining Experience

In this chapter, you learn how it is possible to *learn from experience* by working exercises. In particular, you learn about MACBETH, a procedure that works on précis of Shakespeare's plays. MACBETH *matches* an exercise description to a precedent description, then *transfers explanations* from the precedent to the exercise. The transferred explanation enables MACBETH to deal with the exercise and to construct an *antecedent–consequent rule*, thus performing a sort of *explanation-based learning*.

By way of illustration, you see how MACBETH learns about *causes*, learning, for example, that a weak character and a greedy wife can lead a noble to want to be king. You also see how MACBETH learns to relate *form and function*: given a functional definition for cups, MACBETH uses prior knowledge of other objects, together with physical descriptions of a particular cup, to construct a variety of possible physical descriptions, enabling cup identification.

Once you have finished this chapter, you will see that knowing a lot helps you to learn more.

LEARNING ABOUT WHY PEOPLE ACT THE WAY THEY DO

Teachers constantly supply precedents, give exercises, and expect students to do the exercises and to discover principles that apply to everyday situations. Students must find the correspondence between the precedents and the exercises, use the precedents to deal with the exercises, generalize their work to form principles, and store the principles so that the principles can be retrieved when appropriate. This type of teaching and learning pervades subjects such as management, economics, law, medicine, and engineering, as well as aiding in the development of commonsense knowledge about life in general.

Consider, for example, the following exercise and précis of *Macbeth*:

Greed ———

This is an exercise about a weak noble and a greedy woman. The noble is married to the woman. Explain why the noble is likely to want to be king.

Macbeth ———

This is a story about Macbeth, Lady Macbeth, Duncan, and Macduff. Macbeth is an evil noble, and Lady Macbeth is a greedy, ambitious woman. Duncan is a king, and Macduff is a noble. Lady Macbeth persuades Macbeth to want to be king because she is greedy. She is able to influence him because he is married to her and because he is weak. Macbeth murders Duncan with a knife. Macbeth murders Duncan because Macbeth wants to be king, because Macbeth is evil, and because Duncan is king. Then Lady Macbeth kills herself. Finally Macduff gets angry and kills Macbeth because Macbeth murdered Duncan and because Macduff is loyal to Duncan.

Told by a teacher that *Macbeth* is to be considered a precedent, a human student should establish that the noble corresponds to Macbeth and the woman corresponds to Lady Macbeth. Next, the student should note that the characteristics of the noble and the woman are those that lead to Macbeth's desire to want to be king. From these correspondences, the student should form some sort of rule suggesting that the weakness of a noble and the greed of his wife can cause the noble to want to be king.

In the rest of this section, you learn how a program, MACBETH, can form explanations and learn new rules as well.

Reification and the Vocabulary of Thematic-Role Frames Capture Sentence-Level Meaning

The first step in using a precedent is to prepare a suitable description, cast in a good representation. For the *Macbeth* story, as given, an ordinary semantic net can represent certain characteristics of the people, their motivations, and their consequent actions. For example, Macbeth and Duncan can be denoted by nodes, with a Murder link between, as shown at the top of figure 17.1.

Figure 17.1 In the top part of the figure, Macbeth murders Duncan, as represented in the nodes and links of an ordinary semantic net. In the bottom part of the figure, the reified Murder link is treated as though it were a node with its own descriptive links.

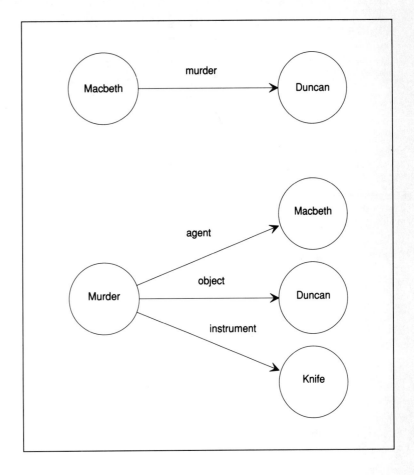

There is more to be said about the murder, however, because Macbeth used a knife. Accordingly, you can think of the Murder link as though it were a node, with descriptive links of its own, as shown at the bottom of figure 17.1.

Treating something abstract and difficult to talk about as though it were concrete and easy to talk about is called **reification**. Thus, the elevation of a link to the status of a describable node is a kind of reification; when a link is so elevated, it is said to be a **reified link**. One notation for reified links is shown at the top of figure 17.2. To prevent illustrations from becoming cluttered, however, it is convenient to drop the circles, along with the redundant Agent and Object links, as shown at the bottom of figure 17.2.

Note that many links denote actions. Accordingly, the vocabulary used to describe links is reminiscent of the thematic-role-frame vocabulary introduced in Chapter 10.

Figure 17.2 Two notations for a reified link describing Macbeth's murder of Duncan.

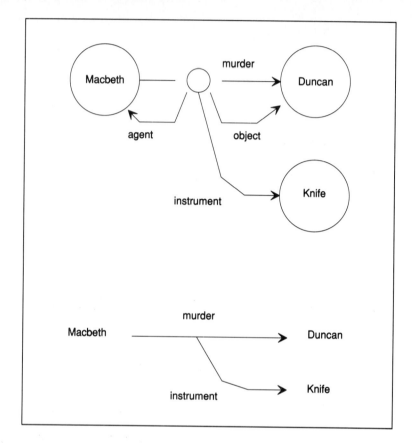

Explanation Transfer Solves Problems Using Analogy

How is it possible to know why an action has occurred or whether an action is likely to occur? How is it possible to know why a relation has come to be or whether it is likely to come to be? The answer to both questions is that Cause links in a precedent situation are likely to identify links that can serve as a basis for justification or prediction. Ultimately, of course, this answer rests on the assumption that, if two situations are similar in some respects, then they are likely to be similar in other respects as well.

To see how MACBETH makes use of precedents, consider the *Macbeth* precedent, shown in semantic-net form in figure 17.3, and the accompanying exercise, *Greed*, shown in figure 17.4.

MACBETH creates an **explanation template** consisting of the Cause links in the precedent and all the links that the Cause links tie together. Thus, the explanation template is a record of how links involving marriage, greed, and weakness have led to a want-to-be-king link in *Macbeth*.

To use the explanation template, MACBETH must determine how the people in the exercise correspond to the people in the precedent. In the

Figure 17.3 The *Macbeth* precedent with Cause links shown in bold.

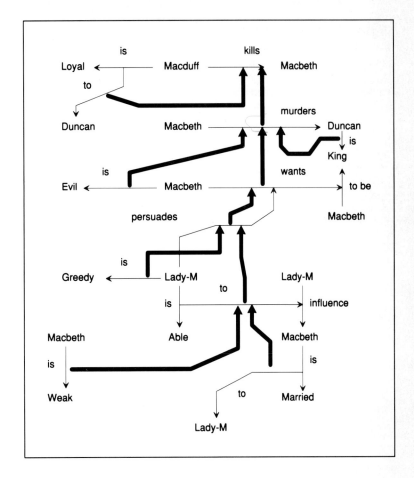

exercise, the noble is weak, and his wife is greedy. In *Macbeth*, Macbeth is weak and his wife, Lady Macbeth, is greedy. Noting these characteristics, MACBETH concludes that the noble corresponds to Macbeth, and that his wife corresponds to Lady Macbeth.

Assuming that similarities among causes in two analogous situations lead to similarities among the consequents of those causes, MACBETH explains the want-to-be-king link in *Greed* by transferring the explanation template from *Macbeth* to *Greed*, as shown in figure 17.5. Once the explanation template taken from *Macbeth* is in place, a chain of overlaid Cause links connects known relations to the want-to-be-king relation, which is the one to be explained.

In this first example, there is only one precedent involved. When a single precedent cannot supply the total explanation template needed, MACBETH attempts to chain together several explanation templates. In the following exercise, for example, it is not known that the noble is weak, as is required for the *Macbeth* precedent to be completely successful:

Figure 17.4 The *Greed* exercise, with dotted links identifying the relation to be explained.

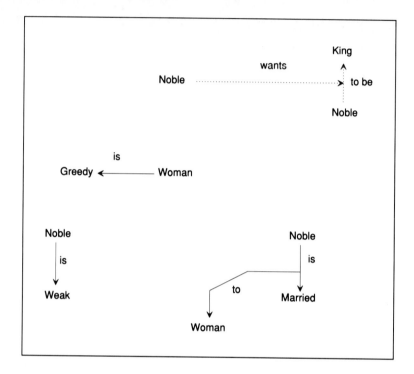

Domination

This is an exercise about a noble and a domineering, greedy woman. The noble is married to the woman. Show that the noble is likely to want to be king.

A second precedent, the *Linda and Dick* story, can help MACBETH to establish that this new noble is also weak, thus working in support of the *Macbeth* precedent:

Linda and Dick

This is a story about Linda and Dick. Linda is a woman, and Dick is a man. Dick is married to Linda. Dick is weak because he is tired. He is tired because Linda is domineering.

Figure 17.6 shows what the *Linda and Dick* story looks like. Figure 17.7 shows how *Linda and Dick* works in support of *Macbeth*: *Macbeth* handles the top part; *Linda and Dick*, handles the bottom; and the two are joined at the link denoting the noble's weakness.

Thus, explanation templates taken from precedents serve to guide MACBETH to the possible causes of the link to be explained. Here, in summary, is the MACBETH procedure expressed in procedural English:

Figure 17.5 The exercise, with an explanation template, taken from *Macbeth*, shown with heavy lines.

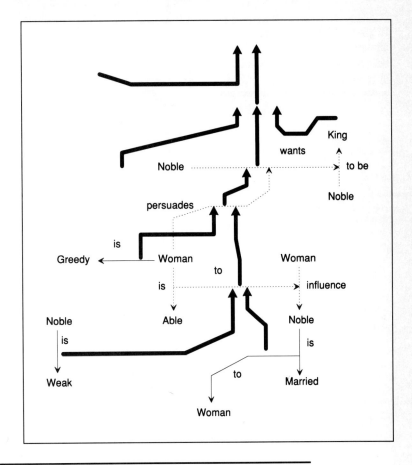

To solve problems with precedents using MACBETH,

▷ Match the exercise to a precedent with a link corresponding to the relation or action to be explained.

▷ Transfer the explanation template from the precedent to the exercise.

▷ Trace through the transferred explanation template. Determine whether the link to be explained is supported by existing links.

　▷ If the desired conclusion is supported, announce success.

　▷ Otherwise, check whether MACBETH can justify needed, but missing, links, using other precedents. If it can, then announce success.

　▷ Otherwise, announce failure.

Figure 17.6 A precedent showing that a person's domineering nature can lead to a spouse's weakness.

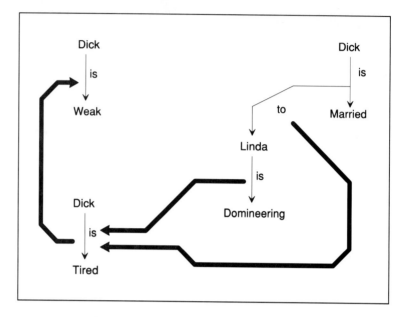

Commonsense Problem Solving Can Generate Rulelike Principles

Whenever explanation templates are used to explain a relation or action, those explanation templates essentially supply an And tree that spans the gap between the relation or action to be explained and relations or actions that are already known. The root node of the And tree corresponds to the relation or action to be explained; the leaf nodes correspond to relations or actions that are already in place; the nodes in between correspond to the links joined by Cause relations in the explanation templates.

If the exercise is a good exercise, the And tree should be a good gap spanner in general, not just in the exercise. Accordingly, MACBETH uses the And tree to commit a new description to memory for future use:

To learn using MACBETH,

▷ Find the And tree implied by the explanation templates used to work the exercise.

▷ Using the climb-tree induction heuristic, generalize the agents and objects that appear in the And tree.

▷ Build a new description using the links that appear in the And tree and the generalized agents and objects.

Because the new description can involve bits of many explanation templates, it is said to be a **recollection**. The word *recollection* is intended to suggest that knowledge is collected in a new way—that is, knowledge is

Figure 17.7 An example illustrating the use of two precedents working together. *Macbeth* establishes, via the heavy lines, that the noble is likely to want to be king, but only if it can be established that the noble is weak. *Linda and Dick* establishes, via the heavy dashed lines, that the noble is likely to be weak by pushing analysis further, ultimately connecting the want-to-be-king link to links that appear in the exercise.

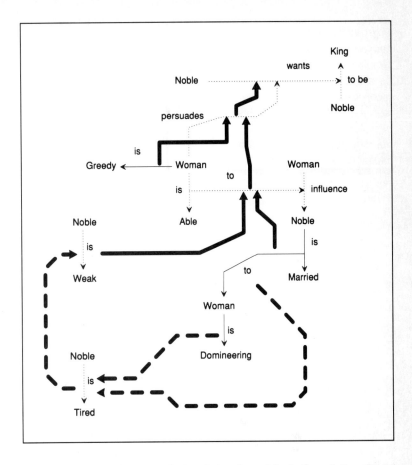

re-collected. In the simple example involving just *Macbeth* and the *Greed* exercise, the recollection synthesized from the precedent and the exercise is illustrated in figure 17.8.

Labeling the root node of the recollection with *then*, and labeling the leaf nodes with *if*, you can see that recollections can be viewed as though they were antecedent–consequent rules of the sort used in rule-based deduction systems:

The Want-To-Be-King Rule
    If   ?noble is weak
             ?noble is married to ?woman
             ?woman is greedy
    Then   ?noble is likely to want to be king

Because recollections are actually represented in the same semantic-net representation as are precedents, they are treated as ordinary precedents by MACBETH. Thus, recollections can contribute to new recollections, just as precedents can.

Figure 17.8 An exercise causes part of the explanation template of a precedent to be extracted, leading to a recollection. The recollection is in the same representation used for the precedent and the exercise. Heavy links are causal links.

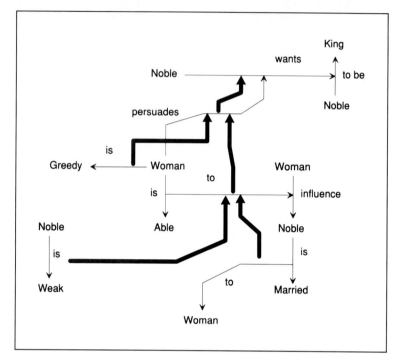

The MACBETH Procedure Illustrates the Explanation Principle

From the problem-solving perspective, MACBETH's job is to explain how an action or relation can be justified or predicted on the basis of precedents. From the learning perspective, however, MACBETH's job is to build on its own explanations, assembling new recollections. This idea is, of course, a good one for people to follow as well:

The **explanation principle**:

▷ If you want to understand a concept, try explaining it to someone else.

The Macbeth Procedure Can Use Causal Chains to Establish Common Context

The MACBETH procedure, as described, happily thinks, by virtue of the *Linda and Dick* story, that a man married to a domineering woman will be weak. But what if the man does not live with the woman? What if the woman is only domineering with respect to her siblings? What if the man is even more domineering?

The usual answer is that precedents such as *Linda and Dick* should be used only in the right **context**, which raises the question of how you can tell whether the context is right. One way—a weak way—is to look for points of general similarity between two situations. It is possible, however, for two situations to be similar in many respects without being similar in the right respects. Worse yet, the analogy-justifying contextual similarities between two situations may be implicit, and may not even be visible in their descriptions.

There is, nevertheless, a way to increase your confidence that a precedent is applicable to an exercise even if many of the Cause links in its explanation template are flimsy and depend on the precedent and the exercise having the same context.

The idea is to turn the problem into an asset. If two situations have different contexts, few matching links lead via Cause links to common consequences. Conversely, if many matching links lead via Cause links to common consequences, you can be increasingly confident that the situations are similar in important ways. If they are similar in important ways, then one is likely to be a good precedent for the other, as expressed in the following principle:

Winston's principle of parallel evolution:

▷ The longer two situations have been evolving in the same way, the more likely they are to continue to evolve in the same way.

To see how MACBETH can use this principle, consider the following exercise:

Domination and Fatigue ─────────────────────

This is an exercise about a noble and a greedy woman. The noble is married to the woman. The noble is tired because the woman is domineering. Show that the noble is likely to want to be king.

As shown in figure 17.9, *Domination and Fatigue* is just like *Domination*, except that the noble is said to be tired, and he is tired because his wife is domineering.

When MACBETH tries to show that this noble is likely to want to be king, MACBETH must once again depend on the *Macbeth* precedent, which leads MACBETH to look for a reason why the noble is weak. Once again, MACBETH must use the *Linda and Dick* precedent. This time, however, *Domination and Fatigue* and *Linda and Dick* both have a Cause link that ties the woman's domineering nature to the man's fatigue. Thus, the explanation template taken from *Linda and Dick* not only spans a gap in *Domination and Fatigue*, but also matches a Cause link that lies just before the gap.

Evidently, the contexts of *Domination and Fatigue* and *Linda and Dick* are the same insofar as the contexts influence the matching Cause links. If

Figure 17.9 This exercise description, for *Domination and Fatigue*, is like the one for *Domination*, except that there are three extra links indicating that the noble is fatigued because the woman is domineering.

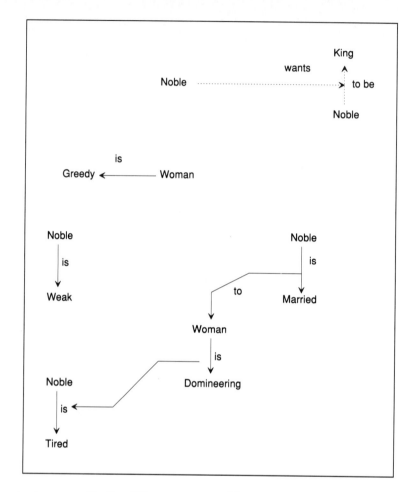

the context were radically different, you would expect no matching Cause links.

Of course, one matching pair of Cause links is not substantial evidence, but it is more evidence than none at all. Furthermore, if the number of parallel Cause links is larger, your expectation that the situations are likely to evolve in parallel increases in proportion.

Accordingly, MACBETH can make use of the following heuristic corollary of Winston's principle of parallel evolution: Given a set of useful-looking precedents, use the one with an explanation template that matches the largest number of Cause links in the exercise.

LEARNING ABOUT FORM AND FUNCTION

Interestingly, the MACBETH procedure also learns what objects look like from functional descriptions and descriptions of particular examples. In

Figure 17.10 A particular object that is likely to be a cup.

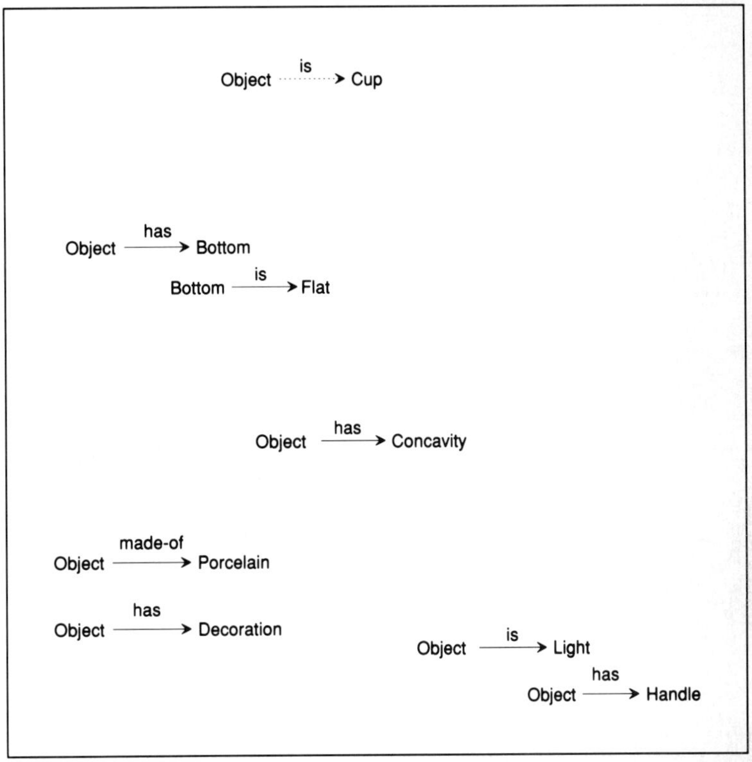

this section, you see how MACBETH can learn what cups look like once it knows what cups are for.

Examples and Precedents Help Each Other

The first step in relating form to function is to describe the function. For MACBETH's benefit, a cup is defined by way of the following English sentences:

A Cup Description ————————————————————
This is a description of an object. The object is a cup because it is stable and because it enables drinking.

In contrast to the functional description, the description of a particular cup, such as the one described below and shown in figure 17.10, concentrates on physical qualities, not functional ones:

A Particular Object ————————————————————
This is an exercise about a light object that is made of porcelain. The object has a decoration, a concavity, and a handle. The object's bottom is flat. Show that the object is a cup.

Now it is time to demonstrate that the functional requirements are met by the physical description. The demonstration requires precedents that relate the cup's functional description to the description of the particular cup. Four precedents are needed. One explains how an object can be stable; another explains how drinking is related to carrying liquids and being liftable; another explains how being liftable is related to being of light weight and having a handle; and still another explains how carrying liquids is related to having a concavity. All contain at least one relation that is irrelevant with respect to dealing with cups; these irrelevant relations are representative of the detritus that can accompany the useful material:

A Brick

This is a description of a brick. The brick is stable because the brick's bottom is flat. The brick is heavy.

A Glass

This is a description of a glass. The glass enables drinking because the glass carries liquids and because the glass is liftable. The glass is pretty.

A Briefcase

This is a description of a briefcase. The briefcase is liftable because it is has a handle and because it is light. The briefcase is useful because it is a portable container for papers.

A Bowl

This is a description of a bowl. The bowl carries liquids because it has a concavity. The bowl contains cherry soup.

With the functional description in hand, together with relevant precedents, MACBETH is ready to go to work. First, MACBETH searches for precedents that are relevant to showing that the object in the exercise is a cup. The functional description is retrieved. Next, MACBETH determines the correspondence between parts of the exercise and the parts of the functional description—a straightforward task in this instance. Now, MACBETH overlays the explanation template of the functional description on the exercise. Tracing through the Cause links in the explanation template raises two questions: Is the observed object stable? Does it enable drinking?

Questioning whether the object is stable leads MACBETH to a second search for a precedent, and the brick precedent is retrieved. The object has a flat bottom, like a brick, so it is likely to be stable.

Next the glass precedent is retrieved to deal with drinking. MACBETH uses the glass precedent to translate the drinking question into a question of carrying liquids and liftability.

Figure 17.11 Evidence supporting the conclusion that a particular object is a cup is drawn from several precedents. Only a few of the links in the precedents supply supporting evidence; the rest are ignored.

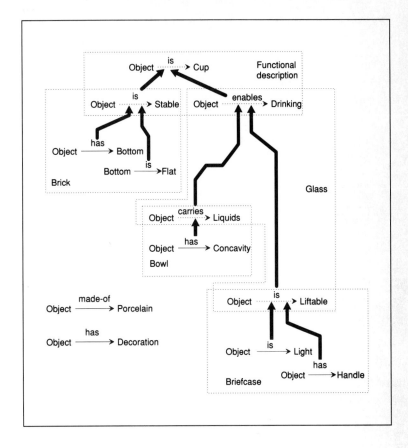

To see whether the object can carry liquids, MACBETH uses the bowl precedent. MACBETH notes that a bowl carries liquids because it has a concavity, just as the example object does.

Next, MACBETH considers the liftability requirement, and retrieves the briefcase precedent. The briefcase precedent indicates that an object is liftable if it is light and has a handle. Because the object is light and has a handle, it must be liftable, completing the explanation of why it can function as a cup.

At this point, MACBETH has supporting evidence for the conclusion that the exercise object is a cup, all of which is summarized in figure 17.11.

Now it is time for MACBETH to build a recollection that deals with what cups look like. Because this new recollection is to be used for identification, rather than for justification or prediction, either the term *identification model* or the term *model* is more appropriate than *recollection*.

MACBETH builds a cup model as it builds justification and prediction explanations, by extracting an And tree from explanation templates. The resulting model, shown as an antecedent–consequent rule, is as follows:

The Cup Model

If	?object has a flat bottom
	?object has a concavity
	?object is light
	?object has a handle
Then	?object is a cup

From this example, it is clear why learning form from function requires a physical example and some precedents, in addition to a functional description:

- The physical example is essential: otherwise, there would be no way to know which precedents are relevant.
- The precedents are essential: otherwise, there would be no way to know which aspects of the physical example are relevant.

Explanation-Based Learning Offers More than Speedup

At first glance, explanation-based learning appears to do no more than to take note of existing Cause links, repackaging them into more directly useful recollections, but not adding anything new. Thus, it would appear that explanation-based learning offers speedup only, for you could always go back to the original precedents in principle.

Looking more deeply, however, you can see that explanation-based learning offers more than mere speedup when the learner has imprecise or faulty knowledge of how individual precedents are allowed to form larger explanations. The reason is that particular exercises, often supplied by a knowledgeable teacher, provide heuristic evidence about which precedents can be stuck together usefully to determine what objects look like. Without that kind of heuristic evidence, a program can chain only through whatever precedents it has, indiscriminately. Such a program could reason that cows are cups on the grounds that they stand stably and enable drinking, thus satisfying the functional description provided for cups.

MATCHING

MACBETH cannot do its job unless it can identify how objects in an exercise correspond to the objects in a precedent. In the *Greed* example, for instance, MACBETH has to know that the noble corresponds to Macbeth and that the woman corresponds to Lady Macbeth. In this section, you learn how a matching procedure can establish that sort of correspondence with reasonable efficiency.

Stupid Matchers Are Slow and Easy to Fool

Consider *Macbeth*, as shown in figure 17.3, and *Greed*, as shown in figure 17.4. The desired correspondence of individuals is as follows:

Macbeth	Greed	Role
Macbeth	The noble	Victim
Lady Macbeth	The woman	Villain

Nothing explicitly identifies the villains and victims, however, so MACBETH must do matching by analyzing how all the individuals fit into the two situations.

The obvious approach, of course, is to try each possible way of pairing off the individuals, scoring each way according to the number of relations that are placed in congruence, and selecting the way with the highest score.

There are two problems, however, with the obvious approach. The first problem is that the number of ways of pairing off the individuals increases with the product of the number of individuals to be paired off. *Macbeth* has four: Macbeth, Lady Macbeth, Duncan, and Macduff; *Greed* has two: the noble and the woman; hence eight pairings would have to be scored, which is not too bad. If each situation has many individuals, however, *not bad* becomes *scary*.

A second, more serious problem, is that accidental, random correspondences can pull the matching process away from the correspondences that produce useful analogies. It might be, for example, that Macbeth in *Macbeth* and the woman in *Greed* share a large number of irrelevant, but mentioned, properties such as hair color and appetite size.

The matcher you learn about here, in contrast, is both more reliable and faster:

- It is driven by the purpose of the match, so it is immune to irrelevant properties.
- It only matches individuals that are relevant to the purpose of the match.

Matching Inexact Situations Reduces to Backward Chaining

The matcher works by using ideas you first learned about in connection with backward chaining through rules. Accordingly, you might find it useful to review Chapter 7 if the forthcoming discussion seems overly telegraphic.

Two key ideas enable the reduction of situation matching to backward chaining:

- You treat the precedent as though it were a source of *antecedent–consequent* rules.
- You use the exercise as though it were a database of assertions.

To see how these ideas help you, first consider the use of *Macbeth* as a source of *antecedent–consequent* rules. On examining figure 17.3, you see that there are five links that are explained by one or more Cause links that tie the first five links to other links. Each of the five explained links is readily transformed into an *antecedent–consequent* rule, with the explained link constituting the consequent, the other links constituting the antecedents, and each individual viewed as a match variable:

R1   If   *?x1* is loyal to *?x2*
                 ?x3 murders *?x2*
       Then   *?x1* kills *?x3*

R2   If   *?x3* is evil
                 ?x3 wants to be king
                 ?x2 is king
       Then   *?x3* murders *?x2*

R3   If   *?x4* persuades *?x3* to want to be king
       Then   *?x3* wants to be king

R4   If   *?x4* is greedy
                 ?x4 is able to influence *?x3*
       Then   *?x4* persuades *?x3* to want to be king

R5   If   *?x3* is weak
                 ?x3 is married to *?x4*
       Then   *?x4* is able to influence *?x3*

The process of converting individual names into match variables is called **variablization**. The following table records how the variablization has been done:

Individual	Variables
Macduff	*?x1*
Duncan	*?x2*
Macbeth	*?x3*
Lady Macbeth	*?x4*

Next, consider the use of *Greed* as a source of assertions. On examining figure 17.5, you see that there are the following assertions only:

The woman is greedy
The noble is weak
The noble is married to the woman

With these assertions, and the five rules, you can now ask whether *Macbeth* supports the assertion, *the noble wants to be king*.

Of the five rules, only rule R3's consequent matches *the noble wants to be king*, creating the following variable bindings:

Variable	Binding
?x3	the noble

Having established the initial variable bindings, backward chaining then attempts to find assertions corresponding to the antecedent of R3 with the variable binding substituted for the variable—namely, *?x4 persuades the noble to want to be king*. Unfortunately, an assertion corresponding to the antecedent of R3 is not found. Accordingly, a rule establishing who persuades the noble to be king must be used. Rule R4 has the right kind of consequent, because that consequent matches the antecedent of R3 exactly.

Now it is time to consider rule R4's antecedents. The first of these is *?x4 is greedy*, which matches the assertion *the woman is greedy*, augmenting the variable bindings:

Variable	Binding
?x4	the woman
?x3	the noble

Alas, there is no assertion corresponding to the second antecedent in R4, with variables replaced by variable bindings, *the woman is able to influence the noble*. Accordingly, further chaining through another rule is necessary. There is, fortunately, a rule that does the job—namely, R5, because the consequent of R5 matches the antecedent of R4 exactly.

Turning to R5's antecedents, assertions are found for both, once variable bindings are substituted for variables, for *Greed* supplies both *the noble is weak* and *the noble is married to the woman*.

At this point, *Macbeth* has found support for the assertion that the noble wants to be king. Also, the pairing of individuals that enables problem solving is obvious, and is captured in the following table of variables, variable bindings, and variable origins:

Variable	Binding in Greed	Origin in Macbeth
?x3	the noble	Macbeth
?x4	the woman	Lady Macbeth

Thus, Macbeth is paired with the noble and Lady Macbeth is paired with the woman, as expected.

Matching Sheds Light on Analogical Problem Solving

From the way matching is done in conjunction with analogical problem solving, you can see that each precedent is, in effect, a repository of implicit antecedent–consequent rules, along with many useless details with respect to any particular purpose. The job of MACBETH, then, is to find and exploit such implicit rules of inference.

SUMMARY

- One way to learn is to piece together explanations from causal chains transferred from precedents to deal with a new problem.

- In general, to reify is to treat something abstract as though it were concrete. To reify a link is treat it as a node so that you can describe it. Reification and the vocabulary of thematic-role frames make it possible to record story plots for use as precedents.

- The MACBETH procedure uses causal chains found in story plots and object descriptions to solve problems and to generate rulelike principles.

- The MACBETH procedure takes overlapping causal chains as evidence of common context.

- The MACBETH procedure uses a matcher that reduces matching to a form of backward chaining. Thus, matching and problem solving are interdigitated.

- Explanation-based learning is particularly beneficial in that teachers can guide students toward appropriate precedent combinations. In the absence of such guidance, a weak student could put together the wrong things, making silly mistakes. Thus, explanation-based learning offers more than speedup.

BACKGROUND

The discussion of MACBETH is based on work by Patrick H. Winston [1980, 1982]. The discussion of MACBETH in the context of form and function is based on work by Winston and his associates [Winston 1980, 1982; Winston, Thomas O. Binford, Boris Katz, and Michael R. Lowry 1983].

The theory was shaped to a great degree by experiments that would have been extraordinarily tedious to perform without the English interface, developed by Boris Katz [1982], by means of which the experimental database was prepared, revised, and revised again. As artificial intelligence progresses beyond toy-world domains, it becomes obvious that databases prepared and accessed using English are necessary for research, not simply for research presentation.

18
Learning by Correcting Mistakes

In this chapter, you learn how a procedure can *repair previously acquired knowledge* by exploiting its own errors. You see that this ability is necessary because to become an expert a program must handle an ever-growing list of unusual cases, and so is forced to do knowledge repair.

In particular, you learn about FIXIT, a procedure designed to resonate with the healthy attitude that errors are valuable knowledge probes, not failures. FIXIT *isolates suspicious relations* that may cause failures, *explains why* those facts cause problems, and ultimately *repairs knowledge*.

By way of illustration, you see how FIXIT deals with a model that incorrectly allows pails to be identified as cups. FIXIT notes that the reason pails are not cups must have something to do with the handles, that cups have to be oriented, that fixed handles enable orientation, and that cups therefore have to have fixed handles, rather than hinged ones.

ISOLATING SUSPICIOUS RELATIONS

In this section, you learn how to use failures to zero in on what is wrong with an identification model. You also learn how to make superficial, ad hoc corrections.

Cups and Pails Illustrate the Problem

The cup-identification model that MACBETH learned in the previous chapter can be used to identify a variety of cups, including porcelain cups and metal cups. Unfortunately, it also allows a variety of pails, including metal pails and wooden pails, to be identified as cups. Such failures lead to the following questions:

- How can a procedure use identification failures to *isolate* suspicious relations that should perhaps prevent a model from being misapplied?
- How can a procedure use precedents to *explain* why those now isolated suspicious relations should prevent a model from being misapplied?
- How can a procedure use explanations to *repair* a model, preventing further misapplication?

Near-Miss Groups Isolate Suspicious Relations

If a pail differs from a cup only in the way the handle is attached, then the pail can act as a near miss. Unfortunately, there may be many differences, both relevant and irrelevant.

Assume, for example, that the porcelain cup in figure 18.1 is known to be a cup, and the metal pail in figure 18.1 is known to be something else, either because a teacher says so or because an attempt to drink from it fails. The pail is metal, but the cup is porcelain; the metal pail is gray, but the porcelain cup is white with balloons painted on the side; perhaps the metal pail carries water, but the porcelain cup carries coffee.

Now assume that the tin cup in figure 18.1 is also known to be a cup, but the wooden pail in figure 18.1 is known to be something else. Each pail differs from the porcelain cup in many ways, and similarly, each pail differs from the tin cup in many ways. It is important, however, that there are fewer ways in which *both* the metal pail and the wooden pail differ from *both* the porcelain cup and the tin cup. In fact, in the example, you are to assume that the cups have fixed handles, whereas the pails have hinged handles, and that nothing else characterizes the way both pails differ from both cups.

Because the model allows all four objects to be identified as cups, when the model is viewed as an antecedent–consequent rule, the antecedent relations must lie in the intersection of all the relation sets describing those four objects. Similarly, the relations, if any, that distinguish the true-success situations from the false-success situations must lie in the union of the two relation subsets shown shaded in figure 18.1.

Because the relations in the true-success set and the false-success set are likely candidates for forming explanations, they are called **suspicious relations**. Also, the situations used to identify the suspicious relations constitute a **near-miss group**, because the situations work together as a group to do the job performed by a single example and a single near miss of the sort discussed in Chapter 16.

Figure 18.1 A near-miss group. The dots represent relations. Suspicious relations are in the shaded area. Some are suspicious because they are in all the true successes, but are not in any of the false successes; others are suspicious because they are in all the false successes, but are not in any of the true successes.

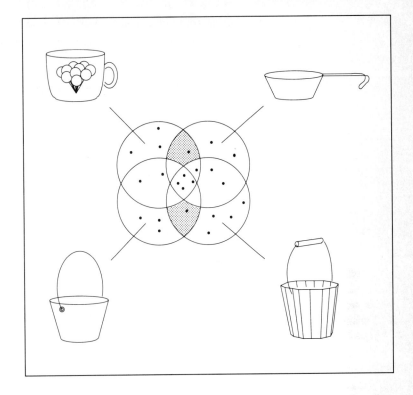

Clearly, isolating suspicious relations is just a simple matter of using set operations on the relations that appear in the true successes and false successes. Here is how the repair procedure, FIXIT, does the work:

To isolate suspicious relations using FIXIT,

▷ To isolate the true-success suspicious relations,

   ▷ Intersect all true successes. Call the result $\bigcap T$.

   ▷ Union all false successes. Call the result $\bigcup F$.

   ▷ Remove all assertions in the union from the intersection. These are the true-success suspicious relations, written mathematically as $\bigcap T - \bigcup F$.

▷ To isolate the false-success suspicious relations,

   ▷ Intersect all false successes. Call the result $\bigcap F$.

   ▷ Union all true successes. Call the result $\bigcup T$.

   ▷ Remove all assertions in the union from the intersection. These are the false-success suspicious relations, written mathematically as $\bigcap F - \bigcup T$.

In general, there will be more than one suspicious relation, but the more true successes and false successes you have, the fewer suspicious relations there are likely to be.

Suspicious Relation Types Determine Overall Repair Strategy

In the example, the *handle is fixed* relation is found in both cups, but it is *not* found in either pail. If a procedure could find a way to include this relation in the model, then the model would enable more discriminating identification. Cups would still be identified, but pails would not be.

Thus, an explanation-free repair would be to include the *handle is fixed* relation in the rule view of the model as a new antecedent condition:

Repaired Cup-Identification Rule
  If   The object has a bottom
          The bottom is flat
          The object has a concavity
          The object is light-weight
          The object has a handle
          The handle is fixed
  Then   The object is a cup

As described, however, the model repair is ad hoc because there is no explanation for why the new antecedent condition should work.

INTELLIGENT KNOWLEDGE REPAIR

In this section, you learn how FIXIT can explain why a particular relation makes an identification rule go wrong, thus enabling FIXIT to make informed repairs.

The Solution May Be to Explain the True-Success Suspicious Relations

Figure 18.2 shows the And tree form of the original, faulty model; figure 18.3 shows the And tree form of the model once repaired by FIXIT.

Comparing the And trees of the faulty and repaired models, you see that the *handle is fixed* relation, which is common to the true successes, now appears in the repaired model tree. There are also two other new relations: *object is manipulable* and *object is orientable*.

The old model was too general, because you cannot be sure you can drink from an object just because it carries liquids and is liftable—it has to be orientable by virtue of having a fixed handle. The new model still allows cups to be identified properly, but the increased specificity of the model prevents pails from being identified as cups.

To make the repair, FIXIT does a breadth-first reexamination of all the relations in the model's And tree, looking for a relation with an explanation

Figure 18.2 A model's And tree before repair. Both cups and pails are identified as cups. The portion of the And tree below the dashed line must be replaced.

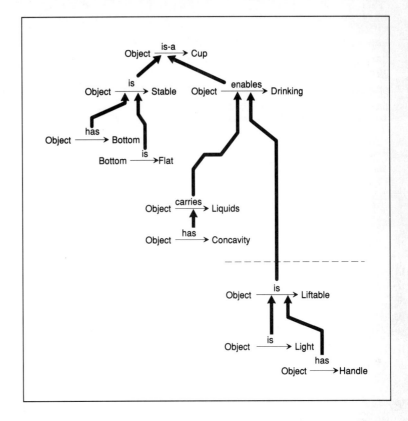

that needs to be replaced. For each relation reexamined, FIXIT looks for precedents that tie the reexamined relation to at least one of the true-success suspicious relations. If such precedents are found, FIXIT replaces the subtree beneath the reexamined relation using those precedents, thus explaining the reexamined relation in a new way.

The new explanation should be as short as possible, because the longer the chain of precedent-supplied Cause links, the less reliable the conclusion. After all, the contributing precedents supply Cause links that are only likely; they are not certain. Consequently, FIXIT initially limits its reexamination effort to the following precedents:

- The precedents MACBETH originally used to learn the model. These are included in the expectation that much of the model will be unchanged, and therefore will be constructable from the original precedents. These original precedents constitute the initial **head set**, so called because they lie at the head end of the chain of Cause links that eventually connects the model to one or more suspicious relations.

- Those precedents in which one of the true-success suspicious relations causes something. These precedents constitute the initial **tail set**, so called to contrast with the head set.

Figure 18.3 A model's And tree after repair. The repaired model allows only cups to be identified as cups. The portion of the And tree below the dashed line has been replaced.

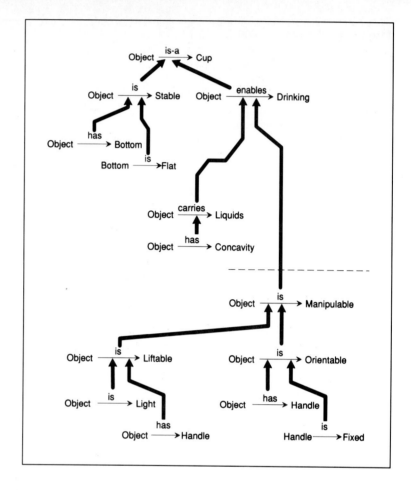

When FIXIT reexamines a relation, it looks for a way to explain that relation using all but one of the precedents in the combined head and tail sets. The exception is the precedent that was used to explain the reexamined relation previously. That precedent is omitted so that FIXIT can explore the hypothesis that it provided an incorrect explanation, leading to the model's defective behavior.

In the cup-and-pail example, the head set consists of the cup's functional description, along with the brick, glass, bowl, and briefcase precedents used by MACBETH. The tail set consist of all those precedents in which the true-success suspicious relation, *handle is fixed*, causes something. Suppose that the *handle is fixed* relation appears in only the door precedent, in which it is tied by a Cause link to *door is orientable*. Then, the tail set consists of the door precedent alone.

Accordingly, when FIXIT reexamines the *object is-a cup* relation, it uses the brick, glass, bowl, briefcase, and door precedents. It does not use the

Figure 18.4 Reexamination fails because the head and tail sets are not connected to one another. Only the relevant parts of the precedents are shown.

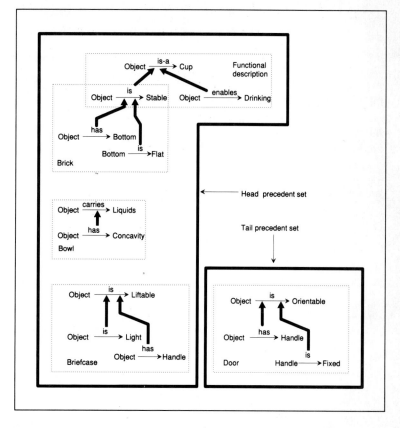

cup's functional description because that is the precedent MACBETH used to explain *object is-a cup* when the model was learned.

At this point, FIXIT's reexamination fails to lead anywhere because the head and tail sets do not connect the reexamined relation, *object is cup*, to the suspicious relation *handle is fixed*.

Similarly, when FIXIT reexamines the *object is stable* relation, it uses the cup's functional description along with the glass, bowl, briefcase, and door precedents, omitting the brick precedent, but fails again. When it reexamines the *object enables drinking* relation, it uses the cup's functional description along with the brick, bowl, briefcase, and door precedents, omitting the glass precedent, but fails again. FIXIT also fails when it reexamines the *object carries liquids* and the *object is liftable* relations. Evidently, more precedents have to be used.

Incorporating True-Success Suspicious Relations May Require Search

Once FIXIT concludes that more precedents have to be considered, it augments the precedents in either the head or the tail sets.

Figure 18.5 A model tree after repair with contributing precedents shown. Note that the straw precedent, having augmented the tail set, bridges the gap between the old model and the suspicious relation, *handle is fixed*. Now only cups are identified as cups; pails are not. Only the relevant parts of the precedents are shown.

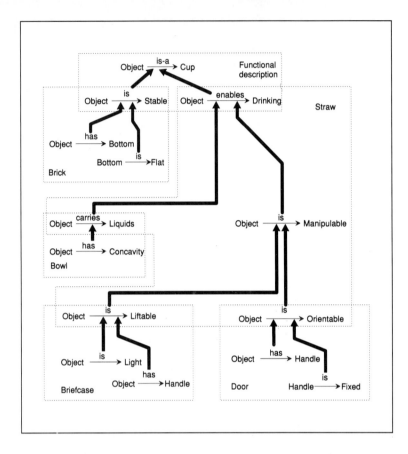

To augment the head set, FIXIT looks for precedents that extend the Cause link chains that lead through the existing head-set precedents. Symmetrically, to augment the tail set, FIXIT looks for precedents that extend the Cause link chains that lead through the existing tail-set precedents.

To keep the number of precedents as small as possible, FIXIT augments only the head or the tail set, whichever has fewer precedents. In the example, FIXIT augments the tail set because it currently has only one precedent, the door precedent. FIXIT adds the straw precedent because *handle is fixed* causes *door is orientable* in the existing door precedent and *straw is orientable* causes *straw is manipulable* in the new straw precedent.

Now FIXIT starts over using the augmented tail set. As before, reexamination fails on the *object is-a cup* relation, and on the first of the relations in the next layer, *object is stable*. But when FIXIT reexamines the *object enables drinking* relation, it succeeds, connecting *object enables drinking* with the *handle is fixed* relation via the new straw precedent and the existing door precedent, as shown in figure 18.5. Of course, all the precedents shown in the figure contain details that are not shown so as to avoid clutter.

Note that the model's And tree is restructured as necessary without reasoning explicitly about wrong or missing nodes and branches. The restructured And tree can be viewed as the following antecedent–consequent rule:

Repaired Cup-Identification Rule
If	The object has a bottom
	The bottom is flat
	The object has a concavity
	The object is light-weight
	The object has a handle
	The handle is fixed
Then	The object is a cup

FIXIT stops as soon as the repaired rule no longer matches the false successes, as the following indicates:

To deal with true-success suspicious relations using FIXIT,

▷ Until the false successes are accounted for,

  ▷ For each relation in the model tree, starting with the root relation and working down, breadth first,

    ▷ Form a head set consisting of all precedents that contributed to the malfunctioning model tree.

    ▷ Form a tail set consisting of all precedents in which one or more true-success suspicious relations cause another relation.

      ▷ Try to find a new explanation for a relation in the model tree using the head set, minus the precedent that explained the relation before, plus the tail set.

      ▷ If an explanation is found, replace that portion of the model that lies beneath the newly reexplained relation.

      ▷ Augment the smaller of the head set and the tail set with other precedents that extend the causal chains found in the set's existing precedents.

The Solution May Be to Explain the False-Success Suspicious Relations, Creating a Censor

The repaired model tree works on all the cup-versus-pail problems, because not one of the pail descriptions contains a *handle is fixed* relation. There remains a danger, however, that a precedent-oriented identification procedure, such as MACBETH would try hard to explain why a pail has a fixed handle, even though it already knows that the pail's description contains a *handle is hinged* relation.

Fortunately, FIXIT can also build recollections such as the following one, expressed as an antecedent–consequent rule:

Hinged-Handle Censor
    If   Handle is hinged
    Then   Handle is not fixed

Once this recollection is created, MACBETH, or any other identification procedure, can use the recollection to stop itself from trying to explain a relation that can be shown to be false by a single Cause link. As before, cups are identified as cups, and pails are not, but now the new recollection blocks useless effort directed at explaining that hinged-handle pails have fixed handles. A recollection so used is called a **censor**.

FIXIT creates censors if it cannot account for the false successes using the true-success suspicious relations. To create censors, FIXIT does a breadth-first reexamination of all the relations in the repaired model tree, looking for precedents that tie the negation of each reexamined relation to a false-success relation. The resulting explanation establishes why the false-success suspicious relation should block identification. This explanation, in turn, permits the creation of a new censor.

Initially, the precedent set is limited to the following, to keep the explanation as short as possible:

- Precedents in which the negation of the reexamined relation is caused by something. These precedents constitute the initial *head set*.
- Precedents in which one of the false-success suspicious relations causes something. These precedents constitute the initial *tail set*.

Here, the idea is to find an explanation for the negation of the reexamined relation that includes at least one of the false-success suspicious relations. If FIXIT finds such a collection of precedents, it creates a new censor from that collection of precedents.

Eventually, FIXIT's breadth-first reexamination tries to explain the *handle is not fixed* relation, given the false-success suspicious relation, *handle is hinged*. At this point, FIXIT uses the suitcase precedent, which happens to find its way into both the head and tail sets, because *handle is hinged* is connected to *handle is not fixed* by a cause relation:

A Suitcase ————————————————————————
This is a description of a suitcase. The suitcase is liftable because it is has a handle and because it is light. The handle is not fixed because it is hinged. The suitcase is useful because it is a portable container for clothes.

With the suitcase precedent, FIXIT has what it needs to generate the appropriate censor.

As before, FIXIT stops as soon as the repaired rule no longer matches the false successes, as the following indicates:

To deal with false-success suspicious relations using FIXIT,

▷ Until the false successes are accounted for,

  ▷ For each relation in the model tree, starting with the root relation and working down, breadth first,

   ▷ Form a head set consisting of all precedents in which the negation of the relation is caused by another relation.

   ▷ Form a tail set consisting of all precedents in which one or more false-success suspicious relations cause another relation.

    ▷ Try to find an explanation for the negation of the relation in the model tree using the head set plus the tail set.

    ▷ If an explanation is found, create a new censor.

   ▷ Augment the smaller of the head set and the tail set with other precedents that extend the causal chains found in the set's existing precedents.

Failure Can Stimulate a Search for More Detailed Descriptions

If there are no suspicious relations in a near-miss group, there are still several ways to correct the situation:

- Although the lack of suspicious relations indicates that there is no common explanation for failure, there may be just a few explanations, each of which is common to a subset of the true successes or the false successes. The problem is to partition situations into groups, inside each of which there is a consistent explanation for failure.

- Assume that a relation that occurs in some, but not all, the true successes is suspicious. See whether that relation can be used to explain the failures. If it can be, ask whether that true-success relation was left out of the other true-success descriptions by oversight.

- The lack of any suspicious relations may indicate that the situations must be described at a finer grain, adding more detail, so that an explicit explanation emerges.

Many good teachers ask their students to describe problems thoroughly before the students start to solve the problems. As a student, FIXIT certainly benefits from thorough descriptions, for thorough descriptions are more likely to contain relations that seem irrelevant at first, but that prove suspicious when several problems are looked at from the perspective of near-miss groups.

SUMMARY

- Sometimes, a learning procedure can make a mistake, leading to a need for knowledge repair. MACBETH, for example, can learn to recognize cups, but initially confounds cups and pails.
- FIXIT uses near-miss groups, consisting of a set of positive examples and a set of negative examples, to isolate suspicious relations.
- Knowledge repair may require FIXIT either to explain true-success suspicious relations, altering an original explanation, or to explain false-success suspicious relations, creating a censor.
- A frustrated attempt to repair knowledge suggests that the right suspicious relations are not in the descriptions, and suggests that more effort should go into creating more detailed descriptions.

BACKGROUND

The near-miss group idea was conceived by Patrick H. Winston; it was first put to use by Kendra Kratkiewicz [1984] when she showed that near-miss groups could pull informative differences out of complicated descriptions of historic conflicts. Subsequently, Satyajit Rao showed how such informative differences could be used to do informed knowledge repairs [Winston and Rao 1990]. Boris Katz suggested the idea of postulating oversights when no suspicious relation emerges from a near-miss group.

The idea of using differences to focus learning appears in the work of Brian Falkenhainer [1988], in which he uses differences between working devices and nonworking devices, plus domain knowledge, to deduce why the nonworking devices fail.

The use of the term *censor* in artificial intelligence has been popularized by Marvin Minsky [1985].

One defect of the approach to learning and knowledge repair described in this chapter is that every concept has to have a name; in many experiments, however, the concepts do not correspond well to English words, forcing us to invent awkward, multiply hyphenated names. An approach to dealing with this defect is explained by Rao [1991].

19

Learning by Recording Cases

In this chapter, you learn how it is possible to deal with problem domains in which good models are impossible to build.

In particular, you see how to *learn by recording cases as is*, doing nothing to the information in those cases until that information is used. First, you learn that you are using the *consistency heuristic* whenever you attribute a feature of a previously observed thing to a new, never-before-seen thing. Next, you learn how it is possible to find nearest neighbors in a feature space quickly using *k-d trees*.

By way of illustration, you see how to find the nearest neighbors of a wooden block, measured by width and height, in time proportional to the logarithm of the number of blocks. You also see how the same ideas make it possible to move a robot's arm without developing complicated motion equations and without obtaining difficult-to-measure arm parameters.

Once you have finished this chapter, you will know how to do nearest-neighbor calculations, and you will understand some of the conditions under which nearest-neighbor calculations work well.

RECORDING AND RETRIEVING RAW EXPERIENCE

In this section, you learn about the consistency heuristic, and you learn to identify the kinds of problems you can solve by recording cases for later use.

The Consistency Heuristic Enables Remembered Cases to Supply Properties

Consider the eight blocks in figure 19.1. Each has a known color, width, and height. Next, suppose you are confronted with a new block of size 1 by 4 centimeters and of unknown color. If you had to guess its color, given nothing else to go on, you would have to guess that the color is the same as that of the block that is most similar in other respects—namely in width and height. In so guessing, you would use the consistency heuristic:

The **consistency heuristic**:

▷ Whenever you want to guess a property of something, given nothing else to go on but a set of reference cases, find the most similar case, as measured by known properties, for which the property is known. Guess that the unknown property is the same as that known property.

Plotting the widths and heights of the cases yields the feature space shown in figure 19.2 and makes it easy to apply the consistency heuristic in the color-guessing situation. No fancy reasoning is needed. Because the width and height of the unknown, labeled U, are closest to the width and height of the orange block, you have to assume that the orange block is the right case, and to guess that block U is orange.

The Consistency Heuristic Solves a Difficult Dynamics Problem

Consider the problem of moving a robot hand along a prescribed path in space at a prescribed speed, as in figure 19.3. To succeed, you clearly need to know how the joint angles should change with time, and what joint torques will produce those joint-angle changes.

Relating the joint angles to manipulator position is a **kinematics** problem. It is relatively easy to derive formulas that relate manipulator position to joint angles. For the joint angles, θ_1 and θ_2, and segment lengths, l_1 and l_2, of the two-dimensional manipulator shown in figure 19.3, the equations are as follows:

$$x = l_1 \cos\theta_1 + l_2 \cos(\pi - \theta_2 - \theta_1),$$
$$y = l_1 \sin\theta_1 + l_2 \sin(\pi - \theta_2 - \theta_1).$$

For the two-joint, two-dimensional manipulator shown in figure 19.3, it is also straightforward, albeit tedious, to derive the inverse formulas relating joint angles to manipulator position:

$$\theta_1 = \tan^{-1}\left(\frac{y}{x}\right) - \tan^{-1}\left(\frac{l_2 \sin\theta_2}{l_1 + l_2 \cos\theta_2}\right)$$
$$\theta_2 = \cos^{-1}\left(\frac{x^2 + y^2 - l_1^2 - l_2^2}{2 l_1 l_2}\right)$$

Figure 19.1 Eight blocks of known color, width, and height. These eight form a set of cases by which color can be guessed for other blocks of known width and height.

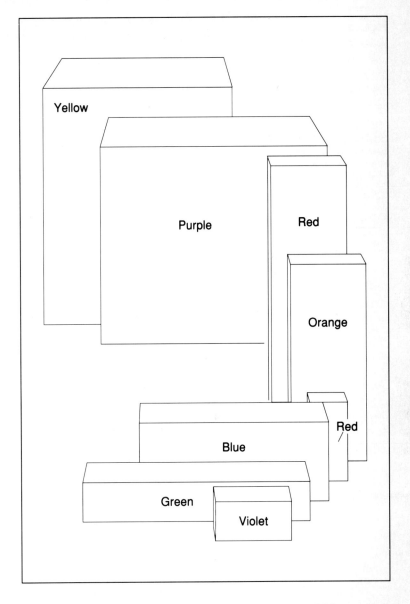

Given formulas for joint angles, you might think it would be easy to move a manipulator: Just chop up the desired trajectory into pieces, determine the necessary joint motions during each piece, and tell the motors about the results. Unfortunately, the only message that motors understand is one that tells them the torque you want them to supply.

Relating joint motions to required motor torques is a *dynamics* problem, which can be unbearably intricate mathematically, even though everything ultimately is just a matter of Newton's second law relating force to

Figure 19.2 A feature space relating the block of unknown color to eight blocks of known color. The color of the unknown, block U, is judged to be the same as the color of the orange block, the one that is closest in width and height.

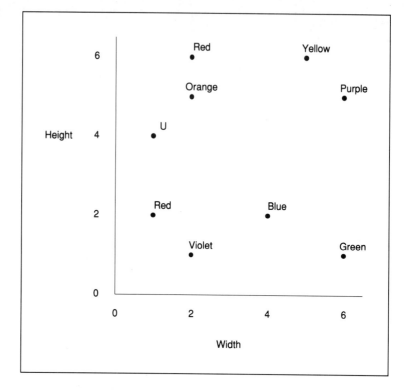

the product of mass and acceleration. The following complicated-looking equations emerge, ignoring gravity, assuming cylindrical links, for the simple two-joint, two-dimensional manipulator shown in figure 19.3:

$$\tau_1 = \ddot{\theta}_1\left(I_1 + I_2 + m_2 l_1 l_2 \cos\theta_2 + \frac{m_1 l_1^2 + m_2 l_2^2}{4} + m_2 l_1^2\right)$$
$$+ \ddot{\theta}_2\left(I_2 + \frac{m_2 l_2^2}{4} + \frac{m_2 l_1 l_2}{2}\cos\theta_2\right)$$
$$- \dot{\theta}_2^2\frac{m_2 l_1 l_2}{2}\sin\theta_2$$
$$- \dot{\theta}_1\dot{\theta}_2 m_2 l_1 l_2 \sin\theta_2,$$
$$\tau_2 = \ddot{\theta}_1\left(I_2 + \frac{m_2 l_1 l_2}{2}\cos\theta_2 + \frac{m_2 l_2^2}{4}\right)$$
$$+ \ddot{\theta}_2\left(I_2 + \frac{m_2 l_2^2}{4}\right)$$
$$+ \dot{\theta}_1^2\frac{m_2 l_1 l_2}{2}\sin\theta_2.$$

where each τ_i is a torque, each $\dot{\theta}_i$ is an angular velocity, each $\ddot{\theta}_i$ is an angular acceleration, each m_i is a mass, each l_i is a length, and each I_i is a moment of inertia about a center of mass.

Figure 19.3 A robot arm throwing a ball. To arrange the throw, you must know the joint angles that produce the straight-line motion shown, and you must know how to apply torques that produce the desired joint angles.

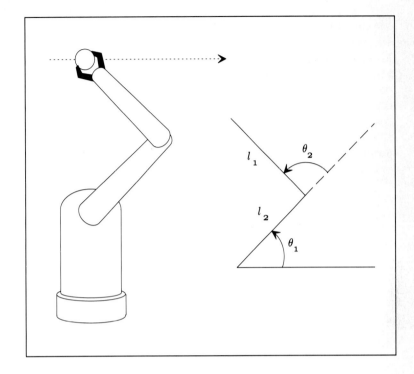

The torque equations for three-dimensional manipulators are much bulkier because six joints are required to place a manipulator at a given position in space with a given orientation. Like the solution for two joints, the real-world solutions demonstrate that the required torques depend, in general, on accelerations, on velocities squared, on velocity products, and on multipliers that depend on joint position:

■ Because there are velocities squared, the torques necessarily involve *centripetal forces.*

■ Because there are products of different velocities, the torques involve *Coriolis forces.*

■ Because there are multipliers that are functions of several angles, the torques involve *variable, cross-coupled moments of effective inertia.*

Even with all this mathematical sophistication, it remains difficult to get satisfactory results with real-world robot arms, and to explain how we can manage to move our biological arms. There are just too many factors to consider and too many measurements to be made with too much precision.

Fortunately, nearest-neighbor calculations in a feature space, together with the notion of practice, provide an alternate approach to robot-arm control. Imagine a giant table with columns for torques, positions, velocities, squared velocities, velocity products, and accelerations:

Figure 19.4 The robot arm shown in figure 19.3 tries to follow a straight line. In the first instance the robot arm does poorly because its table is sparse. In the second and third instances, a table that relates torques to desired path parameters is used, and the robot arm does much better.

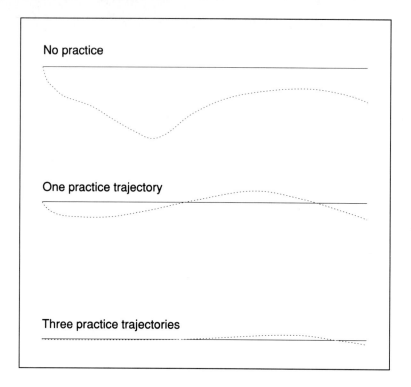

τ_1	τ_2	θ_1	θ_2	$\dot{\theta}_1$	$\dot{\theta}_2$	$\dot{\theta}_1^2$	$\dot{\theta}_2^2$	$\dot{\theta}_1\dot{\theta}_2$	$\ddot{\theta}_1^2$	$\ddot{\theta}_2^2$

Next, suppose you issue a command that causes the robot arm to be waved about more or less randomly. Every so often, you measure the torques, positions, and other indicated parameters, and you record the results in the giant table.

Then, when you want to move the robot arm along a prescribed trajectory, you break up that trajectory into little pieces; treat the giant table as a feature space; look for entries with nearby positions, velocities, squared velocities, velocity products, and accelerations; and interpolate among them to find appropriate torques for the corresponding little piece of trajectory.

You might worry, legitimately, that no table could hold enough entries to fill the feature space densely enough to do a good job, even with an elaborate interpolation method. To combat this density problem, you arrange for practice. The first time that you have the robot try a particular reach or throw motion, it does miserably, because the table relating torques to positions, velocities, and accelerations is sparse. But even though the robot does miserably, it is still writing new entries into its table, and these new entries are closer than old entries to the desired trajectory's positions, velocities, and accelerations. After a few tries, motion becomes smooth and accurate, as shown in figure 19.4, because you are interpolating among the new table entries, and they are much closer to what you want.

FINDING NEAREST NEIGHBORS

In this section, you learn about two relatively fast ways to find nearest neighbors; one is serial, and one is parallel.

A Fast Serial Procedure Finds the Nearest Neighbor in Logarithmic Time

The straightforward way to determine a block's nearest neighbor is to calculate the distance to each other block, and then to find the minimum among those distances. For n other blocks, there are n distances to compute and $n - 1$ distance comparisons to do. Thus, the straightforward approach is fine if n is 10, but it is not so fine if n is 1 million or 1 billion.

Fortunately, there is a better way, one for which the number of calculations is proportional to $\log_2 n$, rather than to n. This better way involves the use of a special kind of **decision tree**. In general, a decision tree is an arrangement of tests that prescribes the most appropriate test at every step in an analysis:

A **decision tree** is a representation

That is a semantic tree

In which

▷ Each node is connected to a set of possible answers.

▷ Each nonleaf node is connected to a test that splits its set of possible answers into subsets corresponding to different test results.

▷ Each branch carries a particular test result's subset to another node.

To exploit the decision-tree idea so as to deal with the block-identification example, you divide up the cases in advance of nearest-neighbor calculation. As illustrated in figure 19.5, all cases are divided first by height alone into two sets, each with an equal number of blocks. In one set, all heights are equal to or greater than 5 centimeters; in the other, equal to or less than 2 centimeters. A 3-centimeter block-free zone separates the two sets.

Next, each of the two sets is divided by width alone. The tall set is divided into one set in which all widths are equal to or greater than 5 centimeters, and another set in which all widths are equal to or less than 2

Figure 19.5 The case sets
are divided horizontally and
vertically until only one block
remains in each set.

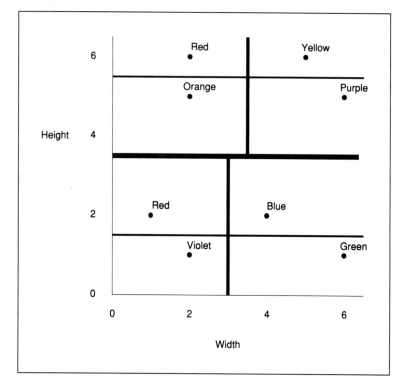

centimeters. Similarly, the bottom set is divided into one set of blocks 2
centimeters or less, and one set of blocks 4 centimeters or greater.

Finally, each of those four sets is divided by height alone, producing
eight sets of just one block each.

The overall result is called a **k-d** tree, where the term *k-d* is used to
emphasize that distances are measured in *k* dimensions:

A **k-d tree** is a representation

That is a decision tree

In which

▷ The set of possible answers consists of points, one of which may
  be the nearest neighbor to a given point.

▷ Each test specifies a coordinate, a threshold, and a neutral zone
  around the threshold containing no points.

▷ Each test divides a set of points into two sets, according to on
  which side of the threshold each point lies.

To determine the nearest neighbor of U, you first note that U's height
is more than 3.5 centimeters, which is the middling height between the

shortest tall block and the tallest short block. From this observation, you conclude that U is more likely, albeit not certain, to be nearer to one of the tall blocks than to one of the short blocks. On this ground, you temporarily ignore the short blocks.

Because the tallest short block is 2 centimeters tall, the distance between U and the tallest short block is at least 2 centimeters, and maybe is more, because the difference in height alone is 2 centimeters, as is evident in the top part of figure 19.6. If U proves to be equal to or less than 2 centimeters from a tall block, your decision temporarily to ignore the short blocks will become a permanent decision. If U is more than 2 centimeters from a tall block, you will have to reconsider the short blocks eventually.

Next, you consider the tall blocks, which are themselves divided into two sets. Because U's width is less than 3.5 centimeters, U is more likely, albeit not certain, to be nearer to one of the narrow tall blocks than to one of the wide tall blocks. On this ground, you temporarily ignore the wide tall blocks.

As illustrated in the middle part of figure 19.6, if U proves to be equal to or less than 4 centimeters from a narrow tall block, your decision temporarily to ignore the wide tall blocks will become a permanent decision, because the width of U differs by 4 centimeters from the width of the narrowest wide tall block.

One more step puts the unknown with the short, narrow, tall blocks, of which there is only one, the orange block, as illustrated in the bottom part of figure 19.6. If U proves to be equal to or less than 2 centimeters from the orange block, there is no need to calculate the distance to the narrow tall red block, which differs from U by 2 centimeters in height alone.

Now it is clear that the nearest block is the orange one, at a distance of 1.41 centimeters, provided that all previous decisions turn out to be justified. In this example, those decisions are justified because 1.41 centimeters is less than 2 centimeters, justifying the rejection of the narrow tall red block; it is less than 4 centimeters, justifying the rejection of the yellow and purple blocks; and it is less than 2 centimeters, justifying the rejection of all the short blocks.

Finding the nearest block is really just a matter of following a path through a decision tree that reflects the way the objects are divided up into sets. As the decision tree in figure 19.7 shows, only three one-axis comparisons are required to guess the nearest neighbor in the example, no matter what the width and height of the unknown are. Once the distance to the guessed nearest neighbor is calculated, only three more comparisons are needed to validate the decisions that led to the guess if it is correct. If you are unlucky, and the guess is wrong, you have to look harder, working down through the sets that have been ignored previously.

In general, the decision tree with branching factor 2 and depth d will have 2^d leaves. Accordingly, if there are n objects to be identified, d will

Figure 19.6 In the top part, unknown U cannot be closer than 2 centimeters to any block in the bottom set, because the height of block U is 4 centimeters and the height of the tallest block in the bottom set is 2 centimeters. In the middle part, the remaining cases are divided into two sets. In one set, all widths are greater than 3.5 centimeters; in the other, less than 3.5 centimeters. Because the width of block U is 1 centimeter and the width of the narrowest block in the right set is 5 centimeters, block U cannot be closer than 4 centimeters to any block in the right set. Finally, in the bottom part, only two cases remain. Because the height of block U is 4 centimeters and the height of the red block is 6 centimeters, block U cannot be closer than 2 centimeters to the red block.

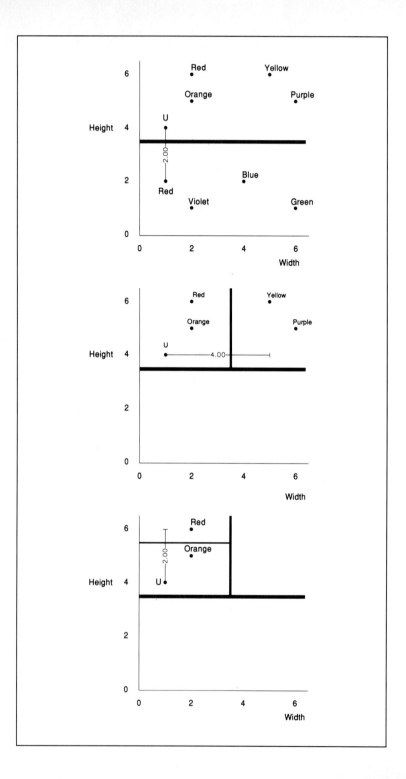

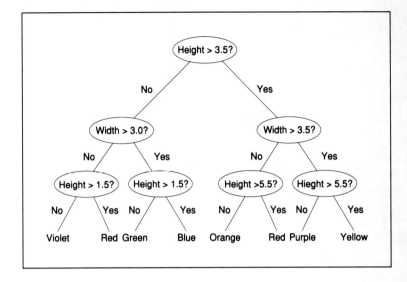

have to be large enough to ensure that $2^d \geq n$. Taking the logarithm of both sides, it is clear that the number of comparisons required, which corresponds to the depth of the tree, will be on the order of $\log_2 n$. If there are eight objects, the saving does not amount to much. If there are 1 billion objects, however, the number of comparisons is on the order of 30, not 1 billion, which is a substantial saving.

Here is the procedure for dividing the cases into sets, building a decision tree along the way:

To divide the cases into sets,

▷ If there is only one case, stop.

▷ If this is the first division of cases, pick the vertical axis for comparison; otherwise, pick the axis that is different from the axis at the next higher level.

▷ Considering only the axis of comparison, find the average position of the two middle objects. Call this average position the threshold, and construct a decision-tree test that compares unknowns in the axis of comparison against the threshold. Also note the position of the two middle objects in the axis of comparison. Call these positions the upper and lower boundaries.

▷ Divide up all the objects into two subsets, according to on which side of the average position they lie.

▷ Divide up the objects in each subset, forming a subtree for each, using this procedure.

Of course, the procedure for finding the nearest neighbor must address the possibility that previously ignored choices will have to be examined. Its common name is the K-D procedure:

To find the nearest neighbor using the K-D procedure,

▷ Determine whether there is only one element in the set under consideration.

    ▷ If there is only one, report it.

    ▷ Otherwise, compare the unknown, in the axis of comparison, against the current node's threshold. The result determines the likely set.

    ▷ Find the nearest neighbor in the likely set using this procedure.

    ▷ Determine whether the distance to the nearest neighbor in the likely set is less than or equal to the distance to the other set's boundary in the axis of comparison:

        ▷ If it is, then report the nearest neighbor in the likely set.

        ▷ If it is not, check the unlikely set using this procedure; return the nearer of the nearest neighbors in the likely set and in the unlikely set.

Parallel Hardware Finds Nearest Neighbors Even Faster

If you happen to have a massively parallel computer, with so many processors that each case can have its own, then none of this fancy search is needed. Each distance measurement can proceed in parallel.

Of course, all the results have to be compared somehow to find the case with the minimum distance from the unknown. One way to do this comparison would be to have neighboring processors compare their results. Then each two-processor minimum would be compared with a neighboring two-processor minimum. Carrying on this way eventually would lead to the global minimum after on the order of $\log_2 n$ sequential steps, where n is the number of distances to be compared. There are better ways, however, that find the minimum distance in constant time on a parallel computer.

SUMMARY

■ The consistency heuristic is the justification for the use of remembered cases as sources of properties for previously unseen objects.

■ Remembered cases can help you to solve many difficult problems, including problems in dynamic arm control.

- The K-D procedure is a fast serial procedure that finds nearest neighbors in logarithmic time.
- Parallel hardware can find nearest neighbors even faster than the K-D procedure can.

BACKGROUND

The discussion of K-D trees is based on the work of Jerome H. Friedman and colleagues [1977].

The discussion of arm control is based on the work of Chris Atkeson [1990]. Atkeson's more recent work does not involve K-D trees, however; instead, he has developed fast hardware that essentially interpolates among all cases.

20

Learning by Managing Multiple Models

In this chapter, you learn about an elegant way to use positive and negative examples to create a *version space*, which in turn helps you to zero in on what it takes to be a member of a class.

The *version-space procedure* can learn quickly as long as there is a stream of noise-free positive and negative examples, there is a fixed number of attributes, and a class-characterizing model can be expressed as a combination of values for those attributes.

By way of illustration, you learn how to extract knowledge from a database that describes the recent habits of a student who sometimes exhibits a mood-depressing allergic reaction.

Once you have finished this chapter, you will see that an ability to handle multiple alternative theories eliminates the need for the negative examples to be near-miss negative examples.

THE VERSION-SPACE METHOD

In Chapter 16, one evolving model was modified each time a new example became available. To prevent mistaken modifications, each new example was required to be only a little different from the current model, thus preventing multiple interpretations and uncertainty about how to modify the model.

In this section, you learn about another way to deal with examples. You prevent mistaken modifications by following each interpretation as long as it remains viable.

Version Space Consists of Overly General and Overly Specific Models

A **version space** is a representation that enables you to keep track of all the useful information supplied by a sequence of learning examples, without remembering any of the examples. A version-space description consists of two complementary trees, one containing nodes connected to overly general models and the other containing nodes connected to overly specific models. Each link between nodes in a version space represents either a specialization or a generalization operation between the models connected to the nodes:

A **version space** is a representation

In which

▷ There is a specialization tree and a generalization tree.

▷ Each node is connected to a model.

▷ One node in the generalization tree is connected to a model that matches everything.

▷ One node in the specialization tree is connected to a model that matches only one thing.

▷ Links between nodes denote generalization and specialization relations between their models.

With writers that

▷ Connect a node with a model

With readers that

▷ Produce a node's model

The key idea in version-space learning is that specialization of the general models and generalization of the specific models ultimately leads to just one, guaranteed-correct model that matches all observed positive examples and does not match any negative examples. You are about to see how the necessary specialization and generalization operations are done, first abstractly, and then in the context of the allergy example.

In figure 20.1(a), you see just two nodes. One represents the most general possible model—the one that matches every possible object. The other represents a very specific model that matches only the description of the first positive example seen.

In figure 20.1(b), you see that the most general model has been specialized such that the new models derived from that most general model all fail to match a new negative example. Each of the new models is to be a small perturbation of the old model from which it was derived.

Also in figure 20.1(b), you see that the most specific model has been generalized such that the new models derived from it are all general enough

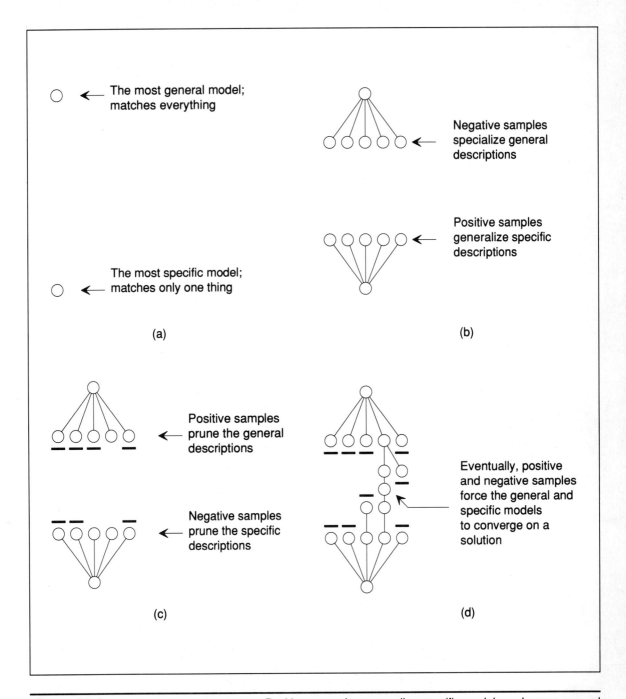

The most general model; matches everything

The most specific model; matches only one thing

(a)

Negative samples specialize general descriptions

Positive samples generalize specific descriptions

(b)

Positive samples prune the general descriptions

Negative samples prune the specific descriptions

(c)

Eventually, positive and negative samples force the general and specific models to converge on a solution

(d)

Figure 20.1 Learning in a version space. Positive examples generalize specific models and prune general models; negative examples specialize general models and prune specific models.

to match a new positive example. Again, each of the new models is to be a small, unique perturbation.

Thus, general models become more specific to prevent match, and specific models become more general to ensure match.

As figure 20.1(c) indicates, however, the trees emerging from the most general model and a specific model do not expand forever. Instead, many branches are pruned away. To see why, consider what happens when you see a negative example. Whenever a specific model matches a negative example, that specific model must be eliminated. The reason is that specific models change only when positive examples are encountered, and positive examples can only make specific models become more general. There is nothing that makes specific models more specific. Hence, if a specific model ever matches a negative example, any other specific model derived from it will match that negative example too.

Symmetrically, each time a positive example is used to generalize the specific models, you need to eliminate those general models that fail to match the positive example. The reason is that general models can only become more specific. Hence, if a general model ever fails to match a positive example, any other general model derived from it will fail to match too.

Eventually, the positive and negative examples may be such that only one general model and one identical specific model survive. When that happens, as shown in figure 20.1(d), no further examples are needed because that sole survivor is sure to be the correct model, assuming that a correct model exists.

Only two details remain. One has to do with what sort of perturbations are allowed to the general and specific models. As emphasized in figure 20.2(a), each time a general model is specialized, that specialization must be a generalization of one of the specific models. Otherwise, no combination of changes could bring the specialization to converge with anything that emerges from the generalization of specific models.

Similarly, each time a specific model is generalized, that generalization must be a specialization of one of the general models. Otherwise, no combination of changes could bring the new generalization to converge with anything that emerges from the specialization of general models.

The other detail is that, each time a general model is specialized, that specialization must not be a specialization of another general model, as suggested in figure 20.2(b). Otherwise, you would be retaining a needlessly specific model in the set of general models.

Generalization and Specialization Leads to Version-Space Convergence

Having learned about version space in abstract terms, let us consider a concrete example. Suppose you are a doctor treating a patient who occa-

Figure 20.2 Each specialization of a general model must be such that it is a generalization of some specific model. Also, each specialization must not be a specialization of some more general generalization.

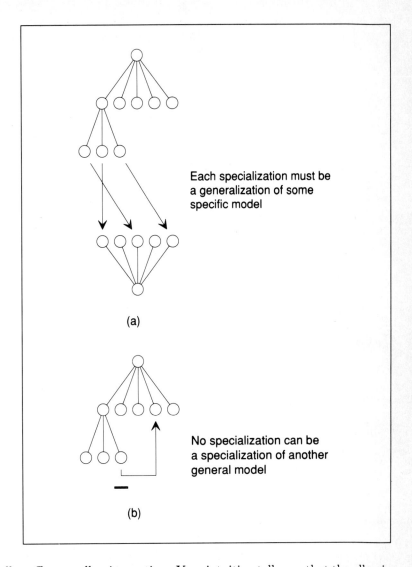

Each specialization must be a generalization of some specific model

(a)

No specialization can be a specialization of another general model

(b)

sionally suffers an allergic reaction. Your intuition tells you that the allergic condition is a direct result of a certain combination of the place where your patient eats, the time of day, the day of the week, and the amount that your patient spends on food. It might be, for example, that eating breakfast on Fridays is the source of your patient's allergy, or perhaps eating something expensive at Sam's is.

One completely specific model in this food world is a list of values for situation-characterizing attributes such as place, meal, day, and cost. One example of such a model is [Sam's, Dinner, Thursday, Expensive]. Such a model, with every attribute value specified, can match only one restaurant–meal–day–cost combination. In contrast, the most general descriptive model does not specify any attribute value. One notation for this general model is a list of question marks, [?, ?, ?, ?], with each question mark signaling that any attribute value in the corresponding position is allowed.

The model [Sam's, ?, ?, Expensive] matches any situation in which your patient eats expensive food at Sam's on any day at any meal. Models such as this one, with mixed attribute values and question marks, lie between those that are completely specific and the completely general model.

Next suppose, so as to keep the example simple, that the only way to generalize a model is to replace one of the attribute values with a question mark. Thus, one generalization of [Sam's, ?, ?, Expensive] is [Sam's, ?, ?, ?]. Similarly, suppose that the only way to specialize a model is to replace a question mark with an attribute value. Thus, one specialization of [Sam's, ?, ?, Expensive] is [Sam's, Dinner, ?, Expensive].

Note that, if your patient eats three meals per day, seven days per week, some cheap and some expensive, at one of three places, you would have to ask your patient to experiment with $3 \times 7 \times 2 \times 3 = 126$ combinations if each combination could, in principle, produce the allergic reaction. But if you happen to believe, somehow, that there is a particular combination of characteristics that produces the allergy in your patient, you can do much better.

Suppose that the examples, in the order analyzed, are as shown in the following table:

Number	Restaurant	Meal	Day	Cost	Reaction
1	Sam's	breakfast	Friday	cheap	yes
2	Lobdell	lunch	Friday	expensive	no
3	Sam's	lunch	Saturday	cheap	yes
4	Sarah's	breakfast	Sunday	cheap	no
5	Sam's	breakfast	Sunday	expensive	no

The first example, a positive one, enables the birth of a version space—the one shown in figure 20.3. It consists of the most general possible model, [? ? ? ?], along with a completely specific model, [Sam's Breakfast Friday Cheap], constructed by straightforward treatment of the positive example itself as a model.

The second example, this time a negative one, forces specialization of the most general model, as shown in figure 20.4. Note that each specialization involves a minimal change to the most general model, [? ? ? ?]. You construct each one by replacing a question mark in the most general model by the corresponding part of the most specific model. This method ensures that each new specialization is a generalization of the most specific model. That, in turn, ensures that specializations of the new general models can eventually converge with generalizations of the existing specific model.

Figure 20.3 A version space is born. It consists of one positive example, together with the most general possible model—the one that matches everything.

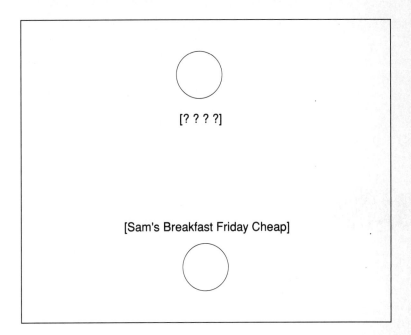

Figure 20.4 A negative example forces specialization of the most general possible model. Each specialization must be a generalization of the single specific model.

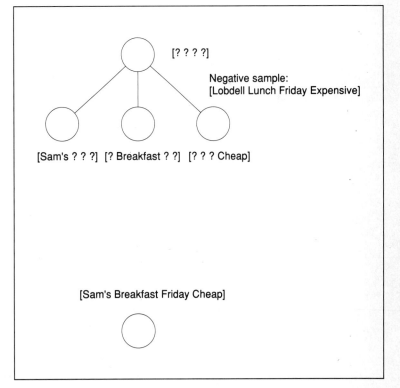

Note that there is one exception. The specialization [? ? Friday ?] does not appear in the version space because it matches the negative example, [Lobdell Lunch Friday Expensive]. After all, the point of specializing the most general description is to prevent a match with the negative example.

Without the requirement that specializations must be generalizations of the specific model, many more specializations would be possible. Given three restaurants, three meals, seven days, and either cheap or expensive meals, there must be $3 + 3 + 7 + 2 = 15$ different ways to specialize [? ? ? ?] by replacing one question mark. Twelve of these 15 possible specializations fail to be generalizations of the specific model.

The third example—another positive one—forces generalization of the most specific model, as shown in figure 20.5. You construct the new model by comparing the existing most specific model with the positive example. In each place where the most specific model differs from the positive example, the existing item in the most specific model is replaced by a question mark. Thus, [Sam's Breakfast Friday Cheap] is compared with [Sam's Lunch Saturday Cheap], producing [Sam's ? ? Cheap]. Thus, the previous most specific model is replaced by a single new generalization that is the same except where the new example positively forces a change.

Note also that [Sam's Lunch Saturday Cheap] cannot possibly match either the general model [? Breakfast ? ?] or any other model that is a specialization of [? Breakfast ? ?]. Accordingly, [? Breakfast ? ?] cannot be on the road toward the ultimate solution, and it is pruned away.

The fourth example—this time another negative one, shown in figure 20.6—forces specialization of any general model that matches it. Because [Sam's ? ? ?] does not match [Sarah's Breakfast Sunday Cheap], however, there is no need to specialize it. Because [? ? ? Cheap] does match [Sarah's Breakfast Sunday Cheap], it requires specialization. As before, the specialization of [? ? ? Cheap] must take the direction of a generalization of a specific model, of which there is only one, [Sam's ? ? Cheap]. Plainly, the only way to specialize [? ? ? Cheap] in the direction of [Sam's ? ? Cheap] is to specialize [? ? ? Cheap] to [Sam's ? ? Cheap], which makes the new general model identical to the only specific model.

Note, however, that this new specialization, [Sam's ? ? Cheap], is also a specialization of another surviving general model—namely, [Sam's ? ? ?]. Accordingly, it is pruned off, because only those specializations that are absolutely forced by the data are to be retained. That way, when the general models and the specific models converge, you can be sure that the positive and negative examples allow no other model.

At this point, only one general model, [Sam's ? ? ?], and one specific model, [Sam's ? ? Cheap], remain. The next example, a negative one, brings them together, as shown in figure 20.7, for [Sam's Breakfast Sunday Expensive] forces a specialization of [Sam's ? ? ?], and the only way to specialize [Sam's ? ? ?] in the direction of [Sam's ? ? Cheap] is to con-

Figure 20.5 A positive example forces generalization of the single specific model. The new, more general specific model is general enough to match both of the positive examples analyzed so far. Also, one general model is pruned.

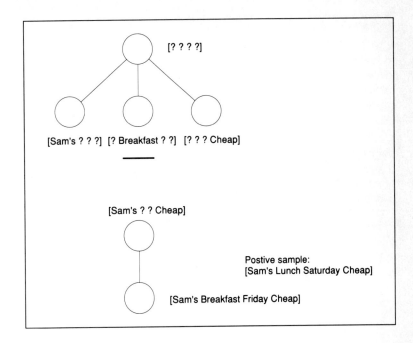

Figure 20.6 Another negative example forces specialization of one of the general models. That new, more specific general model is quickly pruned away, however, for it is a specialization of another general model.

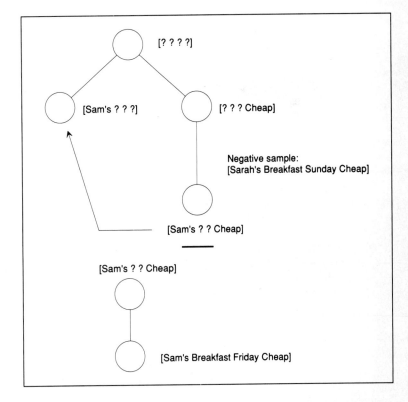

Figure 20.7 Finally, another negative example forces specialization of the only remaining general model. That new, more specific general model is the same as the only specific model. Hence, the general set and the specific set have converged, producing the only possible model that handles the examples properly.

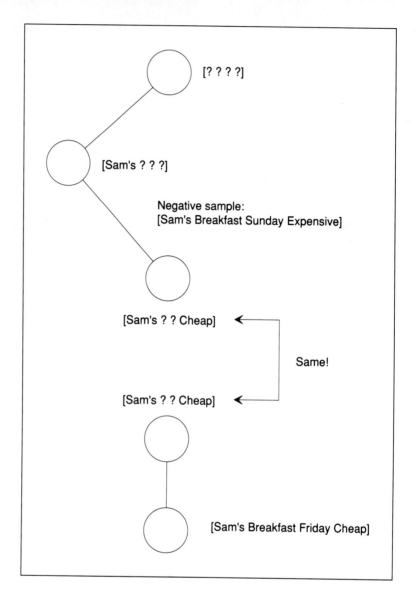

[? ? ? ?]

[Sam's ? ? ?]

Negative sample:
[Sam's Breakfast Sunday Expensive]

[Sam's ? ? Cheap] ←

Same!

[Sam's ? ? Cheap] ←

[Sam's Breakfast Friday Cheap]

struct a new general model that is the same as the existing specific model. Accordingly, learning concludes. Cheap food at Sam's produces the allergy.

VERSION-SPACE CHARACTERISTICS

In this section, you learn that the version-space procedure handles positive and negative examples symmetrically. You also learn that it can do a lot of good even before it converges on a single description.

The Version-Space Procedure Handles Positive and Negative Examples Symmetrically

By way of summary, here is the version-space procedure. Note that positive and negative examples are handled symmetrically.

To respond to positive and negative examples using a version space,

▷ If the example is positive,

    ▷ Generalize all specific models to match the positive example, but ensure the following,

        ▷ The new specific models involve minimal changes.

        ▷ Each new specific model is a specialization of some general model.

        ▷ No new specific model is a generalization of some other specific model.

    ▷ Prune away all general models that fail to match the positive example

▷ If the example is negative,

    ▷ Specialize all general models to prevent match with the negative example, but ensure the following,

        ▷ The new general models involve minimal changes.

        ▷ Each new general model is a generalization of some specific model.

        ▷ No new general model is a specialization of some other general model.

    ▷ Prune away all specific models that match the negative example.

Evidently, the procedure allows multiple specializations as well as multiple generalizations. There is never more than one specialization in the allergy example, because the method used to generalize specializations never produces more than one generalization for each positive example seen. Other generalization methods do not have this characteristic.

The Version-Space Procedure Enables Early Recognition

Once one or more negative examples have been analyzed, you can say with certainty that some examples cannot possibly be positive examples. Just after the first positive and negative examples have been analyzed in the allergy example, there are only three general models. If a combination of attribute values does not match any of them, then it must be a negative example, for none of the three general models can ever become more general.

Thus, you can be sure that [Lobdell Dinner Wednesday Expensive] cannot possibly be a positive example, once you have analyzed [Sam's Breakfast Friday Cheap] and [Lobdell Lunch Friday Expensive], because [Lobdell Dinner Wednesday Expensive] does not match [Sam's ? ? ?], [? Breakfast ? ?], or [? ? ? Cheap].

SUMMARY

- One way to learn is to maintain a set of overly general models and a set of overly specific models in a version space. Then, you can use positive and negative examples to move the two sets together until they converge on one just-right model.
- The version-space procedure enables early recognition before the overly general set and the overly specific set converge.
- The version-space procedure handles positive and negative examples symmetrically. Positive examples generalize the overly specific set and trim down the overly general set. Negative examples specialize the overly general set and trim down the overly specific set.

BACKGROUND

The discussion in this chapter is based on the work of Tom M. Mitchell [1982].

21

Learning by Building Identification Trees

In this chapter, you learn about a method that enables computers to learn by assembling tests into an *identification tree*. You also learn how an identification tree can be transformed into a *perspicuous set of antecedent–consequent rules*.

Identification-tree building is the most widely used learning method. Thousands of practical identification trees, for applications ranging from medical diagnosis to process control, have been built using the ideas that you learn about in this chapter.

By way of illustration, you see how the SPROUTER and PRUNER procedures construct rules that determine whether a person is likely to be sunburned, given a database of sample people and their physical attributes.

Once you have finished this chapter, you will know how to build identification trees, and how to transform them into rules.

FROM DATA TO IDENTIFICATION TREES

In this section, you learn how to build identification trees by looking for regularities in data.

The World Is Supposed to Be Simple

Imagine that you are somehow unaware of the factors that leave some people red and in pain after a few hours on the beach, while other people just turn tanned and happy. Being curious, you go to the beach and start jotting down notes. You observe that people vary in hair color, height, and weight. Some smear lotion on their bodies; others do not. Ultimately, some turn red. You want to use the observed properties to help you predict whether a new person—one who is not in the observed set—will turn red.

One possibility, of course, is to look for a match between the properties of the new person and those of someone observed previously. Unfortunately, the chances of an exact match are usually slim. Suppose, for example, that your observations produce the information that is listed in the following table:

Name	Hair	Height	Weight	Lotion	Result
Sarah	blonde	average	light	no	sunburned
Dana	blonde	tall	average	yes	none
Alex	brown	short	average	yes	none
Annie	blonde	short	average	no	sunburned
Emily	red	average	heavy	no	sunburned
Pete	brown	tall	heavy	no	none
John	brown	average	heavy	no	none
Katie	blonde	short	light	yes	none

Given that there are three possible hair colors, heights, and weights, and that a person either uses or does not use lotion, there are $3 \times 3 \times 3 \times 2 = 54$ possible combinations. If a new person's properties are selected at random, the probability of an exact match with someone already observed is $8/54 = 0.15$, or just 15 percent.

The probability can be lower in practice, because there can be many more properties and many more possible values for each of those properties. Suppose, for example, that you record a dozen unrelated properties for each observed person, that each property has five possible values, and that each property value appears with equal frequency. Then, there would be $5^{12} = 2.44 \times 10^8$ combinations, and even with a table of 1 million observations, you would find an exact match only about 0.4 percent of the time.

Thus, it can be wildly impractical to classify an unknown object by looking for an exact match between the measured properties of that unknown object and the measured properties of samples of known classification.

You could, of course, treat the data as a feature space in which you look for a close match, perhaps using the approach described in Chapter 2. But if you do not know which properties are important, you may find a close match that is close because of the coincidental alignment of irrelevant properties.

An alternative is to use the version-space method described in Chapter 20 to isolate which properties matter and which do not. But you usually have no a priori reason to believe that a class-characterizing model can be expressed as a single combination of values for a subset of the attributes—nor do you have any reason to believe your samples are noise free.

Still another alternative—the one this chapter focuses on—is to devise a property-testing procedure such that the procedure correctly classifies each of the samples. Once such a procedure works on a sufficient number of samples, the procedure should work on objects whose classification is not yet known.

One convenient way to represent property-testing procedures is to arrange the tests involved in an **identification tree**. Because an identification tree is a special kind of decision tree, the specification refers to the decision-tree specification provided in Chapter 19:

An **identification tree** is a representation

That is a decision tree

In which

▷ Each set of possible conclusions is established implicitly
   by a list of samples of known class.

For example, in the identification tree shown in figure 21.1, the first test you use to identify burn-susceptible people—the one at the root of the tree—is the hair-color test. If the result is blonde, then you check whether lotion is in use; on the other hand, if the hair-color result is red or brown, you need no subsequent test. In general, the choice of which test to use, if any, depends on the results of previous tests.

Thus, the property-testing procedure embodied in an identification tree is like a railroad switch yard. Each unknown object is directed down one branch or another at each test, according to its properties, like railroad cars at switches, according to their destination.

The identification tree shown in figure 21.1 can be used to classify the people in the sunburn database, because each sunburned person ends up at a leaf node alone or with other sunburned people. Curiously, however, the identification tree shown in figure 21.2 can be used as well, even though it contains tests that have nothing to do with sunburn susceptibility. The identification tree in figure 21.1 seems more reasonable because you know that hair color and exposure are reasonably congruent with sunburn susceptibility.

The identification tree in figure 21.1 seems to us to be better than the one in figure 21.2, but how can a program reach the same conclusion

Figure 21.1 An identification tree that is consistent with the sunburn database. This tree is consistent with natural intuitions about sunburn. Each checked name identifies a person who turns red.

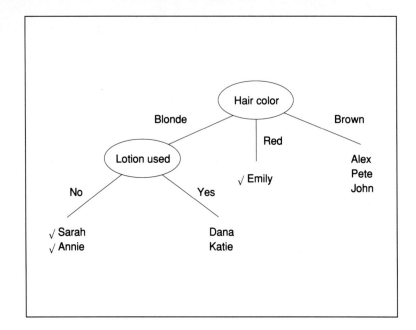

Figure 21.2 Another identification tree that is consistent with the sunburn database, albeit overly large and inconsistent with natural intuitions about sunburn. Each checked name identifies a person who turns red.

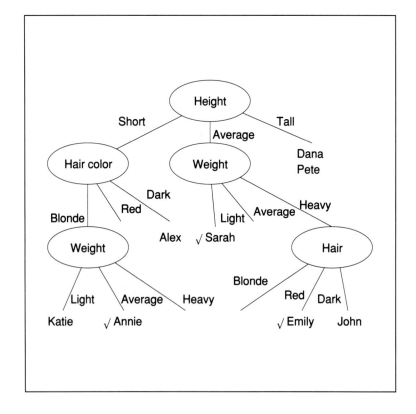

without any prior knowledge of what lotion does or how hair color relates to skin characteristics? One answer is to presume a variation on Occam's razor:

Occam's razor, specialized to identification trees:

▷ The world is inherently simple. Therefore the smallest identification tree that is consistent with the samples is the one that is most likely to identify unknown objects correctly.

Thus, the identification tree in figure 21.1, being smaller than the one in figure 21.2, is the tree that is more likely to identify sunburn-susceptible people.

Consequently, the question turns from *which is the right identification tree* to *how can you construct the smallest identification tree?*

Tests Should Minimize Disorder

Unfortunately, it is computationally impractical to find the smallest possible identification tree when many tests are required, so you have to be content with a procedure that tends to build small trees, albeit trees that are not guaranteed to be the smallest possible.

One way to start is to select a test for the root node that does the best job of dividing the database of samples into subsets in which many samples have the same classification. For each set containing more than one kind of sample, you then select another test in an effort to divide that inhomogeneous set into homogeneous subsets.

Consider, for example, the sunburn database and the four candidates for the root test. As shown in figure 21.3, the weight test is arguably the worst if you judge the tests according to how many people end up in homogeneous sets. After you use the weight test, none of the sample people are in a homogeneous set. The height test is somewhat better, because two people are in a homogeneous set; the lotion-used test is still better, because three people are in homogeneous sets. The hair-color test is best, however, because four people—Emily, Alex, Pete, and John—are in homogeneous sets. Accordingly, you use the hair-color test first.

The hair-color test leaves only one inhomogeneous set, consisting of Sarah, Dana, Annie, and Katie. To divide this set further, you consider what each of the remaining three tests does to the four people in the set. The result is shown in figure 21.4.

This time, there can be no doubt. The lotion-used test divides the set into two homogeneous subsets, whereas both the height and weight tests leave at least one inhomogeneous subset.

Figure 21.3 Each test divides the sunburn database into different subsets. Each checked name identifies a person who turns red. Intuition suggests that the hair-color test does the best job of dividing the database into homogeneous subsets.

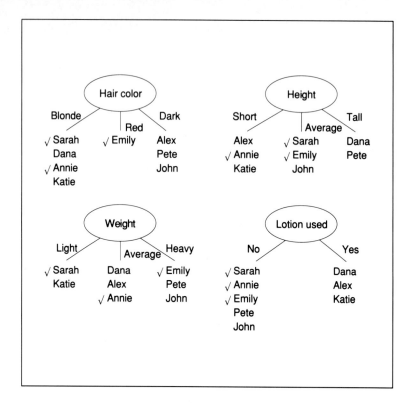

Figure 21.4 Once the blonde-haired people have been isolated, the available tests perform as shown. Each checked name identifies a person who turns red. The lotion-used test plainly does the best job of dividing the blonde-haired set consisting of Sarah, Dana, Annie, and Katie into homogeneous subsets.

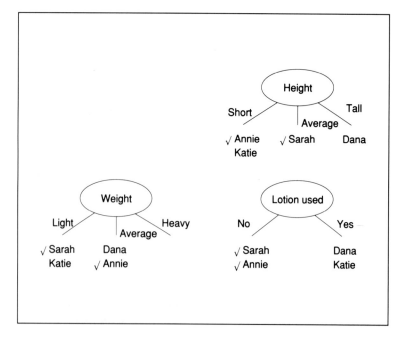

Information Theory Supplies a Disorder Formula

For a real database of any size, it is unlikely that any test would produce even one completely homogeneous subset. Accordingly, for real databases, you need a powerful way to measure the total disorder, or inhomogeneity, in the subsets produced by each test. Fortunately, you can borrow the formula you need from information theory:

$$\text{Average disorder} = \sum_b \left(\frac{n_b}{n_t}\right) \times \left(\sum_c -\frac{n_{bc}}{n_b} \log_2 \frac{n_{bc}}{n_b}\right),$$

where

n_b is the number of samples in branch b,

n_t is the total number of samples in all branches,

n_{bc} is the total of samples in branch b of class c.

To see why this borrowed formula works, first confine your attention to the set of samples lying at the end of one branch b. You want a formula involving n_b and n_{bc} that gives you a high number when a test produces highly inhomogeneous sets and a low number when a test produces completely homogeneous sets. The following formula involving n_{bc} and n_b does the job:

$$\text{Disorder} = \sum_c -\frac{n_{bc}}{n_b} \log_2 \frac{n_{bc}}{n_b}.$$

Although there is nothing sacred about this disorder formula, it certainly has desirable features, which is why information-theory experts use a similar formula to measure information.[†]

To get a feel for the desirable features of the disorder formula, suppose that you have a set that contains members of just two classes, class A and class B. If the number of members from class A and the number of members from class B are perfectly balanced, the measured disorder is 1, the maximum possible value:

$$\text{Disorder} = \sum_c -\frac{n_{bc}}{n_b} \log_2 \frac{n_{bc}}{n_b}$$

$$= -\frac{1}{2} \log_2 \frac{1}{2} - \frac{1}{2} \log_2 \frac{1}{2}$$

$$= \frac{1}{2} + \frac{1}{2}$$

$$= 1.$$

[†]In information theory, the disorder formula is sacred: It is the only formula that satisfies certain general properties. The requirements imposed by heuristic tree building are not so stringent, however.

Figure 21.5 The disorder in a set containing members of two classes A and B, as a function of the fraction of the set belonging to class A. On the left, the total number of samples in both classes combined is two; on the right, the total number of samples in both classes is eight.

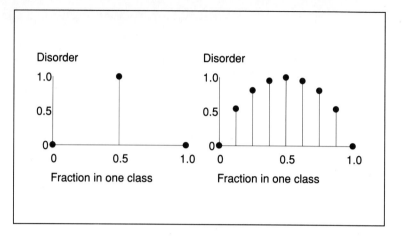

On the other hand, if there are only As or only Bs, the measured disorder is 0, the minimum possible value, because, in the limit, as x approaches zero, $x \times \log_2(x)$ is zero:

$$\text{Disorder} = \sum_c -\frac{n_{bc}}{n_b} \log_2 \frac{n_{bc}}{n_b}$$
$$= -1 \log_2 1 - 0 \log_2 0$$
$$= -0 - 0$$
$$= 0.$$

As you move from perfect balance and perfect homogeneity, disorder varies smoothly between zero and one, as shown in figure 21.5. The disorder is zero when the set is perfectly homogeneous, and the disorder is one when the set is perfectly inhomogeneous.

Now that you have a way of measuring the disorder in one set, you can measure the average disorder of the sets at the ends of the branches under a test. You simply weight the disorder in each branch's set by the size of the set relative to the total size of all the branches' sets. In the following formula, n_b is the number of samples that the test sends down branch b, and n_t is the total number of samples in all branches:

$$\text{Average disorder} = \sum_b \frac{n_b}{n_t} \times (\text{Disorder in the branch } b \text{ set}).$$

Substituting for the disorder in the branch b set, you have the desired formula for average disorder.

Now you can compute the average disorder produced when each test is asked to work on the complete sample set. Looking back at figure 21.3, note that the hair-color test divides those people into three sets. In the blonde set, two people turn red and two do not. In the red-haired set, there is only one person and that person turns red. In the brown-haired set, all three people are unaffected.

Hence, the average disorder produced by the hair-color test when the complete sample set is used is 0.5:

$$\text{Average disorder} = \frac{4}{8}(-\frac{2}{4}\log_2\frac{2}{4} - \frac{2}{4}\log_2\frac{2}{4})$$
$$+ \frac{1}{8} \times 0$$
$$+ \frac{3}{8} \times 0$$
$$= 0.5.$$

Working out the result for the other tests yields the following results:

Test	Disorder
Hair	0.5
Height	0.69
Weight	0.94
Lotion	0.61

Because the hair test clearly produces the least average disorder, the hair test is the first that should be used, which is consistent with the previous informal analysis. Similarly, once the hair test is selected, the choice of another test to separate out the sunburned people from among Sarah, Dana, Annie, and Katie is decided by the following calculations:

Test	Disorder
Height	0.5
Weight	1
Lotion	0

Thus, the lotion-used test is the clear winner. Using the hair test and the lotion-used tests together ensures the proper identification of all the samples.

In summary, to generate an identification tree, execute the following procedure, named SPROUTER:

To generate an identification tree using SPROUTER,

▷ Until each leaf node is populated by as homogeneous a sample set as possible:

  ▷ Select a leaf node with an inhomogeneous sample set.

  ▷ Replace that leaf node by a test node that divides the inhomogeneous sample set into minimally inhomogeneous subsets, according to some measure of disorder.

FROM TREES TO RULES

Once an identification tree is constructed, it is a simple matter to convert it into a set of equivalent rules. You just trace each path in the identification tree, from root node to leaf node, recording the test outcomes as antecedents and the leaf-node classification as the consequent. For the sunburn illustration, the four rules corresponding to the four paths in the identification tree are as follows:

> If   the person's hair color is blonde
>   the person uses lotion
> then   nothing happens

> If   the person's hair color is blonde
>   the person uses no lotion
> then   the person turns red

> If   the person's hair color is red
> then   the person turns red

> If   the person's hair color is brown
> then   nothing happens

In the rest of this section, you learn how to simplify such rule sets so as to increase transparency and to decrease errors.

Unnecessary Rule Antecedents Should Be Eliminated

Once a rule set is devised, you can try to simplify that set by simplifying each rule and then eliminating useless rules. To simplify a rule, you ask whether any of the antecedents can be eliminated without changing what the rule does on the samples.

Two of the rules have two antecedents. For each of the two, you ask whether both antecedents are really necessary. Consider, for example, the two antecedents in the following rule:

> If   the person's hair color is blonde
>   the person uses lotion
> then   nothing happens

If you eliminate the first antecedent, the one about blonde hair, the rule triggers for each person who uses lotion. Three of the sample people use lotion: Dana, Alex, and Katie, none of whom turn red. Because none turn red, it cannot be that hair color matters, so the dropped antecedent that checks for blonde hair is unnecessary. Dropping that antecedent produces the following, simplified rule:

> If   the person uses lotion
> then   nothing happens

Optimizing a Nuclear Fuel Plant

Programs resembling SPROUTER can be used to identify key parameters in chemical processing. Westinghouse used such a program to improve yield at a plant in which uranium hexafloride gas is converted into uranium-dioxide fuel pellets. Approximately six processing steps are required to do the conversion, and among these processing steps, there are approximately 30 controllable temperatures, pressures, and flow rates:

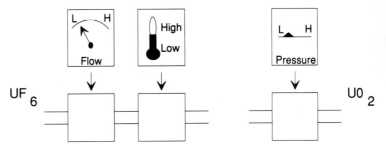

Historically, process engineers noted that yield was high on some days and low on others; of course, they wanted to control the 30 parameters so as to guarantee high yield every day. Unfortunately, no one knew quite what to do. Worse yet, nuclear fuel plants are not something with which to play, so experiments were forbidden.

Fortunately, SPROUTER was able to use plant records to build an identification tree to determine, on the basis of the parameters, when yield is high or low. In the schematic identification tree example that follows, each test decides whether a particular parameter value is high or low with respect to a threshold. Each of the thresholds is determined by SPROUTER itself so as to produce the simplest tree:

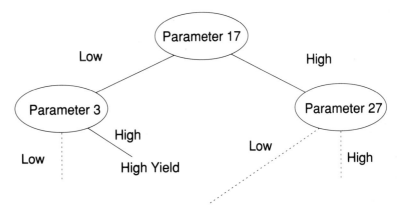

Once such a tree is in hand, it is easy to convert identification into control. You just have to find the shortest path from the root of the tree to one of the high-yield subsets. In this schematic example, you can guarantee high yield by keeping parameter 17 low and parameter 3 high. In the Westinghouse experience, this approach was a spectacular success: Their entire investment was recovered in the first half-day of improved yield.

To make such reasoning easier, it is often helpful to construct what statisticians call a **contingency table**, so called because it shows the degree to which a result is contingent on a property. In the following contingency table you see the number of lotion users who are blonde and not blonde, and the number of lotion users who are sunburned and not sunburned. The table clearly shows that knowledge about whether a person is blonde has no bearing on determining whether the person becomes sunburned given that the person uses lotion.

	No change	Sunburned
Person is blonde	2	0
Person is not blonde	1	0

Now consider the second antecedent in the same rule, the one that checks for lotion. If you eliminate it, the rule triggers whenever the person is blonde. Among the four blonde people, Sarah and Annie, neither of whom use lotion, are both sunburned; on the other hand, Dana and Katie, both of whom do use lotion, are not sunburned. Here is the contingency table:

	No change	Sunburned
Person uses lotion	2	0
Person uses no lotion	0	2

Plainly, the lotion antecedent has a bearing on the result for those people who are blonde. The samples who are blonde are not sunburned if and only if they use lotion. Accordingly, the dropped antecedent does make a difference, and you cannot eliminate it.

Now turn to the other two-antecedent rule; it triggers on blondes who do not use lotion:

> If   the person's hair color is blonde
>   the person does not use lotion
> then   the person turns red

As before, you explore what happens as antecedents are eliminated one at a time. Eliminating the first antecedent produces a rule that looks for people who do not use lotion. Of the five who do not, both blondes are sunburned; among the other three, one is sunburned and two are not:

	No change	Sunburned
Person is blonde	0	2
Person is not blonde	2	1

Evidently the dropped antecedent is important. Without it, you cannot be sure that a person who matches the rule is going to be burned.

Eliminating the second antecedent produces a rule that looks for people who are blonde. Of the four who are, two turn red and two do not:

	No change	Sunburned
Person uses no lotion	0	2
Person uses lotion	2	0

Again, the dropped antecedent is important. You conclude that the rule must remain as is; any simplification makes the rule fail on some of the sample people.

Finally, you need to look at the one-antecedent rules:

> If   the person's hair color is red
> then   the person turns red

> If   the person's hair color is brown
> then   nothing happens

If a rule has one antecedent and that antecedent is dropped, then, by convention, the rule is always triggered. Hence, the contingency tables for the two rules both contain all eight samples:

	No change	Sunburned
Person is red haired	0	1
Person is not red haired	5	2

	No change	Sunburned
Person is brown haired	3	0
Person is not brown haired	2	3

Repeating what you have done with two antecedent rules, you retain the red-hair antecedent in the first of these two rules, as well as the brown-hair antecedent in the second. Of course, these results are obvious in any case, for a rule with no antecedents will work correctly only if all the samples have the same result.

Unnecessary Rules Should Be Eliminated

Once you have simplified individual rules by eliminating antecedents that do not matter, you need to simplify the entire rule set by eliminating entire rules. For the sunburn illustration, the four candidate rules, one of which has been simplified, are as follows:

> If   the person's hair color is blonde
>   the person uses no lotion
> then   the person turns red

> If   the person uses lotion
> then   nothing happens

> If   the person's hair color is red
> then   the person turns red

> If   the person's hair color is brown
> then   nothing happens

In this example, note that two rules have consequents that indicate that a person will turn red, and that two rules have consequents that indicate that nothing will happen. You can replace the two that indicate a person will turn red with a **default rule**, one that is to be used only if no other rule applies. Because there are two possible results in the example, there are two choices:

> If   no other rule applies
> then   the person turns red

> If   no other rule applies
> then   nothing happens

In general, it makes sense to choose the default rule that eliminates as many other rules as possible; in the example, however, because both of the possible conclusions are indicated by two rules, you must use some other, tie-breaking criterion. One obvious tie breaker is to choose the default rule that covers the most common consequent in the sample set, which happens to be that nothing happens. In the example, this produces the following simplified rule set:

> If   the person's hair color is blonde
>   the person uses no lotion
> then   the person turns red

> If   the person's hair color is red
> then   the person turns red

> If   no other rule applies
> then   nothing happens

Another obvious tie breaker is to choose the default rule that produces the simplest rules, perhaps as measured by the total number of antecedents. In the example, this choice produces the following simplified rule set:

> If   the person uses lotion
> then   nothing happens

> If   the person's hair color is brown
> then   nothing happens

> If   no other rule applies
> then   the person turns red

In summary, to convert an identification tree into a rule set, execute the following procedure, named PRUNER:

To generate rules from an identification tree using PRUNER,

▷ Create one rule for each root-to-leaf path in the identification tree.

▷ Simplify each rule by discarding antecedents that have no effect on the conclusion reached by the rule.

▷ Replace those rules that share the most common consequent by a default rule that is triggered when no other rule is triggered. In the event of a tie, use some heuristic tie breaker to choose a default rule.

Fisher's Exact Test Brings Rule Correction in Line with Statistical Theory

Now let us leave the sunburn example to consider the following table, which relates presence or absence of a certain result, R, to the presence or absence of a certain property, P. Suppose that you denote the presence of the result by R_1 and its absence by R_2. Similarly, suppose you denote the presence of the property by P_1 and its absence by P_2. Then you have, in general, the following contingency table:

	R_1	R_2
P_1	l	m
P_2	n	o

Now the question is this: Do the values of l, m, n, and o indicate that knowing about P is relevant to determining R? Consider, for example, the following contingency table:

	R_1	R_2
P_1	1	0
P_2	0	1

On the surface, if you use this table to decide whether to keep an antecedent testing for P in a rule, it seems to indicate that you should keep the antecedent, because, without the antecedent, the rule would misclassify an example. But now consider the following contingency table:

	R_1	R_2
P_1	999	0
P_2	0	1

Without the antecedent testing for P, you would again misclassify a sample, but this time only one sample in 1000, rather than one in two. Is a simplification worth an occasional error? Or is the table entry at the intersection of column P_2 and row R_2 caused by noisy measurement?

And speaking of noise, are two examples really sufficient for you to decide whether an antecedent should be retained? Should you reach the same conclusion with two contingency tables, both of which have the same numbers from a relative point of view, but one of which has 100 times more data, as in the following pair?

	R_1	R_2
P_1	1	0
P_2	0	1

	R_1	R_2
P_1	1000	0
P_2	0	1000

After thinking about such questions, you might decide on a strategy that considers both the sizes of the entries and their relative sizes. To be conservative, if all numbers are small, you probably should get rid of an antecedent rather than treat it as though it were solidly supported. Similarly, if the ratio of l to m is the same or nearly the same as the ratio of n to o, knowing about P is not helpful, and you should probably get rid of the antecedent. On the other hand, if the numbers are large and if l/m is very different from n/o, then knowing about P is quite enlightening, and you should keep the antecedent.

To put this sort of reasoning on solid ground, you should consult a statistician, who might take you through an analysis that leads, in several steps, to **Fisher's exact test**. The following paragraphs sketch those steps.

First, think about your goal. One plausible goal is to determine whether there is a statistical dependence between the result R and the property P. Unfortunately, if there is a statistical dependence, you probably have no clue about which of an infinite number of forms that dependence might take, which means you do not know exactly for what you are to test.

Fortunately, statistical *in*dependence has only one form, making independence much easier to deal with than dependence. Accordingly, your statistician tells you to look for statistical dependence indirectly, through a double negative. Instead of trying to show that the result, R, depends on the property, P, you try to show that it is *un*likely that R does *not* depend on P. Said in another way, your goal is to decide whether your samples cast significant doubt on the independence hypothesis.[†]

Your second step is to ask about the probability of observing a particular combination, l, m, n, o, given that R is independent of P. To

---

[†]A statistician would say that your goal is to perform a significance test on the null hypothesis. I cannot think why.

say something about that probability, however, you have to make more assumptions, because with four things that can vary, the problem is still severely underconstrained, even with independence assumed.

The standard approach is to assume that there is a certain fixed number of samples corresponding to P_1, $S_{P_1} = l + m$, a certain fixed number corresponding to P_2, $S_{P_2} = n + o$, and a certain fixed number corresponding to R_1, $S_{R_1} = l + n$. Of course, these assumptions fix the number corresponding to R_2, $S_{R_2} = m + o$, inasmuch as $S_{P_1} + S_{P_2}$ must be equal to $S_{R_1} + S_{R_2}$.

These extra assumptions are equivalent to saying that the **marginal sums** of the contingency table are constants:

	R_1	R_2	Marginal sum
P_1	l	m	$S_{P_1} = l + m$
P_2	n	o	$S_{P_2} = n + o$
Marginal sum	$S_{R_1} = l + n$	$S_{R_2} = m + o$	$S_{P_1} + S_{P_2} = S_{R_1} + S_{R_2}$

Once you have fixed the size of the marginal sums, you are free to choose a value for only one of l or m or n or o, which then, in cooperation with the marginal sums, determines the rest.

Suppose you pick a value for l, the number of samples with result R_1 and property P_1. Then, your statistician tells you that the following probability formula, grimly full of factorials, provides the probability for your value for l given the marginal sums:

$$p(l|S_{P_1}, S_{P_2}, S_{R_1}, S_{R_2}) = \frac{\frac{S_{P_1}!}{l!(S_{P_1}-l)!} \times \frac{S_{P_2}!}{(S_{R_1}-l)!(S_{P_2}-(S_{R_1}-l))!}}{\frac{(S_{P_1}+S_{P_2})!}{S_{R_1}!(S_{P_1}+S_{P_2}-S_{R_1})!}}.$$

Note that the formula does not involve S_{R_2}, because S_{R_2} is determined by the other marginal sums.

With the formula, you can plot, as in figure 21.6, the probabilities for particular values of l given independence and $S_{R_1} = S_{R_2} = S_{P_1} = S_{P_2} = 10$.

Of course, whenever the values for S_{P_1} and S_{P_2} are unequal, the symmetry disappears—as shown, for example, in figure 21.7.

Your third step is to note that the combined probability of all extremely high and low values of l is low. In the symmetric example—the one with 20 samples—the probability that $l > 7$ is less than 0.025. Also, the probability that $l < 3$ is less than 0.025. Thus, the probability that l is outside the three-to-seven range is less than 0.05, given that the property and the result are independent.

If it is unlikely, however, that the observed value of l is outside the central range, given independence, then, if the observed value actually is outside the central range, independence must not be likely. More precisely, if you say that the property and the result are independent whenever the observed value of l is outside the central range, then the probability of

Figure 21.6 The probability of l samples exhibiting both a certain property and result, given that 10 samples have the property, 10 do not, 10 samples exhibit the result, and 10 do not, for a total of 20 samples.

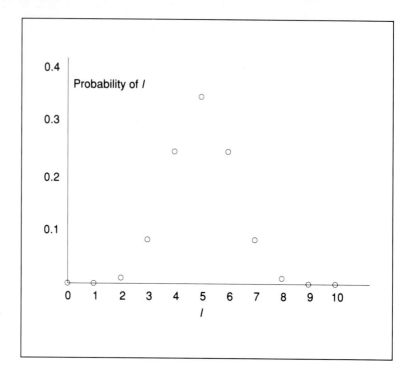

Figure 21.7 The open circles show the probability of l samples exhibiting both a certain property and result, given that 10 samples have the property, 10 do not, 10 samples exhibit the result, and 10 do not, for a total of 20 samples. The filled circles show the probability of l samples exhibiting both a certain property and result, given that 10 samples have the property, 40 do not, 10 samples exhibit the result, and 40 do not, for a total of 50 samples.

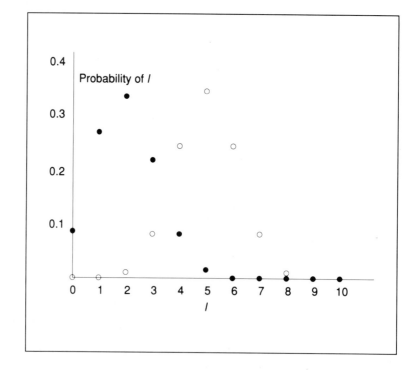

blundering when the property and the result actually are independent is less than 0.05.

Or, saying it still another way, if l lies outside the central range, you can say that the property and the result are statistically dependent with less than a five percent chance of wrongfully ruling out the independence hypothesis. Your statistician says that the observed value is significant at the 5-percent level using Fisher's exact test.

Thus, the following contingency table is seriously unlikely, given independence. Whenever you see such a table, you should retain an antecedent involving a property P.

	R_1	R_2	Marginal sum
P_1	2	8	10
P_2	8	2	10
Marginal sum	10	10	20

On the other hand, the following contingency table is reasonable, given independence. Following your statistician's line of reasoning, you should drop an antecedent involving a property P.

	R_1	R_2	Marginal sum
P_1	4	6	10
P_2	6	4	10
Marginal sum	10	10	20

Not surprisingly, when you use the test on the antecedents in the rules derived from the sunburn example, you eliminate all the antecedents, for there just are not enough data to say that there is significant evidence in favor of rejecting the conservative assumption of independence. On the other hand, were there five times as many data, with all results increased in proportion, you would reinstate all the antecedents that seemed important when reasoning without statistics.

Recall, for example, what happens when you drop the first antecedent in the following rule:

    If   the person's hair color is blonde
              the person uses lotion
    then nothing happens

Given the original data, the contingency table is as follows:

	No change	Sunburned
Person uses lotion	2	0
Person uses no lotion	0	2

With this table, l can be only 0, 1, or 2, and the probabilities are such that the central region covers all three values. There is no value of l such that the independence hypothesis is unlikely.

On the other hand, if there are five times as many data, increased in proportion, then the contingency table is as follows:

	No change	Sunburned
Person uses lotion	10	0
Person uses no lotion	0	10

With this table, l can take on any value from 0 to 10, and the probabilities are such that the central region ranges from 3 to 7. Given $l = 10$, the independence hypothesis is unlikely.

SUMMARY

- According to Occam's razor, the world is simple. Thus, the simplest explanation that covers the data is likely to be the right explanation.
- One way to recognize situations is to apply the sequence of tests dictated by an identification tree. One way to learn is to build an identification tree, keeping it simple in harmony with Occam's razor.
- One way to build a simple identification tree is to use a disorder formula, borrowed from information theory, to determine which tests to include in the tree.
- Once an identification tree is built, you usually should convert it into a simple set of rules so as to make the knowledge embedded in it more comprehensible. To do the conversion, you make a rule for each path through the tree, and then you simplify the resulting set of rules.
- To simplify a set of rules, you first eliminate unnecessary rule antecedents using Fisher's exact test. Then, you eliminate unnecessary rules.

BACKGROUND

The discussion of decision trees is based on the work of Ross Quinlan on ID3 and other decision-tree systems [1979, 1983]. Quinlan has worked out many variations on the same idea using improved measures of tree quality.

Also, Quinlan and Ronald L. Rivest have worked out an alternative approach based on finding a tree that enables identification using the minimum memory [1987].

The discussion of rule extraction from decision trees is also based on Quinlan's work [1986]. A good description of Fisher's exact test is hard to find, but some large libraries have an instructive pamphlet by Finney et al. [1963].

The nuclear-fuel plant application is the work of W. J. Leech and his associates [1986].

22

Learning by Training Neural Nets

In this chapter, you learn how *neuronlike elements, arranged in nets*, can be used to recognize instances of patterns, and you learn how neural nets can learn using the *back-propagation procedure*.

First, you review the most conspicuous properties of real neurons, and learn how those properties are modeled in neural nets.

Next, you learn how the *back-propagation procedure* alters the effect of one simulated neuron on another so as to improve overall performance.

By way of illustration, you see how a simulated neural net can be taught to recognize which people, among six, are acquaintances and which are siblings.

Once you have finished this chapter, you will know how simulated neural nets work, you will understand how the back-propagation procedure improves their performance, and you will understand why working with them remains an art.

SIMULATED NEURAL NETS

A vast literature explains what is known about how real neurons work from every conceivable perspective. Many books and papers explain neurons from the cellular perspective, diving deeply into membrane potentials and ion pumps. Others deal with neurotransmitters and the details of the activity at and near neuron synapses. Still others concentrate on how neurons are connected, tracing the paths taken by neurons as they process

Figure 22.1 A neuron consists of a cell body, one axon, and many dendrites. Dendrites receive inputs from axons of other neurons via excitation or inhibition synapses. Real neurons may have many more dendrites.

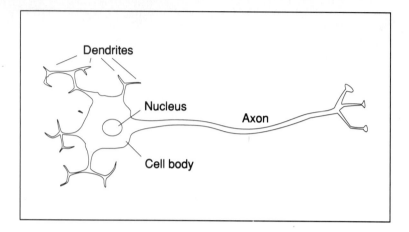

information and carry messages from one place to another. And still others exploit ideas from contemporary engineering, drawing inspiration from subjects as diverse as transmission lines and frequency modulation.

Given this vast literature, the tendency of most people who try to understand and duplicate neural-net function has been to concentrate on only a few prominent characteristics of neurons.

In the rest of this section, you learn what those characteristics are and how they are mimicked in *feed-forward neural nets*. Although feed-forward nets are among the most popular, there are other kinds. For example, in Chapter 23, you learn about *perceptrons*, and in Chapter 24, you learn about *interpolation* and *approximation nets*.

Real Neurons Consist of Synapses, Dendrites, Axons, and Cell Bodies

Most neurons, like the one shown in figure 22.1, consist of a cell body plus one axon and many dendrites. The **axon** is a protuberance that delivers the neuron's output to connections with other neurons. **Dendrites** are protuberances that provide plenty of surface area, facilitating connection with the axons of other neurons. Dendrites often divide a great deal, forming extremely bushy dendritic trees. Axons divide to some extent, but far less than dendrites.

A neuron does nothing unless the collective influence of all its inputs reaches a threshold level. Whenever that threshold level is reached, the neuron produces a full-strength output in the form of a narrow pulse that proceeds from the cell body, down the axon, and into the axon's branches. Whenever this happens, the neuron is said to **fire**. Because a neuron either fires or does nothing, it is said to be an **all-or-none device**.

Axons influence dendrites over narrow gaps called **synapses**. Stimulation at some synapses encourages neurons to fire. Stimulation at others discourages neurons from firing. There is mounting evidence that learning

Figure 22.2 A simulated neuron. Inputs from other neurons are multiplied by weights, and then are added together. The sum is then compared with a threshold level. If the sum is above the threshold, the output is 1; otherwise, the output is 0.

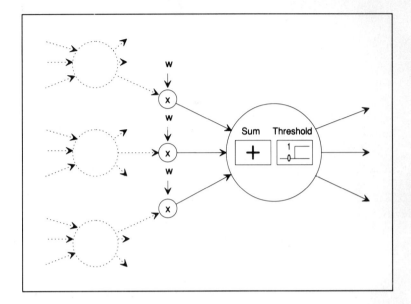

takes place in the vicinity of synapses and has something to do with the degree to which synapses translate the pulse traveling down one neuron's axon into excitation or inhibition of the next neuron.

The number of neurons in the human brain is staggering. Current estimates suggest there may be on the order of 10^{11} neurons per person. If the number of neurons is staggering, the number of synapses must be toppling. In the cerebellum—that part of the brain that is crucial to motor coordination—a single neuron may receive inputs from as many as 10^5 synapses. Inasmuch as most of the neurons in the brain are in the cerebellum, each brain has on the order of 10^{16} synapses.

You can get a better feel for numbers like that if you know that there are about 1.5×10^6 characters in a book such as this one. Also, the United States Library of Congress holds on the order of 20×10^6 books. If each book were about the size of this one, that number of books would contain about 30×10^{12} characters. Accordingly, there are as many synapses in one brain as there would be characters in about 300 such libraries.

Simulated Neurons Consist of Multipliers, Adders, and Thresholds

Simulated neural nets typically consist of simulated neurons like the one shown in figure 22.2. The simulated neuron is viewed as a node connected to other nodes via links that correspond to axon–synapse–dendrite connections.

Each link is associated with a weight. Like a synapse, that weight determines the nature and strength of one node's influence on another. More specifically, one node's influence on another is the product of the influencing neuron's output value times the connecting link's weight. Thus, a large positive weight corresponds to strong excitation, and a small negative weight corresponds to weak inhibition.

Each node combines the separate influences received on its input links into an overall influence using an **activation function**. One simple activation function simply passes the sum of the input values through a **threshold function** to determine the node's output. The output of each node is either 0 or 1 depending on whether the sum of the inputs is below or above the **threshold value** used by the node's threshold function.

Now you can understand what is modeled in these simplified neurons: the weights model synaptic properties; the adder models the influence-combining capability of the dendrites; and comparison with a threshold models the all-or-none characteristic imposed by electrochemical mechanisms in the cell body.

Much of the character of real neurons is not modeled, however. A simulated neuron simply adds up a weighted sum of its inputs. Real neurons may process information via complicated dendritic mechanisms that call to mind electronic transmission lines and logical circuits. A simulated neuron remains on as long as the sum of its weighted inputs is above threshold. Real neurons may encode messages via complicated pulse arrangements that call to mind frequency modulation and multiplexing.

Accordingly, researchers argue hotly about whether simulated neural nets shed much light on real neural activity and whether these nets can perform anything like as wonderfully as the real thing. Many people consider real neural nets to be so different from contemporary simulations, that they always take care to use the qualifiers *simulated* or *real* whenever they use the phrase *neural net*. In the rest of this chapter, however, the word *simulated* is dropped to avoid tedious repetition.

Feed-Forward Nets Can Be Viewed as Arithmetic Constraint Nets

A handy way to do the computation required by a neural net is by arithmetic constraint propagation. Accordingly, you need a representation specification for neurons that builds on arithmetic constraint-propagation nets:

A **neural net** is a representation

That is a arithmetic constraint net

In which

▷ Operation frames denote arithmetic constraints modeling synapses and neurons.

▷ Demon procedures propagate stimuli through synapses and neurons.

And, of course, you need the demon procedures. One moves information across neurons; another moves information from one neuron to another.

When a value is written into a synapse's input slot,

▷ Write the product of the value and the synapse's weight into the synapse's output slot.

When a value is written into a synapse's output slot,

▷ Check the following neuron to see whether all its input synapses' outputs have values.

  ▷ If they do, add the output values of the input synapses together, compare the sum with the neuron's threshold, and write the appropriate value into the neuron's output slot.

  ▷ Otherwise, do nothing.

Feed-Forward Nets Can Recognize Regularity in Data

To get an idea of how neural nets can recognize regularity, consider the neural net shown in figure 22.3. The net is equipped with weights that enable it to recognize properties of pairs of people. Some of the pairs involve siblings, and others involve acquaintances.

Two input connections receive a value of 1 to identify the pair of people under consideration. All other input connections receive values of 0 because the corresponding people are not part of the pair under consideration. Assume that the people in the top group of three are siblings, as are people in the bottom group of three. Further assume that any pair of people who are not siblings are acquaintances.

The nodes just to the right of the input links—the ones labeled H1, H2, and H3—are called **hidden nodes** because their outputs are not observable. The output nodes convey conclusions. The Acquaintances node, for example, receives a value of 1 when the input arrangement corresponds to two people who are acquaintances.

The net is not fully connected so as to simplify discussion: The Robert, Raquel, and Romeo inputs are not connected to the Siblings node, and the Joan, James, and Juliet nodes are not connected to the Acquaintances node.

Any of the first three inputs produces enough stimulation to fire H1, because all the connecting weights are 1.0 and because H1's threshold is 0.5. Similarly, any of the second three produces enough to fire H2. Thus, H1 and H2 act as logical Or gates. At least one of H1 and H2 has to fire because two inputs are always presumed to be on.

Figure 22.3 A neural net that recognizes siblings and acquaintances. All but the two indicated weights are 1.0. Thresholds are indicated inside the nodes.

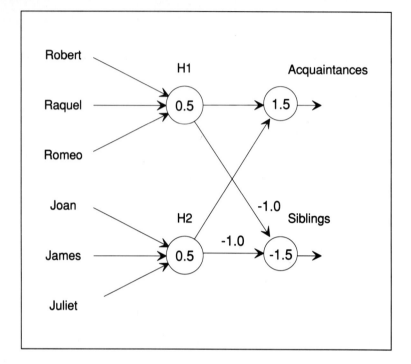

If both H1 and H2 fire, then the weighted sum presented to the Acquaintance node is 2 because both the weights involved are 1.0 and because the Acquaintance node's threshold is 1.5. If only one of H1 and H2 fire, then the Acquaintance node does not fire. Thus, the Acquaintance node acts as a logical And gate: It fires only when the input pair are acquaintances.

On the other hand, if both H1 and H2 fire, then the weighted sum presented to the Siblings node is −2 because of the inhibiting −1 weights. The value −2 is below that node's threshold of −1.5, so the node does not fire. If only one of H1 and H2 fire, then the weighted sum is −1, which is above the Sibling node's threshold of −1.5, so it fires. Thus, the Sibling node fires if and only if the input pair causes exactly one hidden node to fire; this happens only when the input pair are siblings.

Note that each link and node in this example has a clear role. Generally, however, recognition capability is distributed diffusely over many more nodes and weights. Accordingly, the role of particular links and hidden nodes becomes obscure.

HILL CLIMBING AND BACK PROPAGATION

There are surprisingly simple procedures that enable neural-net weights to be learned automatically from training samples. In this section, you learn that hill climbing is one of those simple procedures.

The Back-Propagation Procedure Does Hill Climbing by Gradient Ascent

In the context of neural-net learning, each hill-climbing step amounts to small changes to the weights. The quality measurement is a measurement of how well the net deals with sample inputs for which the appropriate outputs are known.

The hill-climbing procedure explained in Chapter 4 requires you to try each possible step so that you can choose a step that does the most good. If you were to carry that hill-climbing idea over straightforwardly, you would try changing each weight, one at a time, keeping all other weights constant. Then, you would change only the weight that does the most good.

Fortunately, you can do much better whenever the hill you are climbing is a sufficiently smooth function of the weights. In fact, you can move in the direction of most rapid performance improvement by varying all the weights simultaneously in proportion to how much good is done by individual changes. When you use this strategy, you are said to move in the direction of the gradient in weight space and you are said to be doing **gradient ascent**.

The **back-propagation procedure** is a relatively efficient way to compute how much performance improves with individual weight changes. The procedure is called the back-propagation procedure because, as you soon see, it computes changes to the weights in the final layer first, reuses much of the same computation to compute changes to the weights in the penultimate layer, and ultimately goes *back* to the initial layer.

In the rest of this section, you learn about back propagation from two perspectives. The first, heuristic perspective is intended to make the back-propagation procedure seem reasonable; the second, mathematical perspective is intended to validate the heuristic explanation.

First, however, you need to learn about two neural-net modifications required in preparation for back propagation and gradient ascent.

Nonzero Thresholds Can Be Eliminated

You might think that, to learn, you would need separate procedures for adjusting weights and for adjusting thresholds. Fortunately, however, there is a trick that enables you to treat thresholds as though they were weights.

More specifically, a nonzero-threshold neuron is computationally equivalent to a zero-threshold neuron with an extra link connected to an input that is always held at -1.0. As shown in figure 22.4, the nonzero threshold value becomes the connecting weight's value. These threshold-equivalent weights can be changed in the course of learning just like the other weights, thus simplifying learning.

Gradient Ascent Requires a Smooth Threshold Function

Actually, the stair-step threshold function is unsuited for gradient ascent because gradient ascent requires performance to be a smooth function of

Figure 22.4 Thresholds are equivalent to links, with weight values equal to the threshold values, connected to inputs held at −1.0.

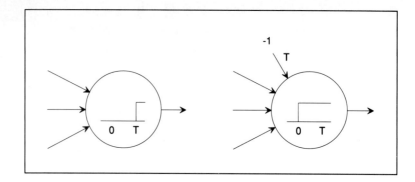

Figure 22.5 The Squashed *S* function and its slope. The slope of the Squashed *S* function approaches 0 when the sum of the inputs is either very negative or very positive; the slope reaches its maximum, 0.25, when the input is 0. Because the slope of the Squashed *S* function is given by a particularly simple formula, the Squashed *S* is a popular threshold function.

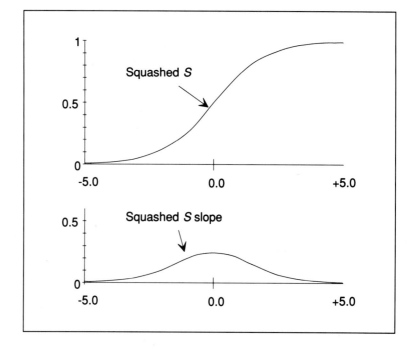

the weights. The all-or-none character of the stair-step produces flat plains and abrupt cliffs in weight space. Thus, the small steps inherent in gradient ascent do nothing almost everywhere, thus defeating the whole procedure.

Accordingly, a squashed *S* threshold function, shown in figure 22.5, replaces the stair-step function. The stair-step threshold function is somewhat more faithful to real neuron action, but the squashed *S* function provides nearly the same effect with the added mathematical advantage of smoothness that is essential for gradient ascent.

To make these modifications to the way neuron outputs are computed, you need only to replace one when-written procedure with another:

When a value is written into a synapse's output slot,

▷ Check the following neuron to see whether all its input synapses' outputs have values.

   ▷ If they do, add the output values of the input synapses together, pass the sum through the squashed S function, determine whether the result is greater than 0, and write the appropriate value into the neuron's output slot.

   ▷ Otherwise, do nothing.

Back Propagation Can Be Understood Heuristically

In this subsection, the back-propagation procedure is explained heuristically, with a minimum of mathematical equipment. If you prefer a briefer, more mathematical approach, skip ahead to the next subsection.

The overall idea behind back propagation is to make a large change to a particular weight, w, if the change leads to a large reduction in the errors observed at the output nodes. For each sample input combination, you consider each output's desired value, d, its actual value, o, and the influence of a particular weight, w, on the error, $d - o$. A big change to w makes sense if that change can reduce a large output error and if the size of that reduction is substantial. On the other hand, if a change to w does not reduce any large output error substantially, little should be done to that weight.

Note that most of the computation needed to compute the change to any particular weight is also needed to compute the changes to weights that are closer to the output nodes. Consider the net shown in figure 22.6. Once you see how to compute a change for a typical weight, $w_{i \to j}$, between a node in layer i and a node in layer j, you see that the required computations involve computations needed for the weights, $w_{j \to k}$, between nodes in layer j and nodes in layer k.

First note that a change in the input to node j results in a change in the output at node j that depends on the slope of the threshold function. Where the slope is steepest, a change in the input has the maximum effect on the output. Accordingly, you arrange for the change in $w_{i \to j}$ to depend on the slope of the threshold function at node j on the ground that change should be liberal only where it can do a lot of good.

The slope of the squashed S function is given by a particularly simple formula, $o(1 - o)$. Thus, the use of the squashed S function as the threshold function leads to the following conclusion about changes to $w_{i \to j}$:

■   Let the change in $w_{i \to j}$ be proportional to $o_j(1 - o_j)$.

Next, the change in the input to node j, given a change in the weight, $w_{i \to j}$, depends on the output of node i. Again, on the ground that change

Figure 22.6 A trainable neural net. Each link has a weight that can be changed so as to improve the net's ability to produce the correct outputs for input combinations in the training set. Threshold-replacing links are not shown.

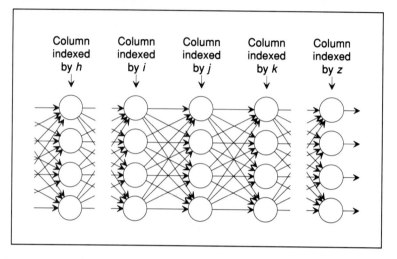

should be liberal only where it can do a lot of good, you arrange for $w_{i \to j}$ to change substantially only if the output of node i is high:

■ Let the change in $w_{i \to j}$ be proportional to o_i, the output at node i.

Putting these considerations together, it seems that the change to a weight, $w_{i \to j}$, should be proportional to o_i, to $o_j(1 - o_j)$, and to a factor that captures how beneficial it is to change the output of node j. To make it easier to write things down, let us agree that the Greek letter β stands for the benefit obtained by changing the output value of a node. Thus, the change to $w_{i \to j}$ should be proportional to $o_i \times o_j(1 - o_j) \times \beta_j$.

Just how beneficial is it to change the output of node j? Imagine first that node j is connected to just one node in the next layer—namely, node k. Then, the reasoning just completed can be reapplied with a slight modification:

■ Because change should be liberal only where it can do substantial good, the change to o_j should be proportional to $o_k(1 - o_k)$, the slope of the threshold function at node k.

■ For the same reason, the change to o_j should be proportional to $w_{j \to k}$, the weight on the link connecting node j to node k.

Of course, node j is connected to many nodes in the next layer. The overall benefit obtained by changing o_j must be the sum of the individual effects, each of which includes a weight, $w_{j \to k}$, a slope $o_k(1 - o_k)$, and the factor β_k that indicates how beneficial it is to change o_k, the output of node k. Thus, the benefit that you obtain by changing the output of node j is summarized as follows:

$$\beta_j = \sum_k w_{j \to k} o_k(1 - o_k)\beta_k.$$

At this point, recall that the change to $w_{i \to j}$ is proportional to β_j. Evidently, the weight change in any layer of weights depends on a benefit calculation, β_j, that depends, in turn, on benefit calculations, β_k, needed to deal with weights closer to the output nodes.

To finish the analysis, you need to answer only one remaining question concerning the benefit you obtain by changing the value of an output node. This value depends, of course, on how wrong the output node's value happens to be. If the difference between d_z, the desired output at node z, and o_z, the actual output at that same node, is small, then the change in the output at node z should be relatively small. On the other hand, if the difference is large, the change in the output at node z should be large. Accordingly, the appropriate change to o_z should be in proportion to the difference, $d_z - o_z$. Recasting this conclusion in the framework of benefit, you have the following:

$$\beta_z = d_z - o_z.$$

Finally, weight changes should depend on a rate parameter, r, that should be as large as possible to encourage rapid learning, but not so large as to cause changes to the output values that considerably overshoot the desired values:

■   Let the change in $w_{i \rightarrow j}$ be proportional to a rate parameter, r, determined experimentally.

Combining all the equations, you have the following **back-propagation formulas**:

$$\Delta w_{i \rightarrow j} = r o_i\, o_j (1 - o_j) \beta_j,$$

$$\beta_j = \sum_k w_{j \rightarrow k}\, o_k (1 - o_k) \beta_k \text{ for nodes in hidden layers,}$$

$$\beta_z = d_z - o_z \text{ for nodes in the output layer.}$$

Once you have worked out the appropriate change in the weights for one input combination, you face an important choice. Some neural-net enthusiasts make changes after considering each sample input. Others add up the changes suggested by individual sample inputs and make actual changes only after all the sample inputs are considered. In the example experiments described later in this chapter, changes are made only after all the sample inputs are considered, because this is the only way that is consistent with the mathematics of gradient ascent described in the following subsection.

Back-Propagation Follows from Gradient Descent and the Chain Rule

The previous subsection provides an heuristic argument leading to the back-propagation formulas. This subsection provides a mathematical argument leading to the same formulas. This mathematical argument rests on two ideas drawn from calculus:

■   Suppose that y is a smooth function of several variables, x_i. Further suppose that you want to know how to make incremental changes to the initial values of each x_i so as to increase the value of y as fast as possible. Then, the change to each initial x_i value should be in proportion to the partial derivative of y with respect to that particular x_i. In other words,

$$\Delta x_i \propto \frac{\partial y}{\partial x_i}.$$

When you make such a change, you are doing **gradient ascent**.

■ Suppose that y is a function of several intermediate variables, x_i, and that each x_i is a function of one variable, z. Further suppose that you want to know the derivative of y with respect to z. You obtain that derivative by adding up the results that you obtained by multiplying each partial derivative of y with respect to the x_i by the derivative of x_i with respect to z:

$$\frac{dy}{dz} = \sum_i \frac{\partial y}{\partial x_i}\frac{dx_i}{dz} = \sum_i \frac{dx_i}{dz}\frac{\partial y}{\partial x_i}.$$

When you compute such a derivative, you are using the **chain rule**.

Now recall that you have a set of weights that you want to improve, and you have a sample set of inputs along with each input's desired output. You need a way to measure how well your weights are performing, and you need a way to improve that measured performance.

The standard way of measuring performance is to pick a particular sample input and then sum up the squared error at each of the outputs. Once that is done for each sample input, you sum over all sample inputs and add a minus sign for an overall measurement of performance that peaks at 0:

$$P = -\sum_s \Big(\sum_z (d_{sz} - o_{sz})^2\Big),$$

where

P is the measured performance,

s is an index that ranges over all sample inputs,

z is an index that ranges over all output nodes,

d_{sz} is the desired output for sample input s at the zth node,

o_{sz} is the actual output for sample input s at the zth node.

Note that the reason that the sum of the squared errors is so popular is that it is the choice that most often leads to pretty and tractable mathematics. Otherwise, something else, such as adding up the absolute errors, would do as well.

Of course, the performance measure, P, is a function of the weights. Thus, you can deploy the idea of gradient ascent if you can calculate the partial derivative of performance with respect to each weight. With these partial derivatives in hand, you can climb the performance hill most rapidly by altering all weights in proportion to the corresponding partial derivative.

First, however, note that performance is given as a sum over all sample inputs. Accordingly, you can compute the partial derivative of performance with respect to a particular weight by adding up the partial derivative of performance for each sample input considered separately. Thus, you can reduce notational clutter by dropping the s subscript, thus focusing on the sample inputs one at a time, with the understanding that each weight will be adjusted by summing the adjustments derived from each sample input. Consider, then, the partial derivative

$$\frac{\partial P}{\partial w_{i \to j}},$$

where the weight, $w_{i \to j}$ is a weight connecting the ith layer of nodes to the jth layer of nodes.

Now your goal is to find an efficient way to compute the partial derivative of P with respect to $w_{i \to j}$. You reach that goal by expressing the partial derivative mostly in terms of computations that have to be done anyway to deal with weights closer to the output layer of nodes.

The effect of $w_{i \to j}$ on performance, P, is through the intermediate variable, o_j, the output of the jth node. Accordingly, you use the chain rule to express the derivative of P with respect to $w_{i \to j}$:

$$\frac{\partial P}{\partial w_{i \to j}} = \frac{\partial P}{\partial o_j} \frac{\partial o_j}{\partial w_{i \to j}} = \frac{\partial o_j}{\partial w_{i \to j}} \frac{\partial P}{\partial o_j}.$$

Now consider $\partial o_j / \partial w_{i \to j}$. You know that you determine o_j by adding up all the inputs to node j and passing the result through a threshold function. Hence, $o_j = f\left(\sum_i o_i w_{i \to j}\right)$, where f is the threshold function. Treating the sum as an intermediate variable, $\sigma_j = \sum_i o_i w_{i \to j}$, you can apply the chain rule again:

$$\frac{\partial o_j}{\partial w_{i \to j}} = \frac{df(\sigma_j)}{d\sigma_j} \frac{\partial \sigma_j}{\partial w_{i \to j}} = \frac{df(\sigma_j)}{d\sigma_j} o_i = o_i \frac{df(\sigma_j)}{d\sigma_j}.$$

Substituting this result back into the equation for $\partial P / \partial w_{i \to j}$ yields the following key equation:

$$\frac{\partial P}{\partial w_{i \to j}} = o_i \frac{df(\sigma_j)}{d\sigma_j} \frac{\partial P}{\partial o_j}.$$

Note that the partial derivative, $\partial P / \partial o_j$ can be expressed in terms of the partial derivatives, $\partial P / \partial o_k$, in the next layer to the right. Because the effect of o_j on P is through the outputs of the nodes in the next layer, the o_k, you can apply the chain rule to calculate $\partial P / \partial o_j$:

$$\frac{\partial P}{\partial o_j} = \sum_k \frac{\partial P}{\partial o_k} \frac{\partial o_k}{\partial o_j} = \sum_k \frac{\partial o_k}{\partial o_j} \frac{\partial P}{\partial o_k}.$$

But you know that you determine o_k by adding up all the inputs to node k and passing the result through a threshold function. Hence, $o_k = f\left(\sum_j o_j w_{j \to k}\right)$ where f is the threshold function. Treating the sum as an intermediate variable, σ_k, and applying the chain rule again, you have the following:

$$\frac{\partial o_k}{\partial o_j} = \frac{df(\sigma_k)}{d\sigma_k}\frac{\partial \sigma_k}{\partial o_j} = \frac{df(\sigma_k)}{d\sigma_k}w_{j\rightarrow k} = w_{j\rightarrow k}\frac{df(\sigma_k)}{d\sigma_k}$$

Substituting this result back into the equation for $\partial P/\partial o_j$ yields the following, additional key equation:

$$\frac{\partial P}{\partial o_j} = \sum_k w_{j\rightarrow k}\frac{df(\sigma_k)}{d\sigma_k}\frac{\partial P}{\partial o_k}.$$

Thus, in summary, the two key equations have two important consequences: first, the partial derivative of performance with respect to a weight depends on the partial derivative of performance with respect to the following output; and second, the partial derivative of performance with respect to one output depends on the partial derivatives of performance with respect to the outputs in the next layer. From these results, you conclude that the partial derivative of P with respect to any weight in the ith layer must be given in terms of computations already required one layer to the right in the jth layer.

To anchor the computation, however, you still have to determine the partial derivative of performance with respect to each output in the final layer. This computation, however, is easy:

$$\frac{\partial P}{\partial o_z} = \frac{\partial}{\partial o_z} - (d_z - o_z)^2$$
$$= 2(d_z - o_z).$$

It remains to deal with the derivative of the threshold function, f, with respect to its argument, σ, which corresponds to the sum of the inputs seen by a node. Naturally, you choose f such that it is both intuitively satisfying and mathematically tractable:

$$f(\sigma) = \frac{1}{1 + e^{-\sigma}}$$
$$\frac{df(\sigma)}{d\sigma} = \frac{d}{d\sigma}\left[\frac{1}{(1+e^{-\sigma})}\right]$$
$$= (1 + e^{-\sigma})^{-2}e^{-\sigma}$$
$$= f(\sigma)(1 - f(\sigma))$$
$$= o(1 - o).$$

Unusually, the derivative is expressed in terms of each node's output, $o = f(\sigma)$, rather than the sum of the inputs, σ. This way of expressing the derivative is exactly what you want, however, because your overall goal is to produce equations that express values in terms of other values to their right.

Finally, weight changes should depend on a rate parameter, r, that should be as large as possible to encourage rapid learning, but not so large as to cause changes to the output values that considerably overshoot the desired values.

Now, at last, you are ready to look at the **back-propagation formulas**. So that they look the same as the back-propagation formulas developed in the previous, heuristic subsection, $\partial P / \partial o$ is written as β, and a factor of 2 is absorbed into the rate parameter, r.

$$\Delta w_{i \to j} = r o_i o_j (1 - o_j) \beta_j,$$

$$\beta_j = \sum_k w_{j \to k} o_k (1 - o_k) \beta_k \text{ for nodes in hidden layers,}$$

$$\beta_z = d_z - o_z \text{ for nodes in the output layer.}$$

Once you compute changes for each sample input combination, the chain rule dictates that you must add up the weight changes suggested by those individual sample input combinations. Then you can make actual changes to the weights.

The Back-Propagation Procedure Is Straightforward

The back-propagation equations are incorporated into the following back-propagation procedure:

To do back propagation to train a neural net,

▷ Pick a rate parameter, r.

▷ Until performance is satisfactory,

   ▷ For each sample input,

      ▷ Compute the resulting output.

      ▷ Compute β for nodes in the output layer using

$$\beta_z = d_z - o_z.$$

      ▷ Compute β for all other nodes using

$$\beta_j = \sum_k w_{j \to k} o_k (1 - o_k) \beta_k.$$

      ▷ Compute weight changes for all weights using

$$\Delta w_{i \to j} = r o_i o_j (1 - o_j) \beta_j.$$

   ▷ Add up the weight changes for all sample inputs, and change the weights.

Because weight changes are proportional to output errors, the outputs will only approach the 1 and 0 values used as training targets; they will never reach those values. Accordingly, performance is usually deemed satisfactory when all outputs that are trained using 1 as the target value actually exhibit values that are greater than 0.9 and all that are trained using 0 as the target value actually exhibit values that are less than 0.1.

BACK-PROPAGATION CHARACTERISTICS

In this section, you learn that back-propagation performance depends critically on your detailed choices and on the nature of the problem to be solved.

Training May Require Thousands of Back Propagations

Changing weights by back propagation is efficient from a computational point of view because the maximum number of additions and multiplications required for the adjustment of any particular weight is on the order of the maximum number of links emanating from a node. Impractically many steps may be required, however.

Consider, for example, the net shown in figure 22.7, which is similar to part of the net shown in figure 22.3. Assume that exactly two of the inputs presented to the net have values of 1, and that the rest have values of 0. The purpose of the net is to determine whether the two people corresponding to the on inputs are acquaintances. The two people are judged to be acquaintances if the output value is greater than 0.9; they are judged to be not acquaintances if the output value is less than 0.1; and the result is considered ambiguous otherwise.

The problem is to adjust the weights in the net, starting from some set of initial values, until all judgments are consistent with the knowledge that everyone knows everyone else, but that Robert, Raquel, and Romeo are siblings and therefore know one another too well to be considered acquaintances, as are Joan, James, and Juliet.

Table 1 expresses the same knowledge by listing the appropriate output in the column labeled A, for acquaintances, for all 15 possible input combinations. The table also has a column for identifying siblings, which is involved in subsequent training.

These sample inputs are just what you need to execute the back-propagation procedure. Suppose, for example, that the value of the rate parameter is 1.0. Further suppose that the back-propagation procedure is given the initial values for thresholds and weights shown in the first column of table 2. Note that the first initial value is 0.1, the second is 0.2, and rest range up to 1.1 in 0.1 increments. These choices constitute a departure from the usual practice of using random numbers for initial values. The reason for the departure is that the use of a regular pattern of initial values makes it easier for you to see how training changes the weights. For the illustrations in this chapter, using random numbers for initial values produces results that are similar to the results for the regular pattern. In fact, just about any numbers will do, as long as they differ from one another.

When all sample inputs produce an appropriate output value, the thresholds and weights are as shown in the second column of table 2. These thresholds and weights are, of course, much different from the ones used earlier during the basic explanation of how neural nets work. The way the

ALVINN Learns to Drive

The ALVINN system learns to drive a van along roads viewed through a television camera. Once ALVINN has been trained on a particular road, it can drive at speeds in excess of 40 miles per hour.

ALVINN, an acronym for autonomous land vehicle in a neural net, contains one hidden layer of nodes, one output layer, and nearly 5000 trainable weights. Each of ALVINN's 960 inputs produce an image intensity recorded on a 30 by 32 photosensitive array. As shown in the following diagram, each of these 960 inputs is connected, via a trainable weight, to all of the five middle-level nodes. And finally, each of the five middle-level nodes is connected, via a trainable weight, to all of the 32 output nodes.

Input retina

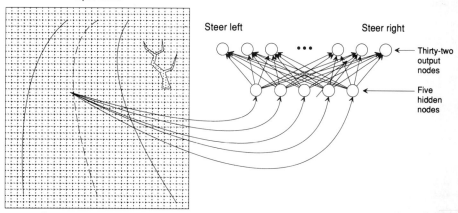

If ALVINN's leftmost output node exhibits the highest output level, ALVINN directs the van's steering mechanism to turn the van sharply left; if the rightmost output node exhibits the highest output level, ALVINN directs the van sharply right; when an intermediate node exhibits the highest output level, ALVINN directs the van in a proportionately intermediate direction.

To smooth out the steering, ALVINN calculates the actual steering direction as the average direction suggested not only by the node with the highest output level but also by that node's immediate neighbors, all contributing in proportion to their output level.

To learn, ALVINN monitors the choices of a human driver. As the human driver steers the van down the training road, periodic sampling of the inputs and the human-selected steering direction provide fodder for back propagation.

One special twist is required, however. Because the human driver does so well, few, if any, of the periodic samples cover situations in which the van is seriously misaligned with the road. Accordingly, monitoring a human driver is not sufficient to ensure that ALVINN can get back on track if the van drifts off track for some reason. Fortunately, however, ALVINN can enrich the set of human-supplied training samples by manufacturing synthetic views from those actually witnessed. Using straightforward geometrical formulas, ALVINN transforms a straight-ahead view of a road seen through the windshield of a well-steered van into a view of what the road would look like if the van were, say, 10° or so off course to the left, thus inviting a right turn that would bring the van back on course.

Figure 22.7 A learning problem involving acquaintances. The task is to learn that anyone in the top group of three is an acquaintance of anyone in the bottom group of three. Threshold-replacing links are not shown.

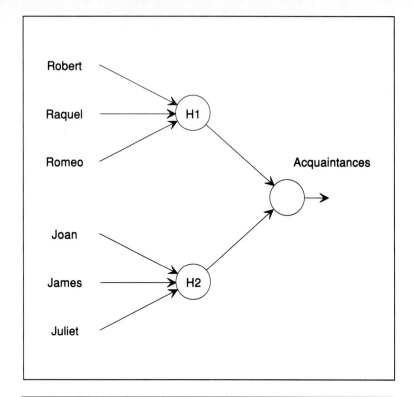

Table 1. Data for the neural-net learning experiments. The first six columns record the possible input combinations. The final two record the corresponding outputs. The column labeled A identifies those pairs of people who are acquaintances; the column labeled S identifies siblings. The first task involves only the acquaintance column; the second task involves both the acquaintance and sibling columns.

Robert	Raquel	Romeo	Joan	James	Juliet	A	S
1	1	0	0	0	0	0	1
1	0	1	0	0	0	0	1
1	0	0	1	0	0	1	0
1	0	0	0	1	0	1	0
1	0	0	0	0	1	1	0
0	1	1	0	0	0	0	1
0	1	0	1	0	0	1	0
0	1	0	0	1	0	1	0
0	1	0	0	0	1	1	0
0	0	1	1	0	0	1	0
0	0	1	0	1	0	1	0
0	0	1	0	0	1	1	0
0	0	0	1	1	0	0	1
0	0	0	1	0	1	0	1
0	0	0	0	1	1	0	1

Table 2. Weight changes observed in training a neural net. Eventually, pairs of people who are acquaintances are recognized. Initial values are changed through back propagation until all outputs are within 0.1 of the required 0.0 or 1.0 value.

Weight	Initial value	End of first task
t_{H1}	0.1	1.99
$w_{Robert \to H1}$	0.2	4.65
$w_{Raquel \to H1}$	0.3	4.65
$w_{Romeo \to H1}$	0.4	4.65
t_{H2}	0.5	2.28
$w_{Joan \to H2}$	0.6	5.28
$w_{James \to H2}$	0.7	5.28
$w_{Juliet \to H2}$	0.8	5.28
$t_{Acquaintances}$	0.9	9.07
$w_{H1 \to Acquaintances}$	1.0	6.27
$w_{H2 \to Acquaintances}$	1.1	6.12

Figure 22.8 Results for a learning experiment. The square root of the average squared error seen at the output nodes is plotted versus the number of back propagations done during staged learning about acquaintances.

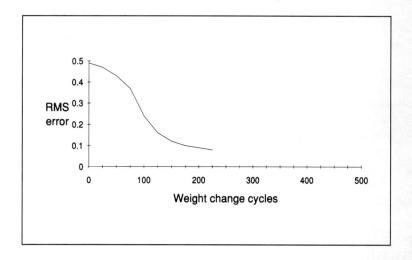

thresholds and weights work for acquaintances is the same, however. Any input in the first group of three pushes H1's output near 1; and any input in the second group pushes H2's output near 1; the Acquaintances node is near 1 only if both H1 and H2 are near 1.

This net training took more than a few steps, however. As shown in figure 22.8, performance becomes satisfactory only after about 225 weight changes. The weights are changed after each complete set of sample inputs is processed with the current weights. Because there are 15 sample inputs, the sample inputs are processed $225 \times 15 = 3375$ times.

Figure 22.9 Learning behavior can depend considerably on the rate parameter. Six different rate parameters, from 0.25 to 8.0, with everything else the same, produced these six results.

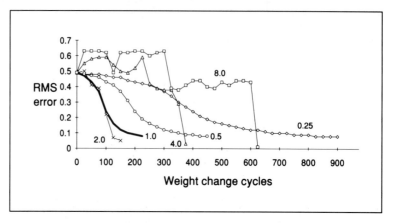

Back Propagation Can Get Stuck or Become Unstable

Now it is time to consider what happens as the rate parameter varies. Specifically, the experiments in the next group repeat the previous experiment, but now the rate parameter varies from 0.25 to 8.0.

You have already seen, in figure 22.8, that the back-propagation procedure can produce a satisfactory solution after about 225 weight changes. For that result, the value of the rate parameter is 1.0. As shown in figure 22.9, decreasing the rate parameter to 0.25 produces a satisfactory solution too, but only after 900 weight changes—about four times as many as for 1.0, as you would expect. Similarly, an intermediate value of 0.5 produces a satisfactory solution after 425 weight changes—about twice as many as for 1.0.

Increasing the rate parameter to 2.0 again reduces the number of weight changes required to produce a satisfactory solution, but now performance is worse, rather than better, for a short time after getting started.

Increasing the rate parameter still further to 4.0 or 8.0 introduces serious instability—errors increase as well as decrease. The reason for the instability is that the steps are so large that the locally computed gradients are not valid.

Thus, a rate parameter of 1.0 produces reasonably rapid solution, but the steps are not so big as to introduce any apparent instability. Accordingly, a rate parameter of 1.0 is used in the rest of the experiments in this chapter. Note, however, that there is no right size for rate parameter in general; the right size depends on the problem you are solving.

Back Propagation Can Be Done in Stages

For further illumination, suppose you add another output node as shown in figure 22.10. The intent is that the output of the new node is to be 1 when the input combination indicates two siblings.

Further suppose that every pair of people who are not acquaintances are siblings, as reflected in the column labeled S, for siblings, in table 1.

Figure 22.10 A learning problem involving acquaintances and siblings. Having learned that anyone in the top group of three is an acquaintance of anyone in the bottom group of three, the net is to learn that each group consists of siblings. Threshold-replacing links are not shown.

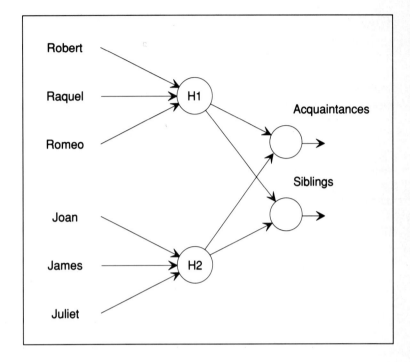

Now you can execute the back-propagation procedure again with the added siblings information. This time, however, you can start with the weights produced by the first experiment; you need new weights for only the new node's threshold and the new connecting links.

When all sample inputs produce an appropriate output value, the weights and thresholds are as shown in the end-of-second-task column of table 3.

As shown by the right portion of the line in figure 22.11, performance becomes satisfactory after about 175 additional weight changes are performed, given a value of 1.0 for the rate parameter. Again, it takes a large number of steps to produce the result, but not so many as required to adjust the weights to recognize acquaintances. This reduction occurs because many of the weights acquired to recognize acquaintances are appropriate for recognizing siblings as well.

Back Propagation Can Train a Net to Learn to Recognize Multiple Concepts Simultaneously

At this point, it is natural to ask what happens when you try to deal with all three output nodes from the very beginning. For this particular example, as shown in figure 22.12, about 425 weight changes produce a satisfactory set of weights, whereas a total of 400 weight changes were required with staged learning. In general, simultaneous learning may be either faster

Table 3. Further weight changes observed in training a neural net. At first, only the acquaintance relation is learned. Then, for the second task, the sibling relation is learned. Dashes indicate that the corresponding weight is not yet present. Initial, random values are changed through back propagation until all outputs are within 0.1 of the required 0.0 or 1.0 value.

Weight	Initial value	End of 1st task	End of 2nd task
t_{H1}	0.1	1.99	2.71
$w_{Robert \rightarrow H1}$	0.2	4.65	6.02
$w_{Raquel \rightarrow H1}$	0.3	4.65	6.02
$w_{Romeo \rightarrow H1}$	0.4	4.65	6.02
t_{H2}	0.5	2.28	2.89
$w_{Joan \rightarrow H2}$	0.6	5.28	6.37
$w_{James \rightarrow H2}$	0.7	5.28	6.37
$w_{Juliet \rightarrow H2}$	0.8	5.28	6.37
$t_{Acquaintances}$	0.9	9.07	10.29
$w_{H1 \rightarrow Acquaintances}$	1.0	6.27	7.04
$w_{H2 \rightarrow Acquaintances}$	1.1	6.12	6.97
$t_{Siblings}$	1.2	–	-8.32
$w_{H1 \rightarrow Siblings}$	1.3	–	-5.72
$w_{H2 \rightarrow Siblings}$	1.4	–	-5.68

Figure 22.11 Results for staged learning. First, the net is taught about acquaintances; then, it is taught about siblings. The square root of the average squared error seen at the output nodes is plotted versus the number of back propagations done during staged learning about acquaintances.

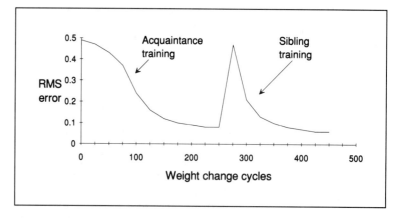

or slower than staged learning. Which method is faster depends on the problem and on the initial weights.

Trained Neural Nets Can Make Predictions

So far, you have learned that you can train a neural net to recognize acquaintances and siblings. In each experiment, however, the training set of

Figure 22.12 The dotted line shows the square root of the average squared error seen at the output nodes during staged learning. The solid line shows the square root of the average squared error seen at the output nodes during simultaneous learning. A little more work is required, in this experiment, if the learning is done in stages.

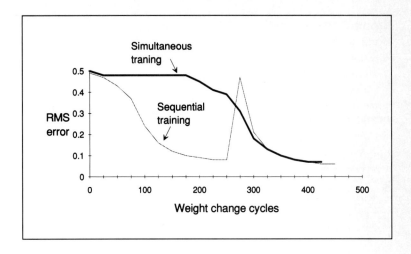

sample input–output combinations included every possible pair of people. Thus, you have yet to see a neural net use what it has learned from sample input–output combinations to predict the correct outputs for previously unseen inputs.

Accordingly, suppose you divide the data shown in table 1 into a **training set** and a **test set**. Let the training set consist of the original data with every fifth sample input–output combination removed. The test set consists of every fifth sample. Thus, you reserve 20 percent of the data for testing whether the neural net can generalize from the data in the training set.

The back-propagation procedure successfully trains the net to deal with all the sample input–output combinations in the training set after only 225 weight changes. That is fewer changes than were required when the net was trained on all the sample input–output combinations, because there are three fewer input–output combinations to be accommodated.

Pleasingly, the trained net also deals successfully with the input–output combinations in the test set, as demonstrated by the following table, in which the d subscript denotes desired value and the o subscript denotes observed value:

Robert	Raquel	Romeo	Joan	James	Juliet	A_d	A_o	S_d	S_o
1	0	0	0	0	1	1	0.92	0	0.06
0	0	1	1	0	0	1	0.92	0	0.06
0	0	0	0	1	1	0	0.09	1	0.91

Excess Weights Lead to Overfitting

Intuitively, you might think that, if one neural net does well, a neural net with more trainable weights would do even better. You must learn to

Figure 22.13 Another neural net for dealing with the acquaintances–siblings problem. This one has too many weights, and illustrates the overfitting problem.

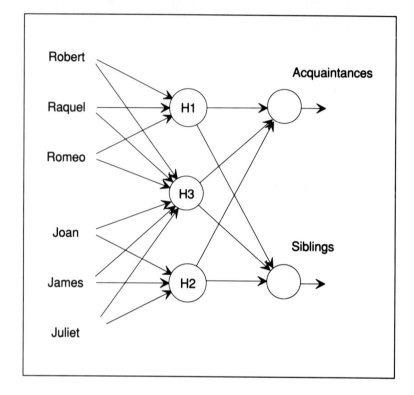

suppress this intuition, because neural nets become erratic and unreliable if they have too many weights.

Consider, for example, the net shown in figure 22.13. Given that it is enriched with a new node and nine new weights—including the one for the new node's threshold—you might think that this net would handle the previous training problem with no difficulty, perhaps converging faster to an equally good solution. In any event, you would think that the additional new weights could do no harm, because the back-propagation procedure conceivably could drive them all toward 0.

The additional new weights do considerable harm, however. The back-propagation procedure requires 300 weight changes to train the net to deal with all the sample input–output combinations. Thus, more weight changes are required by the larger net. Worse still, the performance on the test set now exhibits errors, as demonstrated by the following table:

Robert	Raquel	Romeo	Joan	James	Juliet	A_d	A_o	S_d	S_o
1	0	0	0	0	1	1	0.99	0	0.00
0	0	1	1	0	0	1	0.06 (?)	0	0.94 (?)
0	0	0	0	1	1	0	0.97 (?)	1	0.01 (?)

Figure 22.14 Overfitting is
a consequence of too much
flexibility. Here, a piece of
wood provides a nice fit to the
black dots when forced into
conformance by a few nails.
A steel rod cannot be forced
into any sort of conformance,
however; and a rope can
meander all over the terrain.

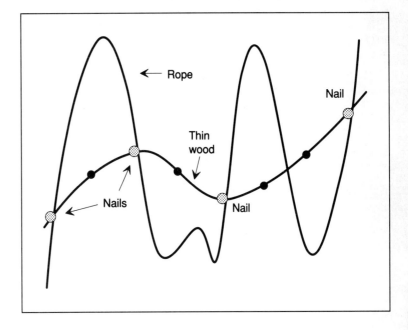

The problem is that the additional weights provide too much flexibility,
making it possible to deal with the training set too easily. To see why both
too little and too much flexibility are bad, consider the points shown in
figure 22.14. You could drive nails into a few points and use those nails to
force a thin piece of wood into a shape that would fit smoothly through all
the points. If you tried to use a heavy steel rod, however, you would find it
too stiff to bend. If you tried to use a rope, you would find it too flexible,
because you could fit the rope to all the nails yet have wild meandering in
between.

The rope is analogous to a neural net with too many trainable weights:
A neural net with too many weights can conform to the input–output
samples in the training set in many ways, some of which correspond to
wild meandering. A net that conforms to the data with wild meandering
is said to exhibit **overfitting**.

To avoid overfitting, you can use one good heuristic: Be sure that the
number of trainable weights influencing any particular output is smaller
than the number of training samples. For the acquaintance–sibling net
shown in figure 22.3, each output value is determined by 11 trainable
weights and there are 12 input–output samples—a dangerously small mar-
gin, but training was successful nevertheless. For the acquaintance–sibling
net shown in figure 22.13, each output value is determined by 19 trainable
weights—an excess of more than 50 percent over the number of training
samples. Overfitting is inevitable.

Neural-Net Training Is an Art

You now know that you face many choices after you decide to work on a problem by training a neural net using back propagation:

- How can you represent information in neural net terms? How can you use neural net inputs to express what you know? How can you use neural net outputs to determine what you want to know?
- How many neurons should you have in your neural net? How many inputs? How many outputs? How many weights? How many hidden layers?
- What rate parameter should you use in the back-propagation formula?
- Should you train your neural net in stages or simultaneously?

The wrong choices lead to poor performance. A small neural net may not learn what you want it to learn. A big net will learn slowly, may get stuck on local maxima, and may exhibit overfitting. A small rate parameter may waste time. A large rate parameter may promote instability or provide poor predictions.

Unfortunately, the proper choices depend on the nature of the samples. Mathematically, you can view the samples as representative glimpses of a hidden function, with one dimension for each input. If there are many inputs, the function's multidimensional character makes the function hard to think about and impossible to visualize.

Accordingly, the best guide to your choices is trial and error, buttressed, if possible, by reference to the choices that have worked well in similar problems. Thus, the successful deployment of neural-net technology requires time and experience. Neural-net experts are artists; they are not mere handbook users.

SUMMARY

- Real neurons consist of synapses, dendrites, axons, and cell bodies. Simulated neurons consist of multipliers, adders, and thresholds.
- One way to learn is to train a simulated neural net to recognize regularity in data.
- The back-propagation procedure is a procedure for training neural nets. Back propagation can be understood heuristically or by way of a mathematical analysis.
- To enable back propagation, you need to perform a simple trick that eliminates nonzero neuron thresholds. You also need to convert stairstep threshold functions into squashed S threshold functions.
- You can teach a neural net, via back propagation, to recognize several concepts. These concepts can be taught one at a time or all at once.
- You must choose a back-propagation rate parameter carefully. A rate parameter that is too small leads to slow training; a rate parameter that is too large leads to instability.

■ An excess of trainable weights, relative to the number of training samples, can lead to overfitting and poor performance on test data.

BACKGROUND

There is a vast literature on the subject of neural nets. For an overview, see *Parallel Distributed Processing*, edited by James L. McClelland and David E. Rumelhart [1986], or *Neurocomputing: Foundations of Research*, edited by James A. Anderson and Edward Rosenfeld [1989].

In the literature on neural nets, the papers by Geoffrey E. Hinton [1989, 1990] and by J. J. Hopfield [1982] have been particularly influential.

The discussion of ALVINN is based on the work of Dean A. Pomerleau [1991]. NETtalk, a system that learns to speak, is another, often cited application of neural nets [Terrence J. Sejnowski and Charles R. Rosenberg 1989].

23

Learning by Training Perceptrons

In this chapter, you learn about *perceptrons*, which can be viewed as a special kind of neural net. In a sense, a perceptron is the simplest possible neural net, because a perceptron has just one neuronlike element. The principal virtue of perceptrons is that they inspired a decade of deep theoretical inquiry.

By way of illustration, you see how a simple perceptron learns to identify digits displayed in a seven-segment digital display.

Once you have finished this chapter, you will know how perceptrons work, you will understand how the *perceptron convergence procedure* improves their performance, and you will understand that there are many tasks that perceptrons simply cannot do.

PERCEPTRONS AND PERCEPTRON LEARNING

Perceptrons, like the simulated neurons introduced in Chapter 22, consist of trainable, multiplicative weights, an adder, and a threshold function. In this section, you learn about how perceptrons are different from the simulated neurons described in Chapter 22 and how they can learn.

Perceptrons Have Logic Boxes and Stair-Step Thresholds

As illustrated in figure 23.1, **perceptrons** are specialized and augmented, relative to ordinary neural nets, according to the following specification:

Figure 23.1 A perceptron. Inputs are all 0s or 1s, as are the outputs of the logic boxes. If the sum of the weighted outputs of the logic boxes is greater than zero, the output of the perceptron is 1 and the perceptron is said to say *yes*, a class has been recognized. Otherwise, the perceptron is said to say *no*, a class is not recognized.

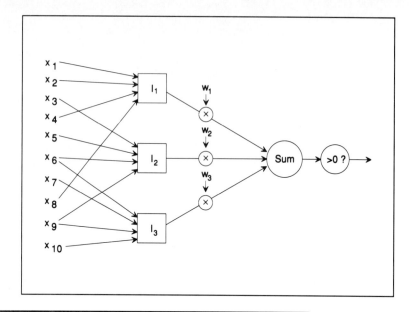

A **perceptron** is a representation

That is a neural net

In which

▷ There is only one neuron.

▷ The inputs are binary: Only 0 and 1 are allowed.

▷ Logic boxes may be interposed between the perceptron's inputs and the perceptron's weights. Each logic box can be viewed as a table that produces an output value of 0 or 1 for each combination of 0s and 1s that can appear at its inputs.

▷ The output of the perceptron is 0 or 1 depending on whether the weighted sum of the logic-box outputs is greater than the threshold.

In Chapter 22, you saw how a nonzero threshold can be converted into the combination of an extra input, an extra weight, and a zero threshold. In this chapter, you analogously convert nonzero thresholds, limiting the need to discuss them.

Expressing what happens in mathematical notation, suppose the output of the ith logic box is l_i; further suppose that ith weight is w_i; and finally, suppose that the threshold is T. Then, the output of the entire perceptron, P is given by the following formula:

$$P = \begin{cases} 1 & \text{if } \sum_i w_i \times l_i > T; \\ 0 & \text{otherwise.} \end{cases}$$

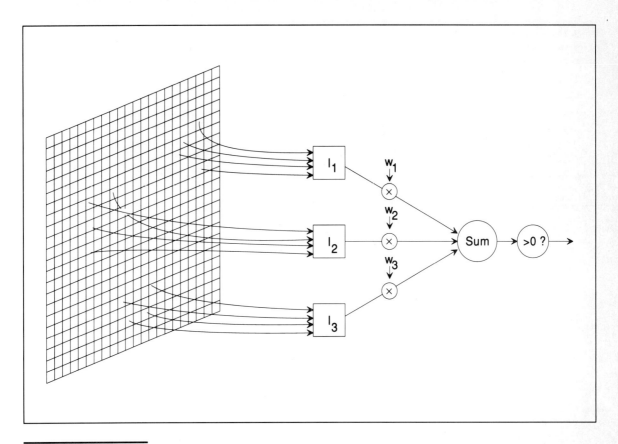

Figure 23.2 Another perceptron. Here the inputs are arranged in a rectangular array with a view toward recognizing a two-dimensional pattern.

Note that, if any one of a perceptron's logic boxes were allowed to look at all of the perceptron's inputs, then there would be no need for any other logic boxes, nor would there be any need for any weights at all, nor would there be any need for a threshold function. Instead, all the combinations of input 0s and 1s would be recorded in the logic box's internal table, along with the appropriate 0-or-1 output.

Of course, the number of entries in the table would have to be 2^n if there are n inputs and all possible combinations of 0s and 1s are to be handled. This exponential relation between the number of entries and the number of inputs makes it impractical for any of a perceptron's logic boxes to look at all the inputs, or even at a substantial fraction of all the inputs, if there are many inputs. Accordingly, each logic box of a perceptron is presumed to look at only a small number of inputs; for example, the logic boxes in the perceptron in figure 23.2 look at a maximum of four inputs:

■ In an **order-limited perceptron** of order n, each logic box looks at n or fewer inputs.

Alternatively, as shown in figure 23.2, a perceptron's inputs may be arranged in a rectangular array, suggestively called a **retina**, when the hoped-

Figure 23.3 A straight-through perceptron.

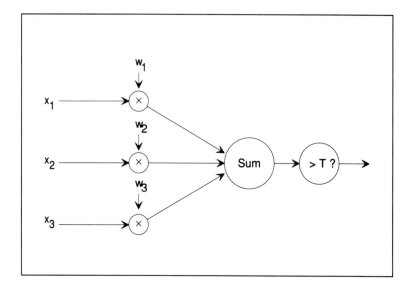

for purpose of the perceptron is to recognize a two-dimensional pattern such as an alphanumeric character. Whenever a perceptron's inputs are so arranged, then you can limit the inputs available to each logic box in another way:

- In a **diameter-limited perceptron** of diameter d, the inputs are assumed to be arranged in a rectangular, retinalike array, and all the inputs to any particular logic box must lie within a circle of diameter d.

Still another limitation is to reduce the logic boxes to a single input, which is passed on to the corresponding multiplier:

- In a **straight-through perceptron**, each logic box has just one input, and the output is always the same as that input.

Alternatively, a straight-through perceptron can be viewed as a perceptron without logic boxes, as illustrated in figure 23.3. The examples in this chapter are straight-through perceptrons because learning examples are easier to follow when there are no logic boxes.

The Perceptron Convergence Procedure Guarantees Success Whenever Success Is Possible

Remarkably, there is a procedure that discovers a successful set of weights for a perceptron given that a successful set of weights exists. Moreover, the procedure is incredibly straightforward. Basically, you start with all weights initially set to 0. Then, you try your perceptron on all samples, one at a time. Whenever your perceptron makes a mistake, you change the weights so as to make the mistake less likely; otherwise, you do nothing.

For the moment, suppose that the perceptron says no, by producing a 0, when it should say yes, by producing a 1. You can make it more likely to say yes the next time if you *increase* the weights attached to those logic boxes that produce 1s at the instant the mistake is made. One way to ensure the eventual discovery of a completely successful set of weights is to increase each such weight by 1.

Symmetrically, whenever the perceptron says yes when it should say no, you *decrease* the weights attached to logic boxes that are producing 1s, with the decrease equal to 1.

In no case do you alter the weights attached to logic boxes that are producing 0s. After all, those weights are multiplied by 0s, so fooling with them cannot possibly change the current result and could make some other correct result wrong.

Finally, to get the effect of a trainable threshold, you add an extra, virtual input, whose value is always assumed to be 1, attached to a logic box that just passes on the input value. With this addition, your perceptron can be viewed as having a threshold of 0, and it says yes whenever the weighted sum of logic-box outputs exceeds 0.

Note that you can talk about the perceptron training procedure more concisely using the language of vectors. The logic-box outputs and the weights, expressed in vector notation, are $(l_1 l_2 \dots l_n)$ and $(w_1 w_2 \dots w_n)$. Adding one to each of the weights attached to logic boxes that are producing 1s is the same as adding the logic box output vector to the weight vector, as in the following description:

To train a perceptron,

▷ Until the perceptron yields the correct result for each training sample, for each sample,

  ▷ If the perceptron yields the wrong answer,

    ▷ If the perceptron says no when it should say yes, add the logic-box output vector to the weight vector.

    ▷ Otherwise, subtract the logic-box output vector from the weight vector.

  ▷ Otherwise, do nothing.

Consider, for example, the straight-through perceptron shown in figure 23.4, and suppose you want to train it to perform a logical Or function starting from scratch. Because the perceptron is a straight-through perceptron, the logic-box output vector, $(l_1 l_2 l_3)$, is the same as the input vector, $(x_1 x_2 x_3)$. Thus, the input samples and corresponding logic-box outputs are as follows for logical Or:

Figure 23.4 A straight-through perceptron with two ordinary inputs and a threshold-replacing input. This one is ready to be trained to recognize the logical Or of its inputs. Note that the always-1 input and corresponding weight take the place of a nonzero threshold.

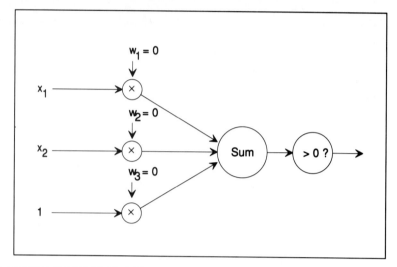

Sample	$x_1 = (l_1)$	$x_2 = (l_2)$	$x_3 = (l_3) = 1$	Desired output
1	0	0	1	0
2	0	1	1	1
3	1	0	1	1
4	1	1	1	1

Cycling through these samples, the perceptron eventually learns logical Or after four changes. The first change occurs following a mistake on the second sample during the first pass. At that time, the weight vector is (0 0 0), so the output is 0, when it should be 1. Accordingly, when the input vector, (0 1 1), is added to the weight vector, the new weight vector is (0 1 1). The next two samples encountered during the first pass both produce a 1, as they should, so there are no further changes during the first pass.

During the second pass, the first sample produces a 1, but should produce a 0. Accordingly, the input vector, (0 0 1) is subtracted from the weight vector, (0 1 1), producing a new weight vector, (0 1 0). With this change, however, the third sample produces a 0 when it should produce a 1. Accordingly, the input vector, (1 0 1), is added to the weight vector, (0 1 0), producing a new weight vector, (1 1 1).

Next, the first sample produces an error again during the third pass. The result should be 0, but it is 1. Subtracting the input vector, (0 0 1), from the weight vector, (1 1 1), leaves a new weight vector, (1 1 0), which subsequently works for all samples.

Because there are only three weights—two for the inputs and one for the threshold—each weight combination can be viewed as a three-dimensional weight vector, as shown in figure 23.5. In general, the weight

Figure 23.5 During perceptron training, the weight vector starts out with all components equal to zero. During learning, its length grows and shrinks.

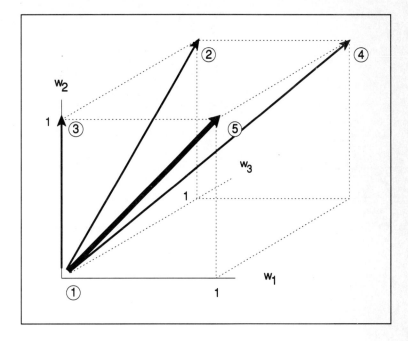

vector grows and shrinks as learning proceeds. In this example, however, the angle between the changing weight vector and the final solution weight always shrinks.

Ordinary Algebra Is Adequate to Demonstrate Convergence When There Are Two Weights

To understand why the perceptron convergence procedure works, let us consider a perceptron with just two weights, w_1 and w_2. There is nothing special about two weights other than that weight combinations can be viewed as simple two-dimensional vectors. Following mathematical convention, boldface type is used for the names of vectors. Thus, **w** is the vector with components w_1 and w_2.

Ordinarily, a weight vector is considered satisfactory as long as $\sum_i w_i \times l_i > 0$ for positive samples and $\sum_i w_i \times l_i \leq 0$ for negative samples. To ensure that the perceptron convergence procedure works, however, you must assume that there is a special weight vector, $\mathbf{w}^*$ that never produces a sum lying in a small zone around 0, of width 2δ. Thus, the $\mathbf{w}^*$ weight vector provides performance only slightly better than satisfactory, because $\sum_i w_i^* \times l_i > \delta$ for positive samples and $\sum_i w_i^* \times l_i < -\delta$ for negative samples.

Notationally, let us agree to label weights with superscripts indicating where they lie in the change sequence. Thus, the initial weights are $w_{1,0}$ and $w_{2,0}$, both of which are 0. After n changes, the weights are $w_{1,n}$ and

$w_{2,n}$. As changes are made, the weight vector can grow, shrink, and move relative to the vector composed of w_1^* and w_2^*.

Now you are ready to understand the key idea. Consider the angle between $\mathbf{w}^*$, the vector with components w_1^* and w_2^*, and $\mathbf{w}_n$, the vector with components $w_{1,n}$ and $w_{2,n}$. You soon see why this angle must lie inside an envelope that must shrink whenever the weight vector changes. Notably, each time the envelope shrinks, the size of the reduction increases. Eventually, there can be no more change because the envelope becomes too small to accommodate the next shrinkage step. But this observation means that no further mistakes are possible either, inasmuch as each mistake produces a weight-vector change and the envelope must shrink whenever the weight vector changes.

All this explanation becomes clearer once you see how an expression for the envelope emerges from the following formula for the cosine of the angle between $\mathbf{w}^*$ and $\mathbf{w}_n$:

$$\cos\theta = \frac{w_1^* w_{1,n} + w_2^* w_{2,n}}{\sqrt{w_1^{*2} + w_2^{*2}}\sqrt{w_{1,n}^2 + w_{2,n}^2}}.$$

By taking advantage of what you know about how the weights change, you can demonstrate that this expression has to be proportional to $\sqrt{n}\delta$.

The first step toward the demonstration is to note the relation between $w_{i,n}$ and $w_{i,n-1}$. For the moment, suppose that a mistake is made such that your perceptron says no when it should say yes. It does so when $\sum_i w_{i,n-1} \times l_i \leq 0$, which leads to the following changes to the weights:

$$w_{1,n} = w_{1,n-1} + l_1,$$
$$w_{2,n} = w_{2,n-1} + l_2.$$

With these equations giving $w_{i,n}$ in terms of $w_{i,n-1}$, the numerator of the cosine expression becomes

$$w_1^* w_{1,n-1} + w_2^* w_{2,n-1} + w_1^* l_1 + w_2^* l_2.$$

By virtue of the original assumption that $\mathbf{w}^*$ always produces correct results, and produces them outside the 2δ no-human's land, you know that $w_1^* l_1 + w_2^* l_2 > \delta$ when the perceptron should say yes. Thus, the numerator of the cosine expression is constrained as follows:

$$w_1^* w_{1,n} + w_2^* w_{2,n} > w_1^* w_{1,n-1} + w_2^* w_{2,n-1} + \delta.$$

Having gone this far, it is easy to see that you can repeat what you have done, this time replacing $w_{i,n-1}$ with $w_{i,n-2}$, producing the following constraint on the cosine's numerator:

$$w_1^* w_{1,n} + w_2^* w_{2,n} > w_1^* w_{1,n-2} + w_2^* w_{2,n-2} + 2\delta.$$

Taking this replacement all the way back to the $w_{i,0}$, both of which are 0, you have the following:

$$w_1^* w_{1,n} + w_2^* w_{2,n} > n\delta.$$

Next, recall that the cosine's denominator is as follows:

$$\sqrt{w_1^{*2} + w_2^{*2}}\sqrt{w_{1,n}^2 + w_{2,n}^2}.$$

Focus, for the moment, on $w_{1,n}^2 + w_{2,n}^2$. Replacing $w_{i,n}$ by $w_{i,n-1} + l_i$ as before, you have this:

$$w_{1,n}^2 + w_{2,n}^2 = \left(w_{1,n-1} + l_1\right)^2 + \left(w_{2,n-1} + l_2\right)^2$$
$$= w_{1,n-1}^2 + w_{2,n-1}^2 + 2(w_{1,n-1}l_1 + w_{2,n-1}l_2) + (l_1)^2 + (l_2)^2.$$

Now note that $w_{1,n-1}l_1 + w_{2,n-1}l_2$ must be 0 or less because the event that started off the change in weight was the perceptron saying no when it should have said yes, which happens only when $w_{1,n-1}l_1 + w_{2,n-1}l_2 \leq 0$. Also note that $(l_1)^2 + (l_2)^2$ must be 2 or less because both l_1 and l_2 must be either 0 or 1. Thus, you have the following constraint on the sum of the squared weights:

$$w_{1,n}^2 + w_{2,n}^2 \leq w_{1,n-1}^2 + w_{2,n-1}^2 + 2.$$

Because $w_{1,0}{}^2 + w_{2,0}{}^2 = 0$, repeated substitution eventually produces the following constraint:

$$w_{1,n}^2 + w_{2,n}^2 \leq 2n.$$

Therefore, the denominator of the cosine expression must be constrained as follows:

$$\sqrt{w_1^{*2} + w_2^{*2}}\sqrt{w_{1,n}^2 + w_{2,n}^2} \leq \sqrt{w_1^{*2} + w_2^{*2}}\sqrt{2n}.$$

Thus, you have one expression that is less than the numerator, and another expression that is greater than or equal to the denominator. Putting both expressions together, you see that the cosine expression is constrained as follows:

$$\cos\theta = \frac{w_1^* w_{1,n} + w_2^* w_{2,n}}{\sqrt{w_1^{*2} + w_2^{*2}}\sqrt{w_{1,n}^2 + w_{2,n}^2}} > \frac{n\delta}{\sqrt{w_1^{*2} + w_2^{*2}}\sqrt{2n}}.$$

Writing this expression in another way, you have the following:

$$\cos\theta > \frac{\delta\sqrt{n/2}}{\sqrt{w_1^{*2} + w_2^{*2}}}.$$

From this inequality, you can see that the cosine of the angle between $\mathbf{w}^*$ and $\mathbf{w}_n$ must increase with each change. For a while, this increase is fine, because as the cosine increases, the angle decreases, so $\mathbf{w}_n$ must be coming closer to congruence with $\mathbf{w}^*$. On the other hand, because a cosine can never be greater than 1, eventually there can be no further weight changes. At this point, no further mistakes are possible, inasmuch as each mistake has to produce a weight change. Thus, the perceptron convergence procedure eventually must produce a set of weights that works on all examples, given the initial assumption that a set of weights exists.

Note, however, that you have assumed so far that the mistake that caused the change was one for which the perceptron said no when it should have said yes. What about when it says yes when it should say no? Fortunately, the constraint is the same, because all the sign changes involved balance out. In particular, the weight changes are negative, rather than positive:

$$w_1, n = w_{1,n-1} - l_1,$$
$$w_2, n = w_{2,n-1} - l_2.$$

Thus, the numerator of the cosine expression becomes

$$w_1^* w_{1,n-1} + w_2^* w_{2,n-1} - w_1^* l_1 - w_2^* l_2.$$

When your perceptron should say no, you know $\mathbf{w}^*$ is such that $w_1^* l_1 + w_2^* l_2 < -\delta$, which is equivalent to $-w_1^* l_1 - w_2^* l_2 > \delta$, which leads to the same constraint as that observed before:

$$w_1^* w_{1,n} + w_2^* w_{2,n} > n\delta.$$

For the denominator, the critical requirement is that

$$w_{1,n}^2 + w_{2,n}^2 \leq w_{1,n-1}^2 + w_{2,n-1}^2 + 2.$$

This inequality must hold, because the relation between $\mathbf{w}_n$ and $\mathbf{w}_{n-1}$ is such that

$$w_{1,n}^2 + w_{2,n}^2 = \left(w_{1,n-1} - l_1\right)^2 + \left(w_{2,n-1} - l_2\right)^2$$
$$= w_{1,n-1}^2 + w_{2,n-1}^2 - 2(w_{1,n-1}l_1 + w_{2,n-1}l_2) + (l_1)^2 + (l_2)^2.$$

Note that $-2(w_{1,n-1}l_1 + w_{2,n-1}l_2)$ has to be less than or equal to 0 because the perceptron says has said yes, requiring that $w_{1,n-1}l_1 + w_{2,n-1}l_2 > 0$. Also, as before, $(l_1)^2 + (l_2)^2$ must be less than 2. From these observations, you can proceed as before to demonstrate that the denominator of the cosine expression is constrained as follows:

$$\sqrt{w_1^{*2} + w_2^{*2}} \sqrt{w_{1,n}^2 + w_{2,n}^2} \leq \sqrt{w_1^{*2} + w_2^{*2}} \sqrt{2n}.$$

Thus, the numerator and the denominator of the expression for the cosine of the angle between $\mathbf{w}^*$ and $\mathbf{w}_n$ are subject to the same restrictions when the perceptron falsely says yes as they are when the perceptron falsely says no.

Vector Algebra Helps You to Demonstrate Convergence When There Are Many Weights

If you happen to be familiar with vectors and the meaning of vector operations, then it is easy to generalize the treatment of two-weight perceptrons to perceptrons with any number of weights.

To begin, let $\mathbf{w}$ be the vector of weights and let $\mathbf{l}$ be a vector of logic-box outputs. Then, using the definition of the dot product of two vectors, $\sum_i w_i \times l_i$ can be rewritten as $\mathbf{w} \cdot \mathbf{l}$. Accordingly, the key assumption made in the analysis of the perceptron convergence theorem is that there is a weight vector, $\mathbf{w}^*$, such that $\mathbf{w}^* \cdot \mathbf{l} > \delta$ if $\mathbf{l}$ is produced by inputs that are supposed to make the perceptron say yes, and $\mathbf{w}^* \cdot \mathbf{l} < -\delta$ otherwise.

Next, the cosine of the angle between $\mathbf{w}^*$ and $\mathbf{w}_n$ is equal to the dot product of the two vectors divided by their lengths:

$$\cos \theta = \frac{\mathbf{w}^* \cdot \mathbf{w}_n}{\|\mathbf{w}^*\|\|\mathbf{w}_n\|}.$$

Now suppose that the mistake that caused the change was one for which the perceptron said no when it should have said yes. This mistake happens when $\mathbf{w}_{n-1} \cdot \mathbf{l} \leq 0$, which leads to the following change to the weight vector:

$$\mathbf{w}_n = \mathbf{w}_{n-1} + \mathbf{l}.$$

Thus the numerator of the cosine expression becomes

$$\begin{aligned} \mathbf{w}^* \cdot \mathbf{w}_n &= \mathbf{w}^* \cdot (\mathbf{w}_{n-1} + \mathbf{l}) \\ &= \mathbf{w}^* \cdot \mathbf{w}_{n-1} + \mathbf{w}^* \cdot \mathbf{l}. \end{aligned}$$

Because $\mathbf{w}^*$ always produces correct results, you know that $\mathbf{w}^* \cdot \mathbf{l} > \delta$, given that the perceptron is supposed to say yes. Thus, the numerator of the cosine expression is constrained as follows:

$$\mathbf{w}^* \cdot \mathbf{w}_n > \mathbf{w}^* \cdot \mathbf{w}_{n-1} + \delta.$$

Repeating produces the following constraint on the cosine's numerator:

$$\mathbf{w}^* \cdot \mathbf{w}_n > n\delta.$$

Now recall that the cosine's denominator is as follows:

$$\|\mathbf{w}^*\|\|\mathbf{w}_n\|.$$

Rewriting the square of $\mathbf{w}_n$'s length, $\|\mathbf{w}_n\|^2$, as a dot product enables the following analysis:

$$\begin{aligned} \|\mathbf{w}_n\|^2 &= \mathbf{w}_n \cdot \mathbf{w}_n \\ &= (\mathbf{w}_{n-1} + \mathbf{l}) \cdot (\mathbf{w}_{n-1} + \mathbf{l}) \\ &= \|\mathbf{w}_{n-1}\|^2 + 2\mathbf{w}_{n-1} \cdot \mathbf{l} + \|\mathbf{l}\|^2. \end{aligned}$$

Next, $\mathbf{w}_{n-1} \cdot \mathbf{l}$ must be 0 or less because the event that started off the change in weight was the perceptron saying no when it should have said yes. Thus, you have the following constraint:

$$\|\mathbf{w}_n\|^2 \leq \|\mathbf{w}_{n-1}\|^2 + \|\mathbf{l}\|^2.$$

Repeated substitution produces the following constraint:

$$\|\mathbf{w}_n\|^2 \leq n\|\mathbf{l}\|^2.$$

Because all the elements of $\mathbf{l}$ are either 0 or 1, $\|\mathbf{l}\|^2$ cannot be larger than the number of logic boxes, $\#\mathbf{l}$. This fact, in turn, means that the denominator of the cosine expression must be constrained as follows:

$$\|\mathbf{w}^*\|\|\mathbf{w}_n\| \leq \|\mathbf{w}^*\|\sqrt{n}\sqrt{\#\mathbf{l}}.$$

Figure 23.6 Seven line
segments are enough to
produce all 10 digits.

Figure 23.6 Seven line segments are enough to produce all 10 digits.

Putting together the constraints on the numerator and the denominator,
the cosine expression evidently is constrained as follows:

$$\cos \theta > \frac{\sqrt{n}\delta}{\|\mathbf{w}^*\|\sqrt{\#1}}.$$

Again, you see that the lower bound on the cosine of the angle between
$\mathbf{w}^*$ and $\mathbf{w}_n$ must increase with each change, and that the lower bound is
proportional to $\sqrt{n}$.

WHAT PERCEPTRONS CAN AND CANNOT DO

In this section, you see that the perceptron convergence procedure can learn
the weights required to identify the digits in digital displays.

Take care, however. The perceptron convergence procedure is so elegant, it is easy to wax enthusiastic about perceptrons, imagining that they
must be enormously powerful, whereas in fact there are simple tasks that
perceptrons cannot do, as you learn in this section.

A Straight-Through Perceptron Can Learn to Identify Digits

As a more elaborate example showing the perceptron convergence procedure in action, consider the problem of recognizing the digits that are often
used in digital displays—the ones that are produced by the turning on of
an appropriate combination of segments from among seven possibilities, as
shown in figure 23.6.

Figure 23.7 A digit-recognizing perceptron. Seven of the inputs are attached to the seven line segments; the eighth is attached to an always-1 input, thus replacing a threshold.

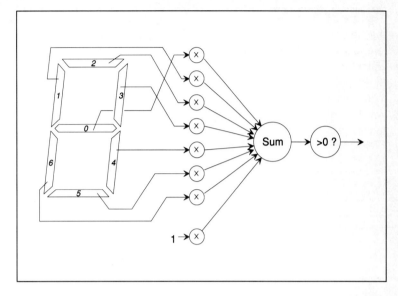

Next, suppose that a hypothetical vision system is able to report which of the seven segments in a display is actually on, thus serving to produce inputs for the straight-through perceptron shown in figure 23.7.

As shown, the seven segment inputs, plus the always-1 input, give you a total of eight inputs with eight corresponding weights that can be changed. The input samples are as follows:

Digit	x_0	x_1	x_2	x_3	x_4	x_5	x_6
0	0	1	1	1	1	1	1
9	1	1	1	1	1	1	0
8	1	1	1	1	1	1	1
7	0	0	1	1	1	1	0
6	1	1	1	0	1	1	1
5	1	1	1	0	1	1	0
4	1	1	0	1	1	1	0
3	1	0	1	1	1	1	0
2	1	0	1	1	0	1	1
1	0	0	0	1	1	0	0

To train a digit-recognizing perceptron to identify 0, you tell it that only the first line should produce a 1. To train it to identify 1, you tell it that only the last line should produce a 1.

Whatever the digit, the perceptron convergence procedure continues to cycle through the samples, making the appropriate adjustment to the weight vector whenever it makes an error, until no further changes are required.

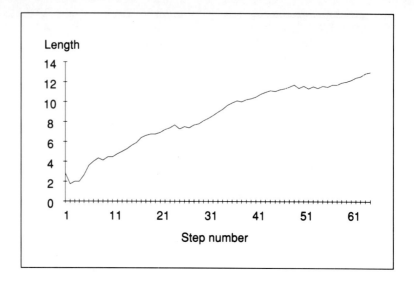

Figure 23.8 The length of the weight vector changes as learning proceeds to produce weight vectors for recognizing 8. Note that the length both increases and decreases on the way toward the final value of the weights.

When the perceptron learns to identify 0, convergence is fast: only two changes are needed. First, because the perceptron immediately fails to identify 0, the first sample of the first pass, the 0 vector, (0 1 1 1 1 1 1 1) is added to the all-0 initial weights. Next, because the perceptron falsely identifies 9, the second sample on the first pass, (1 1 1 1 1 1 0 1) is subtracted. The result is the weight vector (-1 0 0 0 0 0 1 0), which is satisfactory, as 0 is identified and all other digits are rejected. Curiously, this result means that you need to look at only two segments—the ones labeled 0 and 6—to determine whether you have a 0, an assertion that you can verify easily by inspecting figure 23.6.

When the perceptron learns to identify 8, however, convergence is slower than with any other digit. Sixty-five changes are required to produce the final weight vector, (3 3 0 6 -1 -7 4 -7).

Because there are more than three weights in the digit-recognizing perceptron, individual changes in the weight vector cannot be shown as they were in figure 23.5. Nevertheless, you can follow what happens to the length of the weight vector and the angle between the weight vector and its final value. For example, figure 23.8 shows weight-vector changes, and figure 23.9 shows angle changes, as the perceptron learns to identify the digit 8.

Note that both the length of the weight vector and the angle between the weight vector and its final value grow and shrink.

The Perceptron Convergence Procedure Is Amazing

On the surface, it is strange that the perceptron convergence procedure ever succeeds. You would think that, each time it makes a change to improve the handling of one particular sample, that change could ruin what is done

Figure 23.11 Four retinal patterns. The second and third are connected; the first and fourth are not connected.

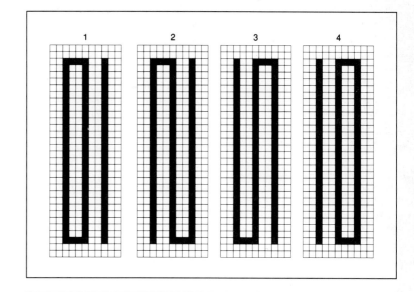

Figure 23.12 A diameter-limited perceptron looks at a retina. Some logic boxes look at the upper part, some look at the lower part, and some in the middle see nothing in either the upper part or the lower part. None look at both the upper and lower parts.

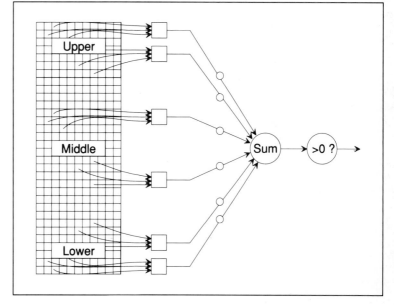

box outputs sum into three parts, one each for the logic boxes that look at the upper, middle, and lower parts of the retina:

$$\sum_{\text{upper}} w_i \times l_i \sum_{\text{middle}} w_i \times l_i \sum_{\text{lower}} w_i \times l_i > 0.$$

Because the logic boxes that contribute to the middle sum do not see any differences among the four patterns in figure 23.12, the middle sum is the same for all four patterns.

On the other hand, the lower sum has to increase, changing the overall sum from negative or zero to positive, as the first pattern is transformed into the second. This increase has to occur because neither of the other sums change and because the unconnected first pattern becomes the connected second pattern.

Similarly, the upper sum has to increase, changing the overall sum from negative or zero to positive, as the first pattern is transformed into the third. This increase has to occur because neither of the other sums change and because the unconnected first pattern becomes the connected third pattern.

Now, what has to happen when the first pattern is transformed into the fourth? Plainly, the lower sum has to increase enough to drive the overall sum positive, because the change witnessed by the lower logic boxes is the same as that witnessed before in the transformation from the first pattern to the second. But the upper sum also has to increase enough to drive the overall sum positive, because the change involved is the same as the one involved in the transformation from the first pattern to the third. Hence, the overall sum has to become positive, indicating that the pattern is not connected. Unfortunately, however, the pattern *is* connected.

This discussion started with an assumption that a perceptron can recognize connectivity, but you see that it cannot even deal with all four of the examples in figure 23.12, providing only that no individual logic box can look at the changes in both the upper part of the retina and the lower part, which is a direct consequence of the fact that the perceptron is diameter limited. Thus, the assumption that a perceptron can recognize connectivity must be wrong.

SUMMARY

- A perceptron is a special kind of one-neuron neural net. In addition to weights, a multiplier, an adder, and a stair-step threshold function, a perceptron has logic boxes between its inputs and its multipliers.
- The perceptron convergence procedure is a training procedure that is guaranteed to succeed whenever successful training is possible.
- Ordinary algebra is adequate to demonstrate the assured success of the perceptron training procedure when there are two weights. Vector algebra helps you to demonstrate the assured success of the perceptron training procedure when there are many weights.
- A straight-through perceptron can learn to identify digits easily, but there are other simple-looking tasks that perceptrons cannot do.

BACKGROUND

The discussion of the perceptron convergence theorem is based on the work of Seymour A. Papert [1961]. The best known work on perceptrons, and the source of much of our understanding of what they can and cannot do, is the book *Perceptrons*, by Marvin Minsky and Seymour A. Papert [1969]. *Perceptrons, Expanded Edition* contains a review by Minsky of contemporary work on neural nets [1988].

24

Learning by Training Approximation Nets

In this chapter, you learn about *interpolation and approximation nets*, which also can be viewed as a two-layer special case of the general notion of neural net. Interpolation and approximation nets have the virtue that you can train them either by *solving linear equations* or by *performing gradient ascent*. They also generalize easily and naturally to do tasks that you might think would require multilevel nets.

By way of illustration, you see how simple interpolation and approximation nets can learn, from experience, to predict how good a vacation will be, given the expected duration of the vacation and the average temperature of the vacation spot during the vacation.

Once you have finished this chapter, you will know how interpolation and approximation nets work, you will understand how to inform them with samples, and you will understand roughly how they might be implemented in biological systems.

INTERPOLATION AND APPROXIMATION NETS

In Chapter 22, you learned that simulated neural nets accept input values and produce output values, or, in the vocabulary of mathematics, how simulated neural nets compute a function.

You train a neural net so as to bring it into conformance with samples relating particular inputs to desired outputs. Thus the function computed by the neural net, through training, becomes more like a desired function, the one that produces the sample input–output combinations. Accordingly, a trained neural net is said to implement an **approximation function**. If a neural net can be trained to do even better, providing exactly correct outputs for all the sample inputs, then the neural net is said to implement an **interpolation function**.

Much is to be gained by looking at neural nets as implementations of approximation functions and interpolation functions. In this section, you learn, for example, that the interpolation–approximation point of view sheds light on the question of how many neurons you need in a neural net. Also, you learn about a mathematically inspired alternative to the biologically inspired stair-step and squashed S threshold functions used in many simulated neural nets.

Gaussian Functions Centered on Samples
Enable Good Interpolations

Suppose you have a black box with several inputs, $x_1, \ldots, x_n$, and one output u. Further suppose that you want to predict the future values of u, given a database of sample input–output combinations. You decide to construct a function of the input values, $y(x_1, \ldots, x_n)$, with the following properties: y's value is exactly equal to the output of the black box whenever the inputs are drawn from one of the sample input–output combinations; and y's value is close to the output of the black box for other inputs.

To learn how to use the samples to construct y, you could launch yourself into the vast literature on the mathematics of interpolation and approximation. Returning, eventually, you would know that reasonable assumptions lead to an interpolation function that is a weighted sum of other functions, f_i:

$$y(x_1, \ldots, x_n) = \sum_{i=1}^{s} w_i f_i(x_1, \ldots, x_n)$$

Although there are many possible forms for the f_i, sophisticated arguments dictate that each f_i must reach its maximum or minimum value when the input values, $x_1, \ldots, x_n$, are close to the input values recorded for the ith input–output sample. As the input values depart from the ith sample's input values, the value of f_i must change.

More precisely, suppose that you treat $x_1, \ldots, x_n$, the current input values, as the coordinates of a vector, $\mathbf{x}$. Further suppose that you treat the input values associated with the ith sample as the coordinates of another vector, $\mathbf{c}_i$. Then, the value of f_i must depend on the size of the difference between $\mathbf{x}$ and $\mathbf{c}_i$:

$$f_i(\mathbf{x}) = g_i(\|\mathbf{x} - \mathbf{c}_i\|)$$

Thus, each sample input, $\mathbf{c}_i$, is a reference point, or **center**, established by the ith input–output sample. Because the value of each f_i depends on only

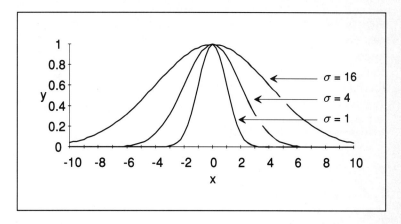

one center, the one established by the ith sample, each f_i can be said to specialize in handling the influence of the ith sample on future predictions.

Now the question is this: Exactly what function should you choose for g_i? The **Gaussian function** is a popular answer for two reasons: the Gaussian function has attractive mathematical properties; and the Gaussian function's hill-like shape is easy to control with a parameter, σ:

$$g_i\left(\|\mathbf{x} - \mathbf{c}_i\|\right) = e^{-\frac{\|\mathbf{x}-\mathbf{c}_i\|^2}{2\sigma}}.$$

Occasionally, σ is called the *width* of the Gaussian because the larger the value of σ, the more the Gaussian spreads out, as shown in figure 24.1. Because a Gaussian function has no sharp boundary, the use of the word *width* is somewhat figurative.

After incorporating hill-like Gaussian functions into the interpolation function, you have the following:

$$y(\mathbf{x}) = \sum_{i=1}^{s} w_i\, e^{-\frac{1}{2\sigma}\|\mathbf{x}-\mathbf{c}_i\|^2}.$$

This interpolation function brings you back to neural nets, because the function can be computed by a two-layer net in which the single node in the second layer computes a weighted sum of the outputs of the first layer nodes, and each of the first-layer nodes computes a Gaussian function centered on a sample input. Such nets are called *interpolation nets*. An example is shown in figure 24.2.

Intuitively, if the value of σ is such that the Gaussian hills are extremely narrow, then only one hill contributes substantially to the output value produced by each sample input. Because the height of each hill is 1, each weight, w_i, must be nearly equal to the output value of the ith input–output sample.

Usually, however, the Gaussian hills have substantial reach, so many may contribute substantially to the output value produced by a particular input vector. Fortunately, as you soon see, it is still easy to compute

Figure 24.2 An interpolation
net. Each first-layer node
responds vigorously to one
particular sample input. The
second-layer node simply adds
up the weighted outputs of the
first layer nodes.

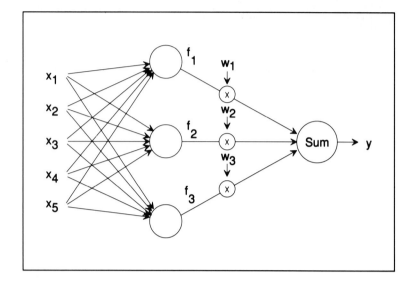

weights such that the proper output is produced for each of the i samples
provided.

In summary, an interpolation net is a special kind of neural net, a point
emphasized by the following specification:

An **interpolation net** is a representation

That is a neural net

In which

▷ There are only two layers of neurons.

▷ Each first-layer neuron computes the Gaussian of the distance between the current input vector and a sample input
vector.

▷ Each second-layer neuron adds its inputs together.

▷ The weights between the two layers are adjusted such that
each second layer neuron's output is exactly the desired
output for each sample input.

Given Sufficient Nodes, Nets Can Interpolate Perfectly

To see how interpolation nets work, suppose that you keep track of how
much you enjoy vacations as a function of their duration. From the data
shown in the following table, it appears that, of your past four vacations,
the brief one was good, the next longer one was best, the one after that
was terrible, and the final one was better again, judged on a scale ranging
from 1 to 10:

Figure 24.3 An interpolation net for predicting vacation ratings given vacation durations.

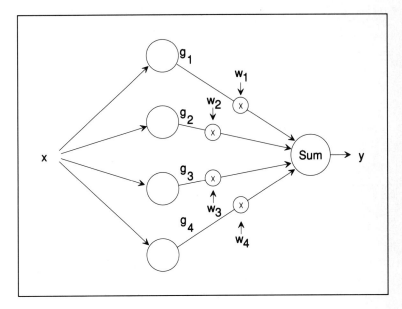

Sample	Duration (days)	Rating (1–10)
1	4	5
2	7	9
3	9	2
4	12	6

Now, suppose you decide to wire up an interpolation net to predict ratings for other vacation durations. Because there are four samples, but just one input variable—the vacation duration—your interpolation net has four nodes and one input, as shown in figure 24.3.

With a narrow-width σ, each sample has only *local* influence; with a wide-width σ, each sample has a *global* influence.

Given a value for σ, it is easy to compute values for the weights such that your interpolation net yields exactly correct results for all the samples. The reason is that the number of weights is the same as the number of sample input–output combinations, and each input–output combination provides an equation involving the unknown weights:

$$y_1 = w_1 e^{-\frac{1}{2\sigma}(x_1-x_1)^2} + w_2 e^{-\frac{1}{2\sigma}(x_1-x_2)^2} + w_3 e^{-\frac{1}{2\sigma}(x_1-x_3)^2} + w_4 e^{-\frac{1}{2\sigma}(x_1-x_4)^2},$$

$$y_2 = w_1 e^{-\frac{1}{2\sigma}(x_2-x_1)^2} + w_2 e^{-\frac{1}{2\sigma}(x_2-x_2)^2} + w_3 e^{-\frac{1}{2\sigma}(x_2-x_3)^2} + w_4 e^{-\frac{1}{2\sigma}(x_2-x_4)^2},$$

$$y_3 = w_1 e^{-\frac{1}{2\sigma}(x_3-x_1)^2} + w_2 e^{-\frac{1}{2\sigma}(x_3-x_2)^2} + w_3 e^{-\frac{1}{2\sigma}(x_3-x_3)^2} + w_4 e^{-\frac{1}{2\sigma}(x_3-x_4)^2},$$

$$y_4 = w_1 e^{-\frac{1}{2\sigma}(x_4-x_1)^2} + w_2 e^{-\frac{1}{2\sigma}(x_4-x_2)^2} + w_3 e^{-\frac{1}{2\sigma}(x_4-x_3)^2} + w_4 e^{-\frac{1}{2\sigma}(x_4-x_4)^2}.$$

Although these equations look a little complicated because of the exponential functions involved, for any given σ, you just have four linear equations in the four unknown weights, w_i, which are easy to solve. Accordingly, the training procedure is simple:

To create an interpolation net,

▷ For each given sample, create a node centered on the sample input. Then, create a equation as follows:

  ▷ Compute the distance between the sample input and each of the node centers.

  ▷ Compute the Gaussian function of each distance.

  ▷ Multiply each Gaussian function by the corresponding node's weight.

  ▷ Equate the sample output with the sum of the weighted Gaussian functions of distance.

▷ Solve the equations for the weights.

The following table gives the values you obtain by solving the equations for three instructive σ choices:

σ	w_1	w_2	w_3	w_4
1	4.90	8.84	0.73	5.99
4	0.87	13.93	−9.20	8.37
16	−76.50	236.49	−237.77	87.55

Given a σ and a corresponding set of weights, you can compute values for the interpolation function and the corresponding net not only for the sample inputs, but for any input. The functions illustrated in figure 24.4 are for the three σ values and the corresponding weights given in the table. Note that the four interpolation functions all intersect when the vacation duration is 4, 7, 9, and 12 days, because each interpolation function has to yield the recorded rating for each of the sample vacation durations.

  With $\sigma = 1$, each Gaussian-computing node has little reach. The weights are positive and are nearly equal to the sample rating values, which is what you would expect.

  With $\sigma = 4$, each Gaussian-computing node has more reach and contributes to the overall rating score for adjacent sample duration values. One of the four weights, w_3, has to be negative to bring the interpolation function down to the rating of 2 required for 9-day vacations.

  Finally, with $\sigma = 16$, each Gaussian-computing node has enormous reach, relative to the separation between sample points. Large weight values, both positive and negative, are required to produce an interpolation function that is equal to the sample ratings at the sample duration values.

Figure 24.4 Gaussian vacation-rating interpolation functions for three σ values. Small σ values produce bumpy interpolation functions reflecting little sample influence outside of local neighborhoods. Larger σ values extend the influence of each sample, but extremely large σ values can make that influence too global. An intermediate σ value produces the heavy line.

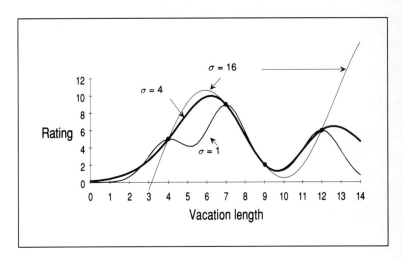

Given Relatively Few Nodes, Approximation Nets Can Yield Approximate Results for All Sample Inputs

If you have many samples, then you have to worry about the number of nodes becoming unreasonably high. The natural approach is to try to approximate the unknown function with a reasonably small number of nodes that are somehow representative, perhaps by picking a few samples at random to serve as node centers.

If you have fewer nodes than samples, however, no choice of weights can ensure that your net yields the correct output for all sample inputs. You can, however, construct nets with fewer nodes than samples, call them **approximation nets** rather than interpolation nets, and look for weight values that yield reasonable approximations.

Too Many Samples Leads to Weight Training

How do you find weights that yield reasonable approximations for all the sample inputs? One way is to use gradient ascent to look for a maximum value for a measure of approximation-net performance. Because the gradient-ascent approach was explained in detail in Chapter 22, the development here only sketches what you need to do.

First, you can measure performance by summing the squared errors for all the sample inputs. Suppose that the actual value of y for a particular sample is y_s, and the desired value is d_s. Then, your goal is to maximize P, a function whose value reaches 0 when there is no error:

$$P = -\sum_s (y_s - d_s)^2.$$

Next, you want to find the partial derivatives of P with respect to each weight, w_i, so that weight changes can be in proportion to those partial derivatives. By invoking the chain rule, as described in Chapter 22, and working through the algebra, you eventually arrive at the following formula for computing weight changes, Δw_i, which includes a rate constant, r, which must be big enough to encourage quick convergence to a satisfactory solution, but small enough to avoid overshoot or instability:

$$\Delta w_i = r \sum_s (d_s - y_s) e^{-\frac{1}{2\sigma} \|x_s - c_i\|^2}.$$

With this formula in hand, you can build an approximation net as follows:

To create an approximation net,

▷ For a few samples, create an interpolation net using the interpolation-net procedure.

▷ Pick a rate constant, r.

▷ Until performance is satisfactory,

  ▷ For all sample inputs,

    ▷ Compute the resulting outputs.

    ▷ Compute Δw_i for each weight.

  ▷ Add up the weight changes for all the sample inputs, and change the weights.

Suppose, for illustration, that you cannot contemplate more than two nodes in your vacation-rating net, forcing you to accept prediction by an approximation net, rather than by an interpolation net. Further suppose that you establish initial values for your two-node net using the samples in the original table for vacations of duration 7 and 12 days, omitting the vacations of duration 4 and 9 days.

Next, you perform gradient ascent, adjusting the weights, using all four samples. The results, after the weights have been adjusted 100 times with a rate constant of 0.1, are summarized in the following table and in figure 24.5. Not surprisingly, w_1 and w_2 drop a bit to reduce the error for 9-day vacations, but they do so at the expense of introducing some error for 7-day and 12-day vacations.

	w_1	w_2	c_1	c_2
Initial values	8.75	5.61	7.00	12.00
Final values	7.33	4.47	7.00	12.00

Once you understand the idea of adjusting the weights to improve performance on sample data, you can take another step forward and adjust the center points as well. All you need to do is to find the partial derivatives of P with respect to the center coordinates. Then, you adjust both the center coordinates and the weights simultaneously.

Figure 24.5 When there are fewer nodes than samples, the approximation function cannot yield the sample outputs for all the sample inputs. Nevertheless, gradient ascent may produce a set of weights that does a reasonable job.

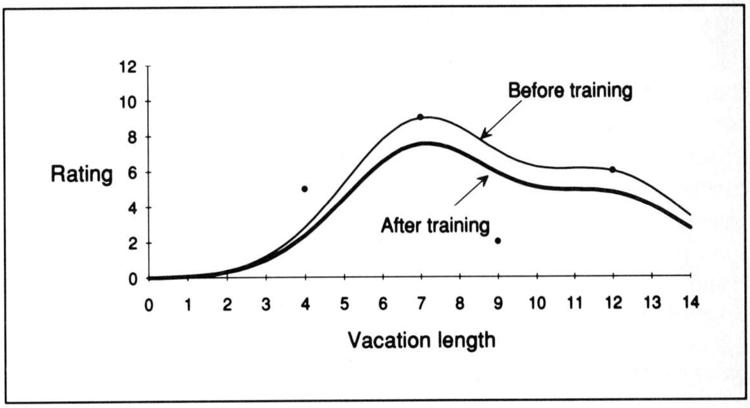

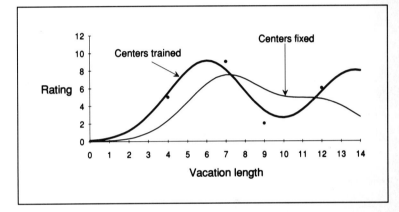

Figure 24.6 When there are fewer nodes than samples, the approximation function cannot yield the sample outputs for all the sample inputs. Adjustments of both weights and centers provides a better approximation than adjustments to either one alone.

If you were to go through the mathematics, you would find that the adjustment formula for the jth component of the ith center is as follows:

$$\Delta c_{ij} = r \sum_s w_i (d_s - y_s) e^{-\frac{1}{2\sigma} \|x_s - c_i\|^2} \frac{1}{\sigma} (x_{sj} - c_{ij}).$$

The results, after both the weights and centers have been adjusted 100 times with a rate constant of 0.1, are summarized in the following table and in figure 24.6. Note that the centers have moved apart so as to accommodate the low value of the rating for the sample duration that lies between them.

	w_1	w_2	c_1	c_2
Initial values	8.75	5.61	7.00	12.00
Final values	9.13	8.06	6.00	13.72

Overlooked Dimensions May Explain Strange Data Better than Elaborate Approximation

So far, the curious rating dip at 9-day vacations has been accommodated, rather than explained. This observation illustrates the folly of concentrat-

Figure 24.7 Predicted vacation ratings versus vacation durations for 73° average temperatures. Wild variation characterizes the approximation function derived ignoring temperature. Of the other two functions, the function derived using Celsius temperature measurement shows more influence from the four samples.

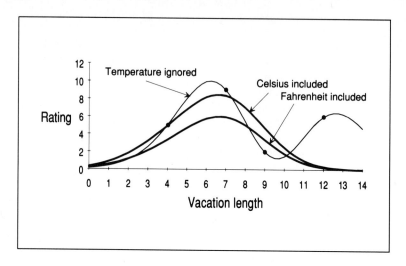

ing on the training scheme to the exclusion of thinking about the problem to be solved. Suppose that your rating really depends on another factor—average temperature, for example. Then, your raw data might look like this:

Sample	Duration	Temperature	Rating
1	4	70	5
2	7	75	9
3	9	45	2
4	12	90	6

There are still four samples, but now there are two inputs for each. Accordingly, you have a two-dimensional problem; solving it yields a net with two inputs (duration and temperature) and one output (rating). Figure 24.7 shows the rating produced by the net as a function of duration for one particular temperature—73°F. Note that the previous dip at 9 days has vanished.

You still must be careful, however, because you are dealing with days on one axis and degrees Fahrenheit on another. If you choose to measure temperature in Celsius instead, you have the following table and the result shown by the Celsius line in figure 24.7:

Sample	Duration	Temperature	Rating
1	4	21	5
2	7	24	9
3	9	7	2
4	12	32	6

Note that the Celsius approximation function is higher than the Fahrenheit approximation function, and all that you have done is to change units. This discrepancy is not really surprising, because the entire idea depends on measuring distances and the numbers involved change when you change units.

Accordingly, you have to be sure that the reach of your Gaussian functions is reasonable in all dimensions. One way to be sure that the reach is correct in all dimensions is to multiply the numbers in each dimension by a reach-adjusting, dimension-dependent scale factor. Then, the scale factor can be trained too.

The Interpolation-Approximation Point of View Helps You to Answer Difficult Design Questions

The interpolation–approximation point of view sheds light on the question of how many neurons you need in a neural net. Evidently, for interpolation, you need one neuron for each of the available samples, plus one that sums the outputs of those sample specialists. For approximation, you can get by with fewer neurons than samples.

Further light is shed on the question of what the neurons should compute. Neither the sample specialists nor the summing neuron should compute the stair-step or squashed S threshold functions described in Chapter 22.

BIOLOGICAL IMPLEMENTATION

Whenever you work with computations performed by simulated neural nets, it is natural to wonder whether there is a plausible biological implementation on which nature may have stumbled during evolution. In this section, you learn about one such implementation.

Numbers Can Be Represented by Position

Because neurons are all-or-none devices, the output of a single neuron cannot represent a number unless the number happens to be 0 or 1. You can use a one-dimensional array of neurons to represent a number, however; you simply arrange for only one neuron in the array to be on, and you take the position of that to be the number you want.

Consider the array of neurons in figure 24.8(a), for example. Among the 16 neurons, the seventh is on, thus representing the number 7.

Neurons Can Compute Gaussian Functions

Let a **Gaussian neuron** be a neuron that just computes a weighted sum of its inputs with weights that approximate a Gaussian function. Once a number is represented by a position in a one-dimensional array of neurons, then a Gaussian neuron can compute the approximate Gaussian of the

Figure 24.8 In (a), you see that position in a one-dimensional array can represent a number. The seventh neuron is the only one on; hence, the number is 7. In (b), you see that neurons can compute the approximate Gaussian of the distance from a center. The two neurons in the second layer respond to the seventh neuron; the one centered on the seventh neuron responds more vigorously.

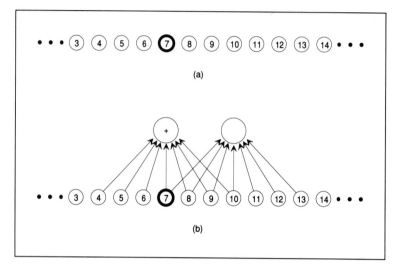

distance of that number relative to any fixed center. The way that this computation works is shown in figure 24.8(b), where a few weights enable the two neurons to be stimulated in proportion to the number represented in the first layer. Plainly, if the seventh neuron is on, a Gaussian neuron directly above it will respond most, but the seventh neuron will have a weighted influence even on other, offset Gaussian neurons. The degree of influence, determined by appropriate weights, falls off with distance in proportion to the Gaussian of that distance.

Gaussian Functions Can Be Computed as Products of Gaussian Functions

At this point, you have a mechanism whereby neurons can compute the Gaussian of a number relative to fixed centers in one dimension. Conveniently, you can use this mechanism in any number of dimensions, even though real neurons have to be wired up in our three-dimensional world. To see why, you need to appreciate an important mathematical property of Gaussian functions of distance. The Gaussian function is a **separable function** because the Gaussian function of distance in n dimensions can be expressed as the product of n Gaussian functions in one dimension:

$$e^{-\frac{1}{2\sigma}\left((x_1-c_1)^2\cdots(x_n-c_n)^2\right)} = e^{-\frac{1}{2\sigma}(x_1-c_1)^2} \times \ldots \times e^{-\frac{1}{2\sigma}(x_n-c_n)^2}.$$

From this property, it is plain that all you need to compute a Gaussian function of distance from a particular n-dimensional center is a multiplier neuron plus the machinery you already have to compute a Gaussian function of distance from a particular one-dimensional center. Figure 24.9 illustrates how this would work for two dimensions.

Thus, all you need to implement an approximation net is a Gaussian neuron and a multiplier neuron. Intriguingly, dendritic trees are well known

Figure 24.9 With the addition of a multiplier neuron, two nets that compute Gaussian functions of one-dimensional distances from centers can compute Gaussian functions of multi-dimensional distances.

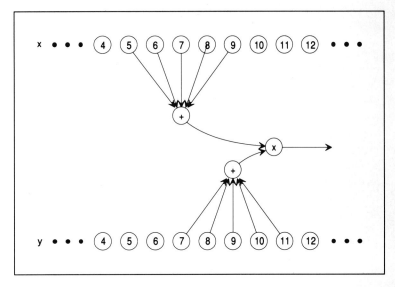

to do Gaussian computations in, for example, the eye's retina, where there are neurons that produce a center-weighted response to small **receptive fields**. There is also some evidence that dendritic trees can perform multiplications. It remains to be seen, however, whether neurons actually perform Gaussian and multiplication functions in contexts well-modeled by approximation nets. It also remains to be seen if there is a plausible neural mechanism for training such nets.

SUMMARY

- Neural nets can be viewed as devices that perform approximations and interpolations.
- An interpolation net is a neural net with one hidden layer and one output layer. Each node in the hidden layer is specialized to a particular sample input, and it computes a Gaussian function of the distance between that sample and the current input. The nodes in the output layer compute weighted sums.
- Interpolation nets can interpolate perfectly, given that one hidden node can be allocated per available sample.
- An approximation net is like an interpolation net, but an approximation net has fewer hidden nodes than there are available samples.
- Although limited to relatively few nodes, approximation nets can yield good approximations for all sample inputs, given appropriate weight training. Training results depend on initial weight and center choices.
- Overlooked dimensions may explain strange data better than does elaborate approximation.
- Certain real neural nets may be performing like approximation nets.

BACKGROUND

This chapter is based largely on the seminal ideas of Tomaso Poggio, worked out to a comprehensive theory by Poggio and Frederico Girosi [1990].

25

Learning by Simulating Evolution

In this chapter, you learn how search can be done using procedures that are inspired by natural evolution. These procedures, commonly called *genetic algorithms*, rest on ideas that are analogous, in some ways, to *individuals*, *mating*, *chromosome crossover*, *gene mutation*, *fitness*, and *natural selection*.

You learn that natural selection often performs terribly when simple selection mechanisms are used. To do better, you need to devise a selection mechanism that takes note of *diversity among individuals*, as well as of individual performance. Such a diversity-noting selection measure can change the way that you think about local maxima. Instead of trying to escape from them, you populate them with sacrificial individuals who themselves get trapped, but who keep other evolving individuals at a distance.

By way of illustration, you see how to construct a genetic algorithm to optimize the quantities of flour and sugar used in the production of cookies. This optimization problem is like many others for which overall performance has a complicated dependence on various controllable factors that include temperatures, pressures, flow rates, and the like.

First, you review the most conspicuous mechanisms involved in evolution. Then, you see how simple procedures may exhibit similar properties.

Once you have finished this chapter, you will know how genetic learning procedures work, when they can be effective, and why they often break down.

SURVIVAL OF THE FITTEST

Every living thing consists of one or more cells, but beyond that, there are exceptions to just about every rule in biology. Nevertheless, certain characteristics of heredity and evolution seem to be universal or nearly so. In this section, you learn about those characteristics.

Chromosomes Determine Hereditary Traits

In higher plants and animals, each cell contains a single nucleus, which, in turn, contains **chromosomes**, often many of them. Late in the nineteenth century, chromosomes were identified as the custodians of the trait-determining factors, traditionally called **genes**, that are passed on when cells divide and when offspring are parented. Genes are strung along chromosomes like cars on a railroad train.

The chromosomes are usually paired, with each parent contributing one chromosome to each pair. The pairs are said to be **homologous**, meaning that, for each gene in one paired chromosome, there is a gene in the other corresponding chromosome that has the same purpose. Cells that contain paired, homologous chromosomes are said to be **diploid** cells.

In preparation for mating, homologous chromosomes are brought together, duplicated, and formed into bundles that look a bit like four ropes twisted together. Somehow, the twisting seems to produce stresses that lead to a great deal of cleavage and reconnection, thereby scrambling the genes on the chromosomes involved. This scrambling is called **crossover**.

Once duplication and crossover occur, there are two complete sets of scrambled chromosome pairs. The sets are herded to opposite ends of the nucleus, whereupon the nucleus divides, initiating the division of the entire cell. The two resulting cells then have the normal number of chromosomes, but they are not ordinary because the chromosomes have undergone crossover.

Next, the cells divide again; unlike in normal cell division, however, there is no chromosome duplication. Instead, one chromosome from each pair ends up in each of the two new cells. These new cells, either eggs or sperm, are said to be **haploid** cells because, in contrast to diploid cells, they exhibit no chromosome pairing.

Mating produces a fertilized, diploid egg, initiating the development of a new individual. Subsequent cell division in the course of development is much simpler. Chromosomes are copied, herded, and assigned to two distinct cells, but there is no crossover.

Occasionally, the chromosome-copying process goes astray, producing an altered gene that is slightly different from the corresponding gene in the contributing parent. This never-before-seen gene is called a **mutation**.

If the purpose of the unmutated gene is to dictate the shape of, say, a crucial enzyme, the mutated gene may dictate a better enzyme; more often, the mutated gene produces either no enzyme or one with greatly diminished activity.

Fortunately, a bad mutation in one chromosome of a diploid pair need not be fatal, because the other, homologous chromosome is generally normal. Inbreeding can lead to tragedy, however, because the same, defective gene may end up on both of the two homologous chromosomes.

In lower plants and animals, chromosomes are paired only briefly, during reproduction. Most often, reproduction involves just one parent, whose chromosomes are copied in preparation for cell division, with the original set of chromosomes going into one of the two new cells, and the copied set going into the other. Occasionally, however, reproduction involves two parents, each of which contributes a set of chromosomes to the other, whereupon homologous chromosomes are paired, crossed, and separated in preparation for cell division.

The Fittest Survive

In his magnum opus, *The Origin of Species*, published in 1859, Charles Darwin championed the principle of **evolution through natural selection**, which subsequently, after much heated argument, became generally accepted among scientists:

- Each individual tends to pass on its traits to its offspring.
- Nevertheless, nature produces individuals with differing traits.
- The fittest individuals—those with the most favorable traits—tend to have more offspring than do those with unfavorable traits, thus driving the population as a whole toward favorable traits.
- Over long periods, variation can accumulate, producing entirely new species whose traits make them especially suited to particular ecological niches.

Of course, every horse breeder knows that traits are passed on and that traits vary; and every horse breeder arranges for faster horses to breed more. Darwin's contribution was to exhibit evidence that the same principles account for the great variation seen in living things.

From a molecular point of view, natural selection is enabled by the variation that follows from crossover and mutation. Crossover assembles existing genes into new combinations. Mutation produces new genes, hitherto unseen.

GENETIC ALGORITHMS

In this section, you learn how it is possible to simulate certain characteristics of heredity and evolution.

Figure 25.1 Cookie quality is dependent on the number of kilograms of flour and sugar per batch. Evidently, the best-quality cookies are produced when there are five kilograms of each, for then the judged quality of the cookies is maximized.

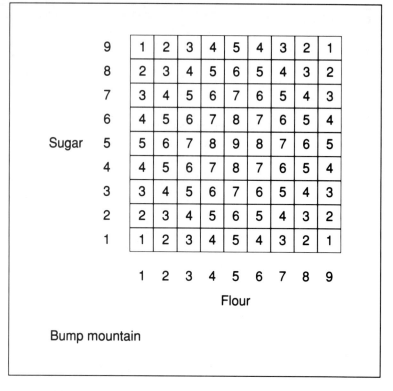

Bump mountain

Genetic Algorithms Involve Myriad Analogs

To understand natural selection from a computational point of view, consider the problem faced by Kookie, a cookie maker, who is trying to optimize the amount of sugar and flour in his cookies.

Essentially, Kookie is trying to find the optimal combination in the two-dimensional space illustrated in figure 25.1. One axis is the number of kilograms of flour per batch, and the other is the number of kilograms of sugar; the quality of the resulting cookies, somehow determined, is given as a function of the other two. In this example, the quality function resembles a smooth bump.

In this illustration, Kookie could, of course, just try every combination, noting that there are only 81, but as the number of options is increased, or as the number of dimensions is increased, brute-force testing eventually becomes impracticable.

Accordingly, assume Kookie wants to find a good combination without trying every combination. Kookie could try one of the search procedures described in Chapter 4. Assume, however, that Kookie is studying artificial intelligence, and he has just learned that search can be performed using **genetic algorithms**. Inspired by the miracle of evolution, Kookie decides to try a genetic algorithm on his cookie problem.

Figure 25.2 A chromosome in the cookie world consists of two numbers, which act as gene analogs. The first determines how much flour to use; the second determines how much sugar to use.

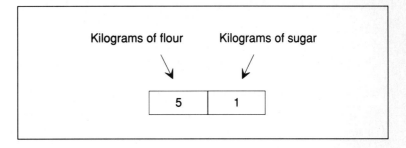

Kilograms of flour   Kilograms of sugar

| 5 | 1 |

To begin, Kookie has to develop analogs to individuals, chromosomes, mutation, crossover, fitness, and natural selection. Analogs for individuals, chromosomes, mutation, and crossover are straightforward, and are easy for Kookie to establish. Kookie first decides that each batch of cookies is an "individual." Then he decides, as illustrated in figure 25.2, that a "chromosome" consists of two "genes," each of which is a number from 1 to 9. The first of these genes prescribes the amount of flour to use, and the second prescribes the amount of sugar. Kookie appears, therefore, to be adhering to the following specification:

A **chromosome** is a representation

In which

▷ There is a list of elements called genes.

▷ The chromosome determines the overall fitness manifested by some mechanism that uses the chromosome's genes as a sort of blueprint.

With constructors that

▷ Create a chromosome, given a list of elements—this constructor might be called the genesis constructor

▷ Create a chromosome by crossing a pair of existing chromosomes

With writers that

▷ Mutate an existing chromosome by changing one of the genes

With readers that

▷ Produce a specified gene, given a chromosome

Next, Kookie decides that each individual will have only one copy of one chromosome, thus following the pattern of lower plants and animals whose chromosomes have no homologous partners except during mating. ·

To mimic chromosome mutation, Kookie selects one of the chromosome's two genes randomly, and alters it randomly by adding or subtracting

1, taking care to stay within the 1-to-9 range. Figure 25.3 illustrates how two chromosomes might evolve through a series of four extremely lucky mutations, producing increasingly high-quality individuals.

Strictly speaking, individuals, which correspond to cookie batches, are the entities that are associated with quality. Chromosomes, which correspond to recipes for the flour and sugar contents of cookies, determine quality indirectly by specifying the characteristics of the individuals. Nevertheless, it is not necessary to be obsessive about the distinction, because the characteristics of individuals are so tightly determined by the nature of the chromosomes. Accordingly, in the rest of this chapter, chromosomes are said to have certain **quality scores**, rather than to produce individuals that have those quality scores. Similarly, chromosomes are said to constitute **populations**, even though it is really the chromosome-determined individuals that constitute populations.

To mimic the crossover involved in mating, Kookie cuts two chromosomes in the middle and rejoins them as illustrated in figure 25.4. Then, Kookie retains both in the hope that at least one will be a fortunate combination. For cookies, the 5-4 chromosome is the fortunate combination, for a 5-4 chromosome is just one mutation step away from the 5-5 combination which yields optimum, quality 9 cookies. On the other hand, the 2-1 chromosome is the unfortunate combination, for a 2-1 chromosome yields horrible, quality 2 cookies.

Of course, with just two genes, there is just one place to cut and rejoin; in general, however, there are many places, and many possible procedures for determining how many places to crossover and where exactly to crossover.

The Standard Method Equates Fitness with Relative Quality

Once Kookie has decided how to mimic mutation and crossover, he must decide on analogs to "fitness" and "natural selection." These choices are far less straightforward, however, for there are many alternative approaches.

In general, the fitness of a chromosome is the probability that the chromosome survives to the next generation. Accordingly, you need a formula that relates the fitness of the ith chromosome, f_i, a probability ranging from 0 to 1, to the quality of the corresponding cookies, q_i, a number ranging from 1 to 9. The following formula, in which the sum is over all candidates, is one possibility:

$$f_i = \frac{q_i}{\sum_j q_j}.$$

Henceforth, the use of this formula is referred to as the **standard method** for fitness computation.

Suppose, for example, that a population consists of four chromosomes, collectively exhibiting 1-4, 3-1, 1-2, and 1-1 chromosomes. By inspecting

Figure 25.3 Two chromosomes undergoing a series of mutations, each of which changes one gene by adding or subtracting 1. Both original chromosomes are 1-1 chromosomes, which produce quality 1 cookies. One final chromosome is a 5-1 chromosome and the other is a 2-4 chromosome, both of which yield quality 5 cookies.

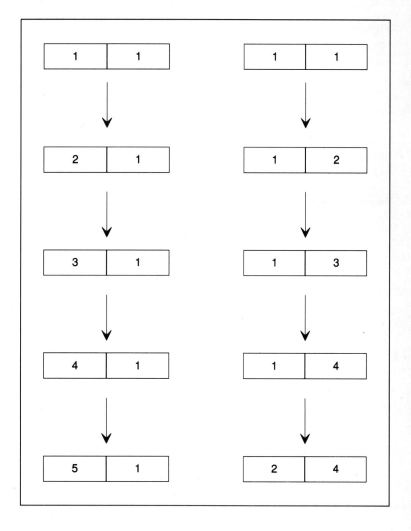

figure 25.1, you can see that their qualities and corresponding fitnesses are as shown in the following table:

Chromosomes	Quality	Standard fitness
1 4	4	0.40
3 1	3	0.30
1 2	2	0.20
1 1	1	0.10

With a fitness analog established, one way that Kookie can mimic natural selection is as follows:

Figure 25.4 Two chromo-somes undergoing crossover, each of which is cut in the mid-dle and reattached to the other chromosome. One of the two original chromosomes is a 5-1 chromosome, and the other is a 2-4 chromosome. One of the two new chromosomes is a 5-4 chromosome, which yields quality 8 cookies.

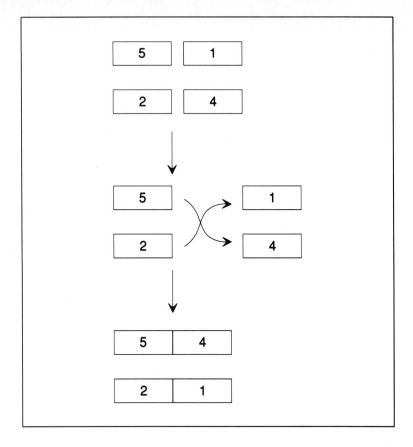

To mimic natural selection in general,

▷ Create an initial "population" of one chromosome.

▷ Mutate one or more genes in one or more of the current chromosomes, producing one new offspring for each chromosome mutated.

▷ Mate one or more pairs of chromosomes.

▷ Add the mutated and offspring chromosomes to the current population.

▷ Create a new generation by keeping the best of the current population's chromosomes, along with other chromosomes selected randomly from the current population. Bias the random selection according to assessed fitness.

Genetic Algorithms Generally Involve Many Choices

Even after Kookie decides to deploy a genetic algorithm using the standard method for computing fitness, many decisions remain.

■ How many chromosomes are to be in the population? If the number is too low, all chromosomes will soon have identical traits and crossover will do nothing; if the number is too high, computation time will be unnecessarily excessive.

■ What is the mutation rate? If the rate is too low, new traits will appear too slowly in the population; if the rate is too high, each generation will be unrelated to the previous generation.

■ Is mating allowed? If so, how are mating pairs selected, and how are crossover points determined?

■ Can any chromosome appear more than once in a population?

Generally speaking, it is helpful to know the shape of the space to be searched, which is a variant of the principle that it is always nice to know the answer before you work the problem.

It Is Easy to Climb Bump Mountain Without Crossover

Recall that the problem is to find an optimum mix of ingredients given the relation between cookie quality and ingredients shown in figure 25.1.

To keep method comparison simple, suppose that Kookie decides to specialize the general method for mimicking natural selection as follows:

■ Kookie starts with a single chromosome located at 1-1.

■ No chromosome is permitted to appear more than once in each generation.

■ A maximum of four chromosomes survive from one generation to the next.

■ Each survivor is a candidate for survival to the next generation, along with any new chromosomes produced.

■ One gene is selected at random in each of the survivors, and is mutated at random. If the mutant is different from any candidate accumulated so far, that mutant is added to the candidates.

■ There is no crossover.

■ The chromosome with the highest score survives to the next generation.

■ The remaining survivors from one generation to the next are selected at random from the remaining candidates, according to the standard method for fitness computation.

Now recall that Kookie not only wants good cookies, but also wants to learn more about how genetic algorithms work. Accordingly, he might propose to improve his cookies 1000 times, starting from a single 1-1 chromosome each time.

If Kookie were to go to all that trouble, he would find the best combination of ingredients, on average, at generation 16. Among 1000 simulation experiments performed by Kookie, the luckiest produced the best combination eight generations after starting at generation 0 with a one 1-1 chromosome, which produces quality 1 cookies:

Generation 0:

Chromosome	Quality
1 1	1

A favorable mutation produced a 1-2 chromosome, which was added to the population, producing two members:

Generation 1:

Chromosome	Quality
1 2	2
1 1	1

The 1-2 chromosome mutated to 1-3, which was added to the population. The 1-1 chromosome mutated to 1-2, which was already in the population. Accordingly, the next generation had just one new member:

Generation 2:

Chromosome	Quality
1 3	3
1 2	2
1 1	1

Now 1-3 mutated to 1-4; 1-2 mutated to 2-2; and 1-1 mutated to 2-1. For the first time, the population exceeded the four-chromosome population limit. Hence, the best plus three more chromosomes had to be selected from the following six:

Chromosome	Quality
1 4	4
2 2	3
1 3	3
2 1	2
1 2	2
1 1	1

The four that happened to be selected, using the standard fitness method, were as follows:

Generation 3:

Chromosome	Quality
1 4	4
1 3	3
1 2	2
2 1	2

Now mutation produced three new chromosomes:

Chromosome	Quality
2 4	5
2 3	4
3 1	3

From the total of seven, four were selected for the next generation:

Generation 4:

Chromosome	Quality
2 4	5
1 4	4
1 3	3
2 1	2

Next, all chromosomes mutated, and the new chromosomes happened to be selected for the next generation:

Generation 5:

Chromosome	Quality
2 5	6
1 5	5
2 3	4
2 2	3

Once again, all chromosomes mutated, but this time one of the existing chromosomes—the 1-5 chromosome—survived to the next generation:

Generation 6:

Chromosome	Quality
3 5	7
1 5	5
3 2	4
1 4	4

This time, 3-5 mutates to 4-5, and 3-2 mutated to 3-1. The other two—1-5 and 1-4—happened to mutate into each other. Accordingly, four chromosomes had to be selected from the following six:

Chromosome	Quality
4 5	8
3 5	7
1 5	5
3 2	4
1 4	4
3 1	3

These were selected:

Generation 7:

Chromosome	Quality
4 5	8
1 5	5
1 4	4
3 1	3

Now 4-5 mutated into 5-5, the optimum, terminating the experiment with the optimum chromosome included in the population:

Generation 8:

Chromosome	Quality
5 5	9
4 5	8
2 5	6
2 1	2

Evidently, for straightforward bumplike terrain, crossover is not at all necessary.

Crossover Enables Genetic Algorithms to Search High-Dimensional Spaces Efficiently

Now suppose Kookie wants to see whether crossover does any good. To decide which chromosomes to cross, Kookie proceeds as follows:

- Kookie considers only the chromosomes that survived from the previous generation.
- For each such chromosome, Kookie selects a mate from among the other survivors. Mate selection is done at random, in keeping with the standard method for computing fitness.
- Each mating pair is crossed in the middle, producing two crossed, offspring chromosomes. If an offspring chromosome is different from any candidate accumulated so far, that offspring chromosome is added to the candidates.

Using this crossover method, Kookie finds the best combination of ingredients on bump mountain, on average, at generation 14, two generations sooner than without crossover.

The reason for this speedup is that crossover can unite an individual that is doing well in the flour dimension with another individual that is doing well in the sugar dimension. If crossover carries a good flour gene and a good sugar gene into a new individual, the new individual has two good genes.

For this crossover improvement to work, of course, the search space must be such that you can search the global maximum by searching for the maximum in each dimension independently. Essentially, crossover reduces the dimensionality of the search space.

Figure 25.5 In this example, the function relating cookie quality to cookie ingredients exhibits a moat. Crossover helps you to jump over.

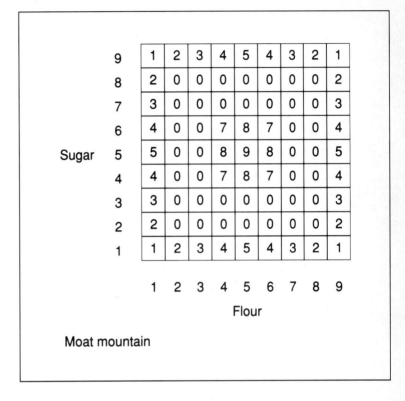

Crossover Enables Genetic Algorithms to Traverse Obstructing Moats

Suspending disbelief, suppose the relation between cookie quality and ingredients is given by the moatlike function in figure 25.5. Under these circumstances, it is not possible for a series of random mutations to lead a population from outside the moat to inside given just one mutation per generation. The reason is that the necessary intermediate chromosomes—the ones producing cookies in the moat—have 0 quality, and hence 0 fitness, and hence 0 chance of surviving to the next generation.

On the other hand, given two well-situated parents, with 1-5 and 5-1 chromosomes, a single mating can create a trans-moat offspring. No zero-fitness intermediates ever need to survive. Evidently, for terrain with moats, crossover can be more than just helpful.

Unfortunately, Kookie still does extremely poorly on moat mountain, even after adding a crossover to each generation, because the population as a whole tends to crawl along the flour axis or up the sugar axis, with all four chromosomes bunching up with 5-1 chromosomes or 1-5 chromosomes. Mutations into the moat die immediately. Mutations that take a chromosome toward 1-1 and beyond tend to die before they get to a favorable position for crossover.

When Kookie tried 1000 times to find the optimum starting with a 1-1 chromosome, he found the best combination, on average, only after 155 generations.

The Rank Method Links Fitness to Quality Rank

The standard method for determining fitness provides you with no way to influence selection. One alternative is to use the **rank method**, which not only offers a way of controlling the bias toward the best chromosome, but also eliminates implicit biases, introduced by unfortunate choices of the measurement scale, that might otherwise do harm.

Basically, the rank method ignores quality measurements except insofar as those measurements serve to rank the candidates from the highest quality to the lowest quality. Then, the fitness of the highest-quality candidate among the ranked candidates is some fixed constant, p. If the best candidate, the one ranked number 1, is not selected, then the next best candidate, the one ranked number 2, is selected with fitness p. This selection process continues until a candidate is selected or there is only one left, in which case that last-ranked candidate is selected, as indicated in the following procedure:

To select a candidate by the rank method,

▷ Sort the n individuals by quality.

▷ Let the probability of selecting the ith candidate, given that the first $i - 1$ candidates have not been selected, be p, except for the final candidate, which is selected if no previous candidate has been selected.

▷ Select a candidate using the computed probabilities.

Suppose, for example, that $p = 0.667$. Next, assume you are interested in the same chromosomes—1-4, 3-1, 1-2, and 1-1—used before to illustrate the standard method, but this time in the context of moat mountain. Further assume that those four chromosomes are augmented by 7-5, which produces quality 0 cookies on moat mountain. The following table and figure 25.6 show the chromosomes' rank fitnesses, along with their standard fitnesses for comparison.

Chromosome	Quality	Rank	Standard fitness	Rank fitness
1 4	4	1	0.40	0.667
1 3	3	2	0.30	0.222
1 2	2	3	0.20	0.074
5 2	1	4	0.10	0.025
7 5	0	5	0.0	0.012

Figure 25.6 Fitnesses for five chromosomes, as measured by both the standard method and the rank method, using quality scores as determined by moat mountain. In contrast to the standard method, the rank method shows nonzero fitness for all chromosomes, even for the one that produces quality 0 cookies.

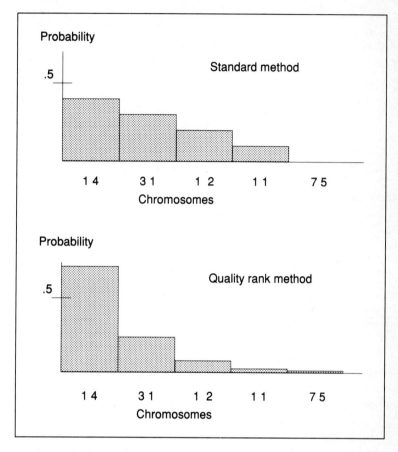

When Kookie tried 1000 times to find the optimum, using the rank method, starting with a 1-1 chromosome, he found the best combination, on average, after 75 generations. Thus, the rank method provides a considerable improvement, on the moat-mountain problem, over the standard method, which takes, on average, 155 generations.

Unfortunately, 75 generations is still a lot through which to work. All four chromosomes still tend to bunch up around either the 5-1 chromosome or the 1-5 chromosomes. Now, however, it is possible to tunnel through the 0-quality moat, because the lowest fitness of any chromosome is determined indirectly, by quality rank, rather than directly, by quality score. Accordingly, no chromosome can have a fitness of 0, whereas with the standard method, chromosomes in the moat have a fitness of exactly 0.

SURVIVAL OF THE MOST DIVERSE

Fitness, as measured so far, ignores **diversity**, which you can think of as the degree to which chromosomes exhibit different genes. Accordingly, chromosomes tend to get wiped out if they score just a bit lower than does a chromosome that is close to the best current chromosome. Even in large populations, the result is uniformity.

On a larger scale, however, unfit-looking individuals and species in nature survive quite well in ecological niches that lie outside the view of other, relatively fit-looking individuals and species:

The **diversity principle**:

▷ It can be as good to be different as it is to be fit.

In this section, you learn that being different can be incorporated into an overall measurement of fitness, and you learn that this observation creates a different perspective on what to do with local maxima.

The Rank-Space Method Links Fitness to Both Quality Rank and Diversity Rank

When you are selecting chromosomes for a new generation, one way to measure the diversity that would be contributed by a candidate chromosome is to calculate the sum of the inverse squared distances between that chromosome and the other, already selected chromosomes. Then, the **diversity rank** of a chromosome is determined by that inverse squared distance sum:

$$\sum_i \frac{1}{d_i^2}.$$

Consider again the set of six candidates that include 5-1, 1-4, 3-1, 1-2, 1-1, and 7-5. The highest-scoring candidate is 5-1. Ranking the other five by quality and inverse squared distances to 5-1 yields the following table:

Chromosome	Score	$\frac{1}{d^2}$	Diversity rank	Quality rank
1 4	4	0.040	1	1
3 1	3	0.250	5	2
1 2	2	0.059	3	3
1 1	1	0.062	4	4
7 5	0	0.050	2	5

One simple way to combine rank by quality and rank by diversity into a combined rank is to rank each chromosome according to the sum of its quality rank and its diversity rank using one or the other of the two rankings to break ties, as indicated in the following procedure:

Figure 25.7 Rank space
enables two chromosomes to
be compared in both quality
and diversity.

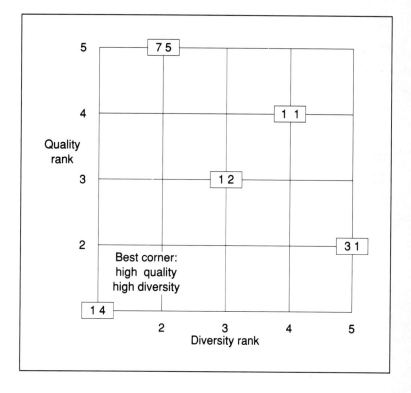

To select a candidate by the rank-space method,

▷ Sort the n individuals by quality.

▷ Sort the n individuals by the sum of their inverse squared
distances to already selected candidates.

▷ Use the rank method, but sort on the sum of the quality
rank and the diversity rank, rather than on quality rank.

Figure 25.7 illustrates this procedure. With diversity rank given by one
axis and quality rank by another, it is natural to call the diagram a **rank
space**, and to refer to the method as the **rank-space method**. Clearly,
it is best to be in the lower-left corner of rank space, where a chromosome
will be if it ranks well in terms of both quality and diversity.

Next, with a combined rank that combines the influence of quality and
diversity, selection can be done as before, setting the fitness of the first
candidate to p. Thus, the rank sum, combined rank, and fitnesses for the
five chromosomes is given by the following table. Note that there is a rank-
sum tie between 3-1 and 7-5. To break the tie, you judge the chromosome
with the better diversity rank to have a better combined rank.

Figure 25.8 Fitnesses for five chromosomes, as measured by the quality-rank method and the rank-space method, using the qualities provided by moat mountain. In contrast to both the standard method and the rank method, the rank-space method takes diversity into account.

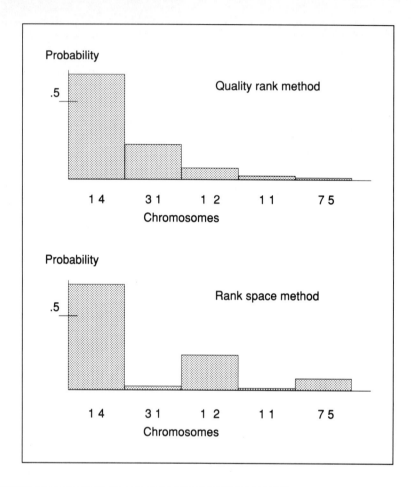

Chromosome	Rank sum	Combined rank	Fitness
1 4	2	1	0.667
3 1	7	4	0.025
1 2	6	2	0.222
1 1	8	5	0.012
7 5	7	3	0.074

Figure 25.8 compares fitness measured by combined rank with fitness measured by quality rank.

Suppose that the most probable chromosome—the 1-4 chromosome—is selected to accompany the 5-1 chromosome into the next generation. Two more remain to be selected. Now, however, the next one selected should be far from both 5-1 and 1-4. Accordingly, instead of measuring the inverse squared distance to just one reference chromosome, you sum the inverse squared distances from both reference chromosomes, 5-1 and 1-4. At this point, the rank sums are all the same, but using diversity rank as the tie breaker yields the following table:

Chromosome	$\sum_i \frac{1}{d_i^2}$	Diversity rank	Quality rank	Combined rank	Fitness
3 1	0.327	4	1	4	0.037
1 2	0.309	3	2	3	0.074
1 1	0.173	2	3	2	0.222
7 5	0.077	1	4	1	0.667

Again suppose that the most probable chromosome—this time the 7-5 chromosome—is selected to accompany the 5-1 and 1-4 chromosomes into the next generation. Then, the ranks relevant to the final choice are determined by the following table; again, you break the rank-sum ties by appealing to diversity rank as the tie breaker. This time, 1-1 is the most probable chromosome:

Chromosome	$\sum_i \frac{1}{d_i^2}$	Diversity rank	Quality rank	Combined rank	Fitness
3 1	0.358	3	1	3	0.111
1 2	0.331	2	2	2	0.222
1 1	0.190	1	3	1	0.667

Figure 25.9 illustrates how all this computation is progressing. Note that the rank-space method tends to maintain diversity relative to the standard method, which would never select 7-5, and to the plain rank method, which would select 7-5 last, rather than third.

In summary, if you assume that the most probable chromosome is selected at each point following the automatic selection of the highest scoring chromosome, 5-1, then 1-4, 7-5, and 1-1 are selected for the next generation, in that order. Had you just examined quality alone, then the order would have been 5-1, 1-4, 3-1, and 1-2.

The Rank-Space Method Does Well on Moat Mountain

If Kookie were to try 1000 times to find the optimum, using the rank-space method, starting with a 1-1 chromosome and $p = 0.66$, he would find the best combination, on average, after about 15 generations. Thus, the rank-space method provides a considerable improvement, on the moat problem, over both the standard method and the rank method. The following table summarizes the improvement:

Figure 25.9 The sequence of three most probable choices drawn from a set of five candidates. Using the rank-space method, selections are made so as to retain diversity.

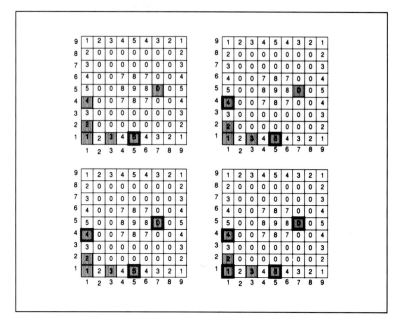

Mountain	Standard method	Quality rank	Rank space
Bump	14	12	12
Moat	155	75	15

Among 1000 simulation experiments performed by Kookie using the rank-space method, the luckiest produced the best combination after just seven generations, after starting at generation 0 with one 1-1 chromosome, which produces quality 1 cookies:

Generation 0:
Chromosome   Quality
1 1   1

At this point, a favorable mutation produced a 2-1 chromosome, which was added to the population, producing two members. Crossover did not add anything during this generation, because there was just one chromosome:

Generation 1:
Chromosome   Quality
2 1   2
1 1   1

Next, mutation added a 3-1 chromosome. Crossover did not add anything during this generation, because both chromosomes in the current population had the same second gene, a 1.

Generation 2:

Chromosome	Quality
3 1	3
2 1	2
1 1	1

Next, mutation added a 2-2 chromosome and a 4-1 chromosome. Again, crossover added nothing. Of the existing and mutated chromosomes, the 2-1 chromosome was lost in forming the third generation:

Generation 3:

Chromosome	Quality
4 1	4
3 1	3
1 1	1
2 2	0

At this point, mutation produces three new chromosomes: 5-1, 1-2, and 2-3. Crossover of the 2-2 and 4-1 chromosomes produced a 2-1 chromosome and a 4-2 chromosome. All the rest of the mutation and crossover results were already in the current population. Accordingly, the next generation was selected from nine chromosomes:

Chromosome	Quality
4 1	4
3 1	3
1 1	1
2 2	0
5 1	5
1 2	2
2 3	0
2 1	2
4 2	0

Of these, the following were retained:

Generation 4:

Chromosome	Quality
5 1	5
3 1	3
1 2	2
2 3	0

Now 5-1 mutated to 6-1, 1-2 mutated to 2-2, 3-1 mutated to 3-2, and 2-3 mutated to 2-4. Also, various crossovers yielded five new chromosomes, 2-1, 1-1, 5-2, 3-2, and 5-3. Accordingly, the next generation was selected from 13 possibilities:

Chromosome	Quality
5 1	5
3 1	3
1 2	2
2 3	0
6 1	4
2 2	0
3 2	0
2 4	0
2 1	2
1 1	1
5 2	0
3 2	0
5 3	0

Of these, four were selected for the next generation, as usual:

Generation 5:

Chromosome	Quality
5 1	5
3 1	3
1 2	2
2 4	0

For the next generation, there was a considerable improvement as a consequence of mating 5-1 with 2-4, which led to a 5-4 chromosome in the next generation:

Generation 6:

Chromosome	Quality
5 4	8
1 4	4
3 1	3
1 2	2

Finally, 5-4 mutated to 5-5 in the final generation:

Generation 7:

Chromosome	Quality
5 5	9
1 4	4
1 2	2
5 2	0

Figure 25.10 shows graphically how this evolution occurred. Note that the rank-space method tends to keep the chromosomes apart. Because there is some randomness in the selection of candidates, however, some bunching still occurred.

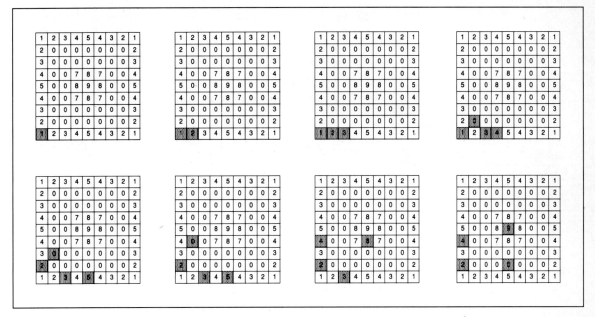

Figure 25.10 The results of a lucky experiment using the rank-space method. The optimum point was found in the seventh generation.

Local Maxima Are Easier to Handle when Diversity Is Maintained

Most approaches to search take the position that local maxima are traps. Accordingly, some approaches involve trap-escaping mechanisms such as backtracking and initially large, ever-shrinking step size. Other approaches involve parallel search with a large number of random starting positions in the hope that one of the parallel searches will get trapped on the local maximum that happens to be the global maximum as well.

In contrast, if a genetic algorithm treats diversity as a component of fitness, then some of the individuals in a population tend to hover around already-discovered local maxima in quality or diversity, driving off other, still peripatetic, individuals. As long as there are enough individuals to populate all the local maxima sufficiently, there is a reasonable chance that one individual will find its way to the global maximum.

The **populate-and-conquer principle**:

▷ Local maxima should be populated, not avoided, when you are seeking a global maximum.

SUMMARY

■ One way to learn may be to imitate natural evolution, using the notion that survival is biased toward the fittest to guide a massive search.

- Chromosomes determine hereditary traits. Genetic learning algorithms modify analogs to chromosomes through analogs to mutation and mating, thus creating new individuals that may be fitter than their parents.

- The standard method for determining fitness equates fitness to a measure of quality. The rank method links fitness to quality rank, thus preventing the particular scale used to measure quality from having deleterious effects.

- The rank-space method links fitness to both quality rank and diversity rank, thus promoting not only the survival of individuals that are extremely fit from the perspective of quality, but also the survival of individuals that are both quite fit and different from other, even more fit individuals.

- It can be as good to be different as it is to be fit. When diversity is maintained, local maxima can be populated, rather than avoided altogether. By embodying this idea, the rank-space method solves problems that are beyond both the standard method and the rank method.

BACKGROUND

The Origin of Species is considered to be among the most influential scientific works of all time [Charles Darwin 1859].

Recently, new light has been shed on evolution by scientists equipped with ideas that have emerged with the dawn of the computer age. In particular, the idea of the importance of neutral mutations is becoming more appreciated. See, for example, the work of Motoo Kimura [1983].

John Holland is one of the pioneers of modern work on natural adaptation algorithms, and is a frequent contributor to the literature [1975, 1986].

An important paper by Jim Antonisse [1989] corrects a long-standing supposition that binary representations are best for genetic algorithms.

Michael de la Maza and Bruce Tidor show how time-varying selective pressure provides a way to maintain diversity on a variety of sample optimization problems, including problems of protein recognition [1991].

A fascinating account of how the speed of evolution can be increased using coevolving parasites appears in a paper by W. Daniel Hillis [1990].

To learn about molecular biology in detail, you should read the comprehensive textbook volumes by James D. Watson et al. [1987].

Part III
Vision and
Language

In part III, you learn about visual perception and language understanding. You learn not only about particular representations and methods, but also about powerful ideas that have been a major source of inspiration for people working in other parts of artificial intelligence.

In Chapter 26, **Recognizing Objects**, you learn how it is possible to *identify objects by constructing custom-tailored templates* from stored two-dimensional image models. You also learn about *methods for solving the correspondence problem*, which enable you to determine the corresponding features in image pairs.

In Chapter 27, **Describing Images**, you learn more about computer vision by learning about the *binocular stereo problem* and the *shape-from-shading problem*.

In Chapter 28, **Expressing Language Constraints**, you learn about the things that linguists think about when they try to explain the nature of language. You also learn about the difference between *competence* and *performance*, and separately, why understanding *language generation* may bear little direct relation to *understanding comprehension*.

In Chapter 29, **Responding to Questions and Commands**, you learn how it is possible to capture the knowledge required to *translate English questions or commands* into *relational-database commands*. Along the way, you see how word-order regularity can be captured in *semantic transition tree grammars*, which are evolutionary descendants of *augmented transition net grammars*.

26

Recognizing Objects

In this chapter, you learn how it is possible to *identify objects by constructing custom-tailored templates* from stored two-dimensional image models. Amazingly, the template-construction procedure just adds together weighted coordinate values from corresponding points in the stored two-dimensional image models. For orthographic projections, the template is perfect—and it is nearly perfect even in perspective projections.

Previously, many researchers thought object identification would have to be done via the transformation of images into explicit three-dimensional descriptions of the objects in the images. The template-construction procedure involves no such explicit three-dimensional descriptions.

The template construction procedure does require knowledge of which points correspond, however. Accordingly, you also learn about *methods for solving the correspondence problem.*

By way of illustration, you see how the linear combination procedure handles similar-looking stylized objects: one is an "obelisk," and another is a "sofa."

Once you have finished this chapter, you will know how the linear combination procedure works, you will appreciate its simple elegance, and you will understand when it is the right approach.

LINEAR IMAGE COMBINATIONS

In this section, you learn how identification can be done by template construction and straightforward matching.

Conventional Wisdom Has Focused on Multilevel Description

Most of the chapters in this book present ideas without providing any explanation about how those ideas emerged. Accordingly, it is easy to imagine that solutions to hard problems improve steadily, whereas, in fact, the march toward solutions to hard problems always seems to involve long periods of little progress, punctuated occasionally by a startling advance.

To appreciate the startling advance associated with the ideas introduced in this chapter, you really need to know that many vision experts believed for years that object identification would require image processing on several descriptive levels, with matching occurring only on the highest:

- At the lowest descriptive level, brightness values are conveyed explicitly in the image.
- The brightness changes in the image are described explicitly in the **primal sketch**.
- The surfaces that are implicit in the primal sketch are described explicitly in the **two-and-one-half–dimensional sketch**.
- The volumes that are implicit in the two-and-one-half–dimensional sketch are described explicitly in the **volume description**.

Information in the primal sketch and the two-and-one-half–dimensional sketch describes what is going on at each point in the original image. Hence, the primal sketch and the two-and-one-half–dimensional sketch often are said to be **viewer centered**.

Unlike the information in the primal sketch and the two-and-one-half–dimensional sketch image, the information in a volume description often is expressed in terms of coordinate systems attached to objects. Such descriptions are said to be **object centered**. Only after constructing a volume description, according to conventional wisdom, can you go into a library and match a description extracted from an image with a remembered description.

Characteristically, conventional wisdom has turned out to be completely wrong. In the rest of this section, you learn that matching can be done at the primal sketch level, rather than at the volume description level.

Images Contain Implicit Shape Information

In elementary geometry, you learned that a polyhedron is an object whose faces are all flat. When you look at a mechanical drawing of a polyhedron, the combination of a front view, a side view, and a top view of that polyhedron is sufficient to give you full knowledge of each vertex's three-dimensional position.

More generally, a few images, each showing a few corresponding vertexes, give you an idea of where those corresponding vertexes are, relative to one another, in three dimensions, even when the images are not the standard front, side, and top views.

For a long time, however, it was not clear how many images and how many vertexes are required to recover where the vertexes are, relative to one another, in three dimensions. Then, in 1979, Shimon Ullman showed that three images, each showing four corresponding vertexes, are almost enough to determine the vertexes' relative positions. All that you need in addition is some source of information about the polyhedron's size, such as the distance between any two vertexes.

Thus, three images carry implicit knowledge of a polyhedron's shape as long as those images all contain at least four corresponding vertexes. If you make the knowledge of shape explicit by deriving the three-dimensional coordinate values of all the vertexes, then you can construct any other image by projecting those vertexes through a suitably placed eye or lens onto a suitably placed biological retina or artificial sensor array.

Knowing that any other image can be constructed via the intermediate step of deriving three-dimensional coordinate values naturally leads to two important questions:

■ Given three recorded images of a polyhedron, are there simple equations that predict the coordinate values of the points in a new, fourth image using only the coordinate values of the corresponding points in the three recorded images?

■ If the answer to the first question is yes, is it possible to determine all the parameters in those simple prediction equations using only the coordinate values of a few of the corresponding points in the recorded images and the new image?

Happily, there are simple equations that predict the coordinate values, and it is possible to determine all the parameters in those simple prediction equations using only a few corresponding points. The coordinate values of the points in a new, fourth image are given by a linear combination of the coordinate values of the points of the three recorded images. Also, you can determine the constants involved in the linear combination by solving a few linear equations involving only a few of the corresponding points. Consequently, when presented with an image of an unidentified polyhedron, you can determine whether it can be an image of each particular polyhedron recorded in a library.

One Approach Is Matching Against Templates

To streamline further discussion, let us agree to call each object-describing image collection a **model**, short for **identification model**, a representation specified loosely as follows:

Figure 26.1 One possible approach to identification is to create templates from models. On the left, you see an object that may be an obelisk; in the middle, you see an obelisk template; and on the right, the two are overlaid. One question is whether the models can consist exclusively of stored two-dimensional images.

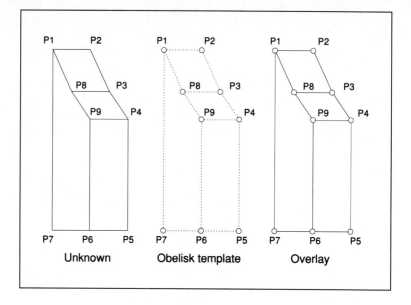

An **identification model** is a representation

In which

▷ An image consists of a list of identifiable places, called **feature points**, observed in an image.

▷ The model consists of several images—minimally three for polyhedra.

Furthermore, let us agree to call each unidentified object an *unknown*. Using this vocabulary of models and unknowns, you want to know whether it is practicable to match an unknown with a model by comparing the points in an image of the unknown with a templatelike collection of points produced from the model. In figure 26.1, for example, the nine points seen in the image of an unknown match the nine points in an overlaid, custom-made obelisk template.

Whenever a general question is hard, it is natural to deal with a special case first. Accordingly, suppose that objects are allowed to rotate around the vertical axis only; there are to be no translations and no rotations about other axes. In figure 26.2, for example, the obelisk shown in figure 26.1 is viewed in its original position, and then is rotated about the vertical axis by 30°, 60°, and 90°.

In each of the images shown in figure 26.2, the obelisk is *projected orthographically* along the z axis. As explained in figure 26.3, the x and y coordinate values for points in the image are exactly the x and y coordinate values of the obelisk's vertexes in three dimensions.

Figure 26.2 An "obelisk" and three orthographic projections of the obelisk, one each for 30°, 60°, and 90° rotations.

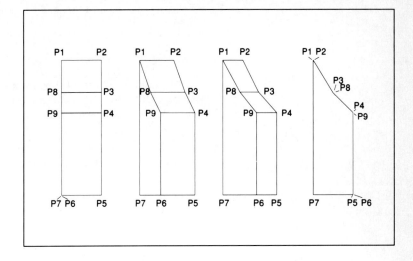

Figure 26.3 Orthographic projection. Light moves along paths parallel to the z axis to an image plane somewhere on the z axis. The x and y coordinate values of the vertexes in an image equal their three-dimensional x and y coordinate values.

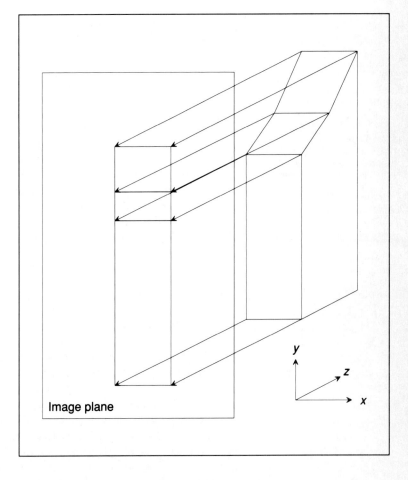

Somewhat unusually, the coordinate system shown in figure 26.3 is a left-handed coordinate system, but most people like to have the distance from the image plane increase with increasing z, which dictates the left-handed arrangement.

Next, note that corresponding points in figure 26.2 are labeled with corresponding numbers. In general, matching points in one image with those in another to establish correspondence may be difficult; for the moment, however, just assume that the necessary matching can be done. You learn about several approaches in the next section.

Now, by way of preview, consider a point that appears with an x coordinate value of x_{I_1} in one obelisk model image, and with an x coordinate value of x_{I_2} in another obelisk model image. Soon, you learn that the x coordinate value of the same point in an observed image is a weighted sum of the coordinate values seen in the model images:

$$x_{I_o} = \alpha x_{I_1} + \beta x_{I_2}.$$

Next you see that α and β can be recovered using a few corresponding points, making it easy to predict where the remaining points should be; providing, ultimately, an identification test.

For One Special Case, Two Images Are Sufficient to Generate a Third

The nature of orthographic projection is such that a point corresponding to a vertex located at (x, y, z) in space is located at (x, y) in the orthographic image. After rotation about the y axis, however, the vertex is no longer at (x, y, z). Although the y coordinate value is unchanged, both the x and z coordinate values change. As demonstrated by some straightforward trigonometry, the coordinate values, after rotation, are determined by the sines and cosines of the rotation angle, θ. More precisely, the new x, y, and z coordinate values, x_θ, y_θ, and z_θ, are related to the old x, y, and z coordinate values by the following equations:

$$x_\theta = x \cos \theta - z \sin \theta,$$

$$y_\theta = y,$$

$$z_\theta = x \sin \theta + z \cos \theta.$$

Because the y coordinate value endures rotation and orthographic projection without change, and because the z coordinate value does not enter into orthographic projection, your interest is exclusively in the fate of the x coordinate value as an object rotates.

To keep the discussion as concrete as possible, assume that the obelisk is rotated from its original position twice, once by θ_{I_1} and once by θ_{I_2}, to produce two model images, I_1 and I_2. What you want to know is what the obelisk looks like when rotated from its original position a third time, by θ_{I_o}, producing image I_o.

Consider a particular point with original coordinate values x, y, and z. In the two model images of the rotated obelisk, the x coordinate values of the same point are x_{I_1} and x_{I_2}. The problem is to find a way of determining x_{I_o} given the known values, x_{I_1} and x_{I_2}. Once you can do this for any particular point, you can do it for all points and thus construct the desired third image of the obelisk. So far, however, you can only relate x_{I_1}, x_{I_2}, and x_{I_o} to the original x and z values and the angles of rotation:

$$x_{I_1} = x \cos \theta_{I_1} - z \sin \theta_{I_1},$$
$$x_{I_2} = x \cos \theta_{I_2} - z \sin \theta_{I_2},$$
$$x_{I_o} = x \cos \theta_{I_o} - z \sin \theta_{I_o}.$$

To understand what these equations can do for you, you need to understand one subtle point. x_{I_1}, x_{I_2}, and x_{I_o} vary from point to point, but θ_{I_1}, θ_{I_2}, and θ_{I_o} do not. The angles do not change as long as you are working with a fixed set of images. Accordingly, if you are trying to solve the equations for x_{I_o} for a fixed set of images, the sines and cosines of the angles are constants.

Better still, the equations are three linear equations in the three unknowns, x_{I_o}, x, and z. From elementary algebra, you know that you can solve three linear equations in three unknowns, leaving x_{I_o} expressed as a weighted sum of x_{I_1} and x_{I_2}:

$$x_{I_o} = \alpha x_{I_1} + \beta x_{I_2}.$$

Describing this expression in mathematical language, x_{I_o} is given by a **linear combination** of x_{I_1} and x_{I_2}, and α and β are called the **coefficients** of the linear combination.

Now, if you only knew the actual values for α and β relating observed points to points in the two model images, you could predict where every point should be from where it appears in the two model images. If the predicted points match the actual points observed, then the observed object matches the model object.

Of course, you could work through the algebra and determine how α and β can be expressed in terms of sines and cosines of θ_{I_1}, θ_{I_2}, and θ_{I_o}. But that would not help you, because you normally do not know any of those angles. You need another approach.

Identification Is a Matter of Finding Consistent Coefficients

You have just learned that there must be constants α and β such that the coordinate values in an observed image are predicted by the equation

$$x_{I_o} = \alpha x_{I_1} + \beta x_{I_2}.$$

Because α and β depend on only the three images, I_1, I_2, and I_o, you need only two linear equations to determine their values.

Fortunately, two sets of corresponding points provide those equations. Suppose, for example, that you have found a point P_1 in the observed image

Figure 26.4 Two unknown
objects compared with
templates made from obelisk
images to fit points P_1 and
P_2. The unknown on the left
is actually an obelisk rotated by
45°. It matches the template of
circles produced from the two
obelisk models. The unknown
on the right—the one that looks
like a jukebox—does not match
the template made for it.

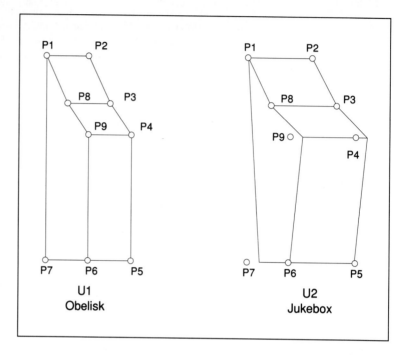

and the corresponding points in the model images. Similarly, suppose you
have found point P_2 and its corresponding points. Then, the x coordinate
values of both points in the observed image must satisfy the following
equations:

$$x_{P_1 I_o} = \alpha x_{P_1 I_1} + \beta x_{P_1 I_2},$$
$$x_{P_2 I_o} = \alpha x_{P_2 I_1} + \beta x_{P_2 I_2}.$$

Now you have two, easily solved equations in two unknowns. The solutions
are, of course,

$$\alpha = \frac{x_{P_1 I_o} x_{P_2 I_2} - x_{P_2 I_o} x_{P_1 I_2}}{x_{P_1 I_1} x_{P_2 I_2} - x_{P_2 I_1} x_{P_1 I_2}},$$
$$\beta = \frac{x_{P_2 I_o} x_{P_1 I_1} - x_{P_1 I_o} x_{P_2 I_1}}{x_{P_1 I_1} x_{P_2 I_2} - x_{P_2 I_1} x_{P_1 I_2}}.$$

Once you have used two of n sets of corresponding points to find α and β,
you can use α and β to predict the positions of the remaining $n-2$ sets of
corresponding points of the observed object:

$$x_{P_i I_o} = \alpha x_{P_i I_1} + \beta x_{P_i I_2}.$$

The predicted point positions then act like a template that the points in the
observed image must match if the object in the image is the same object
seen in the model images.

For the obelisk example, the following table gives the x coordinate
values for points P_1 and P_2 in the images of the obelisk after rotation by
30° and 60°. The table also gives the x coordinate values of corresponding

points on the two unknown objects shown in figure 26.4. The y coordinate values are not shown, because they do not vary from image to image.

	Position in image I_1	Position in image I_2	Position in image U_1	Position in image U_2
x_{P_1}	-2.73	-2.73	-2.83	-3.54
x_{P_2}	0.73	-0.73	0	0.71

Using the x coordinate values, you can calculate what α and β must be for each of the two unknown objects by substituting values from the table into $x_{P_i I_o} = \alpha x_{P_i I_1} + \beta x_{P_i I_2}$. For the first unknown object, you have, for example, the following equations after substitution:

$$-2.83 = \alpha(-2.73) + \beta(-2.73),$$
$$0 = \alpha(0.73) + \beta(-0.73).$$

Solving these equations, you have $\alpha = 0.518315$ and $\beta = 0.518315$. Solving the corresponding equations for the second unknown yields $\alpha = 1.13465$ and $\beta = 0.16205$. You can use these α and β values to predict the x coordinate values for each of the remaining points, with the following results:

	U_1 predicted	U_1 actual	U_2 predicted	U_2 actual
x_{P_1}	-2.83	-2.83	-3.54	-3.54
x_{P_2}	0	0	0.70	0.70
x_{P_3}	1.41	1.41	2.12	2.12
x_{P_4}	2.83	2.83	3.54	4.24
x_{P_5}	2.83	2.83	3.54	3.54
x_{P_6}	0	0	-0.70	-0.70
x_{P_7}	-2.83	-2.83	-3.54	-2.83
x_{P_8}	-1.41	-1.41	-2.12	-2.12
x_{P_9}	0	0	-0.70	0

Evidently, the first unknown is an obelisk, because all predicted points are where they should be, as shown in figure 26.4; the second unknown is not an obelisk, because three predicted points are in the wrong place. Although the second unknown has much in common with the obelisk, the second unknown is wider, and its front and back are tapered, rather than vertical, making it look a bit like a jukebox.

The Template Approach Handles Arbitrary Rotation and Translation

In one special case, you have seen that identification can be done using only two model images together with two points that appear in both of those model images and in an image of an unknown object. The special case is severely restricted, however; only rotation around one axis is permitted.

You have concentrated on the one-axis-rotation special case for two reasons. First, looking at special cases is the sort of thing researchers generally do when they are trying to develop a feel for what is going on. Second, the one-axis-rotation special case is within the reach of straightforward mathematics.

More generally, however, you have to expect that an unknown may have been arbitrarily rotated, arbitrarily translated, and even arbitrarily scaled relative to an arbitrary original position. To deal with these changes, you first have to believe, without proof here, that an arbitrary rotation of an object transforms the coordinate values of any point on that object according to the following equations:

$$x_\theta = r_{xx}(\theta)x + r_{yx}(\theta)y + r_{zx}(\theta)z,$$
$$y_\theta = r_{xy}(\theta)x + r_{yy}(\theta)y + r_{zy}(\theta)z,$$
$$z_\theta = r_{xz}(\theta)x + r_{yz}(\theta)y + r_{zz}(\theta)z.$$

Note that $r_{xx}(\theta)$ is the parameter that shows how much the x coordinate of a point, before rotation, contributes to the x coordinate of the same point after rotation. Similarly, $r_{yz}(\theta)$ is the parameter that shows how much the y coordinate of a point, before rotation, contributes to the z coordinate of the same point after rotation.

If, in addition, the object is translated as well as rotated, each equation gains another parameter:

$$x_\theta = r_{xx}(\theta)x + r_{yx}(\theta)y + r_{zx}(\theta)z + t_x,$$
$$y_\theta = r_{xy}(\theta)x + r_{yy}(\theta)y + r_{zy}(\theta)z + t_y,$$
$$z_\theta = r_{xz}(\theta)x + r_{yz}(\theta)y + r_{zz}(\theta)z + t_z.$$

where the ts are all parameters that are determined by how much the object is translated.

Now you can repeat the development for the one-axis-only special case, only there must be three model images. These three model images yield the following equations relating model and unknown coordinate values to unrotated, untranslated coordinate values, x, y, and z:

$$x_{I_1} = r_{xx}(\theta_1)x + r_{yx}(\theta_1)y + r_{zx}(\theta_1)z + t_x(\theta_1),$$
$$x_{I_2} = r_{xx}(\theta_2)x + r_{yx}(\theta_2)y + r_{zx}(\theta_2)z + t_x(\theta_2),$$
$$x_{I_3} = r_{xx}(\theta_3)x + r_{yx}(\theta_3)y + r_{zx}(\theta_3)z + t_x(\theta_3),$$
$$x_{I_o} = r_{xx}(\theta_o)x + r_{yx}(\theta_o)y + r_{zx}(\theta_o)z + t_x(\theta_o).$$

Plainly, these equations can be viewed as four equations in four unknowns, x, y, z, and x_{I_o}, which can be solved to yield x_{I_o} in terms of x_{I_1}, x_{I_2}, and x_{I_3} and a collection of four constants:

$$x_{I_o} = \alpha_x x_{I_1} + \beta_x x_{I_2} + \gamma_x x_{I_3} + \delta_x,$$

where α_x, β_x, γ_x, and δ_x are the constants required for x-coordinate-value prediction, each of which can be expressed in terms of rs and ts. There is no reason to go through the algebra, however, because, as in the one-axis-only case, there is another way to obtain the values of α_x, β_x, γ_x, and δ_x without knowing the rotations and translations.

Following the development for the one-axis-only special case, you can use a few corresponding points to determine the constants. This time, however, there are four constants, so four points are required:

$$x_{P_1 I_0} = \alpha_x x_{P_1 I_1} + \beta_x x_{P_1 I_2} + \gamma_x x_{P_1 I_3} + \delta_x,$$
$$x_{P_2 I_0} = \alpha_x x_{P_2 I_1} + \beta_x x_{P_2 I_2} + \gamma_x x_{P_2 I_3} + \delta_x,$$
$$x_{P_3 I_0} = \alpha_x x_{P_3 I_1} + \beta_x x_{P_3 I_2} + \gamma_x x_{P_3 I_3} + \delta_x,$$
$$x_{P_4 I_0} = \alpha_x x_{P_4 I_1} + \beta_x x_{P_4 I_2} + \gamma_x x_{P_4 I_3} + \delta_x.$$

Solving these equations for α_x, β_x, γ_x, and δ_x enables you to predict the x coordinate values of any point in the unknown image from the corresponding points in the three model images.

Note, however, that you have to consider the y coordinate values also. There was no need to consider y coordinate values in the one-axis-only special case because rotation was around the y axis, leaving all y coordinate values constant from image to image. In the case of general rotation and translation, the y coordinate values vary as well.

Fortunately, the development of equations for y values follows the development of equations for the x values exactly, producing another, different set of four constants, α_y, β_y, γ_y, and δ_y for the following equation:

$$y_{I_0} = \alpha_y y_{I_1} + \beta_y y_{I_2} + \gamma_y y_{I_3} + \delta_y.$$

Thus, the identification procedure requires three model images for each identity that an object might have:

To identify an unknown object,

▷ Until a satisfactory match is made or there are no more models in the model library,

  ▷ Find four corresponding points in the observed image and in a model's three library images.

  ▷ Use the corresponding points to determine the coefficients, α and β, used to predict the x and y coordinate values of other image points.

  ▷ Determine whether a satisfactory match is made by comparing the predicted x and y coordinate values with those actually found in the observed image.

▷ If a satisfactory match occurs, announce the identity of the unknown; otherwise, announce failure.

Figure 26.5 Three obelisk images. The one on the left has been rotated 30° around the *x* axis relative to the standard initial standing position, pitching it forward; the second has been rotated around the *y* axis; and the third has been rotated around the *z* axis.

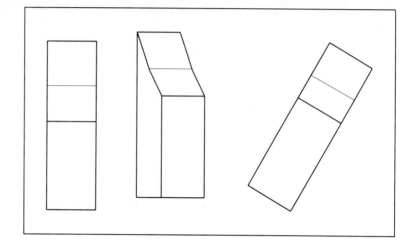

Figure 26.6 Three unknown objects are compared to templates made from obelisk images using the points marked by black circles. The unknown on the left matches the obelisk template. The unknowns resembling a jukebox and a sofa do not match.

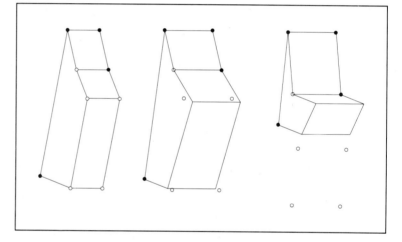

Thus, you need three images, like those in figure 26.5, to have an obelisk model that is good enough to recognize obelisks with unrestricted rotations and translations. With such a model, and knowledge of how four corresponding points in the model correspond to four points in each of the object images shown in figure 26.6, you identify just one of those objects as an obelisk.

The Template Approach Handles Objects with Parts

So far, you have learned that the *x* coordinate value of any point is given by a linear combination of the coordinate values in two or three model images. Now you learn that the *x* coordinate value is given by a linear combination of the coordinate values in several model images, even if an object has parts that move relative to one another.

Figure 26.7 An object with two parts, C_1 and C_2, each of which rotates independently about the y axis.

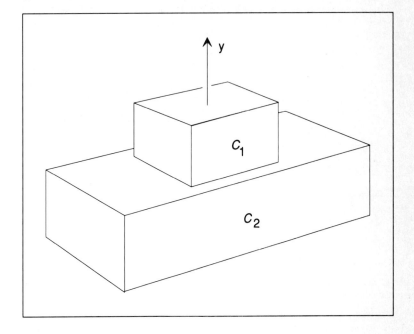

So as to keep the algebra as uncluttered as possible, the explanation is focused on the special case of rotation about the y axis, and the example is the one shown in figure 26.7.

Note that each part is, by itself, one rigid object. Accordingly, the x coordinate value of a point in an observed image, x_{I_o} is determined by two model images and a particular α, β pair specialized to one part of the object, as indicated by elaborate α and β subscripts:

$$x_{I_o} = \alpha_{C_1 I_o} x_{I_1} + \beta_{C_1 I_o} x_{I_2}.$$

The C_1 in the subscripts indicates that the α and β values are for part 1; the I_o subscript indicate that the α and β values transform I_1 and I_2 values into I_o values.

Similarly, x_{I_o} is given by a different α, β pair if the other part is involved:

$$x_{I_o} = \alpha_{C_2 I_o} x_{I_1} + \beta_{C_2 I_o} x_{I_2}.$$

Amazingly, if you have enough images, you do not need to know to which part a point belongs, for there is a set of four coefficients—$\alpha, \beta, \delta, \gamma$—such that the x coordinate value is determined by four model images, four coefficients, and the following equation, no matter to which part the point belongs:

$$x_{I_o} = \alpha x_{I_1} + \beta x_{I_2} + \delta x_{I_3} + \gamma x_{I_4}.$$

To see why, you have to go through a bit of algebra, but in spite of the necessary subscript clutter, there is only one mathematical insight involved: You can solve n independent linear equations in n variables.

Strategically, you need to convince yourself that the four-coefficient equation for x_{I_o}, the one that requires no knowledge of which part is involved, does the same thing as the two-coefficient equation for x_{I_o}, the one that does require knowledge of which part is involved. Said another way, you need to be sure that there is a set of four coefficients, $\alpha, \beta, \delta, \gamma$, such that the following is true if x_{I_o} is a coordinate value of a point on part 1:

$$\alpha x_{I_1} + \beta x_{I_2} + \delta x_{I_3} + \gamma x_{I_4} = \alpha_1 x_{I_1} + \beta_{C_1 I_o} x_{I_2}.$$

Alternatively, the following is true if x_{I_o} is a coordinate value of a point on part 2:

$$\alpha x_{I_1} + \beta x_{I_2} + \delta x_{I_3} + \gamma x_{I_4} = \alpha_{C_2 I_o} x_{I_1} + \beta_{C_2 I_o} x_{I_2}.$$

Focus for now on the case for which x_{I_o} is the x coordinate of a point that belongs to part 1. Because you assume you are dealing with just one part, you know that two model images suffice to determine the x_{I_o} coordinate value of any point in any image. Accordingly, x_{I_3} and x_{I_4} can be determined by x_{I_1} and x_{I_2}, along with an α, β pair suited to the part and the images produced, as indicated by the subscripts:

$$x_{I_3} = \alpha_{C_1 I_3} x_{I_1} + \beta_{C_1 I_3} x_{I_2},$$
$$x_{I_4} = \alpha_{C_1 I_4} x_{I_1} + \beta_{C_1 I_4} x_{I_2}.$$

Evidently, x_{I_o}, given that the point is on part 1, must be determined by the following after substitution for x_{I_3} and x_{I_4}:

$$x_{I_o} = \alpha x_{I_1} + \beta x_{I_2} + \delta(\alpha_{C_1 I_3} x_{I_1} + \beta_{C_1 I_3} x_{I_2}) + \gamma(\alpha_{C_1 I_4} x_{I_1} + \beta_{C_1 I_4} x_{I_2}).$$

Rearranging terms yields the following:

$$x_{I_o} = (\alpha + \delta\alpha_{C_1 I_3} + \gamma\alpha_{C_1 I_4}) x_{I_1} + (\beta + \delta\beta_{C_1 I_3} + \gamma\beta_{C_1 I_4}) x_{I_2}.$$

But you know that $x_{I_o} = \alpha_1 x_{I_1} + \beta_{C_1 I_o} x_{I_2}$. So now you can equate the two expressions for x_{I_o}, yielding the following:

$$\alpha_1 x_{I_1} + \beta_{C_1 I_o} x_{I_2} = (\alpha + \delta\alpha_{C_1 I_3} + \gamma\alpha_{C_1 I_4}) x_{I_1} + (\beta + \delta\beta_{C_1 I_3} + \gamma\beta_{C_1 I_4}) x_{I_2}.$$

For this equation to hold, the coefficients of x_{I_1} and x_{I_2} must be the same, producing two equations in the four coefficients, $\alpha, \beta, \delta, \gamma$:

$$\alpha_1 = \alpha + \delta\alpha_{C_1 I_3} + \gamma\alpha_{C_1 I_4},$$
$$\beta_{C_1 I_o} = \beta + \delta\beta_{C_1 I_3} + \gamma\beta_{C_1 I_4}.$$

Going through exactly the same reasoning, but assuming that x belongs to part 2, produces two more equations in the four coefficients:

$$\alpha_{C_2 I_o} = \alpha + \delta\alpha_{C_2 I_3} + \gamma\alpha_{C_2 I_4},$$
$$\beta_{C_2 I_o} = \beta + \delta\beta_{C_2 I_3} + \gamma\beta_{C_2 I_4}.$$

Now you have four equations in four unknowns, thus fully constraining α, β, δ, and γ. The only $\alpha, \beta, \delta, \gamma$ combination that works, no matter what, is the combination prescribed by those four equations.

Of course, none of this computation would do any good if you had to use the solutions to determine $\alpha, \beta, \delta, \gamma$, for then you would have to know all the particular α, β pairs appropriate to the individual parts and images.

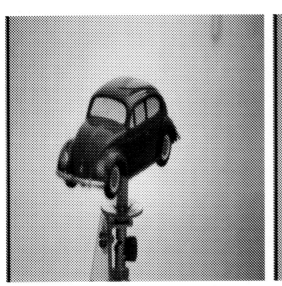

Figure 26.8 Images of two unidentified automobiles. Images courtesy of Ronen Basri.

Fortunately, however, you can use the same idea that proved invaluable before: Given that you know that an appropriate set of coefficients exists, you can create a different set of equations, with easily obtained constants, by looking at four distinct points:

$$x_{P_1 I_o} = \alpha x_{P_1 I_1} + \beta x_{P_1 I_2} + \delta x_{P_1 I_3} + \gamma x_{P_1 I_4},$$
$$x_{P_2 I_o} = \alpha x_{P_2 I_1} + \beta x_{P_2 I_2} + \delta x_{P_2 I_3} + \gamma x_{P_2 I_4},$$
$$x_{P_3 I_o} = \alpha x_{P_3 I_1} + \beta x_{P_3 I_2} + \delta x_{P_3 I_3} + \gamma x_{P_3 I_4},$$
$$x_{P_4 I_o} = \alpha x_{P_4 I_1} + \beta x_{P_4 I_2} + \delta x_{P_4 I_3} + \gamma x_{P_4 I_4}.$$

The Template Approach Handles Complicated Curved Objects

To get a feeling for the power of the template approach, consider the two toy-automobile images shown in figure 26.8. To initiate identification, you have to reduce both to line drawings, as in figure 26.9.

Suppose that each automobile is known to be either an old-model Volkswagen or an old-model SAAB. To determine which it is, you need to match the drawings to constructed-to-order templates. Remarkably, the templates can be made straightforwardly, even though the objects have curved surfaces. All you need to do is to increase the number of images that constitute a model. Instead of the two model images needed for rotation about a vertical axis, you need three. Accordingly, you can form a Volkswagen model by taking three pictures and rendering those pictures as drawings. You can form a SAAB model the same way. Both are shown in figure 26.10.

Figure 26.9 Drawings of
two unidentified automobiles.
Drawings courtesy of Ronen
Basri.

Figure 26.10

Models consist of three
drawings. Above is a
Volkswagen model;
below is a SAAB
model. Drawings
courtesy of Ronen
Basri.

At the top of figure 26.11, the unidentified automobile on the left in
figure 26.9 is shown together with a template manufactured for the drawing
from Volkswagen images. As shown, the fit is just about perfect. At
the bottom of figure 26.11, the unidentified automobile on the right in
figure 26.9 is shown together with a template manufactured for the drawing
from Volkswagen images. The fit is terrible, indicating that the drawing
is not a drawing of a Volkswagen. Had the template been made from the
SAAB model images, however, the fit would have been just about perfect.

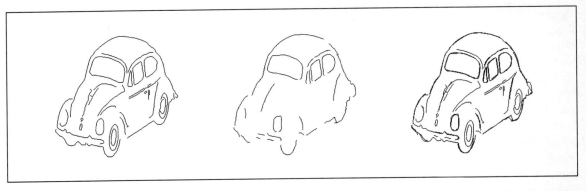

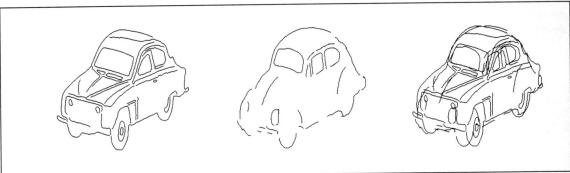

Figure 26.11
Above is a drawing
of a Volkswagen, a
template manufactured
from Volkswagen
images, and the two
images superimposed.
Below is a drawing
of an SAAB, a
template manufactured
from Volkswagen
images, and the
two superimposed.
Drawings courtesy of
Ronen Basri.

ESTABLISHING POINT CORRESPONDENCE

In this section, you learn how it is possible to determine how the points in one image correspond to the points in another, a necessary prerequisite to template construction.

Tracking Enables Model Points to Be Kept in Correspondence

Actually, it is relatively easy to create three images of an object, with known point correspondences, to serve as a model. All you need to do is to move the object slowly, taking many intermediate snapshots between each pair of images that is to be in the model. That way, the difference between adjacent snapshots is so small, corresponding points are always nearest neighbors, and you can track points from one model image to another through the intermediate snapshots, as suggested in figure 26.12.

Only Sets of Points Need to Be Matched

When you are confronted with an unknown object, there can be no such thing as intermediate snapshots lying between the unknown's image and one of the model images. Consequently, matching the points is much harder.

Figure 26.12 Moving an object slowly makes it possible to track points from one model image to another through intermediate snapshots. Corresponding points are always nearest neighbors in adjacent snapshots, even though they are not necessarily nearest neighbors in the model images. Here five obelisk images are shown, with adjacent pairs rotated by $10°$.

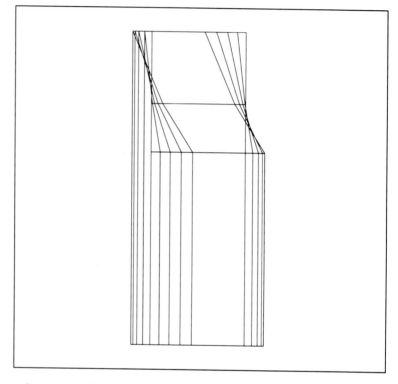

Accordingly, it is important to know that it is enough, in the general case, to establish that sets of points correspond, without knowing exactly how the points in the sets match up individually.

To see why, consider the one-axis-rotation special case again and recall that, for any point, P_i, the following equation holds:

$$x_{P_i I_o} = \alpha x_{P_i I_1} + \beta x_{P_i I_2}.$$

Accordingly, the equation must hold for points P_1 and P_2:

$$x_{P_1 I_o} = \alpha x_{P_1 I_1} + \beta x_{P_1 I_2},$$
$$x_{P_2 I_o} = \alpha x_{P_2 I_1} + \beta x_{P_2 I_2}.$$

Adding these equations produces the following:

$$(x_{P_1 I_o} + x_{P_2 I_o}) = \alpha(x_{P_1 I_1} + x_{P_2 I_1}) + \beta(x_{P_1 I_2} + x_{P_2 I_2}).$$

Repeating for two other points, P_3 and P_4, provides a second equation in the two unknowns, α and β:

$$(x_{P_3 I_o} + x_{P_4 I_o}) = \alpha(x_{P_3 I_1} + x_{P_4 I_1}) + \beta(x_{P_3 I_2} + x_{P_4 I_2}).$$

Note that, wherever $x_{P_1 I_o}$ appears, it is added to $x_{P_2 I_o}$, and vice versa. Similarly, wherever $x_{P_3 I_o}$ appears, it is added to $x_{P_4 I_o}$, and vice versa. Accordingly, there is no harm in confusing $x_{P_1 I_o}$ and $x_{P_2 I_o}$, and there is no harm in confusing $x_{P_3 I_o}$ and $x_{P_4 I_o}$. By adding up the x coordinate values of the points in the sets, you eliminate the need to sort out exactly how the points in the sets correspond. It is enough to know that the points in one set are among the points in the corresponding set.

Thus, for the one-axis-rotation special case, you do not need to find two corresponding points in two images. You need only to find two corresponding sets of points in two images.

The argument generalizes easily. For arbitrary rotation, translation, and scaling, you do not need to find four corresponding points in three images. You need only to find four corresponding sets of points in three images.

Heuristics Help You to Match Unknown Points to Model Points

Once you know that it is enough to find corresponding sets of points, you can use a few heuristics to help you find those corresponding sets. If an object has a natural top and bottom, for example, the points near the top and bottom in any image are likely to form corresponding sets.

Consider the model images and unknown shown in figure 26.13. As before, the 30° and 60° images constitute the model to be checked against the unknown. Earlier, you saw that you can use points P_1 and P_2 to find α and β for the first unknown, using the following equations:

$$-2.83 = \alpha(-2.73) + \beta(-2.73),$$
$$0 = \alpha(0.73) + \beta(-0.73).$$

Any other pair of points would do just as well, of course. Instead of using P_1 and P_2, the points along the top, you could use any two of P_5, P_6, and P_7, the points along the bottom, which produce the following equations:

$$2.83 = \alpha(2.73) + \beta(2.73),$$
$$0 = \alpha(-0.73) + \beta(0.73),$$
$$-2.83 = \alpha(-2.73) + \beta(-2.73).$$

Note that sums of equations are also equations. Thus, you can add together the equations for the top points to get a new equation. Then, you can add together the equations for the bottom points. Thus, you have two more equations in α and β:

$$(-2.83 + 0) = \alpha(-2.73 + 0.73) + \beta(-2.73 - 0.73),$$
$$(2.83 + 0 - 2.83) = \alpha(2.73 - 0.73 - 2.73) + \beta(2.73 + 0.73 - 2.73).$$

Naturally, these new, composed equations have the same solution as do the original equations involving P_1 and P_2—namely, $\alpha = 0.518315$ and $\beta = 0.518315$. Thus, you can use corresponding sets of points to produce equations in α and β, instead of corresponding points. Within the corresponding sets, you do not need to know exactly which point goes with which point.

Still, even finding corresponding sets may be hard. For one thing, the general case requires four sets of corresponding points, not just two. Also,

Figure 26.13 It is sufficient to find sets of corresponding points; it is not necessary to know exactly how the points within the sets correspond.

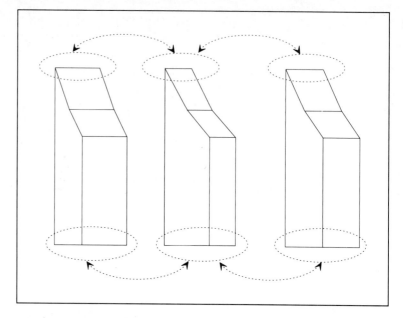

you cannot always expect objects to have a natural standing posture that enables you to identify top and bottom sets.

SUMMARY

- The traditional approach to object identification involves image description, followed by surface description, followed by volume description, followed by matching with library models.

- Amazingly, you can construct a two-dimensional identification template using the two-dimensional image of the object to be identified, plus a few stored two-dimensional image descriptions. Identification becomes a matter of template matching.

- You construct two-dimensional templates by using a few corresponding points to establish position-prediction coefficients.

- For pure rotation of a polyhedron around one axis, two corresponding points in two images are sufficient to establish position-prediction coefficients for an unknown object in a given image. For general polyhedron rotation and translation, you need four points in three images.

- When fully generalized, the template approach handles objects with parts and objects with curved surfaces.

- To use the template approach, you need to be able to identify corresponding features in image sets. Fortunately, you need only to find corresponding sets of points, rather than corresponding points. Sometimes, you can track points as they move, thus maintaining correspondence, rather than establishing correspondence.

BACKGROUND

Identification procedures in which a template is generated and matched to an unknown are called alignment methods. The seminal alignment ideas described in this chapter were developed by Shimon Ullman and Ronen Basri [1989].

27

Describing Images

In this chapter, you learn more about computer vision through discussions of two problems that are better understood than are most problems. The first of these problems, the *binocular stereo problem*, is to find the distance from the viewer to surfaces using two slightly different viewpoints. The second problem, the *shape-from-shading problem*, is to determine surface-direction at each point in an image by exploiting the way surfaces in the image are shaded.

Once you have finished this chapter, you will know that image understanding, like other problems in artificial intelligence, requires the right representation and a thorough understanding of the constraints brought out by that representation.

COMPUTING EDGE DISTANCE

In this section, you learn about a procedure that computes depth from image pairs. First, however, you learn how it is possible to isolate edges in images.

Averaged and Differenced Images Highlight Edges

At the edge between two flat faces, brightness should change sharply from one value to another, as shown in figure 27.1(a). In practice, however, the steplike change generally is corrupted, as in figure 27.1(b), making it hard to determine just where the edge is. One reason is that image input devices do

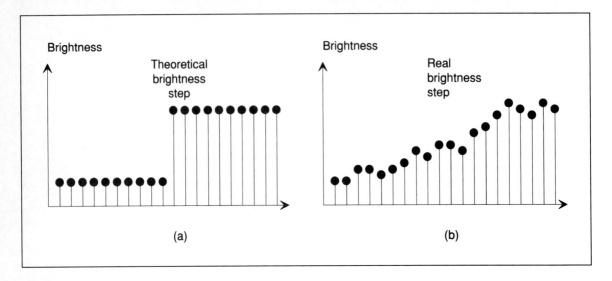

Brightness

Theoretical
brightness
step

(a)

Brightness

Real
brightness
step

(b)

Figure 27.1 The
brightness profile in
part (a) is that of an
ideal edge between
two flat faces. The one
in part (b) is that of a
real edge.

not produce simple clean images. You must cope with variations in brightness sensitivity across the sensor, errors in image coordinate information,
electronic noise, light-source hum, and inability to accept wide variations in
brightness. Another reason is that images are complicated. Edges may be
slightly rounded, rather than sharp, and there may be mutual-illumination
effects, misleading scratches, fingerprints, and dust.

One way to handle noisy edges involves four steps. First, you make an
average-brightness array from the image to reduce the influence of noise.
The following formula illustrates the computation that you do. For simplicity, the formula is a one-dimensional version of what you would use in
two dimensions. I_i is the image brightness at point i, and A_i is the local
average of brightnesses around point i:

$$A_i = \frac{I_{i-1} + I_i + I_{i+1}}{3}.$$

Then, you make an average-first-difference array from the average-
brightness array. To do this, you average the right-neighbor difference,
$A_{i+1} - A_i$, and the left-neighbor difference, $A_i - A_{i-1}$. This computation is equivalent to averaging the right and left neighbors. F_i, then, is
the average first difference of average brightness (and a finite difference
approximation to the first derivative):

$$F_i = \frac{(A_{i+1} - A_i) + (A_i - A_{i-1})}{2} = \frac{A_{i+1} - A_{i-1}}{2}.$$

Next, you make an average-second-difference array by averaging the
first differences of the average-first-difference array. Thus, S_i, is the average
second difference of average brightness:

$$S_i = \frac{(F_{i+1} - F_i) + (F_i - F_{i-1})}{2} = \frac{F_{i+1} - F_{i-1}}{2}.$$

Figure 27.2 The steps in processing edge brightnesses. The brightness change that is to be analyzed is shown in part (a). Part (b) shows the result of averaging. Part (c) shows the averaged differences of part (b), and part (d) shows the averaged differences of part (c). The result in part (d) localizes the step in part (a).

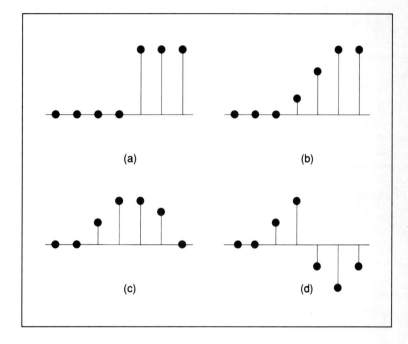

Finally, you work with the resulting array, taking note of peaks, steep slopes, and zero crossings, looking for edge-signaling combinations.

The averaging procedure transforms both perfect and noise-corrupted steps into smoothed steps. The first differencing procedure transforms smoothed steps into bumps; the second differencing procedure transforms bumps into curves that cross zero steeply between positive and negative peaks.

Figure 27.2 shows what these procedures do to a step. The step shown in figure 27.2(a) becomes a smoothed step in 27.2(b), a bump in 27.2(c), and a two-bump curve in 27.2(d).

Somewhat miraculously, the effect of first averaging and then differencing can be combined into one grand averaging procedure. As shown by the following formula, the contribution of each input point, I_j, to an output point O_i varies according to the separation between the input point and the output point. P is the function that expresses how the contribution depends on the separation:

$$O_i = \sum_j P_{j-i} \times I_j.$$

The function P is called a **point-spread function** because it shows how a single isolated nonzero brightness point would spread out its influence in an output image. When outputs are determined from inputs according to this formula, the output is said to be **convolved** by the point-spread function.

Figure 27.3 The first and second differences of an averaging point-spread function. Part (a) shows the averaging function. Part (b) shows the averaged neighboring differences of the point-spread function of part (a); it is also the point-spread function equivalent to averaging followed by the averaging of neighboring differences. Part (c) shows the averaged neighboring differences of the averaged first differences; using the function in part (c) as the point-spread function is equivalent to averaging followed by two differencing steps.

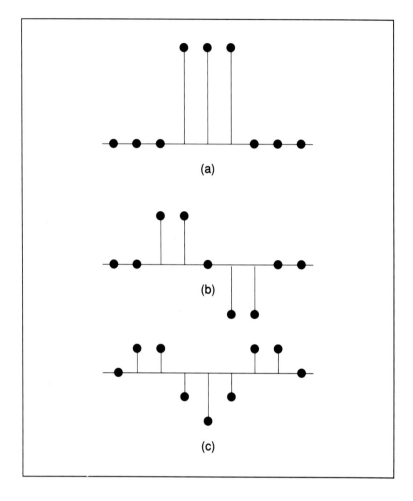

Figure 27.3(a) shows the point-spread function equivalent to three-point, one-dimensional averaging. Figure 27.3(b) shows the point-spread function equivalent to averaging followed by averaging neighboring differences. Figure 27.3(c) shows the point-spread function equivalent to averaging followed by two rounds of averaging neighboring differences.

Of course, the point-spread functions used with real images must combine the influence of many more than seven points. Moreover, they must be two dimensional, not one dimensional. Nevertheless, there are reasonable computational arguments indicating that the peak-and-trough shape of a narrow, two-dimensional point-spread function based on averaging and differencing is essentially correct and is particularly convenient. Here is a synopsis of those computational arguments:

■ Noise should be confronted by convolution with a point-spread function that attenuates high frequencies.

■ A two-dimensional version of the bell-shaped Gaussian function, described in Chapter 24, is a particularly good choice for a point-spread function.

■ Edges should be localized by two rounds of differencing. The noise reduction of the Gaussian convolution cancels the noise enhancement of the differencing procedures.

■ Two-dimensional Gaussian convolution followed by two rounds of two-dimensional differencing is equivalent to convolving with a single point-spread function that looks rather like a Mexican hat, or sombrero. The sombrero shape is a two-dimensional analog to the peak-and-trough shape you have seen in one dimension.

■ The two-dimensional Mexican-hat-shaped point-spread function is approximated closely by the difference between a narrow positive Gaussian point-spread function and a wide negative Gaussian point-spread function.

■ Convolution with two-dimensional Gaussian point-spread functions is equivalent to sequential convolution with two one-dimensional Gaussian point-spread functions, one vertical and the other horizontal. Thus, two-dimensional Gaussian convolution can be made fast. Therefore, sombrero convolution can be fast too.

Multiple-Scale Stereo Enables Distance Determination

Stereo vision uses information from two eyes to determine distance. Stereo vision works because it is easy to find the distance to a visual feature once the feature is found in two images received from two eyes with known separation from each other.

In figure 27.4, you see an image point, two lenses, and two image planes from above. The axes of the lenses are parallel. Both lenses are separated from the image planes by their focal length f, and they are separated from each other by a baseline distance b. The point P is at a distance l from the left lens axis and r from the right. Similarly, P appears on the left image at a distance α from the left lens axis, and in the right image at a distance β from the right lens axis.

An easy way to find the formula relating object distance, d, to α and β is to write two equations derived from similar triangles:

$$\frac{d}{l} = \frac{d+f}{l+\alpha} \qquad \frac{d}{r} = \frac{d+f}{r+\beta}.$$

These equations, with $b = l + r$, are easy to solve, giving the following expression for d:

$$d = \frac{fb}{\alpha + \beta}.$$

Thus, distance to a point is inversely proportional to $\alpha + \beta$, the sum of the shift of the point's position in the two images. This sum is called **disparity**.

Figure 27.4 The geometry of the two eyes involved in stereo vision. The distance to the object is determined by the observed disparity.

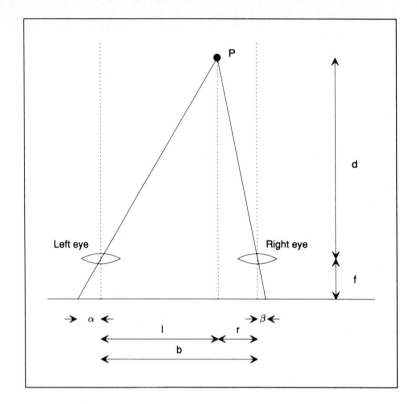

Of course, the real problem in stereo vision is to find corresponding features in the left and right images so that disparity can be measured. There are many different stereo-vision systems that find corresponding features with varying success. To understand them, you must answer several questions:

- With what visual features does the stereo-vision system work?
- How does the system match the visual features in one image with the correct corresponding entities in the other?
- How does the system cope with ambiguous situations in which many equally plausible matches are possible?

As an illustration, you are about to learn about a stereo-vision procedure that focuses on the **zero crossings** in *sombrero-convolved images*. The procedure is based on three assumptions: first, that it is good to work with features that are easy to identify in both images of a stereo pair; second, that it is good to work with features that are easy to localize with good accuracy; and third, that steep zero crossings are easy to identify and to localize.

To see how the procedure works, you should examine figure 27.5, which shows the zero crossings in a narrow horizontal slice of two superimposed sombrero-convolved images. Zero crossings from the right image are shown

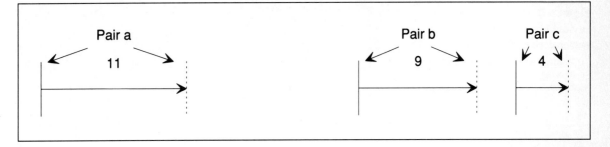

Figure 27.5

Matching with a simple stereo-matching procedure for zero crossings. The zero crossings in a slice are considered matched if they are nearest other-image neighbors.

solid; those from the left image are shown dashed. In the slice, you identify the closest dashed zero-crossing fragment for each solid zero-crossing fragment, and vice versa. Thus, for each image, you find each zero crossing's nearest neighbor in the other image. Two zero crossings are considered matched if they are each other's nearest other-image neighbors and if they are closer than some specified distance from each other. Other zero crossings are ignored.

This discussion is captured in the following procedure. The width, w, involved is the width of the sombrero function's central peak, measured from zero crossing to zero crossing:

To determine initial correspondence,

▷ Find zero crossings using a width w sombrero function.

▷ Divide the image into horizontal slices.

▷ For each horizontal slice in the sombrero-convolved image,

    ▷ Find the nearest neighbors for each zero-crossing fragment in the left image.

    ▷ Find the nearest neighbors for each zero-crossing fragment in the right image.

    ▷ For each pair of zero-crossing fragments that are the closest neighbors of each other, let the right fragment be separated by δ_{initial} from the left. Determine whether δ_{initial} is within a matching tolerance, m. If so, consider the zero-crossing fragments matched with disparity δ_{initial}.

In the example, all pairs match, fortuitously. In general, however, there will be ambiguity and mismatch, for if the width, w, is small enough to give good resolution, there will be too much detail to match well.

To see why a large width eases matching, you should take off your glasses, if you wear them. All the fainter details blur out. Convolution with a wide sombrero function has the same effect. Convolved versions of an arrangement of blocks are shown in figure 27.6. The wider the function is, the more the image is blurred.

Figure 27.6 Images produced
by sombrero convolution using
sombrero functions ranging
from wide to narrow. Courtesy
of W. Eric L. Grimson.

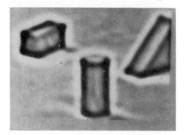

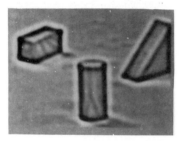

As the sombrero function gets wider, the blurring increases, and the number of zero crossings decreases, as shown in figure 27.7. With fewer zero crossings, the number of accidental mismatches is reduced.

Of course, a large sombrero width also gets rid of just the detail needed to make distance judgments precise. But you can burn this particular candle at both ends by working with more than one sombrero function.

Figure 27.8 shows how. Assume that a wide sombrero function, with width w, produces the zero crossings at the top. Pair a matches with a disparity of 11; pair b matches with a disparity of 9; and pair c matches with a disparity of 4.

Figure 27.7 Drawings
produced by sombrero
convolution. Shown are the
zero crossings found using
sombrero functions ranging
from wide to narrow. Courtesy
of W. Eric L. Grimson.

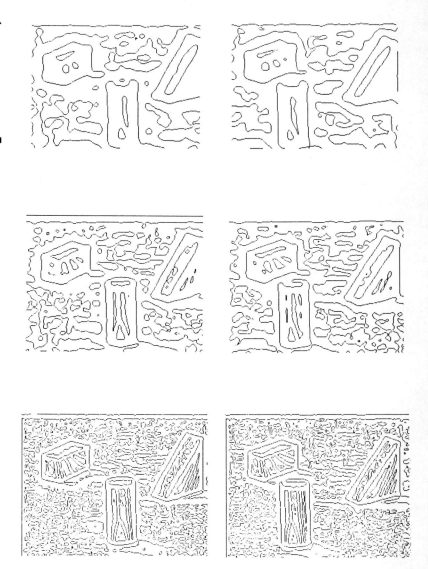

Figure 27.7 Drawings produced by sombrero convolution. Shown are the zero crossings found using sombrero functions ranging from wide to narrow. Courtesy of W. Eric L. Grimson.

Assume that a narrower sombrero function, with width $w/2$, produces the zero crossings in the middle. Because the width is different, the zero crossings are in slightly different places. Note that the dotted line of pair b is equally close to two solid lines, suggesting difficulty.

Now comes the key step. Before matching the width $\frac{w}{2}$ zero crossings, you shift the right-eye, solid-line zero crossings by the disparity obtained at width w. This shifting gives you the zero crossings at the bottom. The shifting places the right-eye, solid-line zero crossings close to the left-eye, dotted-line zero crossings, making matching easy. The final disparities are judged to be 10, 8, and 5.

In summary, here is the procedure for establishing final correspondence; it is a slightly altered version of the previously exhibited procedure for finding initial correspondence:

To determine final correspondence,

▷ Find zero crossings using a sombrero function of reduced width, $\frac{w}{2}$, rather than w.

▷ For each horizontal slice,

    ▷ For each zero-crossing fragment in the left image,

        ▷ Determine the nearest zero-crossing fragment that matched when the sombrero function width was w.

        ▷ Offset the zero-crossing fragment by a distance equal to δ_{initial}, the disparity of the nearest matching zero-crossing fragment found at the lower resolution associated with function width w.

    ▷ Find the nearest neighbors for each zero-crossing fragment in the left image.

    ▷ Find the nearest neighbors for each zero-crossing fragment in the right image.

    ▷ For each pair of zero-crossing fragments that are the closest neighbors of each other, let the right fragment be separated by δ_{new} from the left. Determine whether δ_{new} is within the *reduced* matching tolerance, $\frac{m}{2}$. If so, consider the zero-crossing fragments matched with disparity $\delta_{\text{final}} = \delta_{\text{new}} + \delta_{\text{initial}}$.

Figure 27.8 shows how the procedure works. The zero-crossing fragments from a wide filter match, producing initial disparity estimates of 11, 9, and 4. Using these disparities, you offset the narrow-filter, solid-line fragments, bringing them into close proximity with the dashed-line fragments. Without the offset, one of the narrow-filter, dashed-line fragments would be equally close to two solid-line fragments.

If necessary, you can repeat the match–offset–match cycle many times to zero in on a precise disparity judgment. Generally, however, three or four cycles are sufficient.

Thus, a key idea is to use results on intentionally blurred images to guide work on less blurred images. Sometimes, the idea is called **multiple-scale image analysis**.

COMPUTING SURFACE DIRECTION

In this section, you learn about a procedure that computes surface-direction information from shading. First, however, you learn how surface direction—

Stereo Analysis Determines Elevations from Satellite Images

A system build by the ISTAR company, of Sophia Antpolis, France, determines elevations using a multiple-scale, sombrero-convolution procedure that is similar to the one described in this chapter. The ISTAR system uses image pairs—like the following—produced by the French SPOT satellite.

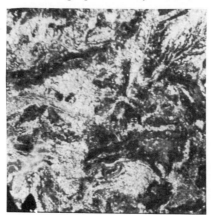 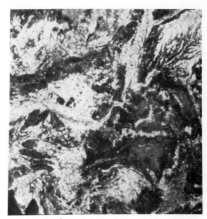

Treating such pairs as stereo images, the ISTAR system convolves, matches, computes disparity, determines distance, and translates distance into a **digital elevation model** that contains an elevation value for every 16 square meters of observed land. The root-mean-square accuracy of the elevation values is 2.5 meters.

The digital elevation model contains the data necessary for making ordinary contour maps. Alternatively, ISTAR can use the data to construct artificial terrain images. To make the following image of a mountain scene in the French Alps, ISTAR used elevation values from the digital elevation model and intensity values from the original satellite images.

Photographs courtesy of ISTAR.

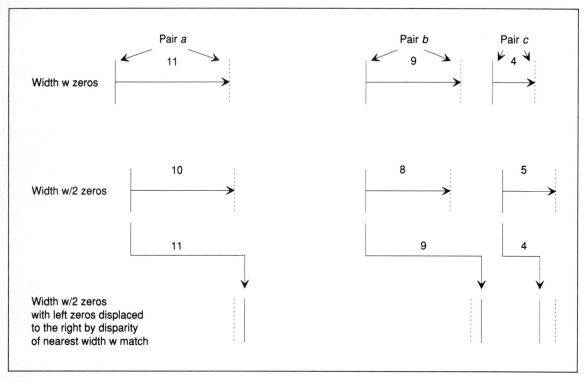

Figure 27.8

Matching with a simple stereo-matching procedure for zero crossings. Initial disparity estimates are made using a wide function. The initial estimates are used to offset the estimates made using a narrow function. Offset narrow-function lines are easy to match.

relative to the viewer and the light source—constrains the brightness of the surface.

Reflectance Maps Embody Illumination Constraints

The amount of light you see reflected from a surface obviously depends on the material covering the surface. In addition, the amount of light you see depends on the various angles shown in figure 27.9: the **emergent** angle e between the surface normal and the viewer direction, the **incident** angle i between the surface normal and the light-source direction, and the **phase** angle g between the viewer direction and the light-source direction.

A **Lambertian surface** is a surface that looks equally bright from all possible viewpoints. The observed brightness depends on only the direction to the light source. The dependence is governed by the following formula, in which E is the observed brightness; ρ is the surface **albedo**, a constant for any particular surface material; and i is the incident angle:

$$E = \rho \cos i.$$

In ordinary English, Lambertian surfaces are those that you would call **matte** or **nonspecular**. Lambertian surfaces are also called **perfect diffusers**.

For some surfaces—that of the earth's moon, for example—the observed brightness varies not as $\cos i$, but as the ratio of $\cos i$ and $\cos e$.

Figure 27.9 This illustration shows a surface-centered view of the relative positions of the viewer and the light source and the relative orientation of the surface. The angles are *e* between the surface normal and the viewer; *i* between the surface normal and the light source; and *g* between the viewer and the light source. For many surfaces, observed brightness is proportional to the cosine of *i* and independent of *e* and *g*.

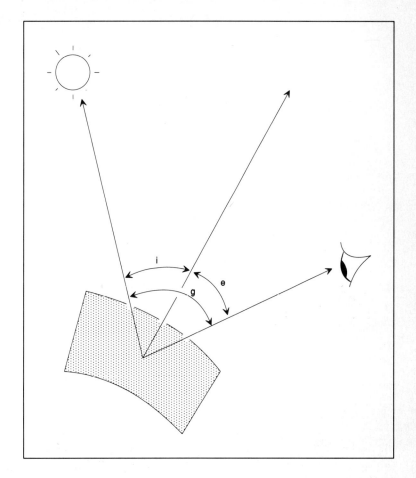

When the moon is full—that is, when the sun is behind the earth—$g = 0$ and $i = e$ for every point. Consequently, $\cos i/\cos e$ is a constant, the observed brightness is constant, there is no dimming at the edges, and the moon looks peculiarly flat.

Most surfaces, however, are more like Lambertian surfaces than they are like the moon. To develop a feel for how Lambertian surfaces reflect light, you could paint a sphere with Lambertian paint and observe this Lambertian sphere as a single-point light source is moved around it. For each light-source position, you could keep notes on the dependence of the brightness on the direction of the surface normal. An easy way to keep these notes is to draw some **isobrightness lines**—lines along which the brightness has a constant value.

Figure 27.10 shows the isobrightness lines for three different light-source directions. On the left light is coming from directly behind the viewer, and the isobrightness lines are concentric circles. The brightest point, with a brightness ρ, is the one for which the surface normal points

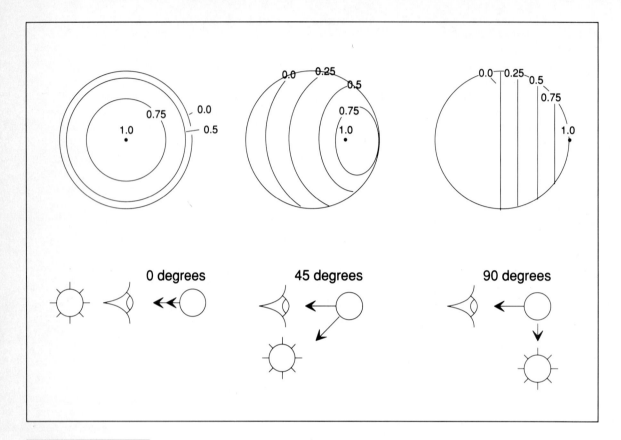

Figure 27.10

Isobrightness lines on
images of Lambertian
spheres illuminated
from three different
directions.

directly at the viewer, because there cos $i = 1$. Brightness shades off toward the sphere's boundary, becoming 0 at the boundary, because cos $i = 0$ at the boundary.

In the middle, however, the circumstances are different because the light-source direction is different. The viewer direction and the light-source direction are now separated by 45°, rather than by 0°. Again, the brightest point has a brightness ρ, but now it is no longer the point for which the surface normal points toward the viewer. As always for Lambertian surfaces, the brightest point is the one for which the surface normal points toward the light source. Note that the line where the brightness is 0, although a circle on the sphere, is not part of a circle in the two-dimensional image of the sphere. The line where the brightness is 0 is sometimes called the **shadow line** or the **terminator**, particularly when we are talking about the earth's moon.

Finally, on the right in figure 27.10, the light is coming in from the right, with the viewer direction and the light-source direction forming a right angle. Now, the brightest point is on the edge of the sphere and the shadow line is straight as seen by the viewer.

The spheres of figure 27.10 are not used in practice to keep track of the relation between surface orientation and brightness. Instead, the iso-brightness lines are projected onto a flat surface, just as they are when someone makes a map of the earth. Projected isobrightness lines are called **reflectance maps**. There are many ways to make reflectance maps because there are many ways to project lines from a sphere to a plane, as you learn from cartographers, who are the custodians of this sort of knowledge.

One especially useful projection takes points on a unit sphere to points on a tangent plane where the coordinate axes are labeled F and G. The projection is done, as shown in figure 27.11, by drawing a straight line from the point on the sphere opposite the viewer, through the point to be projected, to the tangent FG plane. By convention, the FG plane is parallel to the viewer's image plane. Figure 27.11(a) shows what the isobrightness lines of figure 27.11(b) look like when projected onto the FG plane to form FG reflectance maps.

In some circumstances, it is more convenient to use a projection called the PQ projection. Instead of projecting onto a tangent plane from the point on the sphere opposite the viewer, you project onto the plane from the center of the unit sphere, as shown in figure 27.12(a). The location of the PQ plane is the same as for the FG projection; only the projecting point has changed. The isobrightness lines in PQ space extend to infinity, as shown in figure 27.12(b).

Making Synthetic Images Requires a Reflectance Map

Given values for f and g for every point in an image, it is easy to determine the proper brightness at every point using an appropriate FG reflectance map. Consequently, it is easy to synthesize artificial images of what the earth looks like from satellites. All that is required is f and g for every point in the synthetic image and an FG reflectance map corresponding to the desired position for the sun. Determining f and g is straightforward, for f and g can be derived from elevation data.

Creating an FG reflectance map is also straightforward, for you can start out assuming that the earth is covered with Lambertian paint. Figure 27.13 shows two synthetic images for a portion of the Rhone river valley lying in southwestern Switzerland. Note that one corresponds to morning light; the other corresponds to afternoon light.

Surface Shading Determines Surface Direction

So far, you have seen how to use surface direction to predict surface bright-ness. Now, let us go the other way, computing surface direction parameters f and g from perceived brightness.

At first, recovering surface direction by recovering f and g might seem impossible, for the brightness of a small piece of surface determines only a curve in FG space, rather than a single point. In fact, recovery is pos-sible, but only because surfaces vary smoothly for the most part; there

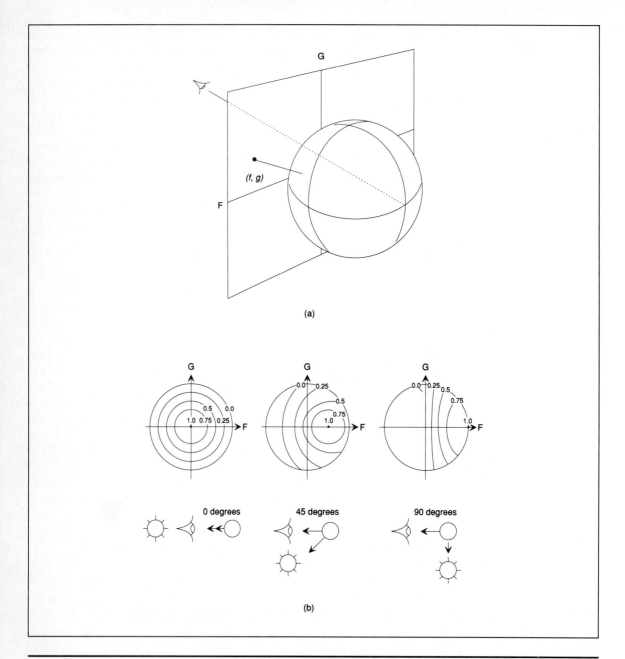

(a)

(b)

Figure 27.11 In part (a), points relating surface direction to observed brightness are projected from the surface of a sphere to the *FG* plane tangent to the sphere and parallel to the image plane. In part (b), isobrightness lines are shown on the *FG* plane for three viewer–light-source combinations. Interestingly, the isobrightness lines are circles and arcs of circles because circles on the unit sphere always map into circles on the *FG* plane.

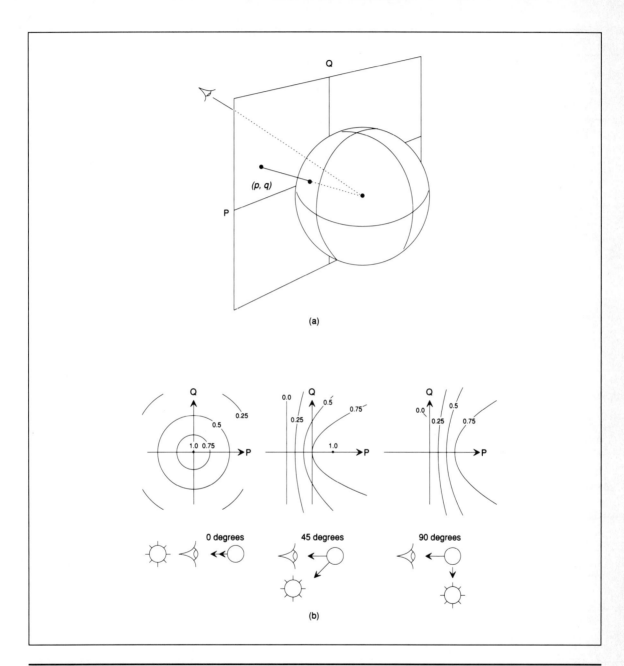

Figure 27.12 In part (a), points relating surface direction to observed brightness are projected from the surface of a sphere to the *PQ* plane tangent to the sphere and parallel to the image plane. In part (b), isobrightness lines are shown on the *PQ* plane for three viewer–light-source combinations. In the *PQ* projection, in contrast to the *FG* projection, the isobrightness lines extend to infinity.

Figure 27.13 Two synthetic images for the same terrain. One corresponds to morning light; the other corresponds to afternoon light. Courtesy of Berthold K. P. Horn.

are few discontinuities in depth or direction. Consequently, there are two constraints to exploit, rather than just one:

- **Brightness:** The surface direction, pinned down by f and g, should not vary much from what the brightness of the surface demands.
- **Surface smoothness:** The surface direction at one point should not vary much from the surface direction at neighboring points.

Each point's calculated f and g values should be some compromise between the values suggested by each of the two constraints. In figure 27.13, brightness suggests that the f and g values of a particular point should lie on the isobrightness line shown. Meanwhile, smoothness suggests that the f and g values should lie near the average of the values at neighboring points.

Intuitively, it makes sense to pick a point somewhere between the average point and the isobrightness line. Two questions remain, however. First, exactly where is somewhere? Second, how do you happen to know the correct values for the neighbors? Here are two reasonable answers:

- Compromise at some point on a line that passes through the average point and that is perpendicular to the isobrightness line.
- Start by assuming that all points with unknown f and g have $f = 0$ and $g = 0$. Find new values for each point by compromising between the average point of the initial values and the isobrightness line. Repeat, using updated values, until f and g values stop changing by more than a specified threshold.

Thus, f and g can be found by relaxation, starting with some assumptions that disappear into oblivion after a few steps. You need some values for

f and g to anchor the process, however. Happily, there usually are some such points. On the occluding boundaries of objects without sharp edges, surface direction is perpendicular to the viewer's line of sight. All such directions project onto a circle of radius 2 in FG space. The exact point on the circle is such that the circle's direction in FG space and the occluding boundary's direction in the image are the same.

To verify that all these assertions make sense, you need to use a little worthwhile—but optional—calculus. Consider two error measures, one capturing departures from smoothness, e_1, and the other capturing departures from predicted brightness, e_2:

$$e_1 = \sum_i \sum_j (f_{i,j} - \bar{f}_{i,j})^2 + (g_{i,j} - \bar{g}_{i,j})^2,$$

$$e_2 = \sum_i \sum_j (E_{i,j} - R(f_{i,j}, g_{i,j}))^2,$$

where

$$\bar{f}_{i,j} = \tfrac{1}{4}(f_{i+1,j} + f_{i,j+1} + f_{i-1,j} + f_{i,j-1}),$$
$$\bar{g}_{i,j} = \tfrac{1}{4}(g_{i+1,j} + g_{i,j+1} + g_{i-1,j} + g_{i,j-1}).$$

The total error is then $e = e_1 + \lambda e_2$, where λ is a constant chosen to put into reasonable balance the two kinds of error. To find values for $f_{i,j}$ and $g_{i,j}$ that minimize the total error, you differentiate with respect to $f_{i,j}$ and $g_{i,j}$, setting the results to zero, producing the following equations:

$$f_{i,j} = \bar{f}_{i,j} + \lambda(E_{i,j} - R(f_{i,j}, g_{i,j}))\left(\frac{\partial R}{\partial f_{i,j}}\right),$$

$$g_{i,j} = \bar{g}_{i,j} + \lambda(E_{i,j} - R(f_{i,j}, g_{i,j}))\left(\frac{\partial R}{\partial g_{i,j}}\right).$$

Set up this way, these equations suggest solution by way of rules relating the values of f and g on the $(n+1)$th iteration, $f_{i,j}^{n+1}$ and $g_{i,j}^{n+1}$, to the values on the nth iteration, $f_{i,j}^n$ and $g_{i,j}^n$:

$$f_{i,j}^{n+1} = \bar{f}_{i,j}^n + \lambda(E_{i,j} - R(f_{i,j}^n, g_{i,j}^n))\left(\frac{\partial R}{\partial f_{i,j}}\right)^n,$$

$$g_{i,j}^{n+1} = \bar{g}_{i,j}^n + \lambda(E_{i,j} - R(f_{i,j}^n, g_{i,j}^n))\left(\frac{\partial R}{\partial g_{i,j}}\right)^n,$$

where $f_{i,j}^0 = 0$ and $g_{i,j}^0 = 0$.

These rules are called **relaxation formulas**. Using these relaxation formulas amounts to improving f and g estimates by taking a step from the previous estimate toward the isobrightness line along a perpendicular to that isobrightness line. The size of the step is proportional to the difference between the observed brightness and that predicted by the current f and g values. The size is also proportional to the error-balancing parameter, λ.

Figure 27.14 A vase and
the surface computed from
it using relaxation. The vase
was designed by the Finnish
architect Alvar Aalto. Courtesy
of Katsushi Ikeuchi.

Procedures using such relaxation formulas are often called **relaxation
procedures**. Sometimes, they are called **cooperative procedures** because they reach for compromises influenced by all the available constraints.

To calculate surface direction using relaxation,

▷ Call the input array the current array. For all nonbound-
ary points, let $f = 0$ and $g = 0$. For all boundary points,
let f and g define a vector of length 2 normal to the boundary.

▷ Until all values are changing sufficiently slowly,

   ▷ For each point in the current array,

      ▷ If the point is a boundary point, do nothing.

      ▷ If the point is a nonboundary point, compute a new
        value for f and g using the relaxation formulas.

   ▷ Call the new array the current array.

Figure 27.14 shows a sample image and the corresponding result.

SUMMARY

■   Much vision research explores the constraints that the world imposes
    on images. Work on binocular stereo and on extracting shape from
    shading are representative successes.

■   A sombrero function combines smoothing and differencing. A sombrero
    function is one mechanism for highlighting edges.

- Stereo vision depends on matching features in one image with features in another. Multiple-scale matching of the zero crossings in sombrero-convolved images is one method.
- You can recover surface direction from shading by compromising between smoothness and brightness constraints.

BACKGROUND

Hans P. Morevec first brought the idea of multiple-scales analysis to stereo [1977]. The first proposal to use zero crossings in stereo was by Marr and Tomaso Poggio [1979]. Their stress on the use of zero crossings was amplified in the work of Ellen C. Hildreth on edge detection [1980].

The stereo correspondence procedure introduced in this chapter is based on that of W. Eric L. Grimson. See Grimson's book *From Images to Surfaces* [1981] for details. Grimson's book also covers his procedure for surface reconstruction between points of known depth. Building on Grimson's results, Demetri Terzopoulos subsequently introduced an improved surface reconstruction procedure that handles discontinuities more accurately, works faster, and allows multiple sources of depth and orientation data [1983].

The ideas of zero crossings and of multiple scales are important in many aspects of vision. One example is the work of Brady on reading printed text [1981]. Another is the work of Andy Witkin on analyzing signals such as those involved in oil-well data logging [1983].

Berthold K. P. Horn is responsible for understanding of the relation between shape and shading [1970, 1984, 1989]. Horn also introduced the needle diagram for surface representation [1982].

There are now several textbooks on vision. *Robot Vision* [1984], by Horn, takes readers on several adventures in applied mathematics, explained beautifully.

28

Expressing Language Constraints

In this chapter, you learn that the goal of most linguists is to understand the constraints that determine how language is generated and understood.

You also learn that linguists often express constraints using trees that show how the words of a sentence fit together. You learn that the trees can be built out of components that are instances of the *X-bar schema*, and that the X-bar schema makes it relatively easy to express various sorts of grammatical constraints, including constraints involving *case marking* and *wh— questions*. In the course of this discussion, you learn what linguists mean when they use words such as *government*, *movement*, *trace*, and *subjacency*.

You also learn that reversing a language-generation procedure is not necessarily the right way to build a language-understanding procedure.

Once you have finished this chapter, you will understand the distinction between *linguistic competence* and *linguistic performance*, and you will understand that linguists work toward an understanding of constraints on human languages, and do not necessarily work toward a model of either language generation or language understanding.

THE SEARCH FOR AN ECONOMICAL THEORY

Linguists, like other scientists, hope for explanations that are simple and concise, yet comprehensive. They have little enthusiasm for explanations limited to simple sentences, for such explanations are too narrow. Similarly, an explanation consisting of multivolume, unrelated discussions of 100 distinct sentence types for each natural language would be too complex, although conceivably it might be comprehensive.

The desire to explain language is ancient. Progress has been slow, however; even today, after centuries of thought, a complete understanding of language seems a long way off. Nevertheless, the rate of progress has accelerated during the recent past, and unifying principles are emerging, as you learn in the rest of this section.

You Cannot Say That

The following sentences are all marked with an asterisk, honoring a standard convention, to signal that they sound strange to native English speakers:

* *She return her book.*
* *Her returned her book.*

Challenged, a native English speaker, equipped with the vocabulary of the English classroom, would say that each of the marked sentences are *unacceptable*. Such sentences are grist for the linguistic mill. A linguist, using the vocabulary of the seminar room, would say that each of the marked sentences violates a well-known linguistic constraint. In the first sentence, the subject fails to agree with the verb. In the second, the wrong type of pronoun appears.

To formulate linguistic constraints, linguists often use sentence pairs in which one sentence sounds natural, but the other is a near miss. The following illustrate:

* *She return her book.*
She returned her book.
* *Her returned her book.*
She returned her book.

Naturally, unearthing the subtler constraints requires more sophisticated near-miss pairs. Often the more sophisticated pairs involve embedded sentences, as illustrated by the following sentences:

* *Would be nice her to return her book.*
It would be nice for her to return her book.

Phrases Crystallize on Words

In elementary school, you doubtlessly learned that words fall into natural categories. *Nouns*, such as *Sarah* or *book*, are words that name things or categories. Many ordinary *verbs*, such as *return*, denote actions; others, such as *love*, establish relations. Eventually, you learned about most of the following categories, albeit differently labeled.

Category	Examples
Determiner	the, this, a
Adjective	big
Adverb	slowly
Noun	Sarah, book
Auxiliary verb	will, have
Verb	return, give
Preposition	to, in
Quantifier	all, every
Complementizer	that, which
Pronoun	she, him, their

Your grammar book also noted that the words in sentences naturally seem to form groups. Consider the following sentence, for example:

Sarah will return her book to the library in the afternoon.

Several prominent word groups denote objects. The first is the one-word group, *Sarah.* The rest are *her book, the library,* and *the afternoon.* Each group contains a noun; in three of the four groups, a determiner accompanies the noun. All four groups are called **noun phrases**.

Prepositions precede two of the four noun phrases, combining with those two noun phrases to form two **prepositional phrases**—namely, *to the library* and *in the afternoon.*

Noun phrases and prepositional phrases are so named because noun phrases crystallize on nouns and prepositional phrases crystallize on prepositions. At the next level, there is another crystallization in which a verb phrase, consisting of the words *return her book to the library in the afternoon,* crystallizes around the verb, *return.* Thus, each of the three phrase types crystallizes around a word belonging to the category for which the phrase is named.

Graphically, trees prove handy whenever you want to describe how the parts of a phrase fit together. In figure 28.1, for example, you see one way to describe the verb phrase *return her book to the library in the afternoon,* along with all its embedded phrases.

Many linguists argue against the sentence tree shown in figure 28.1, however, because it fails to expose properties that are believed by those linguists to be shared among all types of phrases. One proposed alternative is the richer structure shown in figure 28.2 as a better alternative. Instead of just one kind of verb phrase node, there are now three. At the top, you have the node labeled VP, for <u>v</u>erb <u>p</u>hrase, the one whose ultimate descendants are all and only the words that constitute the entire verb phrase. This node is often called the verb's **maximal projection**.

At the bottom, you have the node labeled V, often called the verb phrase's **head node** or *head.* This node's only descendant is the word around which the verb phrase crystallizes.

Figure 28.1 One way to draw the structure of a verb phrase. The triangles, by standard convention, link nodes to word groups whose internal structure is not shown.

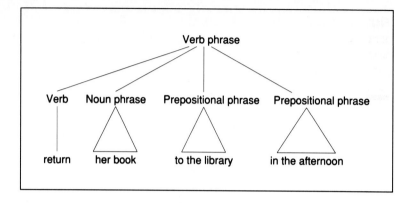

Figure 28.2 A verb phrase represented as a binary sentence tree. The node labeled VP is called the verb's maximal projection. Intermediate nodes are $\overline{V}$ nodes.

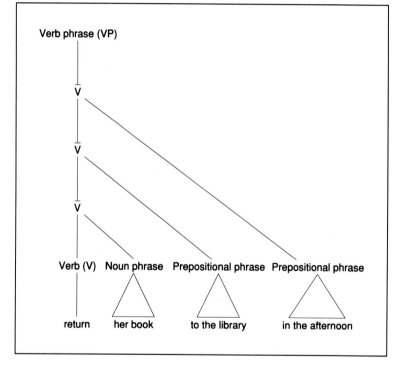

In between is a series of nodes, each of which is labeled $\overline{V}$ (and pronounced *v-bar*). Each $\overline{V}$ node connects exactly one noun phrase or prepositional phrase to the main line between the head node, V, and the verb's maximal projection, the VP node. Thus, the sentence tree is a binary tree in which no node has more than two branches.

Replacement Examples Support Binary Representation

The **binary-tree hypothesis** states that a binary tree is the best kind of tree for representing sentence structure at all levels. One argument

Figure 28.3 Prepositional phrases also have maximal projection nodes, the PP nodes, and intermediate nodes, the $\overline{P}$ nodes.

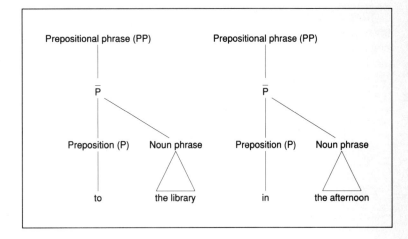

favoring the binary-tree hypothesis centers on sentence combinations such as the following:

Sarah will return her book to the library in the afternoon.
Dana will do so to the store in the morning.
Emily will do so in the morning.
Katlin will do so too.

Using the binary-tree way of describing the sentence structure, you can say that the words *do so* can replace the words under any $\overline{V}$ node or the VP node. Using the more primitive sentence tree shown in figure 28.1, with four branches under the verb phrase node, you would have to say, more awkwardly, that *do so* can replace certain subsets of the verb phrase's direct descendants, but then you would have to explain which subsets. Thus, the *binary branching hypothesis* enables a simpler, more elegant explanation.

Many Phrase Types Have the Same Structure

Forgetting about particular sentences, look at figure 28.2, which shows the structure of verb phrases in general: one VP node at the top, any number of intermediate $\overline{V}$ connectors, and one V node at the bottom connected to a verb.

Interestingly, most prepositional phrases exhibit the same structure: a maximal projection node at the top, an intermediate connector tying in a phrase from the right, and a head node at the bottom connected to a word.

Figure 28.3 shows how the prepositional phrases in *Sarah will return her book to the library in the afternoon* can be drawn so as to conform to the same pattern developed for the verb phrase. Each head node is connected to a preposition, and each $\overline{P}$ node is connected to a noun phrase on the right.

At first, you might think that noun phrases have a different structure: in the sample sentence, the noun phrases have nothing to the right of

Figure 28.4 A noun phrase, like verb phrases and prepositional phrases, has a maximal projection node, the NP node, intermediate nodes, the N̄ nodes, and head nodes, the N.

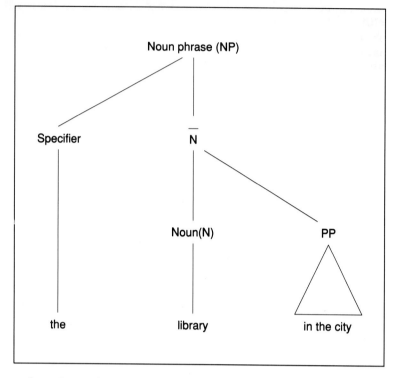

the noun, but three of the four have something to the left—either the determiner *the* or the possessive pronoun *her.* For the structure of noun phrases to look like the structure of prepositional phrases and verb phrases, noun phrases with branches to the right should exist, and, correspondingly, verb phrases and prepositional phrases with branches to the left should exist.

Interestingly, such phrases do exist. Consider, for example, the following noun phrase:

Sarah will return her book to the library in the city.

In this sentence, *in the city* says something about the location of the library. Accordingly, *in the city* demands to be viewed as part of the noun phrase centered on the word *library.* Adhering as much as possible to the pattern established earlier in the discussions of verb phrases and prepositional phrases, you can draw the noun phrase as shown in figure 28.4. Drawn this way, the only difference between a noun phrase and either a verb phrase or a prepositional phrase is the connection of a word coming in from the left at the NP level.

Words or phrases brought in from the right are called **complements**. A word or phrase brought in from the left is called a **specifier**.[†] Thus, *the*

[†]Actually, there are two kinds of sentence constituents that come in from the right

Figure 28.5 Prepositional phrases and verb phrases can have specifiers too.

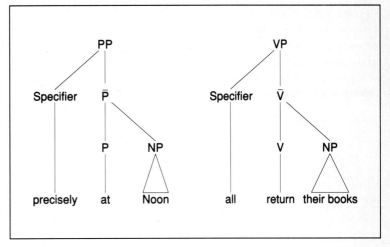

library in the city has both a specifier and a complement. Some other noun phrases, such as *Sarah*, have neither; some have one or the other, but not both.

Note that in some other languages, such as Japanese, words that function like English complements appear to the left of the head and words that function like English specifiers appear to the right.

Now it is time to reexamine verb phrases and prepositional phrases from the noun-phrase perspective, having examined noun phrases from the perspective established by verb phrases and prepositional phrases. The question is whether there can be analogs to the specifiers found in noun phrases; the answer is yes. To see why, consider the following sentence, for example:

Sarah will return her book precisely at noon.

The word *precisely* used this way leads to the structure shown on the left in figure 28.5. Thus, the word *precisely* provides an example of the relatively rare, but not impossible, appearance of a prepositional-phrase specifier.

Similarly, the following sentence contains an example of a relatively rare, but not impossible, appearance of a verb-phrase specifier:

The friends will all return their books.

To see why the word *all* seems to be part of the verb phrase, suppose you ask, *Who will return the books?* One sensible answer, in which *all* and the rest of the sentence are deleted, is as follows:

The friends will.

On the other hand, the following sentence, in which only the word *all* remains, sounds strange:

in English, namely *complements* and *adjuncts*. The distinction is still a matter of considerable debate. In the vocabulary of computation, complements are like required arguments and adjuncts are like optional arguments.

Figure 28.6 The X-bar schema. In English, specifiers enter from the left at the XP level, whereas complements enter from the right at $\overline{\text{X}}$ levels.

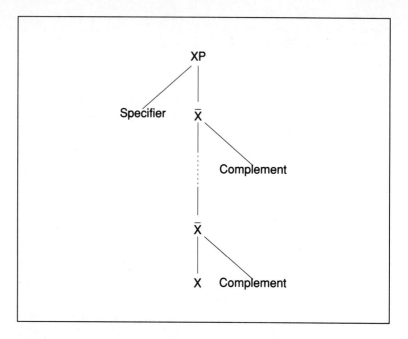

* *The friends will all.*

But then, the following sentences, in which the words *do so* replace part of the sentence, sound acceptable:

The friends will do so.
The friends will all do so.

Treating the quantifier word, *all*, as a verb-phrase specifier, as shown on the right in figure 28.5, you can explain the acceptability or unacceptability of these truncated sentences by the following:

- It is grammatically acceptable to *delete* the words under an entire VP node when answering a question.
- It is grammatically acceptable to *replace* all the words under a VP node or a $\overline{\text{V}}$ node by the words *do so* when answering a question.
- It is *not* grammatically acceptable to *delete* the words under one branch of a VP node, substituting no replacement, leaving the words under another branch stranded.

Thus, verb phrases, noun phrases, and prepositional phrases all conform to the general pattern shown in figure 28.6, although phrases do not need to exhibit all the possible elements. To use a more technical term, the phrases are all instances of the **X-bar schema**.

If you believe that all phrases are best represented as shown in figure 28.6, with a specifier joining the main line from one side and complements joining from the other, you are said to believe in **binary X-bar trees**, which are defined in the following specification:

A **binary X-bar tree** is a representation

That is a tree

In which

▷ There are three general types of nodes: X, $\overline{\text{X}}$, and XP.

▷ Each node has at most two branches.

▷ Leaves are words.

▷ In English, specifiers enter XP nodes from one side; complements enter $\overline{\text{X}}$ nodes from the other. The direction from which specifiers and complements enter is language specific.

▷ The kind of phrase that can serve as a specifier for a particular kind of XP or complement for a particular kind of $\overline{\text{X}}$ depends on the occupant of the head position, X.

The X-Bar Hypothesis Says that All Phrases Have the Same Structure

You may be wondering why you have learned about verb phrases, noun phrases, and prepositional phrases, but have not learned about phrases at a higher level. The reason is that you need the motivation provided by the uniformity of the other phrase types to see the binary structure in sentences, with specifiers on one side and complements on the other. Without that motivation, you would not be likely to conclude, for example, that the following sentences have the same structure:

Sarah will return her book.
Sarah returned her book.

If you are a believer in $\overline{\text{X}}$ theory, however, you may see both of these sentences as instances of an **inflection phrase**, usually abbreviated by IP. As shown in figure 28.7, both sentences are represented as trees under IP nodes. Straightforwardly, the specifiers are the noun phrase, *Sarah,* which sits in what you were taught in elementary school to call the subject position. The complements are the verb phrase, *return her book to the library.*

The difference is in the head position. In the first instance, the head position is occupied by the auxiliary verb *will.* In the second instance, the head position is occupied not by a word, but rather by a word suffix, *—ed.* Both serve to *inflect* the verb, thus supplying **tense** information that indicates when the return takes place. Inflecting a verb by preceding it with the word *will* signals the future; inflecting by adding an *—ed* ending signals the past.

When *will* inflects a verb, you can read the sentence right off the X-bar tree by reciting the words at the leaves in left-to-right order; when *—ed*

Figure 28.7 Simple sentences consist of inflection phrases. Like other phrases, inflection phrases fit the X-bar schema, with a noun-phrase specifier entering the IP node, a verb-phrase complement entering an Ī node, and a head node, I.

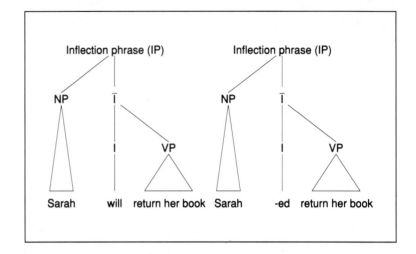

inflects the verb, however, you cannot read it off. Do not be concerned; just remember that the purpose of the X-bar tree is to facilitate the description of constraints, rather than to produce a sentence.

At this point, you might expect to be finished, but there is still one more phrase type that you should learn about. The reason is that you need a way to handle embedded, sentencelike groups, such as the following, in which the previous sentence appears as an embedded inflection phrase:

He said that Sarah will return her book.

Figure 28.8 shows how the embedded inflection phrase becomes part of a **complementizer phrase**, usually abbreviated by CP. The head of the complementizer phrase is the word *that*. The inflection phrase, *Sarah will return her book*, has become a complement of the complementizer phrase. In this example, the complementizer phrase has no specifier.

Some linguists like to have a CP node at the highest level of all sentences, even a simple one such as *Sarah will return her book*. The reason is that the empty specifier and head positions of such a CP node provide convenient landing sites when you want to move a word from one place in a sentence to another to turn the sentence into a question. Suppose, for example, that you analyze the following sentence pair:

Sarah will return her book.
Will Sarah return her book?

The first sentence could be diagramed as a straight inflection phrase, but a popular alternative is to treat it, as shown in figure 28.9, as an inflection phrase embedded in a complementizer phrase with empty specifier and head positions.

Then, a simple movement of the word *will* from the inflection phrase's head position to a landing site in the complementizer phrase's head position, as shown in figure 28.10, describes how the first, declarative sen-

Figure 28.8 A comple-
mentizer phrase. Like other
phrases, complementizer
phrases fit the X-bar schema,
but this one has no specifier.

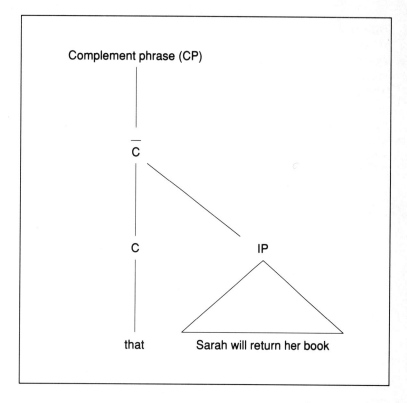

Figure 28.8 A comple-
mentizer phrase. Like other
phrases, complementizer
phrases fit the X-bar schema,
but this one has no specifier.

tence is related to the second, question sentence, *Will Sarah return her book?* Linguists call this particular kind of word movement **head-to-head movement**, and refer to the emptied position as the *trace position* of the moved word, or more simply as the **trace**.

In summary, you have seen a bit of the evidence that verb, prepositional, noun, inflection, and complementizer phrases all can be described by the same binary X-bar schema.

THE SEARCH FOR A UNIVERSAL THEORY

You are unlikely to be a passionate believer in the X-bar hypothesis at this point, given that you have not been exposed to much argument in its favor. You do know that all phrase types can be expressed uniformly using the same $\overline{X}$ schema, with specifiers arriving from one side and complements from the other. And uniformity in any theory lends a certain simple elegance to the theory.

Perhaps more convincingly, you also know that the X-bar schema, specialized to verb phrases, enables the simple expression of the replacement constraint: you can replace the words under a VP node or $\overline{V}$ node by a phrase such as *do so* only if the node has no siblings.

Figure 28.9 Sentences can be viewed as complementizer phrases, but most have empty specifier and head positions.

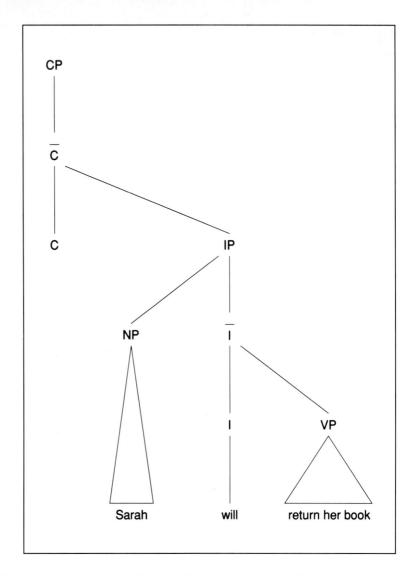

Be assured that you could spend the rest of your life reading papers expressing other constraints in terms of the X-bar schema. One implied claim in all those papers is that the X-bar schema is a good representation; as you learned in Chapter 2, a good representation makes important things explicit and helps you to expose natural constraints.

A Theory of Language Ought to Be a Theory of All Languages

Perhaps the most powerful argument in favor of any language theory is that it covers all human languages, no matter how far they may stand apart from the main stream.

Figure 28.10 An otherwise empty complementizer's head offers a convenient landing site for a moving word.

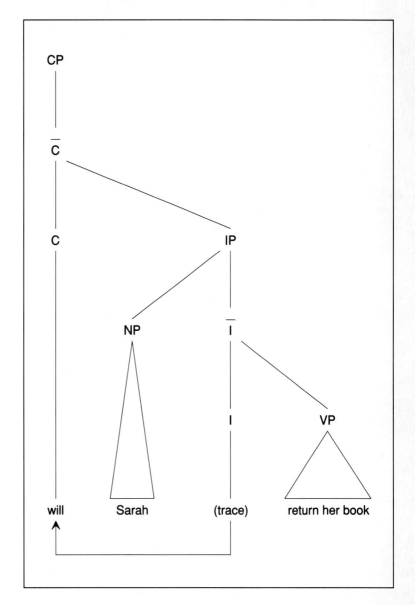

Such a claim is made for the X-bar hypothesis. To be sure, specifiers appear before the head, and complements appear after it, in languages such as English, whereas complements come first, and specifiers come last, in others. Otherwise, however, everything else is arguably the same: there are X nodes, $\overline{\text{X}}$ nodes, and maximal projection XP nodes, and everything crystallizes around the head nodes, the X.

When you learn a particular natural language, you need to learn how specifiers and complements are arrayed around the head, but for any particular kind of phrase, there are only two choices. It is as though you need to establish only which way a particular switch is set.

A Theory of Language Ought to Account for Rapid Language Acquisition

Many linguists think that much of language learning is a matter of establishing which way various switches are set. Everything else, they claim, is carried into each person genetically, thus constituting part of what has come to be called **universal grammar**.

This bias toward built-in knowledge is a consequence of the apparent complexity of language on one hand, and the rapidity with which children acquire it on the other. Much of human knowledge of language constraint must be built in, so the argument goes, for otherwise there would be no way for children to become so facile so fast.

The built-in-knowledge claim resonates with Martin's law, which you learned about in Chapter 16. There, you read that you cannot learn anything unless you almost know it already. Here, analogously, the claim is that you do not actually learn much about language; rather, much of what you need to know is already built in. Or, said another way, much of each individual's linguistic knowledge has been learned only in the sense that universal grammar has been developed through the long process of species evolution.

A Noun Phrase's Case Is Determined by Its Governor

Many linguists believe that the X-bar hypothesis offers the right perspective for determining what is in universal grammar, because it provides a relatively easy way to express constraints.

Constraints on a word's *case* illustrate how the X-bar hypothesis helps. In many languages, albeit not in English, the exact form taken on by a determiner, adjective, or noun varies considerably according to how the word fits into the sentence in which it appears. More precisely, the way a word fits into the sentence establishes the word's **case assignment**. The case assignment, in turn, determines the exact form of the word—a process called **case marking**.

If you have studied Latin, you know that there are seven alternative values for the case property. English is much simpler; it has only three alternatives for case, but only a few words actually exhibit overt case marking. Although sentences cast in older forms of English are richly endowed with case-determined variation, today's English sentences exhibit only dim hints of that variation, except for the use of pronouns, which vary according to case, as shown in the following table, which relates case to person and number:

Person	Number	Nominative	Accusative	Genitive
First	singular	I	me	my
Second	singular	you	you	your
Third	singular	he, she, it	him, her, it	his, her, its
First	plural	we	us	our
Second	plural	you	you	your
Third	plural	they	them	their

From the perspective of grammatical acceptability, you can freely substitute one pronoun for another, as long as both have the same case:

She gave me his book.
I gave them your book.

If you try to substitute one pronoun for another with a different case, however, the result is unacceptable:

She gave me his book.
* *Me gave his she book.*

Thus, pronouns provide a way of exploring how case assignment is constrained. Having done the necessary exploration, you might well choose to express the case-determining constraint in terms of X-bar schemas:

To determine a pronoun's case assignment,

▷ Move upward from the pronoun until you arrive at either an IP node for which the head has tense information, or at an NP node, a PP node, or a CP node.

  ▷ Announce that the pronoun is nominative if the head belongs to an IP node and carries tense information.

  ▷ Announce that the pronoun is accusative if the head is a preposition, verb, or complementizer.

  ▷ Announce that the pronoun is genitive if the head is a noun.

  ▷ Otherwise, the pronoun cannot be assigned case, and the sentence is unacceptable.

Thus, as shown in figure 28.11 for one of the examples, the head of the appropriate phrase determines the case of each pronoun. Casting this observation in technical language, you say that case is determined by the **governing head**, and **government** is a property determined by the structure of the X-bar tree.

Of course, just about any theory can account for the case marking of noun phrases in simple sentences. To test constraints more thoroughly, linguists employ much more complex sentences, typically with embedded

Figure 28.11 Pronoun case assignment is determined by the governing head.

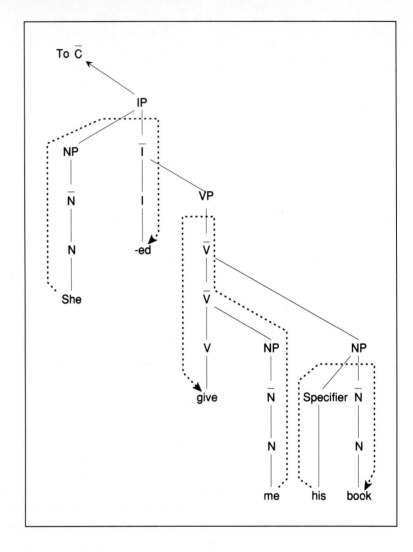

phrases. In general, the more convincingly a constraint accounts for the grammaticality—or lack of grammaticality—of the complex, as well as of the simple sentences, the more believable the constraint is.

The case-assignment constraint, for example, is more believable because it can account for the following sentences, neither of which sounds natural:

∗ *She to give me his book was nice.*
∗ *Her to give me his book was nice.*

As shown in figure 28.12, neither should sound natural because neither *she* in one sentence nor *her* in the other are correctly governed. In both sentences, the verb *give* appears in its infinitive form, which means that

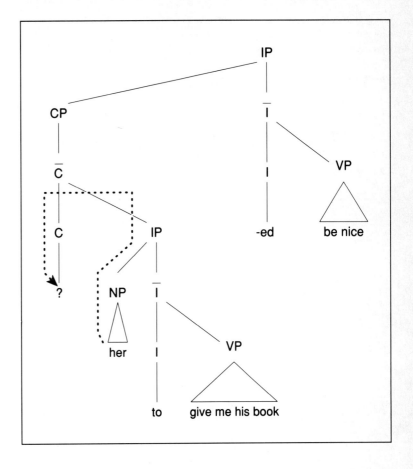

Figure 28.12 A situation in which a pronoun lacks a governor. Accordingly, there is no way to assign case, and the sentence is unacceptable.

there is no tense information. Accordingly, the inflection phrase's head lacks tense and therefore cannot serve as a governor. But the complement phrase has no head, so it also has nothing that can serve as a governor.

Note that you can fix one of the two sentences by inserting the complementizer *for*:

* *For she to give me his book was nice.*
For her to give me his book was nice.

Evidently, a complementizer can serve as a governing head for the specifier of an inflection phrase, as long as the inflection phrase's head does not carry tense information.

In summary, the X-bar schema makes it easy to express one kind of constraint on case assignment, and leads in turn to the introduction of the notion of government, a concept described naturally in terms of the X-bar schema. Note, however, that nothing in language seems simple for long. What the X-bar schema should look like and how government should be defined are matters subject to much refinement and debate. As soon as one linguist builds a wall around a theory with a collection of seemingly unassailable examples, another linguist penetrates the wall with even more unassailable examples.[†]

Subjacency Limits Wh- Movement

Linguists use the X-bar schema to express many constraints, in addition to case-assignment constraints. For a second example, let us turn to interrogative sentences that are formed by substituting a word such as *when* or *whom*—a so-called **wh— word**—for a noun phrase or a prepositional phrase.

Sarah will return the book to Alex in the afternoon.
Sarah will return the book to Alex when?
Sarah will return the book to whom in the afternoon?

You can not only form sentences by substituting a *wh—* word, as illustrated by the previous sentences, but also move the *wh—* word up front as illustrated by the following sentences:

Sarah will return the book to Alex when?
When will Sarah return the book to Alex?
Sarah will return the book to whom in the afternoon?
Whom will Sarah return the book to in the afternoon?

One hypothesis about these sentences, expressed in X-bar terms, is that you can move a *wh—* word to an empty specifier position in a higher-level complement phrase. The *wh—* word starts out on a level lower than that of its landing site in the X-bar tree, but not directly under its landing site. Thus, the *wh—* word is *subjacent to* its landing site, according to the ordinary dictionary definition of the word *subjacent*. Figure 28.13 shows how the subjacent *whom* moves into an empty complement phrase's specifier position in one of the sample sentences.

Note, however, that the movement of the subjacent *wh—* word is constrained; you cannot, for example, pile up *wh—* words:

Whom will Sarah return the book to when?
When will Sarah return the book to whom?
∗ *When whom will Sarah return the book to?*
∗ *Whom when will Sarah return the book to?*

Also, you cannot always move them to separate places:

Whom do you think Sarah will return the book to when?
When do you think Sarah will return the book to whom?
∗ *When do you think whom Sarah will return the book to?*
∗ *Whom do you think when Sarah will return the book to?*

[†]To support their theories, linguists occasionally need to use examples from exotic languages. Among the most popular are Basque, a language spoken on the northwest coast of Spain, and Warlpiri, an aboriginal language spoken by a few hundred native Australians living near Alice Springs.

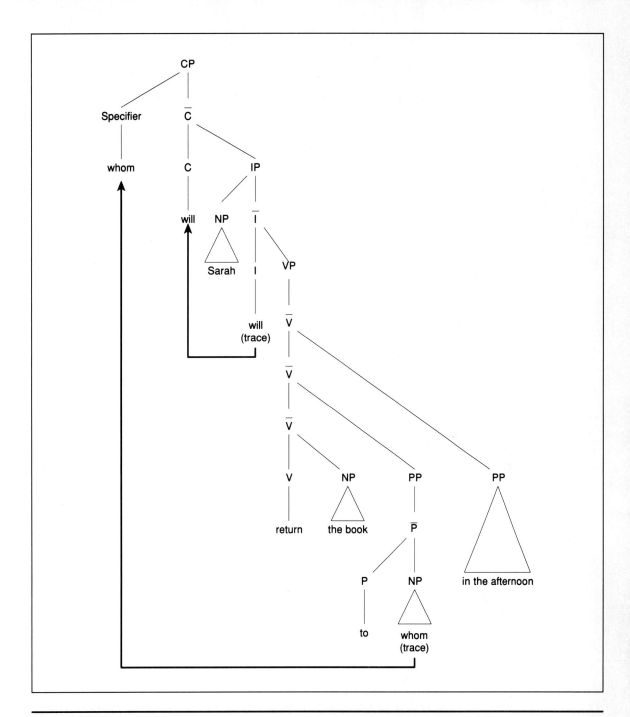

Figure 28.13 Subjacent *wh—* words can move into empty complement phrase's specifier positions.

To account for these and similar movement phenomena, linguists have gathered together some of the contributing factors into the **subjacency principle**. In the context of *wh—* word movement, the subjacency principle says that *wh—* words can move to and through vacant complement-phrase specifier positions, but they cannot move over more than one NP node or IP node in a single bound; also, as subjacent *wh—* words move, they leave behind a connected chain of one or more traces. Positions occupied by traces are not vacant, so you cannot put a *wh—* word into a trace position.

Thus, the following sentence—one of the previous examples—is unnatural, because there is no way to move the *wh—* words without violating the constraint imposed by the subjacency principle:

* *When do you think whom Sarah will return the book to?*

To analyze this sentence in terms of subjacency, you must consider two possibilities: either *whom* can move first, or *when* can. If *whom* moves first, then *when* cannot move at all, as shown in figure 28.14. Here is why: The subjacency constraint says *when* cannot move over the two intervening IP nodes without setting down temporarily in a vacant complement phrase's specifier position, but the only available complement phrase's specifier position is occupied by the previously moved *whom*.

You might think that *when* could move first via an empty complement phrase's specifier position, followed by movement of *whom* into that previously traversed but empty complement phrase's specifier position. This movement does not work, however, because the trace left behind by the movement of *when* keeps the specifier position forever filled, as far as movement is concerned.

Thus, in summary, the X-bar schema makes it relatively easy to express the subjacency constraint on *wh—* word movement, providing a second example of how the X-bar schema can help you to express constraint and illustrating the sort of constraint about which linguists think. In the next section, you learn what you should and should not do with such knowledge.

COMPETENCE VERSUS PERFORMANCE

One way to describe an X-bar structure is to write down the rules that stipulate what sort of branches can appear. For example, an NP node can have either an $\overline{N}$ node or both a determiner and an $\overline{N}$ node as its direct descendants. Using standard notation, the following **rewrite rules** say the same thing:

NP   → $\overline{N}$,
NP   →   determiner — $\overline{N}$.

Many linguists express constraints in the form of rewrite rules, and they talk accordingly of **generative grammars**, as though you could generate actual sentences by using rewrite rules to build a complete sentence tree

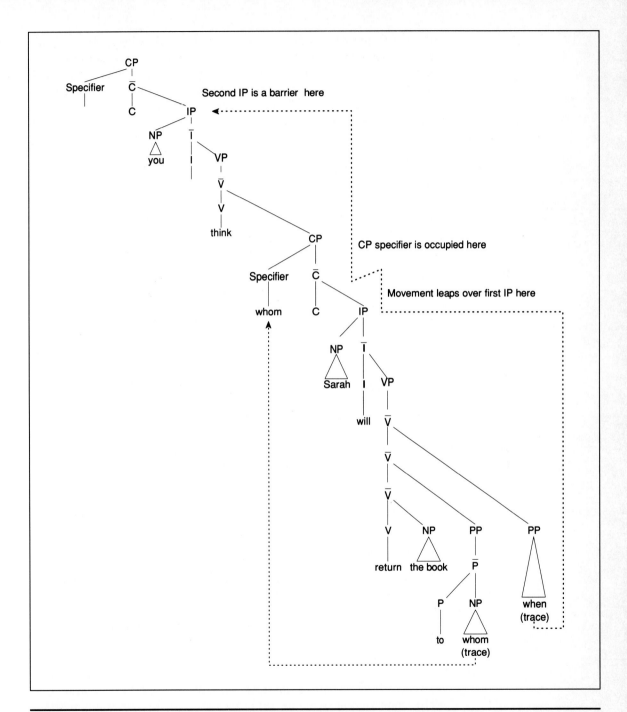

Figure 28.14 Subjacent *wh*— words cannot move over more than one NP node or IP node in a single bound.

under a CP. Superficially, it looks like you have been learning about an explanation for language generation. Do not succumb to this seduction. Few linguists would claim that they are working on a model of the actual computations that produce language. The purpose of sentence trees is to support a concise articulation of the constraints that natural-sounding sentences obey, rather than to provide an explanation for how you produce sentences in your head.

Most Linguists Focus on Competence, Not on Performance

If you try to articulate the constraints that language obey, you are said to be working on a theory of language **competence**. By contrast, if you are working on a program that actually generates language, or that understands language in some sense, you are working on a model of language **performance**.

Nevertheless, it is easy to fall into a mode of thinking that confounds work on competence with work on performance. Worse yet, it is easy to suppose that it would be easy to create a performance model of language understanding by running the rewrite rules of a competence theory backward. If a generative grammar is not supposed to be a performance model, however, trying to reverse the implied computations may not be the best approach to building language-understanding programs.

Moreover, even if generative grammars were performance models, the best path to language understanding programs might not lie in reversing the generation computations.

Analysis by Reversing Generation Can Be Silly

There are several explanations for why language honors grammatical constraints. One is that the constraints make language learnable. Another is that the constraints are manifestations of the speaker's computational limits.

Still another explanation is that the grammatical constraints on language generation force speakers to decorate their utterances with features that help listeners to understand those utterances. It is important, however, that the computations that produce the features may be much different from the computations that use the features.

To see why they might be different, suppose that you have a seeing-eye robot that can tell you a whole lot about what it sees. Further suppose that it has been equipped with something like ZOOKEEPER, the forward chaining, rule-based expert system introduced in Chapter 7. Accordingly, your seeing-eye robot can tell you a whole lot about any zoo animal that happens to be standing in front of it by simply announcing what kind of animal it perceives, presuming that you have a table in your head that relates animal types to animal properties.

Thus, your seeing-eye robot can compress its communication with you by taking advantage of your ability to look up animal properties in an existing table. It goes to a lot of computational trouble to identify the animal, so that you will be spared the trouble of analyzing a longer message.

Note, however, that you do not have to know the rules that your seeing-eye robot uses, and you certainly run no rules backward. You determine what you want to know by table lookup, without reversing your robot's message-producing procedure.

Construction of a Language Understanding Program Remains a Tough Row to Hoe

So what is the problem? Linguists have been working for centuries, with increasing success, to ferret out the constraints honored by native speakers. What remaining obstacles could possibly prevent the quick development of practical language-understanding programs? Here are a few of the most conspicuous ones:

- Although some of the fog that surrounds linguistic constraint is clearing, there are few, if any, points on which linguists universally agree. For on almost any issue, it is easy to find linguists at war against each other, ready to fight it out indefinitely, hurling examples and counterexamples at each other with passion.
- There is no reason to suppose that the emerging principles will be straightforward, simple, and easy to exploit. Evolution has been working on language for a long time, possibly adding patch on top of hack, just as programmers do when in a hurry to make something work. Occam's razor may not apply.
- A sentence do not has to be grammatical to be understood by a person. A really satisfactory language-understanding program should exploit grammatical decoration when exhibited, presuming that the decoration is there to aid understanding, but the program also should survive in the absence of grammar.
- Sentences are full of metaphors. We speak of *a tough row to hoe*, or *fog* surrounding something abstract, or *hurling examples*, or perfectly peaceful people *at war*, or *evolution* personified, or grammar providing a *decoration*, or a program *surviving*. Understanding such metaphors requires understanding the world, not just understanding language per se. Thus, the problem of understanding language is hard to separate from the problem of understanding intelligence in general.

Engineers Must Take Shortcuts

Evidently, the search for a comprehensive theory of language understanding will keep linguists busy for many years. This observation raises important questions about how you can meet engineering goals now, without waiting for many years to pass. One answer—a standard engineering answer—is that you can narrow the focus to specific, limited tasks, hoping that you can handle those tasks with a limited understanding of language phenomena.

One such task, the subject of Chapter 29, is that of connecting human decision makers to the information in relational databases via a natural-language interface.

SUMMARY

- The X-bar hypothesis contends that all phrases conform to a tree structure called the X-bar schema. There is growing evidence that a binary X-bar schema is particularly good as a substrate for expressing linguistic constraint.
- In English, specifiers arrive from the left and complements arrive from the right. The binary X-bar schema seems to be good for other languages as well, but the position of specifiers and complements is language specific.
- A good theory of language ought to be a theory of all languages, and it ought to account for rapid acquisition of language by children.
- A noun phrase's case is determined by that noun phrase's governor. To establish the governor, you climb the X-bar tree, looking for a noun phrase or verb phrase with a head, or an inflection phrase with a tense-exhibiting I node. Inflection phrases in which the verb appears in its infinitive form do not exhibit tense.
- Subjacency limits *wh*— movement to an empty complement phrase's specifier position. If a moving *wh*— word leaps over more than one NP node or IP node, that *wh*— word must be able to touch down in a totally empty complement phrase's specifier position after each leap.
- Most linguists focus on competence, rather than performance. That is, they are interested in discovering constraint, not in building language-generation or language-understanding programs.
- There is no reason to believe that reversing a language-generation procedure would be a good way to construct a language-understanding program.
- Engineers must narrow their focus and take many shortcuts to build practical language-understanding systems today.

BACKGROUND

The chapter is largely based on the extraordinary introductory textbook, *Introduction to Government and Binding Theory*, by Liliane Haegeman [1991]. That book is an introduction to modern linguistic theory as practiced by Noam Chomsky and other leading linguists.

Researchers have begun to make striking progress toward incorporating the principles of modern linguistic theory into language understanding programs. See, for example, the work of Robert C. Berwick and his students [G. Edward Barton 1984, Sandiway Fong and Berwick 1991].

29

Responding to Questions and Commands

In this chapter, you learn how it is possible to capture the knowledge required to *translate English questions or commands* into *relational-database commands*. Thus, you see that, in certain special circumstances, you can arrange for a computer to deal with natural language.

The key idea is to exploit the relatively regular word order and small, domain-specific vocabularies found in the questions and commands typically directed at relational databases. Word-order regularity is captured in *semantic transition-tree grammars*, which are evolutionary descendants of *augmented transition-net grammars*, usually referred to as ATN grammars.[†]

By way of illustration, you see how semantic transition-tree grammars enable programs to translate English questions and commands involving tools into database commands.

You should understand, however, that the ideas involved are just barely strong enough to support database retrieval via natural language. The problem of understanding unconstrained text seems unthinkably difficult, and worse yet, the more you understand about natural language, the more difficult the problems seem.

Once you have finished this chapter, you will be able to make simple extensions to the sample grammar, targeting it, if you like, to another database.

[†]ATN grammars have never been popular with linguists because they are partly specified by unrestricted computer programs, which linguists legitimately argue are a poor representation for linguistic knowledge.

Figure 29.1 A simple transition-net grammar.

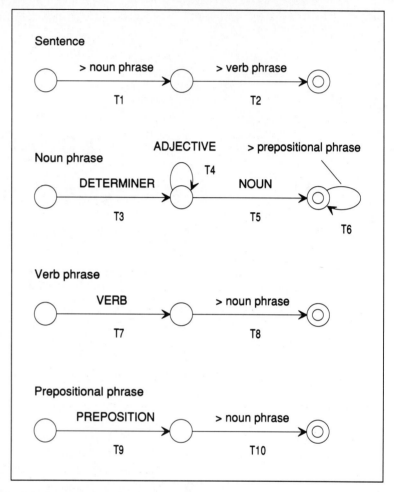

SYNTACTIC TRANSITION NETS

In this section, you learn how syntactic transition-net grammars capture linguistic knowledge about word order in English.

Syntactic Transition Nets Are Like Roadmaps

Generally, a **grammar**, viewed as a representation, is a set of conventions for capturing linguistic knowledge of the sort you learned about in elementary school.

A syntactic transition-net grammar consists of a sentence net and a collection of supporting nets, like those shown in figure 29.1.

Think of those nets as though they were an atlas full of roadmaps, and think of words as directions for driving through those roadmaps. To test a string of words to see whether it constitutes a valid sentence, you try to move along a series of links from the initial node in the sentence net to a terminal node—one with a circle in the center—using the words as directions. If a particular string of words enables you to reach a terminal node, then that string is said to be *accepted* or *recognized* by the transition-net grammar, from which you conclude that the string of words is a *valid sentence* with respect to the grammar.

Consider the sentence net shown in figure 29.1, for example. To move through it, you must first traverse the link labeled > *noun phrase*, which means that you must successfully traverse the noun-phrase net.

To move through the noun-phrase net, you must have a sequence of words starting with a determiner, a word such as *a* or *the*; followed by zero or more adjectives, such as *powerful*, *long*, or *big*; followed by a noun, such as *computer*, *screwdrivers*, or *table*. Each time a word enables you to cross a link, that word is removed from the list of words to be analyzed.

The noun may be followed by a prepositional phrase, such as *on the big table*. The words in prepositional phrases are traversed using the prepositional-phrase net.

Once you have traversed the noun-phrase net, you must move through the verb-phrase net, as indicated by the link labeled > *verb phrase* in the sentence net. Providing that all the words in the sentence are accounted for in traversing the verb-phrase net, your analysis is complete, because you end up at a terminal node, one marked as a double circle.

A Powerful Computer Counted the Long Screwdrivers on the Big Table

To see how such an analysis works on an actual sentence, consider the sentence, "A powerful computer counted the long screwdrivers on the big table." To verify that it is, in fact, a valid sentence, you must determine whether the words specify a path through the grammar. Accordingly, you start to move through the sentence net. Just following the entry node, you encounter a noun-phrase link, labeled T1 in figure 29.1. This sends you off to the noun-phrase net, which in turn requires you to attempt to traverse the determiner link, T3, in the noun-phrase net.

Now it is time to look at the first word in the sentence. It is *a*, one of the words in the determiner class. Having consumed *a* on the determiner link, you are in a position to take either the adjective link, T4, or the noun link, T5.

Assume, by convention, that you always are to try the uppermost of the untried links first. Accordingly, you try the adjective link, T4, consuming the word *powerful*.

Moving on to the next word, *computer*, your attempt to try the adjective link fails, so you try the noun link instead. This time, you succeed, inasmuch as the word *computer* is a noun.

This success brings you to the noun-phrase net's terminal node, where there is the possibility of traversing the prepositional-phrase net.

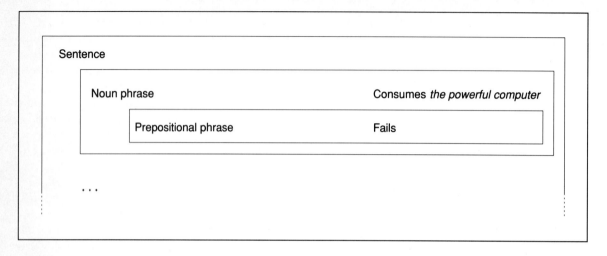

Figure 29.2 The
analysis of a sentence
beginning "The
powerful computer
counted ...." In
this nested-box
diagram, graphical
inside corresponds
to a temporal *during*
relation among the
analyses of the
indicated nets.

Assume, by convention, that you are always to try to traverse the net specified by a link, if a link is available, even if you are at a terminal node. Accordingly, you try the prepositional-phrase link, T6, but you see instantly that the next word, *counted*, is not a preposition. You conclude that the prepositional-phrase net cannot be traversed, so you return to the sentence net.

Figure 29.2 shows what has happened so far, from the point of view of net traversals, using a *nested-box diagram*. By convention, a **nested-box diagram** is a diagram in which graphical *inside* corresponds to temporal *during*. Hence, the noun-phrase net must be traversed *during* the analysis of the sentence net because the box describing the noun-phrase traversal is *inside* the box describing the sentence-net traversal. Similarly, the failing attempt to traverse the prepositional-phrase net occurs during the successful analysis of the noun-phrase net.

Next, you have to see whether the remaining words in the sentence can get you through the verb-phrase net, as required by link T2. After you traverse the link labeled T7 with the verb *counted*, link T8 tells you that you have to look for another noun phrase. This search takes you back to the noun-phrase net again.

You quickly proceed through T3, T4, and T5, with the words *the long screwdrivers*. Then, you try to traverse the prepositional-phrase link, link T6. To get through the corresponding prepositional-phrase net, you need a preposition, as dictated by link T9, and a noun phrase, as dictated by link T10. The word *on* is a preposition, and *the big table* is a noun phrase, so you get through the prepositional-phrase net, and return successfully to the noun-phrase net. As there are no more prepositional phrases, a subsequent attempt to go through the propositional-phrase net fails. You are in a terminal noun-phrase node, however, so the noun-phrase net is traversed successfully.

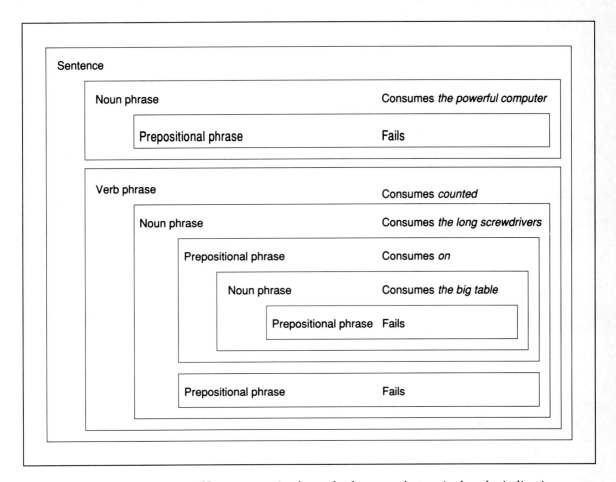

Figure 29.3 Analysis of the sentence, "The powerful computer counted the long screwdrivers on the big table," using a semantic transition-tree grammar. The comments show the words that are consumed as nets are traversed or else indicate failure.

Now you are in the verb-phrase net's terminal node, indicating a successful traversal of a verb-phrase net as well. Having finished with a verb-phrase net, you return to the sentence net, where you find you are, again, in a terminal node. Because there are no more words, you conclude that the sentence is valid with respect to the grammar.

Everything you did during this analysis is summarized, in nested-box form, in figure 29.3.

Such a simple grammar is easy to derail, of course. For example, because the grammar makes no provision for proper names, such as *Hal*, or adverbs, such as *quickly*, it cannot deal with sentences such as "Hal quickly counted the long screwdrivers on the big table."

SEMANTIC TRANSITION TREES

In this section, you learn how it is possible to translate sentences, such as the following, into relational-database commands:

Count the long screwdrivers.
What is the location of the long red screwdriver?

A Relational Database Makes a Good Target

Relational databases, described briefly in Chapter 7 and in more detail in the appendix, consist of one or more *relations*, each of which is a table consisting of labeled columns, called *fields*, and data-containing rows, called *records*. The following example, the tools relation, consists of eight records with entries for the class, color, size, weight, and location fields.

Class	Color	Size	Weight	Location
Saw	black	medium	heavy	pegboard
Hammer	blue	large	heavy	workbench
Wrench	gray	small	light	pegboard
Wrench	gray	large	heavy	pegboard
Screwdriver	blue	long	light	workbench
Screwdriver	black	long	light	toolchest
Screwdriver	red	long	heavy	toolchest
Screwdriver	red	short	light	toolchest

From the perspective of this chapter, the most important characteristic of relational databases is that English descriptions often correspond to simple combinations of the relational-database commands, such as SELECT and PROJECT. For example, you can retrieve the long screwdrivers by first selecting the tools whose class field contains *screwdriver*, and then selecting those tools whose size field contains *long*.

Pattern Instantiation Is the Key to Relational-Database Retrieval in English

Now you are ready to understand the overall semantic transition-tree approach to translating an English question or command into database commands:

■ Use the question or command to select database-oriented patterns.
■ Use the question or command to instantiate and combine the selected patterns.
■ Use the completed pattern to retrieve the database records specified in the question or command.
■ Use the retrieved database items to respond to the question or command.

For the first example, the command "Count the long screwdrivers," there is one key pattern:

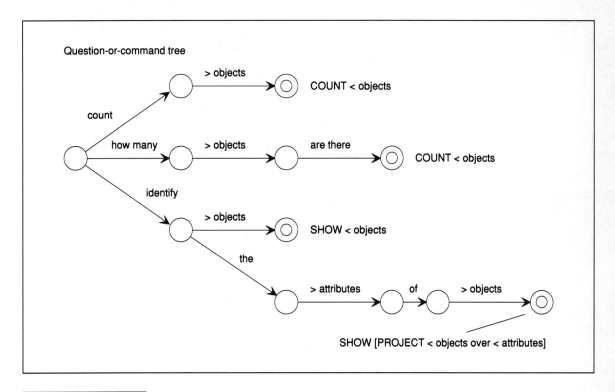

Question-or-command tree

Figure 29.4 The top-level transition tree of a simple semantic grammar.

SELECT < object with < values

Once instantiated, the key pattern looks like this:

SELECT   [SELECT Tools with class = screwdrivers]
         with size = long

When used on the sample database, the instantiated pattern locates long screwdrivers, as required by the original English command.

Moving from Syntactic Nets to Semantic Trees Simplifies Grammar Construction

A few simple changes to the idea of the syntactic transition net are all that you need to construct systems that use English sentences to drive database retrieval. Evidently, you avoid the overwhelming complexity of natural language, as long as you are able to restrict yourself to database-oriented questions and commands, proscribing declaratives.

The resulting changes lead to the idea of the *semantic transition-tree grammar*. An example of such a grammar is shown in figures 29.4 through 29.7.

From those figures, you see that semantic transition-tree grammars differ from the syntactic transition-net grammars in several ways:

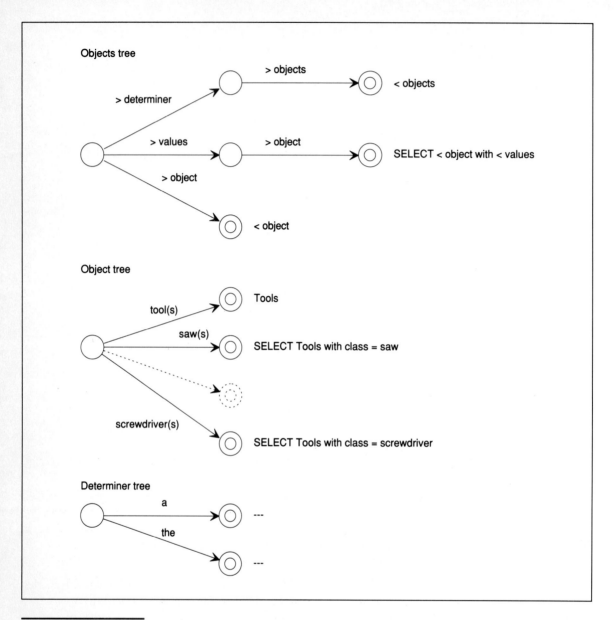

> Objects tree
>
> Object tree
>
> Determiner tree

Figure 29.5 The
semantic transition
trees that enable the
analysis of object
descriptions.

■   Some link transitions require specific words.

For example, a link can be labeled with a word, such as *count*, as in the
top-level tree shown in figure 29.4. This link indicates that the first word
in the sentence must be *count*. A link also can be labeled with a word
followed by *(s)*, such as *tool(s)*, as in the object tree shown in figure 29.5.
This link indicates that the next word must be either the word *tool* or its
plural, *tools*.

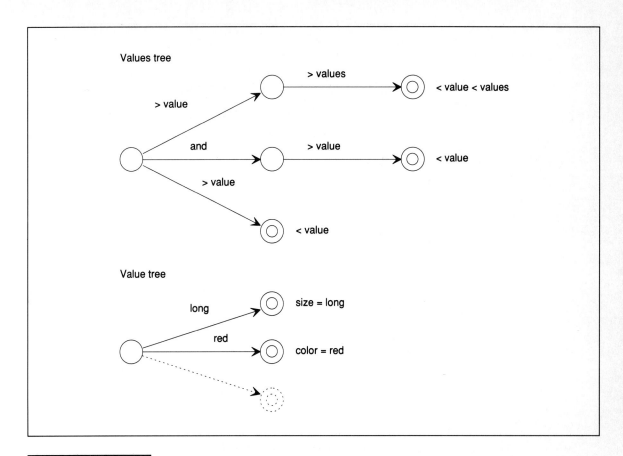

Figure 29.6 The semantic transition trees that enable the analysis of value descriptions.

■ Some link transitions specify phrases semantically, rather than syntactically.

Consider, for example, the objects link and the attributes link in figure 29.4. These links—the ones labeled with > *objects* and > *attributes*—focus on database entries, such as those for screwdrivers and sizes, rather than on linguistic entities, such as nouns and adjectives. Accordingly, both the objects link and the attributes link are said to be semantically specified transitions, reflecting the change in name from *syntactic* grammar to *semantic* grammar.

■ There are no nodes with two inputs.

This characteristic is why we are talking about transition-*tree* semantic grammars rather than transition-*net* syntactic grammars.

Because of the change from nets to trees, there is a one-to-one correspondence between paths and terminal nodes. Accordingly, once you arrive at a terminal node, there is never any question about how you got there, which makes it easy for you to decide which pattern, if any, to use.

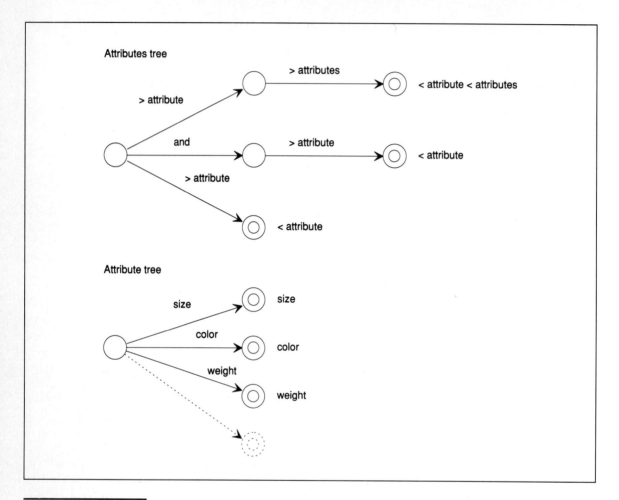

Figure 29.7 The semantic transition trees that enable the analysis of attribute descriptions.

By way of contrast, compare the attribute tree shown in figure 29.7 with the attribute net shown in figure 29.8. In the attribute net, all links converge on one terminal node, so just knowing that you are at that terminal node tells you nothing about how you got there or what you should do. Of course, you could, in principle, keep track of how you got there via some sort of bookkeeping mechanism off to the side, but that alternative would complicate your procedure and diminish your grammar's transparency.

■   Whenever a tree is traversed successfully, the tree's name is considered to be a **tree variable**, and is bound to a pattern located at a terminal node. Accordingly, you can refer to the pattern as the tree variable's binding.

Sometimes, a pattern contains one or more tree variables, each of which is marked by a left bracket, <. Such patterns act like templates.

Figure 29.8 An alternate rendering of the attribute tree. Because the attribute tree is shown as a net, rather than as a tree, this rendering cannot be part of a semantic transition-tree grammar.

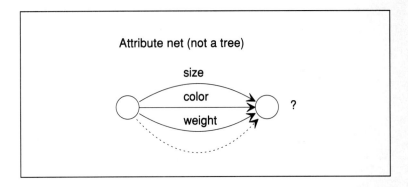

All the paths traversing the objects tree in figure 29.5 lead to template-like patterns. All the paths traversing the object tree and the determiner tree lead to variable-free patterns.

■ Tree variables, marked by left bracket symbols, <, are replaced by their previously established bindings.

For example, the pattern attached to the terminal node of the upper path in the values tree, shown in figure 29.6, contains two marked tree variables, value and values. Whenever this pattern is instantiated, the marked tree variables are replaced by the bindings that were established inside the value tree and the values tree. Thus, the right bracket, >, is a mnemonic preface that is meant to suggest *take processing down* into a subtree, whereas the left bracket, <, is a mnemonic preface meant to suggest *bring a binding up* from a subtree.

Count the Long Screwdrivers

To see how semantic transition trees work together to instantiate patterns, consider the sentence "Count the long screwdrivers." Its analysis, as you will see, is captured by the nested-box diagram shown in figure 29.9.

The top-level tree, the question-or-command tree, is the first used, of course. One link leading out of the entry node is labeled with the word *count*, which matches the first word in the example sentence, taking you to the objects link, whereupon you move your attention to the objects tree.

The objects tree has three links leading out of the entry node, the first of which moves your attention to the determiner tree. Because the next of the remaining words in the sentence is *the*, the determiner tree is traversed successfully. The next link to be traversed in the objects tree is labeled > *objects*, indicating that you should turn your attention to the objects tree again, now on a second level.

At this point, the remaining words are *long screwdrivers*. The word *long* is not a determiner, so the effort to traverse the determiner link fails. Thus, your attention in the objects tree is now focused on the values link.

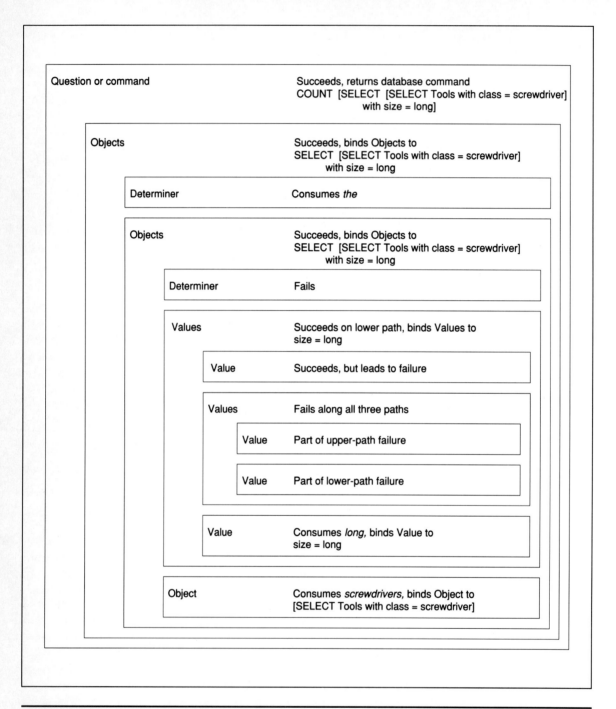

Figure 29.9 The nested-box diagram corresponding to the analysis of "Count the long screwdrivers."

Eventually, you successfully traverse the values tree, consuming the word *long* as you do. To see how you do that, note that you first try to traverse the upper path in the values tree. This attempt requires you to traverse the value tree, which you do easily, consuming the word *long*. Next, however, you must try to traverse the values tree itself on a second level. You fail, however: On that second level, along the upper path, you would need to traverse the value link; along the middle path you would need the word *and*; and along the bottom path you would also need to traverse the value link. Accordingly, you cannot traverse the values tree on a second level, which means, in turn, that you cannot traverse the original values tree along the upper path. You must restore the previously consumed word, *long*, to the remaining words, and try another path from the node where the first alternative happened to be wrong.

You then see that the second path does not work either, because the second path requires the word *and* whereas the first of the remaining words is *long*.

Fortunately, however, the third path requires only the traversal of the value tree, which you have done before and can do again with the word *long*.

Now it is time to think about the consequences of successful traversals. Recall that the successful traversal of a tree causes the tree's name to be bound to the instantiated pattern found at the terminal node. Thus, the successful traversal of the value tree binds value, the tree's name, to the pattern *size = long*.

Similarly, successful traversal of the values tree along the lower path binds the word values to the instantiated form of the pattern *< value*. Because instantiation just replaces tree variables with their bindings, the instantiated form of *< value* is *size = long*. Thus, the tree variables values and value are both bound to *size = long*.

Now recall that all the attention to the values and value trees was launched while you were working on the middle path of the second-level objects tree. Having traversed the values link successfully, you next turn your attention to the object tree, with only the word *screwdrivers* left to be consumed.

Fortunately, there is a link in the object tree labeled with the word *screwdrivers*. Hence, you traversed the object tree successfully, binding the tree variable object to the instantiated pattern, SELECT Tools with class = screwdriver.

At this point, you can see that the meaning of the word *screwdriver*, in this limited context, is captured by a database command that retrieves all the screwdrivers from the tools relation when the database command is executed. After you have traversed the second-level objects tree through the middle path, the tree variable objects is bound to the instantiated form of the pattern, SELECT < object with < values, which is, of course, as follows:

SELECT   [SELECT Tools with class = screwdriver]
           with size = long

Now you see that the meaning of the word *long* is captured by way of the incorporation of the *size = long* pattern—the one found in the value tree—into a database command.

Having traversed the second-level objects tree, you revert your attention to the original objects tree—the one that consumed the word *the* along its upper path. Because the original objects tree just binds the objects tree variable to whatever it is bound to on the next level down, you return your attention to the question-or-command tree with the same binding produced by the second-level objects tree.

Now you have just finished your traversal of the upper path in the question-or-command tree. Instantiating the upper path's pattern produces the following, which delivers the required result when the database command is executed:

COUNT   [SELECT   [SELECT Tools with class = screwdriver]
                      with size = long]

Recursion Replaces Loops

Note that semantic transition trees have no loops of the sort used in syntactic transition nets for adjectives and prepositional phrases. Luckily, no loops are needed, because you can replace loops with trees that use themselves; or said more technically, you can replace loops with recursive tree analysis. The example grammar exhibits this replacement in the objects–object trees, the values–value trees, and the attributes–attribute trees.

To see how such tree pairs handle multiple words, suppose that you are just about to try the values tree and that the remaining words are *long red screwdrivers*. Clearly, you cross the value link on the upper path with the word *long*, leading to another, recursive attempt to cross the values tree, this time with the words *red screwdriver*. This time, after failing on the upper two paths, you succeed on the lower path, successfully traversing the lower level values tree as well as the upper. Figure 29.10 shows how the values tree is traversed in detail.

Thus, you see that the values–value combination handles two word-value sequences successfully. Longer sequences require more recursion—nothing else.

In summary, here are the procedures for traversing semantic transition trees and transition-tree links.

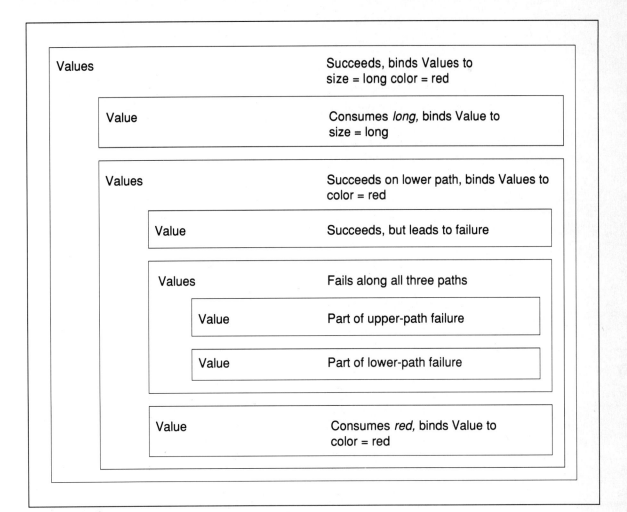

Figure 29.10
Recursion replaces looping in semantic transition trees. Here, the words *long* and *red* are consumed by the values tree and the value tree working together.

To traverse a transition tree,

▷ Determine whether it is possible to reach a success node, denoted by a double circle, via word and subtree links.

   ▷ If it is not possible, announce failure.

   ▷ Otherwise,

      ▷ Instantiate the pattern associated with the double circle. Replace pattern variables, marked by < prefixes, with bindings established as subtree links are traversed.

      ▷ Bind the tree's name to the instantiated pattern.

      ▷ Announce success.

To traverse a link,

▷ If the link is a subtree link, marked by a right bracket, >, and the name of a subtree, try to traverse the subtree. If the traversal is successful, bind the subtree name to the instantiated pattern found at the terminal node of the subtree.

▷ If the link is a word link, the next word in the sentence must be that word. The word is consumed as the link is traversed.

SUMMARY

- A full understanding of natural language lies beyond the present state of scientific knowledge. Nevertheless, it is possible to achieve engineering goals in limited contexts.
- One way to interpret questions and commands, in the limited context of database access, is to use the words in the questions and commands to guide you through a collection of nets or trees. You collect information in the course of the movement that makes it possible for you to instantiate database retrieval patterns.
- Moving from syntactic nets to syntactic trees eliminates loops and simplifies pattern instantiation. Moving from syntactic trees to database-specific semantic trees exposes constraints and simplifies tree construction.
- Some links in semantic transition trees are traversed by individual words. Others require the traversal of a subtree.
- When a subtree is traversed successfully, a pattern is instantiated, and that instantiated pattern becomes the value bound to the subtree's name. When the top-level tree is traversed successfully, a pattern is instantiated, and that instantiated pattern is used to access a database.

BACKGROUND

The notion of an augmented transition net was introduced in a paper by J. Thorne, P. Bratley, and H. Dewar [1968]. Work by Daniel G. Bobrow and Bruce Fraser [1969] and by William A. Woods [1970] developed and popularized the idea soon thereafter. Woods, especially, became a major contributor.

The work of Woods on his LUNAR system, and the work of Terry Winograd on his SHRDLU system [1971], were the precursors to today's commercial language interfaces, for they showed that sentence-analysis procedures

Q&A Translates Questions into Database-Retrieval Commands

The popular Q&A system is one example of a database system with a practical natural-language interface based on the semantic-grammar approach. Q&A's semantic grammar is much more complete than is the one you learned about in this chapter, but it basically provides the same capabilities.

Suppose, for example, that you are an investor. You can use Q&A to keep track of information about the companies in which you are an investor, enabling a dialog:

> Tell me the name of the company that makes Q&A?

Q&A translates the question into a database command aimed at a database containing company and product fields. The response to the database command enables Q&A to print a one-record table:

Company	Product
Semantec	Q&A

> Which product category is Q&A?

Product	Product category
Q&A	Database software

> Count the number of software companies.

Q&A responds with a number. The command is easy to obey for any system based on a semantic grammar, because it is, after all, not much different from the command, "Count the long screwdrivers."

> Which companies in Massachusetts are software companies?

Responding, Q&A prints another table:

Company	Business	City	State
Ascent Technology	Software	Cambridge	MA
Bachman Associates	Software	Burlington	MA
⋮			

> What are the product categories of Ascent Technology's products?

Responding, Q&A prints still another table:

Product	Product category
Aris	Resource allocation
Ferret	Database mining
⋮	

can instantiate search-procedure slots. Woods's work involved questions about moon rocks. Winograd's work involved questions about a simulated world of blocks.

For a good exposition of semantic transition-tree grammars, see work by Gary Hendrix and his associates [Hendrix et al. 1978]. The well-known LIFER system is based on this work, and it led eventually to Q&A, which provides natural-language access to databases.

Appendix
Relational Databases

In this appendix, you learn what a relational database is, and you learn about relational-database operations such as ADD, DELETE, COMBINE, REMOVE, SELECT, PROJECT, and JOIN.

Relational databases are commonly used to store large amounts of data in an orderly, easily manipulated form. This appendix describes the ideas involved in relational databases. Understanding relational database ideas makes it easier to learn about two important topics in artificial intelligence:

- Fast forward chaining using the RETE procedure
- Natural-language access to database information

Relational Databases Consist of Tables Containing Records

A **record** is a collection of named slots, each of which is called a **field**. Fields are usually filled with **field values**. Thus, the record shown in figure A.1 has five fields and five field values. The fields are named class, color, size, weight, and location; the field values are saw, black, medium, heavy, and pegboard.

A record's field names and field values generally constitute a description of one particular object—a tool in this example.

A **relation** is a named set of records, all of which share the same field names. Thus, a relation is a kind of table. The relation shown in figure A.2, the tools relation, contains records describing six tools. A **relational database** is a named set of one or more relations.

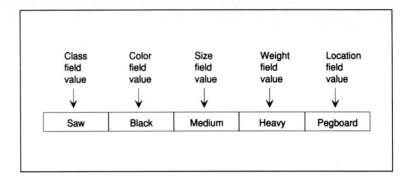

Figure A.1 A record consists of field values for an ordered set of fields.

Figure A.2 A relation consists of field names and records.

Relations Are Easy to Modify

To add or delete records, you use, mnemonically enough, ADD and DELETE. The ADD and DELETE operations are illustrated in figure A.3.

ADD and DELETE handle just one relation and one record at a time. In contrast, COMBINE and REMOVE work with two relations at a time. As shown in figure A.4, COMBINE puts together all the records in two relations to form one new relation; REMOVE removes records from one relation if they happen to appear in another relation as well. Thus, COMBINE and REMOVE operate on relations as though relations were sets.

Records and Fields Are Easy to Extract

To answer questions using a relational database, you generally need to extract some records from a relation using the SELECT operator. SELECT extracts exactly those records whose field values satisfy certain criteria specified in the SELECT operation. In figure A.5, for example, you see that the extracted records all have *screwdriver* as the class field value and *long* as the size field value.

Occasionally, you need to extract fields, rather than relations, using the PROJECT operation. PROJECT extracts exactly those fields specified in

Figure A.3 The tools relation. One record is added, using ADD, and one record is deleted, using DELETE.

Tools

Class	Color	Size	Weight	Location
Saw	Black	Medium	Heavy	Pegboard
Hammer	Blue	Large	Heavy	Workbench
Pliers	Gray	Small	Light	Pegboard
Pliers	Gray	Medium	Light	Pegboard
Wrench	Gray	Small	Light	Pegboard
T-square	Yellow	Medium	Light	Pegboard

DELETE T-square yellow medium light pegboard from Tools

ADD wrench gray large heavy pegboard to Tools

Tools

Class	Color	Size	Weight	Location
Saw	Black	Medium	Heavy	Pegboard
Hammer	Blue	Large	Heavy	Workbench
Pliers	Gray	Small	Light	Pegboard
Pliers	Gray	Medium	Light	Pegboard
Wrench	Gray	Small	Light	Pegboard
Wrench	Gray	Large	Heavy	Pegboard

the PROJECT operation. In figure A.5, for example, the PROJECT operation extracts the color and weight fields, and the relation is said to be *projected* over color and weight.

Relations Are Easy to Combine

Suppose that you have a relation that provides both a class field and a location field. Then, it is easy to see whether there are, for example, any screwdrivers located on the workbench by selecting all records from the relation that have *screwdriver* in the class field and *workbench* in the location field.

Often, you are not so fortunate as to have a single relation with both of the required fields. In figure A.6, for example, you see that the tools1 relation has a class field and the tools2 relation has a location field. Thus,

Figure A.4 COMBINE puts relations together. REMOVE removes all records from one relation that appear in another relation. Thus, REMOVE is an asymmetric operation.

Tools

Class	Color	Size	Weight	Location
Saw	Black	Medium	Heavy	Pegboard
Hammer	Blue	Large	Heavy	Workbench
Pliers	Gray	Small	Light	Pegboard
Pliers	Gray	Medium	Light	Pegboard
Wrench	Gray	Small	Light	Pegboard
Wrench	Gray	Large	Heavy	Pegboard

Screwdrivers

Screwdriver	Blue	Long	Light	Workbench
Screwdriver	Black	Long	Light	Toolchest
Screwdriver	Red	Long	Heavy	Toolchest
Screwdriver	Red	Short	Light	Toolchest

Pliers

Pliers	Gray	Small	Light	Pegboard
Pliers	Gray	Medium	Light	Pegboard

COMBINE Screwdrivers and Tools
REMOVE Pliers from Tools

Tools

Class	Color	Size	Weight	Location
Saw	Black	Medium	Heavy	Pegboard
Hammer	Blue	Large	Heavy	Workbench
Wrench	Gray	Small	Light	Pegboard
Wrench	Gray	Large	Heavy	Pegboard
Screwdriver	Blue	Long	Light	Workbench
Screwdriver	Black	Long	Light	Toolchest
Screwdriver	Red	Long	Heavy	Toolchest
Screwdriver	Red	Short	Light	Toolchest

Figure A.5 A SELECT operation extracts records from a relation, producing a new relation with fewer records. A PROJECT operation extracts fields from a relation, producing a new relation with fewer fields.

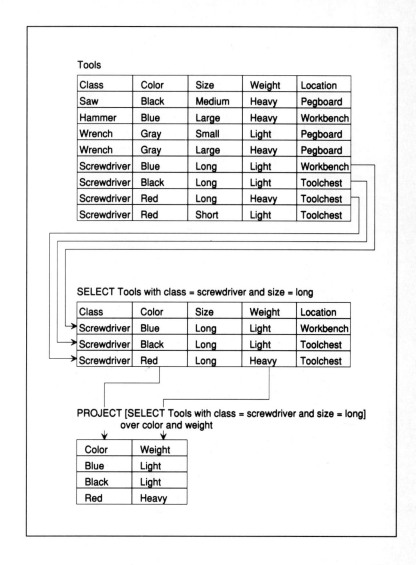

the answer to the screwdrivers-on-the-workbench question is distributed across two relations. To get at the answer, you have to paste together the two relations, which is the job of JOIN, the most complex of the relational-database operations.

The JOIN operation, in the most elementary form, specifies two relations and two fields, one in each relation. In the example shown in figure A.6, the JOIN operation is done using the identifier field in the first relation and the name field in the second relation, and the two relations are said to be joined by their identifier and name fields, both of which record serial numbers in their respective relations. JOIN operations often use such serial-number fields.

To learn how the JOIN operation works, put your finger on the first record in the first relation, noting the field value in the specified field. In the example in figure A.6, the field value in the identifier field of the first record is *saw8*.

Next, you look for relations in the second relation with a matching field value in the second relation's specified field. In the example, the field value in the name field of the first record is *saw8*, which matches.

For each such record, you enter a new record into the result. The new record consists of the matching records concatenated together, as shown in figure A.6.

Once you have finished with the first record in the first relation, you move your finger to the second and subsequent record until you are finished, producing, for example, the seven-field relation shown in figure A.6. From that relation, you can easily select all records with *screwdriver* in the class field and *workbench* in the location field, yielding another new relation with just one record.

Note that the same field value can occur many times in the fields involved in JOIN operations. Thus, a JOIN operation can produce a relation larger than either of those that are joined. After all, a field value in a record in one relation can match the field values in several of the records in a second relation.

Suppose, for example, that the source relation, shown in figure A.7, has just two fields, *name* and *retailer*. Similarly, the properties relation, also shown in figure A.7, has just two fields, *name* and *property*, in the expectation that several records are used for each tool.

To determine which tools purchased from Sears are expensive, you need only to join the two relations over the *name* field that appears in both and then to select the records with *Sears* in the *retailer* field and *expensive* in the *property* field. There is, of course, just one such record in the example.

Note that, whenever the JOIN operation joins two relations that share field names, the JOIN operation prevents ambiguity by concatenating each shared field name with the name of the relations from which the shared field name comes. Thus, the *name* field from the source relation becomes *name.source*, and the *name* field from the properties relation becomes *name.properties*.

Alternatively, of course, you could select the records in the properties relation with *expensive* in the *property* field, join the source relation to the result, and then select the records with *Sears* in the *retailer* field and *expensive* in the *property* field. The JOIN operation involved in this alternative approach is simpler in that only one record is produced for each record in the source relation.

You can also join relations over more than one field, as shown in figure A.8. The result is still a new relation, with corresponding records correctly concatenated.

Tools1

Identifier	Class	Color	Size	Weight
Saw8	Saw	Black	Medium	Heavy
Hammer4	Hammer	Blue	Large	Heavy
Wrench17	Wrench	Gray	Small	Light
Wrench5	Wrench	Gray	Large	Heavy
Screwdriver6	Screwdriver	Blue	Long	Light
Screwdriver3	Screwdriver	Black	Long	Light
Screwdriver1	Screwdriver	Red	Long	Heavy
Screwdriver9	Screwdriver	Red	Short	Light

Tools2

Name	Location
Saw8	Pegboard
Hammer4	Workbench
Wrench17	Pegboard
Wrench5	Pegboard
Screwdriver6	Workbench
Screwdriver3	Toolchest
Screwdriver1	Toolchest
Screwdriver9	Toolchest

JOIN Tools1 and Tools2 with identifier = name

		from Tools1				from Tools2	
Identifier	Class	Color	Size	Weight	Name	Location
Saw8	Saw	Black	Medium	Heavy	Saw8	Pegboard
Hammer4	Hammer	Blue	Large	Heavy	Hammer4	Workbench
Wrench17	Wrench	Gray	Small	Light	Wrench17	Pegboard
Wrench5	Wrench	Gray	Large	Heavy	Wrench5	Pegboard
Screwdriver6	Screwdriver	Blue	Long	Light	Screwdriver6	Workbench
Screwdriver3	Screwdriver	Black	Long	Light	Screwdriver3	Toolchest
Screwdriver1	Screwdriver	Red	Long	Heavy	Screwdriver1	Toolchest
Screwdriver9	Screwdriver	Red	Short	Light	Screwdriver9	Toolchest

Figure A.6 A JOIN operation over fields that contain unique, record-identifying symbols.

Source

Name	Retailer
Saw8	Vanderhoof
Hammer4	Sears

Properties

Name	Property
Saw8	Saw
Saw8	Black
Saw8	Medium
Saw8	Inexpensive
Hammer4	Hammer
Hammer4	Blue
Hammer4	Large
Hammer4	Expensive

JOIN Source and Properties with name = name

from Source		from Properties	
Name.source	Retailer	Name.properties	Property
Saw8	Vanderhoof	Saw8	Saw
Saw8	Vanderhoof	Saw8	Black
Saw8	Vanderhoof	Saw8	Medium
Saw8	Vanderhoof	Saw8	Inexpensive
Hammer4	Sears	Hammer4	Hammer
Hammer4	Sears	Hammer4	Blue
Hammer4	Sears	Hammer4	Large
Hammer4	Sears	Hammer4	Expensive

Figure A.7 Joining the source and properties relations over the *name* field produces multiple records for each record in the source relation.

Tools1

Class	Color	Size	Weight
Saw	Black	Medium	Heavy
Hammer	Blue	Large	Heavy
Wrench	Gray	Small	Light
Wrench	Gray	Large	Heavy
Screwdriver	Blue	Long	Light
Screwdriver	Black	Long	Light
Screwdriver	Red	Long	Heavy
Screwdriver	Red	Short	Light

Tools2

Color	Size	Location
Black	Medium	Pegboard
Blue	Large	Workbench
Gray	Small	Pegboard
Gray	Large	Pegboard
Blue	Long	Workbench
Black	Long	Toolchest
Red	Long	Toolchest
Red	Short	Toolchest

JOIN Tools1 and Tools2 with color=color and size=size

	from Tools1			from Tools2		
Class	Color.tools1	Size.tools1	Weight	Color.tools2	Size.tools2	Location
Saw	Black	Medium	Heavy	Black	Medium	Pegboard
Hammer	Blue	Large	Heavy	Blue	Large	Workbench
Wrench	Gray	Small	Light	Gray	Small	Pegboard
Wrench	Gray	Large	Heavy	Gray	Large	Pegboard
Screwdriver	Blue	Long	Light	Blue	Long	Workbench
Screwdriver	Black	Long	Light	Black	Long	Toolchest
Screwdriver	Red	Long	Heavy	Red	Long	Toolchest
Screwdriver	Red	Short	Light	Red	Short	Toolchest

Figure A.8 A JOIN operation that requires matches in two fields.

All these ideas are summarized in the following specification of the relational-database data structure.

A **relational database** is a data structure

In which

▷ Lexically, there are relations, records, application-specific fields, and application-specific field values.

▷ Structurally, relations contain records, each of which contains a list of values, one for each field.

With constructors that

▷ Define a relation, given a name and a set of field names.

▷ Combine given relations to make a new relation (COMBINE)

With writers that

▷ Add a record to a given relation (ADD)

▷ Delete a record from a given relation (DELETE)

With readers that

▷ Produce a list of records in the relation

▷ Produce a relation with a subset of the records, given a pattern to be matched (SELECT)

▷ Produce a relation with a subset of the fields, given a field specification (PROJECT)

Note that, as specified, a relational database is a data structure; it is not a representation. It becomes a representation once you say something about the semantics involved in a particular relational database.

SUMMARY

- Relational databases consist of tables containing records.
- To add or delete a record from a relation, you use ADD and DELETE. You use REMOVE to eliminate from one relation all records that also appear in another relation.
- To extract a set of pattern-matching records from a relation, producing a new relation, you use SELECT. To extract particular fields from a relation, producing a new relation, you use PROJECT.
- To combine the records in two relations, you use COMBINE. To form a relation consisting of records selected from two source relations and concatenated together, you use JOIN.

Exercises

EXERCISE 1.1

Discuss the following statements:

Part 1 Artificial intelligence is the enterprise of simulating human intelligence.

Part 2 Artificial intelligence is the enterprise of understanding human intelligence.

Part 3 Artificial intelligence is an engineering discipline within computer science.

EXERCISE 1.2

Discuss the following statements:

Part 1 Computers can do only what they are told to do by a programmer.

Part 2 Computers cannot think aesthetically.

Part 3 Intelligence cannot be understood.

EXERCISE 1.3

Discuss the following statement: A working program is prima facie evidence of successful research in artificial intelligence.

EXERCISE 1.4

Discuss the following statement: Artificial intelligence is dangerous because managers are eager to use the ideas of artificial intelligence to eliminate jobs.

EXERCISE 1.5

Discuss the following statements:

Part 1   People in the field of artificial intelligence reject established engineering methods because they believe that methods based on heuristics are better.

Part 2   People in the field of artificial intelligence reject the ideas of psychologists, linguists, and philosophers because they believe that there is no way to explain intelligence without using a computational point of view.

EXERCISE 1.6

Discuss the following statements:

Part 1   Artificial intelligence, viewed as a branch of engineering, is just an amalgam of ideas borrowed from other engineering fields.

Part 2   Artificial intelligence, viewed as a branch of science, is just an amalgam of ideas borrowed from psychology, linguistics, and philosophy.

CHAPTER 2
Semantic Nets and Description Matching

EXERCISE 2.1

Three cannibals and three missionaries are standing on the west bank of a river. A boat is available that will hold either one or two people. If the missionaries are ever outnumbered—on either bank or in the boat—the cannibals will eat them. Your job is to determine a sequence of trips that will get everyone across the river to the east bank.

The exercise is simple to solve once you have the right representation. One such representation is the state space shown in figure E2.1. Nodes in the state space indicate the number of missionaries and cannibals on the west bank. Solid-line arrows indicate trips from west to east; dotted-line arrows indicate trips from east to west. In figure E2.1, a trip with two cannibals from west to east is followed by a trip with one cannibal from east to west.

Because west-to-east trips and east-to-west trips must alternate, any valid sequence of trips must consist of alternating solid-line arrows and dotted-line arrows.[†]

Part 1   Identify the safe points in the state space.

Part 2   Find a path via safe points from the initial state to the desired state. Your path will take you through all the safe points.

[†]This representation is based on work by Saul Amarel [1968].

Figure E2.1 A search space for the missionaries and cannibals.

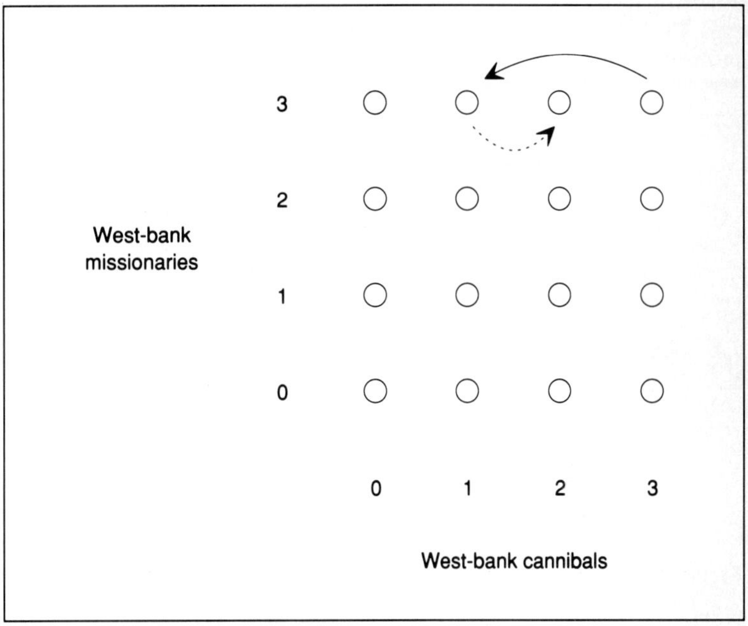

EXERCISE 2.2

Consider cantaloupes, cherries, eggplants, oranges, papayas, and watermelons.

Part 1   Using the pattern-recognition approach, prescribe a two-feature system for differentiating among these fruits.

Part 2   Would your system degrade gracefully as the number of types to be recognized increases? Explain your answer.

EXERCISE 2.3

Write out the rule descriptions in detail to show why the analogy procedure wrongly selects answer 1 in the problem given in figure E2.2.

EXERCISE 2.4

The analogy procedure, as described, cannot solve the problem in figure E2.3. When the A-to-B rule is matched with the C-to-1 rule, x must be associated with l and y with m. Similarly, for C-to-2, the opposite pairing is forced, and you have x associated with m and y with l. But note that, under the associations given, both C-to-1 and C-to-2 give exact match against A-to-B. How could you generalize the analogy procedure so that it could solve the problem correctly?

Figure E2.2 A tricky analogy problem.

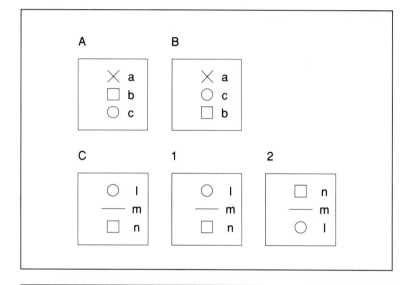

Figure E2.3 An analogy problem that cannot be solved by the analogy procedure, as described.

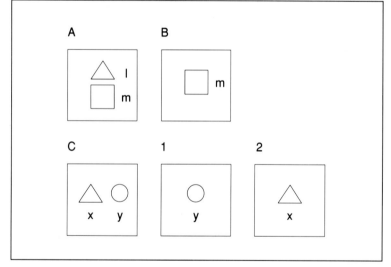

EXERCISE 2.5

As described, summaries are built starting with the most connected abstraction unit in the story to be summarized. Specify two or three other abstraction units with which you might start.

EXERCISE 2.6

One way of describing the similarity between two stories is to name the most connected top-level abstraction unit appearing in both stories. Another is to enumerate all the top-level abstraction units appearing in both stories. Specify two or three other ways to describe similarity.

CHAPTER 3
Generate
and Test,
Means-Ends
Analysis,
and Problem
Reduction

EXERCISE 3.1

You are working quietly with your terminal when you are attacked by an army of ants. Wishing to counterattack, you run to the supermarket and look around wildly, hoping that some useful weapon will catch your eye as you randomly scan the beverages, foods, household cleaners, and other products. You are using the generate-and-test paradigm, of course, but your generator is not likely to have three desired properties. What are those properties?

EXERCISE 3.2

This problem focuses on the use of generate and test in ordinary human activities.

Part 1   Identify the generation and testing procedures that most people use when they decide what to eat in a restaurant. Then, identify the generation and testing procedures that most people use when they decide what holiday gifts to order from a stack of catalogs.

Part 2   Are the generators that you identified complete and nonredundant?

Part 3   Can the generators that you identified be informed?

EXERCISE 3.3

Suppose that you have just installed a new carpet in your bedroom. You discover that the bedroom door will not open until you trim between 1/4 and 1/16 inch off the bottom. Construct a difference-operator table relating a saw, a plane, and a file to the precise amount of wood you need to trim off.

EXERCISE 3.4

Suppose you travel a great deal. At the moment, you figure out how to make each trip using means–ends analysis. It occurs to you that you can speed up your planning using experience. How can you do that?

EXERCISE 3.5

In many problems involving difference-procedure tables, more than one difference may describe how the current state is related to the goal state. In a travel problem, for example, you may need to consider time as well as place.

   Moreover, more than one procedure may be relevant to reducing any particular difference. In a travel problem, for example, you may be able to take either a bus or a taxi.

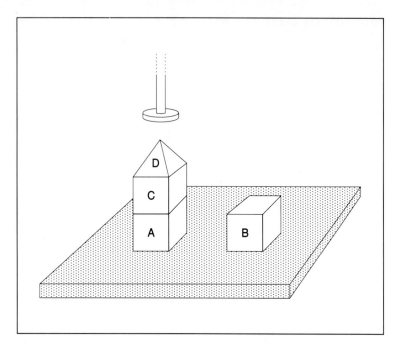

Figure E3.1 An initial situation faced by MOVER.

Part 1   Invent a table-oriented scheme for procedure selection that does the following:

- Combines the evidence from all the observed differences
- Considers the priority of the differences
- Considers the likelihood with which the various procedures reduce the various differences

Part 2   Fill in the following table for traveling from your house to the airport. Assume that buses and taxis are equally reliable for trips that are 1 mile long or less, but buses are more reliable for trips that are longer than 1 mile. Also assume that taxis are faster than buses, and that time considerations have priority over distance considerations. When reliability and time are not issues, you prefer taxis. Cost is not an issue.

	Use taxi	Use bus
More than 1 mile		
1 mile or less		
Adequate time for bus		
Inadequate time for bus		

EXERCISE 3.6

Consider the three-block tower in figure E3.1.

Figure E3.2 A placement
problem.

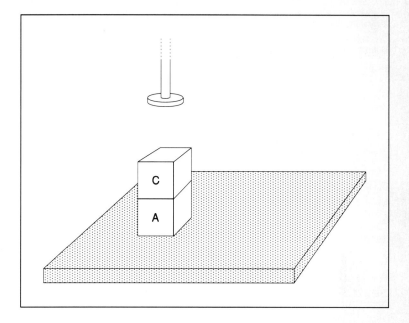

Part 1   Create an And–Or tree reflecting what MOVER does when asked
to put block A on block B.

Part 2   Use the And–Or tree that you constructed in the previous part to
answer the following questions:

- Why did you move D?
- Why did you move C?
- Why did you move A?
- How did you clear the top of A?
- How did you get rid of C?

Part 3   How, in general, would you deal with questions involving *when*?
Use your procedure to deal with the following questions:

- When did you move D?
- When did you move C?
- When did you move A?

EXERCISE 3.7

Consider the situation in figure E3.2.

Part 1   Create an And–Or tree reflecting what MOVER does when asked
to put A on C.

Part 2   How does MOVER blunder?

Part 3   How can you prevent MOVER's blunder?

Figure E4.1 A net to be searched.

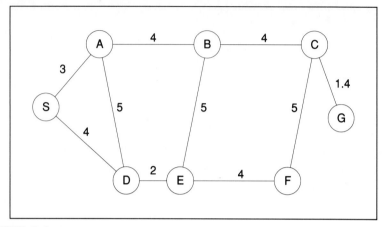

CHAPTER 4
Nets and Basic Search

EXERCISE 4.1

Draw the tree of all loop-free paths that is equivalent to the net shown in figure E4.1. When a node has more than one child, arrange them in alphabetical order.

EXERCISE 4.2

Show how depth-first search would search the net shown in figure E4.1.

EXERCISE 4.3

Show how breadth-first search would search the net shown in figure E4.1.

EXERCISE 4.4

Show how hill climbing would search the net shown in figure E4.1. Use straight-line distances, ranked visually, to sort candidates.

EXERCISE 4.5

Show how beam search, with a beam width of 2, would search the net shown in figure E4.1. Use straight-line distances, ranked visually, to sort candidates.

EXERCISE 4.6

Show how best-first search would search the net shown in figure E4.1. Use straight-line distances, ranked visually, to sort candidates.

EXERCISE 4.7

Given a net with n nodes, what is the maximum number of levels in the corresponding tree?

EXERCISE 4.8

A *map* can be viewed as a semantic net. Provide an informal specification for the map representation.

EXERCISE 4.9

Write a procedure, in procedural English, for best-first search.

EXERCISE 4.10

Write a procedure, in procedural English, for beam search.

<table>
<tr><td>

CHAPTER 5
Nets and
Optimal Search

</td></tr>
</table>

EXERCISE 5.1

Draw the complete search tree produced during branch-and-bound search of the net shown in figure E5.1.

EXERCISE 5.2

Draw the complete search tree produced during a branch-and-bound search with dynamic programming of the net shown in figure E5.1.

EXERCISE 5.3

Construct a family tree for the optimal search techniques.

EXERCISE 5.4

Draw the configuration space for the problem shown in figure E5.1. Use the lower-left corner of the triangle as the reference point. You do need to determine the precise shape of the configuration-space obstacle derived from the circle—a sketch will do.

EXERCISE 5.5

The visibility-graph representation can be described as either a semantic net or a map.

Part 1   Describe the visibility-graph representation in terms of semantic nets.

Part 2   Describe the visibility-graph representation in terms of maps.

CHAPTER 6
Trees and
Adversarial
Search

EXERCISE 6.1

Consider the game tree in figure E6.1. Explore the tree using the ALPHA–BETA procedure. Indicate all parts of the tree that are cut off. Indicate the winning path or paths. Strike out all static values that do not need to be computed.

EXERCISE 6.2

Now consider the tree in figure E6.2, which is the mirror image of the one in figure E6.1.

Explore the tree using the ALPHA–BETA procedure. Indicate all parts of the tree that are cut off. Indicate the winning path or paths. Strike out all static values that to not need to be computed.

Figure E5.1 An obstacle-avoidance problem.

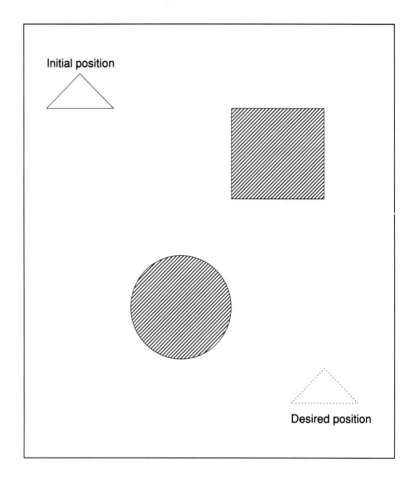

EXERCISE 6.3

Consider the game tree in figure E6.3. Explore the tree using the ALPHA–BETA procedure. Indicate all parts of the tree that are cut off. Indicate the winning path or paths. Strike out all static values that do not need to be computed.

EXERCISE 6.4

Now consider the tree in figure E6.4, which is the mirror image of the game tree in figure E6.3.

Explore the tree using the ALPHA–BETA procedure. Indicate all parts of the tree that are cut off. Indicate the winning path or paths. Strike out all static values that do not need to be computed.

EXERCISE 6.5

Criticize the following statements:

Figure E6.1 A game tree.

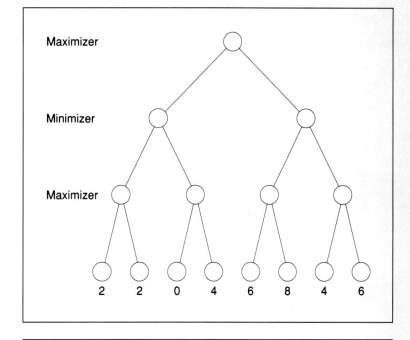

Figure E6.2 The mirror image of the game tree in figure E6.1.

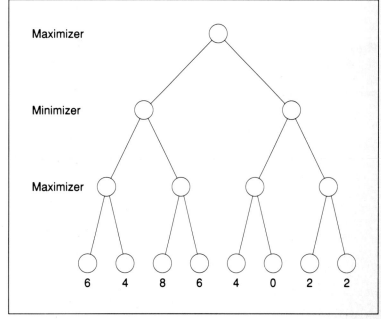

- The alpha–beta theorem demonstrates that no more than $2b^{d/2} - 1$ terminals need to be examined in trees of even depth on the average.
- Given a plausible move generator that always orders the moves per-

Figure E6.3 A four-ply game tree.

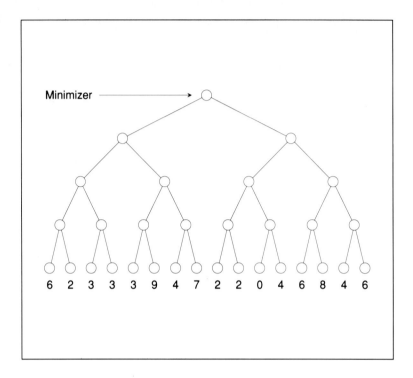

Figure E6.4 The mirror image of the four-play game tree in figure E6.3.

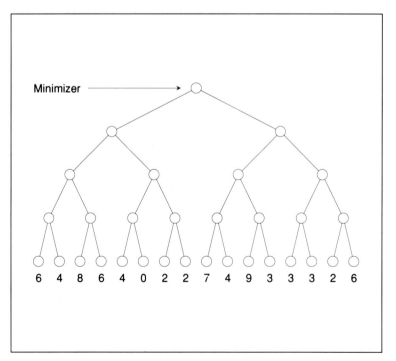

fectly, the ALPHA–BETA procedure gives optimal tree pruning, and only a fool would not use it.

- Unlike straight minimaxing, using the ALPHA–BETA procedure can prevent spectacular moves, such as queen sacrifices leading to checkmate, in chess.

EXERCISE 6.6

Assume that you conspire with an opponent to fix a chess game. You agree to some secret signals that allow you to tell him exactly how to move. The objective is to beat him by as much as possible. How effective is the ALPHA–BETA procedure under these conditions?

CHAPTER 7
Rules and Rule Chaining

EXERCISE 7.1

Assume that the ZOOKEEPER procedure is asked to chain backward from the following hypotheses in the given order:

Ostrich
Penguin
Albatross

Then, consider the following facts about an animal, Splashy:

- Splashy has feathers.
- Splashy lays eggs.
- Splashy does not fly.
- Splashy is black and white.
- Splashy swims.

Assume that nothing else is known to be true.

Part 1   Simulate ZOOKEEPER's behavior so as to determine what kind of animal Splashy is. Take care to use the hypotheses in the specified order. Indicate your answer by showing what is the sequence in which the rules are used, what each rule is trying to do, and whether each rule succeeds.

Part 2   Rework the exercise in the previous part assuming that Splashy has long legs and a long neck. The other properties are unchanged. Why is the result peculiar?

EXERCISE 7.2

You are just starting a quiet evening at home when an old friend calls to announce that he is coming over for dinner. This news being a big surprise, you immediately undertake emergency dinner preparations.

Within a few minutes, you have managed to activate BARTENDER, a rule-based expert system, so that you can select a beverage.

BARTENDER backward chains using rules given next. Note that, when more than one rule has a consequent matching the current problem, those rules are tried in the order given in the list.

Exercise 7.2 is based on an idea contributed by Karen A. Prendergast.

B1   If   expensive wine is indicated
             it is New Year's Eve
     then   choose Bond's Champagne

B2   If   expensive wine is indicated
             entree is steak
     then   choose Chateau Earl of Bartonville Red

B3   If   cheap wine is indicated
             entree is chicken
             guest is not well liked
     then   choose Honest Henry's Apple Wine

B4   If   cheap wine is indicated
             entree is unknown
     then   choose Toe Lakes Rose

B5   If   beer is indicated
             entree is Mexican
     then   choose Dos Equis

B6   If   beer is indicated
     then   choose Coors

B7   If   guest is a health nut
     then   choose Glop

B8   If   guest is a health nut
             carrots are not to be served
     then   choose carrot juice

B9   If   wine is indicated
             guest should be impressed
     then   expensive wine is indicated

B10 If   wine is indicated
     then   cheap wine is indicated

B11 If   guest is sophisticated
     then   wine is indicated

B12 If   entree is Mexican
     then   beer is indicated

B13 If   guest is not well liked
             entree is catered by Death-wish Caterers
     then   beer is indicated

B14   If   entree is anything
      then   choose water

BARTENDER's hypotheses are as follows:

■ Serve Bond's Champagne
■ Serve Chateau Earl of Bartonville Red
■ Serve Toe Lakes Rose
■ Serve Honest Henry's Apple Wine
■ Serve Dos Equis
■ Serve Coors
■ Serve Glop
■ Serve Carrot juice
■ Serve Water

Now here are some facts to assume true, if BARTENDER inquires:

■ Entree is catered by Death-Wish Caterers.
■ Entree is Mexican.
■ Guest is not well liked.
■ Guest is sophisticated.
■ It is New Year's Eve.
■ The entree is chicken.

Assume than nothing else is known to be true.

Part 1   Simulate BARTENDER's behavior for the given facts. Take care to use the hypotheses in the specified order. Indicate your answer by showing the sequence in which the rules are used and whether each succeeds.

Part 2   With some different set of facts, could BARTENDER ever recommend the Chateau Earl of Bartonville Red with a Mexican steak? Explain your answer.

Part 3   With some different set of facts, could BARTENDER ever recommend carrot juice with steak? Explain your answer.

EXERCISE 7.3

BAGGER uses the rule-ordering conflict-resolution strategy. Argue that it also uses the context-limiting conflict-resolution strategy.

EXERCISE 7.4

Simulate BAGGER operating on the following shopping list. To keep your answer manageable, report only which are the successful rule firings and what each rule adds.

Item number	Item	Container type	Size	Frozen?
1	bread	plastic bag	medium	no
2	glop	jar	small	no
3	granola	cardboard box	large	no
4	corn flakes	cardboard box	large	no
5	frozen peas	cardboard carton	medium	yes
6	paper towels	plastic bag	large	no
7	pepsi	bottle	large	no
8	popsicle	paper	small	yes

EXERCISE 7.5

Suppose BAGGER considers whether an item is crushable, as well as the item's other properties. Assuming that only medium items are crushable, add rules to the BAGGER system so that nothing gets crushed.

EXERCISE 7.6

In our version of BAGGER, the steps are activated and deactivated by rules that include antecedents that check the current step. Show how you can eliminate those rules in favor of others that look at what needs to be done, instead of at what the current step is.

EXERCISE 7.7

In the discussion of variable binding, an example in the text uses the following rule:

Parent Rule
    If $?x$ is-a horse
                $?x$ is-a-parent-of $?y$
                $?y$ is fast
    then $?x$ is valuable

Suppose that the first two antecedents are swapped:

Modified Parent Rule
    If $?x$ is-a-parent-of $?y$
                $?x$ is-a horse
                $?y$ is fast
    then $?x$ is valuable

Show what the complete search tree looks like for the same set of assertions used in the text, repeated here for your convenience:

Comet	is-a	horse
Prancer	is-a	horse
Comet	is-a-parent-of	Dasher
Comet	is-a-parent-of	Prancer
Prancer	is	fast
Dasher	is-a-parent-of	Thunder
Thunder	is	fast
Thunder	is-a	horse
Dasher	is-a	horse

EXERCISE 7.8

In the rete example, all antecedents, consequents, and assertions had three elements. What changes would you make to handle assertions of arbitrary length?

EXERCISE 7.9

Design a rete for the following rule. Look for an opportunity to share an operation.

Mule Rule
    If $?x$ is-a horse
             $?x$ is-a-parent-of $?y$
             $?z$ is-a-parent-of $?y$
             $?z$ is-a donkey
    then $?y$ is-a mule

EXERCISE 7.10

Now suppose that you want to use both the rule in the previous exercise together with the Parent Rule given below. Explain how you would design an efficient rete for these two rules.

Parent Rule
    If $?x$ is-a horse
             $?x$ is-a-parent-of $?y$
             $?y$ is fast
    then $?x$ is valuable

**CHAPTER 8
Rules,
Substrates,
and Cognitive
Modeling**

EXERCISE 8.1

Add rules to the ZOOKEEPER system, described in Chapter 7, so that it can recognize porcupines, raccoons, and elephants. Make each rule just strong enough to separate the recognized animal from the others in the zoo, rather than from all possible animals.

EXERCISE 8.2

You have learned that rules with unless and providing assumptions are similar to ordinary antecedent–consequent rules.

Part 1   Recast the following as ordinary antecedent–consequent rules:

Fly Rule
If	*?x* is-a bird
then	*?x* flies
unless	*?x* is-a penguin
providing	*?x* is alive

Bird Rule
If	*?x* flies
then	*?x* is-a bird
unless	*?x* is-a bat
providing	*?x* is alive

Part 2   Explain how the given rules differ from the recast rules from the perspective of a reasoning system operating in ask-questions-later mode.

EXERCISE 8.3

Suppose that you decide to develop a rule-based deduction system to help you choose elective course subjects. Accordingly, you create rules that award points to various subjects. The subject with the highest number of points becomes your first choice. Here is a sample rule:

E0	If	subject is interesting
	add	subject points +10

Create five or six rules that reflect your own taste.

EXERCISE 8.4

According to the text, many rule-based systems are idiot savants.

Part 1   Supply a few reasons why the BAGGER program can be viewed as an idiot.

Part 2   Can you provide BAGGER with a rule that embodies knowledge of *why* potato chips should not be placed at the bottom of a bag? Explain your answer.

EXERCISE 8.5

Part 1   Using SOAR's automatic preference analyzer, determine which of the states, if any, in figure E8.1 should be the next current state. Assume that all states shown are marked *acceptable*, and that one of the states shown is the current state.

Figure E8.1 A state space.

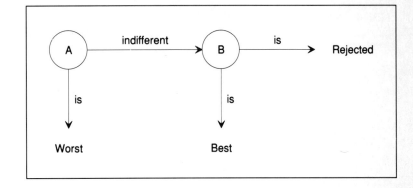

Figure E8.2 Another state space.

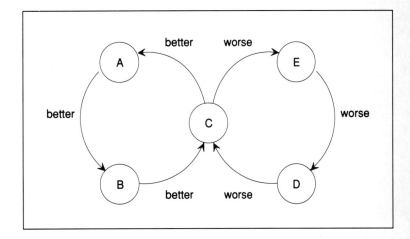

Part 2   Repeat part 1 for the states shown in figure E8.2. Again assume that all states shown are marked *acceptable*, and assume that state A is the current state.

Part 3   Repeat part 1 for the states shown in figure E8.3.

EXERCISE 8.6

Recall that each node in a search tree represents a path. You can use the following search procedure, together with SOAR's automatic preference analyzer, to look for a path from the initial node to a goal node:

Figure E8.3 Still another state space.

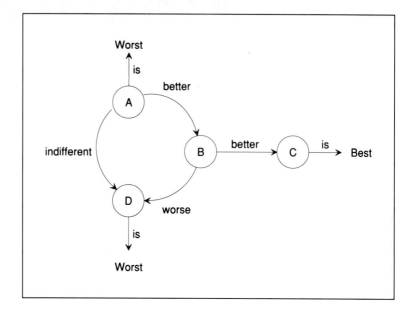

To conduct a search,

▷ Until there is no acceptable node or the goal is reached,

  ▷ If the current node has been expanded already, mark the current node *rejected*. Otherwise, create new nodes by extending the path corresponding to the current node, and add preference links to the new nodes.

  ▷ Use SOAR's automatic preference analyzer to establish a new current node.

Of course, the kind of search performed depends on the preference links inserted. Here is a prescription for preference links that lead to depth-first search:

To insert preference links for depth-first search,

▷ Link all child nodes to their parent with *better* links.

▷ Arrange the child nodes in a random sequence. Link the leftmost node to the adjacent node on its right by a *better* link. Repeat for the other nodes in the child-node sequence up to the rightmost node.

Part 1   Modify the link-insertion procedure such that the search performed is hill climbing.

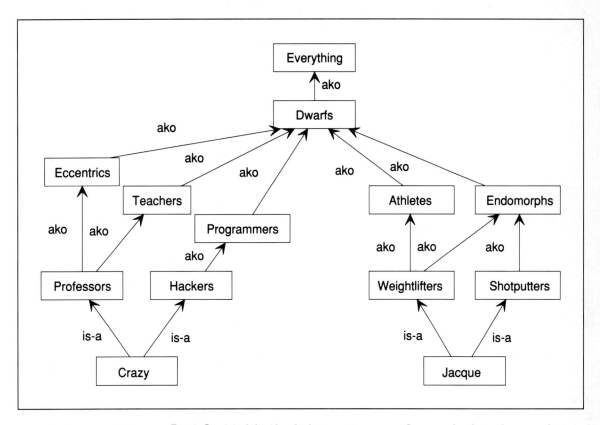

Figure E9.1 A class hierarchy.

Part 2 Modify the link-insertion procedure such that the search performed is breadth first.

EXERCISE 9.1

Suppose, the Crazy class is connected as shown in figure E9.1. Further suppose that you have the following when-constructed procedures, as in the text:

To fill the Income slot when a new Hacker is constructed,

▷ Write High into the slot.

To fill the Income slot when a new Teacher is constructed,

▷ Write Low into the slot.

Part 1 Determine whether Crazy's income is high or low using the topological sorting procedure.

Figure E9.2 A class hierarchy for city dwellers.

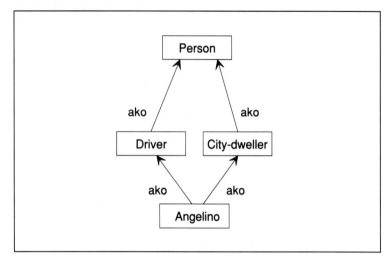

Part 2 Now suppose that you add another when-constructed procedure:

To fill the Income slot when a new Eccentric is constructed,

▷ Write Erratic into the slot.

Will Crazy's income be high, low, or erratic?

EXERCISE 9.2

Compute the class-precedence list for John, who is both a professor and a weight lifter.

EXERCISE 9.3

Consider the class hierarchy shown in figure E9.2.

Part 1 Add the Bostonian class to the hierarchy. Assume that Bostonians are both city dwellers and drivers, but that properties from the city dweller class are to be inherited before those from the driver class.

Part 2 Suppose that Gerry has just left Boston for Los Angeles on sabbatical, making him both a Bostonian and an Angelino. Explain what happens when you try to construct Gerry's class-precedence list.

EXERCISE 9.4

Suppose that a brick can be viewed as a structure, as a toy, or as a gift. Write out with-respect-to procedures for each of these perspectives. Have all your procedures return a reasonable answer when the purpose of a particular instance of a brick is requested.

EXERCISE 9.5

Suggest five heuristics for using news stories to fill slots in wedding frames.

EXERCISE 9.6

If a story writer uses pronouns freely, it may be hard to fill in frames. Consider the following story:

A Birthday Party ―――――――――――――――――――

Robbie and Suzie were going to Marvin's birthday party. *One of them* wanted to buy a kite. "But *he* already has *one*," *he* said to *her*, "if *you* give *him one*, *he* will ask *you* to take *it* back."

In this version, unraveling the pronoun references is difficult. Rewrite the story in the form of news, circumnavigating the pronoun-reference problems.

CHAPTER 10
Frames and Commonsense

EXERCISE 10.1

Consider the following sentence:

Robbie grew plants with fertilizer.

Part 1 Work out the sentence's thematic-role frames.

Part 2 Work out the sentence's action and state-change frames.

EXERCISE 10.2

Consider the following sentences:

Macbeth murdered Duncan.
Macbeth stabbed Duncan.

Part 1 Work out the sentences' thematic-role frames.

Part 2 Work out the sentences' action and state-change frames.

EXERCISE 10.3

Using your answer to the previous exercise, indicate which sentence and which representation you would need to answer the following questions appropriately:

What happened to Duncan's condition?
Who murdered Duncan?
Who was stabbed?
Who did something with a knife?

EXERCISE 10.4

Suppose that you speak a version of English in which the word *give* has only the following meanings:

- *Give1* means to transfer possession of one thing to one recipient.
- *Give2* means to distribute copies of something to many recipients.
- *Give3* means quit.
- *Give4* means to yield.
- *Give5* means to host.
- *Give6* means to infect.
- *Give7* means to emit fumes.
- *Give8* means to return something.

Explain how you would use thematic roles and particles to recognize which meaning is intended, and provide sample sentences exhibiting those recognizable characteristics.

EXERCISE 10.5

Consider the sentence "Suzie comforted Robbie." Reducing the sentence to primitive acts and state changes, and then generating English from the reduced primitive acts and state changes, we have a paraphrase, "Suzie did something that caused Robbie's mood to be happy."

Part 1 Determine what paraphrases would be generated for the following sentences:

Robbie angered Suzie.
Robbie killed a fly.
Robbie opened the door.
Robbie walked to town.
Robbie gorged on ice cream.
Robbie hurled a stone into the stream.

Part 2 Would it be significantly more difficult to generate the paraphrases in another language? Explain your answer.

CHAPTER 11
Numeric
Constraints and
Propagation

EXERCISE 11.1

Show, in summary form, the opinion-net class of representations used to propagate probability bounds through logic constraints. Use the specialization of the value-propagation class of representations to the arithmetic constraint-net class as a model.

EXERCISE 11.2

Consider the arrangement of Or boxes in figure E11.1. Calculate the upper and lower bounds on the output probability, given that the bounds provided for all four inputs are [0.5, 0.5].

Figure E11.1 An opinion net with Or boxes.

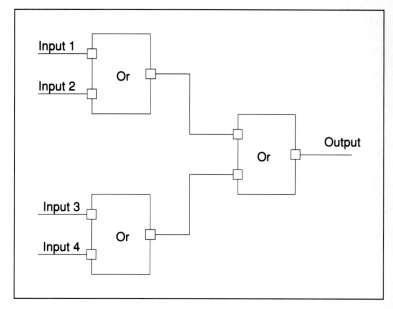

EXERCISE 11.3

Now suppose that the Or boxes in figure E11.1 are actually And boxes. Calculate the upper and lower bounds on the output probability, given that the bounds provided for all four inputs are [0.5, 0.5].

EXERCISE 11.4

The constraint equations for Not boxes are as follows:

$$u(A) \leq 1 - l(\text{not } A),$$
$$l(A) \geq 1 - u(\text{not } A),$$
$$u(\text{not } A) \leq 1 - l(A),$$
$$l(\text{not } A) \geq 1 - u(A).$$

Explain these constraints.

EXERCISE 11.5

Explain the constraint equations for the And box.

EXERCISE 11.6

If you are told that class A and class B are *independent*, you know that the probability that an event is in class A is the same whether or not the event is in class B and vice versa. From the perspective of Venn diagrams, this assertion means that the area of overlap, relative to the total size of class B, is the same as the total area of class A, and that the area of overlap, relative to the total size of class A, is the same as the total size of class B:

$$p(A) = \frac{p(A \text{ and } B)}{p(B)} \qquad \text{and} \qquad p(B) = \frac{p(A \text{ and } B)}{p(A)}$$

Figure E12.1 Two peculiar objects.

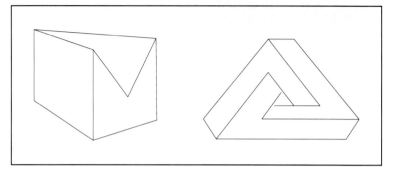

Thus, $p(A \text{ and } B) = p(A) \times p(B)$. Derive constraint equations for Or boxes, given that the inputs are independent.

EXERCISE 11.7

Suppose that the Or boxes in figure E11.1 are actually independent Or boxes. Calculate the upper and lower bounds on the output probability, given that the bounds provided for all four inputs are [0.5, 0.5] as shown.

EXERCISE 11.8

The relaxation procedure for calculating heights from initial altitude estimates used initial altitude estimates of 0 when there was no information. Suggest an alternative that leads to faster convergence.

EXERCISE 11.9

The relaxation procedure for calculating heights from initial altitude estimates converges slowly, because it takes a long time to propagate information through many array points. Suggest a way to use a coarse grid to speed convergence.

CHAPTER 12
Symbolic Constraints and Propagation

EXERCISE 12.1

Decide which of the two objects in figure E12.1 can be labeled using the four-line-label set. Explain.

EXERCISE 12.2

Label the drawings in figure E12.2.

EXERCISE 12.3

Finish labeling figure E12.3, indicating all possible combinations of labels that are consistent with the four-label set.

EXERCISE 12.4

Label the drawing fragment in figure E12.4.

Figure E12.2 A few labeling exercises.

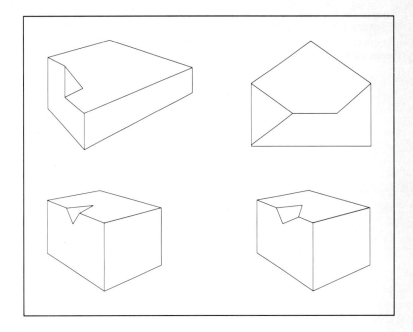

Figure E12.3 A drawing with more than one interpretation.

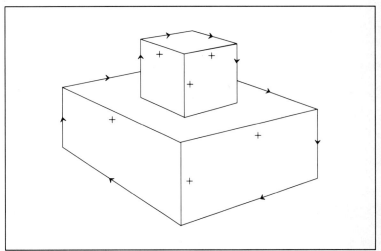

EXERCISE 12.5

Suppose that a robot lives in a world of polyhedra known to have no concave edges.

Part 1   How should the four-line-label theory be modified by this robot to detect impossible objects in the robot's world?

Part 2   What are the physically realizable junctions?

Figure E12.4 A drawing fragment to be labeled.

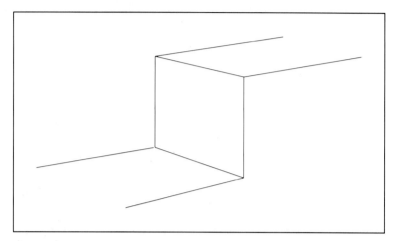

EXERCISE 12.6

What conclusion should be drawn when the Waltz procedure, operating in three-faced-vertex world, eliminates all the labeling possibilities at a junction?

EXERCISE 12.7

Why is it that the Waltz procedure cannot get stuck propagating constraints around some junction loop forever?

EXERCISE 12.8

The number of possible labels for a line is $11 \times 3^2 = 99$, where there are 11 basic line types and 3 states of illumination on either side of each line. Hence, for an L junction, the number of combinatorially possible labels is $11^2 \times 3^4 = 9801$.

Waltz argued that only about 50 labels survive for lines when line type and illumination constraints are considered, giving about $50^2 = 2500$ possible L junction labels.

Ignoring the interaction of line types and illumination states, argue on the basis of region continuity that there can be no more than 1089 possible L junction labels.

EXERCISE 12.9

Suppose that Pat, Terry, and Lynn are students. One wants to be a scientist, another a lawyer, and another a manager. As it happens, one of them reads *Scientific American*, another reads *Business Week*, and another reads *Mercenary World*.

Now assume that X(Pat, Scientist) means "the person who is Pat is not the person who wants to be a scientist," and, symmetrically, "the person

---

Exercise 12.8 is based on an idea contributed by Linda J. Rosentzarat.
Exercise 12.9 is based on an idea contributed by Kenneth D. Forbus.

who wants to be a scientist is not Pat." In this notation, suppose the facts are as follows:

1 X(Pat, Scientist)
2 X(Pat, *Mercenary World*)
3 X(Scientist, *Mercenary World*)
4 X(Terry, *Business Week*)
5 X(Terry, Lawyer)
6 X(Lawyer, *Business Week*)
7 X(Manager, *Scientific American*)
8 X(Manager, *Mercenary World*)

You can represent the possible relations by entries in a table. Each row and column corresponds to names, desired occupations, or magazines read. An *X* entry in the table indicates that the person corresponding to the column entry is not the same as the person corresponding to the row entry, and an *I* denotes that the two are the same. Numbers in the boxes indicate the fact used to establish the entry:

	Scientist	Lawyer	Manager
Pat	X,1		
Terry		X,5	
Lynn			

	Scientific American	*Business Week*	*Mercenary World*
Pat			X,2
Terry		X,4	
Lynn			

	Scientific American	*Business Week*	*Mercenary World*
Scientist			X,3
Lawyer		X,6	
Manager	X,7		X,8

The following rules describe how new table entries can be deduced:

1 If all but one entry in a row are Xs, then the remaining one is an I.
2 If one entry in a row is an I, then all others in the row are Xs.
3 If all but one entry in a column are Xs, then the remaining one is an I.
4 If one entry in a column is an I, then all others in the column are Xs.
5 If you know I(x, y) and X(y, z), then you can conclude X(x, z).

Part 1 For rule 5, write a short English sentence that describes the property of the world that the rule captures.

Part 2 Determine what Terry wants to be, using the rules and the three tables.

EXERCISE 12.10

Consider labeling in interval nets. By looking at all the links in any interval net, trying to reduce the label count at one node at least, you know that the worst-case number of pair examinations is $13 \times \frac{n \times n - 1}{2} \times \frac{n \times n - 1}{2} \times (n - 2)$, which is order n^5. Suppose that you look at all the nodes instead. Does that reduce the worst-case number of pair examinations?

EXERCISE 12.11

Consider the partially labeled nets in figure E12.5.

■ For each net, determine which single label is allowed for the links labeled with question marks.
■ Show how you reach your conclusions.

EXERCISE 12.12

For both of the nets in figure E12.5, suppose that intervals X and Y last 15 minutes, L and M last 30 minutes, and A and B last 1 hour. Further suppose that X finishes at time x_f and that Y starts at time y_s. Determine bounds on $|y_s - x_f|$.

CHAPTER 13
Logic and
Resolution Proof

EXERCISE 13.1

The most popular of the two-argument connectives are &, $\vee$, and $\Rightarrow$. How many two-argument connectives are possible?

EXERCISE 13.2

Show that modus tolens is a special case of resolution.

EXERCISE 13.3

Show the steps required to put the following axioms into clause form:
$$\forall x \forall y [\mathrm{On}(x, y) \Rightarrow \mathrm{Above}(x, y)]$$
$$\forall x \forall y \forall z [\mathrm{Above}(x, y) \& \mathrm{Above}(y, z) \Rightarrow \mathrm{Above}(x, z)]$$

EXERCISE 13.4

The following axiom says that, if x is above y, but is not directly on y, then there must exist some third block, z, in between x and y:
$$\forall x \forall y [\mathrm{Above}(x, y) \& \neg \mathrm{On}(x, y) \Rightarrow \exists z [\mathrm{Above}(x, z) \& \mathrm{Above}(z, y)]]$$
Put the axiom in clause form. Note that you need to introduce a Skolem function.

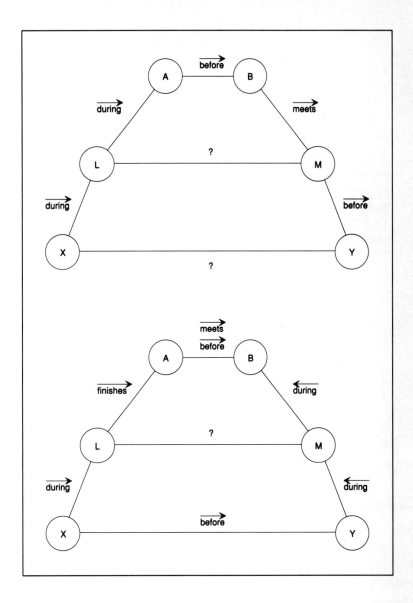

Figure E12.5 Partially labeled interval nets.

EXERCISE 13.5

Suppose that you are given the following axioms:

$$\forall x[\neg\text{Equal}(x, x+1)]$$
$$\text{Equal}(2, 3)$$

Part 1 Show that all apples are oranges.

Part 2 Why were you able to reach a silly conclusion in part 1?

EXERCISE 13.6

Before two clauses are resolved, they must have no variable names in common. Consequently, it might seem superfluous to prohibit replacement of a variable by a term containing that variable. Explain why the prohibition is not superfluous.

CHAPTER 14
Backtracking and Truth Maintenance

EXERCISE 14.1

Consider the activity-planning task described in the text. Suppose that you propose the following activities in the order given:

Planning step	Activity planned
1	Study 6 hours on Tuesday
2	Do not study on Thursday
3	Go out to dinner on Monday
4	Take a walk on Friday
5	Jog on Monday
6	Go out to dinner on Friday

Part 1 Show the contribution in units of each activity to fulfilling your need for exercise, study, and pleasure, and the units charged in money.

Part 2 Indicate at which planning step a problem emerges.

Part 3 Explain whether chronological backtracking would lead to the withdrawal of irrelevant choices.

EXERCISE 14.2

Again consider the activity-planning task described in the text. Suppose that you propose the following activities to yourself in the order given:

Planning step	Activity planned
1	Study 6 hours on Tuesday
2	Do not study on Thursday
3	Go out to dinner on Monday
4	Jog on Friday
5	Jog on Monday
6	Plan no entertainment on Friday
7	Study 2 hours on Wednesday

Part 1 Show the contribution in units of each activity to fulfilling your needs for exercise, study, pleasure, and the units charged in money.

Part 2 Determine which, if any, limit boxes show violations.

EXERCISE 14.3

Now suppose that you add a constraint to the activity-planning task to the effect that the ratio of money spent to pleasure experienced must be less than 8 to 1 each week.

Part 1   Add the necessary limit box to the numeric constraint net shown in the text.

Part 2   Determine whether the new constraint would be violated by the activities planned in the previous exercise.

Part 3   Using nonchronological backtracking, indicate which choices would be reviewed, given the activities planned in the previous exercise. Assume that all activities are planned before the new constraint is added to the constraint net.

EXERCISE 14.4

Suppose that you make an activity plan that suits you just fine. You plan to use it every week, making modifications only when necessary to accommodate unusual circumstances.

Now suppose that you know there is a constraint that limits the relative value of money spent to pleasure experienced, but you do not know how to formulate it. Nevertheless, you can recognize bad combinations when you see them. Describe what you would want to add to a numeric-constraint–propagating system so that you could be sure that you have a satisfactory plan each week, without doing any unnecessary work.

EXERCISE 14.5

Consider the following to be axioms:

$$P \Rightarrow R$$
$$Q \Rightarrow R$$
$$P \vee Q$$

Part 1   Show that R is a theorem using resolution.

Part 2   Repeat part 1, if possible, using the constraint-propagation proof procedure.

CHAPTER 15
Planning

EXERCISE 15.1

Suppose that you have an initial situation in which all of the following assertions hold:

ON(A, B)
ON(B, C)
ON(C, D)
ON(D, Table)

Suppose that your goal is to achieve all the following:

ON(D, Table)
ON(C, Table)
ON(B, Table)
ON(A, Table)

Now, you are to think about constructing a plan for each assertion using the STRIPS approach. Further, suppose that you are to plan for each part of the overall goal in the given order, using breadth-first search, until that part of the goal is satisfied. As you proceed, you are to stay on the lookout for threats.

- You work on the goals one at a time, in the given order.
- You work on each goal using breadth-first search.
- You stay on the lookout for threats at all times, resolving them with ordering constraints.

Part 1 Determine whether it is possible to construct a plan, and whether the resulting plan can be less than optimal. Explain your answer.

Part 2 Repeat part 1, assuming that you must achieve the parts of the overall goal in the opposite order.

EXERCISE 15.2

Consider the arrangement of blocks described by the following assertions:

ON(A, Table)
ON(B, Table)
ON(C, Table)
ON(D, Table)

Suppose that your goal is to achieve all the following, using the STRIPS approach:

ON(A, Table)
ON(B, A)
ON(C, B)
ON(D, C)

Further, suppose that you plan for each part of the overall goal in the given order, using breadth-first search, until that part of the goal is satisfied. As you proceed, you are to stay on the lookout for threats.

Part 1 Determine whether it is possible to construct a plan, and whether the resulting plan can be less than optimal. Also determine whether any threats will have to be resolved.

Part 2 Repeat part 1 assuming that your goal is to achieve the parts of the overall goal in the opposite order.

EXERCISE 15.3

The STRIPS planner explained in the text is a tactical planner in that it checks for only local conflicts. It is not a global planner in that it has no notion of how to avoid conflicts in the first place. To see why it is not a global planner, consider the arrangement of blocks described by the following assertions:

ON(A, B)
ON(B, C)
ON(C, D)
ON(D, Table)

Suppose that the goal is to achieve all the following, using the STRIPS approach:

ON(D, C)
ON(C, B)
ON(B, A)
ON(A, Table)

Part 1   What global heuristics would you use to solve the problem efficiently?

Part 2   Why would the STRIPS planner solve this problem inefficiently?

EXERCISE 15.4

The topological sorting procedure, introduced in Chapter 9, can be adopted to the task of finding a linear ordering of steps, given a complete plan. Explain what you need to do to adapt the topological sorting procedure to find such a linear ordering. Also, explain why the topological sorting procedure is certain to find at least one such linear ordering.

EXERCISE 15.5

Here are some logical expressions for solving blocks-world problems:

$$\forall x \forall y \forall s [\text{CLEAR}(x, s) \& \text{CLEAR}(y, s) \Rightarrow \text{ON}(x, y, \text{PUT-ON}(x, y, s))]$$
$$\forall x \forall y \forall s [\text{ON}(x, y, s) \Rightarrow \neg \text{CLEAR}(y, s)]$$
$$\forall x \forall y \forall s [\text{ON}(x, y, s) \& \text{CLEAR}(x, s) \Rightarrow \text{ON}(x, \text{Table}, \text{PUT-ON}(x, \text{Table}, s))]$$
$$\forall x \forall y \forall s [\text{ON}(x, y, s) \& \text{CLEAR}(x, s) \Rightarrow \text{CLEAR}(y, \text{PUT-ON}(x, \text{Table}, s))]$$

These are the same expressions in clause form:

$$\neg\text{CLEAR}(x_1, s_1) \lor \neg\text{CLEAR}(y_1, s_1) \lor \text{ON}(x_1, y_1, \text{PUT-ON}(x_1, y_1, s_1)) \quad (1)$$
$$\neg\text{ON}(x_2, y_2, s_2) \lor \neg\text{CLEAR}(y_2, s_2) \quad (2)$$
$$\neg\text{ON}(x_3, y_3, s_3) \lor \neg\text{CLEAR}(y_3, s_3) \lor \text{ON}(x_3, \text{Table}, \text{PUT-ON}(x_3, \text{Table}, s_3)) \quad (3)$$
$$\neg\text{ON}(x_4, y_4, s_4) \lor \neg\text{CLEAR}(x_4, s_4) \lor \text{CLEAR}(y_4, \text{PUT-ON}(x_4, \text{Table}, s_4)) \quad (4)$$

The initial state of the world is as follows:

$$\text{ON}(\text{A}, \text{B}, S) \tag{5}$$

$$\text{ON}(\text{B}, \text{C}, S) \tag{6}$$

$$\text{CLEAR}(\text{A}, S) \tag{7}$$

Assume that you also have axioms stating indirectly that certain objects are different; more specifically suppose you have axioms such as Different(A, B), Different(A, C), and Different(B, C). These axioms are used with the following frame axioms:

$$\forall u \forall x \forall y \forall s [\text{CLEAR}(u, s) \& \text{Different}(u, y) \Rightarrow \text{CLEAR}(u, \text{PUT-ON}(x, y, s))]$$

$$\forall u \forall v \forall x \forall y \forall s [\text{ON}(u, v, s) \& \text{Different}(u, x) \Rightarrow \text{ON}(u, v, \text{PUT-ON}(x, y, s))]$$

In clause form, the frame axioms are as follows:

$$\neg\text{CLEAR}(u_8, s_8) \vee \neg\text{Different}(u_8, y_8) \vee \text{CLEAR}(u_8, \text{PUT-ON}(x_8, y_8, s_8)) \tag{8}$$

$$\neg\text{ON}(u_9, v_9, s_9) \vee \neg\text{Different}(u_9, x_9) \vee \text{ON}(u_9, v_9, \text{PUT-ON}(x_9, y_9, s_9)) \tag{9}$$

Part 1   Explain both of the frame axioms in English.

Part 2   Show that the following state can be achieved using set-of-support resolution.

$$\exists s [\text{CLEAR}(\text{C}, s)]$$

A good way to start is to use axiom 4. At each step in the proof, indicate which clauses are being resolved. Rename variables consistently to ensure that the variable names in the clauses that you resolve are mutually exclusive. The proof requires fewer than 10 steps.

Part 3   Repeat using Green's trick to find the plan that achieves the indicated state.

Figure E16.1 A classification
tree for shapes.

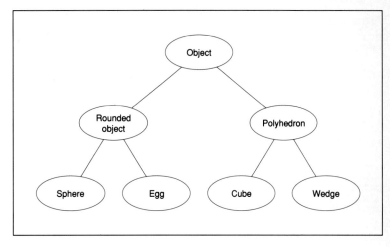

CHAPTER **16**
Learning by
Analyzing
Differences

EXERCISE 16.1

Suppose that you want to teach a Martian about ostriches. You show it an
ostrich that is tall and that has a long neck, long legs, and black feathers.
Next, you select negative examples from a group that includes a penguin,
a tall black crane, a crow, an elephant, a giraffe, a gazelle, and a kiwi.

You want to convey the idea that ostriches cannot fly. Which animal
should you use? What heuristic should the Martian deduce in response?

EXERCISE 16.2

You want to teach a Martian about apples. You assume that the Martian's
perceptual system builds semantic nets with only the following information
in them:

■ An object's color is red, green, blue, purple, white, or black.
■ An object's weight is a number.
■ An object's shape is any one of those in the tree shown in figure E16.1.
■ An object may be inedible, fragrant, or smelly. There are no other
  properties that an object may have.

You elect the following teaching sequence. For each example, note what
heuristic is applied and explain what is learned.

Example	Result	Color	Shape	Weight	Quality
1	positive	red	sphere	4	fragrant
2	positive	red	sphere	4	
3	negative	red	sphere	4	inedible
4	positive	green	sphere	4	
5	positive	green	sphere	7	
6	positive	red	egg	5	
7	negative	red	cube	4	

Figure E16.2 A key with four teeth.

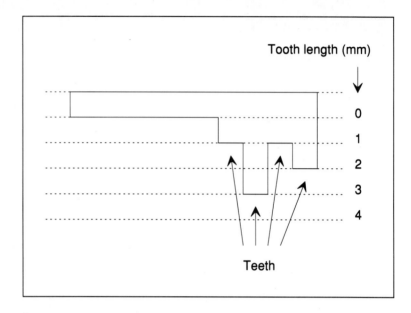

EXERCISE 16.3

Suppose you are trying to open a lock that is known to require an old-fashioned key that has four teeth, each of which protrudes by 0, 1, 2, 3, or 4 millimeters from the shaft of the key. Figure E16.2 shows an example of such a key.

Further suppose that you have wired up a sophisticated lock-picking tool that somehow enables you to sort all available test keys into one of two groups:

■ Group 1 keys are too loose; no tooth protrudes more than it should, and at least one does not protrude far enough.

■ Group 2 keys are too tight; at least one tooth protrudes more than it should; others may not protrude far enough.

Equipped with your lock-picking tool, you sort all available test keys as shown in figure E16.3.

Part 1 Using the test results from only group 1—the too-loose keys—determine an *inner-envelope key* such that

1 Each tooth on the correct key is the same length or longer than the corresponding tooth on the inner-envelope shape.

2 Each tooth on the inner-envelope shape is as long as is justified by the group 1 test results.

Part 2 Use whatever test results you need to determine an *outer-envelope key* such that

1 Each tooth on the correct key is the same length or shorter than the corresponding tooth on the outer-envelope shape.

Figure E16.3 Some too-loose keys and some too-tight keys.

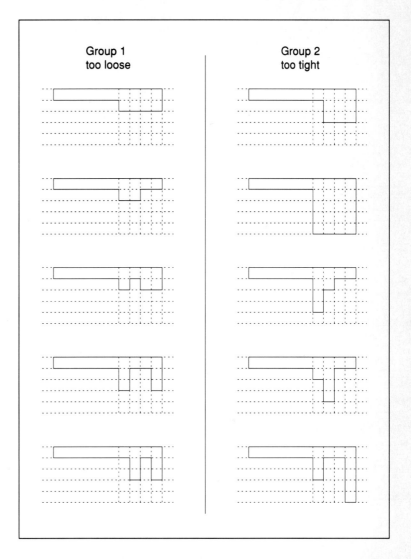

Figure E16.3 Some too-loose keys and some too-tight keys.

2   Each tooth on the outer-envelope shape is as short as is justified by the group 1 and group 2 test results.

EXERCISE 16.4

In the context of the previous exercise identify which of the following could be viewed as a near miss:

- A key with small area.
- A key with large area.
- A key that is entirely within the inner envelope.
- A key that is entirely within the outer envelope.

- A key that has at least one tooth within the inner envelope.
- A key that has exactly one tooth outside the inner envelope.
- A too-tight key that differs from a too-loose key in exactly one tooth.
- A key whose sum of squared tooth differences with respect to the inner envelope is minimal.
- A key whose sum of absolute tooth differences with respect to the outer envelope is minimal.

EXERCISE 16.5

You decide you have had it with computer science; you earn a degree in medicine instead. As a junior resident in a university hospital, you are asked by a department head to study a patient who has a mysterious allergy.

You somehow feel absolutely sure that the allergic reaction is caused by the patient's eating a combination of certain foods over the course of a day. For example, the allergic reaction may be caused by eating apples, eggs, fish, *and* honey during the same day.

Accordingly, you ask the one and only patient with the allergy to write down what he eats every day, and to indicate whether he has an allergic reaction on that day. During 7 days, the patient produces the following data:

Day	Apples	Beef	Cake	Dates	Eggs	Fish	Grapes	Honey	Reaction
1	yes	no	yes	yes	yes	yes	yes	yes	yes
2	no	no	yes	yes	yes	yes	no	no	no
3	yes	no	yes	yes	yes	no	yes	no	yes
4	yes	no	yes	no	no	no	no	no	no
5	yes	no	yes	yes	yes	yes	no	yes	yes
6	yes	yes	no	yes	yes	yes	no	no	no
7	no	yes	no	yes	yes	yes	no	no	no

Part 1   From the positive examples, determine which foods could be involved. Then, using the negative examples and the near-miss idea, determine which foods you can proscribe such that the patient absolutely will not have an allergic reaction if he avoids at least one food from the proscribed group every day.

Part 2   Now suppose that your patient misunderstands your instructions and writes down what he eats on only those days (1, 3, and 5) when he has an allergic reaction. What food or combination of foods would you proscribe such that the patient absolutely will not become allergic, yet is minimally constrained in the face of the data.

Part 3   Explain whether more data will help you to reduce the constraints placed on the patient, given that the patient continues to record what he has eaten only when he has an allergic reaction and that the patient decides whether to eat each food on each day by flipping a coin.

Part 4 Now, suppose you change your mind. You feel absolutely sure that the allergic reaction is caused by the patient's eating any one of certain foods over the course of a day. For example, the allergic reaction may be caused by eating apples *or* eggs *or* fish *or* honey.

From the data, determine which foods could be involved. Then, using the near-miss idea, determine which foods you can proscribe such that the patient absolutely will not have an allergic reaction if he avoids all of them every day.

EXERCISE 16.6

Explain how movement through a similarity net is like solving a geometric analogy problem of the sort described in Chapter 2.

CHAPTER 17
Learning by Explaining Experience

EXERCISE 17.1

Consider the following precedents:

Macbeth ───────────────────────────────
This is a story about Macbeth, Lady Macbeth, Duncan, and Macduff. Macbeth is an evil noble, and Lady Macbeth is a greedy, ambitious woman. Duncan is a king, and Macduff is a noble. Lady Macbeth persuades Macbeth to want to be king because she is greedy. She is able to influence him because he is married to her and because he is weak. Macbeth murders Duncan with a knife. Macbeth murders Duncan because Macbeth wants to be king, because Macbeth is evil, and because Duncan is king. Then, Lady Macbeth kills herself. Finally, Macduff gets angry and kills Macbeth because Macbeth murdered Duncan and because Macduff is loyal to Duncan.

Linda and Dick ───────────────────────────
This is a story about Linda and Dick. Linda is a woman, and Dick is a man. Dick is married to Linda. Dick is weak because he is tired. He is tired because Linda is domineering.

Adam and Eve ─────────────────────────────
This is a story about Adam and Eve and an apple. Adam is greedy because Eve is foolish. Adam wants to eat a forbidden apple because he is greedy. God punishes Adam and Eve because Adam eats the forbidden apple.

Now consider the following problem:

An Exercise ———————————————————

This is a problem concerning a foolish noble and a domineering lady. The noble is married to the lady. Show that the lady may persuade the noble to want to be king.

Show the rule produced by solving the problem using information from the *Macbeth*, *Linda and Dick*, and *Adam and Eve* precedents, as necessary.

EXERCISE 17.2

Given that precedents can, in principle, supply all that you can find in learned recollections, why bother learning recollections?

EXERCISE 17.3

Given that recollections can be given directly, in English, why bother learning them?

EXERCISE 17.4

Consider the *Macbeth* story, as described in the text, and the *Revenge* exercise, based loosely on the characters in *Hamlet*, as told next:

Revenge ———————————————————

This is a exercise concerning Hamlet, the Ghost, Claudius, and Gertrude. Claudius is married to Gertrude. The Ghost was king. Claudius is evil and Claudius wanted to be king. Claudius murdered the Ghost. Hamlet is loyal to the Ghost.

In both *Macbeth* and *Revenge*, someone who wants to be king murders the current king. Thus, Macbeth corresponds to Claudius, Duncan to the Ghost, and Macduff to Hamlet. Show how MATCH produces this pairing of individuals given the task of establishing that *Macbeth* supports the assertion that Hamlet kills Claudius. Be sure to think in terms of the five rules implied in the *Macbeth* story:

R1   If   *?x1* is loyal to *?x2*
                ?x3 murders *?x2*
        Then   *?x1* kills *?x3*

R2   If   *?x3* is evil
                ?x3 wants to be king
                ?x2 is king
        Then   *?x3* murders *?x2*

R3   If   *?x4* persuades *?x3* to want to be king
        Then   *?x3* wants to be king

Figure E18.1 An arch and a near miss.

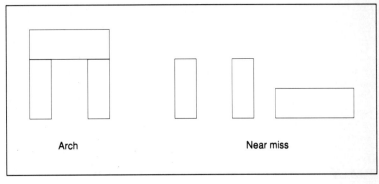

Arch   Near miss

R4   If $?x4$ is greedy
                        $?x4$ is able to influence $?x3$
       Then $?x4$ persuades $?x3$ to want to be king

R5   If $?x3$ is weak
                        $?x3$ is married to $?x4$
       Then $?x4$ is able to influence $?x3$

EXERCISE 17.5

Given that Macbeth marries Lady Macbeth, Lady Macbeth clearly marries Macbeth. Similarly, because Macbeth murders Duncan, it is clear that Macbeth kills Duncan, which makes it clear that Duncan is dead.

How would you arrange for such obvious deductions to be made automatically so that they do not need to be provided explicitly to the MACBETH program in English form?

EXERCISE 17.6

Discuss whether the MACBETH procedure violates Martin's law, as introduced in Chapter 16.

**CHAPTER 18
Learning by
Correcting
Mistakes**

EXERCISE 18.1

In Chapter 16, you learned how the arch concept can be learned from positive and negative samples, assuming that the negative samples are near misses. Sometimes, however, it is difficult to arrange for a negative sample to be different in a way that admits only one interpretation.

In figure E18.1, for example, the near miss can be explained in more than one way: one explanation is that the near miss is not an arch because it loses the *supported-by* relations between the lintel and the posts; another is that it is not an arch because it gains a *right-of* relation between the lintel and both of the posts.

Explain how you can resolve the ambiguity by supplying a second near miss and treating the two near misses as a near-miss group.

Exercise 18.2

Suppose that you have a rule indicating that you enjoy dinner parties attended by George and Sally. However, after you collect more data, you realize that sometimes your rule does not work—it needs repair.

Party	George	Sally	Frank	Ruth	Henry	Donna	Enjoyed?
1	yes	yes	yes	no	yes	no	yes
2	yes	yes	no	yes	yes	no	no
3	yes	yes	yes	yes	no	no	yes
4	yes	yes	no	no	no	yes	no
5	yes	yes	yes	yes	yes	no	yes
6	yes	yes	no	yes	yes	yes	no
7	yes	yes	no	yes	yes	yes	no

Using the near-miss-group idea, analyze the data to determine what changes are likely to improve your rule.

Exercise 18.3

Repeat the previous problem, using the following data:

Party	George	Sally	Frank	Ruth	Henry	Donna	Enjoyed?
1	yes	yes	no	no	yes	no	yes
2	yes	yes	no	yes	yes	yes	no
3	yes	yes	yes	yes	no	no	yes
4	yes	yes	no	no	no	yes	no
5	yes	yes	yes	yes	yes	no	yes
6	yes	yes	no	yes	yes	yes	no
7	yes	yes	no	yes	yes	yes	no

Exercise 18.4

Minimally, only two descriptions are required to learn something as a byproduct of analogical problem solving: an exercise and a precedent. What other sorts of descriptions are involved when knowledge is repaired?

Exercise 18.5

Censors form a sort of fence around each rule. Are there circumstances in which the area bounded by the fence gets bigger as more censors are added? Explain your answer.

Figure E19.1 Unknowns lying at the corners of a space.

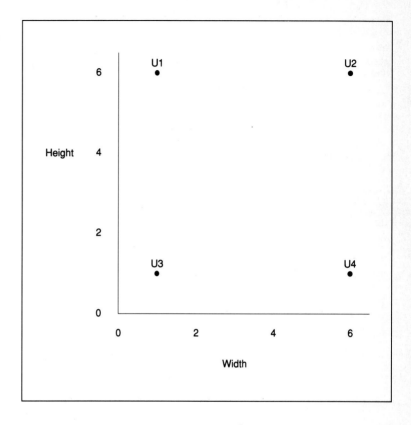

CHAPTER **19**
Learning by
Recording Cases

EXERCISE 19.1

Explain how the consistency principle differs from the notion of object recognition by feature space as introduced as an example of describe and match in Chapter 2.

EXERCISE 19.2

Suppose that all unknowns lie at the corners of the space of precedents, as shown, for example, in figure E19.1. Does finding the nearest neighbors of these blocks in the precedent space shown ever require a review of ignored precedents?

EXERCISE 19.3

Suppose that there is a precedent for every combination of integer widths and heights up to, say, 6×6. Next, suppose that you want to find the nearest neighbor of a block whose dimensions are $m + 1/2 \times n + 1/2$ where m and n are integers ranging from 1 to 5. Does finding the nearest neighbor of any unknown block require any review and correction?

Figure E19.2 A space in which it makes no sense to alternate division axes.

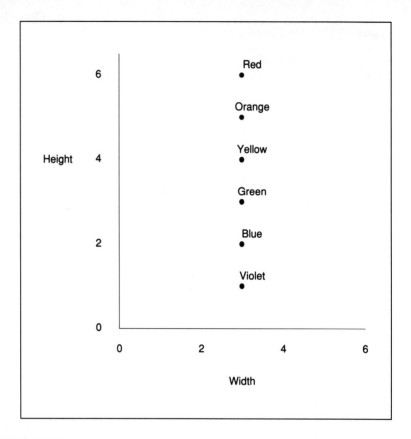

EXERCISE 19.4

Dividing the space of precedents alternately in x and y generally ensures that division always takes place along the axis in which there is the greatest remaining diversity. It does not always do so, however, as illustrated by the space of precedents shown in figure E19.2.

Revise the precedent-division procedure so that division is more likely along the axis in which there is the greatest remaining diversity.

EXERCISE 19.5

Determining that the nearest neighbor of the unknown in figure E19.3 is blue requires some reconsideration. Show the path through the decision tree.

EXERCISE 19.6

If you wish to predict properties, it sometimes makes sense to look at several close neighbors, rather than at just one. But this approach raises the question of what to do when the close neighbors predict differing values. One solution is to let the neighbors vote with equal strength, with victory

Figure E19.3 An unknown for which reconsideration is needed.

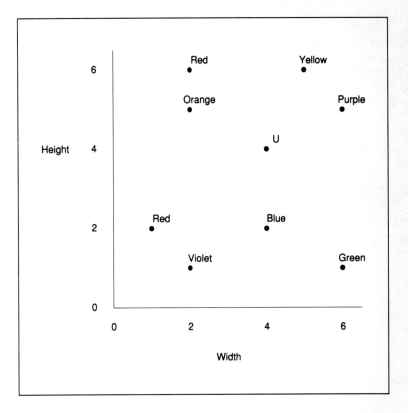

going to the value with the most votes. Another solution is to let the neighbors vote in proportion to a weight, w, that is determined by distance. Here are two possibilities:

■ Each nearby neighbor votes according to the inverse square of its distance, $w = 1/d^2$.

■ Each nearby neighbor votes according to a Gaussian function of the square of its distance, $w = e^{-kd^2}$.

Suppose that three nearby neighbors are used to predict the color of the unknown U in figure E19.4. Determine whether U is orange or red for inverse-square voting and for Gaussian voting with $k = 0.2$ and with $k = 0.4$.

EXERCISE 19.7

Explain how a parallel machine can compute the minimum of a set of numbers in constant time. Make the following assumptions:

■ Each processor contains one number. Each number is represented by n bits, where n is a constant.

■ A central controller can ask whether any processor has a particular bit in its number turned on (or off) in 1 unit of time.

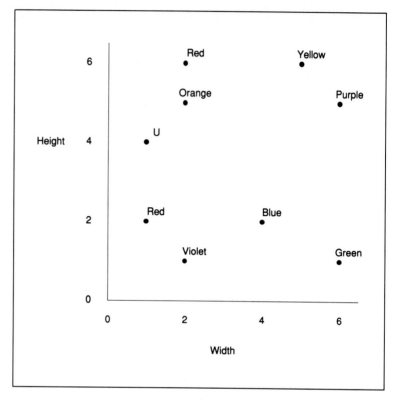

Figure E19.4 More than one nearest neighbor may be used to determine properties.

- The central controller can tell processors with a particular bit in their numbers turned on (or off) that their numbers cannot be the minimum and that they should drop out of contention.
- The central controller can ask a particular processor for its number.

CHAPTER 20
Learning by Managing Multiple Models

EXERCISE 20.1

Explain why, in the allergy example, there is never more than one specific model.

EXERCISE 20.2

Given that there is never more than one specific model, how can you simplify the version-space procedure?

EXERCISE 20.3

Explain why a sample that matches all specific models is guaranteed to be a positive sample. In particular, explain why you can be sure that [Sam's Dinner Wednesday Cheap] is a positive sample once you have analyzed [Sam's Breakfast Friday Cheap] and [Sam's Lunch Saturday Cheap].

EXERCISE 20.4

Suppose that you drop the requirement that the version space start with a positive sample. In particular, suppose that the order of the first two samples in the allergy example are reversed. How does this reversal affect the evolution of the version space? Do you get the same end result?

EXERCISE 20.5

Suppose that the days of the week are arranged in a class hierarchy that distinguishes between workdays and weekend days, as shown in figure E20.1.

How would this class hierarchy affect specialization and generalization operations in the allergy example?

EXERCISE 20.6

Show the development of a version space for the allergy example, given that days are divided into workdays and weekend days.

EXERCISE 20.7

Suppose that the class hierarchy is expanded to include the notion of a long-weekend day; see figure E20.2.

Further suppose that the sequence of samples is the same as before, except for some changes in the day attribute:

Number	Restaurant	Meal	Day	Cost	Reaction?
1	Sam's	breakfast	Saturday	cheap	yes
2	Lobdell	lunch	Saturday	expensive	no
3	Sam's	lunch	Sunday	cheap	yes
4	Sarah's	breakfast	Monday	cheap	no
5	Sam's	breakfast	Sunday	expensive	no

Show how the version-space procedure would handle the samples.

**CHAPTER 21
Learning
by Building
Identification
Trees**

EXERCISE 21.1

Suppose that the sunburn database were to list weight in pounds rather than classifying people as thin, average, or heavy. To handle such numbers, you arrange for SPROUTER to use tests in which numbers are compared to thresholds. Each such test reports that the measured value is either high or low. What thresholds should you try?

Figure E20.1 A class hierarchy for the days of the week.

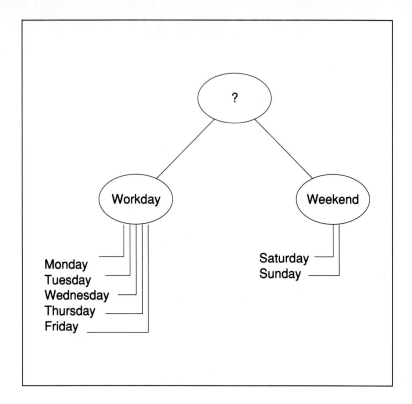

Figure E20.2 A class hierarchy for the days of the week, augmented with the long-weekend class.

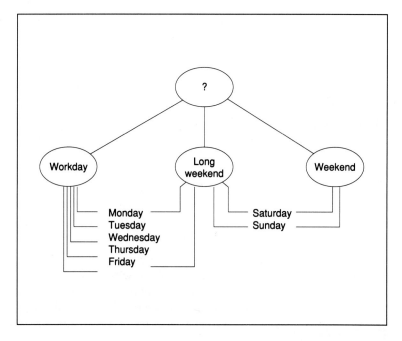

EXERCISE 21.2

Suppose that you are to deal with the situation described in the following table, which gives the history of eight past production runs in a factory setting:

Run	Supervisor	Operator	Machine	Overtime	Output
1	Patrick	Joe	a	no	high
2	Patrick	Samantha	b	yes	low
3	Thomas	Jim	b	yes	low
4	Patrick	Jim	b	no	high
5	Sally	Joe	c	no	high
6	Thomas	Samantha	c	no	low
7	Thomas	Joe	c	no	low
8	Patrick	Jim	a	yes	low

Construct an identification tree using this information so as to determine the factors that influence output.

EXERCISE 21.3

Devise a set of identification rules from the identification tree that you produced in the previous exercise. Do not do any statistical pruning.

EXERCISE 21.4

What would you control in the production problem, introduced in a previous exercise, in order to ensure high output: the supervisor, the operator, the machine, or the overtime?

CHAPTER 22
Learning by Training Neural Nets

EXERCISE 22.1

Consider a neural net with stair-step threshold functions. Suppose that you multiply all weights and thresholds by a constant. Will the behavior change?

EXERCISE 22.2

Consider a neural net with stair-step threshold functions. Suppose that you add a constant to all weights and thresholds. Will the behavior change?

EXERCISE 22.3

Consider the net with stair-step thresholds shown in figure E22.1, which previously appeared in Chapter 22.

Now, suppose you gradually lower all the output-layer thresholds. What happens?

Figure E22.1 A solution to the acquaintances, siblings, and lovers problem.

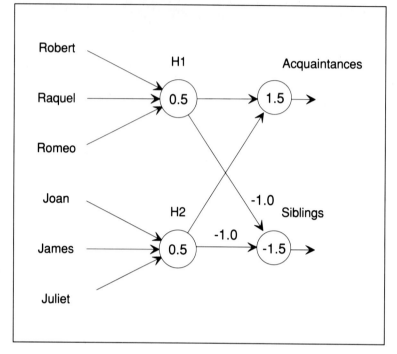

EXERCISE 22.4

For all the illustrations in the text, the root-mean-square error is less than 0.1 at termination. Is it always that low? Explain your answer.

EXERCISE 22.5

Can adding weights slow down back propagation?

EXERCISE 22.6

Suggest a way of changing the learning rate as learning proceeds so as to encourage speed yet discourage instability.

**CHAPTER 23
Learning
by Training
Perceptrons**

EXERCISE 23.1

You learned that the weight vector $(-1\ 0\ 0\ 0\ 0\ 0\ 1\ 0)$ can be used to recognize the digit 0 in a seven-line segment display. Explain why the weight vector $(-3\ 0\ 0\ 0\ 0\ 0\ 3\ 0)$ must work as well.

EXERCISE 23.2

Suppose that you are given two weight vectors for a digit-recognition perceptron. Both vectors, $\mathbf{w}^1$ and $\mathbf{w}^2$, can be used to recognize some particular digit. Suppose that $\mathbf{w}^3 = \mathbf{w}^1 + \mathbf{w}^2$. Can $\mathbf{w}^3$ be used to recognize the same digit?

EXERCISE 23.3

Exhibit a direct procedure that constructs weights for seven-segment digit recognition without using a sequence of training samples. Use your procedure to find suitable weight vectors for recognizing 0 and for recognizing 8.

EXERCISE 23.4

Given the procedure you found in the previous exercise, explain why there cannot be any doubt about the convergence of the perceptron convergence procedure on digit-recognition problems.

EXERCISE 23.5

If there is a satisfactory weight vector for a perceptron, is there is a satisfactory weight vector with integer weights?

CHAPTER 24
**Learning
by Training
Approximation
Nets**

EXERCISE 24.1

The interpolation net described in the text is such that new inputs distant from all Gaussian centers produce output values near 0. *Distant from* means, of course, beyond the effective range of the Gaussian functions' influence.

Suppose that you think that it is strange to have the output value fall toward 0 as an input value moves away from influence of the Gaussian functions. You decide to alter your treatment of a one-input net so that the output value is given as follows:

$$y(x) = \sum_{i=1}^{s} w_i e^{-\frac{1}{2\sigma}\|x - c_i\|^2}$$
$$+ ax$$
$$+ b.$$

Explain what the two additional terms would do for you if there were no Gaussian terms. Then explain what the Gaussian terms provide in addition.

EXERCISE 24.2

Write out a representation for approximation nets using the representation for interpolation nets as a model.

EXERCISE 24.3

Show that the weight change for w_i is given by the following formula:

$$\Delta w_i = r \sum_s (d_s - y_s) e^{-\frac{1}{2\sigma}\|\mathbf{x}_s - \mathbf{c}_i\|^2}.$$

EXERCISE 24.4

Unfortunately, it is difficult to decide what width, σ, to use for the Gaussian functions that appear in approximation nets. If the width is too small, the range of the samples is too short; if the width is too large, the range of the samples is too long.

Fortunately, you can train σ along with weights and centers. Exhibit the appropriate formula for training σ.

EXERCISE 24.5

The Gaussian functions described in the text are **isotropic**, meaning that the distance measured between the observed input values and the Gaussian centers does not depend on the direction in which you must travel to get from one to the other.

Sometimes, however, distance should be measured **anisotropically**, meaning that distance should be measured according to a formula like the following one, in which j denotes a dimension and i denotes a center:

$$\|\mathbf{x} - \mathbf{c}_i\|^2 = \sum_j k_j \times (x_j - c_{ij})^2$$

In qualitative terms, explain how many ks you would have to train and how you would go about training them.

EXERCISE 24.6

As you permit centers to move, and then permit the width of each Gaussian to change, you introduce many more trainable parameters. Suppose that you notice that these introductions make performance deteriorate on a test set of input–output samples. What is the likely cause of the diminished performance?

CHAPTER 25
Learning by Simulating Evolution

EXERCISE 25.1

Determine the minimum number of generations required to reach the top of bump mountain and moat mountain using one initial one-one chromosome, crossover, and the rank-space selection method.

EXERCISE 25.2

Suppose that you are testing various tent designs and tent materials for comfort in winter. The temperature outside the tent is $-40°$. The temperature inside a tent of one design–material combination, warmed by your body heat and a small stove, is 5° C. Other tents produce temperatures of 10° C and 15° C.

Part 1   Compute the fitness of each combination using the standard fitness method with inside temperature as the measure of quality.

Figure E25.1 Two difficult terrains for genetic algorithms.

Pole Mountain

0	0	0	0	0	0	0	0	0
0	0	0	0	0	0	0	0	0
0	0	0	0	0	0	0	0	0
0	0	0	0	0	0	0	0	0
0	0	0	0	9	0	0	0	0
0	0	0	0	0	0	0	0	0
0	0	0	0	0	0	0	0	0
0	0	0	0	0	0	0	0	0
0	0	0	0	0	0	0	0	0

Random Foothills

1	6	8	3	1	2	7	0	4
5	8	7	2	7	0	2	3	0
7	6	2	5	8	8	2	0	6
8	7	6	4	5	5	1	6	7
6	1	1	7	9	2	0	5	7
7	2	7	2	1	0	1	0	2
6	0	2	5	3	8	2	0	8
7	7	6	1	7	3	8	6	4
4	5	4	4	3	5	5	6	5

Part 2 Now suppose that you have lost your Celsius thermometer, reducing you to measuring temperature with an old Fahrenheit thermometer. Recalculate the fitness of each combination with the 41° F, 50° F, and 59° F temperatures.

Part 3 Recall that the fitness computed by the standard method determines the probability that a combination will be selected for the next generation. For both the Celsius and Fahrenheit measurements, compute the ratio of the highest probability to the lowest probability. Then, comment on why your results argue against the use of the standard method.

EXERCISE 25.3

Consider the pole mountain and random foothills configurations shown in figure E25.1. Random foothills was produced by placing a 9 at the central position and random numbers at other positions.

Explain why neither configuration is handled well by the standard genetic-algorithm method. Then, explain whether one configuration is significantly harder to handle than the other is.

EXERCISE 25.4

Suppose that you are using the rank method to select candidates. Recall that the probability of picking the first-ranked candidate is p. If the first candidate is not picked, then the probability of picking the second-ranked candidate is p, and so on, until only one candidate is left, in which case it is selected.

Part 1 Suppose that you have five candidates. You decide to select one using the rank-space method with $p = 0.25$. Compute the probabilities for each of the five as a function of rank.

Part 2 What is peculiar about the probabilities that you computed in part 1?

Part 3 Can you avoid the peculiarity you observed in part 2 by restricting the probability to a particular range?

EXERCISE 25.5

Suppose that you are using the rank method to select candidates. You want to select a candidate from among the ranked candidates such that all have an equal chance of being selected. With what probability should you pick the first-ranked candidate, from among those still under consideration, such that all have an equal chance?

EXERCISE 25.6

Another method for determining fitness, the *fixed-ratio method*, focuses on the ratio of the fitness of the chromosome producing the highest-quality result to that of the chromosome producing the lowest-quality result. Specifically, the ratio of these fitnesses is to be a constant, r; the fitness of all other chromosomes are to be strung out proportionately in between; and the sum of all fitnesses, as usual, must be equal to 1:

$$P(q_{max}) = rP(q_{min})$$

$$P(q) = P(q_{min}) + \frac{q - q_{min}}{q_{max} - q_{min}} \times \left[P(q_{max}) - P(q_{min}) \right],$$

$$\sum P(q) = 1.$$

Determine a formula for $P(q)$.

CHAPTER 26
Recognizing Objects

EXERCISE 26.1

Consider the thin triangle shown in figure E26.1 from above and from an observation point down the $-z$ axis.

The x-axis coordinates of the triangle's three points, both as is and after rotation around the y axis by an unknown angle, are given by the following table:

View	Position of point A	Position of point B	Position of point C
As is	−1.0	0	3.0
Rotated	−1.48	0.26	2.38

Now suppose that you see three objects from the same distant point down the $-z$ axis. They too are thin triangles, but they are not necessarily the same as the model triangle. Nevertheless, you somehow establish, for each object seen, how its points must correspond to those of the model if it is to be the model triangle. Once this correspondence is established, you have the following table:

Figure E26.1 A triangle to be identified.

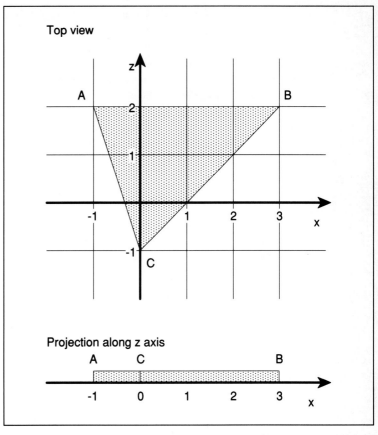

Object	Position of point A	Position of point B	Position of point C
1	−2.36	1.59	0
2	−1.86	2.59	0.49
3	−1.86	1.59	0.49

Determine which of the objects observed from a distant point on the z axis in figure E26.1 could be the same as the model triangle.

EXERCISE 26.2

Is it possible for an image to be identified falsely with a model? In particular, is it possible for something to be recognized falsely as the model triangle in the previous exercise?

EXERCISE 26.3

For problems involving pure rotation, you learned that two corresponding points in two model images provide enough information to predict the positions of other corresponding points. Suppose that you have a situation involving rotation around the y axis and translation along the x axis. How many corresponding points in how many model images would you need to predict the positions of other corresponding points?

EXERCISE 26.4

Suppose that you have a model of a thin triangle consisting of two images, one being the triangle in standard position and one being rotated around the y axis. Next, you see three points that you believe belong to the thin triangle after further rotation around the y axis and translation along the x axis. Can you construct a template for identification? Explain your answer.

EXERCISE 26.5

Show that the x and z coordinate values of a point on an object, after rotation by θ around the y axis, are given by the following formulas:

$$x_\theta = x \cos \theta - z \sin \theta$$
$$z_\theta = x \sin \theta + z \cos \theta$$

Hint: The vector $[x, \ z]$ can be viewed as the sum of $[x, \ 0]$ and $[0, \ z]$.

EXERCISE 26.6

Determine the values of α and β in the formula $x_{I_o} = \alpha x_{I_1} + \beta x_{I_2}$ in terms of rotation angles for the special case of pure rotation around the y axis.

CHAPTER 27
Describing Images

EXERCISE 27.1

This exercise explores the stereo procedure invented by Hans P. Morevec.

Part 1 Suppose that you want to find that part of the right image that best matches a particular small square patch, $\mathcal{P}$, of the left image. You propose to find it by maximizing the following measure of correlation:

$$\max_{X,Y} \sum_{\mathcal{P}} L_{i,j} \times R_{i+X,j+Y},$$

where the $L_{i,j}$ are left-image intensities and the $R_{i+X,j+Y}$ are right-image intensities in a patch offset by X and Y.

After some experiments, you determine that your measure is flawed: Your procedure tends to get sucked toward those parts of the right image with high average intensity. How would you fix this problem?

Part 2 Matching by correlation works best in areas that have high variability. Morevec calls such areas *interesting*. Suggest a measure for locating interesting areas.

Figure E27.1 Some zero crossings to be matched. (a) Edge fragments from a wide filter. (b) Edge fragments from a narrow filter.

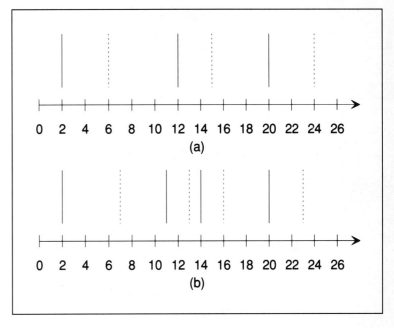

(a)

(b)

Part 3 Unfortunately, for high resolution, you would like to correlate using small areas, but to avoid local maxima in the correlation measure, you would like to correlate using large areas. How can you get the best of both small and large areas?

EXERCISE 27.2

Consider the zero crossings found with wide and medium sombrero filters shown in figure E27.1. Note that there are fewer lines in the coarse-scale result.

Part 1 Match the coarse-scale zero crossings.

Part 2 Match the fine-scale zero crossing. Ignore the previous results from coarse-scale matching.

Part 3 Match the fine-scale zero crossings. Exploit the results from coarse-scale matching in part 1.

Part 4 What are the disparities?

EXERCISE 27.3

Note that, for the PQ projection, the projecting line is normal to the surface of the sphere, because it goes through the center of the sphere. This observation makes it easy to write an expression for a surface-normal vector corresponding to the (p, q) point on the PQ plane. Show that the surface normal is given by $(p, q, -1)$.

Exercise 27.2 is based on an idea contributed by Ellen C. Hildreth.

EXERCISE 27.4

In addition to the surface-normal vector, $(p, q, -1)$, two other vectors are of consummate interest. One of these vectors points to the light source. This vector will correspond to some particular values of p and q. Let us call these values p_s and q_s, where the s is to suggest s̲un, corresponding to the vector pointing to the sun, $(p_s, q_s, -1)$. Another interesting vector is the one pointing to the viewer; this vector is $(0, 0, -1)$.

   With surface-normal, sun, and viewer vectors in hand, you can derive useful formulas relating the emergent, incident, and phase angles to p and q.

Part 1   Show that the following formula holds:

$$\cos i = \frac{pp_s + qq_s + 1}{\sqrt{p^2 + q^2 + 1}\sqrt{p_s^2 + q_s^2 + 1}}.$$

Part 2   Derive formulas similar to that in part 1, but for $\cos e$ and $\cos g$.

EXERCISE 27.5

Recall that the brightness of a Lambertian surface is $\rho \cos i$. If the light source is directly behind the viewer, $p_s = 0$ and $q_s = 0$. Exploiting the general formula for $\cos i$, we have this formula relating brightness to p and q:

$$E = \rho \cos i$$

$$= \rho \times \frac{1}{\sqrt{p^2 + q^2 + 1}}.$$

This value is a constant when $p^2 + q^2 + 1$ is a constant. But, because $p^2 + q^2 + 1 = c$ is an equation for a circle on the PQ plane, we conclude that the isobrightness lines on a PQ reflectance map are circles when the light source is behind the viewer. Show that the shadow line, when present, is straight.

EXERCISE 27.6

Examine a basketball in a room illuminated by a single small light source to your rear.

Part 1   How does the intensity of light on the basketball vary?

Part 2   Why does the full moon look flat?

EXERCISE 27.7

Part 1   Should people with flat-looking faces use dark or light makeup to make their faces look less flat?

Figure E27.2 A scanning
electron microscope.

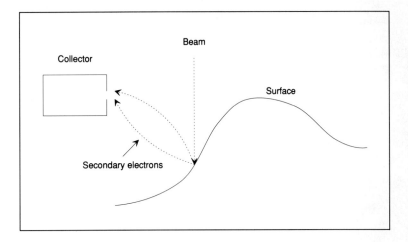

Part 2   Suppose Martians generally have spherical heads and Lambertian
skin. The really beautiful Martians have egg-shaped heads, with the long
axis of the egg horizontal and pointed in the direction the Martian is looking. Describe where you would advise a Martian with a spherical head
to place dark makeup, given that the Martian wishes to look like it has
an egg-shaped head. You may assume that the light source is behind the
viewer at all times.

EXERCISE 27.8

A scanning electron microscope works because beam electrons crash into
surfaces, whereupon secondary electrons are emitted, collected, and counted, as suggested in figure E27.2.

   The steeper the surface, the greater the number of electrons emitted. In
fact, when the electron beam hits a surface perpendicularly, the secondary
electron emission goes to 0. For our purposes here, assume that the actual
observed brightness, E, is given by $E = \rho \sin i$, where i is the incident
angle. Curiously, pictures made with a scanning electron microscope do
not impress people as weird, in spite of the strange reflectance function
involved.

   Suppose the electron beam is scanned across a surface with the cross
section shown in figure E27.3. Sketch the resulting image intensity.

EXERCISE 27.9

You have learned a well-kept secret that there are three oddly shaped mountains of unknown origin somewhere on the equator. When seen from the
side, these mountains look as shown in figure E27.4(a).

   Alphonse, an intrepid explorer, arranges a flight to go directly above
these mountains so that he can photograph them. Wishing to capture them
in their glory, he arranges the overflight for noon, when the sun is directly
overhead. His flight path is shown in figure E27.4(b).

Figure E27.3 A surface cross-section for the scanning electron microscope.

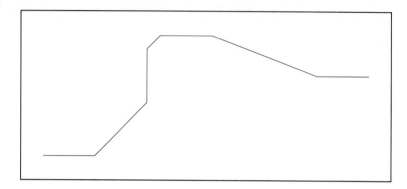

Figure E27.4 Three mountains. (a) Side view. (b) Top view.

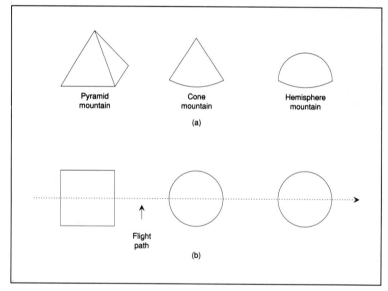

Part 1   Using three PQ spaces, indicate the surface normals exhibited by each of the three mountains.

Part 2   Alphonse is disappointed by the view; two of the mountains look the same! Describe what he sees, assuming that the mountains are made of a Lambertian material.

EXERCISE 27.10

A surface patch has unknown albedo, ρ. It is illuminated at different times from three separate light sources. For surfaces with $\rho = 1.0$, the three lights yield reflectance maps as shown in figure E27.5. The brightness observed when the various lights are on is as follows:

$$I_1 = 0.2 \qquad I_2 = 0.1 \qquad I_3 = 0.1$$

Part 1   Draw lines in PQ spaces representing loci where I_1/I_2 is equal to 2, 3, and 4. Similarly, draw lines for I_2/I_3 equal to 0.5, 1, and 2.

Figure E27.5 Three
reflectance maps.

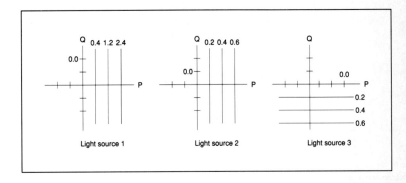

Part 2   What is the value of ρ?

EXERCISE 28.1

Draw the X-bar trees for the verb phrases in the following sentences, but
do not bother to show the internal structure of the prepositional phrases:

Sarah will go to the park by car.
Sarah will go to the park by the river.

EXERCISE 28.2

The text shows an X-bar tree for the following sentence:

Will Sarah return her book?

Using that X-bar tree as a guide, draw the X-bar tree for the following
sentence, taking care to account for the word *when*:

When will Sarah return her book?

EXERCISE 28.3

The text provides an X-bar diagram for the following sentence:

Whom will Sarah return the book to in the afternoon?

Draw an X-bar diagram for the following related sentence:

Who will return the book to Alex in the afternoon?

EXERCISE 28.4

Consider the following sentence:

Whom will Sarah return the book to in the afternoon?

In the text, the X-bar tree of the sentence shows the word *whom* moving
into a complement phrase's empty specifier position, where it is governed
by the word *will*, which has also moved from another position. Accordingly,
you might think that *whom* is accusative by virtue of having a complement

phrase's head as its governor. But then you have no explanation for the following sentence, in which a nominative pronoun appears:

Who will return the book to Alex in the afternoon?

How can you explain why one pronoun is accusative and the other is nominative?

EXERCISE 28.5

Consider the following sentences:

Sarah returned to the library on the corner in the afternoon.
∗ Sarah returned to the library in the afternoon on the corner.

Part 1   Assuming that the phrase *on the corner* has not moved into position, explain why one sentence is grammatical and the other is not. Use the perspective provided by X-bar schema in your explanation.

Part 2   Explain why it is not plausible to suppose that *on the corner* has not just moved into position from some other, reasonable place. Use semantic considerations in your explanation.

**CHAPTER 29
Responding to
Questions and
Commands**

EXERCISE 29.1

The sample semantic transition-tree grammar can handle sentences with a single object-describing word sequence such as this:

Identify the short screwdrivers.

The grammar cannot handle sentences such as the following, in which there are multiple object-describing word sequences:

Identify the short screwdrivers and the small wrenches.

Extend the grammar to handle multiple object-describing word sequences. Do this by creating a new tree named List-of-object-descriptions, which has Objects links. Do not make any changes to the Objects tree itself.

Note that you need the COMBINE database command, which combines all the records from two relations into one new relation.

EXERCISE 29.2

The sample semantic transition-tree grammar does not allow much flexibility with respect to phrasing. With only a minimal change to the Question-or-command tree, generalize the grammar so that all the following commands and questions are handled:

Identify the screwdrivers.
What are the long screwdrivers?
Show me the long blue screwdrivers.
List the light long blue screwdrivers.

EXERCISE 29.3

Extend the sample semantic transition-tree grammar so that it can deal with phrases that indicate location, as in the following examples:

Count the long screwdrivers in the toolchest.
Count the long screwdrivers on the pegboard.
Count the long screwdrivers on the table.

EXERCISE 29.4

You have seen the nested-box description of how the word sequence *long red* is analyzed. Draw the nested-box description showing how the word sequence *heavy long red* is analyzed.

EXERCISE 29.5

Suppose that you work for a railroad, which maintains a database of all the cars currently in a particular yard:

Type	Owner	Size	State	Track
Tank	P&PU	medium	full	one
Gondola	TP&W	large	full	two
Hopper	IC	small	empty	one
Hopper	IC	large	full	one
Box	TP&W	long	empty	two
Box	P&PU	long	empty	three
Box	SF	long	full	three
Box	SF	short	empty	three

How would you change the sample semantic transition-tree grammar so that it can deal with this database, instead of with the one containing descriptions of tools?

Bibliography

This bibliography contains items directly cited in the chapters, as well as some related items of special interest. To keep length manageable, I generally list only the earliest publication together with the most recent or most easily accessible publication for each concept.

Abelson, Harold, and Andrea diSessa, *Turtle Geometry*, MIT Press, Cambridge, MA, 1981.

Aikins, Janice, "A Theory and Methodology of Inductive Learning," *Artificial Intelligence*, vol. 20, no. 3, 1983.

Allen, James F. and C. Raymond Perrault, "Analyzing Intention in Utterances," *Artificial Intelligence*, vol. 15, 1980.

Allen, James F., "Towards a General Theory of Action and Time," *Artificial Intelligence*, vol. 23, 1984.

Allen, James F., "Maintaining Knowledge About Temporal Intervals," *Communications of the ACM*, vol. 26, no. 11, 1983.

Allen, James, "Recognizing Intentions from Natural Language Utterances," in *Computational Models of Discourse*, edited by J. Michael Brady and Robert C. Berwick, MIT Press, Cambridge, MA, 1983.

Altay, Güvenir, H. and G. W. Ernst, "Learning Problem Solving Strategies Using Refinement and Macro Generation," *Artificial Intelligence*, vol. 44, 1990.

Amarel, Saul, "On Representation of Problems of Reasoning about Actions," in *Machine Intelligence 3*, edited by Donald Michie, Edinburgh University Press, Edinburgh, Scotland, 1968.

Ambler, A. P., H. G. Barrow, C. M. Brown, R. M. Burstall, and R. J. Popplestone, "A Versatile System for Computer Controlled Assembly," *Artificial Intelligence*, vol. 6, no. 2, 1975.

Anderson, James A. and Edward Rosenfeld, *Neurocomputing: Foundations of Research*, MIT Press, Cambridge, MA, 1989.

Antonisse, Jim, "A New Interpretation of Schema Notation that Overturns the Binary Encoding Constraint," *Proceedings of the Third International Conference on Genetic Algorithms*, 1989.

Atkeson, Christopher G., "Memory-Based Approaches to Approximating Continuous Functions," *Proceedings of the Workshop on Nonlinear Modeling and Forecasting*, 1990.

Bailey, David Lee, "Similarity Networks as a Means of Indexing and Retrieving Descriptions," BS Thesis, Department of Electrical Engineering & Computer Science, Massachusetts Institute of Technology, Cambridge, MA, 1986.

Bajcsy, Ruzena (editor), *Representation of Three-Dimensional Objects*, Springer-Verlag, New York, 1982.

Ballard, Dana H., and Christopher Brown, *Computer Vision*, Prentice-Hall, Englewood Cliffs, NJ, 1982.

Barlow, H. B., "Summation and Inhibition in the Frog's Retina," *Journal of Physiology*, vol. 119, 1953.

Barr, Avron, Edward A. Feigenbaum, and Paul R. Cohen, *The Handbook of Artificial Intelligence* (Three Volumes), William Kaufman, Los Altos, CA, 1981.

Barrow, Harry G. and Jay M. Tenenbaum, "Interpreting Line Drawings as Three-Dimensional Surfaces," *Artificial Intelligence*, vol. 17, 1981.

Barrow, Harry G., and Jay M. Tenenbaum, "Recovering Intrinsic Scene Characteristics from Images," in *Computer Vision Systems*, edited by A. Hanson and E. Riseman, Academic Press, New York, 1978.

Barrow, Harry G., and Jay M. Tenenbaum, "Computational Vision," *Proceedings of the IEEE*, vol. 69, no. 5, 1981.

Barrow, Harry G., "VERIFY: A Program for Proving Correctness of Digital Hardware Designs," *Artificial Intelligence*, vol. 24, 1984.

Barry, M., D. Cyrluk, D. Kapur, J. L. Mundy and V.-D. Nguyen, "A Multi-Level Geometric Reasoning System for Vision," *Artificial Intelligence*, vol. 37, 1988.

Barton, G. Edward, Jr., Robert C. Berwick, and Eric Sven Ristad, *Computational Complexity and Natural Language*, MIT Press, Cambridge, MA, 1987.

Barton, G. Edward, Jr., "Toward a Principle-Based Parser," Report 788, Artificial Intelligence Laboratory, Massachusetts Institute of Technology, Cambridge, MA, 1984.

Basri, Ronen, "The Recognition of Three-Dimensional Objects from Two-Dimensional Images," PhD Thesis, Weizmann Institute of Science, 1990.

Baudet, Gerard M., "On the Branching Factor of the Alpha–Beta Pruning Algorithm," *Artificial Intelligence*, vol. 10, no. 2, 1978.

Beckman, Lennart, Anders Haraldson, Osten Oskarsson, and Erik Sandewall, "A Partial Evaluator, and Its Use as a Programming Tool," *Artificial Intelligence*, vol. 7, no. 4, 1976.

Berliner, H. J., G. Goetsch, M. S. Campbell and C. Ebeling, "Measuring the Performance Potential of Chess Programs," *Artificial Intelligence*, vol. 43, 1990.

Berliner, Hans J. and Murray S. Campbell, "Using Chunking to Solve Chess Pawn Endgames," *Artificial Intelligence*, vol. 23, 1984.

Berliner, Hans J., "An Examination of Brute-Force Intelligence," *Seventh International Joint Conference on Artificial Intelligence*, Vancouver, Canada, 1981.

Berliner, Hans J., "Some Necessary Conditions for a Master Chess Program," *Third International Joint Conference on Artificial Intelligence*, Stanford, CA, 1973.

Berliner, Hans J., "A Chronology of Computer Chess and Its Literature," *Artificial Intelligence*, vol. 10, no. 2, 1978.

Berliner, Hans J., "Computer Backgammon," *Scientific American*, vol. 242, no. 9, 1980.

Berliner, Hans J., "Chess as Problem Solving: The Development of a Tactics Analyzer," PhD Thesis, Carnegie–Mellon University, Pittsburgh, PA, 1975.

Berliner, Hans J., "Backgammon Computer Program Beats World Champion (Performance Note)," *Artificial Intelligence*, vol. 14, 1980.

Berliner, Hans J., "The B* Tree Search Algorithm: A Best-First Proof Procedure," *Artificial Intelligence*, vol. 12, 1979.

Berwick, Robert C., and Amy Weinberg, *The Grammatical Basis of Linguistic Performance*, MIT Press, Cambridge, MA, 1983.

Berwick, Robert C., "Introduction: Computational Aspects of Discourse," in *Computational Models of Discourse*, edited by J. Michael Brady and Robert C. Berwick, MIT Press, Cambridge, MA, 1983.

Berwick, Robert C., *The Acquisition of Syntactic Knowledge*, MIT Press, Cambridge, MA, 1985. Based on a PhD thesis, Massachusetts Institute of Technology, Cambridge, MA, 1982.

Bibel, Wolfgang, "A Comparative Study of Several Proof Procedures," *Artificial Intelligence*, vol. 18, 1982.

Binford, Thomas O., "Survey of Model-Based Image Analysis Systems," *International Journal of Robotics Research*, vol. 1, no. 1, 1982.

Binford, Thomas O., "Inferring Surfaces from Images," *Artificial Intelligence*, vol. 17, 1981.

Binford, Thomas O., "Visual Perception by Computer," *Proceedings of the IEEE Conference on Systems Science and Cybernetics, Miami*, 1971.

Bledsoe, W. W., "Non-Resolution Theorem Proving," *Artificial Intelligence*, vol. 9, no. 1, 1977.

Bledsoe, Woodrow W., K. Kunen and R. E. Shostak, "Completeness Results for Inequality Provers," *Artificial Intelligence*, vol. 27, 1985.

Bobrow Daniel G., Ronald M. Kaplan, Martin Kay, Donald A. Norman, Henry Thompson, and Terry Winograd, "GUS, A Frame-Driven Dialog System," *Artificial Intelligence*, vol. 8, no. 2, 1977.

Bobrow, Daniel G. and Patrick J. Hayes, "Artificial Intelligence: Where Are We," *Artificial Intelligence*, vol. 25, 1985.

Bobrow, Daniel G., and Allan Collins, *Representation and Understanding*, Academic Press, New York, 1975.

Bobrow, Daniel G., and Bruce Fraser, "An Augmented State Transition Network Analysis Procedure," *First International Joint Conference on Artificial Intelligence*, Washington, D. C., 1969.

Bobrow, Daniel G., and Terry Winograd, "An Overview of KRL, a Knowledge Representation Language," *Cognitive Science*, vol. 1, no. 1, 1977.

Bobrow, Daniel G., "Qualitative Reasoning About Physical Systems: An Introduction," *Artificial Intelligence*, vol. 24, 1984.

Boden, Margaret A., *Artificial Intelligence and Natural Man*, Basic Books, New York, 1977.

Boley, Harold, "Directed Recursive Labelnode Hypergraphs: A New Representation-Language," *Artificial Intelligence*, vol. 9, no. 1, 1977.

Booker, L. B., D. E. Goldberg and John H. Holland, "Classifier Systems and Genetic Algorithms," *Artificial Intelligence*, vol. 40, 1989.

Brachman, Ronald J., "On the Epistemological Status of Semantic Networks," in *Associative Networks: Representation and Use of Knowledge by Computers*, edited by Nicholas V. Findler, Academic Press, New York, 1979.

Brady, J. Michael (editor), *Computer Vision*, North-Holland, Amsterdam, 1981.

Brady, J. Michael, and Robert C. Berwick (editors), *Computational Models of Discourse*, MIT Press, Cambridge, MA, 1983.

Brady, J. Michael, John M. Hollerbach, Timothy L. Johnson Tomás Lozano-Pérez, and Matthew T. Mason (editors), *Robot Motion: Planning and Control*, MIT Press, Cambridge, MA, 1982.

Brady, J. Michael, "Representing Shape," in *Robotics*, edited by Lester Gerhardt and J. Michael Brady, Springer-Verlag, New York, 1983.

Brady, Michael, "Artificial Intelligence and Robotics," *Artificial Intelligence*, vol. 26, 1985.

Brand, D., "Analytic Resolution in Theorem Proving," *Artificial Intelligence*, vol. 7, no. 4, 1976.

Bratko, Ivan, PROLOG *Programming for Artificial Intelligence* (second edition), Addison-Wesley, Reading, MA, 1990.

Brooks, Rodney A., and Tomás Lozano-Pérez, "A Subdivision Algorithm in Configuration Space for Findpath with Rotation," *Eighth International Joint Conference on Artificial Intelligence*, Karlsruhe, Germany, 1983.

Brooks, Rodney A., "Planning Collision Free Motions for Pick and Place Operations," *International Journal of Robotics Research*, vol. 2, no. 4, 1983.

Brooks, Rodney A., "Solving the Find-Path Problem by Good Representation of Free Space," *IEEE Transactions on Systems, Man, and Cybernetics*, vol. SMC-13, 1983.

Brooks, Rodney A., "Intelligence Without Representation," *Artificial Intelligence*, vol. 47, 1991.

Brooks, Rodney A., "Symbolic Reasoning Among Three-Dimensional Models and Two-Dimensional Images," *Artificial Intelligence*, vol. 17, 1981. Based on a PhD thesis, Stanford University, Stanford, CA, 1981.

Brou, Philippe, "Finding the Orientation of Objects in Vector Maps," PhD Thesis, Department of Electrical Engineering & Computer Science, Massachusetts Institute of Technology, Cambridge, MA, 1983.

Brown, Malloy F., "Doing Arithmetic without Diagrams," *Artificial Intelligence*, vol. 8, no. 2, 1977.

Buchanan, Bruce G. and Edward A. Feigenbaum, "Dendral and Meta-Dendral: Their Applications Dimension," *Artificial Intelligence*, vol. 11, 1978.

Buchanan, Bruce G., and Edward H. Shortliffe, *Rule-Based Expert Programs: The* MYCIN *Experiments of the Stanford Heuristic Programming Project*, Addison-Wesley, Reading, MA, 1984.

Buchanan, Bruce G., and Richard O. Duda, "Principles of Rule-Based Expert Systems," *Advances in Computers*, vol. 22, 1983.

Bundy, Alan, Bernard Silver and Dave Plummer, "An Analytical Comparison of Some Rule-Learning Programs," *Artificial Intelligence*, vol. 27, 1985.

Bundy, Alan, "Will It Reach the Top? Prediction in the Mechanics World," *Artificial Intelligence*, vol. 10, no. 2, 1978.

Campbell, A. N., V. F. Hollister, Richard O. Duda, and Peter E. Hart, "Recognition of a Hidden Mineral Deposit by an Artificial Intelligence Program," *Science*, vol. 217, no. 3, 1982.

Carbonell, Jaime G., "Learning by Analogy: Formulating and Generalizing Plans from Past Experience," in *Machine Learning: An Artificial Intelligence Approach*, edited by Ryszard S. Michalski, Jaime G. Carbonell, and Tom M. Mitchell, Tioga Publishing Company, Palo Alto, CA, 1983.

Card, Stuart, Thomas P. Moran, and Allen Newell, *The Psychology of Human–Computer Interaction*, Lawrence Erlbaum Associates, Hillsdale, NJ, 1983.

Chapman, David, "Planning for Conjunctive Goals," *Artificial Intelligence*, vol. 32, 1987.

Charniak, Eugene, Christopher K. Riesbeck, and Drew V. McDermott, *Artificial Intelligence Programming*, Lawrence Erlbaum Associates, Hillsdale, NJ, 1980.

Charniak, Eugene, "Toward a Model of Children's Story Comprehension," PhD Thesis, Department of Electrical Engineering & Computer Science, Massachusetts Institute of Technology, Cambridge, MA, 1972.

Charniak, Eugene, "Motivation Analysis, Abductive Unification, and Non-monotonic Equality," *Artificial Intelligence*, vol. 34, 1988.

Charniak, Eugene, "A Common Representation for Problem-Solving and Language-Comprehension Information," *Artificial Intelligence*, vol. 16, 1981.

Charniak, Eugene, "On the Use of Framed Knowledge in Language Comprehension," *Artificial Intelligence*, vol. 11, 1978.

Chester, Daniel, "The Translation of Formal Proofs into English," *Artificial Intelligence*, vol. 7, no. 3, 1976.

Chomsky, Noam, *Syntactic Structures*, Mouton, The Hague, 1957.

Chomsky, Noam, *Lectures on Government and Binding*, Foris, Dordrecht, Holland, 1981.

Clancey, William J., "The Epistemology of a Rule-Based Expert System: A Framework for Explanation," *Artificial Intelligence*, vol. 20, 1983.

Clancey, William J., "Heuristic Classification," *Artificial Intelligence*, vol. 27, 1985.

Clark, Keith L., and Sten-Åke Tärnlund, *Logic Programming*, Academic Press, New York, 1982.

Clarke, M. R. B. (editor), *Advances in Computer Chess 1*, Edinburgh University Press, Edinburgh, Scotland, 1977.

Clarke, M. R. B. (editor), *Advances in Computer Chess 2*, Edinburgh University Press, Edinburgh, Scotland, 1980.

Clocksin, William F., and Christopher S. Mellish, *Programming in Prolog*, Springer-Verlag, New York, 1981.

Clowes, Maxwell, "On Seeing Things," *Artificial Intelligence*, vol. 2, no. 1, 1971.

Cohen, Brian L., "A Powerful and Efficient Structural Pattern Recognition System," *Artificial Intelligence*, vol. 9, no. 3, 1977.

Cohen, Brian L., "The Mechanical Discovery of Certain Problem Symmetries," *Artificial Intelligence*, vol. 8, no. 1, 1977.

Colmerauer, A., H. Kanoui, R. Pasero, and P. Roussel, "Un Système de Communication Homme-Machine en Français," Report II, Groupe d'Intelligence Artificielle, Université Aix-Marseille, 1973.

Colmerauer, Alain, "Prolog and Infinite Trees," in *Logic Programming*, edited by Keith L. Clark and Sten-Åke Tärnlund, Academic Press, New York, 1982.

Connell, Jonathan H. and Brady, Michael, "Generating and Generalizing Models of Visual Objects," *Artificial Intelligence*, vol. 31, 1987.

Cormen, Thomas H., Charles E. Leiserson, and Ronald L. Rivest, *Introduction to Algorithms*, MIT Press, Cambridge, MA; and McGraw-Hill, New York, 1990.

Darwin, Charles, *The Origin of Species*, John Murray, 1859.

Davis, Ernest, "Constraint Propagation with Interval Labels," *Artificial Intelligence*, vol. 32, 1987.

Davis, Larry S., and Azriel Rosenfeld, "Cooperative Processes for Low-level Vision: A Survey," *Artificial Intelligence*, vol. 17, 1981.

Davis, Martin, "The Mathematics of Non-Monotonic Reasoning," *Artificial Intelligence*, vol. 13, 1980.

Davis, Randall and Reid G. Smith, "Negotiation as a Metaphor for Distributed Problem Solving," *Artificial Intelligence*, vol. 20, 1983.

Davis, Randall, and Douglas B. Lenat, *Knowledge-Based Systems in Artificial Intelligence*, McGraw-Hill, New York, 1982.

Davis, Randall, and Jonathan King, "An Overview of Production Systems," in *Machine Intelligence 8*, edited by Edward W. Elcock and Donald Michie, John Wiley and Sons, New York, 1977.

Davis, Randall, and Reid G. Smith, "Negotiation as a Metaphor for Distributed Problem Solving," *Artificial Intelligence*, vol. 20, no. 1, 1983.

Davis, Randall, Bruce G. Buchanan, and Edward H. Shortliffe, "Production Rules as a Representation for a Knowledge-Based Consultation Program," *Artificial Intelligence*, vol. 8, no. 1, 1977.

Davis, Randall, Howard Austin, Ingrid Carlbom, Bud Frawley, Paul Pruchnik, Rich Sneiderman, and Al Gilreath, "The Dipmeter Advisor: Interpretation of Geological Signals," *Seventh International Joint Conference on Artificial Intelligence*, Vancouver, Canada, 1981.

Davis, Randall, "Expert Systems: Where Are We? And Where Do We Go from Here?," Report AIM-665, Artificial Intelligence Laboratory, Massachusetts Institute of Technology, Cambridge, MA, 1982.

Davis, Randall, "Teiresias: Applications of Meta-Level Knowledge," in *Knowledge-Based Systems in Artificial Intelligence*, edited by Randall Davis and Douglas B. Lenat, McGraw-Hill, New York, 1982. Based on a PhD thesis, Stanford University, Stanford, CA, 1976.

Davis, Randall, "Diagnostic Reasoning Based on Structure and Behavior," *Artificial Intelligence*, vol. 24, 1984.

de Kleer, Johan and Brian C. Williams, "Diagnosing Multiple Faults," *Artificial Intelligence*, vol. 32, 1987.

de Kleer, Johan and John S. Brown, "Theories of Causal Ordering," *Artificial Intelligence*, vol. 29, 1986.

de Kleer, Johan and John S. Brown, "A Qualitative Physics Based on Confluences," *Artificial Intelligence*, vol. 24, 1984.

de Kleer, Johan, "Causal and Teleological Reasoning in Circuit Recognition," Report TR-529, Artificial Intelligence Laboratory, Massachusetts Institute of Technology, Cambridge, MA, 1979.

de Kleer, Johan, "Qualitative and Quantitative Knowledge in Classical Mechanics," PhD Thesis, Department of Electrical Engineering & Computer Science, Massachusetts Institute of Technology, Cambridge, MA, 1975.

de Kleer, Johan, "An Assumption-Based TMS," *Artificial Intelligence*, vol. 28, 1986.

de Kleer, Johan, "How Circuits Work," *Artificial Intelligence*, vol. 24, 1984.

de Kleer, Johan, "Using Crude Probability Estimates to Guide Diagnosis," *Artificial Intelligence*, vol. 45, 1990.

de la Maza, Michael and Bruce Tidor, "Increased Flexibility in Genetic Algorithms: The Use of Variable Boltzmann Selective Pressure to Control Propagation," *Proceedings of the ORSA CSTS Conference: Computer Science and Operations Research: New Developments in Their Interfaces*, 1991.

Dean, Thomas L. and Drew V. McDermott, "Temporal Data Base Management," *Artificial Intelligence*, vol. 32, 1987.

Dean, Thomas L. and Mark Boddy, "Reasoning About Partially Ordered Events," *Artificial Intelligence*, vol. 36, 1988.

Dechter, R. and J. Pearl, "Network-Based Heuristics for Constraint-Satisfaction Problems," *Artificial Intelligence*, vol. 34, 1988.

Dechter, Rina, Itay Meiri and Judea Pearl, "Temporal Constraint Networks," *Artificial Intelligence*, vol. 49, 1991.

DeJong, Gerald F., II, "A New Approach to Natural Language Processing," *Cognitive Science*, vol. 3, no. 3, 1979.

Dennett, Daniel C., "Recent Work in Philosophy of Interest to AI," *Artificial Intelligence*, vol. 19, 1982.

Dennett, Daniel C., "Recent Work in Philosophy II," *Artificial Intelligence*, vol. 22, 1984.

Dietterich, Thomas G. and Ryszard S. Michalski, "Inductive Learning of Structural Descriptions," *Artificial Intelligence*, vol. 16, no. 3, 1981.

Dietterich, Thomas G. and Ryszard S. Michalski, "Discovering Patterns in Sequences of Events," *Artificial Intelligence*, vol. 25, 1985.

Donald, B. R., "A Search Algorithm for Motion Planning with Six Degrees of Freedom," *Artificial Intelligence*, vol. 31, 1987.

Donald, Bruce R., "A Geometric Approach to Error Detection and Recovery for Robot Motion Planning with Uncertainty," *Artificial Intelligence*, vol. 37, 1988.

Doyle, Jon and Michael P. Wellman, "Impediments to Universal Preference-Based Default Theories," *Artificial Intelligence*, vol. 49, 1991.

Doyle, Jon and Ramesh S. Patil, "Two Theses of Knowledge Representation: Language Restrictions, Taxonomic Classification, and the Utility of Representation Services," *Artificial Intelligence*, vol. 48, 1991.

Doyle, Jon, "A Truth Maintenance System," *Artificial Intelligence*, vol. 12, 1979.

Duda, Richard O., and Peter E. Hart, *Pattern Recognition and Scene Analysis*, John Wiley and Sons, New York, 1973.

Duda, Richard O., Peter E. Hart, and Nils J. Nilsson, "Subjective Bayesian Methods for Rule-Based Inference Systems," Report TR-124, Artificial Intelligence Center, SRI International, Menlo Park, CA, 1976.

Duda, Richard O., Peter E. Hart, Nils J. Nilsson, and Georgia L. Sutherland, "Semantic Network Representations in Rule Based Inference Systems," in *Pattern Directed Inference Systems*, edited by Donald A. Waterman and Frederick Hayes-Roth, Academic Press, New York, 1978.

Dyer, Michael G., *In-depth Understanding: A Computer Model of Integrated Processing for Narrative Comprehension*, MIT Press, Cambridge, MA, 1983.

Ernst, George, and Allen Newell, GPS: *A Case Study in Generality and Problem Solving*, Academic Press, New York, 1969.

Etzioni, Oren, "Embedding Decision-Analytic Control in a Learning Architecture," *Artificial Intelligence*, vol. 49, 1991.

Evans, Thomas G., "A Heuristic Program to Solve Geometric Analogy Problems," in *Semantic Information Processing*, edited by Marvin Minsky, MIT Press, Cambridge, MA, 1968. Based on a PhD thesis, Massachusetts Institute of Technology, Cambridge, MA, 1963.

Fahlman, Scott E, *NETL: A System for Representing and Using Real-World Knowledge*, MIT Press, Cambridge, MA, 1979. Based on a PhD thesis, Massachusetts Institute of Technology, Cambridge, MA, 1979.

Falkenhainer, Brian, Kenneth D. Forbus and Dedre Gentner, "The Structure-Mapping Engine: Algorithm and Examples," *Artificial Intelligence*, vol. 41, 1990.

Falkenhainer, Brian, "The Utility of Difference-Based Reasoning," *National Conference on Artificial Intelligence*, 1988.

Faltings, B., "Qualitative Kinematics in Mechanisms," *Artificial Intelligence*, vol. 44, 1990.

Faugeras, O. D., E. Le Bras-Mehlman and J. D. Boissonat, "Representing Stereo Data with the Delaunay Triangulation," *Artificial Intelligence*, vol. 44, 1990.

Feigenbaum, Edward A., and Julian Feldman, *Computers and Thought*, McGraw-Hill, New York, 1963.

Feigenbaum, Edward A., and Pamela McCorduck, *The Fifth Generation*, Addison-Wesley, Reading, MA, 1983.

Feigenbaum, Edward A., "The Art of Artificial Intelligence: Themes and Case Studies in Knowledge Engineering," *Fifth International Joint Conference on Artificial Intelligence*, Cambridge, MA, 1977.

Fikes, Richard E., and Nils J. Nilsson, "STRIPS: A New Approach to the Application of Theorem Proving to Problem Solving," *Artificial Intelligence*, vol. 2, 1971.

Fikes, Richard E., Peter E. Hart, and Nils J. Nilsson, "Learning and Executing Generalized Robot Plans," *Artificial Intelligence*, vol. 3, 1972.

Fillmore, C. J., "The Case for Case," in *Universals in Linguistic Theory*, edited by E. Bach and R. Harms, Holt, Rinehart, and Winston, New York, 1968.

Findler, Nicholas V. (editor), *Associative Networks: Representation and Use of Knowledge by Computers*, Academic Press, New York, 1979.

Finkel, Raphael A., and John P. Fishburn, "Parallelism in Alpha–Beta Search," *Artificial Intelligence*, vol. 19, no. 1, 1982.

Finney, D. J., R. Latscha, B. M. Bennet, and P. Hsu, *Tables for Testing Significance in a 2 × 2 Contingency Table*, Cambridge University Press, 1963.

Follett, Ria, "Synthesizing Recursive Functions with Side Effects," *Artificial Intelligence*, vol. 13, no. 3, 1980.

Fong, Sandiway, and Robert C. Berwick, *Parsing with Principles and Parameters*, MIT Press, Cambridge, MA, 1992.

Forbus, Kenneth D., "Qualitative Process Theory," Report AIM-664, Artificial Intelligence Laboratory, Massachusetts Institute of Technology, Cambridge, MA, 1982.

Forbus, Kenneth D., "Qualitative Reasoning About Physical Processes," *Seventh International Joint Conference on Artificial Intelligence*, Vancouver, Canada, 1981.

Forbus, Kenneth D., "Qualitative Process Theory," *Artificial Intelligence*, vol. 24, 1984.

Forgy, Charles L., "RETE: A Fast Algorithm for the Many Pattern/Many Object Pattern Match Problem," *Artificial Intelligence*, vol. 19, no. 1, 1982.

Frankot, Robert T. and Rama Chellappa, "Estimation of Surface Topography from SAR Imagery Using Shape from Shading Techniques," *Artificial Intelligence*, vol. 43, 1990.

Freeman, P., and Allen Newell, "A Model for Functional Reasoning in Design," *Second International Joint Conference on Artificial Intelligence*, London, 1971.

Freuder, Eugene C., "Synthesizing Constraint Expressions," *Communications of the ACM*, vol. 21, no. 11, 1978.

Freuder, Eugene C., "A Computer System for Visual Recognition Using Active Knowledge," PhD Thesis, Department of Electrical Engineering & Computer Science, Massachusetts Institute of Technology, Cambridge, MA, 1976.

Freuder, Eugene C., "A Sufficient Condition for Backtrack-Free Search," *Journal of the Association for Computing Machinery*, vol. 29, no. 1, 1982.

Freuder, Eugene C., "On the Knowledge Required to Label a Picture Graph," *Artificial Intelligence*, vol. 15, 1980.

Frey, Peter W. (editor), *Chess Skill in Man and Machine* (second edition), Springer-Verlag, New York, 1983.

Friedman, Jerome H., Jon Louis Bentley, and Raphael Ari Finkel, "An Algorithm for Finding Best Matches in Logarithmic Expected Time," *ACM Transactions on Mathematical Software*, vol. 3, no. 3, 1977.

Funt, V. Brian, "Problem-Solving with Diagrammatic Representations," *Artificial Intelligence*, vol. 13, no. 3, 1980.

Gardin, Francesco and Bernard Meltzer, "Analogical Representations of Naive Physics," *Artificial Intelligence*, vol. 38, 1989.

Gaschnig, John, "Performance Measurement and Analysis of Certain Search Algorithms," Report CMU-CS-79-124, Department of Computer Science, Carnegie–Mellon University, Pittsburgh, PA, 1979.

Gelperin, David, "On the Optimality of A*," *Artificial Intelligence*, vol. 8, no. 1, 1977.

Genesereth, Michael R., "The Use of Design Descriptions in Automated Diagnosis," *Artificial Intelligence*, vol. 24, 1984.

Gentner, Dedre and Kenneth D. Forbus, "A Note on Creativity and Learning in a Case-Based Explainer," *Artificial Intelligence*, vol. 44, 1990.

Gentner, Dedre, and Albert L. Stevens (editors), *Mental Models*, Lawrence Erlbaum Associates, Hillsdale, NJ, 1983.

Gentner, Dedre, "Structure-Mapping: A Theoretical Framework for Analogy," *Cognitive Science*, vol. 7, no. 2, 1983.

Gentner, Dedre, "The Structure of Analogical Models in Science," Report 4451, Bolt, Beranek and Newman, Cambridge, MA, 1980.

Gillogly, James J., "The Technology Chess Program," *Artificial Intelligence*, vol. 3, no. 3, 1972.

Goldberg, David E., *Genetic Algorithms in Search Optimization and Machine Learning*, Addison-Wesley, Reading, MA, 1989.

Goldstein, Ira P., "Summary of MYCROFT: A System for Understanding Simple Picture Programs," *Artificial Intelligence*, vol. 6, no. 3, 1975. Based on a PhD thesis, Massachusetts Institute of Technology, Cambridge, MA, 1973.

Gordon, Jean and Edward H. Shortliffe, "A Method for Managing Evidential Reasoning in a Hierarchical Hypothesis Space," *Artificial Intelligence*, vol. 26, 1985.

Green, Claude Cordell, *The Application of Theorem Proving to Question-answering Systems*, Garland, New York, 1980. Based on a PhD thesis, Stanford University, Stanford, CA, 1969.

Green, Claude Cordell, "Theorem Proving by Resolution as a Basis for Question Answering," in *Machine Intelligence 4*, edited by Bernard Melzer and Donald Michie, Edinburgh University Press, Edinburgh, Scotland, 1969.

Greiner, Russell, "Learning by Understanding Analogies," *Artificial Intelligence*, vol. 35, 1988.

Griffith, Arnold K., "A Comparison and Evaluation of Three Machine Learning Procedures as Applied to the Game of Checkers," *Artificial Intelligence*, vol. 5, no. 2, 1974.

Grimson, W. Eric L., *From Images to Surfaces*, MIT Press, Cambridge, MA, 1981. Based on a PhD thesis, Massachusetts Institute of Technology, Cambridge, MA, 1980.

Grimson, W. Eric L., *Object Recognition by Computer: The Role of Geometric Constraints*, MIT Press, Cambridge, MA, 1990.

Grimson, W. Eric L., "The Combinatorics of Object Recognition in Cluttered Environments Using Constrained Search," *Artificial Intelligence*, vol. 44, 1990.

Grosz, Barbara J., Douglas E. Appelt, Paul A. Martin and Fernando C. N. Pereira, "TEAM: An Experiment in the Design of Transportable Natural-Language Interfaces," *Artificial Intelligence*, vol. 32, 1987.

Grosz, Barbara J., "Natural Language Processing," *Artificial Intelligence*, vol. 19, no. 2, 1982.

Guzman, Adolfo, "Computer Recognition of Three-Dimensional Objects in a Visual Scene," PhD Thesis, Department of Electrical Engineering & Computer Science, Massachusetts Institute of Technology, Cambridge, MA, 1968.

Haas, Andrew R., "A Syntactic Theory of Belief and Action," *Artificial Intelligence*, vol. 28, 1986.

Haegeman, Liliane, *Introduction to Government and Binding Theory*, Basil Blackwell Ltd, Oxford, 1991.

Hall, Roger P., "Computational Approaches to Analogical Reasoning: A Comparative Analysis," *Artificial Intelligence*, vol. 39, 1989.

Hammond, K.J., "Explaining and Repairing Plans that Fail," *Artificial Intelligence*, vol. 45, 1990.

Hanks, Steve and Drew McDermott, "Nonmontonic Logic and Temporal Projection," *Artificial Intelligence*, vol. 33, 1987.

Haralick, Robert M., Larry S. Davis, and Azriel Rosenfeld, "Reduction Operations for Constraint Satisfaction," *Information Sciences*, vol. 14, 1978.

Hart, Peter E., Richard O. Duda, and M. T. Einaudi, "PROSPECTOR: A Computer-Based Consultation System for Mineral Exploration," *Mathematical Geology*, vol. 10, no. 5, 1978.

Hart, Peter E., "Progress on a Computer Based Consultant," *Fourth International Joint Conference on Artificial Intelligence*, Tbilisi, Georgia, USSR, 1975.

Hayes, Patrick J., "In Defense of Logic," *Fifth International Joint Conference on Artificial Intelligence*, Cambridge, MA, 1977.

Hayes, Patrick J., "The Naive Physics Manifesto," in *Expert Systems in the Micro-Electronic Age*, edited by Donald Michie, Edinburgh University Press, Edinburgh, Scotland, 1979.

Hayes-Roth, Barbara, "A Blackboard Architecture for Control," *Artificial Intelligence*, vol. 26, 1985.

Hayes-Roth, Frederick, Donald A. Waterman, and Douglas B. Lenat (editors), *Building Expert Systems*, Addison-Wesley, Reading, MA, 1983.

Hayes-Roth, Frederick, "Using Proofs and Refutations to Learn from Experience," in *Machine Learning: An Artificial Intelligence Approach*, edited by Ryszard S. Michalski, Jaime G. Carbonell, and Tom M. Mitchell, Tioga Publishing Company, Palo Alto, CA, 1983.

Hedrick, L. Charles, "Learning Production Systems from Examples," *Artificial Intelligence*, vol. 7, no. 1, 1976.

Hendrix, Gary G., Earl D. Sacerdoti, Daniel Sagalowicz, and Jonathan Slocum, "Developing a Natural Language Interface to Complex Data," *ACM Transactions on Database Systems*, vol. 8, no. 3, 1978.

Henon, Michel, "Numerical Study of Quadratic Area-Preserving Mappings," *Quarterly of Applied Mathematics*, vol. 17, 1969.

Hewitt, Carl E., and Peter de Jong, "Open Systems," Report AIM-691, Artificial Intelligence Laboratory, Massachusetts Institute of Technology, Cambridge, MA, 1982.

Hewitt, Carl E., "PLANNER: A Language for Proving Theorems in Robots," *First International Joint Conference on Artificial Intelligence*, Washington, D. C., 1969.

Hewitt, Carl E., "Viewing Control Structures as Patterns of Passing Messages," *Artificial Intelligence*, vol. 8, no. 3, 1977.

Hildreth, Ellen C., "The Measurement of Visual Motion," PhD Thesis, Department of Electrical Engineering & Computer Science, Massachusetts Institute of Technology, Cambridge, MA, 1983.

Hildreth, Ellen C., "The Detection of Intensity Changes by Computer and Biological Vision Systems," *Computer Vision, Graphics, and Image Processing*, vol. 22, 1983. Based on MS thesis, Massachusetts Institute of Technology, Cambridge, MA, 1980.

Hildreth, Ellen C., "Computations Underlying the Measurement of Visual Motion," *Artificial Intelligence*, vol. 23, 1984.

Hillis, W. Daniel, "Co-Evolving Parasites Improve Simulated Evolution as an Optimizing Procedure," *Physica*, 1990.

Hillis, W. Daniel, "The Connection Machine," Report AIM-646, Artificial Intelligence Laboratory, Massachusetts Institute of Technology, Cambridge, MA, 1981.

Hillis, W. Daniel, "A High Resolution Imaging Touch Sensor," *International Journal of Robotics Research*, vol. 1, no. 2, 1982. Based on MS thesis, Massachusetts Institute of Technology, Cambridge, MA, 1981.

Hinton, Geoffrey E., "Connectionist Learning Procedures," *Artificial Intelligence*, vol. 40, 1989.

Hinton, Geoffrey E., "Mapping Part–Whole Hierarchies Into Connectionist Networks," *Artificial Intelligence*, vol. 46, 1990.

Hobbs, Jerry R., and Stanley J. Rosenschein, "Making Computational Sense of Montague's Intensional Logic," *Artificial Intelligence*, vol. 9, no. 3, 1977.

Hofstadter, Douglas R., *Gödel, Escher, Bach: The Eternal Golden Braid*, Vintage Books, New York, 1980.

Holland, John H., K. J. Holyoak, R. E. Nisbett, and P. R. Thagard, *Induction: Processes of Inference, Learning, and Discovery*, MIT Press, Cambridge, MA, 1986.

Holland, John H., *Adaptation in Natural and Artificial Systems*, The University of Michigan Press, Ann Arbor, MI, 1975.

Holland, Stephen W., Lothar Rossol, and Mitchell R. Ward, "CONSIGHT-I: A Vision-Controlled Robot System for Transferring Parts from Belt Conveyors," in *Computer Vision and Sensor-based Robots*, edited by George G. Dodd and Lothar Rossol, Plenum Press, New York, 1979.

Hollerbach, John, "Dynamics," in *Robot Motion: Planning and Control*, edited by J. Michael Brady, John M. Hollerbach, Timothy L. Johnson, Tomás Lozano-Pérez, and Matthew T. Mason, MIT Press, Cambridge, MA, 1982.

Hollerbach, John, "A Recursive Lagrangian Formulation of Manipulator Dynamics and a Comparative Study of Dynamics Formulation Complexity," in *Robot Motion: Planning and Control*, edited by J. Michael Brady, John M. Hollerbach, Timothy L. Johnson, Tomás Lozano-Pérez, and Matthew T. Mason, MIT Press, Cambridge, MA, 1982.

Hollerbach, John, "Hierarchical Shape Description of Objects by Selection and Modification of Prototypes," MS Thesis, Department of Electrical Engineering & Computer Science, Massachusetts Institute of Technology, Cambridge, MA, 1976.

Hopfield, J. J., "Neural Networks and Physical Systems with Emergent Collective Computational Abilities," *Proceedings of the National Academy of Sciences*, vol. 79, 1982.

Horaud, Radu and Michael Brady, "On the Geometric Interpretation of Image Contours," *Artificial Intelligence*, vol. 37, 1988.

Horn, Berthold K. P. and Michael J. Brooks (editors), *Shape from Shading*, MIT Press, Cambridge, MA, 1989.

Horn, Berthold K. P., "The Binford–Horn Line Finder," Report AIM-285, Artificial Intelligence Laboratory, Massachusetts Institute of Technology, Cambridge, MA, 1971.

Horn, Berthold K. P., *Robot Vision*, MIT Press, Cambridge, MA, and McGraw-Hill, New York, 1984.

Horn, Berthold K. P., "Obtaining Shape from Shading Information," in *Psychology of Computer Vision*, edited by Patrick H. Winston, MIT Press, Cambridge, MA, 1975. Based on a PhD thesis, Massachusetts Institute of Technology, Cambridge, MA, 1970.

Horn, Berthold K.P., "Understanding Image Intensities," *Artificial Intelligence*, vol. 8, no. 2, 1977.

Horn, Berthold K.P., "Sequins and Quills: Representations for Surface Topography," in *Representation of Three-Dimensional Objects*, edited by Ruzena Bajcsy, Springer-Verlag, New York, 1982.

Hsu, Teng-hsiung, Thomas Anantharaman, Murray Campbell, and Andreas Nowatzyk, "A Grandmaster Chess Machine," *Scientific American*, vol. 263, no. 4, 1990.

Hubel, D. H., and T. N. Wiesel, "Receptive Fields, Binocular Interaction and Functional Architecture in the Cat's Visual Cortex," *Journal of Physiology*, vol. 160, 1962.

Huffman, David, "Impossible Objects as Nonsense Sentences," in *Machine Intelligence 6*, edited by Bernard Meltzer and Donald Michie, Edinburgh University Press, Edinburgh, Scotland, 1971.

Hummel, Robert A., and Steven W. Zucker, "On the Foundations of Relaxation Labeling Processes," *IEEE Transactions on Pattern Analysis and Machine Intelligence*, vol. PAMI-5, no. 3, 1983.

Hunt, Earl B., *Artificial Intelligence*, Academic Press, New York, 1975.

Huyn, Nam, Rina Dechter and Judea Pearl, "Probabilistic Analysis of the Complexity of A*," *Artificial Intelligence*, vol. 15, 1980.

Ikeuchi, K., "Shape from Regular Patterns," *Artificial Intelligence*, vol. 22, 1984.

Ikeuchi, Katsushi, and Berthold K. P. Horn, "Numerical Shape from Shading and Occluding Boundaries," *Artificial Intelligence*, vol. 17, 1981.

Inoue, Hirochika, "Force Feedback in Precise Assembly Tasks," Report AIM-308, Artificial Intelligence Laboratory, Massachusetts Institute of Technology, Cambridge, MA, 1974.

Kahn, Kenneth, and Anthony G. Gorry, "Mechanizing Temporal Knowledge," *Artificial Intelligence*, vol. 9, no. 1, 1977.

Kanade, Takeo, "A Theory of Origami World," *Artificial Intelligence*, vol. 13, no. 3, 1980.

Kanade, Takeo, "Recovery of the Three-Dimensional Shape of an Object from a Single View," *Artificial Intelligence*, vol. 17, 1981.

Kant, Elaine, "On the Efficient Synthesis of Efficient Programs," *Artificial Intelligence*, vol. 20, 1983.

Kaplan, Jerrold., "Cooperative Responses from a Portable Natural Language Query System," in *Computational Models of Discourse*, edited by J. Michael Brady and Robert C. Berwick, MIT Press, Cambridge, MA, 1983.

Kaplan, Ronald M., "Augmented Transition Networks: Psychological Models of Sentence Comprehension," *Artificial Intelligence*, vol. 3, no. 2, 1972.

Karp, Richard M. and Judea Pearl, "Searching for an Optimal Path in a Tree with Random Costs," *Artificial Intelligence*, vol. 21, 1983.

Katz, Boris, and Patrick H. Winston, "A Two-Way Natural Language Interface," in *Integrated Interactive Computing Systems*, edited by P. Degano and Erik Sandewall, North-Holland, Amsterdam, 1982.

Katz, Boris, "Using English for Indexing and Retrieving," in *Artificial Intelligence at MIT: Expanding Frontiers (Two Volumes)*, edited by Patrick H. Winston and Sarah Alexandra Shellard, MIT Press, Cambridge, MA, 1990.

Kautz, Henry A. and Bart Selman, "Hard Problems for Simple Default Logics," *Artificial Intelligence*, vol. 49, 1991.

Keene, Sonya E., *Object-Oriented Programming in* COMMON LISP, Addison-Wesley, Reading, MA, 1989.

Kimura, Motoo, *The Neutral Theory of Molecular Evolution*, Cambridge University Press, Cambridge, England, 1983.

Kirsh, David, "Foundations of AI: The Big Issues," *Artificial Intelligence*, vol. 47, 1991.

Kirsh, David, "Today the Earwig, Tomorrow Man?," *Artificial Intelligence*, vol. 47, 1991.

Knuth, Donald E., and Ronald W. Moore, "An Analysis of Alpha–Beta Pruning," *Artificial Intelligence*, vol. 6, no. 4, 1975.

Korf, R. E., "Real-Time Heuristic Search," *Artificial Intelligence*, vol. 42, 1990.

Kornfeld, William A., and Carl E. Hewitt, "The Scientific Community Metaphor," *IEEE Transactions on Systems, Man, and Cybernetics*, vol. SMC-11, no. 1, 1981.

Kowalski, Robert, *Logic for Problem Solving*, North-Holland, Amsterdam, 1979.

Kratkiewicz, Kendra, "Improving Learned Rules Using Near Miss Groups," BS Thesis, Department of Electrical Engineering & Computer Science, Massachusetts Institute of Technology, Cambridge, MA, 1984.

Kuipers, Benjamin J., "Commonsense Reasoning About Causality: Deriving Behavior from Structure," *Artificial Intelligence*, vol. 24, 1984.

Kuipers, Benjamin J., "Qualitative Simulation," *Artificial Intelligence*, vol. 29, 1986.

Kulikowski, Casimir A., and Sholom M. Weiss, "Representation of Expert Knowledge for Consultant," in *Artificial Intelligence in Medicine*, edited by Peter Szolovits, Westview Press, Boulder, CO, 1982.

Laird, John E., Alan Newell and Paul S. Rosenbloom, "SOAR: An Architecture for General Intelligence," *Artificial Intelligence*, vol. 33, 1987.

Langley, Pat and Jan M. Zytkow, "Data-Driven Approaches to Empirical Discovery," *Artificial Intelligence*, vol. 40, 1989.

Langley, Pat, Gary L. Bradshaw, and Herbert A. Simon, "Rediscovering Chemistry with the BACON System," in *Machine Learning: An Artificial Intelligence Approach*, edited by Ryszard S. Michalski, Jaime G. Carbonell, and Tom M. Mitchell, Tioga Publishing Company, Palo Alto, CA, 1983.

Lathrop, Richard Harold, "Efficient Methods for Massively Parallel Symbolic Induction: Algorithms and Implementation," PhD Thesis, Department of Electrical Engineering & Computer Science, Massachusetts Institute of Technology, Cambridge, MA, 1990.

Lauriere, Jean-Louis, "A Language and a Program for Stating and Solving Combinatorial Problems," *Artificial Intelligence*, vol. 10, no. 1, 1978.

Lee, Chia-Hoang and Azriel Rosenfeld, "Improved Methods of Estimating Shape from Shading Using the Light Source Coordinate System," *Artificial Intelligence*, vol. 26, 1985.

Lee, Kai-Fu and Sanjoy Mahajan, "A Pattern Classification Approach to Evaluation Function Learning," *Artificial Intelligence*, vol. 36, 1988.

Lee, Kai-Fu and Sanjoy Mahajan, "The Development of a World Class Othello Program," *Artificial Intelligence*, vol. 43, 1990.

Leech, W. J., "A Rule Based Process Control Method with Feedback," *Proceedings of the International Conference and Exhibit, Instrument Society of America*, 1986.

Lehnert, Wendy G., Michael G. Dyer, Peter N. Johnson, C. J. Yang, and, Steve Harley, "BORIS: An Experiment in In-Depth Understanding of Narratives," *Artificial Intelligence*, vol. 20, no. 1, 1983.

Lehnert, Wendy, "Plot Units and Narrative Summarization," *Cognitive Science*, vol. 5, no. 4, 1981.

Lenat, Douglas B. and Edward A. Feigenbaum, "On the Thresholds of Knowledge," *Artificial Intelligence*, vol. 47, 1991.

Lenat, Douglas B. and John S. Brown, "Why AM and EURISKO Appear to Work," *Artificial Intelligence*, vol. 23, 1984.

Lenat, Douglas B. and R. V. Guha, *Building Large Knowledge-Based Systems*, Addison-Wesley, Reading, MA, 1990.

Lenat, Douglas B., "The Ubiquity of Discovery," *Artificial Intelligence*, vol. 9, no. 3, 1977.

Lenat, Douglas B., "AM: Discovery in Mathematics as Heuristic Search," in *Knowledge-Based Systems in Artificial Intelligence*, edited by Randall Davis and Douglas B. Lenat, McGraw-Hill, New York, 1982. Based on a PhD thesis, Stanford University, Stanford, CA, 1977.

Lesser, Victor R., and Lee D. Erman, "A Retrospective View of the Hearsay-II Architecture," *Fifth International Joint Conference on Artificial Intelligence*, Cambridge, MA, 1977.

Lettvin, Jerome Y., R. R. Maturana, W. S. McCulloch, and W. H. Pitts, "What the Frog's Eye Tells the Frog's Brain," *Proceedings of the Institute of Radio Engineers*, vol. 47, 1959.

Levesque, Hector J., "Foundations of a Functional Approach to Knowledge Representation," *Artificial Intelligence*, vol. 23, 1984.

Levesque, Hector J., "Making Believers Out of Computers," *Artificial Intelligence*, vol. 30, 1986.

Levesque, Hector J., "All I Know: A Study in Autoepistemic Logic," *Artificial Intelligence*, vol. 42, 1990.

Levi, Giorgio, and Sirovich Franco, "Generalized and/or Graphs," *Artificial Intelligence*, vol. 7, no. 3, 1976.

Levy, David, *Chess and Computers*, Computer Science Press, Woodland Hills, CA, 1976.

Lindsay, Peter H. and Donald A. Norman, *Human Information Processing*, Academic Press, New York, 1972.

Lindsay, Robert, Bruce G. Buchanan, Edward A. Feigenbaum, and Joshua Lederberg, *Applications of Artificial Intelligence for Chemical Inference: The DENDRAL Project*, McGraw-Hill, New York, 1980.

Lowe, David G., "Three-Dimensional Object Recognition from Single Two-Dimensional Images," *Artificial Intelligence*, vol. 31, 1987.

Lozano-Pérez, Tomás, "Robot Programming," Report AIM-698, Artificial Intelligence Laboratory, Massachusetts Institute of Technology, Cambridge, MA, 1982.

Lozano-Pérez, Tomás, "Spatial Planning: A Configuration-Space Approach," *IEEE Transactions on Computers*, vol. 71, no. 7, 1983. Based on a PhD thesis, Massachusetts Institute of Technology, Cambridge, MA, 1980.

Mackworth, Alan K. and Eugene C. Freuder, "The Complexity of Some Polynomial Consistency Algorithms for Constraint Satisfaction Problems," *Artificial Intelligence*, vol. 25, 1985.

Mackworth, Alan K., "Consistency in Networks of Relations," *Artificial Intelligence*, vol. 8, no. 1, 1977.

Mackworth, Alan K., "Interpreting Pictures of Polyhedral Scenes," *Artificial Intelligence*, vol. 4, no. 2, 1973.

Marcus, Mitchell P., *A Theory of Syntactic Recognition for Natural Language*, MIT Press, Cambridge, MA, 1980. Based on a PhD thesis, Massachusetts Institute of Technology, Cambridge, MA, 1977.

Marcus, Sandra and John McDermott, "SALT: A Knowledge Acquisition Language for Propose-and-Revise Systems," *Artificial Intelligence*, vol. 39, 1989.

Marr, David, and Tomaso Poggio, "A Theory of Human Stereo Vision," *Proceedings of the Royal Society of London*, vol. 204, 1979.

Marr, David, "Artificial Intelligence: A Personal View," *Artificial Intelligence*, vol. 9, no. 1, 1977.

Marr, David, *Vision*, W. H. Freeman, San Francisco, CA, 1982.

Martelli, Alberto, "On the Complexity of Admissible Search Algorithms," *Artificial Intelligence*, vol. 8, no. 1, 1977.

Martin, William A., "Descriptions and the Specialization of Concepts," Report TM-101, Laboratory for Computer Science, Massachusetts Institute of Technology, Cambridge, MA, 1978.

Mason, Matthew T., "Compliance and Force Control for Computer Controlled Manipulators," *IEEE Transactions on Systems, Man, and Cybernetics*, vol. SCM-11, no. 6, 1981. Based on MS thesis, Massachusetts Institute of Technology, Cambridge, MA, 1979.

Mason, Matthew T., "Manipulator Grasping and Pushing Operations," PhD Thesis, Department of Electrical Engineering & Computer Science, Massachusetts Institute of Technology, Cambridge, MA, 1982.

Mayhew, John E. W., and John P. Frisby, "Psychophysical and Computational Studies Towards a Theory of Human Stereopsis," *Artificial Intelligence*, vol. 17, 1981.

Mazlack, Lawrence, J., "Computer Construction of Crossword Puzzles Using Precedence Relationships," *Artificial Intelligence*, vol. 7, no. 1, 1976.

McAllester, David A., "Conspiracy Numbers for Min-Max Search," *Artificial Intelligence*, vol. 35, no. 3, 1988.

McAllester, David A., "An Outlook on Truth Maintenance," Report AIM-551, Artificial Intelligence Laboratory, Massachusetts Institute of Technology, Cambridge, MA, 1980.

McAllester, David A., "Conspiracy Numbers for Min-Max Search," *Artificial Intelligence*, vol. 35, 1988.

McAllester, David and David Rosenblitt, "Systematic Nonlinear Planning," *National Conference on Artificial Intelligence*, 1991.

McCarthy, John, and Patrick J. Hayes, "Some Philosophical Problems from the Standpoint of Artificial Intelligence," in *Machine Intelligence 4*, edited by Bernard Melzer and Donald Michie, Edinburgh University Press, Edinburgh, Scotland, 1969.

McCarthy, John, "Circumscription: A Form of Non-Monotonic Reasoning," *Artificial Intelligence*, vol. 13, 1980.

McCarthy, John, "Epistemological Problems of Artificial Intelligence," *Fifth International Joint Conference on Artificial Intelligence*, Cambridge, MA, 1977.

McCarthy, John, "Applications of Circumscription to Formalizing Common-Sense Knowledge," *Artificial Intelligence*, vol. 28, 1986.

McClelland, James L. and David E. Rumelhart (editors), *Parallel Distributed Processing* (Two Volumes), MIT Press, Cambridge, MA, 1986.

McCorduck, Pamela, *Machines Who Think*, W. H. Freeman, San Francisco, CA, 1979.

McDermott, Drew and Ernest Davis, "Planning Routes Through Uncertain Territory," *Artificial Intelligence*, vol. 22, 1984.

McDermott, Drew, and Jon Doyle, "Non-Monotonic Logic I," *Artificial Intelligence*, vol. 13, 1980.

McDermott, Drew, "A General Framework for Reason Maintenance," *Artificial Intelligence*, vol. 50, 1991.

McDermott, John, "R1: A Rule-Based Configurer of Computer Systems," *Artificial Intelligence*, vol. 19, no. 1, 1982.

McDonald, David D., "Natural Language Generation as a Computational Problem," in *Computational Models of Discourse*, edited by J. Michael Brady and Robert C. Berwick, MIT Press, Cambridge, MA, 1983.

Michalski, Ryszard S. and Patrick H. Winston, "Variable Precision Logic," *Artificial Intelligence*, vol. 29, 1986.

Michalski, Ryszard S., and Richard L. Chilausky, "Learning by Being Told and Learning from Examples: An Experimental Comparison of the Two Methods of Knowledge Acquisition in the Context of Developing an Expert System for Soybean Disease Diagnosis," *International Journal of Policy Analysis and Information Systems*, vol. 4, no. 2, 1980.

Michalski, Ryszard S., and Robert E. Stepp, "Learning from Observation: Conceptual Clustering," in *Machine Learning: An Artificial Intelligence Approach*, edited by Ryszard S. Michalski, Jaime G. Carbonell, and Tom M. Mitchell, Tioga Publishing Company, Palo Alto, CA, 1983.

Michalski, Ryszard S., Jaime G. Carbonell, and Tom M. Mitchell (editors), *Machine Learning: An Artificial Intelligence Approach*, Tioga Publishing Company, Palo Alto, CA, 1983.

Michalski, Ryszard S., "Pattern Recognition as Rule-Guided Inductive Inference," *IEEE Transactions on Pattern Analysis and Machine Intelligence*, vol. 2, no. 4, 1980.

Michalski, Ryszard S., "A Theory and Methodology of Inductive Learning," *Artificial Intelligence*, vol. 20, no. 3, 1983.

Michalski, Ryszard S., "A Theory and Methodology of Inductive Learning," *Artificial Intelligence*, vol. 20, 1983.

Michie, Donald (editor), *Expert Systems in the Micro-Electronic Age*, Edinburgh University Press, Edinburgh, Scotland, 1979.

Michie, Donald, *On Machine Intelligence*, John Wiley and Sons, New York, 1974.

Michie, Donald, "Chess with Computers," *Interdisciplinary Science Reviews*, vol. 5, no. 3, 1980.

Miller, G. A., E. Galanter, and K. H. Pribram, *Plans and the Structure of Behavior*, Holt, Rinehart, and Winston, New York, 1960.

Minker, Jack, Daniel H. Fishman, and James R. McSkimin, "The Q* Algorithm: A Search Strategy for a Deductive Question-Answering System," *Artificial Intelligence*, vol. 4, no. 3&4, 1973.

Minsky, Marvin (editor), *Semantic Information Processing*, MIT Press, Cambridge, MA, 1968.

Minsky, Marvin, "A Framework for Representing Knowledge," in *Psychology of Computer Vision*, edited by Patrick H. Winston, MIT Press, Cambridge, MA, 1975.

Minsky, Marvin, "Plain Talk about Neurodevelopmental Epistemology," *Fifth International Joint Conference on Artificial Intelligence*, Cambridge, MA, 1977.

Minsky, Marvin, *The Society of Mind*, Simon & Schuster, New York, 1985.

Minsky, Marvin, "K-lines: A Theory of Memory," *Cognitive Science*, vol. 4, no. 1, 1980.

Minsky, Marvin, "Matter, Mind, and Models," in *Semantic Information Processing*, edited by Marvin Minsky, MIT Press, Cambridge, MA, 1968.

Minton, Steven, Jaime G. Carbonell, Craig A. Knoblock, Daniel R. Kuokka, Oren Etzioni and Yolanda Gil, "Explanation-Based Learning: A Problem Solving Perspective," *Artificial Intelligence*, vol. 40, 1989.

Minton, Steven, "Quantitative Results Concerning the Utility of Explanation-Based Learning," *Artificial Intelligence*, vol. 42, 1990.

Mitchell, T. M., R. M. Keller, and S. T. Kedar-Cabelli, "Explanation-Based Generalization: A Unifying View," *Machine Learning*, vol. 1, no. 1, 1986.

Mitchell, Tom M., "Generalization as Search," *Artificial Intelligence*, vol. 18, no. 2, 1982. Based on a PhD thesis, Stanford University, Stanford, CA, 1978.

Mitchell, Tom M., "Generalization as Search," *Artificial Intelligence*, vol. 18, 1982.

Montanari, Ugo and Francesca Rossi, "Constraint Relaxation May Be Perfect," *Artificial Intelligence*, vol. 48, 1991.

Moore, James A., and Allen Newell, "How Can Merlin Understand?," in *Knowledge and Cognition*, edited by L. Gregg, Lawrence Erlbaum Associates, Hillsdale, NJ, 1974.

Moore, Robert C., "Semantical Considerations of Nonmonotonic Logic," *Artificial Intelligence*, vol. 25, 1985.

Morevec, Hans P., "Towards Automatic Visual Obstacle Avoidance," *Fifth International Joint Conference on Artificial Intelligence*, Cambridge, MA, 1977.

Moses, Joel, "Symbolic Integration," PhD Thesis, Department of Electrical Engineering & Computer Science, Massachusetts Institute of Technology, Cambridge, MA, 1967.

Mostow, Jack, "Design by Derivational Analogy: Issues in the Automated Replay of Design Plans," *Artificial Intelligence*, vol. 40, 1989.

Nagel, Hans-Hellmut, "On the Estimation of Optical Flow: Relations Between Different Approaches and Some New Results," *Artificial Intelligence*, vol. 33, 1987.

Nau, Dana S., "An Investigation of the Causes of Pathology in Games," *Artificial Intelligence*, vol. 19, no. 3, 1982.

Nevatia, Ramakant, and Thomas O. Binford, "Description and Recognition of Curved Objects," *Artificial Intelligence*, vol. 8, no. 1, 1977.

Nevatia, Ramakant, *Machine Perception*, Prentice-Hall, Englewood Cliffs, NJ, 1982.

Newborn, M. M., "The Efficiency of the Alpha–Beta Search on Trees with Branch-Dependent Terminal Node Scores," *Artificial Intelligence*, vol. 8, no. 2, 1977.

Newell, Allen, and Herbert A. Simon, *Human Problem Solving*, Prentice-Hall, Englewood Cliffs, NJ, 1972.

Newell, Allen, John C. Shaw, and Herbert A. Simon, "Preliminary Description of General Problem Solving Program-I (Gps-I)," Report CIP Working Paper 7, Carnegie Institute of Technology, Pittsburgh, PA, 1957.

Newell, Allen, *Unified Theories of Cognition*, Harvard University Press, Cambridge, MA, 1990.

Nilsson, Nils J., *Principles of Artificial Intelligence*, Tioga Publishing Company, Palo Alto, CA, 1980.

Nilsson, Nils J., "Logic and Artificial Intelligence," *Artificial Intelligence*, vol. 47, 1991.

Nilsson, Nils J., "Probabilistic Logic," *Artificial Intelligence*, vol. 28, 1986.

Nishihara, H. Keith, "Intensity, Visible-surface, and Volumetric Representations," *Artificial Intelligence*, vol. 17, 1981. Based on a PhD thesis, Massachusetts Institute of Technology, Cambridge, MA, 1978.

Norman, Donald A., "Approaches to the Study of Intelligence," *Artificial Intelligence*, vol. 47, 1991.

O'Gorman, Frank, "Edge Detection Using Walsh Functions," *Artificial Intelligence*, vol. 10, no. 2, 1978.

Ogden, C. K., *Basic English: International Second Language*, Harcourt, Brace, and World, New York, 1968.

Ohlander, Ronald B., Keith Price, and D. Raj Reddy, "Picture Segmentation Using a Recursive Splitting Method," *Computer Graphics and Image Processing*, vol. 8, 1979.

Ohlander, Ronald B., "Analysis of Natural Scenes," PhD Thesis, Carnegie–Mellon University, Pittsburgh, PA, 1975.

Palay, Andrew J., "The B* Tree Search Algorithm: New Results," *Artificial Intelligence*, vol. 19, no. 2, 1982.

Papazian, Pegor, "Principles, Opportunism and Seeing in Design: A Computational Approach," MS Thesis, Department of Architecture, Massachusetts Institute of Technology, Cambridge, MA, 1991.

Papert, Seymour A., "Some Mathematical Models of Learning," *Proceedings of the Fourth London Symposium on Information Theory*, 1961.

Papert, Seymour, and Cynthia Solomon, "Twenty Things to Do with a Computer," Report AIM-248, Artificial Intelligence Laboratory, Massachusetts Institute of Technology, Cambridge, MA, 1971.

Papert, Seymour, *Mindstorms*, Basic Books, New York, 1981.

Papert, Seymour, "Uses of Technology to Enhance Education," Report AIM-298, Artificial Intelligence Laboratory, Massachusetts Institute of Technology, Cambridge, MA, 1973.

Pastre, D., "Automatic Theorem Proving in Set Theory," *Artificial Intelligence*, vol. 10, no. 1, 1978.

Patil, Ramesh S., Peter Szolovits, and William B. Schwartz, "Causal Understanding of Patient Illness," *Seventh International Joint Conference on Artificial Intelligence*, Vancouver, Canada, 1981.

Patil, Ramesh, "Causal Representation of Patient Illness for Electrolyte and Acid-Base Diagnosis," PhD Thesis, Department of Electrical Engineering & Computer Science, Massachusetts Institute of Technology, Cambridge, MA, 1981.

Paul, Richard P., *Robot Manipulators: Mathematics, Programming, and Control*, MIT Press, Cambridge, MA, 1981.

Pearl, Judea, "Knowledge versus Search: A Quantitative Analysis Using A*," *Artificial Intelligence*, vol. 20, no. 1, 1983.

Pearl, Judea, "Distributed Revision of Composite Beliefs," *Artificial Intelligence*, vol. 33, 1987.

Pearl, Judea, "Embracing Causality in Default Reasoning," *Artificial Intelligence*, vol. 35, 1988.

Pearl, Judea, "Fusion, Propagation, and Structuring in Belief Networks," *Artificial Intelligence*, vol. 29, 1986.

Pednault, E. P. D., Steven W. Zucker, and L. V. Muresan, "On the Independence Assumption Underlying Subjective Bayesian Updating," *Artificial Intelligence*, vol. 16, no. 2, 1981.

Pentland, Alex P., "Shading into Texture," *Artificial Intelligence*, vol. 29, 1986.

Pentland, Alex P., "Perceptual Organization and the Representation of Natural Form," *Artificial Intelligence*, vol. 28, 1986.

Pereira, Fernando C. N., and David H. D. Warren, "Definite Clause Grammars for Language Analysis: A Survey of the Formalism and a Comparison with Augmented Transition Networks," *Artificial Intelligence*, vol. 13, no. 3, 1980.

Pereira, Fernando C. N. and Martha E. Pollack, "Incremental Interpretation," *Artificial Intelligence*, vol. 50, 1991.

Pitrat, Jacques, "A Chess Combination Program which Uses Plans," *Artificial Intelligence*, vol. 8, no. 3, 1977.

Poggio, Tomaso A., and Frederico Girose, "Networks for Approximation and Learning," *Proceedings of the IEEE*, vol. 78, no. 9, 1990.

Pomerleau, Dean, A., "Efficient Training of Artificial Neural Networks for Autonomous Navigation," *Neural Computation*, vol. 3, no. 1, 1991.

Pomerleau, Dean, A., "Neural Network Based Vision for Precise Control of a Walking Robot," *Machine Learning*, 1992.

Pople, Harry E., Jr., "Heuristic Methods for Imposing Structure on Ill-Structured Problems: The Structuring of Medical Diagnostics," in *Artificial Intelligence in Medicine*, edited by Peter Szolovits, Westview Press, Boulder, CO, 1982.

Pople, Harry E., Jr., "On the Mechanization of Abductive Logic," *Third International Joint Conference on Artificial Intelligence*, Stanford, CA, 1973.

Popplestone, R.J., A. P. Ambler and I. M. Bellos, "An Interpreter for a Language for Describing Assemblies," *Artificial Intelligence*, vol. 14, 1980.

Pylyshyn, Zenon W., "Literature from Cognitive Psychology," *Artificial Intelligence*, vol. 19, no. 3, 1982.

Quinlan, J. Ross and Ronald Rivest, "Inferring Decision Trees Using the Minimum Description Length Principle," Report TM-339, Laboratory for Computer Science, Massachusetts Institute of Technology, Cambridge, MA, 1987.

Quinlan, J. Ross, "Inferno: A Cautious Approach to Uncertain Inference," *The Computer Journal*, vol. 26, no. 3, 1983.

Quinlan, J. Ross, "Learning Efficient Classification Procedures and their Application to Chess End Games," in *Machine Learning: An Artificial Intelligence Approach*, edited by Ryszard S. Michalski, Jaime G. Carbonell, and Tom M. Mitchell, Tioga Publishing Company, Palo Alto, CA, 1983.

Quinlan, J. Ross, "Discovering Rules by Induction from Large Collections of Examples," in *Expert Systems in the Micro-Electronic Age*, edited by Donald Michie, Edinburgh University Press, Edinburgh, Scotland, 1979.

Quinlan, J. Ross, "Simplifying Decision Trees," Report AIM-930, Artificial Intelligence Laboratory, Massachusetts Institute of Technology, Cambridge, MA, 1986.

Raibert, Marc H., and Ivan Sutherland, "Machines that Walk," *Scientific American*, vol. 248, no. 1, 1983.

Rao, Satyajit, "Knowledge Repair," MS Thesis, Department of Electrical Engineering & Computer Science, Massachusetts Institute of Technology, Cambridge, MA, 1991.

Raphael, Bertram, *The Thinking Computer*, W. H. Freeman, San Francisco, CA, 1976.

Reiter, R., "A Logic for Default Reasoning," *Artificial Intelligence*, vol. 13, 1980.

Reiter, Raymond and Alan K. Mackworth, "A Logical Framework for Depiction and Image Interpretation," *Artificial Intelligence*, vol. 41, 1990.

Reiter, Raymond, "A Theory of Diagnosis from First Principles," *Artificial Intelligence*, vol. 32, 1987.

Requicha, Aristides A., "Representations for Rigid Solids: Theory, Methods, and Systems," *ACM Computing Surveys*, vol. 12, no. 4, 1980.

Rich, Charles and Richard C. Waters, *The Programmer's Apprentice*, Addison-Wesley, Reading, MA, 1990.

Rich, Charles, and Howard E. Shrobe, "Initial Report on a LISP Programmer's Apprentice," *IEEE Transactions on Software Engineering*, vol. SE-4, no. 6, 1978.

Rich, Elaine, *Artificial Intelligence*, McGraw-Hill, New York, 1983.

Richards, Whitman (editor), *Natural Computation*, MIT Press, Cambridge, MA, 1988.

Richter, Jacob, and Shimon Ullman, "A Model for the Temporal Organization of the X- and Y-Type Receptive Fields in the Primate Retina," *Biological Cybernetics*, vol. 43, 1982.

Rieger, Chuck, "On Organization of Knowledge for Problem Solving and Language Comprehension," *Artificial Intelligence*, vol. 7, no. 2, 1976.

Roberts, R. Bruce, and Ira P. Goldstein, "The FRL primer," Report AIM-408, Artificial Intelligence Laboratory, Massachusetts Institute of Technology, Cambridge, MA, 1977.

Robinson, J. A., "A Machine-Oriented Logic Based on the Resolution Principle," *Journal of the Association for Computing Machinery*, vol. 12, no. 1, 1965.

Robinson, J. A., "The Generalized Resolution Principle," in *Machine Intelligence 3*, edited by Donald Michie, Elsevier, New York, 1968.

Rosenbloom, Paul S., John E. Laird, Alan Newell and Robert McCarl, "A Preliminary Analysis of the Soar Architecture as a Basis for General Intelligence," *Artificial Intelligence*, vol. 47, 1991.

Rosenbloom, Paul S., "A World-Championship-Level Othello Program," *Artificial Intelligence*, vol. 19, no. 3, 1982.

Rosenfeld, Azriel (editor), *Multiresolution Image Processing and Analysis*, Springer-Verlag, New York, 1983.

Rosenfeld, Azriel, and Avinash C. Kak, *Digital Picture Processing*, Academic Press, New York, 1976.

Rosenfeld, Azriel, Robert A. Hummel, and Steven W. Zucker, "Scene Labeling by Relaxation Operators," *IEEE Transactions on Systems, Man, and Society*, vol. 6, 1976.

Ruth, Gregory R., "Intelligent Program Analysis," *Artificial Intelligence*, vol. 7, no. 1, 1976.

Sacerdoti, Earl D., "Planning in a Hierarchy of Abstraction Spaces," *Artificial Intelligence*, vol. 5, no. 2, 1974.

Sacks, Elisa P., "Automatic Qualitative Analysis of Dynamic Systems Using Piecewise Linear Approximations," *Artificial Intelligence*, vol. 41, 1990.

Sacks, Elisa P., "Automatic Analysis of One-Parameter Planar Ordinary Differential Equations by Intelligent Numeric Simulation," *Artificial Intelligence*, vol. 48, 1991.

Sacks, Elisa P., "A Dynamic Systems Perspective on Qualitative Simulation," *Artificial Intelligence*, vol. 42, 1990.

Salisbury, J. Kenneth, Jr., and B. Roth, "Kinematic and Force Analysis of Articulated Mechanical Hands," *Journal of Mechanisms, Transmissions, and Automation in Design*, vol. 105, 1983.

Salisbury, J. Kenneth, Jr., and John J. Craig, "Articulated Hands: Force Control and Kinematic Issues," *International Journal of Robotics Research*, vol. 1, no. 1, 1982.

Salisbury, J. Kenneth, Jr., "Kinematic and Force Analysis of Articulated Hands," PhD Thesis, Stanford University, Stanford, CA, 1982.

Samuel, Arthur L., "Some Studies in Machine Learning Using the Game of Checkers II. Recent Progress," *IBM Journal of Research and Development*, vol. 11, no. 6, 1967.

Samuel, Arthur L., "Some Studies in Machine Learning Using the Game of Checkers," *IBM Journal of Research and Development*, vol. 3, no. 3, 1959.

Schank, Roger C. and C. J. Rieger III, "Inference and the Computer Understanding of Natural Language," *Artificial Intelligence*, vol. 5, 1974.

Schank, Roger C. and David B. Leake, "Creativity and Learning in a Case-Based Explainer," *Artificial Intelligence*, vol. 40, 1989.

Schank, Roger C., and Kenneth Colby (editors), *Computer Models of Thought and Language*, W. H. Freeman, San Francisco, CA, 1973.

Schank, Roger C., "Conceptual Dependency: A Theory of Natural Language Understanding," *Cognitive Psychology*, vol. 3, no. 4, 1972.

Schank, Roger C., *Dynamic Memory*, Cambridge University Press, Cambridge, England, 1982.

Schubert, L. K., "Extending the Expressive Power of Semantic Networks," *Artificial Intelligence*, vol. 7, no. 2, 1976.

Sejnowski, Terrence J. and Charles R. Rosenberg, "NETtalk: a Parallel Network that Learns to Read Aloud," in *Neurocomputing: Foundations of Research*, edited by James A. Anderson and Edward Rosenfeld, MIT Press, Cambridge, MA, 1989. Based on a technical report that appeared in 1986.

Selfridge, Mallory, "A Computer Model of Child Language Learning," *Artificial Intelligence*, vol. 29, 1986.

Selman, B. and H. A. Kautz, "Model-Preference Default Theories," *Artificial Intelligence*, vol. 45, 1990.

Shannon, Claude E., "Programming a Digital Computer for Playing Chess," *Philosophy Magazine*, vol. 41, 1950.

Shannon, Claude E., "Automatic Chess Player," *Scientific American*, vol. 182, no. 48, 1950.

Shirai, Yoshiaki, "Analyzing Intensity Arrays Using Knowledge about Scenes," in *Psychology of Computer Vision*, edited by Patrick H. Winston, MIT Press, Cambridge, MA, 1975.

Shoham, Yoav and Drew McDermott, "Problems in Formal Temporal Reasoning," *Artificial Intelligence*, vol. 36, 1988.

Shoham, Yoav , "Temporal Logics in AI: Semantical and Ontological Considerations," *Artificial Intelligence*, vol. 33, 1987.

Shoham, Yoav, "Chronological Ignorance: Experiments in Nonmonotonic Temporal Reasoning," *Artificial Intelligence*, vol. 36, 1988.

Shortliffe, Edward H., and Bruce G. Buchanan, "A Model of Inexact Reasoning in Medicine," *Mathematical Biosciences*, vol. 23, 1975.

Shortliffe, Edward H., Mycin: *Computer-Based Medical Consultations*, Elsevier, New York, 1976. Based on a PhD thesis, Stanford University, Stanford, CA, 1974.

Shostak, Robert E., "Refutation Graphs," *Artificial Intelligence*, vol. 7, no. 1, 1976.

Sidner, Candace L., "Focusing in the Comprehension of Definite Anaphora," in *Computational Models of Discourse*, edited by J. Michael Brady and Robert C. Berwick, MIT Press, Cambridge, MA, 1983.

Simmons, Robert, "Semantic Networks: Their Computation and Use for Understanding English Sentences," in *Computer Models of Thought and Language*, edited by Roger Schank and Kenneth Colby, W. H. Freeman, San Francisco, CA, 1973.

Simon, Herbert A., and Joseph B. Kadane, "Optimal Problem-Solving Search: All-or-None Solutions," *Artificial Intelligence*, vol. 6, no. 3, 1975.

Simon, Herbert A., "The Structure of Ill Structured Problems," *Artificial Intelligence*, vol. 4, 1973.

Simon, Herbert A., *The Sciences of the Artificial*, MIT Press, Cambridge, MA, 1969.

Simon, Herbert A., "Search and Reasoning in Problem Solving," *Artificial Intelligence*, vol. 21, 1983.

Slagle, James R., "A Heuristic Program that Solves Symbolic Integration Problems in Freshman Calculus," in *Computers and Thought*, edited by Edward A. Feigenbaum and Julian Feldman, McGraw-Hill, New York, 1963. Based on a PhD thesis, Massachusetts Institute of Technology, Cambridge, MA, 1961.

Sloman, A., "Interactions Between Philosophy and Artificial Intelligence: The Role of Intuition and Non-Logical Reasoning in Intelligence," *Artificial Intelligence*, vol. 2, 1971.

Stallman, Richard M. and Gerald J. Sussman, "Forward Reasoning and Dependency-Directed Backtracking in a System for Computer-Aided Circuit Analysis," *Artificial Intelligence*, vol. 9, no. 2, 1977.

Stefik, M., "Inferring DNA Structures from Segmentation Data," *Artificial Intelligence*, vol. 11, 1978.

Stefik, Mark, "Planning with Constraints (MOLGEN: Part 1 and Part 2)," *Artificial Intelligence*, vol. 16, no. 2, 1980.

Stepankova, Olga, and Ivan M. Havel, "A Logical Theory of Robot Problem Solving and Language Comprehension," *Artificial Intelligence*, vol. 7, no. 2, 1976.

Stepp, Robert E. and Ryszard S. Michalski, "Conceptual Clustering of Structured Objects: A Goal-Oriented Approach," *Artificial Intelligence*, vol. 28, 1986.

Stevens, Albert L., R. Bruce Roberts, Larry S. Stead, Kenneth D. Forbus Cindy Steinberg, and Brian C. Smith, "Steamer: Advanced Computer Aided Instruction in Propulsion Engineering," Report 4702, Bolt, Beranek and Newman, Cambridge, MA, 1981.

Sugihara, Kokichi, "Mathematical Structures of Line Drawings of Polyhedrons: Toward Man-Machine Communication by Means of Line Drawings," *IEEE Transactions on Pattern Analysis and Machine Intelligence*, vol. PAMI-4, 1982.

Sugihara, Kokichi, "Quantitative Analysis of Line Drawings of Polyhedral Scenes," *Proceedings of the Fourth International Joint Conference on Pattern Recognition, Kyoto, Japan*, 1978.

Sussman, Gerald J. and Guy L. Steele Jr, "CONSTRAINTS: A Language for Expressing Almost Hierarchical Descriptions," *Artificial Intelligence*, vol. 14, 1980.

Sussman, Gerald J. and Richard M. Stallman, "Heuristic Techniques in Computer Aided Circuit Analysis," *IEEE Transactions on Circuits and Systems*, vol. CAS-22, no. 11, 1975.

Sussman, Gerald J., Terry Winograd, and Eugene Charniak, "MICRO-PLANNER Reference Manual," Report AIM-203A, Artificial Intelligence Laboratory, Massachusetts Institute of Technology, Cambridge, MA, 1971.

Sussman, Gerald J., *A Computer Model of Skill Acquisition*, Elsevier, New York, 1975. Based on a PhD thesis, Massachusetts Institute of Technology, Cambridge, MA, 1973.

Szolovits, Peter (editor), *Artificial Intelligence in Medicine*, Westview Press, Boulder, CO, 1982.

Szolovits, Peter, Lowell B. Hawkinson, and William A. Martin, "An Overview of OWL, a Language for Knowledge Representation," Report TM-86, Laboratory for Computer Science, Massachusetts Institute of Technology, Cambridge, MA, 1977.

Szolovits, Peter, "Compilation for Fast Calculation over Pedigrees," *Cytogenetics and Cell Genetics*, vol. 59, 1992.

Tanimoto, Steven L., *The Elements of Artificial Intelligence*, Computer Science Press, 1990.

Tate, Austin, "Generating Project Networks," *Fifth International Joint Conference on Artificial Intelligence*, Cambridge, MA, 1977.

Tenenbaum, Jay M., and Harry G. Barrow, "Experiments in Interpretation-Guided Segmentation," *Artificial Intelligence*, vol. 8, no. 3, 1977.

Terzopoulos, D., A. P. Witkin and M. Kass, "Constraints on Deformable Models: Recovering Three-Dimensional Shape and Nonrigid Motion," *Artificial Intelligence*, vol. 36, 1988.

Terzopoulos, Demetri, "The Computation of Visible-Surface Representations," PhD Thesis, Department of Electrical Engineering & Computer Science, Massachusetts Institute of Technology, Cambridge, MA, 1983.

Tesauro, G. and T.J. Sejnowski, "A Parallel Network that Learns to Play Backgammon," *Artificial Intelligence*, vol. 39, 1989.

Thorne, J., P. Bratley, and H. Dewar, "The Syntactic Analysis of English by Machine," in *Machine Intelligence 3*, edited by Donald Michie, Edinburgh University Press, Edinburgh, Scotland, 1968.

Touretzky, David S., "BoltzCONS: Dynamic Symbol Structures in a Connectionist Network," *Artificial Intelligence*, vol. 46, 1990.

Tversky, Amos, "Features of Similarity," *Psychological Review*, vol. 84, no. 4, 1977.

Ullman, Shimon and Ronen Basri, "Recognition by Linear Combinations of Models," *IEEE Transactions on Pattern Analysis and Machine Intelligence*, vol. 13, no. 10, 1991.

Ullman, Shimon and Ronen Basri, "Recognition by Linear Combinations of Models," Report AIM-1152, Artificial Intelligence Laboratory, Massachusetts Institute of Technology, Cambridge, MA, 1989.

Ullman, Shimon, *The Interpretation of Visual Motion*, MIT Press, Cambridge, MA, 1979. Based on a PhD thesis, Massachusetts Institute of Technology, Cambridge, MA, 1977.

Ulrich, Karl T., "Computation and Pre-Parametric Design," PhD Thesis, Department of Electrical Engineering & Computer Science, Massachusetts Institute of Technology, Cambridge, MA, 1988.

VanLehn, Kurt Alan, "Felicity Conditions for Human Skill Acquisition: Validating an AI-based Theory," PhD Thesis, Department of Electrical Engineering & Computer Science, Massachusetts Institute of Technology, Cambridge, MA, 1983.

VanLehn, Kurt, "Learning One Subprocedure per Lesson," *Artificial Intelligence*, vol. 31, 1987.

Vere, Steven A., "Relational Production Systems," *Artificial Intelligence*, vol. 8, no. 1, 1977.

Waltz, David, "Natural Language Access to a Large Data Base: An Engineering Approach," *Fourth International Joint Conference on Artificial Intelligence*, Tbilisi, Georgia, USSR, 1975.

Waltz, David, "Understanding Line Drawings of Scenes with Shadows," in *Psychology of Computer Vision*, edited by Patrick H. Winston, MIT Press, Cambridge, MA, 1975. Based on a PhD thesis, Massachusetts Institute of Technology, Cambridge, MA, 1972.

Waters, Richard C., "The Programmer's Apprentice: Knowledge Based Program Editing," *IEEE Transactions on Software Engineering*, vol. SE-8, no. 1, 1982.

Watson, James D., Nancy H. Hopkins, Jeffrey W. Roberts, Joan Argetsinger Steitz, and Alan M. Weiner, *Molecular Biology of the Gene* (fourth edition), Benjamin/Cummings Publishing Company, Menlo Park, CA, 1987.

Webb, Jon A., and J. K. Aggarwal, "Structure from Motion of Rigid and Jointed Objects," *Artificial Intelligence*, vol. 19, no. 1, 1982.

Webber, Bonnie L., "So What Can We Talk about Now," in *Computational Models of Discourse*, edited by J. Michael Brady and Robert C. Berwick, MIT Press, Cambridge, MA, 1983.

Weiss, Solomon M., Casimir A. Kulikowski and Saul Amarel, "A Model-Based Method for Computer-Aided Medical Decision-Making," *Artificial Intelligence*, vol. 11, 1978.

Weizenbaum, Joseph, *Computer Power and Human Reason*, W. H. Freeman, San Francisco, CA, 1976.

Weld, Daniel S., "Exaggeration," *Artificial Intelligence*, vol. 43, 1990.

Weld, Daniel S., "The Use of Aggregation in Causal Simulation," *Artificial Intelligence*, vol. 30, 1986.

Weld, Daniel S., "Comparative Analysis," *Artificial Intelligence*, vol. 36, 1988.

Weyhrauch Richard W., "Prolegomena to a Theory of Mechanized Formal Reasoning," *Artificial Intelligence*, vol. 13, 1980.

White, Barbara Y. and John R. Frederiksen, "Causal Model Progressions as a Foundation for Intelligent Learning Environments," *Artificial Intelligence*, vol. 42, 1990.

Wilks, Yorick A., *Grammar, Meaning, and the Machine Analysis of Language*, Routledge and Kegan Paul, London, 1972.

Wilks, Yorick, and Eugene Charniak, *Computational Semantics*, North-Holland, Amsterdam, 1976.

Wilks, Yorick, "A Preferential, Pattern-Seeking, Semantics for Natural Language Inference," *Artificial Intelligence*, vol. 6, 1975.

Wilks, Yorick, "Making Preferences More Active," *Artificial Intelligence*, vol. 11, 1978.

Williams, Brian C., "Qualitative Analysis of MOS Circuits," *Artificial Intelligence*, vol. 24, 1984.

Winograd, Terry, "Extended Inference Modes in Reasoning by Computer Systems," *Artificial Intelligence*, vol. 13, 1980.

Winograd, Terry, "Towards a Procedural Understanding of Semantics," *Revue Internationale de Philosophie*, vol. 3, 1976.

Winograd, Terry, *Understanding Natural Language*, Academic Press, New York, 1972. Based on a PhD thesis, Massachusetts Institute of Technology, Cambridge, MA, 1971.

Winograd, Terry, *Language as a Cognitive Process, Volume I: Syntax*, Addison-Wesley, Reading, MA, 1983.

Winograd, Terry, "Frame Representations and the Declarative/Procedural Controversy," in *Representation and Understanding*, edited by Daniel G. Bobrow and Allan Collins, Academic Press, New York, 1975.

Winston, Patrick H. and Sarah Alexandra Shellard, *Artificial Intelligence at MIT: Expanding Frontiers* (Two Volumes), MIT Press, Cambridge, MA, 1990.

Winston, Patrick H. and Satyajit Rao, "Repairing Learned Knowledge Using Experience," in *Artificial Intelligence at MIT: Expanding Frontiers (Two Volumes)*, edited by Patrick H. Winston and Sarah Alexandra Shellard, MIT Press, Cambridge, MA, 1990.

Winston, Patrick Henry (editor), *The Psychology of Computer Vision*, McGraw-Hill, New York, 1975.

Winston, Patrick Henry and Richard Henry Brown (editors), *Artificial Intelligence: An MIT Perspective* (Two Volumes), MIT Press, Cambridge, MA, 1979.

Winston, Patrick Henry, and Berthold K. P. Horn, LISP, Third Edition, Addison-Wesley, Reading, MA, 1989.

Winston, Patrick Henry, and Karen A. Prendergast (editors), *The AI Business: The Commercial Uses of Artificial Intelligence*, MIT Press, Cambridge, MA, 1984.

Winston, Patrick Henry, Thomas O. Binford, Boris Katz, and Michael R. Lowry, "Learning Physical Descriptions from Functional Definitions, Examples, and Precedents," *Proceedings of the National Conference on Artificial Intelligence, Washington, D. C.*, 1983.

Winston, Patrick Henry, "Learning by Creating and Justifying Transfer Frames," *Artificial Intelligence*, vol. 10, no. 2, 1978.

Winston, Patrick Henry, "Learning and Reasoning by Analogy," *Communications of the ACM*, vol. 23, no. 12, 1980.

Winston, Patrick Henry, "Learning New Principles from Precedents and Exercises," *Artificial Intelligence*, vol. 19, no. 3, 1982.

Winston, Patrick Henry, "Learning Structural Descriptions from Examples," in *Psychology of Computer Vision*, edited by Patrick H. Winston, MIT Press, Cambridge, MA, 1975. Based on a PhD thesis, Massachusetts Institute of Technology, Cambridge, MA, 1970.

Winston, Patrick Henry, "Learning by Augmenting Rules and Accumulating Censors," Report AIM-678, Artificial Intelligence Laboratory, Massachusetts Institute of Technology, Cambridge, MA, 1982.

Winston, Patrick Henry, "The MIT Robot," in *Machine Intelligence 7*, edited by Bernard Meltzer and Donald Michie, Edinburgh University Press, Edinburgh, Scotland, 1972.

Witkin, Andy, "Scale-Space Filtering," *Eighth International Joint Conference on Artificial Intelligence*, Karlsruhe, Germany, 1983.

Woodham, Robert J., "Analysing Images of Curved Surfaces," *Artificial Intelligence*, vol. 17, 1981. Based on a PhD thesis, Massachusetts Institute of Technology, Cambridge, MA, 1978.

Woods, William A., and Ronald M. Kaplan, "The Lunar Sciences Natural Language Information System," Report 2265, Bolt, Beranek and Newman, Cambridge, MA, 1971.

Woods, William A., "Transition Network Grammars for Natural Language Analysis," *Communications of the ACM*, vol. 13, no. 10, 1970.

Woods, William A., "What's in a Link?," in *Representation and Understanding*, edited by Daniel G. Bobrow and Allan Collins, Academic Press, New York, 1975.

Yip, Kenneth Man-kam, "KAM: Automatic Planning and Interpretation of Numerical Experiments Using Geometrical Methods," PhD Thesis, Department of Electrical Engineering & Computer Science, Massachusetts Institute of Technology, Cambridge, MA, 1989.

Zucker, Steven W., Azriel Rosenfeld, and Larry S. Davis, "General Purpose Models: Expectations About the Unexpected," *Fourth International Joint Conference on Artificial Intelligence*, Tbilisi, Georgia, USSR, 1975.

Index

725

Colophon

Camera-ready copy for this book was created by the author using TeX, Donald E. Knuth's computer typesetting language, with additional macros written by Daniel C. Brotsky, Jerry Roylance, and the author. It is said that Knuth started thinking about computer typesetting after looking at the first edition of this book, which was one of the earliest books typeset by a computer.

Source files were processed using PCTeX, a product of Personal TeX, Inc., of Mill Valley, California. Conversion of the TeX DVI files to the PostScript printer language was done using DVIPSONE, a product of Y&Y, of Carlisle, Massachusetts. The drawings were prepared using Designer, a product of Micrographics, Inc., of Richardson, Texas. The production of film from PostScript files was done by Chiron, Inc., of Cambridge, Massachusetts.

The principal type family is Computer Modern, and the body type is 10-point Computer Modern Roman. Titles are set in Frutiger Black. Type in illustrations is set in Helvetica.